Macs®

ALL-IN-ONE

5th Edition

**by Joe Hutsko, Barbara Boyd,
Jesse Feiler, and Doug Sahlin**

A Wiley Brand

Macs® All-in-One For Dummies®, 5th Edition

Published by: **John Wiley & Sons, Inc.,** 111 River Street, Hoboken, NJ 07030-5774, www.wiley.com

Copyright © 2020 by John Wiley & Sons, Inc., Hoboken, New Jersey

Published simultaneously in Canada

For general information on our other products and services, please contact our Customer Care Department within the U.S. at 877-762-2974, outside the U.S. at 317-572-3993, or fax 317-572-4002. For technical support, please visit https://hub.wiley.com/community/support/dummies.

Wiley publishes in a variety of print and electronic formats and by print-on-demand. Some material included with standard print versions of this book may not be included in e-books or in print-on-demand. If this book refers to media such as a CD or DVD that is not included in the version you purchased, you may download this material at http://booksupport.wiley.com. For more information about Wiley products, visit www.wiley.com.

Library of Congress Control Number: 2019954080

ISBN 978-1-119-60798-4 (pbk); ISBN 978-1-119-60805-9 (ebk); ISBN 978-1-119-60807-3 (ebk)

Manufactured in the United States of America

V10015918_112719

Contents at a Glance

Introduction 1

Book 1: Getting Started with Your Mac 5
CHAPTER 1: Starting to Use Your Mac 7
CHAPTER 2: Getting Acquainted with the Mac User Interface 23
CHAPTER 3: Making Your First Connections 57
CHAPTER 4: Working with Files and Folders 83
CHAPTER 5: Managing Apps on the Dock, Launchpad, and Desktop 127
CHAPTER 6: Changing How Your Mac Looks, Sounds, and Feels 165

Book 2: Using the Internet 205
CHAPTER 1: Browsing the Web with Safari 207
CHAPTER 2: Corresponding with Mail 249
CHAPTER 3: Chatting with Messages and FaceTime 293
CHAPTER 4: Using Apple Pay and Apple Card 307
CHAPTER 5: Moving Around with Maps 311

Book 3: Beyond the Basics 323
CHAPTER 1: Backing Up and Restoring Your Data 325
CHAPTER 2: Protecting Your Mac against Local and Remote Threats 349
CHAPTER 3: Networking Your Mac and Connecting Peripherals 385
CHAPTER 4: Sharing Files and Resources on a Network 403
CHAPTER 5: Running Windows on a Mac 421
CHAPTER 6: Maintenance and Troubleshooting 427

Book 4: Using Your Mac as a Media Center 441
CHAPTER 1: Getting Acquainted with Media on Your Mac 443
CHAPTER 2: Tuning In and Listening with Music 455
CHAPTER 3: Enjoying Podcasts, News, and TV 491
CHAPTER 4: Reading and Listening to Books on Your Mac 505
CHAPTER 5: Looking at Photos 515

Book 5: Taking Care of Business 547
CHAPTER 1: Managing Contacts 549
CHAPTER 2: Staying on Schedule with Calendar 573

CHAPTER 3: Creating Documents with Pages 607

CHAPTER 4: Presenting with Keynote 649

CHAPTER 5: Crunching with Numbers 695

CHAPTER 6: Getting the Most Out of Pages, Numbers, and Keynote 727

Index... 739

Table of Contents

INTRODUCTION 1

About This Book 1

Foolish Assumptions 2

Icons Used in This Book 3

Beyond the Book 4

Where to Go from Here 4

BOOK 1: GETTING STARTED WITH YOUR MAC 5

CHAPTER 1: **Starting to Use Your Mac** 7

Examining Different Mac Models 7

    The Mac mini and Mac Pro 9

    The iMac 9

    The MacBook Air and MacBook Pro 10

Starting Your Mac 11

Turning Off Your Mac 13

    Putting your Mac to sleep 13

    Shutting down your Mac 16

    Restarting your Mac 18

Understanding Mac Processors 19

Exploring Your Mac's Inner Workings 20

CHAPTER 2: **Getting Acquainted with the Mac User Interface** 23

Looking at Menus, Dialogs, and Windows 24

    Exploring the menu bar 25

    Understanding menu commands 26

    Working with dialogs 26

    Managing windows 27

Mastering the Mouse, Trackpad, and Keyboard 32

    Using the mouse 33

    Operating the trackpad 34

    Examining the parts of the keyboard 36

Getting to Know the Parts of the Desktop 43

    The Dock 44

    The Finder 46

Getting to Know Siri 48

    Exploring a basic Siri interaction 49

    Using complex Siri commands 51

    Configuring Siri 53

    Empowering Siri 53

Getting Help 54

CHAPTER 3: **Making Your First Connections** 57

Setting Up an Internet Connection 58
  Ethernet connection 58
  Wireless (Wi-Fi) access 59
Establishing Your Apple Identity 63
  Creating an Apple ID during Mac setup 64
  Using two-factor authentication 65
  Creating an Apple ID in iCloud 66
Keeping Your Data in iCloud 71
  Configuring iCloud preferences 72
  Syncing with your other devices 74
  Using the iCloud website 75
Setting Up Email and Social Network Accounts 77
  Adding accounts 77
  Gathering your account information 78
  Configuring your account 79

CHAPTER 4: **Working with Files and Folders** 83

Getting to Know the Finder 84
  Handling devices 85
  Understanding folders 86
  Setting Finder preferences 88
Navigating the Finder 90
  Opening a folder 90
  Working with tabs 90
  Jumping to a specific folder 91
  Jumping back and forth 92
  Moving to a higher folder 92
  Following the folder path 93
Organizing and Viewing Folders 93
  Selecting items in the Finder 94
  Using Icon view 94
  Using List view 96
  Using Column view 97
  Using Gallery view 98
  Changing your view options 99
  Using Quick Look to view file contents 100
Creating Folders 102
  Creating a folder from the Finder menu 102
  Creating a folder from Save or Save As 102
Playing Tag: Classify Files and Folders for Quick Access 105
  Setting tag preferences 105
  Tagging existing files and folders 105
  Tagging new files 107
  Finding your tagged files 107

Manipulating Files and Folders 107
    Renaming files and folders 108
    Copying a file or folder 110
    Moving a file or folder. 111
    Grouping files. 112
Archiving Files and Folders. 112
    Creating a Zip file. 113
    Creating a DMG file 114
    Deleting files and folders 116
Searching Files. 117
    Using Spotlight. 118
    Spotlight Preferences 120
    Using Smart Folders 121
    Creating a Smart Folder with Spotlight 122
Deleting a File or Folder 123
    Retrieving a file or folder from the Trash. 124
    Emptying the Trash. 124

CHAPTER 5: **Managing Apps on the Dock, Launchpad, and Desktop** 127
Launching an App 128
    From the Dock 129
    From Launchpad 131
    From the Apple menu's Recent Items. 132
    From the Finder. 133
    With Spotlight. 134
    Opening documents 134
Switching among Applications. 137
Quitting Apps 139
    Closing a document. 139
    Shutting down an app. 139
    Force-quitting an app 140
Creating Alias Icons. 142
Working with Dock Aliases. 143
    Adding file and folder aliases to the Dock 144
    Rearranging icons on the Dock 146
    Removing icons from the Dock 147
Organizing Multiple Desktops with Spaces 148
    Creating Desktops. 148
    Switching Desktops. 150
    Moving app windows to different Desktops 150
    Setting Mission Control preferences 151
Acquiring New Apps 152
    Shopping in the App Store 153
    Downloading apps from the App Store 156

Installing Applications...158
Updating Applications and System Software 158
Uninstalling Applications 160
    Uninstalling an app 160
    Removing app alias icons from the Dock and Desktop.........162
    Removing user setting files 162
Paying Attention to App Security...............................163

CHAPTER 6: **Changing How Your Mac Looks, Sounds, and Feels** 165
Changing the Desktop and Screen Saver........................166
    Choosing a Desktop image 166
    Customizing the screen saver 168
Changing the Display and Appearance 171
    Changing the screen resolution 171
    Using Night Shift 172
    Changing the colors of the user interface 173
Changing the Date and Time....................................175
Adjusting Sounds...178
Noticing Notifications 181
Working in Split-View Mode.....................................186
Using Your Mac's Accessibility Features........................187
    Mitigating vision limitations...............................188
    Compensating for hearing limitations 191
    Interacting with ease......................................192
Enabling Switch Control..198
Speaking with Your Mac..199
    Setting up the microphone 200
    Setting up Speakable Items 201

BOOK 2: USING THE INTERNET 205

CHAPTER 1: **Browsing the Web with Safari**....................207
Browsing Websites 208
    Going on Safari 208
    Visiting websites 209
    Reading in Reader 217
    Using tabbed browsing.....................................218
    Setting your Safari home page 222
    Searching within a web page...............................223
Organizing Your Website Experience 223
    Using bookmarks..224
    Creating a Reading List....................................230
    Displaying favorites in Top Sites 232

Storing Personal Info and Keeping It Private. .234
    Using AutoFill to track passwords and more. 234
    Protecting your web-browsing privacy. 236
Saving and Sharing Web Pages 238
    Saving a web page as a file. 239
    Saving a photo from the web. . . . .,240
    Sharing a web page. 241
    Printing a web page. 242
Viewing and Playing Multimedia Files 243
    Listening to streaming audio. 243
    Viewing PDF files 243
Downloading Files. 244
Using Extensions 246

CHAPTER 2: **Corresponding with Mail**. 249
Adding an Email Account to Mail. 250
Looking at the Mail Window 254
Writing Emails 257
    Creating a new email 257
    Replying to or forwarding a message. 259
    Customizing your messages 261
    Sending a file or photo attachment 266
    Spelling and grammar checking 270
Receiving and Reading Email. 271
    Retrieving email. 271
    Reading email. 273
    Viewing and saving file attachments 274
    Adding an email address to Contacts. 275
    Adding an email contact to your VIPs list. .276
Organizing Email 276
    Searching through email 277
    Organizing email with mailbox folders. 278
    Deleting a mailbox folder. 280
    Automatically organizing email with smart mailboxes 280
    Automatically organizing email with rules. 282
    Flagging your messages 283
Dealing with Junk Email 284
    Filtering junk email 285
    Using advanced filter rules. 287
    Using blocked sender rules 289
Deleting and Archiving Messages 290
    Deleting messages 290
    Retrieving messages from the Trash folder 291
    Emptying the Trash folder 292
    Archiving messages. 292

CHAPTER 3: **Chatting with Messages and FaceTime** 293
Getting Started in Messages 294
Setting up a Messages account 294
Keeping up appearances 294
Chatting with Others 296
Initiating a text chat 297
Initiating an audio or a video chat 299
Sharing files and photos 301
Saving or deleting your conversations 301
Making Calls with FaceTime 302
Signing in to FaceTime 303
Making a call with FaceTime 303
Receiving a FaceTime call 305

CHAPTER 4: **Using Apple Pay and Apple Card** 307
Paying for Purchases with Apple Pay 308
Using Apple Card 309

CHAPTER 5: **Moving Around with Maps** 311
Wherever You Go, There You Are 312
Finding your location 312
Navigating the Maps interface 314
Asking for Directions 315
Finding what you seek 315
Sharing what you find 318
Dropping a pin 320
Getting directions 320

BOOK 3: BEYOND THE BASICS 323

CHAPTER 1: **Backing Up and Restoring Your Data** 325
Using iCloud for Your Data 326
Understanding Different Backup Options 328
Backing up with external hard drives 329
Storing backups on USB flash drives 330
Storing backups off-site 331
Blasting into the Past with Time Machine 332
Setting up Time Machine 332
Skipping files you don't want to back up 336
Retrieving files and folders 337
Understanding Versions 342
Restoring your entire backup 342
Moving Your Backup from an Old Mac to a New Mac 344
Working with Data-Recovery Programs 345
Getting Rid of What You No Longer Need 348

CHAPTER 2: **Protecting Your Mac against Local and Remote Threats** 349

Locking Down Your Mac 350
Using Passwords 350
  Changing your password 351
  Applying password protection 353
Using Touch ID 356
  Setting up Touch ID 357
  Using Touch ID 357
Encrypting Data with FileVault 358
  Setting up FileVault 358
  Turning off FileVault 361
Using Firewalls 362
  Configuring the Mac firewall 362
  Buying a more robust firewall 365
Selecting Privacy Settings 366
Creating Multiple Accounts 368
  Adding a new user account 369
Defining Parental Controls 371
  Activating a Sharing Only account 377
  Switching between accounts 379
  Deleting an account 381
A Few Final Security Tips 383

CHAPTER 3: **Networking Your Mac and Connecting Peripherals** 385

Creating a Wired Network 386
Creating a Wireless Network with a Router 390
Connecting and Choosing a Printer 393
Biting into Bluetooth 395
  Configuring Bluetooth on your Mac 396
  Pairing a Bluetooth device 398
  Sharing through Bluetooth 400

CHAPTER 4: **Sharing Files and Resources on a Network** 403

Sharing Files with People Near and Far 404
  Using AirDrop 404
  Using a network 407
Sharing Printers 415
Seeing Your Screen from Afar 416
  Enabling screen sharing 416
  Starting a screen-sharing session with another Mac 417

CHAPTER 5: **Running Windows on a Mac** 421

Working with BYOD and a Heterogeneous
Computer Environment 422

Using Boot Camp. 423

Setting up Boot Camp Assistant 423

CHAPTER 6: **Maintenance and Troubleshooting** 427

Shutting Down Frozen or Hung-Up Programs 428

Handling Startup Troubles. 430

Resetting the System Management Controller 430

Resetting NVRAM and PRAM 431

Booting up in Safe Mode 431

Uninstalling apps. 433

Repairing and Maintaining Storage Drives 434

Running First Aid 434

Booting from another Mac through a Thunderbolt cable. 436

Using the Recovery Disk. 437

Removing Jammed CDs or DVDs. 438

BOOK 4: USING YOUR MAC AS A MEDIA CENTER 441

CHAPTER 1: **Getting Acquainted with Media on Your Mac** 443

Using Your Apple ID to Enjoy and Share Media 443

Media Sharing 444

Family Sharing 445

Getting into the Media Apps in macOS Catalina. 453

CHAPTER 2: **Tuning In and Listening with Music** 455

Getting to Know the Music App. 456

The sidebar. 457

The Music window. 458

Working with Playlists. 458

Ordinary playlists. 459

Smart Playlists 461

Genius playlists, shuffles, or mixes. 466

Organizing Your Music 468

Adjusting Music Preferences 470

Playing Audio with Music 474

Listening to CDs. 474

Importing a CD's audio tracks into Music 476

Importing digital audio files. 478

Searching your Music library 478

Playing digital audio files 479

Burning an audio CD. 482

Listening to the Radio. 484
    Playing Music Radio. 484
Shopping at the iTunes Store 485
    Downloading media from Music. 488

CHAPTER 3: **Enjoying Podcasts, News, and TV** 491
Finding and Playing Podcasts 491
    Exploring podcasts 492
    Listening to or watching podcasts 492
    Setting Podcast Preferences 494
Reading the News: Extra, Extra, Read All about It! 496
    Reading the daily news. 496
    Following a publisher or channel 498
    Saving and sharing stories 498
    Setting News preferences 499
Watching TV on Your Mac 500

CHAPTER 4: **Reading and Listening to Books on Your Mac** 505
Thumbing through Books 505
    Finding something to read at Apple Books 507
    Adding books and files from other sources 509
    Reading by screen light. 510
    Sorting your books 513

CHAPTER 5: **Looking at Photos** 515
Understanding Digital Photography. 515
Transferring Digital Images to the Mac 517
    Retrieving photos using Photos. 518
    Moving photos from other folders into Photos 520
Organizing Your Photo Library 521
    Tagging images 521
    Using the Keyword Manager 523
    Manually adding information to photos 524
    Creating a Smart Album 525
    Creating folders 526
    Deleting photos, albums, and folders 527
    Mapping your images. 528
    Creating Memories 530
    Finding images. 531
    Creating a slideshow. 531
Capturing Photos with Photo Booth. 534
Editing Photos with Photos 537
Sharing Photos. 541
    Printing photos 541
    Sending photos in a message 542
    Using Photo Stream 543

BOOK 5: TAKING CARE OF BUSINESS 547

CHAPTER 1: **Managing Contacts** 549

Setting Up Contacts 550
Viewing Contacts 550
Designing your Contacts template 551
Entering contacts 553
Working with Contacts 560
Searching contacts 561
Editing a card 561
Deleting a contact 562
Creating groups 562
Sharing Your Contacts 568
Sending one contact at a time 568
Exporting multiple cards 569
Printing your Contacts 570

CHAPTER 2: **Staying on Schedule with Calendar** 573

Getting Acquainted with Calendar 574
Working with Multiple Calendars 576
Creating a new calendar 577
Accessing calendars from other accounts 578
Subscribing to online calendars 580
Importing Calendar data 582
Creating a new calendar group 582
Moving a calendar or group 584
Renaming and deleting calendars and groups 584
Creating and Modifying Events 585
Viewing events 585
Creating an event 585
Editing an event 587
Moving an event 594
Deleting an event 595
Finding Events 595
Color-coding events 595
Selectively hiding events 595
Checking for today's events 596
Checking events for a specific date 596
Searching for an event 597
Exporting Calendar data 598
Sharing your calendars 598
Backing up Calendar data and restoring a backup file 600
Printing a Calendar file 601

Organizing Tasks with Reminders..............................602
    Creating new Reminders tasks 602
    Making new lists 605

CHAPTER 3: **Creating Documents with Pages**....................607

Working with Document Templates............................608
    Choosing a template.....................................608
    Replacing placeholder text..............................610
    Replacing placeholder photos and graphics 611
    Adding pages or sections to your document. 614
    Moving around your document 616
Working with Text 617
    Editing text 617
    Formatting text 618
    Adjusting line spacing, justification, and margins............620
Creating and Placing Text Boxes............................629
    Creating a text box 629
    Moving a text box 630
    Resizing a text box.....................................630
    Uniting text boxes 631
Using Styles 631
    Using a paragraph style.................................632
    Using an image style...................................633
    Using a text box style 634
Creating Charts and Tables 635
    Adding and removing a chart 635
    Adding a table 637
    Adding shapes..638
    Arranging objects......................................640
    Wrapping text around an object..........................641
Polishing Your Document..................................642
    Spell-checking a document 642
    Finding and replacing text 644
Saving Your Documents on Your Mac or iCloud.................645
Printing Your Documents..................................646
Exporting to a Different File Format..........................646

CHAPTER 4: **Presenting with Keynote**............................649

Creating a Presentation 650
    Choosing a theme and saving your presentation..............651
    Opening an existing file 653
    Finding your way around Keynote 654
    Adding slides 656

Manipulating Text 658
     Entering text. 658
     Inserting text boxes. 659
     Editing text 659
     Formatting text and text boxes 660
Adding Shapes, Charts, and Tables. 667
     Inserting predefined shapes 667
     Aligning and arranging objects 669
     Adding a chart 670
     Adding a table 672
Adding Media Files 674
     Adding sound. 674
     Adding photos or movies 676
Rearranging Slides. 678
     Creating groups of slides 678
     Deleting a slide. 680
     Skipping a slide 680
Creating Transitions and Effects 680
     Creating a slide transition 681
     Creating text and graphic effects 682
     Adding hyperlinks to your presentation 685
Using Masters to Customize Themes. 686
Polishing Your Presentation. 687
     Viewing a presentation. 688
     Rehearsing a presentation. 688
     Preparing for your big event 689
     Controlling your presentation remotely 690
     Letting others run your presentation. 692

CHAPTER 5:   **Crunching with Numbers** 695
Understanding the Parts of a Numbers Spreadsheet 696
Creating a Numbers Spreadsheet. 699
     Creating a new spreadsheet with a template 699
     Opening an existing file 700
Working with Sheets 701
     Adding a sheet 702
     Deleting a sheet. 702
     Adding or removing a table 702
     Resizing a table 703
     Changing the appearance of a table. 703
     Inserting headers and resizing rows and columns. 704
Typing Data into Tables 706
     Formatting numbers and text 707
     Entering formulas 710

Formatting data entry cells 713
Sorting data 717
Deleting data in cells. 718
Adding a chart 718
Naming sheets, tables, and charts 720
Making Your Spreadsheets Pretty. 720
Adding a text box. 721
Adding media. 721
Sharing Your Spreadsheet 722
Printing a spreadsheet 722
Exporting a spreadsheet 723
Sharing files directly from Numbers. 725

CHAPTER 6: Getting the Most Out of Pages,
Numbers, and Keynote. 727
Collaborating with Keynote, Pages, and Numbers. 728
Inserting Media from Other Sources 731
Copying and Pasting. 732
Modifying Photos. 732
Masking a photo 733
Making parts of a picture transparent with Instant Alpha 735
Using Adjust Image 735
Adding Comments. 737
Finding More Templates. 738

INDEX. 739

Introduction

Whether you're a beginner, an intermediate user, or a seasoned computer expert, you can find something in *Macs All-in-One For Dummies,* 5th Edition. This book is divided into five minibooks so you can focus on the topics that interest you and skip over the ones that don't. We explored every menu and button of the Mac, its operating system, as well as Apple's Pages, Numbers, and Keynote applications and other built-in applications and wrote about most of them, focusing on the functions and features we think you'll use frequently or that will help you get the most out of your Mac and the applications.

About This Book

This book begins by focusing on the basics for all the aspects of using a Mac with the latest operating system, macOS Catalina. We start at the very beginning, from turning on your Mac, using the mouse and trackpad with multitouch gestures, and organizing your virtual desktop. We segue to creating your Apple ID and connecting your Mac to the Internet. In true *For Dummies* style, we show you step by step how to conduct all your online activities from setting up email accounts to having video chats. We introduce you to more advanced but important tasks, such as protecting your Mac and your personal information; networking your Mac with other Macs, peripherals, and devices; and installing Windows on your Mac!

The fun begins when we explore Apple's apps to manage tasks, such as editing and organizing your digital photos and videos, adding music to your Mac, and even reading books and watching movies. Along the way, we tell you how to share your finds and creations with people you know.

This book also shows you how to use and take advantage of the applications included with Catalina, which provides word processing, desktop publishing, a presentation app, and a spreadsheet app for calculating formulas and displaying your data as 3D charts. Whether you use a Mac for work, school, or just for fun, you'll find that with the right software apps, your Mac can meet all your computing needs.

If you're migrating to a Mac from a Windows PC, this book can ease you into the Mac way of computing and show you how to install Windows on your Mac so you can still use your favorite Windows programs. By running Windows on a Mac, you can turn your Mac into two computers for the price of one.

If you're new to the Mac, you'll find that this book introduces you to all the main features of your Mac. If you're already a Mac user, you'll find information on topics you might not know much about. After reading this book, you'll have the foundation and confidence to delve deeper into your Mac's bundled apps as well as others you can find at the App Store.

This book is a reference, which means you don't need to read the chapters in order from front cover to back, and you're not expected to commit anything to memory — there won't be a test on Friday. You can dip into the book wherever you want, to find answers to your most pressing questions. If you're short on time, you can safely skip sidebars (the text in gray boxes) and anything marked with the Technical Stuff icon without missing anything essential to the topic at hand.

To help you navigate this book efficiently, we use a few style conventions:

>> *Control-click* means to hold the Control key and click the mouse. If you're using a mouse that has a left and right button, you can right-click rather than Control-click. If you have one of Apple's trackpads, tap with two fingers. You find complete explanations of the multitouch gestures in Book 1, Chapter 2.

>> When we refer to the Apple menu — the menu that appears when you click the Apple icon in the very upper-left corner of your Mac's screen — we use this apple symbol: . When we talk about menu commands, we use a command arrow, like this: Choose ⟹Recent Items ⟹Calendar. That just means to click the Apple menu; then, when it appears, slide your pointer down to Recent Items and drag slightly to the right to open a submenu from which we want you to click Calendar.

Finally, within this book, you may note that some web addresses break across two lines of text. If you're reading this book in print and want to visit one of these web pages, simply key in the web address exactly as it's noted in the text, pretending as though the line break doesn't exist. If you're reading this as an e-book, you've got it easy — just click the web address to be taken directly to the web page.

Foolish Assumptions

In writing this book, we made a few assumptions about you, dear reader. To make sure that we're on the same page, we assume that

>> You know something, but not necessarily a whole lot, about computers, and you want to find out the basics of using a Mac or doing more with your Mac than you are already.

>> You have at least a general concept of this wild and crazy thing called the Internet — or more precisely, the phenomenon known as *the web* (or, more formally, the World Wide Web).

>> You'll turn to the introductory chapters if you find yourself scratching your head at such terms as *double-click, drag and drop, scroll,* and *Control-click* — or any other terms that sound like things we assume that you know but you don't.

>> You appreciate the speed at which technology-based products like the Mac (and the programs you can run on it) can change in as little as a few months, with newer, sleeker, faster models and app versions replacing previous versions.

>> You can traverse the web to find updated information about the products described throughout this book.

>> You know that keeping up with the topic of all things high-tech and Mac (even as a full-time job, as it is for us) still can't make a guy or gal the be-all and end-all Mac Genius of the World. You will, therefore, alert us to cool stuff you discover in your Mac odyssey so that we can consider including it in the next edition of this book.

>> You're here to have fun, or at least try to have fun, as you dive into The Wonderful World of Mac.

Icons Used in This Book

To help emphasize certain information, this book displays different icons in the page margins.

TIP

The Tip icon marks tips (duh!) and points out useful nuggets of information that can help you get things done more efficiently or direct you to something helpful that you might not know. Sometimes Tips give you a second, or even third, way of doing the task that was pointed out in the step.

REMEMBER

Remember icons mark the information that's been mentioned previously but is useful for the task at hand. This icon often points out useful information that isn't quite as important as a Tip but not as threatening as a Warning. If you ignore this information, you can't hurt your files or your Mac, but it may make the task at hand easier.

TECHNICAL STUFF

This icon highlights interesting information that isn't necessary to know but can help explain why certain things work the way they do on a Mac. Feel free to skip this information if you're in a hurry, but browse through this information when you have time. You might find out something interesting that can help you use your Mac.

WARNING

Watch out! This icon highlights something that can go terribly wrong if you're not careful, such as wiping out your important files or messing up your Mac. Make sure that you read any Warning information before following any instructions.

Beyond the Book

In addition to the material in the print or e-book you're reading right now, this product also comes with some access-anywhere goodies on the web. Although the Mac uses menus for just about everything, the menu commands have key combination counterparts. We put together a table of the most common key commands that you can print and keep near your Mac. You also find a table that shows you how to type foreign letters and common symbols and one that summarizes the multitouch gestures. To help you stay up to date with the latest Mac news, we provide a list of Mac websites with hot links, which you can simply click to go to the site. To find the Cheat Sheet for this book, just go to www.dummies.com and type **Macs All-in-One For Dummies Cheat Sheet** in the Search box.

Where to Go from Here

For Dummies books aren't meant to be read cover to cover. However, this book flows from task to task, chapter to chapter, in an order that would be logical if you're learning the Mac for the first time. In that case, feel free to start at Book 1, Chapter 1 and go through the Book 1 chapters to familiarize yourself with how the Mac is organized and how you can make it do what you want it to do. Then mix it up, moving on to fun tasks, such as making FaceTime video calls (Book 2, Chapter 3) or designing a flyer with Pages (Book 5, Chapter 3), and then bounce back to a crucial task, such as backing up (Book 3, Chapter 1).

If you're computer intuitive, you could start with Book 1, Chapter 3 to get your Apple ID and Internet connection set up, and then move in the direction you want, whether it's learning about more advanced system functions in Book 3 or organizing and editing your images using Photos.

If you're familiar with the Mac but want to brush up on the latest macOS — Catalina — read about Notification Center in Book 1, Chapter 6; Maps in Book 2, Chapter 5; Books in Book 4, Chapter 4; and the completely updated Pages, Numbers, and Keynote apps in Book 5, Chapters 3–6.

1

Getting Started with Your Mac

Contents at a Glance

CHAPTER 1: Starting to Use Your Mac 7

Examining Different Mac Models 7
Starting Your Mac 11
Turning Off Your Mac 13
Understanding Mac Processors 19
Exploring Your Mac's Inner Workings 20

CHAPTER 2: Getting Acquainted with the Mac User Interface 23

Looking at Menus, Dialogs, and Windows 24
Mastering the Mouse, Trackpad, and Keyboard 32
Getting to Know the Parts of the Desktop 43
Getting to Know Siri 48
Getting Help 54

CHAPTER 3: Making Your First Connections 57

Setting Up an Internet Connection 58
Establishing Your Apple Identity 63
Keeping Your Data in iCloud 71
Setting Up Email and Social Network Accounts 77

CHAPTER 4: Working with Files and Folders 83

Getting to Know the Finder 84
Navigating the Finder 90
Organizing and Viewing Folders 93
Creating Folders 102
Playing Tag: Classify Files and Folders for Quick Access 105
Manipulating Files and Folders 107
Archiving Files and Folders 112
Searching Files 117
Deleting a File or Folder 123

CHAPTER 5: Managing Apps on the Dock, Launchpad, and Desktop 127

Launching an App 128
Switching among Applications 137
Quitting Apps 139
Creating Alias Icons 142
Working with Dock Aliases 143
Organizing Multiple Desktops with Spaces 148
Acquiring New Apps 152
Installing Applications 158
Updating Applications and System Software 158
Uninstalling Applications 160
Paying Attention to App Security 163

CHAPTER 6: Changing How Your Mac Looks, Sounds, and Feels 165

Changing the Desktop and Screen Saver 166
Changing the Display and Appearance 171
Changing the Date and Time 175
Adjusting Sounds 178
Noticing Notifications 181
Working in Split-View Mode 186
Using Your Mac's Accessibility Features 187
Enabling Switch Control 198
Speaking with Your Mac 199

Chapter 1

Starting to Use Your Mac

Apple offers several different kinds of Macs, and understanding how your Mac is different from the others can help you navigate this book more quickly, gathering the information you need and skipping the rest. Before you can use your Mac, you have to start it up — which makes perfect sense — so we tell you how to do that. Now, get ready for the counterintuitive part: After you have your Mac up and running, you can just leave it on.

In this chapter, we cover current Mac models and how they're different and alike, show you how to start and restart your Mac (and give you an idea of what goes on behind the scenes), and then tell you how to put it to sleep and shut it down completely. Sprinkled throughout this chapter is technical information about the various Mac models and what goes on inside that makes your Mac tick, but we make our explanations as clear and simple as possible. At the end of the chapter, we introduce you to Mac processors and show you how to find out precisely which features your Mac has.

Examining Different Mac Models

Apple's Macintosh computer — Mac for short — enjoys the reputation of being the easiest computer to use in the world. Macs are so dependable, durable, and beautifully designed that they incite techno-lust in gadget geeks like us and ordinary Joes alike. For those doubly good reasons, you probably won't buy a new Mac to replace your old one because you *have* to, but because you *want* to.

The Macintosh has been around since 1984, and since that time, Apple has produced a wide variety of Mac models. Although you can still find and use older Macs (although many are not compatible with the latest and greatest OS or applications), chances are, if you buy a newer Mac, it will fall into one of three categories:

>> **Desktop:** Mac mini or Mac Pro, which require a separate display (monitor), keyboard, and mouse or trackpad.

>> **All-in-one desktop:** iMac or iMac Pro, which house the display and computer in one unit and require a keyboard and mouse or trackpad.

>> **Notebook:** MacBook Air or MacBook Pro, which have built-in keyboards, trackpads that work like a mouse at the touch of your fingertips, and bright displays. A clamshell design lets you close and tote them in your backpack, messenger bag, or briefcase.

All the newest Mac models have at least one Thunderbolt/USB port to connect peripheral hardware, such as external drives and displays. They're also engineered for Wi-Fi and Bluetooth connections, which are used for data transfer and peripheral connectivity.

The Thunderbolt port, standard on all newer Macs, is a data-transfer protocol used to connect peripheral devices, such as displays, speakers, or hard drives. Thunderbolt transfers data faster than either USB or FireWire. The latest iteration, Thunderbolt 3, uses the same ports and connectors as the new version of USB (called USB-C).

Because most data transfer and storage happens online or with flash drives, optical disc drives (which play CDs and DVDs) have become almost obsolete and have been removed from all the Mac models sold today. If you still use CDs or DVDs, you can buy an external CD/DVD drive. You can also connect to an older computer on a network and access its optical disc drive.

Mac mini, Mac Pro, and iMac models use an external wireless or wired (usually USB) keyboard and a mouse or trackpad (sold separately from the mini and Pro). Apple's Magic Trackpad lets you use the multitouch gestures — such as swipe, pinch, and flick — to control the cursor and windows on whichever Mac desktop model you choose. If you use a trackpad, you don't need a mouse, but you can use both if you prefer.

By understanding the particular type of Mac that you have and its capabilities, you'll have a better idea of what your Mac can do. We highlight those capabilities in the sections that follow. No matter what the capabilities of your Mac are, chances are, it will work reliably for as long as you own it.

The Mac mini and Mac Pro

The biggest advantages desktop Macs (the Mac mini and Mac Pro) offer are that you can choose the type of display to use and place it anywhere you want on your desk — as long as you have a cable that can reach. The Mac mini, however, is small enough to hide under your desk or situate in a corner of your desktop.

The Mac mini started as a lower-priced version of the Mac, designed for people who wanted an inexpensive Mac for ordinary uses, such as word processing and writing, sending email, browsing the web, and playing video games. At the same time, it packs a fast Intel Core i3, i5 or i7 processor, with up to 64GB of memory, and between 128 gigabytes (GB) and 2 terabytes (TB) of storage, and an assortment of the latest ports and slots for audio, video, and USB connections — nothing to sneeze at. Alternatively, it can function as a terrific, cost-effective server for home or small-business networks. With the latest iterations of the Mac mini, everything has been updated to the latest hardware with power to manage industrial-strength tasks, including everything from home automation to sound and image editing (including artificial reality).

The Mac Pro was completely remodeled and released in December 2013 with a new model coming in the fall of 2019. The 2013 version of this higher-priced professional-version Mac boasts ports to connect multiple monitors and lots of expandability for up to 64GB of memory and up to 1TB of flash storage, as well as greater graphics and processing capabilities with the latest Intel Xeon processor and dual graphics processors.

The iMac

The all-in-one design of the iMac is an evolutionary result of the original — 1984-era — Mac design. The iMac is available in two varieties — iMac 21 with a 21-inch monitor, and iMac 27 with a 27-inch monitor. Both models feature a built-in display, speakers, and FaceTime camera. The standard display is LED-backlit, but you can specify a Retina 4K display. You can configure up to 1TB of storage for an iMac 21 or 3TB of storage for an iMac 27. You choose flash storage instead of a hard drive, or a fusion drive, which combines a flash drive with a conventional hard drive, depending on your need for speed or space. On iMac models, you can connect external speakers and a second external display.

Recently, Apple launched a high-powered extension to the iMac line: iMac Pro. The iMac Pro is a powerhouse that features a more vibrant 5K Retina display, a faster processor, and more memory, with up to 4TB of storage.

The advantage of the iMac's all-in-one design is that you have everything you need in a single unit. The disadvantage is that if one part of your iMac fails (such as the display or speaker), you can't easily replace the failed part, although in our experience, Apple responds quickly and professionally to problems with its products.

The MacBook Air and MacBook Pro

MacBook Air and MacBook Pro are the notebook members of the Mac family. All the MacBook models run on rechargeable battery packs or external power. If you need to take your Mac everywhere you go, you can choose from the ultralight MacBook Air or one of the MacBook Pro models.

Although both MacBook Air and MacBook Pro have full-size keyboards, neither includes the extra numeric keypad found on most external keyboards (but not on Apple's standard wireless keyboard) or on larger Windows notebooks. Also, instead of a mouse, the MacBook uses a built-in trackpad, which responds to all the multitouch gestures you can use to control the cursor and windows on your Mac.

TIP

If you find the keyboard or trackpad of your notebook Mac too clumsy to use, you can always plug an external keyboard and mouse into your notebook, or use a wireless keyboard and mouse.

The MacBook Air is a featherweight computer with a 1.66 GHz i5 processor, and can be configured with up to 1TB of flash storage and up to 16GB of memory.

The MacBook Pro models can be configured to include up to a 2.4 GHz 8-core i9 processor, up to 32GB of memory, and up to 4TB of flash storage. MacBook Pro computers now include a Touch Bar above the keyboard. It lets you tap icons that change as you work with your Mac so that the function button or tools that you need appear when you need them.

The MacBook Air comes with a 13-inch LED-backlit screen, and the MacBook Pro models come in two screen sizes: 13 inch and 15 inch.

TECHNICAL
STUFF

Apple's Retina display uses a liquid crystal display (LCD) with a pixel density of 227 pixels per inch (PPI). At this density, the human eye doesn't distinguish the individual pixels at a normal distance. All MacBook Pros have the Retina display, as do some iPad and iPhone models. The MacBook Air and other desktop models sport an LED-backlit screen.

Starting Your Mac

Here's the simple way to start your Mac — the way you'll probably use 99 percent of the time: Press the Power button.

Depending on the type of Mac you have, the Power button may be in back (Mac mini and iMac), front (Mac Pro), above the keyboard (MacBook Air and MacBook Pro), or at the right of the Touch Bar. Some Apple displays have a Power button that commands the computer it's connected to.

TIP

With the Touch Bar, you have Touch ID so that your touch turns on the Mac and logs you in as well.

A few seconds after you press the Power button, your Mac chimes to let you know that it's starting. (Techie types say *booting up,* a term derived from the phrase "to lift yourself up by the bootstraps.")

The moment electricity courses through, your Mac's electronic brain immediately looks for instructions embedded inside a special read-only memory (ROM) chip. While your computer is reading these instructions (also known as *firmware*), it displays the Apple logo on the screen and a progress bar to let you know that the computer is working and hasn't forgotten about you.

The firmware instructions tell the computer to make sure that all its components are working; most often, they are. However, if some part of your computer (say, a memory chip) is defective, your computer will stop at this point.

WARNING

Unless you know something about repairing the physical parts of a Mac, this is the time to haul your Mac to the nearest Apple Store or authorized repair shop, call Apple Support (800-275-2273 in the United States), or go to http://support. apple.com.

REMEMBER

Sometimes a Mac may refuse to start correctly because of software problems. To fix software problems, check out Book 3, Chapter 6, which explains how to perform basic troubleshooting on a Mac.

After your computer determines that all components are working, the last set of instructions on the chip tells the computer, "Now that you know all your parts are working, load an operating system."

When you unpack your Mac and turn it on for the very first time, it asks you to type your name and make up a password to create an account for using your Mac. You use this name and password in the following situations:

>> When you wake or restart your Mac, if you activate those types of privacy settings (see Book 3, Chapter 2)

>> When you install new apps or update the system software

>> When you change some settings in System Preferences

>> When you switch from one user to another, if you set up your Mac to work with multiple users (see Book 3, Chapter 2)

This username and password are different than your Apple ID, which you use for iCloud and making Music Store, App Store, and Apple Books purchases. You can learn about creating an Apple ID in Book 1, Chapter 3.

To guide you through the process of setting up a Mac for the first time, a special application called Setup Assistant runs, which asks for your time zone, the date, and whether you want to transfer files and applications from another Mac to your newer one. If you've just upgraded to a new Mac, you don't have to reinvent the wheel and set up everything again. You can migrate settings from your old Mac to your new Mac.

Normally, you need to run through this initial procedure only once, but you also have to perform it if you reinstall your operating system (OS). We explain reinstalling the OS in Book 3, Chapter 6. The most important part of this initial procedure is remembering the password you choose because you'll need it to log in to your account, change some of the settings in System Preferences, or install new software.

An *operating system* is the program that controls your computer and is almost always stored on your computer's built-in hard drive (rather than on an external drive). On the Mac, the operating system is named macOS (pronounced *mac oh ess*) and is followed by a version number, such as 10.14.

Apple code-names each version of macOS. The current version is macOS Catalina 10.15. Early versions of macOS were named after big cats, such as Mountain Lion, Snow Leopard, and Jaguar. Now, they're named after places in California.

After the operating system loads and you log in, you can start using your computer to run other applications to do things such as design a poster, send an email, browse the web, calculate your yearly budget, or play a game — you know, all the cool things you bought your Mac for in the first place.

Turning Off Your Mac

You can choose one of three different ways — sleep, shut down, or restart — to turn off your Mac (or let it rest a bit). In this section, we explain when and why you would want to use each option and, of course, how.

Putting your Mac to sleep

If you're taking a short break from working on your Mac, you don't have to always turn it off and then turn it back on again when you want to use it. To conserve energy, put your Mac to sleep instead of leaving it running while you're away. When you put your Mac to sleep, it shuts down almost every power-draining component of your Mac and draws only a teensy trickle of power. The great part, though, is that you can instantly wake it up by touching the keyboard, clicking the mouse, swiping the trackpad, or opening the lid (if you use a MacBook Air or Mac-Book Pro). Presto change-o! Your Mac immediately returns to the same state you left it in, without making you wait to power on as if it were completely shut down.

To put your Mac to sleep, you can go manual or automatic:

>> **Manual:** If someone walks into your office and you want to hide that secret project you're working on, you may want to put your Mac to sleep manually.

>> **Automatic:** So you don't have to remember to put your Mac to sleep when you stop using it (to take a phone call or go out to lunch) you can adjust your Mac's settings so that it automatically falls asleep after a certain amount of time.

WARNING

If your Mac is doing a task, such as sending an email or downloading a file, let it finish the task before putting it to sleep.

To put your Mac to sleep manually, choose one of the following actions:

>> **Choose ⌘⇨Sleep.** The ⌘ menu is in the upper-left corner of the screen.

>> **Press and hold the Power button.** (If you're having trouble finding your way around the keyboard, see Book 1, Chapter 2.) Then, when a dialog appears, as shown in Figure 1-1, click the Sleep button (or press the S key on your Mac's keyboard). *Note:* This does not work on models with Touch ID.

>> **Press Option+⌘+Power Button.** This puts your Mac to sleep instantly without a dialog appearing. This is a useful option if you're shopping online for your wife's anniversary present and she walks into the room.

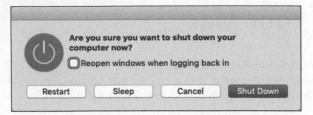

FIGURE 1-1:
Put your
computer to sleep.

>> **Press ⌘+Option+Eject.** If your MacBook doesn't have a disc drive, it doesn't have an Eject key, so this option doesn't work. This option also doesn't work on models with Touch ID.

>> **If you have a MacBook, just close its lid.** When a MacBook is sleeping, you can safely move it without worrying about jarring the built-in hard drive that spins most of the time your MacBook is awake and in use.

To put your Mac to sleep automatically, you set the amount of time your Mac sits idle before it goes to sleep. Which sleep options you see depend on what type of Mac you're using:

>> **Desktops:** On desktop Macs, you can adjust when your Mac puts the display to sleep and when it puts the computer to sleep.

>> **Notebooks:** Your Mac knows whether it's using battery power or the power adapter, and you can adjust when the display and computer sleep in both instances.

Follow these steps to adjust how your computer sleeps automatically:

1. **Choose ⌥⇨System Preferences, and then click the Energy Saver icon that looks like a light bulb.**

   The Energy Saver window appears, as shown in Figure 1-2. If you have a MacBook, you'll see separate tabs with appropriate information for when you're using the battery or power adapter.

   When powered by the battery, you may want your Mac to go to sleep after a short time (say, 5 minutes) to make the battery charge last longer. Then, when your Mac is connected to a power source, you could set it longer: say, after 15 minutes.

2. **Drag the Turn Display Off After slider to the amount of time you want your Mac to sit idle before it goes to sleep.**

   The exact time is shown above the timescale (on the right) as you move the slider.

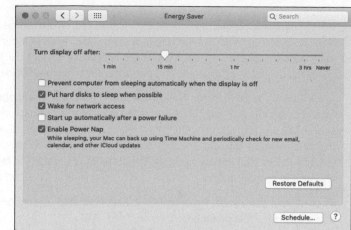

Energy Saver

FIGURE 1-2:
Use the Energy
Saver System
Preferences to
put your Mac on
a sleep schedule.

TIP

This setting puts the hard drive to sleep. You may want to set a longer time interval for Computer Sleep than for Display Sleep (the following step) because it takes your Mac slightly longer to wake from Computer Sleep than Display Sleep.

3. **Drag the Turn Display Off After slider to the amount of time you want your Mac to sit idle before the screen saver plays.**

This setting puts the display to sleep. A *screen saver* is an image that appears when your Mac is inactive after the time interval you set here. It hides whatever you were working on from peering eyes when you're away from your Mac. You can find out how to choose a special image for your screen saver and set a password for it in Book 1, Chapter 6.

TIP

If you perform tasks such as downloading large files, select the Prevent Computer from Sleeping When Display Is Off check box and set a time interval to turn the display off. This way, your Mac continues to do the task at hand even though the display is sleeping.

4. **(For MacBook) Select the Show Battery Status in Menu Bar check box (in the lower-left corner).**

This displays an icon at the top of your Mac's screen indicating how much charge is left on your battery.

5. **(Optional) Select the check boxes next to the other options to set when your Mac goes to sleep or wakes.**

For instance, If you access your Mac remotely, select the Wake for Wi-Fi Network Access check box so your Mac will wake when you try to retrieve files and data from your Mac.

Select Enable Power Nap so your Mac continues to perform some functions while it's sleeping. When Power Nap is on, your Mac receives incoming email, automatically updates any apps you share with other devices (such as Contacts, Calendar, and Notes), and performs Time Machine backups.

The MacBook has two Power Nap settings: one for Battery and one for Power Adapter. By default, Power Nap is on when your Mac is connected to a power source but off when running on the battery. To change either, click the Battery or Power Adapter tab and select, or deselect, the Power Nap check box. When you use Power Nap in Battery mode, the activities are limited to receiving email and updating shared data.

To see if your Mac model supports Power Nap, visit http://support.apple.com and search for *about power nap*.

6. **(Optional) Click the Schedule button and adjust those settings as desired.**

   A pane opens that lets you schedule the days and times you want your Mac to start or wake up and go to sleep. This is convenient if you don't want to accidently leave your Mac on when you leave your home or office or you do want to find it awake and waiting for you when you arrive.

7. **Save your setting by choosing System Preferences ⇨ Quit System Preferences or clicking the Close (red) button in the upper-left corner of the Energy Saver dialog box.**

To wake a sleeping desktop or all-in-one Mac or a MacBook with the lid open, click the mouse button or tap any key. To keep from accidentally typing any characters into a currently running application, press a noncharacter key, such as Shift or an arrow key. To wake your closed and sleeping MacBook, just open its lid. You can wake a sleeping MacBook with the lid open by swiping the trackpad or pressing any key.

TECHNICAL STUFF

Depending on which Mac model you own, you may notice a built-in combination power/sleep indicator light that softly pulses like a firefly when your Mac is sleeping. On the MacBook Pro, the power/sleep indicator light is on the front edge below the right wrist rest. On the Mac mini, the indicator light is in the lower-right corner. No such light is anywhere on the iMac or the latest MacBook Air, which appear to be totally in the dark when they're asleep.

Shutting down your Mac

When you shut down your Mac, open applications are automatically closed, Internet and network connections are disconnected, and logged-in users are logged out. It may take a few minutes for your Mac to shut down. You know your Mac is shut down completely when the screen is black, the hard drive and fan are silent, and there are no blinking lights anywhere. Here are a few circumstances when you'd want to shut down your Mac:

>> **Taking an extended break:** When you won't be using it for an extended length of time. Turning your Mac completely off can extend its useful life, waste less energy, and save you a few bucks on your yearly energy expense.

>> **Traveling:** When you're traveling with your Mac and putting your MacBook Air, MacBook Pro, or Mac mini in your wheeled carry-on bag.

TIP

Putting your Mac to sleep is fine if you're carrying your MacBook in a laptop bag or backpack. If you're going through a security line in an airport or other location, sleep is actually exactly what you want so that when the inspector checks your computer, one touch will bring it to life. Security guards may ask you to turn on a computer that is turned off.

>> **Repairing hardware:** If you own a Mac that is user serviceable, and you want to open the computer to install a new battery, additional memory, or a video graphics card.

>> **Restarting:** To resolve weird situations, such as unresponsive or slow-running applications, because your Mac runs a number of behind-the-scenes file-system housekeeping chores every time you start it. (See the next section for instructions.)

Here are the ways to shut down your Mac:

>> **Choose ⌘⇨Shut Down.** A confirmation dialog appears (as shown in Figure 1-3) asking whether you're sure you want to shut down.

TIP

Select the Reopen Windows When Logging Back In check box if you want everything you're working on to open when you turn on your Mac the next time.

Click the Shut Down button (or Cancel if you change your mind). If you don't click either option, your Mac will shut down automatically after 1 minute.

>> **Press and hold the Power button.** When a dialog appears (refer to Figure 1-1), click the Shut Down button or press the Return key.

FIGURE 1-3:
Click Shut Down
to turn off your
computer.

> **Are you sure you want to shut down your computer now?**
> If you do nothing, the computer will shut down automatically in 50 seconds.
> ☐ Reopen windows when logging back in
>
> [Cancel] [Shut Down]

WARNING

Make sure that your MacBook Air or MacBook Pro is completely shut down before closing the lid, or it may not shut down properly. Even more problematic, it may not start up properly when you next try to turn it on.

TIP

To shut down without seeing those bothersome dialogs, do this: Hold the Option key and then choose ⇨ Shut Down. This bypasses the confirmation prompt asking whether you're sure that you want to shut down.

WARNING

You have one more option for shutting down your Mac, but proceed with caution. Press and hold ⌘+Control and then press the Power button to perform a *force shutdown*, which forces all running applications to shut down immediately. However, this route should never be your first choice when shutting down. Use a force shutdown as your last resort only if your Mac — your *Mac*, not just a stubborn application — is unresponsive and appears to have frozen. If a single application is freezing or acting flaky, force-quit (close) that single application instead of shutting down your entire computer. (See Book 3, Chapter 6 for information about how to force-quit a single application.) Performing a force shutdown can cause you to lose any changes you've made since the last time you saved them, so use force shutdown only as a last resort.

Restarting your Mac

Sometimes your Mac can act sluggish, or applications may fail to run. If that happens, you can shut down and immediately restart your Mac, which essentially clears your computer's memory and starts it fresh.

To restart your computer, you have three choices:

>> **Press the Power button.** Then, when a dialog appears, click the Restart button (refer to Figure 1-1) or press the R key.

>> **Choose ⇨ Restart.**

>> **Press Control+⌘+Eject.**

When you restart your computer, your Mac closes all running applications; you have the chance, though, to save any files you're working on. After you choose to save any files, those applications are closed, and then your Mac will shut down and boot up again.

Understanding Mac Processors

The *processor* acts as the brain of your Mac. A computer is only as powerful as the processor inside. Generally, the newer your computer, the newer and more powerful its processor and the faster it will run.

REMEMBER

The type of processor in your Mac can determine the applications (also known as *apps* or *software*) your Mac can run. Before you buy any software, make sure that it can run on your computer.

To identify the type of processor used in your Mac, choose ⇨ About This Mac. An About This Mac window appears, listing your processor (see Figure 1-4).

FIGURE 1-4:
The About This Mac window identifies the processor used in your Mac.

The Intel family of processors includes (from slowest to fastest) the Core Solo, Core Duo, Core 2 Duo, dual-core i3, dual-core i5, quad-core i7, and quad- and six-core Xeon. Every processor runs at a specific speed, so, for example, a 2.0 gigahertz (GHz) Core 2 Duo processor is slower than a 2.4 GHz Core 2 Duo processor. If understanding processor types and gigahertz confuses you, just remember that the most expensive computer within a product line is usually the fastest.

Talk to your friendly Apple reseller to get suggestions for which Mac to buy. Or talk or chat online with someone at the Apple Store (http://store.apple.com). The tasks you plan to do with your Mac determine the processor speed that will meet your needs. For example, if you plan to mostly write books, surf the web, and use productivity apps like Calendar and Contacts, a low-end processor is probably sufficient. If, instead, you're a video editor or game developer, you want the fastest processor you can afford.

Click each tab at the top of the About This Mac window to open panes that show more information about your Mac: Overview, Displays, Storage (shown in Figure 1-5), and Memory. These tabs provide information about your Mac in clear, well-designed graphics (this is Apple, after all). For example, in Figure 1-5, you see a Mac with the built-in Flash Storage that is standard on some Macs; you also see an external disk drive, which is subdivided into two sections (Backup and Current). The different types of files are color-coded.

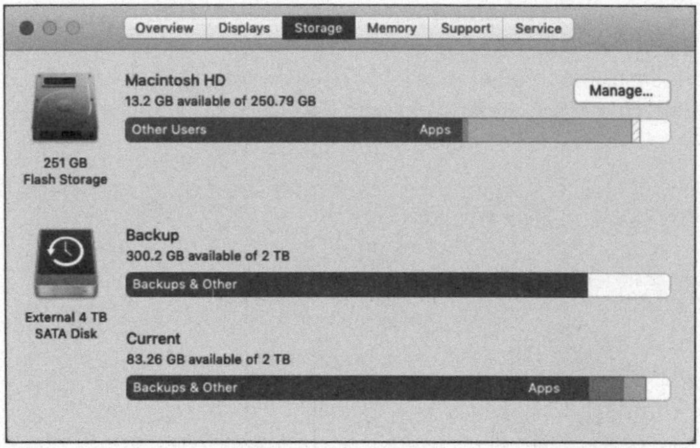

FIGURE 1-5:
The Storage pane of the About This Mac window tells you how your Mac's storage is being used.

Click the Support tab for links to the Help Center and user manuals. Click the Service tab to access links to information about your Mac's warranty and AppleCare protection.

Exploring Your Mac's Inner Workings

By looking at your Mac, you can tell whether it's an all-in-one design (iMac), a notebook (MacBook Air or MacBook Pro), or a desktop unit that lacks a built-in screen (Mac mini or Mac Pro). However, looking at the outside of your Mac can't tell you the parts used on the inside or the details regarding what your Mac is capable of. You may need to look at the hardware information in the System Report window when you want to know about the health of your MacBook's battery or the type of graphics card in your Mac Pro.

To identify the parts and capabilities of your Mac, follow these steps:

1. **Choose ⇨ About This Mac.**

The About This Mac window appears.

2. **Click System Report.**

The System Report window appears.

3. **Click the disclosure triangle to the left of the Hardware option in the category pane on the left (as shown in Figure 1-6) to view a list of hardware items.**

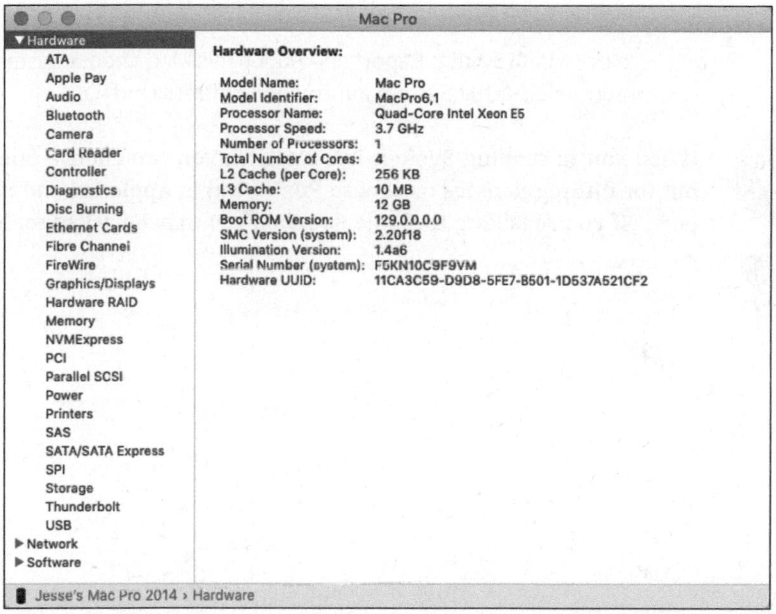

FIGURE 1-6:
The System
Report
identifies the type
and capabilities
of the hardware
in your Mac.

If the list of hardware items (such as Bluetooth, Memory, and USB) already appears under the Hardware category, skip this step.

Clicking a disclosure triangle toggles to open or close a list of options.

TIP

You can also click the disclosure triangle next to Network or Software in the category pane on the left to see information about networks you're connected to or software installed on your Mac. (You can learn more about networking your Mac in Book 3, Chapter 3; we tell you how to install software in Book 1, Chapter 5; and we cover uninstalling software in Book 1, Chapter 5.)

4. **Click a hardware item, such as Audio, Disc Burning, or Memory.**

The right pane of the System Report window displays the capabilities of your chosen hardware.

Don't worry if the information displayed in the System Report window doesn't make much sense to you. The main idea here is to identify a quick way to find out about the capabilities of your Mac, which can be especially helpful if you have a problem in the future and a technician asks for information about your computer.

5. **When you finish scouting the contents of the System Report window, you can simply close it (click the red circle in the upper-left corner) to return to About This Mac.**

   To close both System Report and About This Mac, choose System Information⇨Quit System Information or Press cmd+Q.

When you're running System Information, you can choose File⇨Print to print it out for future reference or choose File⇨Send to Apple to send it to Apple for support. (If you're talking to Apple Support, you may be asked to do this.)

IN THIS CHAPTER

» Perusing menus, dialogs, and windows

» Using the mouse, trackpad, and keyboard

» Getting familiar with the parts of the Desktop

» Saying hello to Siri

» Getting help with your Mac

Chapter **2**

Getting Acquainted with the Mac User Interface

Theoretically, using a computer is simple. In practice, using a computer can cause people to suffer a wide range of emotions from elation to sheer frustration and despair.

The problem with using a computer stems mostly from two causes:

» Not knowing what the computer can do

» Not knowing how to tell the computer what you *want* it to do

In the early days of personal computers (PCs), this communication gap between users and computers arose mostly from ordinary people trying to use machines designed by engineers for other engineers. If you didn't understand how a computer engineer thinks (or doesn't think), computers seemed nearly impossible to understand.

Fortunately, Apple has mostly solved this problem with the Mac. Instead of designing a computer for other computer engineers, Apple designed a computer for ordinary people. And what do ordinary people want? Here's the short (but definitely important) list:

>> Reliability

>> Ease of use

From a technical point of view, what makes the Mac reliable is its operating system, macOS. An operating system (OS) is nothing more than an application that makes your computer work.

An OS works in the background. When you use a computer, you don't really notice the operating system, but you do see its *user interface* (UI) — which functions like a clerk at the front desk of a hotel: Instead of talking directly to the housekeeper or the plumber (the OS), you always talk to the front desk clerk, and the clerk talks to the housekeeper or plumber on your behalf.

Apple designed a UI that everyone can understand. You control your Mac with multitouch gestures applied to the trackpad or mouse, making the UI even more intuitive and literally hands-on.

In this chapter, we explain what you see on the screen when you turn your Mac on. Then we explain how to use a mouse, trackpad, and keyboard to control your Mac. We introduce the Dock, Finder, and Dashboard. We introduce to Siri, your very own virtual assistant. And we tell you how to get help from your Mac if you need it.

Chances are, if you work with a computer, you know how to click and drag and open menus, but we explain it step by step in the beginning in case this is your first time using a computer. After all, we were all newbies once. The layout and gestures you read about in this chapter apply to almost everything you'll ever do with your Mac.

Looking at Menus, Dialogs, and Windows

The Mac UI acts like a communication pathway between you and the OS, serving three purposes:

>> To display all the options you can choose

>> To display information

>> To accept commands

This section tells you how menus and windows serve those three purposes.

REMEMBER

One of the most crucial parts of the Mac UI is an application called the *Finder*, which displays files stored on your Mac. You find out more about the Finder later in this chapter.

Exploring the menu bar

The menu bar runs across the top of your Mac's screen. The menu bar is always accessible and almost always visible, and it provides a single location where you can find nearly every possible command you may need for your computer or the app you're using. The menu bar consists of three parts: the Apple menu, the app menus, and menulets.

Figure 2-1 identifies the parts that appear on the left side of the menu bar:

>> **The Apple menu (🍎):** This menu always appears on the menu bar and gives you one-click access to commands for controlling or modifying your Mac.

>> **The app menus:** Here's where you find the name of the active app along with several menus that contain commands for controlling that particular app and its data. (If you don't run any additional apps, your Mac always runs the Finder, which you find out more about in this chapter.)

App menus

Apple menu

FIGURE 2-1:
The left side of
the menu bar.

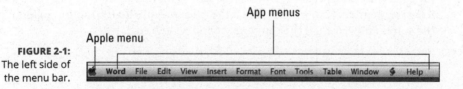

🍎   Word   File   Edit   View   Insert   Format   Font   Tools   Table   Window   💲   Help

On the right side of the menu bar, you see the menulets, shown in Figure 2-2. *Menulets* are mini menus that open when you click the icons on the right end of the menu bar. They give you quick access to specific System Preferences settings, such as Date & Time, Network, or Sound.

Menulets

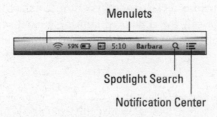

Spotlight Search

Notification Center

FIGURE 2-2:
The menulets.

The icons on the right end of the menulets open menus that perform one or more system functions, such as providing fast access to Wi-Fi controls or battery status (MacBook models). The two icons to the right open Spotlight Search and Notification Center.

TIP

If you don't want a menulet cluttering up the menu bar, you can typically remove it by holding down the ⌘ key, moving the pointer over the icon you want to remove, dragging (moving) the mouse pointer off the menu bar, and then releasing the mouse button. If a menulet cannot be removed from the menu bar, a circle with a line through it appears. If you've removed a menulet and decide you want it back on the menu bar, you can display it again by choosing that option in the menulet's section of System Preferences. For example, you can display or hide the Bluetooth menulet in the Bluetooth section of System Preferences.

Understanding menu commands

Each menu on the menu bar contains a group of related commands. The File menu contains commands for opening, saving, and printing files; the Edit menu contains commands for copying or deleting selected items; and the View menu gives you options for what you see on the screen. The number and names of different menus depend on the application.

To give a command to your Mac, drag your finger across the trackpad or move the mouse so the pointer points to the menu you want. Then tap the trackpad or click the mouse to call up a drop-down menu listing all the commands you can choose. Drag the pointer (with your finger on the trackpad or with the mouse) to highlight the command you want the computer to follow and click it.

Working with dialogs

When your Mac needs information from you or wants to present a choice you can make, it typically displays a *dialog* — essentially a box that offers a variety of choices. Some common dialogs appear when you choose the Print, Save, and Open commands.

Some dialogs (particularly Print and Save) often appear in a condensed version, but you can blow them up into an expanded version, as shown in Figure 2-3. For example, to switch between the expanded and the condensed version of the Save dialog, click the upward- or downward-pointing arrow (near the pointer in Figure 2-3).

FIGURE 2-3:
When expanded,
the Save dialog
offers more
options.

The arrow points down when you're looking at the condensed version of the dialog; click it to expand the dialog. The arrow points up when you're looking at the expanded version of the dialog; click it to condense the dialog.

TIP

Whether expanded or condensed, every dialog displays buttons that let you cancel the command or complete it. To cancel a command, you have three choices:

» Click the Cancel button.

» Press Esc.

» Press ⌘+. (period).

To complete a command, you also have two choices:

» Click the button that represents the command that you want to complete, such as Save or Print.

» Press Return to choose the default button, which appears in blue.

Managing windows

Every app needs to accept, manipulate, and/or display data, also referred to as *information*. A word processor lets you type and edit text, a spreadsheet app lets you type and calculate numbers, and a presentation app lets you display text and pictures. To help you work with different types of information (such as text, pictures, audio files, and video files), every app displays information inside a rectangular area called a *window*. Figure 2-4 shows two app windows.

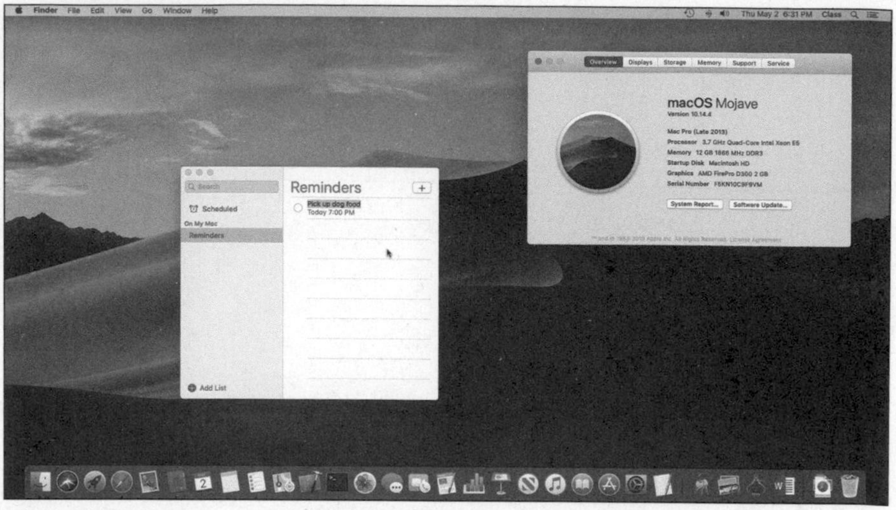

FIGURE 2-4:
Multiple apps
can display
in windows
onscreen at the
same time.

Dividing a screen into multiple windows offers several advantages:

>> Two or more apps can display information on the screen simultaneously.

>> A single app can open and display information stored in two or more files or display two or more views of the same file.

>> You can copy (or move) data from one window to another. If each window belongs to a different app, this action transfers data from one app to another.

Of course, windows aren't perfect. When a window appears on the screen, it might be too big or too small, be hard to find because it's hidden behind another window, or display the beginning of a file when you want to see the middle or end of it. To control the appearance of a window, most windows provide built-in controls, as shown in Figure 2-5. The following sections show you what you can do with these controls.

Moving a window with the title bar

The title bar of every window serves two purposes:

>> It identifies the filename that contains the information displayed in the window.

>> It provides a place to grab when you want to drag (move) the window to a new location on the screen, which we explain in the sections "Using the mouse" and "Operating the trackpad," later in this chapter.

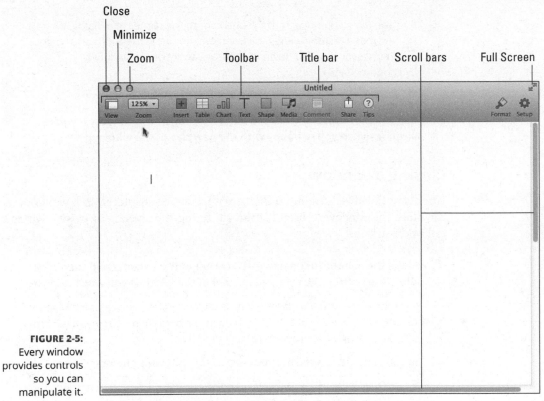

Close

Minimize

Zoom — Toolbar — Title bar — Scroll bars — Full Screen

FIGURE 2-5:
Every window
provides controls
so you can
manipulate it.

Resizing a window

Sometimes a window may be in the perfect location, but it's too small or too large for what you want to do at that moment. To change the size of a window, follow these steps:

1. **Move the pointer over any corner or edge of the window to reveal a resizing handle.**

The resizing handle looks like a dash with arrows on both ends if you can make the window larger or smaller; it has just one arrow if the window has reached its size limits and can only be made smaller (or larger).

2. **Hold down the mouse or trackpad button with one finger or your thumb and drag the mouse, or a second finger on the trackpad, to move the resizing widget.**

- *If you have a two-button mouse,* hold down the left mouse button.

- *If you have a trackpad,* you can also tap when the pointer becomes a resizing widget, and then drag in the direction you want the window to grow or shrink.

- *If you have a trackpad,* move your cursor to the corner of a dialog. When it becomes a resizing widget, click and drag to resize the width and height simultaneously. Hold down the Shift key to resize the window proportionately.

   The window grows or shrinks while you drag or swipe.

3. **Release the mouse or trackpad button (or tap in the window if you're swiping) when you're happy with the new size of the window.**

Closing a window

When you finish viewing or editing any information displayed in a window, you can close the window to keep it from cluttering the screen. To close a window, follow these steps:

1. **Move the pointer to the upper-left corner of the window and then click the Close button (the little red button) of the window you want to close.**

   If you haven't saved the information inside the window, such as a letter you're writing with a word-processing application, the application displays a confirmation dialog that asks whether you want to save it.

2. **In the dialog that appears, click one of the following choices:**

   - *Don't Save:* Closes the window and discards any changes you made to the information inside the window.

   - *Cancel:* Keeps the window open.

   - *Save:* Closes the window but saves the information in a file. If this is the first time you've saved this information, another dialog appears, giving you a chance to name the file and to store the saved information in a specific location on your hard drive.

REMEMBER

Computers typically offer two or more ways to accomplish the same task, so you can choose the way you like best. As an alternative to clicking the Close button, you can click inside the window you want to close and then choose File⇨Close or press ⌘+W.

Minimizing a window

Sometimes you may not want to close a window, but you still want to get it out of the way so it doesn't clutter your screen. In that case, you can minimize or hide the window, which tucks it onto the Dock. (We explain the features and functions of the Dock a bit later in this chapter.)

To minimize a window, choose one of the following methods:

>> Click the Minimize button — the yellow button in the upper-left corner — of the window you want to tuck out of the way.

>> Click the window you want to minimize and choose Window⇨Minimize Window (or press ⌘+M).

>> Double-click the window's title bar.

To open a minimized window, choose ⬤⇨Recent Items and then click the minimized app or document in the list, or click the minimized window on the Dock, as we explain in the section "The Dock," later in this chapter.

Zooming a window

If a window is too small to display information, you can instantly make it bigger by using the Zoom button — the green button in the upper-left corner of most windows. (When you move the mouse over the Zoom button, a plus sign appears inside.) Clicking the Zoom button a second time shrinks the window to its prior size.

REMEMBER

Zooming a window makes the window — not the contents — grow larger. Many apps have sliders or menus that increase or decrease the size of the contents: 100 percent is the actual size; a lower percentage (such as 75 percent) shows more information at a smaller size; and a higher percentage (such as 200 percent) shows less information but may be easier on your eyes. Most word-processing applications have an option for Page Width.

Employing full-screen view

Most Apple apps and many third-party apps offer full-screen view. When available, the full-screen button (a line with an arrow on each end) appears in the upper-right corner of the title bar of the app window. When you click the full-screen button, the application fills the screen, and the menu bar is hidden from view. Hover the pointer at the very top of the screen to reveal the menu bar so you can point and click to use the menus. Move the pointer back to the window, and the menu bar disappears again. Press the Esc key or Control+⌘+F to return to normal view or click the full-screen button again, which you find by hovering the pointer over the upper-right corner.

TIP

If you use several applications in full-screen view, swipe left or right with four fingers across the trackpad or Control+→ or Control +← to move from one application to another. This is only for different desktops.

Scrolling through a window

No matter how large you make a window, it may still be too small to display all the information contained inside. If a window isn't large enough to display all the information inside it, the window lets you know by displaying vertical or horizontal scroll bars.

You can scroll what's displayed in a window two ways:

>> **Mouse or trackpad scrolling:** See the sections "Using the mouse" and "Operating the trackpad," later in this chapter, to learn how to use both the mouse and the trackpad. With either one, moving two fingers or the mouse up and down and left and right moves the contents of the window up and down, left and right.

>> **Scroll bars:** You can move the contents by

- *Dragging the scroll box:* Click and drag the gray oval scroll box in the scroll bar to move up/down or right/left in the window. This scrolls through a window faster than mouse or trackpad scrolling.

- *Clicking in the scroll bar:* Scrolls up/down or right/left in large increments or directly to the spot where you click.

    Although the scroll bar is the size of the window, it represents the length, or width, of the document; if you want to jump to page 25 of a 100-page document, click and hold in the upper quarter of the vertical scroll bar; to go to page 90, click and hold near the bottom of the scroll bar.

You can adjust the scroll bar's appearance — or eliminate the scroll bar altogether — which we explain in Book 1, Chapter 6.

Depending on your Mac model, your Mac's keyboard may have dedicated Page Up and Page Down keys, which you can press to scroll up and down. Not seeing Page Up and Page Down keys on your Mac or MacBook keyboard doesn't mean they aren't there. To use your Mac's invisible Page Up and Page Down keys, see the "Arrow and cursor control keys" section, later in this chapter.

Mastering the Mouse, Trackpad, and Keyboard

To control your Mac, you use the mouse or trackpad and the keyboard. Using the mouse or trackpad and the keyboard, you can choose commands, manipulate items on the screen, or create such data as text or pictures.

Using the mouse

A typical mouse looks like, and is about the size of, a bar of soap. The main purpose of the mouse is to move a pointer on the screen, which tells the computer, "See what I'm pointing at right now? That's what I want to select." To select an item on the screen, you move the mouse (which, in turn, makes the onscreen pointer move), put the pointer on that item, and then press and release (click) the mouse button, or press down the upper-left side of the mouse if you have a mouse, such as the Apple Magic Mouse, that doesn't have visible buttons.

The whole surface of the wireless Apple Magic Mouse uses touch-sensitive technology that detects your fingertip gestures just like the MacBook trackpads.

These are the basic mouse gestures to use with either mouse:

>> **Clicking (single-clicking):** This is the most common activity with a mouse. With the Magic Mouse, move the mouse and tap anywhere on the surface. If you have an older mouse with buttons, pressing the left mouse button, or the left side of the mouse, is *clicking*.

>> **Double-clicking:** If you point at something and tap twice in rapid succession on the surface (that is, you *double-click* it), you can often select an item and open it at the same time. (If you're using an older mouse, click the left mouse button or the mouse's single button twice in rapid succession to double-click.)

>> **Dragging:** Another common activity with the mouse is *dragging* — pointing at an item on the screen, holding down the left mouse button or the Magic Mouse's invisible single center button to select the item, moving the mouse (which drags the item in the direction you move the mouse), and then releasing the button. Clicking and dragging is often the way to open menus, too.

>> **Control-clicking/right-clicking:** Holding down the Control key while you click, or clicking the right button on the mouse, commonly displays a menu of commands (known as a *contextual menu* or *shortcut menu*) at the point you clicked to do something with the item that the mouse is pointing at. For example, in some apps (such as Pages), right-clicking a misspelled word displays a list of properly spelled words to choose from. Or, in Microsoft Word, access a list of synonyms by right-clicking a correctly spelled word and then dragging on the contextual menu to Synonyms, as shown in Figure 2-6.

On the Magic Mouse, hold down the Control key and tap to click. To simulate a right-click with a single-button mouse, hold down the Control key and click the mouse button. On a two-button mouse, click the right button.

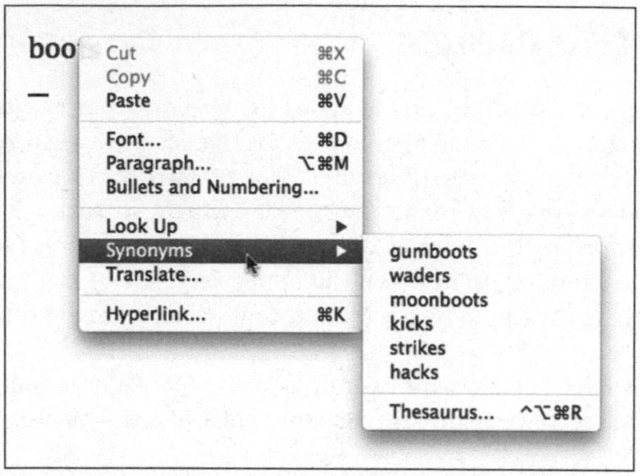

FIGURE 2-6:
Right-clicking
typically
displays a list of
commands.

boo	Cut	⌘X
	Copy	⌘C
—	**Paste**	⌘V
	Font...	⌘D
	Paragraph...	⌥⌘M
	Bullets and Numbering...	
	Look Up	▶
	Synonyms	▶
	Translate...	
	Hyperlink...	⌘K

gumboots
waders
moonboots
kicks
strikes
hacks

Thesaurus...   ^⌥⌘R

TIP

You can set up the Magic Mouse to function like an old-style two-button mouse by choosing ⇨ System Preferences. Click Mouse in the Hardware section and then select the Secondary Click check box. You can even choose left or right side, making it more natural if you're left-handed.

>> **Scrolling:** The surface of the Magic Mouse has the sensitivity of a trackpad, so you can move a finger up or down to scroll up and down the onscreen image (say, a word-processing document or a web page). Hold down the Control key while you scroll with one finger to zoom in on items on the screen.

>> **Swipe:** Swipe two fingers left and right on the Magic Mouse surface to move back and forth through web pages or to browse photos in Photos.

REMEMBER

If you don't like the mouse that came with your Mac, you can always buy a replacement mouse or a *trackball*, which looks like a golf ball embedded in a switch plate; you rotate the trackball with your fingers or palm to move the pointer instead of moving the entire mouse across your desk or mousepad. Some mice are ergonomically molded to be a better fit for the shape of your hand, so find a mouse that you like and connect it via the USB port of your Mac. Or, get a wireless mouse that connects to your Mac using your Mac's Bluetooth wireless connection feature.

Operating the trackpad

All current MacBook models sport trackpads that can do more than most advanced multi-button mice. If you have a desktop model or find the trackpad on a MacBook model inconvenient, you can opt for the Magic Trackpad, which will give you all the multitouch gestures explained in this section.

Thanks to the trackpad's smart sensing abilities, *point-and-click* has a whole new meaning because you're often using your index (or pointer) finger to move the pointer and then tapping once on the trackpad to click. A double-tap is the same as a double-click. Other gestures you can use with the trackpad are as follows:

>> **Scroll:** To move what you see on the screen up/down or left/right, slide or swipe two fingers up and down or left and right across the trackpad. The items in the window follow the movement of your fingers, the window contents move up when you move your fingers up.

>> **Rotate:** Move the window contents 360 degrees by placing two fingers on the trackpad and making a circular motion.

>> **Swipe:** Swipe the tips of three or four fingers across the trackpad to perform various tasks:

- Swipe up with three or four fingers to open Mission Control (see Book 1, Chapter 5), and then tap to close it or tap a different window to switch to it. You can also swipe down with three fingers to return to the previous window.

- Swipe left and right with three or four fingers to switch between full-screen applications or Desktops (see Book 1, Chapter 5).

REMEMBER

The default for swiping left or right is three fingers. To change to four fingers, choose ⇧app ⇧System Preferences ⇧Trackpad and then from the More Gestures tab choose Swipe Left or Right with Four Fingers from the Swipe between Full-Screen Apps pop-up menu.

>> **Pinch:** Place three fingers and your thumb slightly open on the trackpad, and then bring them together as if picking up a small item; doing so opens Launchpad (see Book 1, Chapter 5). Tap to close it or tap an icon to open a different app.

>> **Unpinch:** Place three fingers and your thumb together on the trackpad and open them to move everything off the Desktop. Pinch to bring everything back.

>> **Control-click:** Hold down the Control key and tap the trackpad or tap with two fingers.

>> **Click and drag:** Move the pointer to a menu, window title bar, file, folder, or just on the Desktop. Press and hold your thumb on the trackpad. Then, with another finger, drag down to open a menu, drag the title bar of an open window to move the window, or drag a closed file or folder to move the file or folder. On the Desktop, or if your windows are in Icon view (as explained in Book 1, Chapter 4), drag around multiple objects, as if you were lassoing them, to select a group. Click and drag across text to select it in an app you can type in, such as a word-processing or email app.

>> **Two-finger tap:** Tap the trackpad once with two fingers to Control-click/
right-click.

>> **Two-finger double-tap:** Tap the trackpad twice with two fingers to zoom in
on a web page.

>> **One-finger drag:** Move the pointer to the title bar of a window and move it
around on the Desktop with three fingers.

TIP

Choose ⬦ System Preferences and then click Mouse or Trackpad to specify how
you want to use the mouse or trackpad and to see examples of how the multitouch
gestures work, as shown in Figure 2-7.

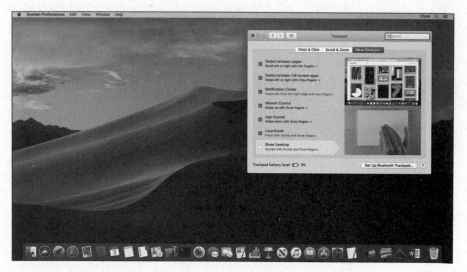

FIGURE 2-7:
See multitouch
gestures in
action in System
Preferences.

Examining the parts of the keyboard

The primary use of the keyboard is to type information. However, you can also
use the keyboard to select items and menu commands — sometimes more quickly
than using the mouse. Figure 2-8 shows how the keyboard groups related keys.
The next few sections cover each group of keys in detail.

Function and special feature keys

Depending on your particular keyboard, you may see 12 to 20 function and special feature keys running along the top of the keyboard. These keys are labeled F1
through F12/F19, along with an Esc key — short for Escape — and an Eject key
that looks like a triangle on top of a horizontal line.

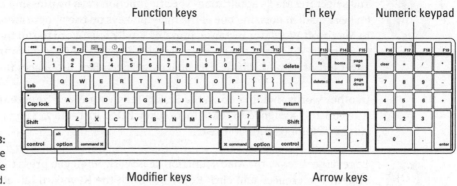

Function keys   Cursor control keys

Fn key   Numeric keypad

FIGURE 2-8:
The separate
parts of the
keyboard.

Modifier keys   Arrow keys

On Mac models made after April 2007, the function number appears in the lower-right corner of the key and a larger icon represents the special feature task that happens when you press the key to do things, such as turn down the screen brightness (F1) or play and pause music you're listening to in Music (F8). Although the icons on each of these special feature keys are self-evident, check out Table 2-1 to find out what all your Mac's special features keys do when you press them.

TABLE 2-1

Mac Assigned Commands

Function Key	What It Does
F1	Decreases display brightness
F2	Increases display brightness
F3	Displays Mission Control
F4	Displays Launchpad (displays Dashboard on older Macs)
F5	Decreases keyboard backlight brightness
F6	Increases keyboard backlight brightness
F7	Video and audio rewind
F8	Video and audio play/pause
F9	Video and audio fast-forward
F10	Mutes sound
F11	Decreases sound volume
F12	Increases sound volume

You select the Mac's application-specific function keys by pressing and holding the Fn key and *then* pressing one of the function keys on the upper row of the keyboard. In Microsoft Word, for instance, pressing Fn+F7 tells Word to run the spell checker; pressing Fn+F5 opens the Find and Replace dialog. The Fn key is often found at the lower left of a Mac keyboard; if you have a Touch Bar, it replaces the Fn key.

In other words, holding down the Fn key tells your Mac, "Ignore the special feature controls assigned to that function key listed in Table 2-1 and just behave like an old-fashioned function key."

TIP

To reverse the way the Mac's function keys work when you press them, choose ⇨ System Preferences and click Keyboard. Click the Keyboard tab at the top of the window, and then select the check box next to Use All F1, F2, Etc. Keys as Standard Function Keys. When you activate this option, you *must* hold down the Fn key to perform the commands shown in Table 2-1, but you don't have to hold down the Fn key to use app-specific function keys.

Here are some additional tips for getting the most out of the function and special feature keys:

>> **Shortcut commands:** As for the other keys — F1–F7 and (possibly) F13–F19 — holding the Fn key and pressing these keys can carry out shortcut commands on a by-application basis.

>> **Escape and Eject:** The Esc key often works as a "You may be excused" command. For example, if a drop-down menu appears on the screen and you want it to go away, press the Esc key. The Eject key ejects a CD or DVD from your Mac. (If your MacBook Pro or Air came without a disc drive, there's no Eject key.)

TECHNICAL
STUFF

Originally, function keys existed because some applications assigned commands to different function keys. Unfortunately, every application assigned different commands to identical function keys, which sometimes made function keys more confusing than helpful. You can assign your own commands to different function keys, but just remember that not every Mac will have the same commands assigned to the same function keys. (Not everyone thinks exactly as you, as amazing as that may seem.) To customize which function keys perform which commands, choose ⇨ System Preferences, click Keyboard, and then click the Keyboard Shortcuts tab at the top of the window; adjust your Mac's keyboard shortcuts to your heart's content.

Typewriter keys

When you press a typewriter key, you're telling the Mac what character to type at the cursor position, which often appears as a blinking vertical line on the screen.

TIP

You can move the cursor by pointing to and clicking a new location with the mouse or by pressing the arrow keys, as explained in the upcoming "Arrow and cursor control keys" section.

TIP

Just because you don't find a character labeled on your keyboard doesn't mean you can't type that character. Holding down Shift, Option, or Shift+Option while pressing another key on the keyboard results in different symbols or letters, such as uppercase letters or the symbol for a trademark or square root.

To see all the key combinations, follow these steps:

1. **Choose ⇨ System Preferences and then click Keyboard.**

2. **Click the Keyboard tab and then select the Show Keyboard & Emoji Viewers in Menu Bar check box.**

3. **Close System Preferences.**

   A menulet for the Keyboard & Emoji Viewers appears in the menu bar at the top of your screen.

4. **Click the Keyboard & Emoji Viewers icon and then click Show Keyboard Viewer.**

   A graphic representation of the keyboard appears on your screen, as shown in Figure 2-9.

FIGURE 2-9: Keyboard Viewer.

5. **Hold down the Shift, Option, or Shift+Option keys.**

   The keyboard changes to show the letter or symbol that will be typed when you hold down Shift, Option, or Shift+Option and type a letter or number.

   Refer to the Cheat Sheet for more information about typing special characters. (Turn to the Introduction of this book for instructions on accessing the Cheat Sheet.)

In addition to keys that type letters and characters, you'll find keys that don't type anything but nevertheless play an important role:

>> **Delete:** Appears to the right of the +/= key. The Delete key deletes any characters that appear to the left of the cursor. If you hold down Delete, your Mac deletes any characters to the left of the cursor until you lift your finger.

>> **Tab:** This key indents text in a word processor and moves from cell to cell in a spreadsheet app, but it can also move from text box to text box in a form, like when you type a shipping address for an online merchant.

>> **Return:** Moves the cursor to the next line in a word processor, but can also choose a default button (which appears in blue) on the screen. For example, the Print button is the default button in the Print dialog, so pressing Return in the Print dialog sends your document to the printer.

TIP

The Return key is also entitled Enter, which is handy for first-time Mac users used to a PC keyboard.

TIP

Press ⌘+Tab to revert to the last open application you used. This keyboard shortcut also displays an icon for each application you have open. Click the desired icon to work in that application or use the arrow keys to scroll between applications.

Modifier keys

Modifier keys are almost never used individually. Instead, modifier keys are usually held down while tapping another key. Included in the modifier keys category are the function keys mentioned in a few of the previous sections (which you use in combination with the Fn key), along with the Shift, Control, Option, and ⌘ keys.

Here's an example of how modifier keys work. If you press the S key in a word-processing document, your Mac types the letter *s* on the screen. If you hold down a modifier key, such as the ⌘ key, and then press the S key, the S key is modified to behave differently. In this case, holding down the ⌘ key followed by the S key (⌘+S) tells your word-processing application to issue the Save command and save whatever you typed or changed since the last time you saved the document.

Most modifier keystrokes involve pressing two keys, such as ⌘+Q (the Quit command), but some modifier keystrokes can involve pressing three or four keys, such as Shift+⌘+3, which saves a snapshot of what you see on your screen as an image file, which is commonly referred to as a *screenshot*.

The main use for modifier keys is to help you choose commands quickly without fumbling with the mouse or trackpad to use menu commands. Every application includes dozens of such keystroke shortcuts, but Table 2-2 lists the common keystroke shortcuts that work the same in most apps.

TABLE 2-2

Common Keystroke Shortcuts

Command	Keystroke Shortcut
Copy	⌘+C
Cut	⌘+X
Paste	⌘+V
Open	⌘+O
New	⌘+N
Print	⌘+P
Quit	⌘+Q
Save	⌘+S
Select All	⌘+A
Undo the previous command	⌘+Z
Redo the previous command	⌘+Y

Most Mac apps display their keystroke shortcuts for commands directly on their drop-down menus, as shown in Figure 2-10.

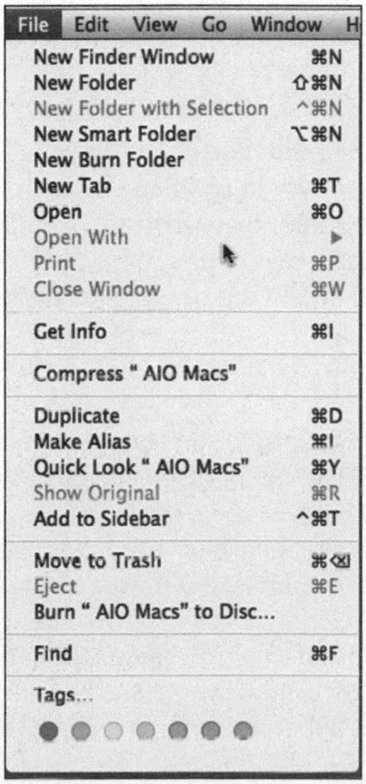

FIGURE 2-10: Most drop-down menus list shortcut keystrokes for commonly used commands.

The Caps Lock key, when active (as indicated by the green light on the key), lets you type in all capital letters but doesn't affect the function of modifier keys combined with letters.

Most Mac apps display their keystroke shortcuts for commands directly on their drop-down menus (refer to Figure 2-10).

Instead of describing the modifier keys to press by name (such as Shift), most keystroke shortcuts displayed on menus use cryptic graphics. Figure 2-11 displays the different symbols that represent shortcut commands.

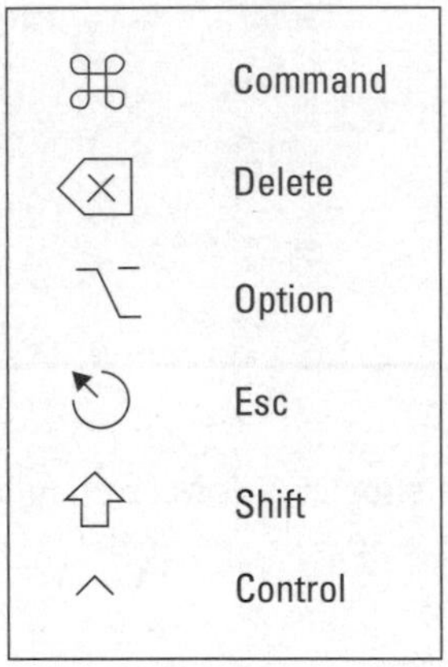

⌘	Command
⌫	Delete
⌥	Option
↺	Esc
⇧	Shift
⌃	Control

FIGURE 2-11: A guide to symbols for keystroke commands.

Numeric keypad

The numeric keypad appears on the right side of the keyboard (if your keyboard has one!) and arranges the numbers 0–9 in rows and columns like a typical calculator keypad. It also features other keys that are useful for mathematical calculations. The main use for the numeric keys is to make typing numbers faster and easier than using the numeric keys on the top row of the typewriter keys.

Arrow and cursor control keys

The pointer becomes a cursor when you use the keyboard to enter data in any type of app or even when naming a file. The cursor often appears as a vertical blinking line and acts like a placeholder. Wherever the cursor appears, that's where your next character will appear if you press a keyboard key. You can move the cursor with the mouse or trackpad, or you can move it with the arrow keys.

The up arrow moves the cursor up, the down arrow moves the cursor down, the right arrow moves the cursor right, and the left arrow moves the cursor left. (Could it be any more logical?) Depending on the application you're using, pressing an arrow key may move the cursor in different ways. For example, pressing the right arrow key in a word processor moves the cursor right one character, but pressing that same right arrow key in a spreadsheet may move the cursor to the adjacent cell on the right.

On some Mac keyboards, you may see four additional cursor control keys: Home, End, Page Up, and Page Down. Typically, pressing the Page Up key scrolls up one screen, and pressing the Page Down key scrolls down one screen. Many applications ignore the Home and End keys, but some applications let you move the cursor with them. For example, Microsoft Word uses the Home key to move the cursor to the beginning of a line or row and the End key to move the cursor to the end of a line or row, and ⌘+Home/End moves the cursor to the beginning or end, respectively, of a document.

TECHNICAL STUFF

Just because you may not see the Home, End, Page Up, and Page Down keys on your Mac keyboard doesn't mean those command keys aren't there. For example, on the MacBook, holding down the Fn key and then pressing the left arrow key acts as the Home key, which moves the cursor to the start of the line that the cursor is in. Pressing Fn+→ jumps the cursor to the end of the current line, Fn+← moves the cursor to the beginning of the current line, Fn+↑ scrolls the text up one page, and Fn+↓ scrolls the text down one page. Also, ⌘+Fn+←/→ moves the cursor to the beginning or end, respectively, of the document. Because seeing is believing, try it on your own Mac keyboard — even if you don't see keys bearing those actual labels.

To the left of the End key on a full keyboard, you may find a smaller Delete key. Like the bigger Delete key, this smaller Delete key also deletes characters one at a time. The difference is that the big Delete key erases characters to the *left* of the cursor, but the small Delete key, sometimes labeled Del, erases characters to the *right* of the cursor. If your keyboard lacks the Del key, you can hold down the Fn key while pressing the Delete key to erase characters to the right of the cursor.

Getting to Know the Parts of the Desktop

Consider your physical desk: You keep the things you use most frequently, like a calculator or day planner, out in the open so you can grab them easily. Likewise, if you start leaving documents about, sooner or later there are so many that you can't see the surface, so you divvy up the documents and place related ones in folders, keeping only the most pertinent folders on your desk and putting the others in a filing cabinet to be pulled out when needed.

The theory behind the Mac Desktop — the screen you see most of the time — is the same. Windows open on the screen display the documents or files you're working on. Windows cover part of — or, when you use a full-screen app, all of — the Desktop. File and app icons are like those documents and tools you keep on your physical desk. Unfortunately, the more icons you store on the Desktop, the more cluttered it appears, making it harder to find anything — just like your physical desk. Organizing your app and files into folders makes things easier to find and your virtual desktop more orderly. In addition, you can place frequently used apps and files on the Dock, which is a quickly accessed area of the Desktop.

The Desktop generally shows an icon that represents your hard drive — think of it as your filing cabinet. If you have any additional storage devices attached to your Mac (such as an external hard drive, a CD or DVD drive, or a USB flash drive), you typically see icons for those storage devices on your Desktop, too. We describe the menu and menulets at the beginning of this chapter. Here we take a look at the other parts of the Desktop: the Dock and the Finder.

TIP

The cool thing about the virtual Mac Desktop is that you can have more than one, and we explain how to do that in Book 1, Chapter 5.

The Dock

The *Dock* is a rectangular strip that contains app, file, and folder icons. It lies in wait just out of sight either at the bottom or on the left or right side of the Desktop. When you hover the pointer in the area where the Dock is hiding, it appears, displaying the app, file, and folder icons stored there. When you use your Mac for the first time, the Dock already has icons for many of the preinstalled apps, as well as the Downloads folder and a Trash icon. You click an icon to elicit an action, which is usually to open an app or file, although you can also remove the icon from the Dock or activate a setting so that app opens when you log in to your Mac. We tell you about working with apps in the Dock in Book 1, Chapter 5; here, we tell you how to change the Dock's appearance.

When you open an app that isn't on the Dock, a temporary icon appears there; when you quit that app, the icon disappears from the Dock. You can add icons to the Dock for apps, folders, or files you use frequently. To help keep your icons organized, application icons appear on the left side of a divider and file icons on the right side, as shown in Figure 2-12.

FIGURE 2-12:
The Dock.

Applications

Files

By default, the Dock appears at the bottom of the screen, and the icons have a standard size. Like most things on your Mac, however, the Dock is flexible, and you can move it to the left or right of the screen and modify the size of the icons. If you move the Dock to the side of the screen, the application icons are above the divider, and the file icons are below.

The Dock occupies a fixed amount of real estate at the bottom of your screen. Unless you magnify the Dock, the app and file icons shrink each time you add more app and file icons to it. (We explain how to customize the icons on the Dock in Book 1, Chapter 5.) Fortunately, the name of the application above the pointer appears to tell you what application it is, and you can turn on magnification in the Dock section of Preferences, which makes Dock icons zoom in size when you move the pointer over them (refer to Figure 2-12).

To make changes to the Dock's appearance, follow these steps:

1. **Choose System Preferences and then click Dock.**

The Dock preferences pane, shown in Figure 2-13, appears.

2. **Drag the Size slider to adjust the size of the Dock.**

When you decrease the size of the Dock, the icons shrink as well. In our humble opinion, the best option is to drag the size slider to Large, especially if you have a lot of app icons parked on the dock.

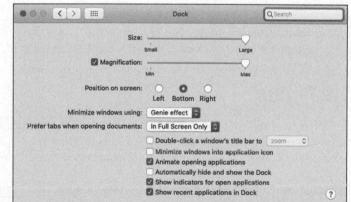

FIGURE 2-13: Control the appearance and position of the Dock.

3. **Select (or clear) the Magnification check box.**

4. **Drag the Magnification slider to adjust the magnification of the Dock.**

Magnification makes the icons appear larger as you move the pointer over them, which is especially helpful if you have a small Dock with a lot of items on it.

REMEMBER

5. **Click the radio button for your preferred location for the Dock: Left, Bottom, or Right.**

6. **From the Prefer Tabs When Opening Documents drop-down list, select how you want apps and files to open when clicked in the Dock:**

   - *Genie Effect:* When you open or minimize a file or app, it exits and enters the Dock like a genie being pulled in and out of a magic lamp.

   - *Scale Effect:* Files or apps exit and enter the Dock in a simple, linear fashion.

7. **Select the check boxes next to the other display choices to turn them on or off, as you prefer.**

8. **Click the Close button of the Dock preferences pane.**

When you click the Minimize window button (the yellow button in the upper-left corner of an app), a minimized window icon on the Dock actually displays the contents of that window, and sometimes continues playing the content. If you squint hard enough (or have a large enough screen), you can see what each minimized window contains. Reopen minimized windows as you would any other file or app, hover the pointer over the window and then click; the window pops back up on the Desktop.

REMEMBER

If you select the Minimize Windows into Application Icon check box in the Dock preferences pane (refer to Figure 2-13), any windows you minimize will be kept with the app icon. Click and hold the app icon; then select the name of the file that was in the window to open it.

If you have multiple monitors, you can move the Dock from one monitor to the other. No matter where the Dock is, it still has the same behavior.

The Finder

The Finder is an app that lets you find, copy, move, rename, delete, and open files and folders on your Mac. You can run apps directly from the Finder, although the Dock makes finding and running apps you use frequently much more convenient.

The Finder runs all the time. To switch to the Finder, do one of the following:

>> Click an area of the Desktop outside any open windows.

>> Click the Finder icon on the Dock. The Finder icon is the one with a blue Picasso-like face. It's located on the far left of the Dock, if your Dock is on the bottom of your Desktop, or on the top of the Dock, if your Dock is on the left or right side of your Desktop.

You know you're in the Finder because the app menu at the upper left of the screen is Finder, as opposed to Pages, System Preferences, or some other app name.

Open a new Finder window by choosing File⇨New Finder Window or by right-clicking the Finder icon in the Dock and choosing New Finder Window. You can open as many Finder windows as you want, although it's common just to have one Finder window open and several tabs within that window for the folders and devices you want quick access to.

Because the Finder helps you manage the files stored on your hard drive, a Finder window consists of two panes and multiple tabs, as shown in Figure 2-14.

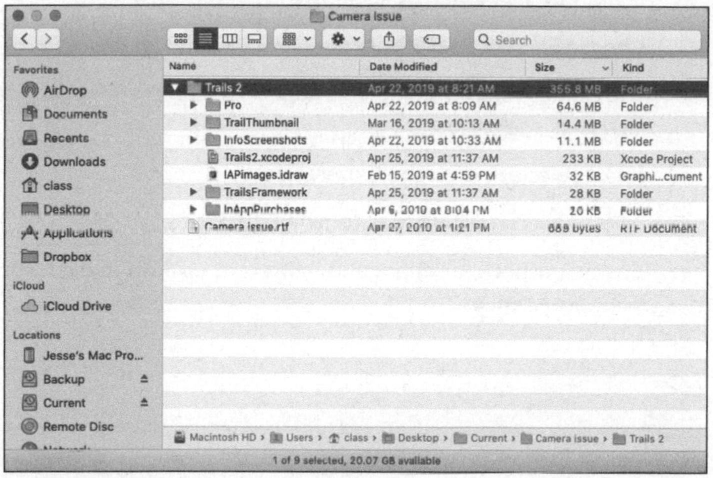

FIGURE 2-14:
The Finder displays panes and tabs to help you navigate to different parts of your hard drive.

The left pane — the *Sidebar* — displays up to four different categories:

>> **Favorites:** Lists things like Applications, Desktop, Documents Downloads, Movies, Music, and pictures. You can customize what appears in the Favorites section of your Finder Sidebar, as shown in Book 1, Chapter 4.

>> **iCloud:** Lists iCloud Drive, which is a cloud storage you can set up to share documents across all your devices (iPhone, iPad, and so on).

>> **Locations:** Lists your Mac, as well as all the storage devices connected to your Mac, such as hard drives, external drives, and CD/DVD drives. Again, you can customize what appears in the Locations section of your Finder Sidebar in the Finder preferences.

>> **Tags:** Lists tags you can apply to files; clicking a tag shows all the files tagged with that criteria.

Getting Acquainted with the Mac User Interface

The right pane of the Finder displays the contents of an item selected in the Side-bar. For example, if you click a hard drive icon in the Sidebar, the right pane displays the contents of that hard drive. All apps and files displayed in a Finder window or tab appear as icons with text labels, regardless of which type of view you chose to view the Finder window.

You find out how to use and customize the Finder, as well as create tabs, tags, and folders in the Finder, in Book 1, Chapter 4.

TIP

You can change what your Mac displays on the Desktop. To do so, follow these steps:

1. **Switch to the Finder by clicking the Finder Dock icon.**

2. **Choose Finder⇨Preferences.**

    The Finder Preferences window appears. When the Window opens, the section last used is selected.

3. **If not selected, click the General icon.**

    A list of options appears, as show in Figure 2-15.

4. **Check, uncheck, or change the different options in each section to suit your preferences.**

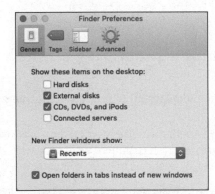

FIGURE 2-15: Select what you want to see on the Desktop in the Finder Preferences window.

Getting to Know Siri

If you have an iPhone or iPad, you're probably already familiar with Siri. Siri is the virtual assistant that's built into many Apple devices, including the Mac. Siri for the Mac was first introduced with the Mac OS Sierra operating system.

REMEMBER

The Mac Mini and Mac Pro do not have built in microphones. To use Siri on either machine, you need a compatible external USB microphone. Once the microphone is attached, you can set up the microphone sensitivity on the Input tab of Audio Preferences.

A *virtual assistant* is software that can respond to verbal commands. A basic virtual assistant needs to have the ability to respond to commands such as "What time is it?" A more sophisticated virtual assistant can pull together information from several sources.

In this section, we give you an example of how Siri can function for you, walk you through some complex Siri commands, and show you how to configure Siri and get Siri working for you.

Exploring a basic Siri interaction

Here's an example of Siri in action. You can ask, "What time is it?" (You see how to set up Siri so it can wait for your requests shortly.)

Siri (on your Mac) responds by repeating your question and, if possible, providing an answer, as shown in Figure 2-16.

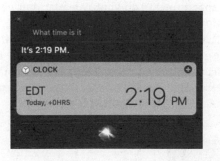

FIGURE 2-16:
Asking Siri what time it is.

You can ask Siri to perform tasks such as reminding you to do something, as shown in Figure 2-17. When you ask Siri to schedule an appointment for you, you have the option to change or remove the appointment if something is wrong.

In Figure 2-18, you can see that we asked Siri to remind us not only to walk the dog but to do it "tomorrow morning at 8:30." Siri knows what today is, so it can set an appointment for "tomorrow" on the correct date in our calendar. Siri also interprets "morning" as 8:30 a.m.

FIGURE 2-17:
Siri can remind
you when to
perform a task.

FIGURE 2-18:
Siri can respond
to complex
requests.

You can tell Siri to make appointments on your calendar, but your virtual assistant can also give you information about those appointments. For example, in Figure 2-19, you can see that we asked Siri to tell us what appointments we have "next Thursday," and the response is that we don't have any. Importantly, the response shows that Siri has interpreted "next Thursday" as "May 16, 2019." Siri can make mistakes in interpreting "next" or "this" when referring to dates, so providing the exact date allows you to verify that it's correct.

FIGURE 2-19:
Siri can work
with contexts.

A good example of using "next" is shown in Figure 2-20, when we asked what the next holiday is. Because Siri has access to our calendar and we have default holidays listed, Siri can tell us that the next holiday is Saint Florian's Day.

If by some chance you're not familiar with Saint Florian's Day, you can ask Siri for information, as shown in Figure 2-21. Siri can look up the holiday on the web.

FIGURE 2-20:
Siri can tell us the
next holiday in
our calendar.

FIGURE 2-21:
Siri can look up
information on
the web.

Using complex Siri commands

After you use Siri for a while, you'll get a sense for what works. Siri can learn, in the sense that you can allow Siri to have access to your data. You'll also see what types of commands work. You don't have to be too fussy, because Siri can help you formulate queries and commands in ways that it can act upon.

REMEMBER

When you ask Siri to perform a task or look up information, speak slowly and clearly. Do not turn away from the computer when you speak as the microphone on most Mac computers (except the Mac Mini and Mac Pro, which do not have built-in microphones) is in the top center of the display frame.

For example, in Figure 2-22, you can see Siri responding to a question that it can't answer ("Let me know when my doctor's appoint is" in the case where there is no doctor's appointment in the calendar).

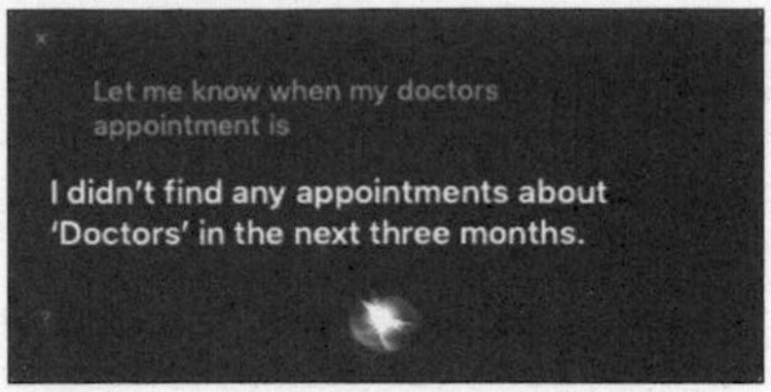

FIGURE 2-22:
Siri can handle
complex
commands that
may not have a
simple answer.

In a case like this, where you don't have an appointment for Siri to report, you could go into your calendar to create one, or you can make the appointment with Siri instead of using the keyboard. Note that the information that we've given to Siri is incomplete, as shown in Figure 2-23. We didn't specify the time, and Siri asked us for that information.

FIGURE 2-23:
Siri can ask for
missing data.

You can reformulate your request (see Figure 2-24) or just provide the missing data. Many people find that while they're using Siri in this way, Siri is, in effect, training *them* to formulate requests in the ways that Siri can manage. In addition, Siri itself is learning about you.

FIGURE 2-24:
We've learned
to formulate a
request for Siri.

Configuring Siri

Siri is a virtual assistant — some very advanced software — but you can control how it appears. Choose ⌘➪System Preferences, and then click Siri. As shown in Figure 2-25, you can choose the language and voice for Siri to use, as well as the keyboard shortcut to activate Siri on your Mac.

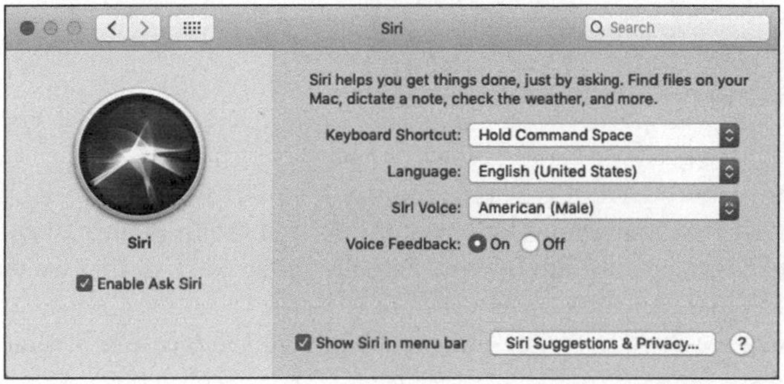

FIGURE 2-25: Configure Siri from System Preferences.

Click the Siri Suggestions & Privacy button at the lower right of the dialog to control which of your data Siri can access (see Figure 2-26).

FIGURE 2-26: You can control the data to which Siri has access.

Empowering Siri

The more you use Siri, the more you'll see what you can do with it. One of the most interesting aspects of Siri is how it handles voice recognition. There's an example of this in Figure 2-27, where we asked Siri to tell us when our last appointment with our friend Uta was. You can see at the top of Figure 2-27 that Siri interpreted "Uta" (pronounced oo-tah) as "water."

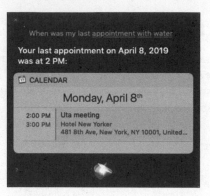

FIGURE 2-27:
Siri can look up
unknown words
by sound.

The name "water" was unrecognized, so Siri was able to look for words that it *knows* that may sound like "water." As you see in Figure 2-27, Siri took a known word that sounds like Uta and actually found the meeting we were looking for!

Now, we can use Siri or our mouse to find the location of that meeting (refer to Figure 2-27).

REMEMBER

Relying on speech to interact with a computer is sometimes a strange or even difficult experience at first, but when you get used to it, you'll see how simple it can be.

WARNING

Siri and speech are not appropriate for every situation. There are some places where you don't want to annoy people or let them know what you're doing (for example, when you're working on your Mac in a coffee shop). For all the many cases where you *can't* use speech or Siri, you *can* use menus, dialogs, and windows, as always.

TIP

If you need a break, and you're a fan of the rock group Queen, say the following to Siri, "I see a little silhouetto of a man." Then sit back and listen.

Getting Help

Theoretically, the Mac should be so easy and intuitive that you can teach yourself how to use your computer just by looking at the screen. Realistically, the Mac can still be confusing and complicated — otherwise, there would be no need for this book! We've done our best to give you steps and tips to handle any Mac task you come across, but we've probably missed a few things. And sometimes it may just help to read the same task explained in a different way. So, any time you're confused when using your Mac and you can't find the answers in this book, try turning to your Mac for help with your Mac!

Your Mac offers two types of help:

» **It can point out specific menu commands to choose for accomplishing a specific task.** For example, if you want to know how to save or print a file, Mac Help will point out the Save or Print command so you know which command to choose.

» **It can provide brief explanations for how to accomplish a specific task.** By skimming through the brief explanations, you can (hopefully) figure out how to do something useful.

Here's how you can access both types of help:

1. **Click the Help menu at the far-right end of the menu bar for any application you're running.**

   Or you can switch to the Finder by clicking the Finder icon on the Dock, and then click Help.

   A Search text box appears.

2. **Begin typing a word or phrase.**

   If, for instance, you want help with printing a document, type **print**. While you type, a list of possible topics appears.

   Help topics for the application you're running appear first under the Menu Items category, followed by the Help Topics category.

3. **Move your pointer over a Menu Items topic.**

   A floating arrow points to the command on a menu to show you how to access your chosen topic for the application you're running, as shown in Figure 2-28.

4. **If you want to read a Help article on a specific subject, click one of the topics under Help Topics.**

   If you're accessing Help from the Finder, you're taken to a page from the macOS User Guide, as shown in Figure 2-29. You can also access the macOS User Guide in the Finder by choosing Help⇔macOS Help.

   If you're accessing Help from a third-party application, like Microsoft Word, you're taken to that application's Help documentation.

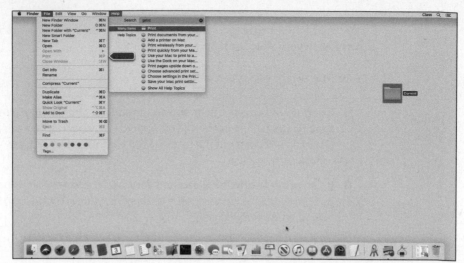

FIGURE 2-28:
macOS Help
shows you
how to access
a particular
command.

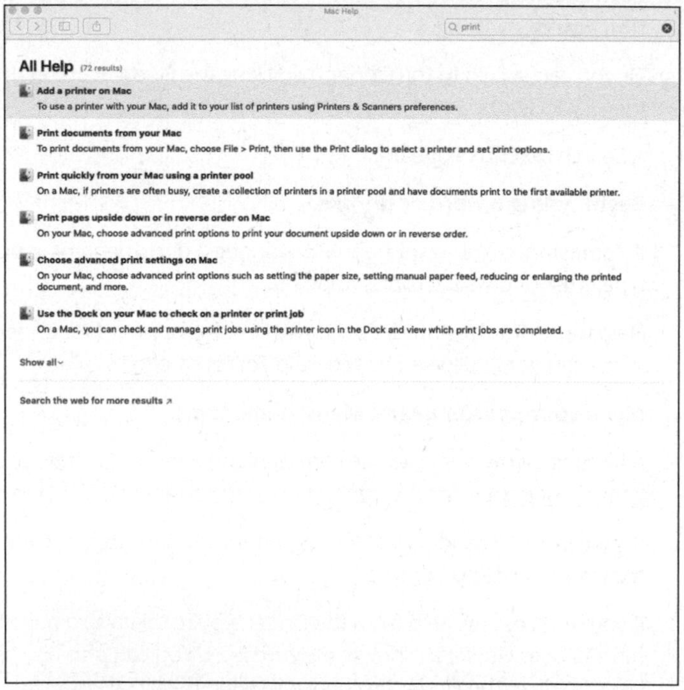

All Help (72 results)

Add a printer on Mac
To use a printer with your Mac, add it to your list of printers using Printers & Scanners preferences.

Print documents from your Mac
To print documents from your Mac, choose File > Print, then use the Print dialog to select a printer and set print options.

Print quickly from your Mac using a printer pool
On a Mac, if printers are often busy, create a collection of printers in a printer pool and have documents print to the first available printer.

Print pages upside down or in reverse order on Mac
On your Mac, choose advanced print options to print your document upside down or in reverse order.

Choose advanced print settings on Mac
On your Mac, choose advanced print options such as setting the paper size, setting manual paper feed, reducing or enlarging the printed document, and more.

Use the Dock on your Mac to check on a printer or print job
On a Mac, you can check and manage print jobs using the printer icon in the Dock and view which print jobs are completed.

Show all ⌄

Search the web for more results ↗

FIGURE 2-29:
The macOS
User Guide.

Chapter **3**

Making Your First Connections

For most people, an Internet connection is no longer an option but a necessity. You can use a computer all by itself, but to get the most out of your Mac, you need an Internet connection. An Internet connection gives you access to the World Wide Web, but equally important, it lets you use the Mail, FaceTime, Messages, and Maps apps; shop in the iTunes app, the App Store and Apple's Book Store; sync Calendar, Contacts, Notes, and more across different devices; plus share photos and documents with iCloud and other Apple and third-party apps.

In this chapter, we explain how to connect your Mac to the Internet. Then we walk you through creating an Apple ID, which you use for iCloud, FaceTime, and shopping in the iTunes app, the App Store, and the Apple Book Store. After you have an Apple ID, we show you how to set up iCloud and explain the various iCloud options. At the end of this chapter, we explain how to add email accounts from other providers, such as Office 365 and Google, as well as social networks like Facebook and LinkedIn. Many apps that came with your Mac access information from these accounts, so setting them up at the beginning makes your Mac experience easier down the road.

Setting Up an Internet Connection

From a technical point of view, to connect to the Internet, your Mac must connect to another computer, run by a company called an Internet service provider (ISP), through which your Mac actually connects to the Internet. The ISP may offer one or both of the following connections:

>> Broadband, which travels across fiber, digital service (DSL) phone lines, digital terrestrial television cable service, cellular data, or satellite connections

>> Analog or dial-up, which is generally too slow to do more than send and receive simple text email messages

Most likely you already have a broadband Internet connection in your home either through your cable or phone service provider, but if you don't, ask around to find out what's available in your area. Some providers, including Xfinity (Comcast) and AT&T, let you connect to the Internet when you're away from home through Wi-Fi *hotspots*, which provide Internet access in public locations.

Many phone accounts let you use your iPhone or other smartphone as a mobile hotspot. This may incur additional charges, so check with your carrier before relying on your phone's hotspot as your primary Internet connection.

TIP

If you live in an area where Internet service is unavailable or limited to dial-up, check into using a cellular data modem or satellite Internet service.

Regardless of the type of broadband service, to connect your Mac to an ISP, you have two options:

>> **Ethernet:** You connect your Mac physically to the modem with an Ethernet cable.

>> **Wireless:** Your Mac connects to the modem wirelessly. A wireless connection is a wonderful thing — you can connect other computers and devices wirelessly, such as your phone and tablet.

Ethernet connection

A broadband Ethernet connection is the fastest way to connect to the Internet. Essentially, you connect a modem to the digital cable or DSL outlet, and then connect one end of an Ethernet cable to the modem and the other end to the Ethernet port of your Mac. (If you have a MacBook Air or a newer MacBook Pro, you need a USB-to-Ethernet adapter.) After you connect your Mac to the modem, you can usually start using the Internet right away.

To confirm your connection, choose ●⇨System Preferences, click the Network icon, and look for "Ethernet Connected" in the list of services. For more information about setting up a network and sharing a single Internet connection with multiple computers, see Book 3, Chapter 3.

You can usually lease a modem from your ISP or purchase one separately, although you want to be sure the one you purchase meets your ISP's specifications (check with your provider). Each modem comes with its own instructions, which you should refer to when setting up your Ethernet connection.

TECHNICAL STUFF

When you connect your Mac to a broadband modem by using your Mac's Ethernet port, your Mac can recognize the Internet connection right away through the Dynamic Host Configuration Protocol (DHCP): Your Mac automatically figures out the proper settings to connect to the Internet without making you type a bunch of cryptic numbers and fiddle with confusing technical standards.

Your Mac can also connect to your broadband modem wirelessly if the modem you buy (or rent from your ISP) has a built-in Wi-Fi router, which your Mac's built-in AirPort Wi-Fi feature can access. (See the next section for more on AirPort.)

TIP

New networking technologies — referred to as *mesh Wi-Fi systems* — let you create efficient networks with a variety of clients. If you're setting up a new network, check with your ISP or carrier to see what your options are, because they may have changed since the last time you checked.

Wireless (Wi-Fi) access

Wireless broadband access is popular because it allows you to connect to the Internet without stringing cables through your house to trip over. Every new and recent Mac comes with a built-in wireless capability.

You then connect to a wireless network, whether in your home or at another location if you're using a MacBook that you can take wherever you go. Public libraries and many coffeehouses offer free wireless Internet access, as do many hotels and motels, which is handy when you're traveling. Your ISP may offer Wi-Fi *hotspots*, which let you access the Internet in public locations where they offer service. You can set up your own wireless network at home or work (see Book 3, Chapter 3) by using a wireless router that lets several computers and other Wi-Fi-able gadgets (such as video game consoles, iPhones, iPads, and some printers) share a single Internet connection.

Choosing a wireless router

A *wireless router* connects to your modem — cable, DSL, cellular, or satellite — and broadcasts radio signals to connect your Mac wirelessly to the Internet. Most cable and DSL modems come with built-in Wi-Fi transmitters, giving you one device that does the job of two Wi-Fi devices.

If you choose to use a separate Wi-Fi router to connect to your modem, you can find excellent compatible devices on Apple's website at www.apple.com/shop/mac/mac-accessories/networking. (Apple discontinued its AirPort Time Capsule, AirPort Extreme, and AirPort Express in 2018.)

Here are the key considerations in purchasing a router:

>> **Speed:** The brand name of your wireless router is less important than the speed offered by the router, which is determined by the wireless standard the router uses. A *wireless standard* simply defines the wireless signal used to connect to the Internet.

>> **Compatibility:** To connect to a wireless network, you need to make sure that your router and your Mac's built-in wireless use the same wireless standard. (See Table 3-1.) All new and recent Macs connect preferably to Wi-Fi routers that use the 802.11ac standard but are compatible with all five types of the wireless network standards.

REMEMBER

The 802.11ac standard, which is the most common at the time of writing, offers good range and high speed.

Table 3-1 lists the different wireless standards in use today.

TABLE 3-1

Wireless Standards and Router Speeds

Wireless Standard	Speed	Indoor Range
802.11a	Up to 54 Mbps	30 meters (98 feet)
802.11b	Up to 11 Mbps	35 meters (114 feet)
802.11g	Up to 54 Mbps	35 meters (114 feet)
802.11n	Up to 248 Mbps	70 meters (229 feet)
802.11ac	Up to 1.3 Gbps	90 meters (295 feet)

The upload/download speed of wireless standards is measured in megabits per second (Mbps) — or, with the super-fast 802.11ac, gigabits per second (Gbps), although this maximum speed is rarely achieved in normal use. The speed and range of a wireless Internet connection also degrade with distance and obstacles, such as walls or heavy furniture that stand between the Wi-Fi router and your Mac. The 802.11g standard also suffers interference from peripherals (such as wireless keyboards) that use the 2.4 GHz band. The 802.11ac standard uses 5 GHz signals, which make it almost impervious to interference and also uses a beaming (instead of broadcasting) technology, so it targets devices that are connected to it.

TIP

The most important words in Table 3-1 are *Up to.* The actual speed you get is dependent on many variables, including how many people are using a cable system at the time you're using it, as well as a variety of other sometimes obscure factors. If a cable comes into your house (where it would be connected to a modem), windstorms can cause the cable's connection to vary, but not necessarily fail. There are also reports that some wireless connections are degraded by wet leaves on large trees.

TIP

If you're using lots of devices on your Wi-Fi networks or the signal is weak in certain areas of your house, consider purchasing one or more Wi-Fi boosters.

Connecting to a Wi-Fi network

Each router or modem will have its own set of instructions, which you should refer to when setting up your Wi-Fi network at home or in your office. In general, you connect the router to the modem that's connected to the DSL, digital terrestrial, or satellite outlet, turn the router on, and then access the router administration tools through a web browser (Safari on your Mac) to set up the network name and password.

You can connect your Mac to a wireless network (say, at a café or a Wi-Fi network in your home) by following these steps:

1. **Click the Wi-Fi icon in the right corner of the menu bar to open a pull-down menu displaying a list of any Wi-Fi networks within range of your Mac, and then select the network name you want to connect to, as shown in Figure 3-1.**

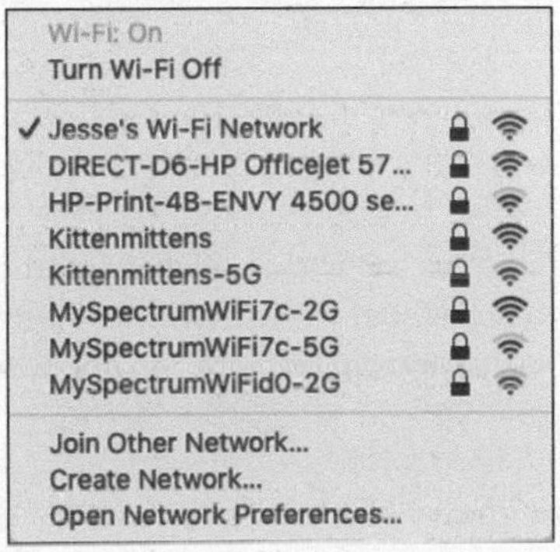

> Wi-Fi: On
> **Turn Wi-Fi Off**
>
> ✓ Jesse's Wi-Fi Network 🔒 📶
> DIRECT-D6-HP Officejet 57... 🔒 📶
> HP-Print-4B-ENVY 4500 se... 🔒 📶
> Kittenmittens 🔒 📶
> Kittenmittens-5G 🔒 📶
> MySpectrumWiFi7c-2G 🔒 📶
> MySpectrumWiFi7c-5G 🔒 📶
> MySpectrumWiFid0-2G 🔒 📶
>
> Join Other Network...
> Create Network...
> Open Network Preferences...

FIGURE 3-1:
See nearby
Wi-Fi networks.

(sidebar) Making Your First Connections

If you see WiFi: Off when you click the Wi-Fi icon on the menu bar, choose Turn WiFi On and then click the Wi-Fi menu icon again to display a list of any nearby wireless networks (refer to Figure 3-1).

If you don't see the Wi-Fi icon on the menu bar, choose ⌘ ⇨ System Preferences, click the Network icon, and then select the Show Wi-Fi Status in Menu Bar check box.

A lock icon to the left of the network's signal strength indicates a *secured* (also known as *encrypted*) wireless network that is protected by a password. You must know what password to enter when prompted if you try to connect to a secured network.

You can enter the name of a network you want to join, as shown in Figure 3-2. You'll be asked to enter a password if the network is secure.

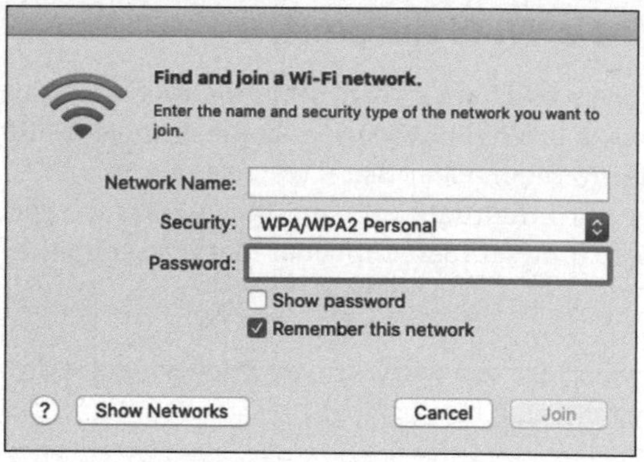

Find and join a Wi-Fi network.

Enter the name and security type of the network you want to join.

Network Name:

Security: WPA/WPA2 Personal

Password:

☐ Show password

☑ Remember this network

(?) Show Networks   Cancel   Join

FIGURE 3-2:
A secure Wi-Fi network requires a password to connect to it.

2. **(Optional) Select the following options on the password dialog prompt:**

- *Show Password:* Displays actual characters you type instead of dots that hide your password. With long, mixed-character case-sensitive passwords, it can be helpful to see what you type — just make sure that no one is looking over your shoulder.

- *Remember This Network:* Remembers that you have connected to the selected network before and then connects to it automatically whenever you're within range of its signal. This option is handy if the network is at a place you visit frequently, such as a friend or relative's house or your workplace. (If you chose to remember more than one wireless network in the same location, your Mac always connects to the one with the strongest signal first.)

The Wi-Fi icon on the menu bar shows black bars to indicate the strength of the Wi-Fi network signal your Mac is connected to. Like with mobile phone reception (and gold), more bars are better.

You're now free to choose any activity that requires an Internet connection, such as running Safari to browse the news on *The New York Times* website (www.nytimes.com) or launching Messages to partake in a video chat with a friend who's also connected to the Internet and signed in to Messages.

WARNING

When you connect to a wireless network that doesn't require you to enter a password, your Mac essentially broadcasts any information you type (such as credit card numbers or passwords) through the airwaves. Although the likelihood of anyone actually monitoring what you're typing may be small, tech-savvy engineers or hackers can "sniff" wireless signals to monitor or collect information flowing through the airwaves. Whenever you connect to a public Wi-Fi network, assume that a stranger is peeking at your data and type only such data that you're comfortable giving away to others. Connecting to a secured network that requires you to type a password to connect to it can lessen the likelihood that anyone is monitoring or collecting what you're typing.

Cellular data modem

If you're on the move a lot with your MacBook and go to places that don't have Wi-Fi service, a cellular data modem may be a good solution. These devices, which look like flash drives or small mobile phones, hold a SIM card just like the one in your smartphone, and they use your selected cellular carrier to connect to the cellular broadband data network. And, like your mobile phone, you don't have to plug into the phone line. With 3G, 4G, and LTE network availability, service is acceptable for simple tasks: reading and sending email, surfing the web, or even watching a short video. Some cellular data modems are freestanding and can support Wi-Fi connections for three to five devices at a time. Others are *plug-and-play:* You plug the device into your Mac's USB port, enter the associated password (provided by the modem and cellular service provider), and *voilà!* You're online.

TIP

Many smartphones, including the latest versions of the Apple iPhone, enable you to use the device to create a Wi-Fi hotspot. This option is handy when there is no Wi-Fi available. This uses your phone's cellular service to connect to the Internet. You can then connect your MacBook to your phone's hotspot network. Note that this option may incur data charges from your cellular phone service provider.

Establishing Your Apple Identity

When you first turn on your Mac (or install an upgrade to the operating system), a series of questions and prompts appear, including a prompt to sign in to your Apple ID account or create a new Apple ID.

An Apple ID identifies you and your devices in all things Apple that you do: registering new products, purchasing media and apps from the iTunes Store, the Book Store, and the App Store, as well as signing in to your iCloud account.

iCloud is Apple's remote syncing and storage service. See the "Keeping Your Data in iCloud" section for more information on why you might want to use iCloud.

You might already have an Apple ID — in which case you can either skip this section or continue reading for information on adding an iCloud account to the mix. You can use the same Apple ID for everything, iCloud and Apple Music included, or create separate Apple IDs for separate accounts. *Note:* If you've used Apple products long enough that you still have one of the very old Apple IDs that isn't an email address, you do have to set up a new account to use iCloud.

In the next sections, we explain two ways to create an Apple ID.

TIP

If you don't have an email address or want to create an @icloud.com email as your Apple ID and use it for all your Apple interactions, set up a new Apple ID from within iCloud in System Preferences (we show you how to do that in the next section), not during the Mac setup. When you set up an Apple ID during the Mac setup, you must use an existing non-Apple domain email address — because if you have an Apple domain email address, that is your Apple ID and you use that to sign in.

Creating an Apple ID during Mac setup

When you first turn on your Mac, the onscreen dialog prompts you to sign in with your Apple ID or create a new one. Read through these steps to see what to expect:

1. **Click one of the following on the opening screen:**

- *Sign In with Apple ID:* Type in your existing Apple ID and password and then click Continue.

- *Create Apple ID:* The Apple ID website (https://appleid.apple.com) opens. Type the information requested in the fields on the form: Use an existing email address as your Apple ID, choose three security questions and answers, and provide your date of birth and an optional rescue email that's different than your Apple ID email. Complete the form with your mailing address (so the products you order online can be shipped to you), select your preferred language from the pop-up menu, select the email you want to receive from Apple, type the Captcha word, select the check box to concede your agreement to the Terms of Service, and finally, click the Create Apple ID button.

- *Use Separate ID for iCloud and Apple Music:* The iCloud icon is highlighted in the center of the screen. Enter the Apple ID you use with iCloud or click Create Apple ID, which takes you to the Apple ID website as we explain in the previous bullet. Click Continue. The iTunes and App Stores icons are highlighted; type in the Apple ID you use with them or click Create Apple ID and repeat as above. (Using separate Apple IDs is not necessary.)

REMEMBER

If you want to create an Apple ID with an @icloud.com suffix, click Don't Sign In and confirm your choice by clicking the Skip button in the dialog that appears. Go to the next section to create an Apple ID and email address in iCloud.

2. **If you sign in with an existing Apple ID, you are prompted to do the following:**

- Turn on Find My Mac, which we suggest you do.

- Choose three security questions and answers.

- Agree to the Terms of Service.

The message in the window lets you know your Mac is being set up, and then the Desktop appears.

Using two-factor authentication

Online security is a bigger concern than ever these days. There are three highly recommended techniques for keeping yourself safe online:

>> You can use yourself (that is, your fingerprint or face). This is called *biometric security*. Touch ID, which is available on the latest MacBooks, can implement a biometric feature.

>> Devices with cameras that support FaceID can use your face for login.

>> Two-factor authentication requires you to use two devices to log in. It is highly secure, and don't panic: You don't need two Macs (but they will work). If you happen to have your iPad or iPhone nearby, you can use it for authentication. This means that you need to authenticate yourself to your iPhone and your Mac.

To set up two-factor authentication, you need to provide the alternate device information to be used during login. If you're using the same Apple ID on both your Mac and your iPhone or iPad, the Apple ID is used automatically. You can also provide the phone number of your phone.

Here's what two-factor authentication looks like after you've established two devices with the same Apple ID or provided your phone number and turned the two-factor authentication on when you're setting up your iCloud account. This is an example of a case in which you're logging in to your Mac and using your iPhone as the second factor (the process is the same if you log in to your iPhone and use your Mac as the second factor).

1. **Log in to your Mac with your Apple ID as usual.**

   You receive an automated message on your iPhone, as shown in Figure 3-3. It contains a six-digit verification code that can only be used once. (This code is sent either to your Apple ID devices or to your phone.)

FIGURE 3-3: Log in and receive a verification code on your iPhone.

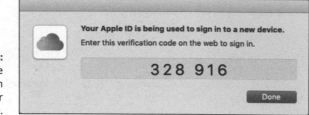

Your Apple ID is being used to sign in to a new device.
Enter this verification code on the web to sign in.

328 916

Done

2. **On your Mac, enter the code that appeared on your phone, as shown in Figure 3-4.**

   If you want an alternate verification code, you can ask for it by clicking Didn't Get a Verification Code, as shown in Figure 3-4.

3. **If you're asked if you trust the browser (see Figure 3-5), click Trust.**

Creating an Apple ID in iCloud

We find creating and using an @icloud.com email address as your Apple ID convenient because you need remember only one password for all your interactions with Apple, and we like to think there's added security for the information you sync across devices using iCloud when using an Apple domain rather than Google mail, Yahoo!, or one of the other email service providers. (For more info on the benefits of iCloud, see the next section.)

TIP

If you use the iCloud email only for exchanges with Apple, notifications about product updates or invoices don't get lost in the shuffle of myriad messages in a more active email account.

FIGURE 3-4:
Enter your
verification code
on your Mac.

FIGURE 3-5:
Verify that you
trust the browser.

Here we show you how to create an Apple ID with iCloud and then segue into managing your iCloud preferences in the next section.

1. **Choose ⬄ System Preferences or click the System Preferences icon on the Dock. Then click the Internet Accounts button.**

   The Internet Accounts window opens.

2. **Click the iCloud button in the left column.**

   The iCloud preferences window opens.

3. **Click Create Apple ID.**

4. **Enter your Date of Birth, and then click Next.**

   The Create an Apple ID window opens, as shown in Figure 3-6.

5. **Select the Get a Free iCloud Email Address link.**

   This appears right below the "This will be your new Apple ID" message.

6. **Type in your email address, first name, last name, and password.**

   Your password must be at least eight characters and contain at least one number, one uppercase letter, and one lowercase letter.

7. **(Optional) Select the check box for Apple News & Announcements information.**

8. **Click Next.**

   If someone else already uses the name you chose, you're prompted to type an alternative. It may take a few tries to find an unused name.

9. **Select three security questions and answers from the pop-up menus that appear on the next window.**

10. **Type in a rescue email, which is different than the iCloud email address you just created.**

    Apple uses this address to communicate with you in the event you completely forget your iCloud email address and password. There are various services that let you create an email address that is free, like Gmail; however, check that "free" doesn't mean that you're allowing access to your data in exchange for the email account.

11. **Click Next.**

12. **Select the check box to confirm that you read and agree to the Terms of Service, and then click Continue.**

13. **The iCloud activation screen opens, as shown in Figure 3-7.**

    Leave both check boxes checked.

FIGURE 3-7: Activate iCloud syncing and Mac locating features.

14. **Click Next.**

    You're asked to provide security features for your account. These features change from time to time as Apple tightens security. Among the options you may be asked for are passphrases you can use, as well as a device that you can use to confirm access (known as two-factor authentication, covered in the preceding section).

    Figure 3-8 shows some of the security mechanisms in use at the time of this writing.

15. **When requested, type a mobile phone number that will be used to send approval codes to your mobile phone when you access iCloud Keychain from another device.**

    This adds additional security to iCloud Keychain access.

Making Your First Connections

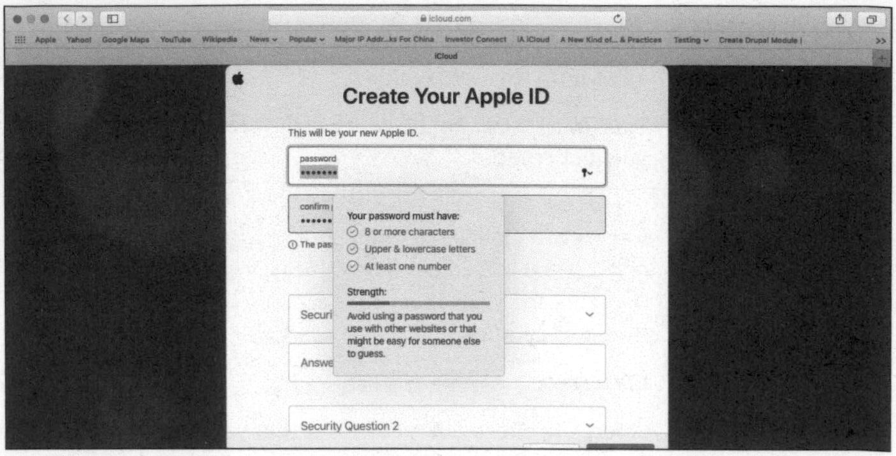

FIGURE 3-8:
Create an Apple
ID security
code here.

16. **Click Next.**

iCloud opens, as shown in Figure 3-9.

A list of Apple apps that work with iCloud appears, and check marks indicate which are active. The data in checked apps can sync across all devices — computers, iPhones, iPads, iPod touches — that sign in to the same iCloud account. Some apps have options that you can use to refine what is or isn't allowed for that app when it interacts with iCloud.

FIGURE 3-9:
Sync apps with
iCloud across all
your devices.

YOUR LEGACY APPLE ID

New Apple IDs take the form of an email address. If you have an Apple ID that you created several years ago, it may be in the form of a name, such as barbaradepaula. If your Apple ID isn't an email address, you can continue to use it for iTunes, App, and Book Store purchases, though. Just know that you have to create a different Apple ID for iCloud because that service requires the email address ID format.

Keeping Your Data in iCloud

iCloud remotely stores and syncs data that you access from various devices — your Mac and other Apple devices, such as iPhones, iPads, and iPods, and PCs running Windows. Sign in to the same iCloud account on different devices, and the data for activated apps *syncs*; that is, you find the same data on all your devices, and when you make a change on one device, it shows up on the others. iCloud works with the following Apple apps and the data within them:

>> Contacts (known as Address Book in earlier versions of Mac OS X)

>> Calendar (known as iCal in earlier versions of Mac OS X)

>> Reminders

>> Mail

>> Notes

>> Safari bookmarks, reading list, tabs, and viewing history

>> Photos from both Photos and Aperture

>> Music and television shows

>> iWork apps (Pages, Numbers, and Keynote)

>> Preview

>> TextEdit

>> Keychain

>> GarageBand

TIP

iCloud also works with third-party iCloud–enabled apps, such as iA Writer.

Here are some situations where iCloud can make your life easier:

>> You want to back up the songs you add to the Music app and TV show collections.

>> You use both a Mac and an iOS device, such as an iPhone, iPad, or iPod touch.

>> You want to access Contacts, Calendar, and Mail from more than one computer — Mac or Windows — say, one for work and one at home.

>> You keep a calendar that other people need to see and maybe even edit.

>> You want to activate Find My Mac to keep tabs on your Mac's location and relocate it should it be lost or stolen.

The initial setup on your Mac or the creation of an iCloud Apple ID as explained previously activates your iCloud account and places a copy of the data from Mail, Contacts, Calendar, Notes, Reminders, and Safari from your Mac to the cloud (that is, the Apple data storage equipment). Here, we show you how to work with the iCloud preferences, sync devices, and sign in to and use the iCloud website.

TIP

If you use a Windows PC in addition to your Mac, you can download the iCloud Control Panel 3.0 for Windows at https://support.apple.com/en-us/HT204283, which enables iCloud storage and syncing in Windows. You then access the iCloud apps through iCloud.com and Microsoft Outlook.

Configuring iCloud preferences

You can choose which apps you want to use with iCloud and how they can be used. For example, you may want to keep Contacts and Calendars synced across all your devices but prefer that Notes stay separate because you use Notes on your iPhone for shopping lists that you don't need on your Mac. Here's how to customize how you work with iCloud:

1. **Choose ❖⇨System Preferences and then click the Internet Accounts button.**

The Internet Accounts window appears.

2. **If you haven't signed in to iCloud, click the Sign In button, enter your Apple ID and password, and click Sign In.**

3. **Click iCloud.**

The iCloud window appears displaying your iCloud account information.

4. **Click the Options button that is to the right of the iCloud Drive icon.**

The iCloud Drive options window appears (see Figure 3-10). This window enables you to choose which documents are stored in iCloud.

FIGURE 3-10:
Specify which documents are stored in your iCloud drive.

5. **Specify which documents you want to store in your iCloud drive.**

Click the check mark that corresponds to each app that contains documents that you want to store in your iCloud drive.

6. **(Optional) Click the Manage button in the lower right to see the data that occupies your allotted iCloud storage, as shown in Figure 3-11.**

Click each item in the list on the left to see the files for each. Backups (top of this list) keeps the backups of your iOS devices — *not your Mac*. iCloud keeps documents and data for iCloud-enabled apps but *does not back up your entire Mac*. See Book 3, Chapter 1 to learn about backing up your Mac.

7. **(Optional) Click the Buy More Storage button.**

A free iCloud account gives you 5 gigabytes (GB) of storage — but songs purchased from the Apple Music Store or up to 25,000 tracks in iTunes Match (if you're subscribed) plus photos in PhotoStream don't count toward that amount. In PhotoStream, iCloud stores up to 1,000 photos from the last 30 days. You can purchase additional storage for a yearly subscription fee if necessary, as shown in Figure 3-12.

If you decide to purchase additional storage, click the desired storage amount and then click Next. Follow the onscreen instructions to add your personal and payment information.

FIGURE 3-11:
Manage storage
for the apps
you want to
use with iCloud.

FIGURE 3-12:
Upgrade
and increase
your iCloud
storage here.

8. **Click Done.**

9. **Click the Close button in the upper left to quit System Preferences.**

Syncing with your other devices

The only reason this topic has a heading is so it stands out because it couldn't be simpler. To sync iCloud app specific documents, such as Pages documents, and data from apps such as Calendar and Contacts with your iOS devices, do the following:

1. **Tap Settings on the Home screen of the device you want to sync with iCloud.**

2. **Tap iCloud.**

3. **Sign in to your iCloud account.**

4. **Tap the apps you want to use to the on position.**

   The data in each app is automatically synced between your Mac and your iOS device.

REMEMBER

You must have an Internet connection to use iCloud.

Using the iCloud website

To manage your data on iCloud, you can go to the iCloud website. Follow these steps:

1. **Click the Safari icon on the Dock or from Launchpad. (See Book 2, Chapter 1 to read about using Safari.)**

2. **Type** www.icloud.com **in the URL field in Safari.**

   The iCloud website opens with the sign in fields.

3. **Type in your Apple ID or the email you used when you set up your iCloud account (see Figure 3-13), and then type your password.**

FIGURE 3-13:
Signing in to an iCloud account.

4. (Optional) Select the Keep Me Signed In check box if you want to stay connected to iCloud even when you go to other websites or quit Safari.

5. Press the Enter key or click the arrow button.

Your name appears in the upper-right corner, and icons that take you to your activated services appear in the window, as shown in Figure 3-14.

FIGURE 3-14: Click the icons to go to the data you want.

6. Click any of the icons to go to the app you want.

7. From the app window, click the cloud button in the upper-left corner to return to the opening iCloud web page.

8. Click the arrow to the right of your name and choose Sign Out to close iCloud.com.

Note that when you sign out, you have the option to trust the browser you're using and won't need to trust the browser the next time you sign into the iCloud website.

Setting Up Email and Social Network Accounts

Even if you've created an Apple ID and set up iCloud, you may use a different account for email and associated services such as calendars and contacts. Additionally, you might want to link contacts and events from your social networks to Contacts and Calendar. You can sync the data between apps on your Mac (such as Mail, Calendar, and Contacts) and the online apps (such as Google or Twitter). Here we show you how to add accounts to your Mac and activate the services and data you want to share.

Adding accounts

Many email accounts offer contact and calendar management, and even note-taking services, too. Your email address and password identify and give you access to your account. The three types of email accounts you can set up are

>> POP (Post Office Protocol)

>> IMAP (Internet Message Access Protocol)

>> Exchange

A POP email account usually transfers (moves) email from the POP server computer to your computer. An IMAP or Exchange email account stores email on its server, which allows access to email from multiple devices. Most individuals have POP accounts, whereas many corporations have IMAP or Exchange accounts. If your organization has other types of accounts, you can talk to them about setting them up. One of the advantages of the bring your own device (BYOD) movement is that IT departments now have more information about setting up Macs.

You can use dozens of email applications, but the most popular one is the free Mail app that comes with your Mac. If you don't like Mail, you can download and install a free email app, such as Thunderbird (www.mozilla.org/en-US/thunderbird) or Mailsmith (www.mailsmith.org).

REMEMBER

You can access your email from Mail (or a different email app) on your Mac, from a web browser on your Mac, or on another computer, such as at your friend's house or in an Internet café. When you use a web browser, you go to the email provider's website.

Gathering your account information

To make Mail work with your email account or link Contacts and Calendar to a social network account like Facebook or Twitter, you need to gather the following information:

>> **Your username (also called an *account name*):** Typically a descriptive name (such as nickyhutsko) or a collection of numbers and symbols (such as nickyhutsko09). Your username plus the name of your email provider or ISP defines your complete email address, such as nickyhutsko@gmail.com or lilypond@comcast.net.

>> **Your password:** Any phrase that you choose to access your account. If someone sets up an email account for you, he might have already assigned a password that you can always change later.

For Mail, you might also need the following two bits of information, so have them handy if you can:

>> **Your email account's incoming server name:** The mail server name of the computer that contains your email message is usually a combination of POP or IMAP and your email account company, such as pop.comcast.net or imap.gmail.com.

>> **Your email account's outgoing server name:** The name of the outgoing mail server that sends your messages to other people. The outgoing server name is usually a combination of SMTP (Simple Mail Transfer Protocol) and the name of the company that provides your email account, such as `smtp.gmail.com` or `smtp.comcast.net`.

REMEMBER

If you don't know your account name, password, incoming server name, or outgoing server name, ask the company that runs your email account or search on the provider's website. If you're unable to find the information, chances are you might still be able to set up your email account on your Mac, thanks to the Mail app's ability to detect the most popular email account settings, such as those for Gmail or Yahoo!.

Configuring your account

After you collect the technical information needed to access your account, you need to add it to the Internet Accounts on your Mac by following these steps:

1. **Choose ⌘⇨System Preferences or click the System Preferences icon on the Dock or from Launchpad.**

   Click the Internet Accounts button.

2. **Click the plus sign at the bottom of the window to reveal a list of other accounts you can add, as shown in Figure 3-15.**

FIGURE 3-15: Add accounts from those listed.

3. **Click the name of the account you want to add, such as Google, Exchange, Yahoo!, or AOL.**

If the type of email account you want to add is not listed (for example, if you have an email account from your company's domain or your personal domain such as StoogeCurly@mydomain.com), click the Add Another Account button and choose the type of account you want to add.

If you choose Add Another Account, choose one of the following options: @ Mail account (if you have an email account from your own domain), CalDAV account, CardDAV account, LDAP account, or Game Center account. After choosing an option, an account information window opens, similar to Figure 3-16.

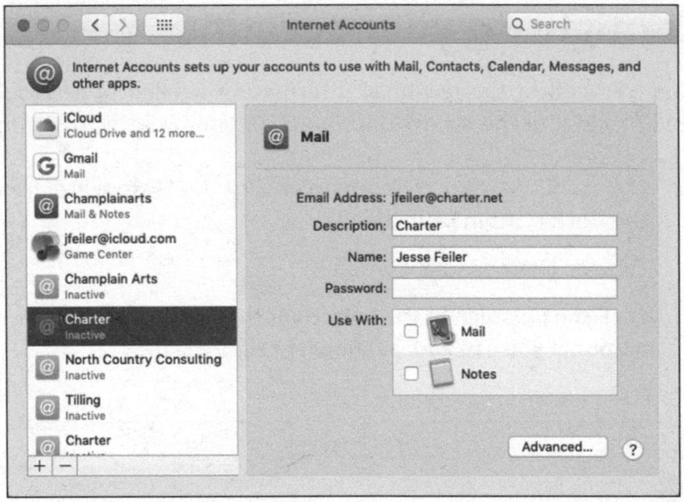

FIGURE 3-16:
Activate the account.

4. **Type your name, email address, and password, and any other requested information (each type of account is slightly different).**

A Set Up button will appear when you've provided all the information. If a button such as Set Up doesn't appear, make sure you've provided all the requested information.

5. **Click Set Up when you're done.**

Your account is verified and a list of services appears, such as Contacts or Calendar.

6. **Click the services you want to use.**

For example, if you choose Contacts, all the entries in your Contacts app will be stored in iCloud.

As you add accounts, they appear in the list on the left of the window (refer to Figure 3-15).

7. **(Optional) Edit or delete accounts:**

- *Edit:* Click an account to edit the services it provides: for example, to add Notes to your Gmail account or deactivate Contacts from Facebook.

- *Delete:* Click an account and then click the minus sign to delete it from your Mac.

8. **Click the Close button to quit System Preferences.**

REMEMBER

After you add an account, you access its contents in other apps, such as Mail, Contacts, Calendar, and Safari.

IN THIS CHAPTER

» **Using the Finder**

» **Organizing and viewing folders**

» **Tagging files and folders**

» **Searching with Spotlight**

» **Setting up Smart Folders**

» **Deleting files and folders**

Chapter **4**

Working with Files and Folders

When you need to organize stuff scattered around the house, one strategy would be to toss everything in the middle of the floor. However, it's probably easier to take a more organized approach by storing off-season clothes in one box, retired gadgets in another box (to be taken to the local recycling center or your favorite charity), bills in one file folder, and new books you want to read — or your e-book reader — on your nightstand.

Computers work in a similar way. Although you *could* dump everything on the top level of your hard drive, it's more helpful to divide your hard drive in a way that can help you sort and arrange your stuff in an orderly, easy-to-get-to fashion. Instead of boxes or shelves, the Mac uses *folders* (which tech-types like Joe also refer to as *directories*). In a nutshell, a folder lets you store and organize related files.

This chapter is dense with information, but familiarizing yourself with the way your Mac organizes documents, applications, and files will make everything you do on your Mac a lot easier. We tell you several ways to do the same thing so you can choose the way that's easiest for you to do and remember. We begin by explaining the *Finder*, which is the tool you use to organize your files and folders. Next, we show you how to create and manage folders. We also tell you about *tags,* a feature added in OS X Mavericks, which helps you quickly identify and find folders and files. Later in the chapter, we shine a light on your Mac's search tool, Spotlight Search, as well as on how files and folders work on iOS devices (the same as on your Mac but with one significant difference). At the end of the chapter, we spell out the procedure for deleting files and folders.

Getting to Know the Finder

The *Finder* manages drives, devices, files, and folders on your Mac. To access the Finder, click the Finder icon (the smiley face icon on the far left or top) on the Dock. The Finder is divided into three parts, as shown in Figure 4-1:

» A *toolbar* that runs across the top of the window and contains buttons that you use to control and manage the files and folders in the Finder.

» A left pane showing the *Sidebar,* which is where you find a list of connected storage devices as well as commonly used folders.

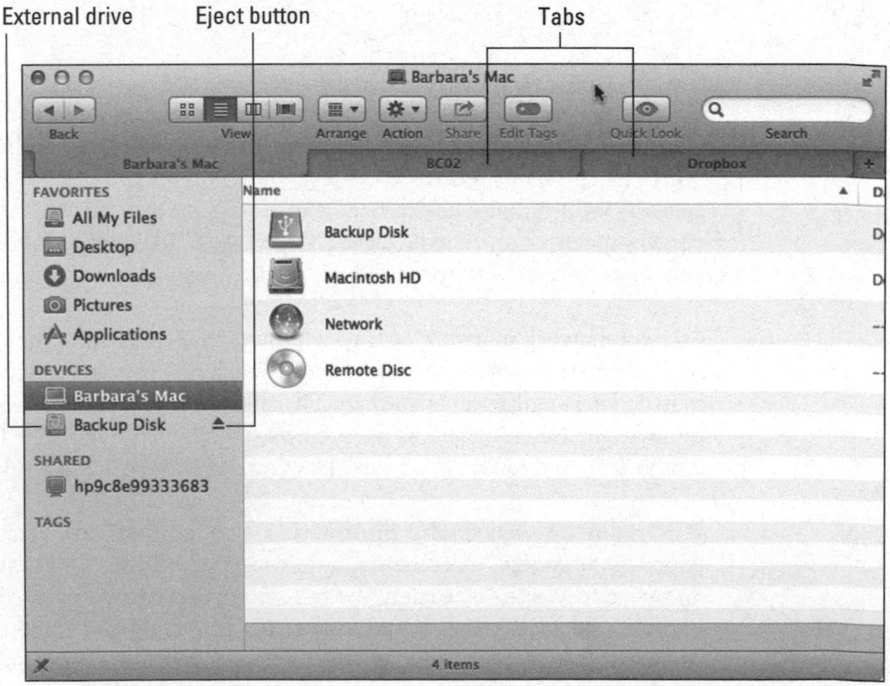

FIGURE 4-1:
The Finder displays the files, folders, and devices connected to your Mac.

>> A right pane showing the contents of the selected drive or folder (or search results if one was performed). If you switch to List, Column, or Cover Flow view, which we explain in the section "Organizing and Viewing Folders," the right pane also shows a hierarchy of files — and even other folders — stored inside folders.

The right pane may be further divided into *tabs*, which are essentially panes within the pane that display different folders open simultaneously, although only the one in view on top is active.

TIP

You can choose to hide or show either or both the toolbar and Sidebar by choosing the appropriate command from the Finder's View menu.

Handling devices

The Devices category of the Sidebar lists your Mac (Barbara's Mac in Figure 4-1) and any devices, remote or cabled, connected to your Mac, as well as any mounted disk images, which can appear when you download software updates or large files.

When you click your Mac in the Device category of the Sidebar, you see the internal hard disk drive (HDD) or solid state drive (SSD), which is named Macintosh HD by default. This is the drive that your Mac boots from. If your desktop Mac has a second hard drive installed, it appears in the Devices list.

The other devices listed here are those that you plug into your Mac, such as an external hard drive, a USB flash drive, or a digital camera. One external drive, Backup Disk, is connected in Figure 4-1. These removable devices can be connected and disconnected at any time.

To connect a removable device to your Mac, just plug it in with the appropriate FireWire, Thunderbolt, or USB cable. The icon for the device appears in the Devices list and on the Desktop.

You can eject a removable drive when you no longer need to access it or want to take it with you. Ejecting a removable hard drive or USB flash drive removes its icon from the Finder and Desktop and allows you to then safely disconnect it from your Mac.

WARNING

If you physically try to disconnect a removable drive before you eject it, your Mac might mess up the data on that drive. Always eject removable drives before physically disconnecting them.

To remove a removable device from a Mac, do one of the following:

>> Click the Finder icon on the Dock to open the Finder window, and then click the Eject button next to the connected drive you want to remove in the Finder window Sidebar.

>> Click the device icon on the Desktop and choose File⇨Eject.

>> Click the device icon and press ⌘+E.

>> Control-click the device icon and choose Eject from the shortcut menu that appears.

>> Drag the device icon to Trash on the Dock (it turns into an Eject button); then let go of the mouse.

If the removable device is a CD/DVD, your Mac ejects it. If the removable device is plugged into a USB (Universal Serial Bus) port (or a FireWire port on an older Mac), you can then physically disconnect the device.

Understanding folders

All the data you create and save by using an application (such as a word-processing document or a photograph you copy from your digital camera to your Mac's hard drive) is stored as a *file*. Although you can store files on any storage device, the more files you store on a device, the harder it is to find the one file you want at any given time (but wait to read about Spotlight later in this chapter for a great way to find things). Much like you would place related paper documents in a manila folder rather than stack them willy-nilly on your desk, folders on your Mac help you organize and manage electronic files on a storage device in a logical way. You can even store folders inside other folders.

Initially, every Mac hard drive contains the following folders:

>> **Applications:** Contains all the apps installed on your Mac. When you open Launchpad, you also see all the apps that are stored in the Applications folder.

>> **Library:** Contains data and settings files used by applications installed on your Mac, fonts, and plug-ins used by applications such as Internet web browsers.

>> **System:** Contains files used by the OS X operating system. You shouldn't change this folder.

Never delete, rename, or move any files or folders stored in the Library or System folders, or else you might cause your Mac (or at least some apps on your Mac) to stop working. Files in the Library and System folders are used by your Mac to make your computer work. If you delete or rename files in either

WARNING

folder, your Mac might not operate the way it's supposed to — or (worse) grind to a halt.

>> **Users:** Contains any files that you — and anyone else who uses your Mac — create and save, including documents, pictures, music, and movies.

Home folders are kept in the Users folder; each account on your Mac is assigned a Home folder when the account is set up. (See Book 3, Chapter 2 for more information about creating accounts.) The Home folder has the same name as the account and shouldn't be renamed. The Home folder of the user who is logged in looks like a little house.

Each Home folder automatically contains the following folders when an account is set up. Notice that these folders have icons on them.

>> **Desktop:** Contains any application and document icons that appear on your Mac's Desktop.

>> **Documents:** Contains any files you create and save by using different applications. (You'll probably want to organize this folder by creating multiple folders inside it to keep all your files organized in a logical, easy-to-manage way.)

>> **Downloads:** Contains any files you download from the Internet. After being downloaded, you'll want to move them to an appropriate folder or, if you download apps, install them.

>> **Library:** Contains folders and files used by any applications installed on your Mac. (***Note:*** There are three Library folders: one stored on the top level of your hard drive, another inside that Library folder, and one hidden inside your Home folder, which you can see by holding the Option key and choosing Go ⇨ Library.)

>> **Movies:** Contains video files created by iMovie and certain other applications for playing or editing video, such as Final Cut Pro X or QuickTime Player.

>> **Music:** Contains audio files, such as music tracks stored in Music, or created by GarageBand or another audio application, such as Audacity or Logic Pro X.

>> **Pictures:** Contains digital photographs, such as those you import into Photos.

>> **Public:** Provides a folder that you can use to share files with other user accounts on the same Mac, or with other users on a local area network (LAN).

Every drive (such as your hard drive) can contain multiple folders, and each folder can contain multiple folders. A collection of folders stored inside folders stored inside other folders is a *hierarchy*. It's important to know how to view and navigate through a folder hierarchy to find specific files, and we tell you how to do that in the "Navigating the Finder" section later in this chapter.

Setting Finder preferences

As you look at the figures in this book, you might say to yourself, "My Finder doesn't look like that." You probably have different Finder preferences than we do. You can choose the items you see in the Finder Sidebar and also how the Finder behaves in certain situations by setting the Finder preferences to your liking. Follow these steps, and remember you can always go back and change them later if you think of a better setup:

1. **Click the Finder icon on the Dock.**

A Finder window opens.

2. **Choose Finder ⇨ Preferences.**

The Finder Preferences window opens.

3. **Click the General button at the top, if it isn't selected.**

4. **Select the check boxes next to the items you want to see on your Desktop.**

You can select any or all of the following: Hard Disks, External Disks, CDs, DVDs, and iPods, and/or Connected Servers.

5. **From the New Finder Windows Show pop-up menu, choose which window you want to open when you open the finder.**

6. **(Optional) Select the Open Folders in Tabs Instead of New Windows check box if you want this option in the Action menu, which you find in the Finder Toolbar.**

You can have more than one folder open simultaneously. They can be opened in separate windows, which tend to clutter the Desktop, or in separate tabs within one Finder window. See the section "Working with tabs" to learn about tabs.

7. **Click the Sidebar button.**

The Sidebar preferences pane opens, as shown in Figure 4-2.

8. **Select the check boxes next to the items you want to see in the Finder Sidebar.**

When the Finder is open, you can show and hide the items in each category by clicking the Show/Hide button that appears when you hover to the right of the category title in the Sidebar.

FIGURE 4-2:
Choose the items
you want to
see listed in the
Finder Sidebar.

9. **Click the Advanced button to choose to activate one or more of the following options:**

- *Show All Filename Extensions* displays the file extension on every filename on your Mac. File extensions are the two or more letters after a file name, such as .doc or .xls.

- *Show Warning before Changing an Extension* opens a dialog if you save a file as a different type, such as saving a .doc file as .txt.

- *Show Warning before Removing from iCloud Drive* displays a warning dialog when you delete a file from your iCloud drive.

- *Show Warning before Emptying the Trash* gives you time for second thoughts before you empty the trash.

- *Remove Items from the Trash after 30 Days* automatically empties any file in the Trash older than 30 days.

You can also set the search level for Spotlight search, which we discuss in the "Spotlight Preferences" section, later in this chapter.

10. **Click the red Close button in the upper-left corner to close the window.**

Working with Files and Folders

Navigating the Finder

To access files stored on your Mac, navigate the different folders and devices by using the Finder. First choose a connected drive or device, and then you can open and exit folders or jump between specific folders. We explain each method throughout these sections.

REMEMBER

To open the Finder, click the Finder icon on the Dock or click the background of your Desktop and choose File⇨New Finder Window. The Finder opens to the folder or device you specified in Finder preferences. The Finder opens when you double-click a folder, too, but it opens at the level of that specific folder, not at the highest point of the Finder hierarchy. See the section "Working with tabs" to learn about opening more than one Finder window or tab at a time.

Opening a folder

When you open the Finder and click a device, the Finder displays all the files and folders stored on that device. To open a folder (and move down the folder hierarchy), you have several choices:

>> Double-click the folder.

>> Click the folder and choose File⇨Open.

>> Click the folder and press ⌘+O.

>> Click the folder and press ⌘+↓.

>> Click the folder, and then click the Action button that looks like a gear on the toolbar and choose Open in New Tab or Open in New Window (depending on whether you select the Open Folders in Tabs Instead of New Windows option from Finder⇨Preferences⇨General) or double-click the folder to open it in the existing tab or window.

>> Control-click the folder and choose Open in New Tab/Window from the shortcut menu that appears.

REMEMBER

Each time you open a folder within a folder, you're essentially moving down the hierarchy of folders stored on that device.

Working with tabs

Tabs are a way of having several folders open in one pane at the same time so you don't have to close and open folders to switch between them or use the Back and Forward buttons. To open a folder in a new tab, click the folder, click the Action button, and choose Open in New Tab, as shown in Figure 4-3.

FIGURE 4-3:
Tabs help you
navigate through
folders on the
Finder.

TIP

Hold down the Option key while clicking the Action button, and Open in New Tab becomes Open in New Window.

If you want to open a new tab as if it were a new Finder window, click the Add Tab button (the plus sign) on the far right end of the tabs. The Finder opens to the device or folder you specified from Finder➪Preferences➪General. You only see the Add Tab button when two or more tabs are open; if you don't see it, choose File➪New Tab or Open in New Tab from the Action menu.

To close a tab, hover over the left end until you see the "x" and then click it.

When you hide, close, or minimize the Finder window and reopen it from the Dock, your tabs are still in place. If, instead, you click the Desktop and choose File➪New Finder Window, you won't see your tabs, but you can still access them by clicking the Finder icon on the Dock.

Jumping to a specific folder

By moving up and down the folder hierarchy on a device, you can view the contents of every file stored on a device. However, you can also jump to a specific folder right away by choosing one of these options:

» Click the tab you opened for that folder.

» Choose a folder from the Go menu — for example, choose Go➪Utilities — or press ⌘+Shift+U to open the Utilities folder. Other folders listed on the Go menu can also be accessed by pressing the appropriate shortcut keys, which appear next to the folder name on the menu.

Working with Files and Folders

>> Click a folder displayed in the Sidebar.

>> Use the Go ⇨ Recents command to jump to a recently opened folder. (Using this command sequence displays a submenu of the last ten folders you visited.)

>> To open the Library folder, press Option+Go and then choose Library.

REMEMBER

If you display the contents of a folder in List, Column, or Cover Flow views, you can view folder hierarchies directly in the Finder. (You find out more about using the List, Column, and Cover Flow views later in the "Organizing and Viewing Folders" section.)

Jumping back and forth

While you navigate from one folder to the next, you might suddenly want to return to a folder for a second look. To view a previously viewed folder, you can choose the Back command in one of three ways:

>> Click the Back arrow.

>> Choose Go ⇨ Back.

>> Press ⌘+[.

After you use the Back command at least once, you can choose the Forward command, which reverses each Back command you chose. To choose the Forward command, pick one of the following ways:

>> Click the Forward arrow.

>> Choose Go ⇨ Forward.

>> Press ⌘+].

Moving to a higher folder

After you open a folder, you might want to go back and view the contents of the folder that encloses the current folder. To view the enclosing folder (and move up the folder hierarchy), choose one of the following:

>> **Choose Go ⇨ Enclosing Folder.**

>> **Press ⌘+↑.**

Each of these options changes the tab, if you're using tabs.

Following the folder path

Click the Finder icon on the Dock and then choose View⇨Show Path Bar. Displayed at the bottom of the Finder window is the series of folders that lead to the folder you're currently viewing. Double-click any of the folders in the series to switch to that folder's view. If you misplace or can't find a file, click in the Search field of the Finder window, and then type the name of the file or a word or phrase it contains. Click the file you seek from the list of matches that appears, and then use the Path Bar to see where it's hiding.

REMEMBER

The Back command is not the same thing as the Enclosing Folder command. If you open an external drive and then switch to the Utilities folder on your hard drive, the Back command returns the Finder to the external drive, but the Go⇨Enclosing Folder command opens the Applications folder where Utilities resides.

Organizing and Viewing Folders

The Finder shows the contents stored on a device, such as a hard drive, which acts like a giant folder. To move, copy, or delete items within that folder or any of its subfolders, you first have to select the item(s), and we tell you how to do that. If your Mac's hard drive contains a large number of files and folders, trying to find a particular file or folder can be frustrating so we show you how to search for and tag files and folders. To organize a folder's contents, the Finder can display the contents of a folder in four views, which we discuss throughout this section. You can also preview files, and we tell you how to do that here as well.

To switch to a different view in the Finder, choose View and then choose As Icons, As Lists, As Columns, or As Cover Flow — or just click one of the view buttons on the toolbar shown in Figure 4-4.

Selecting items in the Finder

No matter how you view the contents of a folder, selecting items remains the same. You always have to select an item before you can do anything with it, such as copy or delete it. You can select items three ways:

>> Select a single item (file or folder) by clicking it.

>> Select multiple items by holding down the ⌘ key and clicking each item.

>> Selecting a range of contiguous items by clicking alongside the first item you want to select and then dragging the mouse up or down to the last item you want to select. Or, in List, Column, or Cover Flow view, click the first item, holding the Shift key, and then click the last item; all items in between the first and last are selected.

Using Icon view

Icon view displays all files and folders as icons (refer to Figure 4-4). To organize files in Icon view, you can manually drag icons where you want, or you can have your Mac automatically arrange icons based on certain criteria, such as name or date modified.

To arrange icons within Icon view manually, follow these steps:

1. **Move the pointer over an icon you want to move.**

   You can select two or more icons by holding down the ⌘ or Shift key and clicking multiple icons.

REMEMBER

2. **Click and drag the mouse.**

   Your selected icon(s) moves when you move the mouse.

3. **Release the mouse button when you're happy with the new location of your icon(s).**

TIP

When you arrange icons manually, they might not align with one another. To fix this problem, make sure that no items are selected and then choose View⇨Clean Up to straighten them up.

Manually arranging icons can be cumbersome if you have dozens of icons you want to arrange. As a faster alternative, you can arrange icons automatically in Icon view by following these steps:

1. **Click the Group button, which is the fifth button from the right on the toolbar of the Finder window to open the pop-up menu, or choose View⇨Clean Up By.**

2. **Choose one of the following options:**

   - *Name:* Arranges icons alphabetically.

   All the following arrangements create sections to group like files and folders.

   - *Kind:* Arranges items alphabetically by file extension, clustering together documents, images, and music tracks, for instance.

   - *Application:* Groups items by application type.

   - *Date Last Opened:* Puts files and folders you opened today in the Today section, those you opened yesterday in the Yesterday section, and so on for the Previous 7 Days, Previous 30 Days, and Earlier.

   - *Date Added:* Same type of sorting as Date Last Opened but by when you added the file or folder. Added files may be ones that were copied or downloaded from another source as well as files or folders you created.

   - *Date Modified:* Arranges the most recently modified items at the top of the window and divides the others in the time intervals as Date Last Opened.

   - *Date Created:* Arranges the most recently created items at the top of the window and divides the others in the time intervals as with Date Last Opened.

- *Size:* Arranges the largest sized files and folders at the top of the window. Files are grouped by size divisions, such as From 100MB to 10GB, From1MB to 100MB, and From 10KB to 1MB.

- *Tags:* Arranges icons alphabetically by Tag color assigned to a file. Icons with no tags appear near the top of the window, followed by icons with blue tags, Important tags, red tags, orange tags, gray tags, purple tags, Work tags, yellow tags, and green tags. Your Finder may not display all these tags. You can add or delete tags by choosing Finder ⇨ Preferences and clicking the Tags icon, and then choosing which icons are displayed in the Finder Sidebar.

TIP

If you don't see the buttons we describe in the toolbar, choose View ⇨ Customize Toolbar. Click and drag the buttons you want to see from the bottom pane to the Finder toolbar. To delete those you don't want to see, simply click and drag them down to the bottom pane, and they disappear in a puff of virtual smoke.

Using List view

By default, List view displays each item by name, size, date it was last modified, and the kind of item it is, such as a folder or a PDF (Portable Document Format) file. The biggest advantages of List view are that it always displays more items in the same amount of space than the Icon view, it displays hierarchies of folders as indented items (shown in Figure 4-5), and you can select items from multiple folders at the same time.

FIGURE 4-5:
List view displays items in rows and folders as hierarchies.

You can change the width of the columns by hovering the cursor over the line between two headers until it becomes a vertical line crossed by a double-ended arrow. Click and drag left or right to make the columns wider or narrower. Rearrange the order of the columns by clicking and dragging the header title. Only the Name column must remain as the first column. Additionally, if you click a column heading in List view (such as Name or Date Modified), the Finder sorts your items by that column in ascending or descending order. The order in which the files are displayed is indicated by an up arrow (ascending order) or a down arrow (descending order).

When you view your Macintosh HD in List view, user folders are identified by a folder icon and a triangle symbol (which Apple officially refers to as a *disclosure triangle*) pointing to it. Clicking that triangle symbol expands that folder to display its contents — files, more folders, whatever. Clicking the triangle again collapses that folder to hide its contents. If you click a folder with a disclosure triangle, and then select Option+→, the top level folder and all folders contained within it open. Choose Option+← to collapse and close all the folders.

When you expand more than one folder, List view makes it easy to move files and folders from one folder to another. Select multiple folders or files at one time by holding down the ⌘ key and clicking each item you want to select. When you're done selecting folders and/or files, you can then click and hold on one of the selected items and drag them all to wherever you want to move them — to another folder in that view, to the Desktop, or to the Trash on the Dock. If you have another folder, device, or drive open in a separate tab, drag the items to the tab. Then when the tab is highlighted, release the mouse or trackpad button, and the items will be moved to that folder, device, or drive.

TIP

If you don't have many files or folders (or you just like everything sort of thrown together), the Finder has an All My Files option, which displays documents from your user account on your Mac, in the view you choose, sorted by the criteria selected from the Arrange pop-up menu.

Using Column view

Column view initially displays files and folders in a single column. As with List view, all folders display a disclosure triangle next to the folder name. (Okay, okay, in List view, the triangle is just to the left of the folder name, and Column view has the triangle at the far right, but you get the idea.) Clicking a folder displays the contents of that folder in the column to the right, as shown in Figure 4-6.

When you reach an application, document file, or image the rightmost column shows a preview of the application, document, or image.

You can adjust the width of the columns by clicking and dragging the short, vertical lines at the bottom of the column divider. You can rearrange the order of the columns by dragging the headers, as in List view.

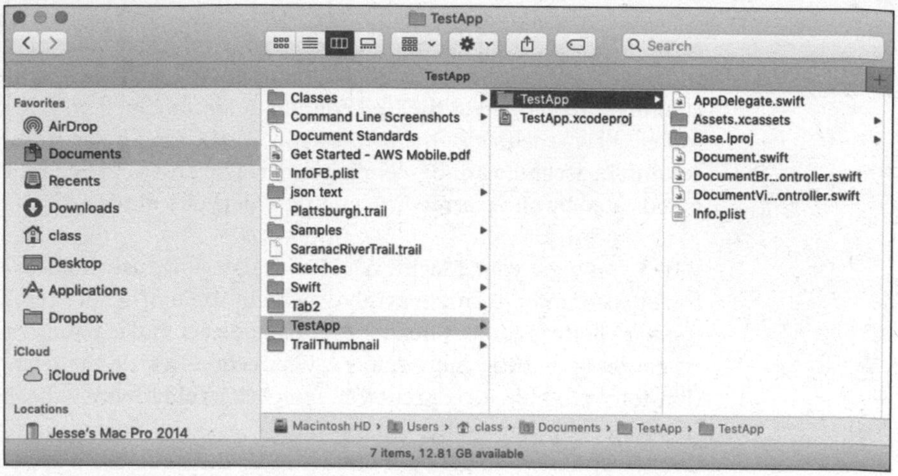

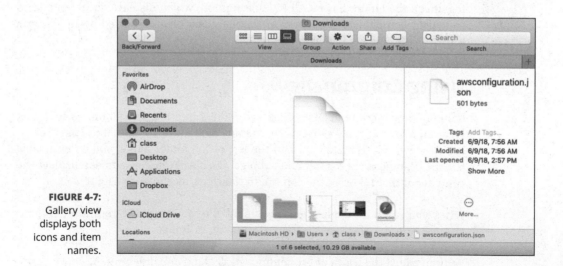

FIGURE 4-6:
Column view displays the folder contents in adjacent columns.

TIP

In any view, click the Group button to change the sorting criteria.

Using Gallery view

Gallery view combines List view with the graphic elements of Icon view, as shown in Figure 4-7. In the Finder, Gallery view lets you choose files or folders by flipping through enlarged icons of those files or folders, which can make finding a particular file or folder easier. This can give you an enlarged view of the contents of a file. As you can see in Figure 4-7, you can get an inside look at a variety of files.

FIGURE 4-7:
Gallery view displays both icons and item names.

Changing your view options

In any view of the Finder or any folder — Icon, List, Column, or Gallery — you can change the view options. You can also choose to make one style view the default for every folder you open in a Finder window or you can set different views for different folders. From any of the four views, choose View⇨Show View Options.

The View Options window opens, shown in Figure 4-8, displaying these choices from left to right:

>> **Icon view:** Scale the size of the icons and the grid spacing, adjust the text size and position, and add color to the background.

>> **List view:** Set the same options. Choose small or large icons, the text size, and the columns you want to see displayed.

>> **Column view:** Choose the text size and whether you want to see icons and the preview column.

>> **Gallery view:** Choose the size of the thumbnails you want to see.

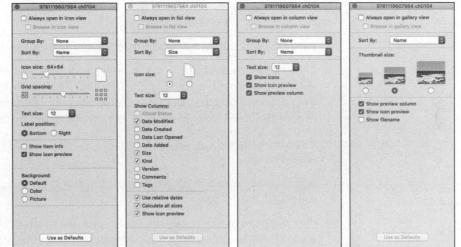

FIGURE 4-8: Use View Options to customize how you view the Finder and folders.

In any of the View Options windows, you can choose how to arrange or sort the folders and files.

>> **Always Open in Icon/List/Column/Gallery View:** Select this option if you want to see the selected folder in that view.

Working with Files and Folders

>> **Browse in Icon/List/Column/Gallery View:** You want subfolders of this folder to open in the same view.

>> **Use as Defaults:** You want the Finder and any folders to always open with this view (not available in Column view).

Using Quick Look to view file contents

Quick Look enables you to see the contents of a file for many file types without having to run the application you would normally use to create, view, and save it. Just select a file icon and then click the Quick Look view button (or press the spacebar) to display an enlarged preview icon of the selected file, as shown in Figure 4-9. You have four options to close the Quick Look display:

>> Click the Close button in the upper-left corner.

>> Press the spacebar.

>> Press the Escape key.

>> Click the app button to open the file. The associated app is listed on the button at the top of the Quick Look window. The Quick Look window offers many options for working with the image:

● Resize the window by clicking and dragging any edge or corner.

● Click the full-screen button in the upper-right corner to isolate the Quick Look window from everything on the Desktop. In full screen view, click the Exit Full Screen button to keep the window open but return to the Finder, or click the Close button to close the window and return to the Finder.

● If you use a trackpad, pinch and spread to zoom the contents of the Quick Look window.

● Scroll up and down and left and right on documents that are longer or wider than the window.

● Click the Share button to send the file to someone as an attachment to an email in Mail, an instant message in Message, or to another computer on the same network with AirDrop. Some files can also be shared on Facebook, Twitter, or Flickr.

● (Available for some file types) Choose File ⇨ Print to immediately print the image.

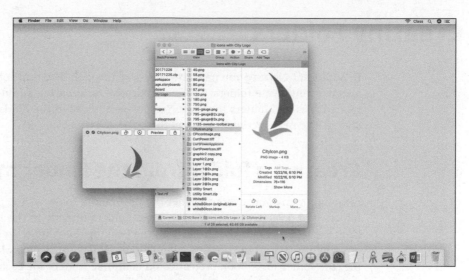

FIGURE 4-9:
Click a file icon
and press the
spacebar to
preview the file's
contents with
Quick Look.

The Quick Look view behaves differently, depending on the type of file you're peeking into:

>> A recognizable audio file plays in its entirety, so you can hear its contents.

>> A full-size picture file appears in a window, so you can see what the picture looks like.

>> A recognizable movie file plays in its entirety, so you can see and hear its contents.

>> PDF files and HTML files (web pages) appear in a scrollable window that lets you read their contents.

>> A document file (created by other applications, such as spreadsheets and word processors) is scrollable if in a format that Quick Look recognizes, or displays the first screen of its contents along with a listing of its name, size, and date of last modification.

>> A folder appears as an icon listing its name, size, and last modified date.

>> An application icon is displayed along with a name, size, and last modified date.

TIP

If you don't have the app that a file was created in, chances are that you can view it as an image by using the Preview app. From Preview, you can search, copy, and print — but not edit — image and PDF documents. Click the Preview icon from Launchpad. Choose File⇨Open, and then click the file you want to view in the Chooser, which looks and functions like the Finder.

Creating Folders

In addition to letting you navigate your way through different folders, the Finder also lets you create folders. The main purpose for creating a folder is to organize related files and folders together. You create a folder in the Finder or the Save As dialog. The next sections walk you through each method.

Creating a folder from the Finder menu

Although many Mac users consider the Documents folder as the repository for all folders and documents, we tend to create folders directly in the Home folder and keep the folders for active projects on the Desktop. Each folder relates to a project or category and often contains subfolders and files in the subfolders. For example, the folder for a book project could comprise folders for each chapter, which contain the word processing and image files for the respective chapter. You can create and organize your files and folders in a way that makes sense to you — and that's the beauty of the modern, flexible computer interface called Mac. To create a folder from the Finder menu, follow these steps:

1. **Click the Finder icon on the Dock.**

    The Finder appears.

2. **In the Sidebar of the Finder, click the location (for example, Macintosh HD) or device (such as an external USB flash drive) where you want to create a folder.**

3. **Navigate to and open the folder where you want to store your new folder, such as the Documents or Home folder or Desktop.**

4. **Choose File ⇨ New Folder (or press Shift+⌘+N).**

    An untitled folder icon appears with its name selected.

5. **Type a descriptive name for your folder and then press Return.**

    Your new folder is christened and ready for use.

Creating a folder from Save or Save As

The Finder isn't the only way to create a new folder. When you save a file for the first time or save an existing file under a new name, you can also create a new folder to store your file at the same time. You use the Save As command, which is the Duplicate command in apps that support Versions, such as Pages or Numbers. (To find out more about Mac's version control feature, see the nearby sidebar,

"Saving multiple versions of documents.") To create a folder from the Save or Save As dialog, follow these steps:

1. **Create a new document in any application, such as Microsoft Word or Apple Pages.**

2. **Choose File⇨Save if this is the first time you're saving the document.**

   If you've already saved the document, choose Save As or Duplicate; choosing Save at this point only saves changes to the current document without opening a dialog.

   A Save As dialog appears, as shown in Figure 4-10.

3. **Click the arrow button to the right of the Save As field.**

   The Save As dialog expands to display your Mac's storage devices and common folders in a Finder-like presentation.

4. **In the Sidebar of the dialog, click the location where you want to create a folder and open the folder where you want to create a new folder.**

5. **Click the New Folder button (or Shift+⌘+N).**

   A New Folder dialog appears, as shown in Figure 4-11.

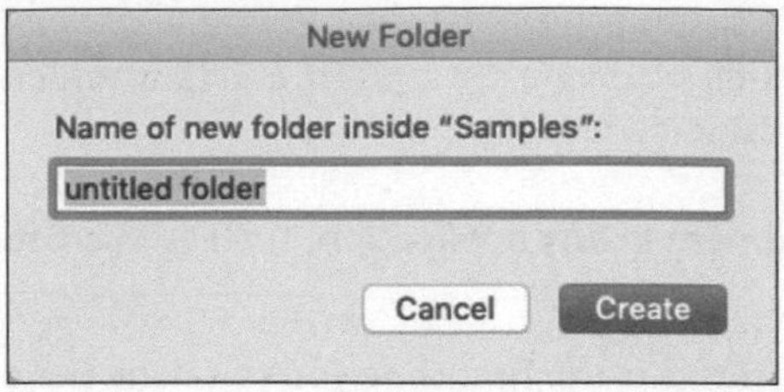

New Folder

Name of new folder inside "Samples":

untitled folder

Cancel   **Create**

FIGURE 4-11:
Name your
folder.

6. **Type a name for your folder in the dialog's text box and then click Create.**

A new folder is created in the location you specified.

This name can't be identical to the name of any existing folder in that location.

REMEMBER

7. **In the main window of the Save As dialog, type a name for your document in the Save As text box and click Save.**

Your new document is stored in your new folder.

SAVING MULTIPLE VERSIONS OF DOCUMENTS

If you're using an app that supports Versions, such as Pages or Numbers, Versions keeps your current document, creates a snapshot of the changed document, and saves a version of the changed document once per hour. The new version doesn't have a different name but a timestamp that shows when each was saved. Instead of opening several files, you access the different versions from within the app and restore an older version if you don't like the changes you made to a more recent version.

To see the previous versions of a document, choose File⇨Revert To. The current document appears on the left and a stack of previous time-stamped versions appears on the right. Scroll through the stack to access a previous version, and click Restore when you find the version you want to use. Even when you close the document, the interim versions remain so you can always retrieve a version from older (better) times.

The first time you save a document you create, you see the Save option in the File menu, just as you always do. After you save the document for the first time, you see the Save a Version option in the File menu. Versions automatically saves a copy of an open file you're working on once per hour. If you want to save a version in the interim, choose File⇨Save a Version.

If you want to save a copy of the document and create a new folder in which to place it, choose File⇨Duplicate, and then choose File⇨Save. Create a folder as explained previously and save the duplicated document in the newly created folder.

Playing Tag: Classify Files and Folders for Quick Access

You may have noticed the Tags button in the Finder preferences window. *Tags* provide a way to identify files, in addition to the name. Although every file should have a unique name (you can have duplicates if they're stored in different folders but we don't recommend this), you can apply the same tag to many files or folders and then search for or view files by tag. You can add tags to new files when you save them for the first time or add tags to existing files and folders — and then with a click, access everything attached to a single tag.

You can simply tag a file or folder by a color, but then you have to remember what each color means. Tags become more effective when you name the colors and add other named tags. You can also assign a color to the named tags, but your choices are limited to the seven predetermined colors.

Setting tag preferences

To give more meaningful names to the colored tags, click the Desktop outside a window and then choose Finder ➪ Preferences ➪ Tags. Click the color name of one of the tags to select it, and then type a new name. For example, Green could become Garden Ideas. Do two other tasks in the Tags preferences:

>> **Display tags in the Sidebar.** Select the check box next to the tags you want to appear in the Finder Sidebar. When you click the tag in the Sidebar, all files with that tag will appear in the right pane of the Finder window.

>> **Access tags from the Finder menu.** Drag tags from the list to the box at the bottom of the window to designate favorite tags that you want to see in the Finder's File menu.

>> **Change tag colors.** Click the colored circle next to a tag name and choose a different color or no color from the list.

Tagging existing files and folders

If you have thousands of files on your Mac, you probably won't go through and tag them all, but you may want to tag those files that you access frequently or are related to a project. To tag an existing file or folder:

1. Click the Finder icon on the Dock to open a Finder window.

2. Click and scroll through the folders and files to find the one you want to tag.

3. **Click the file or folder once to select it (double-clicking would open it).**

4. **Click the File menu and then do one of the following:**

- *Click a color from the tags at the bottom of the menu.* The tag is added to your folder or file.

- *Click Tags to see more tag options or create a new tag name.* The Tags window opens, as shown in Figure 4-12. Type a new tag name or click Show All (at the bottom of the Tags list) to see all the tags you use and click one from that selection. When you type a new tag name, it appears in the Tags list.

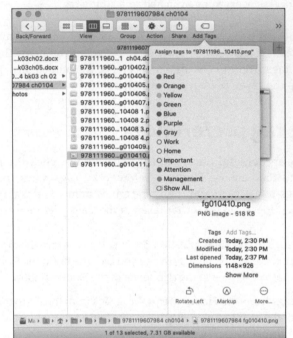

FIGURE 4-12:
Descriptive tags
help you find files
and folders fast.

Or, click the Add Tags button in the Finder window toolbar and click the tag you want to add to the file or folder (click Show All if you don't see all your existing tags) or type a name to create a new tag.

5. **Click or create other tags you wish to add to the file or folder.**

You can add as many text tags as you want. You are limited to the seven preset colors, although you can use the same color for more than one tab. Go to Finder ⇨ Preferences ⇨ Tags and click the colored circle next to a tag to change a tag's color.

6. **(Optional) To delete tags from a file or folder, click the file or folder once, and then click the Edit Tags button in the Finder window toolbar. Click to place the pointer to the right of the tag you want to delete and then press the Delete key.**

Tagging new files

When you create a new file of any kind, you save it at some point with a name and location. The Save and Save As dialogs have Tag fields where you tag the new file with an existing tag or tags, or create a new tag that you can then use for other files as well. From the app, choose File⇨Save or Save As and then click the Tags field. The list of colored tags appears, and the Show All option is at the bottom. Click the tag you want to use from the list or type a new tag to add it to the Show All list.

Finding your tagged files

To find files with the same tag, click Finder on the Dock and then click the tag in the Sidebar (or click All Tags and then click the tag you want). All files and folders with that tag appear in the contents pane on the right side of the Finder window.

If you don't see Tags in the Sidebar, choose Finder⇨Preferences⇨Sidebar, and make sure the check box next to Tags is selected. Then, click the Tags button, and click the check box next to the Tags you want to see listed in the Sidebar — although clicking All Tags will open a list that shows all your tags, including those you choose not to see in the Sidebar.

Manipulating Files and Folders

After you create a file (by using an application such as a word processor) or a folder (by using the Finder or a Save As dialog from an application), you might need to change or edit the name of that file or folder to correct a misspelling or to change the name altogether. Additionally, you might need to move or copy that file or folder to a new location or delete it altogether.

REMEMBER

To make sure that you're copying, moving, or changing the correct file, you may want to open it first. However, this can take time, and a faster way to view the contents of a file is to click that file in the Finder window and then click the Quick Look icon (or press the spacebar) to take a peek into the file's contents (refer to Figure 4-9).

Renaming files and folders

Keep these rules in mind when naming and renaming files and folders.

>> **Number of characters:** File and folder names can't be longer than 255 characters.

>> **Character restrictions:** You can't use certain characters when naming files or folders, such as the colon (:). Additionally, some applications might not let you use the period (.) or slash (/) characters in a filename.

>> **Duplicate folder names:** One folder can't have the same name as another folder in that same location. For example, you can't store two folders named Tax Info in one folder (such as the Documents folder). You can, however, store two folders with the same name in two different locations — and if you try to move one of them to the same place as the other, your Mac asks whether you want to merge the two folders into one folder with the same name or replace one with the other.

>> **Duplicate filenames:** You can store two identically named files in different folders. If you try to move a file into a folder that already contains a file with the same name, a confirmation dialog asks whether you want to replace the older file with the new one or keep the new one with a numeric suffix appended to the name.

>> **File extensions:** You can also store identically named files in the same location if (and only if) a different application created each file. That means you can have a word processor document named My Resume and a spread-sheet file also named My Resume stored in the same folder.

TECHNICAL STUFF

A file's complete name consists of two parts: a name and a file extension. The name is any arbitrary descriptive name you choose, but the file extension identifies the type of file. An application file actually consists of the .app file extension, a Microsoft Word file consists of the .doc or .docx file extension, a Pages file consists of the .pages file extension, and a Keynote file consists of the .key file extension.

Therefore, a My Resume file created by Microsoft Word is actually named My Resume.doc, or My Resume.docx, and the identically named file created by Pages is actually named My Resume.pages.

TIP

To view a file's extension, click that file and choose File⇨Get Info (or press ⌘+I). An Info window appears and displays the file extension in the Name & Extension text box, as shown in Figure 4-13. To view the file extensions for this file, deselect the Hide Extension check box. To view extensions for all files in the Finder, follow the instructions as explained in the earlier section, "Setting Finder preferences." You can also add tags to a file in its Info window.

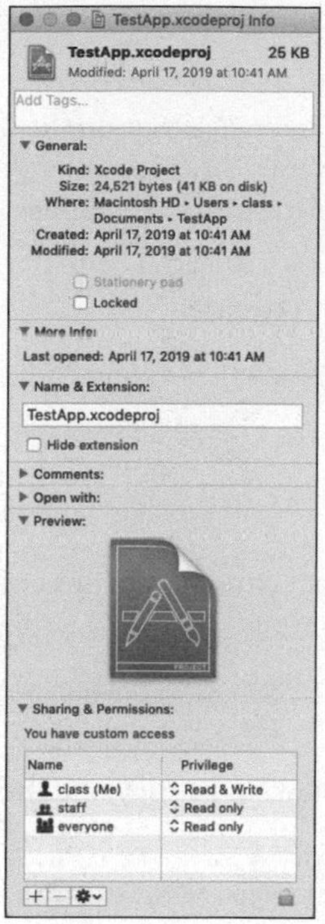

FIGURE 4-13:
Display file
extensions or not.

REMEMBER

Folders don't need file extensions because file extensions identify the type of file, and folders can hold a variety of different types of files.

For a fast way to rename a file or folder, follow these steps:

1. **Click a file or folder that you want to rename and then press Return.**

   The file or folder's name appears highlighted.

WARNING

When editing or typing a new name for a file, changing the file extension can confuse your Mac and prevent it from properly opening the file because it can no longer identify which application can open the file. Don't modify or remove the file extension.

2. **Type a new name (or use the left- and right-arrow keys and the Delete key to edit the existing name) and then press Return.**

   Your selected file or folder appears with its new name.

Working with Files and Folders

Copying a file or folder

At any time, you can copy a file or folder and place that duplicate copy in another location. When you copy a folder, you also copy any files and folders stored inside. To copy a file or folder, you can use either menus or the mouse.

Using menus to copy a file or folder

To copy a file or folder by using menus, follow these steps:

1. **Click the Finder icon on the Dock.**

    The Finder appears.

2. **Navigate to (and open) the folder that contains the files or folders you want to copy.**

    Use the Sidebar and the various other navigation techniques we outline earlier in this chapter to find what you want.

3. **Select one or more files or folders you want to copy and then choose Edit ⇨ Copy (or press ⌘+C).**

4. **Navigate to (and open) the folder where you want to store a copy of the file or folder.**

5. **Choose Edit ⇨ Paste (or press ⌘+V).**

    You have your own cloned file or folder right where you want it.

REMEMBER

You can also create an alias of a file or folder, as we explain in Book 1, Chapter 5. An *alias* — a shortcut — points to the actual file or folder, acting like a remote control for opening the file. Because it points to the actual file (and not a copy), changes you make are saved. If you work with a copy, you can make changes that don't interfere with the original version, so be careful.

Using the mouse or trackpad to copy a file or folder

Using the menus to copy a file or folder is simple, but some people find clicking and dragging items with the mouse to be more intuitive. You can drag between two separate devices (such as from a flash drive to a hard drive) or between different folders on the same device.

1. **Click the Finder icon on the Dock.**

    The Finder shows its face.

2. **Navigate to the folder that contains the file you want to copy and double-click the folder to open it.**

3. **Click the folder and choose File ⇨ New Tab.**

   A new Tab appears showing Recents. Alternatively, you can choose File New Window, and a window containing Recents appears.

4. **Click the new tab or window and navigate to the folder where you want to move the file.**

5. **Using your mouse, click to select one or ⌘-click to select multiple files or folders.**

6. **Hold the Option key and drag your selected file(s) and/or folder(s) to the second tab.**

WARNING

   To simply move a file or folder to a new location on the same device without making a copy, drag it to its new location without holding down the Option key.

   A green plus sign appears near the pointer while you drag the mouse.

7. **Release the mouse button when the second tab is highlighted.**

   When you hear the Basso sound effect, the selected files and folders have been successfully copied to the folder you selected.

REMEMBER

Dragging a file or folder to a new location on the same device (such as from one folder to another on the same hard drive) always moves that file or folder (unless you hold down the Option key, which ensures that the original stays where it is and a copy is created in the new location). On the other hand, dragging a file or folder from one device to another (such as from a USB flash drive to a hard drive) always copies a file or folder — unless you use the ⌘ key, which creates a copy on the destination drive and deletes the original.

Moving a file or folder

Files and folders can be moved within the Finder following similar steps as for copying — just don't hold down the Option key.

However, thanks to your Mac's *spring-loaded folders* feature, you can also move files and folders without opening a second tab. Drag and hold the file or folder you want to move over the icon of the device or folder you want to copy to, and wait a moment or two until the folder springs open. (You can keep springing folders open this way until you reach the one you want.) Let go of the mouse button to move the file or folder. To adjust how long it takes for folders to spring open, choose Preferences ⇨ Accessibility and click the Pointer Control tab; then drag the Spring-Loading Delay slider to adjust how quickly or slowly folders spring open when you hover over them with a selected file or folder.

REMEMBER

Don't release the mouse button until you're sure you're moving the file to the desired folder. If in doubt, don't release the mouse button to leave things the way they were.

Grouping files

You can select several files from different locations and move them into a folder by holding the ⌘ key and clicking each file, or by holding the Shift key while clicking the first and last file in a list to select all the files between the first and last file selected. Click and hold one of the selected files and begin to drag them toward the folder where you want to place them. They will be grouped together, and the number of files appears in a red circle on top of the group. Drag the group over the folder where you want to place them until the folder is highlighted, and then release them.

If you want to create a new folder for a group of files, select the files as we describe in the previous paragraph. From the folder, choose File⇨New Folder with Selection. A new folder is created called New Folder with Items, which you can rename as explained previously in the "Renaming files and folders" section. If the grouped files are from the Desktop, invoke the command from the Desktop and the new folder appears there.

REMEMBER

Create a new folder, open that folder in a new tab, and then drag selected files and folders to the new folder in the new tab. All the selected items are moved to the new folder. Hold down the Option key if you want to copy the files to the new folder without moving the originals.

Archiving Files and Folders

Files and folders take up space. If you have a bunch of files or folders that you don't use, yet want or need to save (such as old tax information), you can archive those files. *Archiving* grabs a file or folder (or a bunch of files or folders) and compresses them into a single file that takes up less space on your hard drive than the original file(s), unless you're archiving files that don't compress, such as JPEG, videos, and some audio.

After you archive a group of files, you can delete the original files. If necessary, you can later "unpack" the archive file to retrieve all its files.

You have two common ways to archive files and folders:

>> **Creating Zip files:** Zip files represent the standard archiving file format used on Windows computers. (By the way, Zip isn't an acronym. It just sounds speedy.)

>> **Creating DMG files:** DMG files (DMG is shorthand for *disk image*) are meant for archiving files to be shared only with other Mac users. Generally, if you want to archive files that Windows and Mac users can use, store them in the Zip file format. If you want to archive files just for other Mac users, you can use the ZIP or DMG file format. If you want to share the disk image with computers that use a different operating system, use the Disk Utility found on your Mac to create a Hybrid disk image, as explained in the section "Creating a DMG file."

TECHNICAL
STUFF

The ZIP file format is faster and creates smaller archives than the DMG file format. However, the DMG file format offers more flexibility by allowing you to access individual files in the archive without having to unzip everything the way you must with a Zip file. Most people use Zip archives to store data. The most popular way to use DMG files is for storing and distributing software.

Creating a Zip file

1. **Click the Finder icon on the Dock.**

   The Finder comes to the fore.

2. **Navigate to (and open) the folder that contains the file or folder you want to archive.**

3. **Select one or more Items you want to archive.**

4. **Choose File ⇨ Compress.**

   If, for instance, you select three items in Step 3, the Compress command displays Compress 3 items.

   After invoking this command, an archive file named Archive.zip appears in the folder that contains the items you selected to compress. If you compress a named folder, the Zip file has the same name as the folder with the .zip extension. You can see both in Figure 4-14.

TIP

To rename a Zip file with the terribly original name of Archive.zip, right-click the file and choose Rename from the context menu.

REMEMBER

To open a Zip file, just double-click it. Doing so creates a folder inside the same folder where the Zip file is stored. Now you can double-click this newly created folder to view the contents that were stored in the Zip file.

Working with Files and Folders

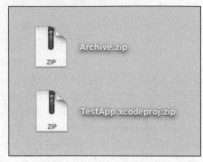

FIGURE 4-14:
Zip files appear
with a zipper
icon.

Archive.zip

TestApp.xcodeproj.zip

Creating a DMG file

Although Zip files are handy for storing files, DMG files more often are used to compress and store large items, such as the contents of an entire folder, CD, or hard drive. To create a DMG file, follow these steps:

1. Click the Finder icon on the Dock.

The Finder appears.

2. Create a new folder, and then move or copy the files you want to store in the DMG file.

3. Choose Go ➪ Utilities and double-click the Disk Utility application icon.

The Disk Utility application loads and displays its window.

4. Choose File ➪ New Image ➪ Image from Folder.

The Select Folder to Image dialog appears.

5. Using the Select Folder to Image dialog, navigate to and select the folder containing the files you chose in Step 2.

6. Click Image.

The New Image from Folder dialog appears, as shown in Figure 4-15.

7. In the Save As text box, enter a name for your disk image file.

Alternatively, you can accept the name of the folder.

8. (Optional) Add any tags that might help you find the file later.

9. (Optional) From the Where pop-up menu, choose a folder or device to store your disk image.

The disk image will be saved to the Desktop by default.

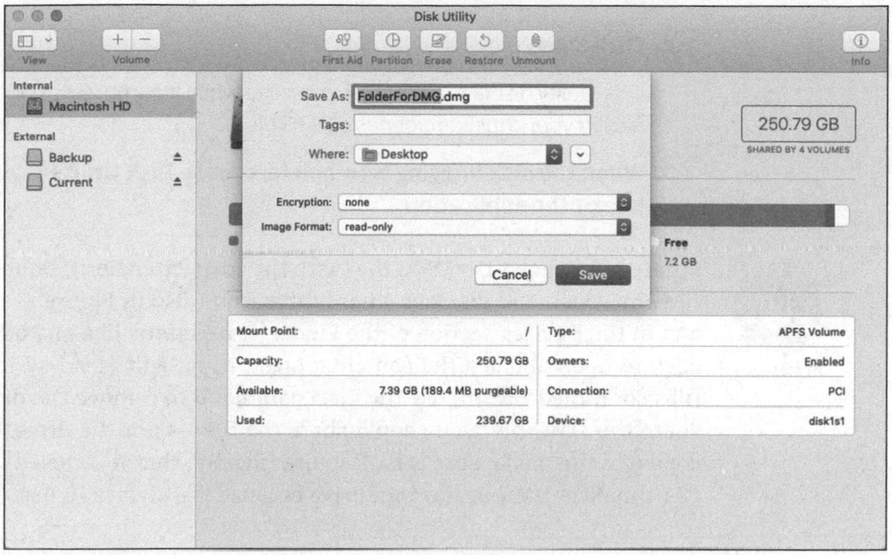

FIGURE 4-15:
Name and define
the location
of your disk
image file.

10. **Open the Image Format pop-up menu and choose one of the following:**

- *Read-Only:* Saves files in the DMG file, but you can never add more files to this DMG file later.

- *Compressed:* Same as the Read-Only option except that it squeezes the size of your DMG file to make it as small as possible.

- *Read-Write:* Saves files in a DMG file with the option of adding more files to this DMG file later.

- *DVD/CD Master:* Saves files for burning to an audio CD or a video DVD.

- *Hybrid Image (HFS + ISO/UDF):* Saves files in a DMG file designed to be burned to a CD/DVD for use in computers that can recognize Hierarchical File Structure (HFS), ISO 9660 (International Organization for Standardization), or Universal Disk Format (UDF) for storing data on optical media. (Most modern computers can recognize HFS and UDF discs, but older computers might not.) Also saves files in a DMG file designed for transfer over the Internet.

11. **(Optional) From the Encryption pop-up menu, choose None, 128 bit AES, or 256-bit AES encryption.**

If you choose encryption, you have to define a password that can open the DMG file.

AES stands for *Advanced Encryption Standard,* the American government's latest standard for algorithms that scramble data. Choose one of these options if you want to prevent prying eyes from viewing your disk image file's contents (unless you share the password with those you trust).

Working with Files and Folders

12. **Click Save.**

Disk Utility displays a progress message while it compresses and stores the files in your chosen folder as a DMG file.

13. **When the disk imaging is complete, choose Disk Utility ⇨ Quit Disk Utility to exit the application.**

REMEMBER

Figure 4-16 shows the DMG file (with the .dmg extension). Double-clicking a DMG file unpacks it and displays a hard drive icon (also in Figure 4-16) on the Desktop and in the Devices section of the Finder. It functions like any other drive: Double-click to open and see the contents; open, copy, edit (read-write files), and print files contained within; use the Eject command to remove the drive. If you want to share the DMG file, you should share the file — not the drive. When you make a copy of a file, make sure it isn't in use (ideally, that it's closed). For example, you can't make a DMG of the boot drive because it's always in use.

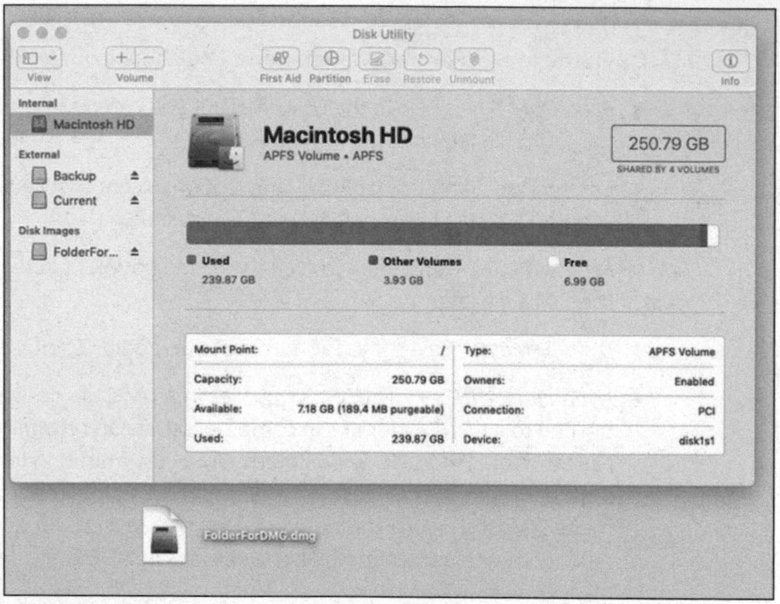

FIGURE 4-16:
Creating a disk image from a folder creates a DMG file.

Deleting files and folders

Like garages, basements, and attics, after a while your Mac probably has stuff that you can throw away, get rid of, or just plain delete. You can delete single files, single folders that contain multiple files, or multiple files and folders together with these steps:

1. **In a Finder window or on the desktop, select the single or multiple files or folders you want to delete in one of the following ways:**

   - Click the single file or folder.

   - Click and drag around a group of contiguous files or folders in a window or on the desktop to select them. As you drag, you'll see a marquee around the items you're selecting. Release the mouse button or track when the files or folders have a gray border around them.

   - Shift-click the first and last of a group of contiguous files or folders.

   - ⌘-click multiple non-contiguous files or folders.

2. **Click File ⇨ Move to Trash or drag the selected files to the Trash icon on the Dock or press ⌘+Delete.**

   The files and folders are moved to the Trash file. From here, you can still retrieve your files and folders.

3. **When you're sure you want to eliminate the files and folders from your Mac's hard drive, click the Desktop, and choose Finder ⇨ Empty Trash.**

   After choosing this command a dialog appears asking you if you want to permanently delete the items in Trash.

4. **Click Empty Trash.**

   A sound like crumpling paper plays and — *voilà!* — the trash is empty.

Searching Files

No matter how organized you try to be, there's a good chance you might forget where you stored a file. To find your wayward files quickly, you can use the Spotlight feature.

In Spotlight, just type a word or phrase to identify the name of the file you want or a word or phrase stored inside that file. Then Spotlight displays a list of files that matches what you typed. Say you want to find all the files related to your baseball collection. Type **baseball**, and Spotlight would find all files that contain *baseball* in the filename — or in the file itself, if it's one your Mac can peer into (such as a Word document or an Excel spreadsheet). If you type **image:baseball**, Spotlight will show you only the image files that have *baseball* in the name.

Using Spotlight

Spotlight searches for text that matches all or part of a filename and data stored inside of a file. *Hint:* When using Spotlight, search for distinct words. For example, searching for *A* will be relatively useless because so many files use *A* as part of the filename and in the content. However, searching for *ebola* will narrow your search to the files you most likely want.

Spotlight searches your entire computer. To restrict a search to a specific folder, be sure to check out the next section.

To use Spotlight, follow these steps:

1. **Click the Spotlight icon, which looks like a magnifying glass in the upper-right corner of the menu bar.**

   Alternatively, press ⌘+Spacebar.

   If your application is open in full-screen mode, move the pointer up to the upper-right corner of your screen so the menulets appear, where you can click the Spotlight icon.

2. **Type a word or phrase in the text box next to the magnifying glass icon.**

   While you type, Spotlight displays the files that match your text, dividing by file type. If you click one of the matching files, a quick view window opens, as shown in Figure 4-17.

FIGURE 4-17:
Click a matching file in the Spotlight list to see a preview.

3. Click a file to open it or click Show All in Finder at the top of the list to see the entire list of matches in a Finder window.

Narrow your search by setting more limited criteria in the Show All in Finder window.

The previous steps enable you to search your entire computer for files. However, you can narrow your search to a specific device or drive attached to your computer. To search a device or drive attached to your computer, follow these steps:

1. Click the device you want to search.

2. Enter the word or phrase you want to search for in the text field next to the Spotlight magnifying glass.

A list of files and/or folders appears.

3. Click the plus button next to Save on the right side to open two criteria fields, as shown in Figure 4-18.

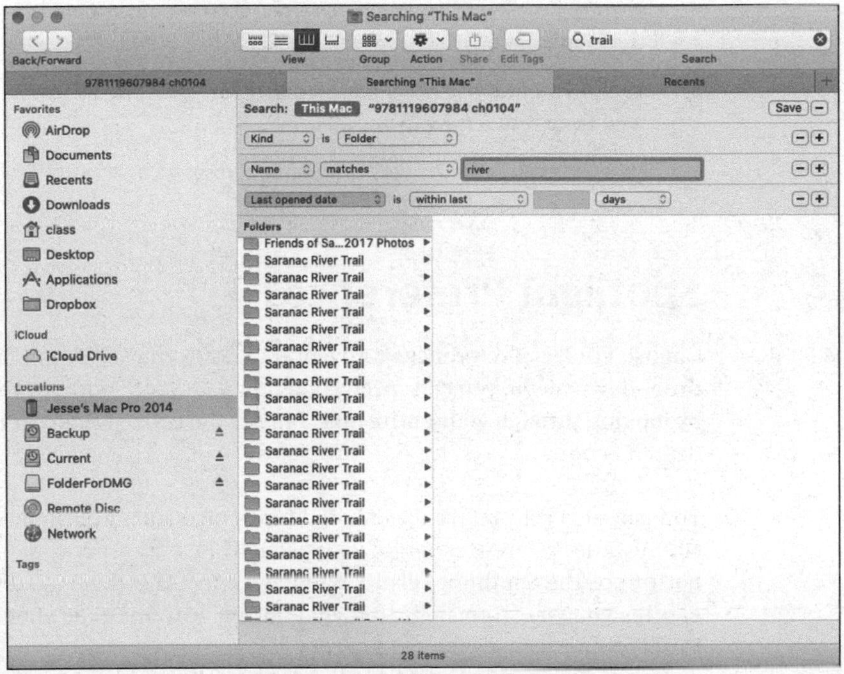

FIGURE 4-18.
Use specific criteria to narrow your search.

4. **In the first field, choose from Kind, Name, Contents, Visibility, and Creation and Modification Dates. Click Other to open a window that lets you choose more specific attributes to search by.**

   For example, if you're searching for images that match a specific word or phrase, choose Kind and then from the Is drop-down menu, choose Image.

5. **Enter information in the successive field (or fields) or pop-up menus to complete the search criteria, and then type the word or words in the file(s) you're seeking.**

   For example, if you choose Name in the first field, the second field enables you to select Matches, Contains, Begins With, and so on.

   Continuing with our image scenario, the default option for the third menu is all, but you can narrow down your search by choosing a specific image type: JPEG, TIFF, GIF, PNG, or BMP.

6. **Repeat Steps 3–5 to add another rule for the search criteria.**

7. **(Optional) Click Save to save this search criteria to use again in the future.**

   A button named after the search word appears next to the other searchable device names.

8. **When you find the file you're looking for, click the item to open it or drag and drop it to a new location.**

   You can even drop the files in an AirDrop box on a different Mac. Read about AirDrop in Book 3, Chapter 4.

Spotlight Preferences

Choose Finder ⇨ Preferences ⇨ Advanced, and from the When Performing a Search drop-down menu, you can specify whether you want Spotlight to perform searches by looking through your entire Mac, only in the active folder, or using the Previous Search Scope.

You can also set preferences for the types of results Spotlight gives you. Choose ⇨ System Preferences and click Spotlight or click Spotlight Preferences at the bottom of the Spotlight results window. Select the check boxes next to the categories you want Spotlight to include when searching, as shown in Figure 4-19. Deselect check boxes next to types of categories you want Spotlight to ignore. For example, you may not want applications to be included in your search results.

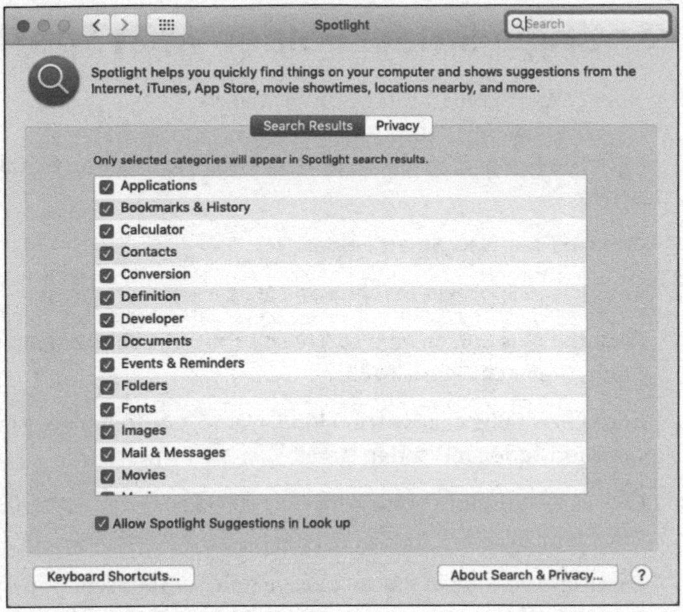

FIGURE 4-19:
Set Spotlight
Preferences to
obtain better
search results.

You can also prevent Spotlight from searching specific locations. To do this, click the Privacy tab, and then drag a folder or disk to the window shown in Figure 4-20. In this figure, we've added the Downloads folder, which will not be included in future Spotlight searches.

Using Smart Folders

Spotlight can make finding files and folders fast and easy. However, if you find yourself searching for the same types of files repeatedly, you can create a *Smart Folder,* which essentially works behind the scenes with Spotlight to keep track of a bunch of files that share one or more common characteristics. For example, you can tell a Smart Folder to store info about only those files that contain *rose* in the filename or the file; and from now on, you can look in that Smart Folder to access all files and folders that match *rose* without having to type the words in the Spotlight text box.

Think of Smart Folders as a way to organize your files automatically. Rather than take the time to physically move and organize the files, you can have Smart Folders do the work for you.

TECHNICAL
STUFF

A Smart Folder doesn't physically contain any files or folders. Instead, it contains only links to files or folders. This saves space by not duplicating files.

Working with Files and
Folders

Creating a Smart Folder with Spotlight

To create a Smart Folder, follow these steps:

1. Click the Finder icon on the Dock or click the Desktop to make the Finder active.

2. Choose File ➪ New Smart Folder.

3. Click in the Spotlight text box and type a word or phrase.

4. Click the plus button next to Save on the right side to open two criteria fields. (Refer to Figure 4-18.)

5. In the first field, choose from Kind, Name, Contents, Visibility, and Creation and Modification Dates.

Click Other to open a window that lets you choose more specific attributes to search by.

6. Enter information in the successive field (or fields) or pop-up menus to complete the search criteria, and then type the word or words in the file(s) you're seeking.

7. Repeat Steps 4–6 to add more criteria, which leads to more specific results.

8. Click the Save button that appears underneath the Spotlight text box.

A Save As dialog appears, as shown in Figure 4-20.

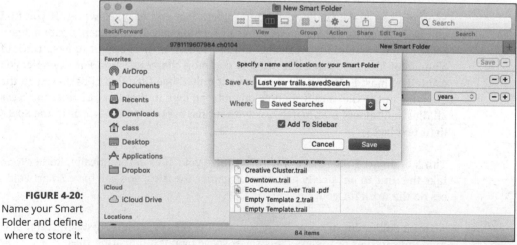

FIGURE 4-20:
Name your Smart Folder and define where to store it.

9. **Click in the Save As text box and type a descriptive name for your Smart Folder.**

10. **Choose a location to store your Smart Folder from the Where pop-up menu (or click the down arrow and navigate to the location where you want to save your Smart Folder).**

11. **(Optional) Select or deselect the Add to Sidebar check box.**

    Select the check box if you want the Smart Folder to appear in the Sidebar in the Favorites section. Deselect the check box if you don't want to see your Smart Folder in the Sidebar.

12. **Click Save.**

    Your Smart Folder appears in your chosen location. Instead of displaying an ordinary folder icon, Smart Folder icons always show a gear inside a folder.

REMEMBER

After you create a Smart Folder, it automatically keeps your list of files and folders up to date at all times. If you create new files or folders that match the criteria used to define a Smart Folder, that new file or folder name will appear in the Smart Folder automatically. Delete a file, and the Smart Folder deletes its link to that file as well.

Deleting a File or Folder

To delete a file or folder, you first have to place that item in the Trash. But putting an item in the Trash doesn't immediately delete it. In fact, you can retrieve any number of files or folders you've "thrown away." Nothing is really gone — that is, permanently deleted — until you empty the Trash.

WARNING

Deleting a folder deletes any files or folders stored inside. Therefore, if you delete a single folder, you might really be deleting 200 other folders containing files you might not have meant to get rid of, so always check the contents of a folder before you delete it, just to make sure it doesn't contain anything important.

To delete a file or folder, follow these steps:

1. **Click the Finder icon in the Dock, and then navigate to (and open) the folder that contains the file or folder you want to delete.**

2. **Select the file or folder (or files and folders) that you want to delete.**

3. **Choose one of the following:**

- Choose File ➪ Move to Trash.
- Drag the selected items onto the Trash icon in the Dock.
- Press ⌘+Delete.
- Control-click a selected item and choose Move to Trash from the shortcut menu that appears.

Retrieving a file or folder from the Trash

When you move items to the Trash, you can retrieve them again as long as you haven't emptied the Trash since you threw them out. If the Trash icon in the Dock appears filled with a pile of crumbled up paper, you can still retrieve items from the Trash. If the Trash icon appears empty, there are no files or folders there that you can retrieve.

To retrieve a file or folder from the Trash, follow these steps:

1. **Click the Trash icon in the Dock.**

   A Finder window appears, showing all the files and folders you deleted since the last time you emptied the Trash.

2. **Select the item (or items) you want to retrieve, drag them onto a device or folder in which you want to store your retrieved items, and then release the mouse button.**

TIP

To put the deleted file back in the same location from which it was deleted, in the Finder window that appears after you click the Trash icon, select the file, and then click the Actions icon that looks like a gear and from the drop-down menu, choose Put Back.

Emptying the Trash

Every deleted file or folder gets stored in the Trash, where it eats up space on your hard drive until you empty the Trash. When you're sure that you won't need items you trashed any more, you can empty the Trash to permanently delete the files and free up additional space on your hard drive.

To empty the Trash, do one of the following:

>> Click the Finder icon in the Dock (or click the Desktop) and choose Finder ⇨ Empty Trash.

>> Control-click the Trash icon in the Dock and choose Empty Trash from the shortcut menu that appears.

>> If you want to examine the files in the Trash bin before deleting them, Control-click the Trash icon and choose Open from the pop-up menu. This opens a Finder window and shows all the files in the Trash.

>> Click the Finder icon (or the Desktop) and press ⌘+Shift+Delete.

A dialog appears, asking whether you're sure that you want to remove the items in the Trash permanently. Click OK (or Cancel).

IN THIS CHAPTER

» Launching apps and opening documents

» Switching between apps

» Closing out of a document or app

» Using aliases

» Organizing the Dock

» Working with Mission Control

» Shopping at the App Store

» Installing, updating, and uninstalling apps

» Staying safe when working with apps

Chapter **5**

Managing Apps on the Dock, Launchpad, and Desktop

After you power on your Mac and have macOS up and running, you have to use apps (*applications*; or software or programs) to actually do anything with your Mac, such as write a report with a word-processing app such as Pages, edit a video, play a game, browse the web, or read and write email. The number of apps you can load and run simultaneously is limited mostly by your Mac's memory and processing resources. Like most computers today, the operating system manages multiple apps at the same time, swapping them in and out of the processor as needed. The real limitation on the number of apps you can run simultaneously is your patience as the machine uses its resources to move apps and data around.

This chapter explains how to run, install, and uninstall apps for your Mac. Most of the time, you start or launch an app from the Dock (which we introduce to you in Book 1, Chapter 2) or Launchpad, which we show you in this chapter. We explain how to use and organize both in this chapter. We also show you three other ways to open apps. Although your Mac comes with many great preinstalled apps, we give you pointers for finding new apps and take you window-shopping in the App Store (purchasing is optional).

Launching an App

Running an app is also referred to as *launching* an app or *starting up* an app.

To start an app, you can choose any of the six most common methods. Don't worry if some of the terms here are new to you; we show you how to do each throughout this chapter:

>> Click an app or document icon on the Dock.

>> Double-click an app or document icon in the Finder from the Applications folder. Many apps are stored in folders. To drill down to the actual app, click the down-pointing arrow to open the folder, and then choose the file with the .app extension (for example, Microsoft Word.app).

To open the Applications folder from a Finder window, choose Go⇨Applications.

>> Click an alias of the app or document in any of the locations just listed.

>> Click Launchpad on the Dock (or open it with the F4 key on newer keyboard and click the icon for the app you want to open). The Launchpad icon looks like a rocket.

>> If you have a Trackpad, pinch your thumb and three fingers to open the Launchpad, and then click the desired app icon.

>> Choose an app name from the Apple () menu's Recent Items.

>> Find the app with the Spotlight Search feature and then select it to run.

The *Dock* is the strip of animated icons that are displayed on the bottom of your Mac's screen (on the left or right side if you changed the Dock's position) by choosing ⇨System Preferences and clicking Dock.

TIP

You can hide the Dock by choosing ⌘⇨System Preferences, and then clicking the Dock icon. Click the Automatically Hide and Show the Dock check box, and the Dock will be hidden until you hover over the bottom of your screen (or right or left side if you changed the position). Hiding the Dock is a handy way to gain screen real estate if you're working on a small laptop.

Optionally, the Dock identifies running apps by displaying a black dot underneath the icon of each running app. You can run multiple apps and display multiple windows showing active files created with those apps, but only one window is active, and therefore only one app is active. The *active app* is the one that is front and center on your screen, ready to accept any data or commands you give. The window of the active app may be on top of any other app windows that are open, or it could be next to other windows if you have a large screen or are working with multiple displays.

TIP

When you attach a device, such as a digital camera or a mobile phone, an app such as Photos or Music may launch automatically, depending on the settings you choose.

From the Dock

To run an app from the Dock, move the pointer over the app icon that you want to run and click. (What? Were you expecting something difficult?) The Dock contains icons that represent some (but not all) of the apps installed on your Mac. When you turn on your Mac for the first time, you see that the Dock already includes a variety of apps that Apple thinks you might want to use right away. However, you can always add or remove app icons to/from the Dock (that's next in this section).

You can use the Dock in several ways:

>> **To gain one-click access to your favorite apps**

>> **To see which apps are running:** You see a dot under, or next to, the app icon (see Figure 5-1) if you turn on the Dock indicator lights in Dock Preferences. (We tell you how to adjust Dock Preferences in Book 1, Chapter 2.)

You can turn on indicators for open apps in System Preferences. In Figure 5-1, you see that Mail is running (note the dot beneath the icon) and Safari is also running (note its dot). The other apps represented by icons in the Dock are not running. Furthermore, because the Mail label is shown, you can tell that the mouse is hovering over Mail.

FIGURE 5-1:
The Dock
identifies running
apps with a dot.

>> **To switch between different apps quickly:** Clicking a running app's Dock icon makes it easy to switch among all the apps that are open at the same time. So, if you want to switch to the Photos app from the Mail app, you just click the Photos app icon in the Dock. Doing so immediately displays the Photos window(s) and displays the Photos app name in the Application menu on the menu bar at the top of the screen. (Clicking the Photos app icon brings Photos to the forefront, but the Mail app doesn't close or quit on you; it just moseys to the background, waiting for its turn to step into the limelight again.)

>> **To see which windows you have minimized:** *Minimized* windows are tucked out of sight but are still open. By default, you see a miniature version of the minimized window on the right (or lower) end of the dock. Simply click it to bring it back to full size.

You won't see minimized windows if the Minimize Windows into Application Icon option is selected in Dock Preferences; click the app icon to open the minimized windows of documents created in the app. (We tell you how to adjust Dock Preferences in Book 1, Chapter 2.)

>> **To view a specific app window:** Just click the icon in the Dock.

>> **To go to a specific window of a running app:** Click the window if it's visible. If it isn't visible, click the app's icon in the Dock; all its windows should be visible.

>> **To perform specific tasks of an app:** Bring the app forward with a click on the icon in the Dock and then use Siri or the commands in the menu bar to do whatever you want to do.

>> **To hide all windows that belong to a specific app:** Bring the app forward and then choose application⇨Hide <*app name*> to hide all windows associated with the app. To reveal the windows, click the app in the Dock or Launchpad.

>> **To hide all windows of other apps currently open:** Choose application⇨ Hide Others. To reveal hidden windows of all apps currently open, choose application⇨Show All.

You can add or remove app icons to or from the Dock so it contains only the apps you use most often, and you can arrange the icons in the Dock to suit yourself and make starting apps even easier. The following sections give you all you need to know about the relationship between the Dock and its icons.

From Launchpad

If the app you want to open isn't stored on the Dock, you can go to Launchpad, which shows all apps that are in the Applications folder. Click the Launchpad icon (which looks like a rocket) on the Dock.

If you removed the Launchpad icon like we did, press the shortcut key (F4), to open Launchpad, as shown in Figure 5-3. If you use a trackpad, with three fingers and your thumb slightly open, place your fingers and thumb on the trackpad and bring them together as if you were to pick up a small object. *Voilà!* Launchpad launches. (Sorry, but there's no default mouse equivalent although if you have a multi-button mouse, you can assign that function to one of the buttons.)

To add other keyboard shortcuts, you can go to System Preferences and choose Shortcuts from the Keyboard preferences tab, as shown in Figure 5-2. As with all the shortcuts, put a check box in the shortcut you want to set. Then, at the right (in the field showing None in Figure 5-2), there will be a blank space where the keyboard combination you press down will be shown. That's all there is to it.

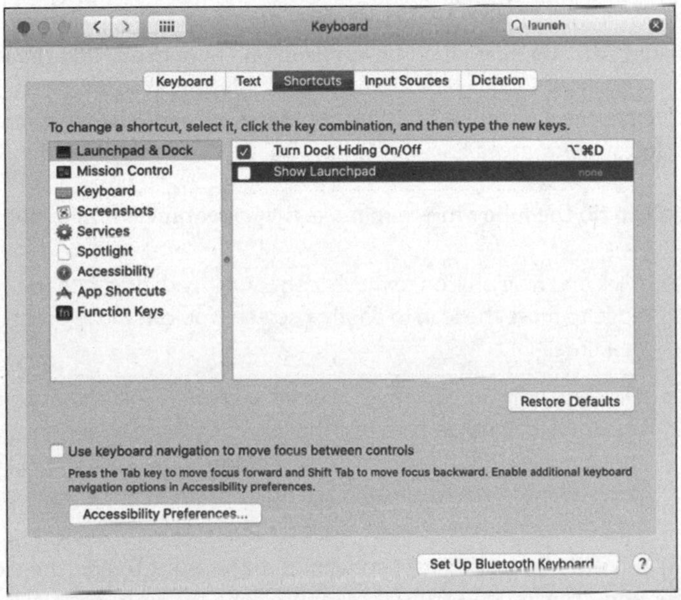

FIGURE 5-2: Change keyboard shortcuts for Launchpad and other options,

No matter how you get there, Launchpad will show you your apps, as you see in Figure 5-3.

Launchpad shows all the apps that are in the Applications folder, using multiple screens depending on how many apps are installed on your Mac. That means all the apps that came with your Mac and all apps you install have an icon on Launchpad.

FIGURE 5-3:
Apps stored in
the Applications
folder on your
Mac appear on
Launchpad.

You can have multiple Launchpad screens. To move from one Launchpad screen to another, hold the mouse button and move the mouse left or right, swipe left and right with two fingers on the trackpad, or use ⌘+→ or ⌘+←.

To open an app, just click the app icon on Launchpad, and the app opens.

To leave the Launchpad without opening an app, simply click anywhere on the background or press Esc.

You can do the following to manage the appearance of Launchpad:

» Click and drag an icon to move it on Launchpad; drag it to the very right or left edge to move the icon to another screen. You can move only one icon at a time.

» Click and drag one icon over another to create a folder that holds both icons, and then drag other icons into the folder. Click the folder once to open it, and then double-click the name to highlight the name and type in a new name. To remove an icon from a folder, just drag it from its folder onto Launchpad.

TIP

You can drag an icon from Launchpad to the Dock to add the icon to the Dock, or drag and drop an icon from the Applications folder to the Dock to add the icon to the Dock.

From the Apple menu's Recent Items

This one's a no-brainer: Choose ➪ Recent Items and then choose the app you want to run from the list of recently run apps. You can also choose a recently created or viewed document or other file to automatically launch the associated app and load the document or file.

From the Finder

Because an app's icon might not appear on the Dock, you have to be able to access icons another way. The Launchpad shows apps stored in the Applications folder, but the Finder can help you find any applications that are stored in another folder.

REMEMBER

You can store an app icon in any folder on your hard drive, but you should store apps in the Applications folder.

TIP

Resist the temptation to get cute about organizing your apps. Apps today often consist of several components, many of which you may not see. Renaming files can launch a cascade of unpleasant issues. At the very least use your favorite search engine to search on a phrase like "Can I rename Mac Photos app to something else?"

To run an app from the Finder, follow these steps:

1. **Click the Finder icon on the Dock and then click the Applications folder in the Finder window's Sidebar to display the apps installed on your Mac.**

2. **Scroll through the Applications folder window until you see the app icon you want and then double-click the icon to run the app.**

   (You might have to double-click a folder that contains an app icon and then double-click the app icon.) Alternatively, you can single click the app icon and then choose File⇨Open or press a keyboard shortcut, such as ⌘+O or ⌘+↓.

   Your chosen app appears, typically with a blank window, ready for you to do something application-y, such as typing text. Other apps, such as Music, may be filled with brightly colored icons.

TIP

Typing the first letter of an app file or document you're looking for in any Finder window will instantly jump to and select the first icon that matches the letter you type. For instance, to locate Safari in the Applications folder quickly, press S to jump to and select Safari (or another app icon whose name starts with S that might come before Safari, if one is present).

REMEMBER

If you're having trouble understanding how the Finder works, go to Book 1, Chapter 2 to read a brief introductory overview and Book 1, Chapter 4 to learn all the nitty-gritty Finder details.

With Spotlight

As an alternative to clicking an app's Dock or Launchpad icon, or locating an app or document by clicking through folders, you can use your Mac's handy Spotlight feature to quickly open apps or documents for you. We explain Spotlight in detail in Book 1, Chapter 4. You can use Spotlight to run apps and open documents in two ways:

>> **Via Finder:** Click the Finder icon on the Dock, click in the Search text box, type all or part of a document or app name (or the contents of a document you want to open), select the app, and then press Return, or you can double-click the document or app you want to open from the list of results.

>> **From the menu bar:** Click the Spotlight icon in the far-right corner of your Mac's menu bar (or press ⌘+Spacebar) and begin typing the first few letters of the app or file name (or contents of a file) you're looking for. Move the pointer to the app or document you want to open and double-click it.

Opening documents

A file on the Mac appears as a graphically descriptive icon with a name. Icons can represent applications and documents or a link, known as an *alias*, to either of those.

>> *Application files* actually do something, such as let you play a game of chess, or send, receive, and organize your email.

>> *Document files* hold data created by applications, such as a report created in a word processing app, a budget created in a spreadsheet app, or a movie created in a video-editing app.

>> *Application icons* are often distinct enough to help you identify the type of app they represent. For example, the Launchpad app icon appears as a rocket launching against a gray background, the Photo icon appears as a sort of color wheel, and the Mail application icon (for sending and receiving email) appears as a postage stamp.

>> *Document icons* often appear as a dog-eared page showing a thumbnail image of the content and the suffix of the file type stamped on the bottom, such as *web*, *docx*, or *html*, as shown in Figure 5-4. Folders look like folders, and image files such as JPG, PNG, or TIFF may appear as thumbnails of the image.

>> *Alias icons* represent links to app icons or document icons. You find out more about alias icons in the "Creating Alias Icons" section, later in this chapter.

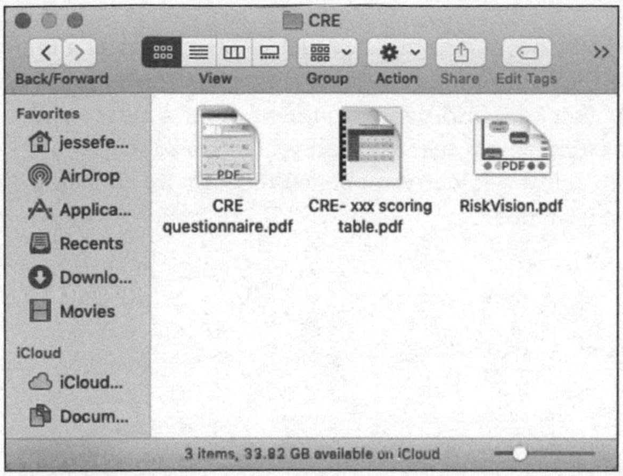

FIGURE 5-4:
Document icons may display thumbnails of their content.

When you double-click an app icon in the Finder, you start (that is, *run* or *launch*) that particular app. If you want to use your newly opened app to work on an existing file, you then have to search for and open that file by using the app's File⇨Open command.

As an alternative to starting an app and then having to find and open the file you want to work with, the Mac gives you the option of double-clicking the document icon you want to open. This opens the app with your chosen document ready for action.

You have several ways to find and open a document stored in the Documents folder, which is stored in your Home folder but can be accessed from the Dock, the Finder sidebar, and the Desktop window as follows:

>> Control-click the Documents icon on the Dock and then choose Open in New Tab, or Show in Enclosing Folder (or click and hold the Documents icon to see the folders and documents inside it, and then double-click the one you want to open).

>> Click the Finder icon on the Dock and then click the Documents folder in the Sidebar to open the Documents window.

>> Click the Desktop and press ⌘+Shift+D to open the Finder Desktop window. Then click the Documents icon in the Sidebar.

>> Click the Finder icon on the Dock and then click the location of the folder that contains your document, such as Desktop or the Home Icon. Double-click the folder to see the documents within.

>> Type the document name or a word or phrase it contains in the Spotlight Search field in the Finder window or menu bar.

If you store your document files in other folders, such as a folder that's specific to a project with all related files in that folder (but you're not working in that folder right now), you can find your document with a new feature: Recents. Choose Finder⇨Go⇨Recents to see just that: recent files (see Figure 5-5). You also have the option to select a folder you opened recently by choosing Finder⇨Go⇨Recent Folders⇨folder name.

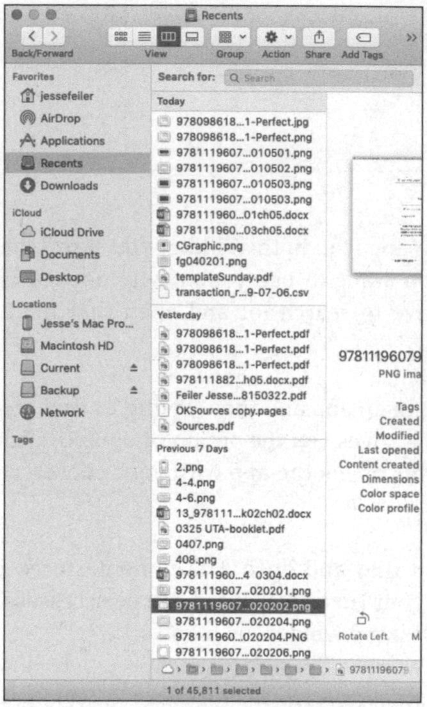

FIGURE 5-5:
See Recent files.

Scroll through the documents wherever you find them — Documents folder, Spotlight Search results, or another folder — and double-click your document file when you find it to open it.

Your Mac loads the application that created the document (if it's not already running) and displays your chosen document in a window. If your Mac can't find the application that created the document, it might load another application, or it might ask you to choose an existing application on your Mac that can open the document.

Sometimes if you double-click a document icon, an entirely different application loads and displays your file. This can occur if you save your file in a different file format. For example, if you save a Keynote presentation as a PDF document, it will open with Preview (or whatever app you've selected to open PDF documents with).

Switching among Applications

When you run multiple applications, multiple windows from different apps clutter your screen, much like covering a clean tabletop with piles of different papers. To help keep your screen organized, you can switch between different apps (say, a word processor and a web browser) as well as switch to different windows displayed by the same app (such as a word processor displaying a window containing a letter of resignation and a second window containing a résumé).

Your Mac offers quite a few different ways to switch among different apps, including using the Dock, using the Application Switcher, clicking a window of a different app, using Mission Control, or by hiding apps or entire Desktops, which we explain in the section "Organizing Multiple Desktops with Spaces," later in this chapter.

We discuss the first three ways of switching between running apps in the following list:

>> **Using the Dock:** Refer to the section "From the Dock" earlier in this chapter to review this method.

>> **Using the Application Switcher:** Press ⌘+Tab to open the Application Switcher, which displays icons of all active applications, even if the windows are closed or you hid the app with the *app menu*⇨Hide *app* command (see Figure 5-6). Hold the ⌘ key to keep the Application Switcher open and then press the Tab key to move left to right from one running application to the next, as shown in Figure 5-6. When you release the ⌘ key, the chosen application moves to the front of your screen.

Pressing the Shift key while holding down ⌘ and pressing Tab will move the selection from right to left. You can also press ⌘+Tab and then let go of the Tab key and use the arrow keys to navigate left and right.

If an application has several files open in different windows, the Application Switcher just switches you to that application, but you still have to find the specific window to view.

>> **Clicking different windows:** A fast but somewhat clumsier way to switch between applications is to rearrange your windows so you can see two or more windows at one time. To switch to another window, click anywhere inside that window.

>> **Going to Mission Control:** To see all the open windows on your Desktop, as well as the Dashboard and other Desktops Spaces (which we get to in just a bit), press F3, swipe up on the trackpad with three or four fingers, or use the Mission Control icon in Launchpad (it may be at the upper right) to open Mission Control, as shown in Figure 5-7. Then click the window you want to work in.

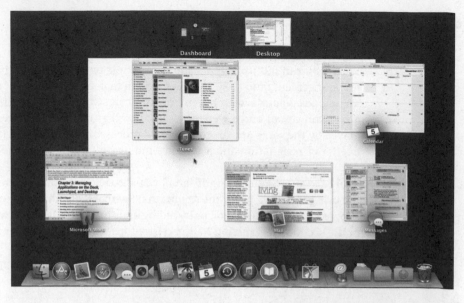

FIGURE 5-6:
The Application
Switcher displays
icons of running
applications.

FIGURE 5-7:
Mission Control
shows everything
that's open on
your Desktop.

TIP

To choose how many fingers you need to open Mission Control, click System Preferences on the Dock and select Trackpad from the list (you have this choice only if you use a trackpad). Click the More Gestures tab, and then choose Swipe Up with Three Fingers or Swipe Up with Four Fingers from the pop-up menu, which you see when you click the disclosure triangle.

TIP

If you want to switch between two or more open windows from the same app, press ⌘ +` (that's the accent grave character, which lives on the key to the left of numeral 1 on most keyboards).

You can control the keyboard combinations, so your Mac may be set to a different combination. Use System Preferences to get to the Mission Control panel and check or change your keyboard shortcuts (refer to Figure 5-2).

Quitting Apps

When you shut down an app, you also shut down all document windows that app may have open. However, if you simply close a document in an open app, the app keeps running.

REMEMBER

If you leave apps running when you shut down your Mac or log out of your account, in the dialog that appears you can choose to automatically reopen the running apps when you start your Mac the next time, letting you pick up where you left off.

Closing a document

If you want to stop working with or viewing a specific document but want to keep the application running, you can close just that particular document. You have three different ways to close a document window:

>> Choose File➪Close.

>> Press ⌘+W.

>> Click the red Close button of the document window.

TIP

If you click the yellow button, the window is hidden on the Dock but isn't closed. Click the document or app icon on the Dock to quickly reopen it.

If you try to close a window before saving the file, a confirmation dialog appears, asking whether you want to save your file.

Shutting down an app

When you finish using an app, shut it down to free up your Mac's memory to run other apps. The more apps you have running at the same time on your Mac, the slower your Mac can become, so always shut down apps if you don't need them anymore.

Today's operating systems are designed to be able to stay in the background without using computer resources whenever possible, so shutting down apps for performance reasons is not a concerning as it was in the past. Nevertheless, it's not a bad habit to get into because you may want to force data to be saved (and credentials *not* to be visible for a running app).

To shut down an app, you have three choices:

» Click the application menu and choose Quit (such as Photos⇨Quit Photos to shut down the Photos application).

» Press ⌘+Q.

» Control-click the app icon on the Dock and choose Quit from the contextual menu that appears.

REMEMBER

If you try to shut down an application that displays a window containing a document that you haven't saved yet, a confirmation dialog appears asking whether you want to save your file.

Force-quitting an app

Despite the Mac's reputation for reliability, there's always a chance that an app will crash, freeze, or hang, which are less-than-technical-terms for an app screwing up and not reacting when you click the mouse or press a key. When an app no longer responds to any attempts to work or shut down, you might have to resort to a last-resort procedure known as a *force-quit.*

WARNING

If you force-quit an app, you will lose any data you changed between the time of your last save and right before the app suddenly froze or crashed. For instance, say you're typing a sentence and then perform a force-quit press before pressing ⌘+S to save it — that sentence would be missing the next time you reopen that document.

As the name implies, force-quitting makes an app shut down whether it wants to or not. Here are the two easiest ways to force-quit an app:

» **Choose ⌥⇨Force Quit (or press ⌘+Option+Esc).** The Force Quit Applications dialog appears, as shown in Figure 5-8. Frozen or crashed applications might appear in the Force Quit Applications dialog with the phrase Not Responding next to its name. Just click the application you want to force-quit and then click the Force Quit button. If you select Finder, the Force Quit button reads Relaunch.

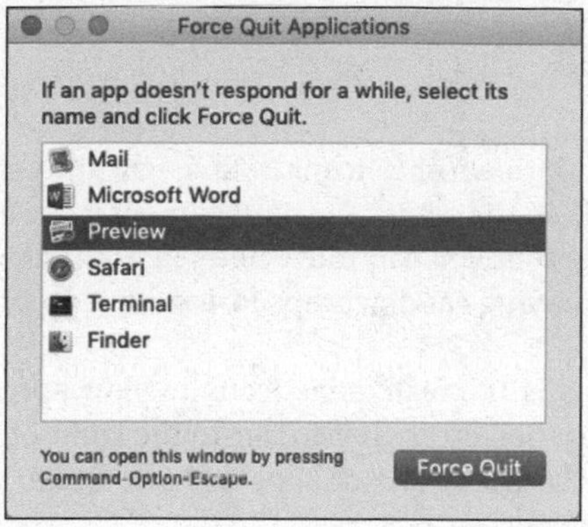

FIGURE 5-8:
The Force Quit dialog shows you all running applications.

>> **Control-click an app icon on the Dock and choose Force Quit from the shortcut menu that appears.** If the app hasn't really crashed or if your Mac thinks the app hasn't crashed, you won't see a Force Quit option in this pop-up menu. In that case, you may want to wait a minute or so to give your Mac time to correct the seemingly hung-up app. If you wait awhile, and the app still appears stuck but you don't see the Force Quit option, hold down the Option key, Control-click an app icon on the Dock, and then choose Force Quit.

TIP

Most apps present you with the original and a recovered version of the document you were working on before a force-quit. Look at both to determine which is the most recent or most correct version, and then proceed as follows, depending on which file is the better one:

>> **Original file:** Save the file by choosing File⇨Save. If you're not happy with the original document, click the Close button (the red button in the upper-left corner) of the recovered file. When asked whether you want to save it, click Don't Save.

>> **Recovered file:** Close the original file, and then click the window of the recovered file to make it active. Choose File⇨Save and give the recovered file the same name as the original file. Click Replace when asked in the confirmation dialog.

TIP

If the documents you're comparing are lengthy, and were created in an app that lets you compare versions, save the original and recovered versions using different names, compare both version in the app, and continue with the one you like best.

Creating Alias Icons

An *alias icon* acts like a link to another icon. Double-clicking an alias icon works identically to double-clicking the actual app or document icon. The biggest advantage of using alias icons is that you can move and place alias icons anywhere you want without physically moving (and perhaps losing) an app or document.

TIP

One way to use alias icons is to create alias icons to your app icons, store those alias icons in a folder, and then store that folder to the right of the divider on the Dock. This gives you easy access to lots of apps without cluttering the Dock.

You can do the following things with alias icons:

>> **Create an alias icon.** Click the Finder icon on the Dock, scroll through your folders and files, and then click the one you want to select. Choose File➪ Make Alias. (You can also Control-click it and choose Make Alias, or press ⌘+Control+A.) A copy of your chosen icon appears in the window. Notice that the new icon has an arrow in the bottom corner and *alias* is added to its name, as shown in Figure 5-9.

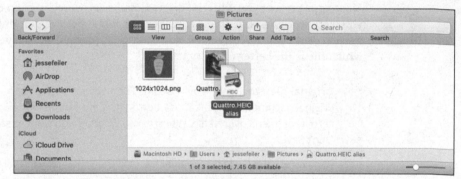

FIGURE 5-9: An arrow identifies an alias icon.

>> **Move an alias icon.** Because it's pointless to store the original icon and the alias icon in the same location, store the alias icon in a new location. To move an alias icon, click it to select it and then drag it to the Desktop, the Dock, or the folder you want to move it to.

>> **Create and move an alias icon in one step.** Press Option+⌘ when you click the icon you want to create an alias of, and then drag it to the new position. The alias is created and positioned in the new location.

» **Delete an alias icon.** Simply Control-click it and choose Move to Trash from the context menu, or move the pointer over the icon and press ⌘+Delete. Note that deleting an alias icon never deletes the original icon — meaning that if you delete an alias icon that represents an app, you never delete the actual application. The only way to delete an application or document is to delete the original application or document icon.

TIP

You can store alias icons on the Desktop for fast access or in specific folders to organize applications and documents without moving them to a new location. (Essentially, the Dock replaces the need to place alias icons on the Desktop, and Smart Folders duplicate the process of creating and storing alias icons in a folder. You can delve into Smart Folders in Book 1, Chapter 4.)

Working with Dock Aliases

The Dock includes several apps already installed on your Mac, but if you install more apps, you might want to add their icons to the Dock as well. One way to add an app icon to the Dock is to click and drag the icon onto the Dock.

When you drag an app icon to the Dock, you aren't physically moving the app from the Applications folder onto the Dock; you're just creating a link, or *alias*, from the Dock to the actual app (which is still safely stashed in its folder). Here's how that's usually done:

1. **Click the Finder icon (the Picasso-like faces icon) on the Dock, choose File⇨New Finder Window and then click the Applications folder in the Finder window's sidebar.**

The Finder displays the contents of the Applications folder. Alternatively, you can click the Applications icon on the dock to view the contents of the Applications folder.

2. **Drag the desired app to the Dock.**

To drag an app, move the pointer over the icon of the app you want to move, click and hold the mouse button or trackpad, drag the pointer where you want to place the icon on the Dock, and then release the mouse button.

Make sure that you drag app icons on the Dock to the left of the divider, which appears as a gap near the Trash icon. To the left of the divider, you see app icons. To the right of the divider, you can store file or folder icons.

Your chosen app icon now has its own place on the Dock.

Be careful not to drag the application icon to the Trash bin unless you really want to delete it from your hard drive.

You can also add an app icon to the Dock when the app is open. Remember that the Dock displays the icons of all running apps at all times, but when you exit an app, that app's icon — if it's not a Dock resident — will disappear from the Dock. To give a running app Dock residency, Control-click the running app's icon on the Dock — or click and hold down on the app icon — and choose Options⇨Keep in Dock from the shortcut menu, as shown in Figure 5-10. Now when you exit from this app, the app icon remains visible on the Dock.

As you can see in Figure 5-10, various other shortcuts are available. For example, you can move immediately to any of the files open in the app, quit from the app, and, if you want, you can hide the app.

FIGURE 5-10:
Dock icons have shortcut menus.

Adding file and folder aliases to the Dock

You can always find the files and folders you want by using the Finder. However, you might find that switching to the Finder constantly just to access the contents of a particular folder can be tedious. As a faster alternative, you can store aliases to files and folders directly on the Dock.

Accessing files from the Dock

If you have a file that you access regularly, consider placing an icon for that file directly on the Dock. That way, the file icon remains visible at all times (whenever the Dock is visible), giving you one-click access to your frequently used files. To place a file icon on the Dock, follow these steps:

1. **Click the Finder icon on the Dock and navigate to the folder containing the file you use frequently.**

2. **Drag the file to the Dock into any space to the left of (or above) the Trash icon.**

   The icons on the Dock slide apart to make room for the icon. To open this file, just click its file icon, which looks like a thumbnail version of the original.

You can add more than one icon, but too many will clutter up the Dock. If you've got lots of files you'd like to access from the Dock, consider making Stacks, as we show you in the next section.

REMEMBER

A file icon on the Dock is just an alias or link to your actual file. If you drag the file icon off the Dock to delete it from the Dock, your physical file remains untouched.

Creating Stacks on the Dock

Rather than clutter the Dock with multiple app or file icons, consider storing a folder on the Dock. A folder icon, when stored on the Dock, is a *Stack*. After you create a Stack on the Dock, you can view its contents by clicking the Stack.

TIP

To load the app or open the file, you can click the stack on the Dock and then click the app or file icon. The downsides include losing the shortcut menus for the items in the stack and not being able to open a document in an app other than the one in which it was created.

To store a Stack on the Dock, follow these steps:

1. **Click the Finder icon on the Dock to open a new Finder window, and then navigate to a folder you use frequently.**

2. **Drag the folder to the Dock into any space to the right of (or above) the divider.**

   The Dock icons slide apart to make room for your Stack to give your folder a place all its own.

Alternatively, you can create a new folder anywhere. In the folder, create aliases for the apps or documents you use frequently, and then drag that folder to the dock as outlined in the previous steps.

Opening files stored in a Stack

After you place a Stack on the Dock, you can view its contents — and open a file in that Stack — by following these steps:

1. Click a Stack folder on the Dock.

The files and folders in the stack appear as a stack of single icons neatly arranged in an arc above the icon. At the top of the stack is a link telling you how many more can be accessed from the Finder. Click the link to view all the files in a Finder window. If a file contained in the folder represented by the Stack is open, the icon shows a piece of paper emerging from the folder.

2. Click the file you want to open.

Your chosen file opens.

Or, click Open in Finder link to see the files in a Finder window.

TIP

Control-click (two-finger tap on a trackpad) a Stack icon to display a shortcut menu of options you can choose to customize the way a Stack folder appears on the Dock (as a Stack or Folder) and how its contents are displayed when you click it, as shown in Figure 5-11.

FIGURE 5-11:
Control-click a Stack to display a shortcut menu.

Rearranging icons on the Dock

After you place app, file, and folder icons on the Dock, you may want to rearrange their order. How you rearrange your Dock is up to you! To rearrange icons on the Dock, click the icon that you want to move, drag the mouse (or your finger on the trackpad) sideways (or up and down) to move the icon to its new position, and then release the mouse or trackpad button.

Rearranging icons is handy when you have two or more apps that work in conjunction with each other. For example, if you use Grammarly to check the grammar in documents you create, position the icon near the Word app and Pages app icons.

You notice that while you move an icon, its neighbors move to the side to show you where the icon will appear when you let go of the mouse button. Neat effect, right?

TIP

You can rearrange icons on the Dock how you want, but one icon you can't move or remove is the Finder icon, which won't budge no matter how hard you try to drag it from its Number One position on the Dock.

Removing icons from the Dock

Right from the get-go, you might see icons on the Dock for apps that you rarely use. Or, you might think having the Launchpad icon on the Dock is redundant because opening the Launchpad is a quick operation. Rather than let those icons take up precious Dock real estate, get rid of them and make room for the icons of apps and files you use frequently. It's like keeping salt and pepper on the counter and the mustard seed in the cupboard. You have two ways of removing an icon from the Dock:

>> Click the icon that you want to remove from the Dock, drag it away from the Dock over to the edge of the screen, and then release the mouse button. Your unwanted application icon disappears in an animated puff of smoke.

>> Control-click the app or file icon and choose Options⇨Remove from Dock from the shortcut menu. (This doesn't work for folders or stacks.)

Note: Removing an icon from the Dock doesn't remove or delete the actual file. To remove apps, see the "Uninstalling Applications" section, later in this chapter.

REMEMBER

Here are two things you can't do with icons on the Dock:

>> You can never remove the Finder and Trash icons from the Dock.

>> You can't remove an app icon from the Dock if the app is still running.

Organizing Multiple Desktops with Spaces

Spaces multiplies your Mac's single display into as many as 16 separate virtual screens, or Desktops. The main purpose of Spaces is to help organize multiple applications running at the same time. Rather than cram multiple application windows on a single screen (Desktop), Spaces lets you store multiple applications in separate Desktops. One Desktop might contain only Internet applications, such as Safari and Mail, whereas a second Desktop might contain only Microsoft Word and the Mac's built-in Dictionary application. Each Desktop can have its own desktop picture and a customized Dock.

If one application has multiple windows open, you can store each application window on a separate Desktop. For example, if you have a word processor and open a personal letter and a business letter, you could store the personal letter's window on one Desktop and the business letter's window on a second Desktop.

You manage each Space individually, but you can see all of them and move windows from one Space to another in Mission Control, or by swiping left or right with three fingers.

Your Mac comes with one Desktop, also called a Desktop Space or Space, plus the Dashboard (see Book 1, Chapter 2). You can see both by opening Mission Control, which is where you create additional Desktops. Apps in full-screen view, which you activate by clicking the full-screen button in the upper right corner, act as a Space, too.

Creating Desktops

1. **Open Mission Control by using one of these methods:**

- Press F3.

- Press Control+Shift+↑.

- Click the Mission Control icon on the Dock, which resides next to the Finder icon and looks like a miniature screen with three open windows.

- Swipe up on the trackpad with three or four fingers (the number of fingers that opens Mission Control is determined in the Trackpad section of System Preferences).

2. **Click or tap the plus sign in the upper-right corner (if you have the Dock on the right, the plus sign will be in the upper-left corner).**

A new Desktop Space appears with the name Desktop 2. Subsequent desktops will be named Desktop 3, Desktop 4, and so on up to Desktop 16, as shown in Figure 5-12.

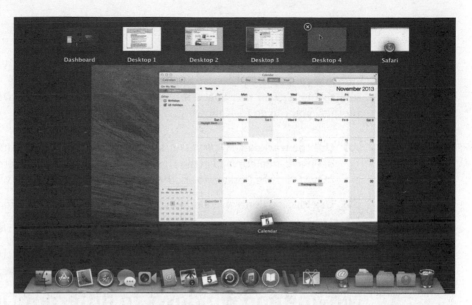

FIGURE 5-12:
Create additional desktops from Mission Control.

You can give each Desktop Space a personal desktop image and Dock. Open Mission Control and click the Desktop you want to work in. Then do the following:

» **Set the picture for that Desktop.** Navigate to the desktop for which you want to set the picture and go to ⌘⇨System Preferences and click Desktop and Screensaver, as explained in Book 1, Chapter 6.

» **Choose which icons you want on the Dock for that Desktop.** Click and hold an icon on the Dock and choose Options⇨System This Desktop (to use the icon only on this Desktop), All Desktops (to use the icon on every Desktop), or None (to not use this icon on the Dock in any Space), as shown in Figure 5-13.

WARNING

All the changes you make to an individual desktop disappear when you remove that desktop from Spaces.

FIGURE 5-13:
Use the Options for each app icon on the Dock to customize each Desktop.

Switching Desktops

Apps used in full-screen mode are treated as Desktop Spaces. When you create multiple Desktops and/or use applications in full-screen mode, you want to be able to move from one Space to another. To move from one Desktop Space to another, you can do the following:

>> **Use the trackpad.** Swipe left or right with three or four fingers (the number of fingers is determined in the Trackpad section of System Preferences) to move from one Desktop to another.

>> **Use Mission Control.** Enter Mission Control and click the Desktop you want.

>> **Switch between Desktops.** Hold the Control key and press the left- or right-arrow keys.

Moving app windows to different Desktops

When you run an app, it appears on the Desktop you're working in. For example, if you're on Desktop 1 and you run the Safari web browser, Safari appears on Desktop 1. Unless you choose the All Desktops option from the Safari icon on the Dock or turn off the related option in Mission Control preferences (see the next section), when you try to open Safari on another Desktop, you are sent back to Desktop 1. You can choose the All Desktops option, or you can move an app's window from one Desktop to another, so that the window appears where you want, by doing one of the following:

>> **Move the window via Mission Control.** Go to Mission Control and click the Desktop that has the window you want to move. That Desktop is now active. Go to Mission Control again and drag the window from the active Desktop, which appears in the center of the screen, to the thumbnail (among those across the top of the screen) of the Desktop where you want to move the window.

>> **Control-click and choose the Desktop from the menu.** Go to Mission Control and click the Desktop where you want the window to be. On the Dock, control-click the app that correlates to the app of the window you want to move, and then choose Options⇨Assign to This Desktop. The window moves. For example, say you have a Word document window open on Desktop 3, and you want to move it to Desktop 6. Click Desktop 6 and then control-click the Word icon on the Dock. Choose Options⇨Assign to This Desktop (refer to Figure 5-13).

>> **Drag the window to the desired Desktop.** From the Desktop, click the title bar of the window you want to move and drag to the far left or right edge of the screen until it shifts to the neighboring Desktop. Release the mouse or trackpad button or keep going until you reach the Desktop you want to move the window to.

Setting Mission Control preferences

Mission Control lets you choose some of the ways you view and interact with it. Choose System Preferences and click the Mission Control icon, or Control-click System Preferences on the Dock and choose Mission Control (see Figure 5-14).

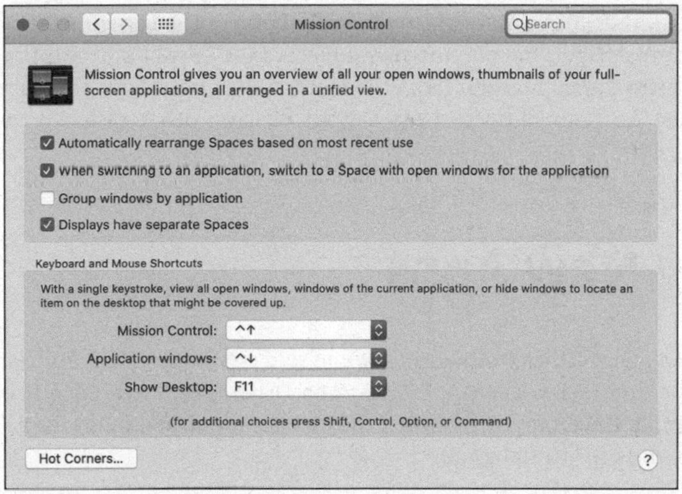

FIGURE 5-14: Set Mission Control preferences.

Select the check boxes next to the features you want to activate:

>> **Automatically Rearrange Spaces Based on Most Recent Use:** Moves your Desktop Spaces around so the most frequently used are first. If you're a creature of habit and like to find things where you put them, leave this check box deselected.

>> **When Switching to an Application, Switch to a Space with Open Windows for the Application:** When you open an app, your Desktop scrolls automatically to the Desktop that has a window open and uses that app. If this option is deselected, when you click an app on a Desktop, it opens on that Desktop even if the app is already open on another Desktop. And, just clicking the app

icon on the Dock moves you from one window on a Desktop to another window of the same app on another Desktop.

>> **Group Windows by Application:** When you have multiple windows of multiple apps open and go to Mission Control, the windows are grouped by app.

>> **Displays Have Separate Spaces:** If you use multiple displays, this option lets you have different Spaces for each display.

In the Keyboard and Mouse Shortcuts section of the Mission Control preferences dialog (Preferences ⇨ Mission Control), you can use the pop-up menus to set keyboard (left column) or mouse command (right column) shortcuts to access Mission Control, to see Application Windows, to Show Desktop, and to Show Dashboard.

Click the Hot Corners button to assign one of the screen's four corners to Mission Control. Open the pop-up menu next to the corner you want to assign to Mission Control, and choose it from the menu. When you move the pointer to that corner, Mission Control opens. You can also assign other tasks to the remaining three corners.

Acquiring New Apps

In ancient times (until 2016), Apple sold computers with built-in optical drives for CDs and DVDs. The Apple USB SuperDrive is still available from Apple, but most people have moved to digital media that requires no hardware. There are several reasons for this change:

>> Mechanical devices (such as disk drives) are prone to failures over time (think of it as the digital version of aches and pains).

>> Digital media is much less expensive to produce and ship than CDs and DVDs.

>> Digital media is much more robust than physical media.

You can shop for apps in the App Store. Many are free, but there are also paid apps.

This area is changing rapidly, but here is a brief rundown of the app options:

>> **Free:** Some apps are free. That's all there is to it. Many free apps have options or upgrades you can purchase in app.

>> **Subscription:** This functions like any kind of subscription — you get an update periodically for the cost of your subscription. When you purchase a subscription, your Apple ID credit card is charged for each period, and you can stop a subscription at any time (except after it has just renewed).

Some subscriptions are updates to an app's data (just like a magazine subscription). Other subscriptions use a model generally known as *software as a service* (SaaS). These subscriptions enable certain options in an app (for example, editing tools) for a repeating period of time.

>> **Freemium:** This model starts with a free version of an app. Then you can add on premium levels with new functionality or options. This is also referred to as "try before you buy."

Other pricing, use, and distribution models are in the works.

Shopping in the App Store

If you have a new Mac or you've upgraded to macOS Catalina, the App Store app is on your Mac — you can find the App Store icon on the Dock.

The App Store is a great place to look for new apps to add to your Mac. In this section and the next section, we give you a quick rundown of how the store is organized and how to purchase and download applications from the App Store.

REMEMBER

Like the Music Store, the App Store is an online service, so you need to have an active Internet connection to browse, purchase, and/or download applications.

Although you can browse the App Store as much as you want, you need an Apple ID. You can use your iTunes Apple ID or an iCloud Apple ID, or set up a new Apple ID by choosing Account⇨Sign In and then clicking the Create New Apple ID button, as shown in Figure 5-15, and then follow the onscreen instructions, which basically ask for an email address and a password. You need a credit card or iTunes Store card to purchase apps.

Sign In to the iTunes Store

If you have an Apple ID and password, enter them here. If you've used the iTunes Store or iCloud, for example, you have an Apple ID.

Apple ID: example@icloud.com

Forgot Apple ID or Password?

Create New Apple ID   Cancel   Sign In

FIGURE 5-15:
Setting up a new
Apple ID.

When you first click the App Store from the Dock or Launchpad, a window opens similar to the one shown in Figure 5-16.

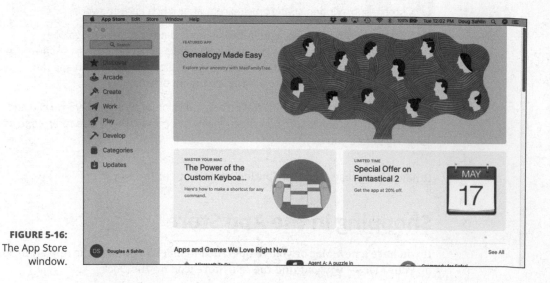

FIGURE 5-16:
The App Store window.

The opening window of the App Store is divided into two sections. The left side contains different categories such as Discover, Arcade, Create, Work, Play, and so on. Click a link to see apps in that category. The right side shows a featured app and tips on how to achieve certain tasks in the macOS, and as shown in Figure 5-16. Below the tips, you find the following:

>> **Apps and Games We Love Right Now:** This section contains a list of featured apps and games. These are probably the equivalent of paid ads. Click a link to learn more about the featured software and purchase it if it floats your boat.

>> **Ready, Set, Play:** This section features apps for people who like to play games.

>> **Top Free Games and Apps:** This section features the most popular free games and apps. Click a link to learn more about the app and possibly add it to your treasure trove of apps.

>> **Top Paid Games and Apps:** This section features the most popular paid games and apps. Click a link to learn more about the app or purchase it.

>> **Editor's Choice:** This section features apps Apple staff currently like.

>> **Quick Links:** This section has links that, when clicked, give you more information about in-app purchases and other App Store information.

You can change the view of the opening window by clicking the links in the left column.

When you find an app that interests you, click the app name or icon to open the app information screen. You'll see the name and description for the current version of the app, and also these items, as shown in Figure 5-17:

>> **Price/Buy App button:** Click the price and the button morphs to Get. Click Buy App to purchase the application. If you're perusing free apps, the button is Get/Install.

>> **Link to developers' website:** Click to go to those websites.

>> **Sample images:** In the center of the window, you see several sample images that you can click through to see what the app looks like and get an idea of how it works.

>> **Ratings and Reviews:** Users can give a simple star rating, from zero to five, or write a review. Reviews, (Not shown in the figure), help you decide if the item is worth downloading or purchasing.

>> **Information box:** Check here for the category, release date, version number, language used, an age-appropriate rating, and system requirements.

>> **More By:** Lists other apps by the same developer.

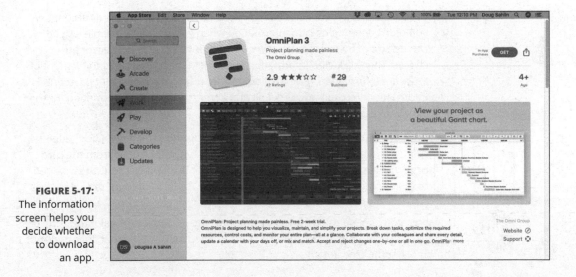

FIGURE 5-17:
The information screen helps you decide whether to download an app.

The information on the app you're reviewing for purchase may be slightly different. For example, if this is an upgrade or revision from a previous version of the app, you'll see a section called What's New. And, of course, the whole thing may change when Apple decides to try something different.

Downloading apps from the App Store

When you find something you like, click the price or the Get button, follow the prompts, and it's downloaded to the Applications folder and you find the icon on Launchpad on your Mac. Some apps have "in-app purchases," which you buy while using the app. Examples of in-app purchases are additional functions or features, chips for online poker games, or music for instrument apps.

You can switch over to Launchpad to see the app downloading or updating and pause or resume the download if you want. Some app downloads and updates are so quick that you won't have any reason to pause and resume. If, however, the power goes out or your Wi-Fi router dies in the middle of the download, when you're back up and running, clicking the app on Launchpad will resume the download at the point it was interrupted. Choose Store ➪ Check for Unfinished Downloads to prompt completion.

Of course, when you buy, you have to pay from your Apple ID account. This happens two ways:

>> **Credit Card:** Enter your credit card information into your Apple ID account. If you didn't enter credit card information when you created an Apple ID, you can do so by choosing Store ➪ View My Account. This displays recent purchases. Then click View Information and click Manage Payments to the right of Payment Information. A window opens that displays your current payment information. To change it, click Edit and enter the payment information for the card you're going to use going forward.

>> **Redeem Gift Card:** This option appears on your Account page. Click Redeem Gift Card to open the Redeem Code window. Type in the code from the card or certificate and click Redeem. The amount of the card or certificate is added to your account and appears to the left of the Apple ID account tab.

However you choose to pay for your app purchases, a prompt asks for your password to confirm your intent before making the final purchase. (This may not be shown for some free apps.)

WHEN YOUR APP CUP RUNNETH OVER

Because you have a physical limit on the amount of software and data you can install on your Mac, you have three choices when you're running out of room for your apps:

- **More hard drive space:** You can get another hard drive (an external drive or a larger internal drive) to store big byte-consuming files, such as videos or graphic heavy documents, so you can keep installing more apps.

- **Cloud storage:** You can move things off your computer to a remote storage site such as iCloud, Dropbox, or SugarSync. Cloud storage is free until you exceed 5GB.

- **Purging:** You can delete some apps or files that you don't want or need, which makes room for more apps that you do want and need.

Notwithstanding these points, in general if you don't have enough room to install an app, you probably don't have enough room, period. There are many suggestions as to the amount of unused disk space you should normally have — having 30 percent of your disk free is usually enough to run your apps smoothly. Yes, 30 percent of your disk free for installations and running of apps.

If you ever have a problem with a purchase, follow these steps:

1. Go to http://reportaproblem.apple.com.

2. Enter the Apple ID and password that you used to buy the item; then click Sign In.

3. Click Report a Problem next to the item that you need help with.

4. Choose your problem from the menu.

5. Follow the onscreen steps.

TIP

If you want to limit the types of downloads that others who use your Mac can make, you can set up separate user accounts and apply Parental Controls. If you apply Parental Controls to your account, those controls apply to you as well. See Book 3, Chapter 2.

Installing Applications

The most common place to install software is inside the Applications folder, so you should specify that folder when installing software. Some apps store their app icon inside the Applications folder plain as day, but others hide their application icons within another folder.

TECHNICAL STUFF

An application icon actually represents a folder containing multiple files. Hiding these details from you and letting you treat a folder of files as a single application icon ensures that you can't accidentally delete or move a single crucial file that the entire application needs to work. For the technically curious, you can see the hidden files tucked inside an application by Control-clicking the application icon and choosing Show Package Contents from the shortcut menu. You're free to look around, but we strongly advise that you don't delete, move, modify, or rename any of the files you see because doing so might render the application inoperable.

Updating Applications and System Software

Developers are constantly working to improve and enhance their applications or fix bugs that have been pointed out by disgruntled customers. Likewise, when Apple offers an operating system upgrade, developers must update their apps to make them compatible with the new OS. You want to keep your applications up to date to take advantage of these improvements.

You see a badge on the App Store icon on the Dock to let you know when any applications you downloaded from the App Store have been updated. Simply click the Update button on the App Store, and the updates will be downloaded.

You can set up your Mac to automatically check for updates to OS X and apps downloaded from the App Store by choosing ⇨System Preferences, and then choosing Software Update. Select the Automatically Keep My Mac Up to Date check box (see Figure 5-18), which tells your Mac to check for updates without any further instructions from you. You can also leave the box deselected and check manually by choosing ⇨App Store⇨Updates, as shown in Figure 5-19, but we suggest that you let your Mac worry about checking for updates for you.

Select the other options that you want to activate:

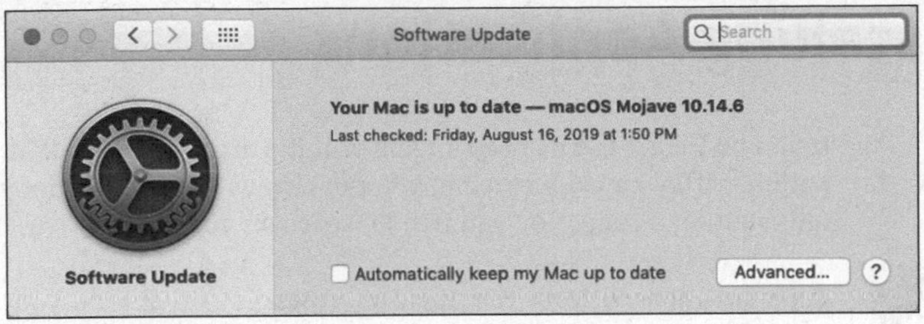

FIGURE 5-18:
Let Software
Update check
automatically for
system software
updates.

If you have more than one Mac, you may want to select the last check box so that when you download purchases on one Mac, they are automatically downloaded on other Macs that are signed in to the same Apple ID account in the App Store.

When new software is available, a message arrives, as shown in Figure 5-19.

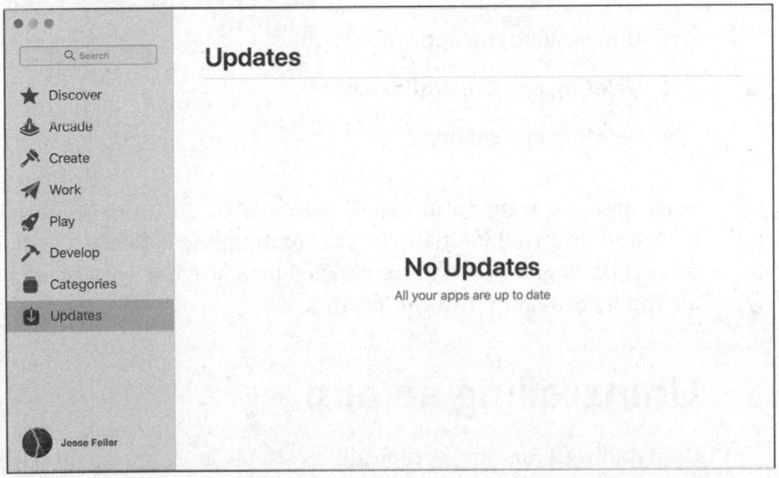

FIGURE 5-19:
Your Mac tells
you when
updates are
available.

Apps you download or install from other sources may also have automatic software updates available. You usually find them either under the Help menu or in the Application menu. If you're having problems with a particular application, go to the developer's website to check for an update. If you're having a problem, others folks probably are, too, and an update can often be the remedy.

Uninstalling Applications

If you no longer use or need an app or if it's an old version that is no longer compatible with your OS X version, you can always remove it from your hard drive. By uninstalling an app, you can free up space on your hard drive.

REMEMBER

Apps downloaded from the App Store remain available in your purchase records even if you remove them from your hard drive. You can download them again in the future, as long they are still available.

WARNING

Don't uninstall an app from a non–App Store source unless you have the original disc or the website from which you downloaded it offers a lifetime download policy. Otherwise, you may have to purchase the app again.

Uninstalling an app can involve three parts, which we explain in detail:

>> **Uninstalling the app**

>> **Deleting app icons/alias icons**

>> **Deleting app settings**

If an app you want to uninstall comes with an uninstaller application, double-click it to uninstall your app instead of dragging it to the Trash. However, the next few sections give you a more detailed look at what's involved when you uninstall an app by dragging it to the Trash.

Uninstalling an app

Uninstalling a Mac app is typically as simple as dragging and dropping its app icon into the Trash. If you've purchased an app in the App Store, you can remove it via Launchpad, and we explain how later in this section. Apps that are preinstalled on your Mac are extremely difficult to remove; we suggest that you don't try to remove them.

To uninstall an app, follow these steps:

1. **Make sure that the application you want to uninstall isn't running. If it is running, shut it down by choosing the Quit command (⌘+Q).**

2. **Click the Finder icon on the Dock.**

    The Finder appears.

3. **Click the Applications folder in the Finder Sidebar to display the apps installed on your Mac, and then click the app icon you want to uninstall.**

If the app is in a folder, open the folder before deleting it. Many companies that sell applications store them all in a folder (Microsoft Office is a good example of this). If the folder contains multiple apps, select the desired app and go to Step 4. If the folder contains an uninstaller for the program you want to remove, run it and say, "Adios" to the program.

4. **Choose File ⇨ Move to Trash.**

Alternatively, you can also drag the app icon or folder to the Trash icon on the Dock, or press ⌘+Delete to move the app icon or folder to the Trash.

TIP

In some cases, you might be prompted for your administrator password when you move an application file to the Trash. If so, type in your password and then click OK or press Return.

The Trash icon displays an image showing the Trash filled with crumpled papers.

WARNING

Before emptying the Trash, make sure that you want to permanently delete any other apps or documents you might have dragged into the Trash. After you empty the Trash, any files contained therein are deleted from your hard drive forever.

5. **Choose Finder ⇨ Empty Trash.**

Alternatively, you can Control-click the Trash icon and choose Empty Trash, or press ⌘+Shift+Delete to empty the Trash. The keyboard shortcut only works when you're applying it from the desktop.

Adiós, application!

TIP

From Launchpad, you can delete apps purchased in the App Store. Press the Option key, and all the icons begin to wiggle and jiggle. Those you can delete from the Launchpad have an X on the upper left of the icon. Click the X. A confirmation dialog asks whether you really want to delete the app. Click Delete if you do; click Cancel if you don't.

Today's apps often are complex, and they may involve more than one file. Their settings or preferences can be stored separately from the app itself (and usually are). When you want to remove an app, your first step should be to see if there is an uninstaller available. If an uninstaller is not available in the app's folder, your favorite search engine may be your best friend here. Run an uninstaller before you remove the app. In fact, removing the app itself may be the final step that the uninstaller takes when you run it.

Well-behaved apps let you delete them and their supporting files easily. However, not all apps are well behaved, and it's possible to find remnants of apps on your Mac. These remnants may cause problems later, so be sure to do a backup before removing any app.

Better yet, before buying and installing an app, check the documentation or the product support link to get removal instructions. Don't install something you can't remove unless you're very certain you want it installed forever.

Removing app alias icons from the Dock and Desktop

After you uninstall an app, it's also wise to remove all Dock or alias icons because those icons will no longer work. To remove an app icon from the Dock, click the app icon that you want to remove, drag the icon up and away from the Dock, and then release the mouse button. Your chosen app disappears in a puff of animated smoke.

TIP

If you created multiple alias icons of an app, click the Finder icon to open a new Finder window, click in the Spotlight text box, and then type the name of the app you uninstalled followed by the word *alias*, such as **PowerPoint alias** or **Stickies alias**. The Finder will display the location of the specified alias icons. Click each alias icon you want to delete, and then press ⌘+Delete to move them to the Trash. *Au revoir!*

REMEMBER

Deleting the alias is *not* the same as deleting the app because the alias is only a pointer to the app, not the app itself. Removing the alias is useful to eliminate clutter but won't eliminate the app.

Removing user setting files

Almost every app creates special user setting files that contain custom settings and preferences for the app, such as the default font used to type text when you use the app or your choice of toolbar icons displayed by the app. When you uninstall an app by dragging it to the Trash, the app's user setting files remain on your computer.

The more unnecessary files you have cluttering your hard drive, the slower your Mac might perform because it needs to keep track of these unused files even though it isn't using them anymore. To keep your Mac in optimum condition, you should delete the user setting files of apps you uninstall from your computer. You can do that manually or you can buy an app to do it for you automatically. We explain both ways.

Manually removing user setting files

Manually removing user setting files requires deleting individual files or entire folders from your Mac's hard drive. This process isn't difficult although it can be tedious.

WARNING

If you feel squeamish about deleting files that you don't understand, don't delete them without an expert's help. If you delete the wrong files, you could mess up the way your Mac works.

Automatically removing user setting files

Because manually deleting user setting and preference files might seem scary and intimidating, you may prefer to remove these files automatically. To do so, you have to buy and install a special uninstaller app. When you run an uninstaller app, you tell it which app you want to uninstall. Then the uninstaller app identifies all the files used by that application.

Popular uninstaller apps include

>> **AppZapper:** www.appzapper.com

>> **Spring Cleaning:** http://my.smithmicro.com/

>> **Uninstaller:** http://macmagna.free.fr

Paying Attention to App Security

Apple makes it easy to keep your Mac free from the worst malware hazards. If you look at the Security & Privacy pane of System Preferences, you'll see one of the key safeguards (see Figure 5-20): You can choose to allow installation of apps only from the App Store or from known and identified developers. (This tool is called *Gatekeeper.*)

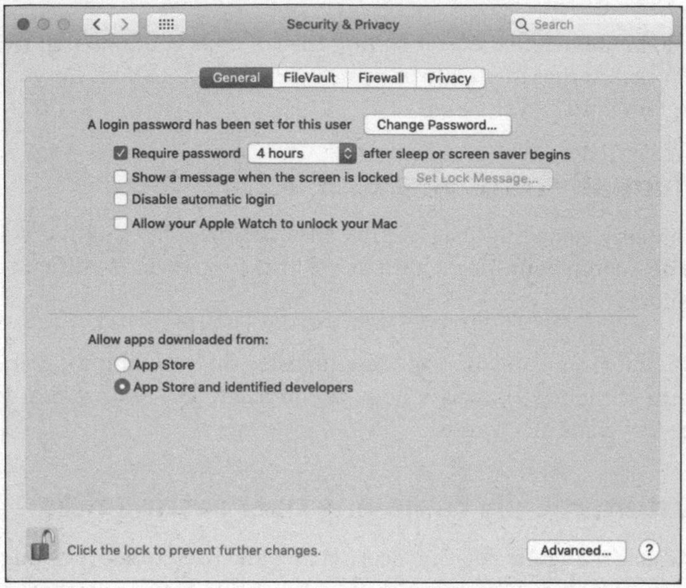

FIGURE 5-20:
This option
ensures that only
software checked
by Apple can be
installed.

All apps from known and identified developers are checked by Apple before they're released. The checks are designed for two critical security concerns:

>> Does the app run and does it run as described in the documentation?

>> Does the app contain code that could cause damage to the device or to other apps?

Note that there is another category of apps that you can install: If you're part of an organization such as a school or a corporation, the organization may have the ability to install apps on devices it owns.

IN THIS CHAPTER

» **Changing the Desktop and screen saver**

» **Setting the date and time**

» **Adjusting alert sounds**

» **Working in split-screen mode**

» **Making your Mac more accessible**

» **Talking to your Mac**

» **Listening to your Mac**

Chapter 6

Changing How Your Mac Looks, Sounds, and Feels

The desktop user interface functions the same way regardless of the Mac model you have, but that doesn't mean they all have to look and feel the same. To personalize your Mac, you can change the way it looks and even how it behaves.

By customizing your Mac — and adjusting how it works to make things easier on your eyes, ears, or hands — you can stamp it with your personality and truly turn your Mac into a personal computer that feels like it's working with you and for you, rather than against you.

When you have a choice about how an application or function looks or responds, the Preferences sections are where you go to specify your choices. There are two places to find preferences on your Mac:

>> **System Preferences** gathers all the preferences settings for your Mac operating system in one place. This is where you set up your Mac's appearance, connect to a network or printer, and establish the type of notifications

you want to receive for incoming information such as an email message or Facebook update. You read about keyboard, mouse, and trackpad preferences in Book 1, Chapter 2.

>> *Application menu*⇨**Preferences** lets you set application-specific preferences. In Book 1, Chapter 4, you can read all about Finder preferences.

In this chapter, we discuss the System Preferences. We show you how to customize your Desktop image, set up screen savers, and adjust the screen resolution. We explain how to use Notification Center and how to set the date and time. At the end of the chapter, we show you how to set Accessibility Preferences, which are the preferences you can choose to make working with your Mac easier if you have trouble with your vision, hearing, or movement.

REMEMBER

If you share your Mac with other people and set up separate user accounts as explained in Book 3, Chapter 2, some system preference settings, such as Network or Date & Time apply to all users, while others, such as Desktop, as well as app preferences, are specific to the user who sets them.

Changing the Desktop and Screen Saver

The Desktop fills the screen in the absence of any application windows, and the Screen Saver is the image that runs across the screen when your Mac sleeps. You set preferences for both from the same window, and we explain how to do that in the next few sections.

Choosing a Desktop image

Generally, the Desktop displays a decorative background image. Your Mac comes with a variety of images, but you can display any image, such as a photo captured with a digital camera or a favorite picture you downloaded from the Internet. To choose your Desktop image, follow these steps:

1. **Control-click anywhere on the Desktop and choose Change Desktop Background.**

   Or you can click the System Preferences icon on the Dock and choose Desktop & Screen Saver from the pop-up menu.

   The Desktop & Screen Saver preferences pane appears, as shown in Figure 6-1.

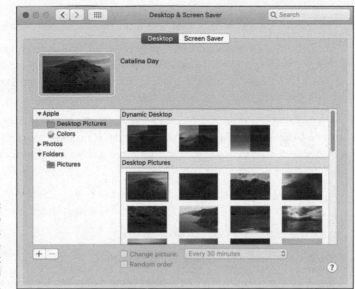

FIGURE 6-1:
Desktop
preferences
let you choose
a different
background
image or color.

2. **Choose one of the following options from the pop-up menu to the right of the thumbnail of the current desktop image.**

- *Fill Screen:* This option fills the screen with the selected image. The image may be cropped if the image aspect ratio is different from that of the screen.

- *Fit to Screen:* This option fits the entire image to the screen. If the aspect ratio does not match that of the screen, there will be white space on the left and right side of the image.

- *Stretch to Fill Screen:* This option fills the screen with the image, but it may increase the width or height nonproportionately if the image aspect ratio does not match that of the screen.

- *Center:* This option centers the image to the screen without resizing it. If you choose a small image, there will be white space around the image.

- *Tile:* This option tiles the image across the screen. In our humble opinion, this option is the best if you choose a small image for your desktop eye candy.

3. **Click one of the following to choose the Desktop image (click the disclosure triangle next to Apple if you don't see the first two choices):**

- *Desktop Pictures* to browse images bundled with macOS.

- *Colors* to pick a solid background color.

- *Folders* for access to photos stored in your Pictures folder.

4. **Choose the image or color that you want to adorn your Desktop.**

- *Use a personal photo.* Click the disclosure triangle next to Photos and then scroll through the choices. Click Photos to see all the photos you have stored or click successive disclosure triangles, such as Events or Places, to narrow your choices to specific albums in those sections.

- *Use something from your Pictures folder (inside Folders).* These are images downloaded from a website or from a digital camera. Images stored in separate folders inside the Pictures folder will not initially be visible; click the folder to see images inside.

- *Click the Add (+) button in the lower-left corner and use the dialog that appears to navigate to the folder that contains the image you want to use.*

5. **Click the image or color you want to use.**

6. **(Optional) Choose the Change Picture option.**

   This option changes the desktop image using one of images from the folder you choose in Step 4. From the pop-up menu, choose how often you want the picture to change. If you choose the Random Order option, the images will change randomly instead of changing from image to image in the order in which they appear in the originating folder.

7. **Click the Close button in the upper-left corner of the window. (Or choose System Preferences⇨Quit or press ⌘+Q to close the System Preferences window.)**

You can now choose from several dynamic desktop images. These images change their coloring so that it matches the time on your computer. In other words, if it's the middle of the night where you are, the dynamic images will be dark and may even show the moon. These effects are quite striking and make your Mac experience quite immersive — if it's the middle of the night on your desk it's the middle of the night in real life. Other people find this distracting. No matter which camp you're in, you can choose dynamic desktop images or not. It's a simple mouse click in preferences.

Customizing the screen saver

A *screen saver* is an animated image that appears onscreen after a fixed period when your Mac doesn't detect any keyboard, trackpad, or mouse activity. When selecting a screen saver, you can choose an image to display and the amount of time to wait before the screen saver starts.

TIP

For an eco-friendlier alternative to using the screen saver, check out the Energy Saver setting described in the section about putting your Mac in Sleep mode in Book 1, Chapter 1.

To choose a screen saver, follow these steps:

1. **Choose ⌘⇨System Preferences from the Finder menu and click the Desktop & Screen Saver icon.**

    Or you can Control-click the System Preferences icon on the Dock and choose Change Desktop Background from the pop-up menu.

    The Desktop & Screen Saver preferences pane appears.

2. **Click the Screen Saver tab.**

    The Screen Saver preferences pane (shown in Figure 6-2) appears.

3. **Click one of the screen saver styles and behaviors shown in the left column.**

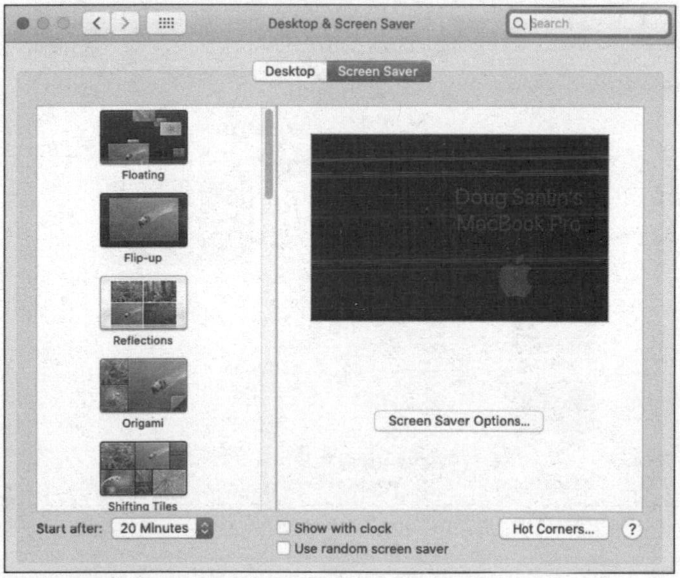

FIGURE 6-2: You can choose your screen saver on the Screen Saver pane.

4. **Open the Start After pop-up menu to specify an amount of time to wait before your screen saver starts.**

    Opting for a short amount of time can mean the screen saver starts while you're reading a web page or document, so you might have to experiment a bit to find the best time for you.

5. **(Optional) Select the Show with Clock check box to display the time with your screen saver.**

6. **(Optional) Use Random Screen Saver.**

    macOS displays a different screen saver each time your computer goes to sleep.

7. (Optional) Enable Hot Corners.

a. Click the Hot Corners button (shown previously in Figure 6-2).

b. Open one (or each) of the four pop-up menus and choose a command that your Mac will carry out when you move your pointer to the specified corner, as shown in Figure 6-3.

Two common uses for a hot corner are to turn on the screen saver, or to put your Mac's display to sleep to save energy, but you can use them for any of the options from each corner's pop-up menu, as shown in Figure 6-3. For your convenience, the pop-up menu that opens when you configure a hot corner is shown below the dialog.

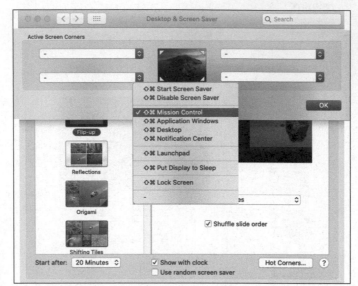

FIGURE 6-3:
Each pop-up menu defines a function for a hot corner.

TIP

You can define multiple hot corners to do the same task, such as defining the two top corners to start the screen saver and the two bottom corners to put the display to sleep.

c. Click OK to close the Active Screen Corners dialog.

8. Click the Close button in the Desktop & Screen Saver preferences pane.

TIP

You can customize the layout of the System Preferences window by choosing View⇨Customize. Clear the check box next to the items you don't want to see. You still see all the preferences in the Show All menu and the System Preferences menu accessed from the Dock.

Changing the Display and Appearance

Because you'll be staring at your Mac's screen every time you use it, you might want to modify how the screen displays information. Some changes you can make include changing the Desktop size (resolution), or selecting another color scheme of your various menus, windows, and dialogs. The next sections show you how.

TIP

This section focuses on changing the appearance of your Mac and its behaviors. Some apps let you change the appearance of the individual app.

Changing the screen resolution

The display defines the screen resolution, measured in *pixels*, which are the dots that make up an image. The higher the display resolution, the more pixels you have and the sharper the image — but everything on your screen might appear smaller.

REMEMBER

Selecting your Mac display's highest resolution generally puts your Mac's best face forward, so to speak, when it comes to making everything look sharp and correct on your screen.

To change the screen resolution, follow these steps:

1. **Choose ⌘⇨System Preferences and click the Displays icon, or click the System Preferences icon on the Dock and choose Displays from the menu that opens.**

The Display preferences pane opens, as shown in Figure 6-4. Depending on your Mac model, the image may be different.

2. **Click the Display tab (if it isn't already selected) and select one of the following:**

- *Default for Display:* Sets the resolution to an optimal size.

- *Scaled:* Choose a specific resolution to make objects appear larger onscreen or to make them smaller so you see more objects onscreen.

3. **Choose a resolution.**

Your Mac immediately changes the resolution so you can see how it looks. If you don't like the resolution, try again until you find one that's easy on your eyes.

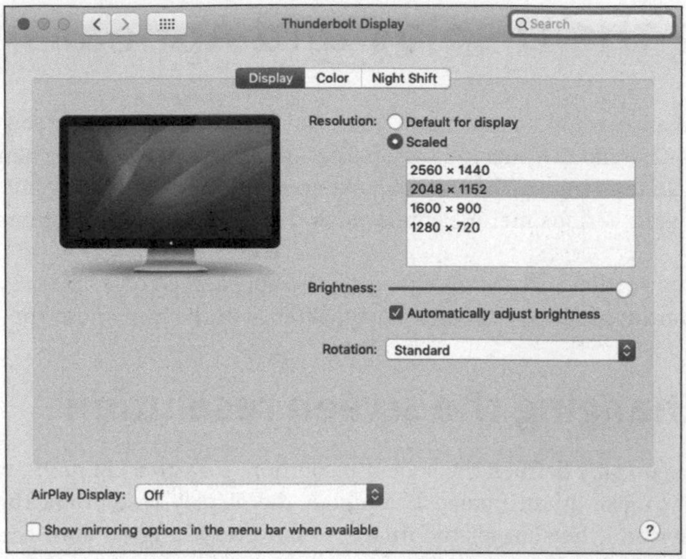

FIGURE 6-4:
The Display
preferences.

4. Adjust brightness.

Move the brightness slider to adjust the luminosity of your screen or select the Automatically Adjust Brightness check box to have your Mac adjust the screen brightness based on the ambient light.

5. (Optional) Adjust color.

Click the Color tab, click the Calibrate button, and then follow the steps that appear to tweak the way your Mac displays colors; click the Done button when you reach the final step to return to the Display preferences pane.

6. Click the Close button in the System Preferences window when you're happy with the screen resolution.

**TECHNICAL
STUFF**

The AirPlay Display menu will be active when external monitors or displays are available on the same network. A Detect Displays button appears when you hold down the Option key. Do this and then click the display in the pop-up menu to connect your Mac to it. After you connect another display, hold down the Option key while clicking Scaled to adjust the resolution for that display.

Using Night Shift

The Night Shift tab lets you schedule a shift in the general colors of the screen. Research has shown that the normal blueish screen display (referred to as "cool" colors) can interfere with sleep, so you may get a better night's sleep by using a display that is biased toward the yellow end of the palette ("warm") rather than blue.

As you see in Figure 6-5, you can set Night Shift to be active at specific times of day depending on the clock or on sunrise and sunset.

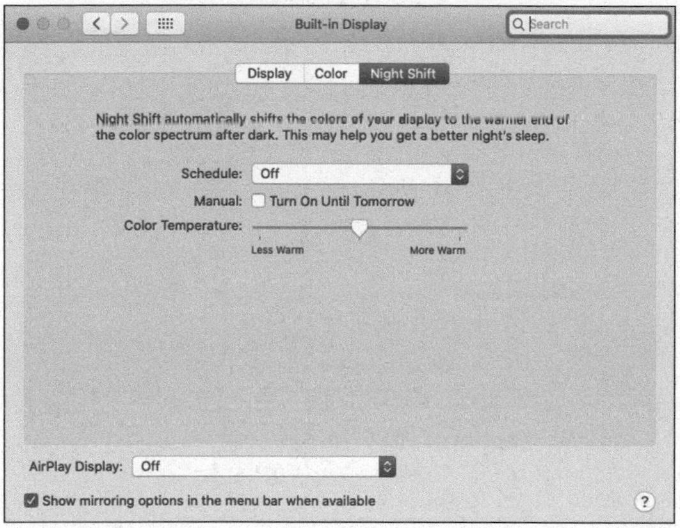

FIGURE 6-5:
Get a better night's sleep with Night Shift.

Changing the colors of the user interface

Another way to change the appearance of the screen is to modify the colors used in windows, menus, and dialogs. To change the color of these user interface items, follow these steps:

1. **Choose ⌘⇨ System Preferences and click the General icon.**

Or, Control-click the System Preferences icon on the Dock and choose General from the menu that opens.

The General preferences pane appears, as shown in Figure 6-6.

2. **Choose from Light, Dark, or Auto overall appearance.**

The Light option uses lighter colors for buttons, menus, and windows. With the Dark option, buttons, menus, and windows appear dark. With the third option, macOS periodically adjusts the appearance of buttons, menus, and windows throughout the day based on ambient lighting.

3. **From the Highlight Color pop-up menu, choose your color variations.**

The Accent color radio buttons define the colors that normally show up on windows, buttons, and so on. The Highlight Color pop-up menu defines the color of items that you select.

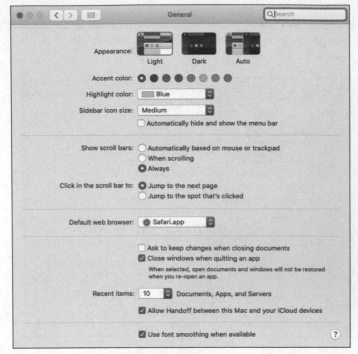

FIGURE 6-6:
Use Appearance
preferences to
modify colors.

4. **From the Sidebar Icon Size pop-up menu, choose the size of icons in the Sidebar of the Finder window.**

5. **Select the radio buttons and check boxes to adjust how the scroll bars work.**

   These changes will be seen only in applications that support these features. Choose from these three:

   - *Automatically Based on Mouse or Trackpad* reveals scroll bars only when the window is smaller than its contents. This gives you a visual clue that there's more than meets the eye.

   - *When Scrolling* uses a shadowy black oblong that appears only when you are hovering over the right edge of the window if you're scrolling up and down, or on the bottom of the window if you're scrolling left to right. The advantage is that scroll bars don't take up precious window real estate.

   - *Always* puts right side and bottom scroll bars on your windows whether you need them or not.

   And then choose one of these options when you click in the scroll bar:

   - *Jump to the Next Page* moves your document up or down one page when you click above or below the scroller in the scroll bar.

- *Jump to the Spot That's Clicked* takes you to the position in your document more or less in relation to where you clicked the scroll bar. If you click near the bottom of the scroll bar, the window jumps toward the end of the document.

6. **Choose your default web browser.**

   You can always open another one that you installed on your system.

7. **(Recommended) Select the Close Windows When Quitting an Application check box to only open the app (and no windows) when you restart an app.**

TIP

   By default, when you quit an app, windows that are open in that app close. Then, when you restart the app, the windows that were open when you quit automatically reopen.

8. **From the Recent Items pop-up menu, choose how many items you want to appear in the Recent Items list under the menu.**

9. **Select the LCD Font Smoothing When Available check box to make fonts appear smoother.**

10. **Accept the default, Allow Handoff between This Mac and Your iCloud Devices.**

   This option allows you to continue work you started on your Mac on another iOS device that is connected to iCloud with the same Apple ID. For example, you could start work on a Pages document and then continue on your iPad. We advise you to accept this option.

11. **Click the Close button to close the General preferences pane.**

TIP

To move quickly between one System Preferences pane and another, click and hold the Show All button to reveal a pop-up menu that lists all the preferences items in alphabetical order.

Changing the Date and Time

Keeping track of time might seem trivial, but knowing the right time is important. That way, your Mac can determine when you created or modified a particular file, and keep track of appointments you've made through applications, such as Reminders and Calendar.

Of course, keeping track of time is useless if you don't set the right time to begin with. To set the proper date and time, follow these steps:

1. **Choose ➪ System Preferences and click the Date & Time icon.**

    Or, Control-click the System Preferences icon on the Dock and choose Date & Time from the menu that opens.

    The Date & Time preferences pane appears, as shown in Figure 6-7.

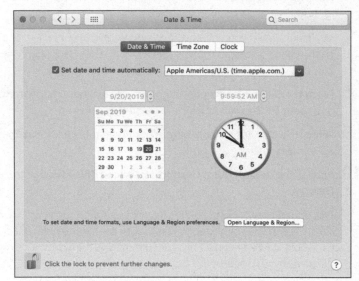

FIGURE 6-7:
Set the clock in
your Mac.

2. **Click the Lock button to make changes.**

    A dialog appears prompting you to enter your admin password to make changes.

3. **Enter your password and click Unlock.**

    Time is on your side.

4. **Select (or deselect) the Set Date & Time Automatically check box.**

    If you select this check box, open the drop-down list to choose a location.

    This feature works only if you're connected to the Internet. If you aren't connected to the Internet, click the calendar to pick a date and click the clock to set the time.

    You can use a different method to set the time. Instead of selecting the Set Date & Time Automatically check box, click the Time Zone tab at the top of the window and then click near your home city on the map.

You can also click in the Closest City field and begin typing the name of the city nearest you in the same time zone, or click the drop-down list and select the city nearest you.

5. **(Optional) On the Time Zone tab, click Set Time Zone Automatically Using Current Location if you want the clock to change automatically when you travel to a different time zone.**

    This feature works when you have an Internet connection and have turned on Location Services.

6. **Click the Clock tab and select (or deselect) the Show Date and Time in Menu Bar check box, as shown in Figure 6-8.**

    If selected, this displays the time on the right side of the menu bar. After you make your selection, you can select the other options to change the appearance of the clock, such as choosing between a digital or an analog clock, and choosing whether to show the day of the week (Digital option only).

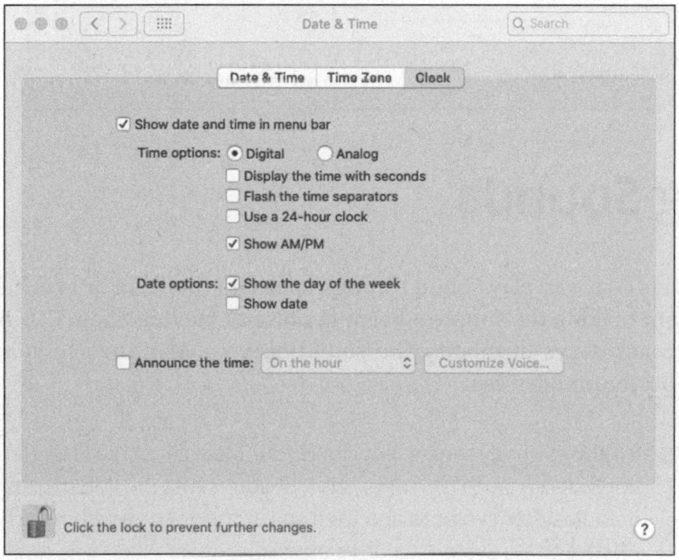

FIGURE 6-8:
Pick the type of clock you want.

7. **Select (or deselect) the Announce the Time check box if you want your Mac to recite the time by using a synthesized voice every hour, half-hour, or quarter hour.**

    The associated pop-up menu lets you specify when announcements are made; click the Customize Voice button to choose what kind of voice is used and how quickly and loudly it utters the time.

8. **Click the Lock button to save your changes and close the Date & Time preferences pane.**

TIP

Click the Language & Region icon in System Preferences to change the time and date format based on your language and region. Use the pop-up menus as shown in Figure 6-9.

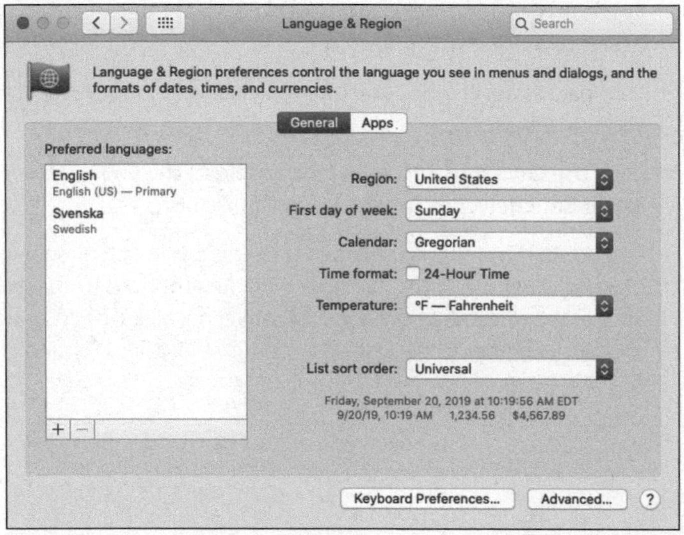

FIGURE 6-9:
The Language & Region preferences provide time and date formatting options.

Adjusting Sounds

Every Mac can play sound through speakers (built-in or external) or headphones, from making the simplest beeping noise to playing audio CDs like a stereo. Three primary ways to modify the sound on your Mac involve volume, balance, and input/output devices.

>> **Volume:** Simply means how loud your Mac plays sound by default. Many applications, such as iTunes, also let you adjust the volume, so you can set the default system volume and then adjust the volume within each application, relative to the system volume, as well.

>> **Balance:** Defines how sound plays through the right and left stereo speakers. By adjusting the balance, you can make sound louder coming from one speaker and weaker coming from the other.

>> **Input/output:** Depending on your equipment, you might have multiple input and output devices — speakers and headphones as two distinct output devices, for example. By defining which input and output device to use, you can define which one to use by default.

To modify the way your Mac accepts and plays sound, follow these steps:

1. **Choose ⌘⇨System Preferences and click the Sound icon.**

Or, Control-click the System Preferences icon on the Dock and choose Sound from the menu that opens.

The Sound preferences pane appears, as shown in Figure 6-10.

2. **Choose a sound effect.**

Click the Sound Effects tab (if it isn't already selected) and scroll through the list to choose the sound your Mac will play when it needs your attention, such as when you're quitting an application without saving a document.

TIP

In the last section of this chapter, "Speaking with Your Mac," we tell you how to hear a spoken warning when your Mac wants to alert you to something.

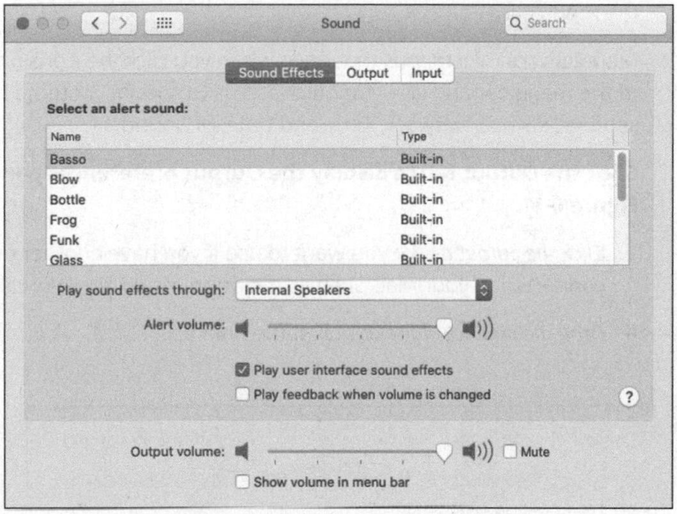

FIGURE 6-10:
Use Sound Effects preferences to define audible alerts.

3. **(Optional) From the Play Sound Effects Through pop-up menu, choose whether your Mac plays sounds through its built-in Internal Speakers or through another set of speakers you might have connected to your Mac.**

4. **(Optional) Drag the Alert Volume slider to the desired location to set how loudly (or softly) your Mac will play the alert when it needs to get your attention.**

5. (Optional) Select (or deselect) either of the following check boxes:

- *Play User Interface Sound Effects:* Lets you hear such sounds as the crinkling of paper when you empty the Trash or a whooshing sound if you remove an icon from the Dock.

- *Play Feedback When Volume Is Changed:* Beeps to match the sound level while you increase or decrease the volume.

6. (Optional) Drag the Output Volume slider or press the volume-up and volume-down keys on the keyboard.

Output volume defines the maximum volume that sound-playing applications can emit, so if you set Output volume at 75 percent and then play a song in iTunes with the iTunes volume at 50 percent, the song plays at 37.5 percent of the Mac's maximum output capacity.

7. (Optional) Select (or deselect) the Show Volume in Menu Bar check box.

When selected, you can see and adjust your Mac's volume from the *menulet* in the menu bar.

Menulets are mini menus that open when you click the icons on the right end of the menu bar and give you quick access to specific System Preferences settings, such as Network, Time and Date, or Sound.

REMEMBER

8. Click the Output tab to display the Output preferences pane, as shown in Figure 6-11.

- *Click the output device* you want to use if you have another output option connected to your Mac, such as headphones, external speakers, or Apple TV.

- *Drag the Balance slider* to adjust the balance.

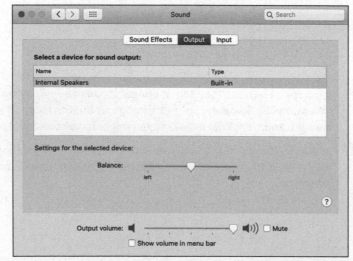

FIGURE 6-11:
Adjust volume and balance of sound output from apps like Music.

9. Click the Input tab to open the Input preferences pane, as shown in Figure 6-12.

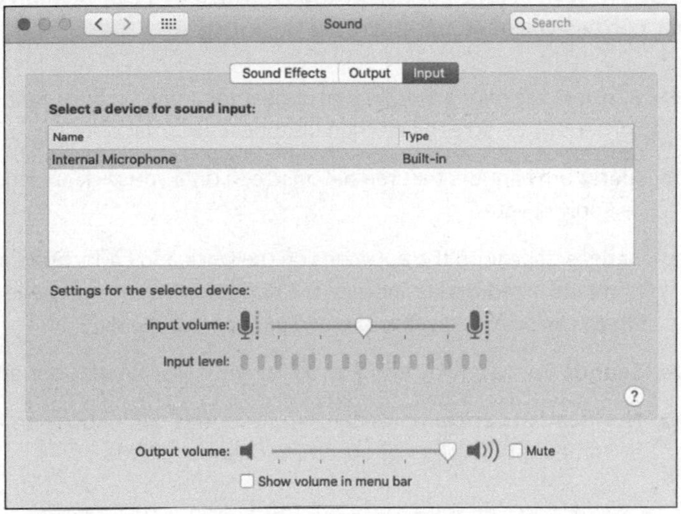

FIGURE 6-12:
Input preferences let you define how to record sound.

10. Click the input device you want your Mac to use to receive sound.

For instance, you might choose a built-in microphone or the line in port as your input device.

Your Mac may not have a Line In port — the MacBook Air does not.

Drag the Input Volume slider to adjust the default input volume.

11. Click the Close button to close the Sound preferences pane when you finish making adjustments.

TECHNICAL STUFF

If you connect a USB microphone or headset to your Mac, macOS detects the hardware and give you options for controlling input and output in the Sound Preferences pane.

Noticing Notifications

When your Mac wants to tell you or remind you of something, it alerts you. It used to be those alerts were few and far between, but today with bells ringing for birthdays, beeps telling you you've got mail, and banners flying across the screen with the latest tweet, your Mac can sound like a noisy traffic jam. From Notification Center, you can define how you want to be alerted by any app that might generate an alert. It's managed in System Preferences, and you view the Notification Center by clicking its button at the far right end of the status bar.

There are several types of notifications, which you can turn on or off for each app that notifies you of something:

>> **Banners** are mini-windows that appear for a few seconds in the upper-right corner of your screen and then disappear automatically.

>> **Alerts** are banners that remain onscreen until you click an action button, such as Reply or Later.

>> **Badges** appear on the app icons on the Dock and Launchpad as white numbers in red circles, indicate the number of items that need attending, which can be messages to be read or apps to update.

>> **Sounds** play to let you know an app or your Mac needs your attention.

>> **Notification Center** holds items from various apps, such as a Facebook post by someone you follow or upcoming calendar events.

To personalize how you receive notifications, do the following:

1. Choose ⇨ System Preferences or click the System Preferences icon on the Dock or from Launchpad.

2. Click the Notifications icon.

The Notifications preferences window opens, as shown in Figure 6-13. Your preferences window may look slightly different based on the apps you have installed on your Mac.

The list that runs down the left of the window shows notification options for each app. Do Not Disturb is at the top of the heap. Other applications are listed in alphabetical order. Beneath each app is a description of the type of notification given (for example, Calendar notifications are badges, sounds, and alerts). Off is displayed beneath applications for which you have not allowed notifications.

3. In the list that runs down the left of the Notifications preferences window, click an app and choose how you want to be notified when that app has information for you.

Figure 6-14 shows the notification options for Calendar.

• *Click the Calendar alert style you prefer.* Choose None, Banners, or Alerts.

• *Select the check boxes for the type of notifications you want.* If you select Show in Notification Center, use the pop-up menu to choose how many recent notifications you want to see.

FIGURE 6-13:
Manage how your
Mac alerts you.

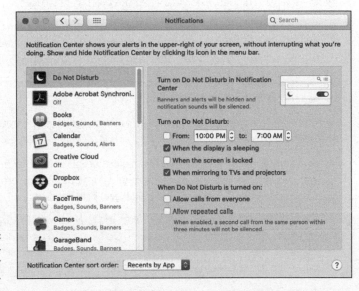

FIGURE 6-14:
Setting notifica-
tIon options for
the Calendar app.

TIP

If you deselect Show in Notification Center, the app will have the word *Off* below the application name in the Notification Center section of the list on the left of the preferences window.

4. **Click the next app in the list and set your preferences.**

   Some apps have additional choices:

   - *Mail:* Choose if you want to show an alert when new mail arrives.

   - *Messages:* Choose if and when you want to see a message preview.

5. **Open the Sort Notification Center sort order pop-up menu and choose one of the following options:**

   - *Recents,* which displays items in Notification Center in the chronological order in which they arrived

   - *Recents by App,* which displays the most recent notifications, sorted by application.

   - *Manually by App,* in which case you click and drag the apps in the preferences list into the order you wish them to appear in Notification Center

6. **(Optional) Click Do Not Disturb, as shown in Figure 6-15, to schedule an interruption-free work or rest time.**

   When Do Not Disturb is on, you don't hear any alert sounds and notification banners remain hidden. Choose the features you want to use:

   - *Turn on Do Not Disturb:* Select this check box and then use the arrows to set the From and To times to schedule a daily fixed time of silence. Deselect the check box to deactivate scheduled Do Not Disturb time.

   - *When the Display Is Sleeping:* Selecting this check box prevents notifications when the display is sleeping.

   - *When the Screen Is Locked:* Selecting this check box disables notifications when the screen is locked.

   - *When Mirroring to TVs and Projectors:* Selecting this check box prevents interruptions such as a banner that might come across the projection screen during your multi-million dollar deal presentation.

   - *When Do Not Disturb Is Turned On:* Select the check boxes for the types of FaceTime calls you want to allow when Do Not Disturb is turned on. Choose Everyone or Favorites if you want to allow some or all FaceTime calls. Click Allow Repeated Calls if you want insistent callers to get through.

7. **Click the Close button to exit System Preferences.**

   To see how your settings affect the Notification Center, click the Notification Center button, the right-most button of the menu bar that looks like three horizontal lines to display notifications, as shown in Figure 6-16.

TIP

From the Notifications window, you can also enable Night Shift and Do Not Disturb by clicking the buttons.

8. **After reviewing the Notifications Center, click the Desktop to close Notification Center.**

REMEMBER

Click the button on the right side of the task bar any time you want to see notifications.

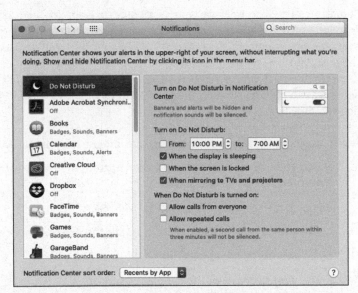

FIGURE 6-15: This dialog is your ticket to peace and quiet when you want it.

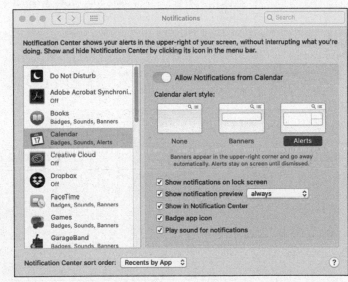

FIGURE 6-16: Consider yourself notified.

TIP

To disable notifications while you're doing something important like writing the next Great American Mystery Novel, press Option and click the Notification Center button to enable Do Not Disturb. Click the button again to disable Do Not Disturb.

Working in Split-View Mode

Sometimes it's nice to have your work side-by-side, so you can seamlessly go from one program to another without switching desktops. This feature has been available for Mac users since Mac OS X El Capitan. If you've used this feature in the past, you'll be happy to know that the Apple software design gurus have made it easier to use. If you've never worked in Split-View mode, we're about to show you a way to seamlessly increase your productivity. To work in Split-View mode, do the following:

1. **Launch an Apple app such as Pages, Numbers, Keynote, or Safari.**

2. **Hover your cursor over the Full Screen button, the green button on the upper-left side of the interface.**

   A pop-up menu appears, as shown in Figure 6-17.

3. **Choose which side of the screen you want the app to appear on.**

4. **Open another Apple application.**

5. **Pause your cursor over the Full Screen button.**

   The pop-up menu previously shown in Figure 6-17 appears.

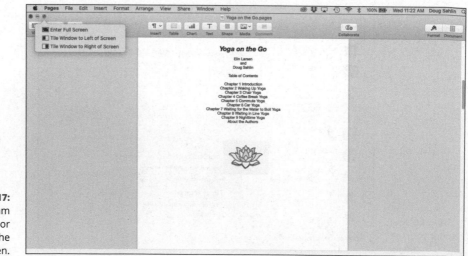

FIGURE 6-17:
Tiling a program to the left or right side of the screen.

6. **Choose the side of the screen that is opposite the side you choose in Step 3.**

   macOS displays the programs in Split-View mode. Figure 6-18 shows Pages on the left side of the screen and Safari on the right.

7. **To switch from one app to another, click inside that application's window.**

8. **To exit Split-View mode, click the Full Screen button on either application.**

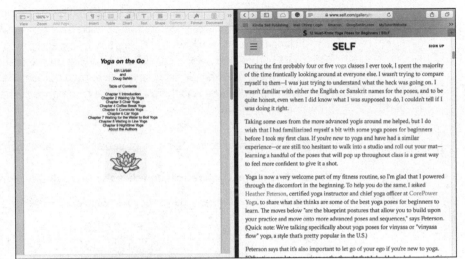

FIGURE 6-18: Working in Split-View mode.

Using Your Mac's Accessibility Features

Not everyone has perfect eyesight, hearing, or eye-hand coordination. If you have trouble with your vision, hearing, or ability to use the keyboard, trackpad, or mouse (or all three), using a computer can be difficult. That's why every Mac comes with special Accessibility features that you can turn on and modify for your needs. These features fall under three categories — seeing, hearing, and interacting — all of which we introduce you to on the following pages. If you're interested in getting the most out of the Accessibility features, especially VoiceOver and Switch Control, we recommend that you read Apple's extensive instructions for all the Accessibility features on both the Help menu and online at www.apple.com/support/accessibility.

TIP

Click the question mark button in the lower-right corner of any System Preferences pane to open help for that preference.

Mitigating vision limitations

Every Mac includes three options to help the visually impaired:

» **Display:** Inverts the color of the screen so you see white or light colored text on a dark background.

» **Zoom:** Sets up keyboard shortcuts so you can enlarge (zoom) the screen.

» **VoiceOver:** Allows your Mac to read text, email, and even descriptions of the screen in a computer-generated voice. VoiceOver can speak more than 30 languages and analyzes text paragraph by paragraph, so the reading is more natural and, well, humanlike. You can set up preferences for specific activities: for example, reading headlines at a quicker speaking rate than the article itself. And there are special commands to make browsing web pages easier.

To modify the vision assistance features of your Mac, follow these steps:

1. **Choose ⌾ System Preferences and click the Accessibility icon.**

The Accessibility preferences pane, shown in Figure 6-19, opens.

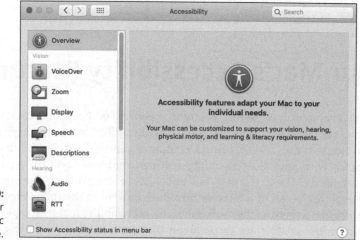

FIGURE 6-19:
Set options for making your Mac easier to use.

2. Click VoiceOver.

The VoiceOver Preferences appear. You have three options:

- *Enable VoiceOver:* Click this check box to enable VoiceOver, which provides spoken or Braille descriptions of items on the screen. This option also provides control of the computer via the keyboard.

- *Open VoiceOver Training:* Click this button to listen to the Mac's digital computer voice show you how to use the VoiceOver option.

- *Open VoiceOver Utility:* Click this button to open a dialog with options for the VoiceOver Utility. This dialog is divided into a series of sections such as Verbosity, Speech, Navigation, Web, and so on. For example, in Speech, you choose a computer voice you like and the rate at which the voice speaks to you. Choose voice and Rate options from the drop-down menus.

3. Click Zoom.

The Zoom section of the Accessibility Preferences dialog appears, as shown in Figure 6-20.

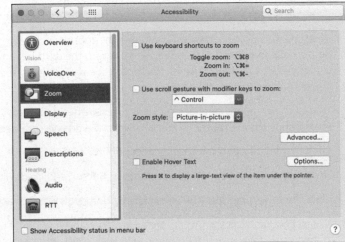

FIGURE 6-20: Setting Zoom Accessibility Preferences.

4. Set the following Zoom Accessibility Preferences:

- *Use Keyboard Shortcuts to Zoom:* Choose this option to use the default macOS shortcuts for zooming in or out. After choosing this option, you can make tasks easier (for example, when logging in you can use a shortcut to enlarge the password text field).

- *Use Scroll Gesture with Modifiers to Zoom:* Choose this option to use gestures on a trackpad or the scroll wheel on a mouse to zoom. Choose one of the following modifiers: the Control key, the Option key, or the ⌘ key.

- *Zoom Style:* Choose one of the following options from the drop-down menu: Full Screen, Split Window, or Picture-in-Picture. Experiment with this setting to see which option you prefer.

- *Advanced:* Click this button to open the Advanced Zoom Preferences dialog, which is divided into two tabs: Appearance and Controls. On the Appearance tab, you choose how the screen moves when zoomed in, and other options that make the computer easier to view. Smooth Images is selected by default, but you can also choose Invert Colors, Flash Screen When a Notification Appears out of the Zoomed Area of the Screen, Follow Keyboard Focus, and Keep Zoom Window Stationary.

  On the Controls tab, you set options for modifier keys and whether to use trackpad gestures to zoom. On this tab, you also set maximum and minimum zoom.

- *Enable Hover Text:* Choose this option, and text is enlarged when you hover your cursor over it. Click the Advanced button to open another dialog, which enables you to set the size of hover text, the font, and activation modifier.

TIP
In our humble opinion, the best way to set the zoom options is to plant your butt in your computer chair and experiment with the different options until you come up with a combination that makes it easy for you to see text and images when using your favorite programs.

TIP
The zooming options can be particularly helpful when working with photo editing apps or when aligning several objects in a drawing or page layout app.

5. **Click Display to open the Display accessibility options.**

   The dialog is divided into three tabs: Display, Cursor, and Color Filters.

6. **Click the following tabs and select the options you want to activate:**

   - *Display tab:* Select the Invert Colors check box to switch to display white text on a black screen. If you choose Invert Colors, don't enable Night Shift. You can also increase contrast, reduce motion when you open applications or switch desktops, or reduce the transparency that is apparent with some backgrounds. The last option makes it easier to read text.

   - *Cursor tab:* On this tab, you can change the cursor size. Shaking the mouse pointer to locate it is enabled by default. This option enlarges the cursor when you shake the mouse from side to side or move a finger quickly on the trackpad.

- *Color Filters tab:* On this tab, if you enable color filters, you can convert the display to grayscale, or choose one of four color filters. Again our advice is to experiment with the different options to see which one you prefer.

TIP

Click Show Accessibility Status in the Menu Bar to access an Accessibility menu that shows which features are activated.

7. **Click the Close button or press ⌘+Q to quit System Preferences or go on to the next section to set up other Accessibility functions.**

Compensating for hearing limitations

To adjust for hearing impairments, you can have your Mac flash the screen to catch your attention and set up subtitles and closed captioning to appear when those options are available. Follow these steps to manage these two Hearing options:

1. **Choose ⊄⇨System Preferences and click the Accessibility icon.**

2. **Click Speech.**

   The Speech Accessibility dialog appears. In this section of Accessibility Preferences, you can choose your preferred system voice, specify the speaking rate, and choose to enable announcements when an alert is displayed or an app needs your attentions. You can also choose to have text read aloud when a keyboard shortcut (Option+Esc by default, but you can change it) is pressed. You can also choose for the computer to speak items under your cursor, for example, the name of a folder or button.

TIP

If you visit websites or view documents with lots of visual content, you can choose to have an audio description play when available in the Descriptions tab of Accessibility preferences.

3. **Click Audio.**

   The Audio section of Accessibility Preferences appears.

4. **Select the Flash the Screen When an Alert Sound Occurs check box.**

   This option flashes the screen when an alert sound is played.

5. **(Optional) Select the Play Stereo Audio as Mono check box to remove the stereo effect from music or other stereo-enabled sounds your Mac plays.**

REMEMBER

Use the Sound Preferences to adjust the volume of alerts and other audible output, as we explain in the earlier section, "Adjusting Sounds."

6. **Click the Captions button to select how you want to see subtitles or closed captioning, when those services are available.**

   Make the appropriate selections from the options shown in Figure 6-20.

- *Style for Subtitles and Captions:* Click one of the choices in the list, as shown in Figure 6-21, to see how it will appear and if you want to select it. Or click the plus button to create a custom subtitle style. In the window that opens, type a name for your new subtitle; choose the typeface, size, and color from the pop-up menus; and then click Done. The new subtitle style is added to the list.

- *Prefer Closed Captions and SDH (Synchronous Digital Hierarchy):* Select this check box if you want to see those types of captions rather than subtitles.

7. **Click the Close button or press ⌘+Q to quit System Preferences or go on to the next section to set up other Accessibility functions.**

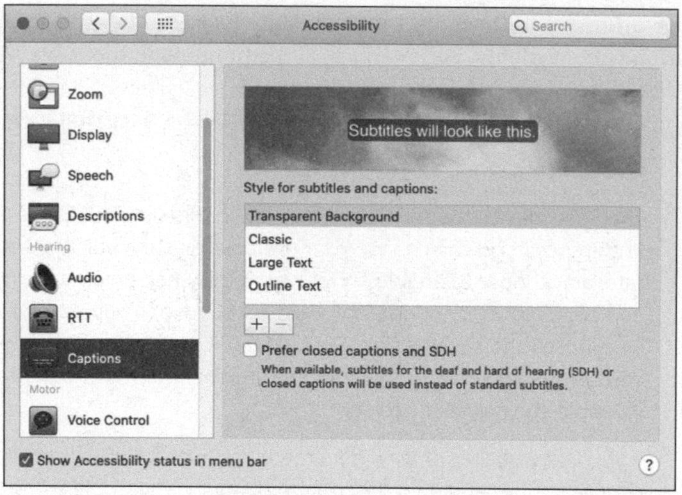

FIGURE 6-21:
Create custom subtitle styles here.

If you're watching movies, TV shows, or other video in one of your Mac's media player applications (such as iTunes, QuickTime, or DVD Player), you may have closed caption options available, depending on the source of the video. Some apps have controls for subtitles and closed captioning within their menus.

REMEMBER

Interacting with ease

If you have physical limitations or find eye–hand coordination challenging, your Mac offers several options to improve your control of the user interface. You find each of the following under the Interacting section of the Accessibility preferences.

Easing keyboard limitations

If you have physical limitations using the keyboard, the Mac offers two solutions: Sticky Keys and Slow Keys. Sticky Keys can help you use keystroke shortcuts, such as ⌘+P (Print), which usually require pressing two or more keys at the same time. By turning on Sticky Keys, you can use keystroke shortcuts by pressing one key at a time in sequence. Press the modifier key first, such as the ⌘ key, and it "sticks" in place and waits until you press a second key to complete the keystroke shortcut.

The Slow Keys feature slows the reaction time of the Mac every time you press a key. Normally when you press a key, the Mac accepts it right away, but Slow Keys can force a Mac to wait a long time before accepting the typed key. That way, your Mac will ignore any accidental taps on the keyboard and patiently wait until you hold down a key for a designated period before it accepts it as valid.

To turn on Sticky Keys or Slow Keys, follow these steps:

1. **Choose ⌘⇨System Preferences and click the Accessibility icon.**

2. **Click Keyboard in the left pane of the window.**

   The Keyboard Accessibility Preference has two sections, Hardware and Accessibility Keyboard, as shown in Figure 6-22.

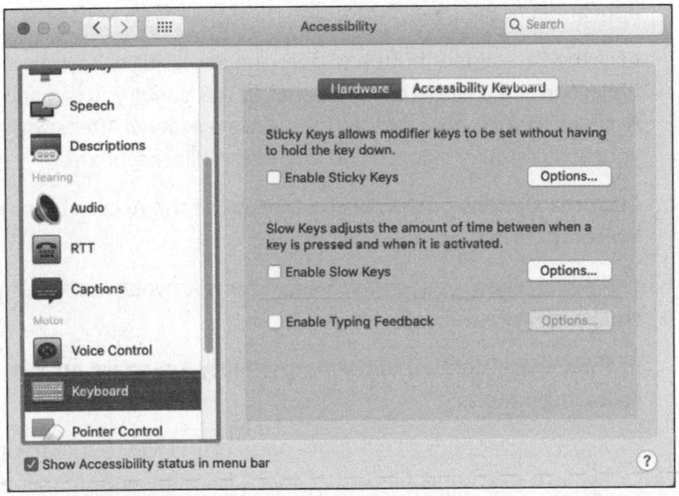

FIGURE 6-22: Keyboard preferences let you adjust keyboard behavior.

3. **In the Hardware section, you have the following options:**

   • *Enable Sticky Keys:* Click this check box to enable the Sticky Keys option. After enabling this option, click the Options button to open another window with these options: Press the Shift Key Five Times to Toggle Sticky Keys, which lets you turn the feature on and off from the keyboard; Beep When a Modifier Key Is Set, which causes a beep to sound after a modifier key like Option or ⌘ is set, after which you can press the next key of the keyboard shortcut; or Display Pressed Key on Screen, which displays a modifier key like ⌘ or Alt on screen. By default, the key is displayed on the upper right of the screen, but you can choose another option from the drop-down menu.

- *Enable Slow Keys:* Click this check box to create a slight delay between when a key is clicked and when it's activated. Click the Options button and you can click the Use Click Key Sounds check box, which makes a sound like a typewriter when a key is clicked. You also vary the delay between when a key is clicked and when it's recognized by macOS by dragging the Acceptance Delay Slider.

- *Enable Typing Feedback:* Click this check box, and then click Options. Here, you can have a voice echo the keys you press and words you type. You also have the option to echo selection changes and modifier keys.

4. **Click the Accessibility Keyboard button.**

   The Accessibility Keyboard section of the Keyboard Accessibility Preferences appears. In this section, click Enable Accessibility Keyboard, and a virtual keyboard appears on your screen. When you press a key, it's highlighted on the Accessibility Keyboard. You can also click a key from the Accessibility Keyboard to add it to a document or email you're creating. As you type, word suggestions appear below the Dwell buttons on the Accessibility keyboard.

TIP

   Click the Panel Editor button to open the Accessibility Keyboard Active Panel Collection and create a custom panel. In this panel, you can add buttons, to the Accessibility Keyboard that perform certain actions. After saving your changes, your customizations appear on the accessibility keyboard.

5. **Click the Options button at the bottom of the Accessibility Keyboard Preferences dialog.**

   The dialog refreshes and has three sections for your Accessibility Keyboard, as shown in Figure 6-23.

6. **In the General section of the Accessibility Keyboard option, choose the following options:**

- *Appearance:* Choose Dark (dark background, white characters) or Light (white background, black characters) from the pop-up menu.

- *Fade Panel after ___ Seconds of Inactivity:* Choose this option and then choose how many seconds from the pop-up menu. If you choose this option, you specify the opacity by which it fades by dragging the Fade By slider.

FIGURE 6-23:
Setting your
Accessibility
Keyboard
options.

- *Play Key Sounds:* Choose this option and the computer voice will tell you which key you've pressed. If you choose this option, choose whether the sound should be played on Mouse Down or Mouse Up.

- *Insert and Remove Spaces Automatically:* Choose this option and macOS will manage content after punctuation marks, inserting or deleting spaces based on content.

- *Capitalize Sentences Automatically:* Choose this option and macOS will automatically capitalize the first character of a word entered after a period.

TIP

Click the Keyboard Preferences button to display a dialog box that offers more options for customizing the Accessibility Keyboard such as adding keyboard and emoji viewers in the menu bar, replacing text, shortcuts, and more. You can also enable dictation from this panel. By default, there is a Dwell menu at the top of the Accessibility Keyboard.

The Dwell buttons enable you to perform an action when you select a Dwell button and then hover your cursor over an object. From left to right the Dwell buttons are:

- *Left-click:* Performs a left-click after you dwell on the button and then dwell on an item.

- *Double-click:* Performs a double-click after you dwell on the button and dwell on an item.

- *Right-click:* Performs a right-click after you dwell on the button and then dwell on an item.

- *Drag and Drop:* Dwell on the button to activate, and then dwell on an item to activate drag; then reposition the item and dwell again to release the item.

- *Scroll Menu:* Dwell on the button and then dwell on an item that can be scrolled, such as a web page.

- *Options Menu:* Dwell on this button to show the other dwell options in a circular menu.

- *Pause:* Dwell on this button to deactivate dwell controls when doing something like watching a video. To reactivate dwell, dwell on another button.

You can also use the Hot Corners option to activate your favorite dwell options when dwelling over a corner.

TIP

7. **Click the Close button or press ⌘+Q to quit System Preferences or go on to the next section to set up other Accessibility functions.**

Choosing mouse and trackpad options

If you have physical limitations using the mouse or trackpad, you can turn on the Mouse Keys feature, which lets you control the mouse through the numeric keys. To set up Pointer Control, follow these steps:

1. **Click the Accessibility icon in System Preferences and then click Pointer Control in the list on the left pane of the window.**

   The Mouse and Trackpad section of Pointer Control preferences appears, as shown in Figure 6-24.

2. **Drag the sliders to specify Double-Click Speed and Spring-Loading Delay.**

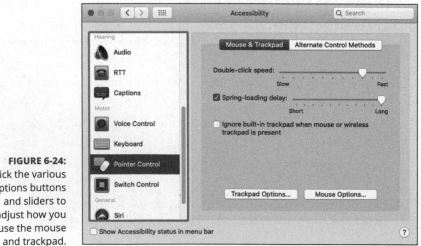

FIGURE 6-24: Click the various options buttons and sliders to adjust how you use the mouse and trackpad.

3. **(Optional) Click the Ignore Built-In Trackpad When Mouse or Wireless Trackpad Is Present check box.**

Don't click this check box if you don't have a mouse or wireless trackpad present. If you do, you won't be able to use your computer and will have to hold down the Start button to force-restart your Mac.

4. **Click the Trackpad Options button if you use a trackpad.**

This opens a dialog that enables you to set scrolling speed and choose an option from the Scrolling pop-up menu. Your choices are: With Inertia or Without Inertia. Click the Enable Dragging check box and then choose one of the following options from the pop-up menu: Without Drag Lock, With Drag Lock, or Three-Finger Drag.

5. **Click the Mouse Options button.**

A dialog appears enabling you to change the scrolling speed with a slider.

6. **Click the Alternate Control Methods button.**

The dialog refreshes, giving you Mouse Keys options and Alternate Pointer Actions, as shown in Figure 6-25.

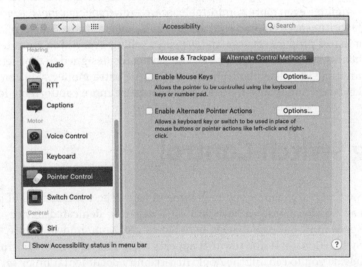

FIGURE 6-25: Exploring Alternate Control Method options.

7. **If you enabled Mouse Keys, click Options and choose from the following:**

- *Press the Option Key Five Times to Toggle Mouse Keys On or Off:* Lets you turn the Mouse Keys feature on or off from the keyboard.

- *Ignore Built-In Trackpad When Mouse Keys Is On* (only Macs with trackpads): Disables the trackpad when you turn on Mouse Keys.

    If you select this check box, you have to use the mouse keys to deselect it and use the trackpad again.

- *Initial Delay:* Drag the slider to define how long the Mac waits before moving the pointer with the numeric key. A short value means that the Mac may immediately move the pointer as soon as you press a number or letter key. A long value means that you must hold down a key for a longer period before it starts moving the pointer. Choose a long value if you use a compact keyboard so you can type normally without moving the mouse and move the mouse without typing a series of the same letter.

- *Maximum Speed:* Drag the slider to adjust how fast the Mouse Keys feature moves the pointer with the keyboard.

8. **Click the OK button to close the Mouse Keys options.**

9. **Click the Close button or press ⌘+Q to quit System Preferences or go on to the next section to set up other Accessibility functions.**

TIP

To find different types of keyboards and mice designed to make controlling your computer even more comfortable, search for *ergonomic input devices* by using your favorite search engine, such as Google, Yahoo!, or Bing. Search results will contain a list of product reviews and websites selling everything from left-handed keyboards and mice to foot pedals and keyboards designed to type letters by pressing multiple keys like piano chords. For a little extra money, you can buy the perfect keyboard and mouse that can make your Mac more comfortable for you to use.

Enabling Switch Control

Switch Control allows you to command your Mac with a series of switches, which can be the mouse, a keyboard, or a separate dedicated device. Experience and space limit our explanation here but to give you an idea, Figure 6-26 shows the Switch Control Home row that appears when Enable Switch Control is selected. We advise you to consult the Apple Accessibility documentation or set up an appointment with a Genius at an Apple Store to best take advantage of these functions.

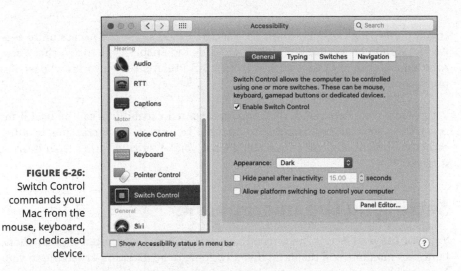

FIGURE 6-26:
Switch Control commands your Mac from the mouse, keyboard, or dedicated device.

Speaking with Your Mac

Your Mac offers voice command, dictation, and speech capabilities. The Speakable Items feature lets you control your Mac by using spoken commands, and the Dictation & Speech functions let you dictate to your Mac or have your Mac read text or alert you when something happens (for example, when a dialog pops up onscreen). Speakable Items are part of the Accessibility functions; Dictation & Speech share an icon in the System Preferences window. We talk about both here.

DICTATING AND SPEAKING TO YOUR MAC AND TALKING TO SIRI

You may think these are two separate processes, but, in fact, they're quite different. You can use your voice and the Mac's built-in microphone to ask your Mac to carry out tasks. For example, when you're dictating some text to Pages or to a text field in Keynote, you can issue editing commands such as "Delete last sentence." Dictating text and speaking commands let you use your voice instead of a keyboard or trackpad.

On the other hand, when you're talking to Siri, you often aren't asking Siri to do something that you could do with the keyboard ("Delete last sentence" for example). Instead, you're asking Siri to do a higher-level task than typing or erasing. For example, you may say, "Siri, what time is my next appointment?"

This chapter deals with dictation and speaking to your Mac. For more about talking to Siri, see Book 1, Chapter 2.

TIP

If you prefer, you can type commands to Siri. To do so, in the Accessibility section of System Preferences, click Siri and click the Enable Type to Siri check box. After enabling Type to Siri, click the Open Siri Preferences button to choose Siri preferences.

TIP

Your Mac's voice command, dictation, and speech capabilities can be useful for controlling your Mac or listening to text you've written to catch typos or other errors you might miss by only reading what you've written rather than hearing it aloud.

Setting up the microphone

You can use your Mac's built-in microphone; there is also often a microphone built into monitors and displays. If you're going to be dictating or talking to your Mac, make sure the microphone is turned on and you know where it is. If you speak directly to the microphone, your voice will be picked up much better than if you're looking out the window on a busy street. Look at the mic.

And make sure it's turned on. Open System Preferences by choosing ⟐ System Preferences, and then click Sound. For the purpose of setting up your microphone, click the Input tab, shown in Figure 6-27.

You can adjust the input volume as you want. In Figure 6-27, you see that the sound is coming from a display that has a built-in microphone.

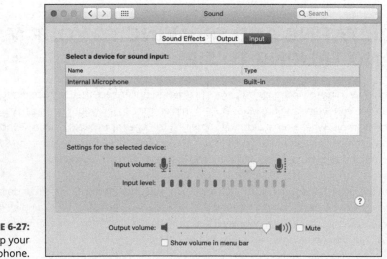

FIGURE 6-27:
Set up your
microphone.

Note that you may have several input devices, but in this window you select only one of them to be used.

When it comes to output, this example shows several devices, as you see in Figure 6-28.

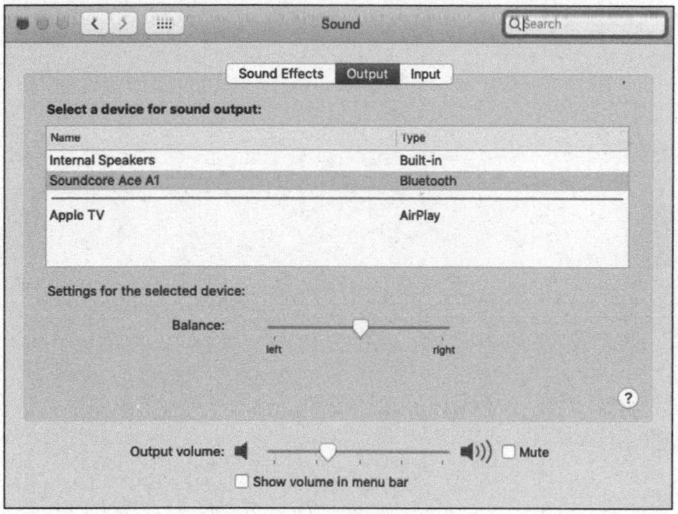

FIGURE 6-28: Choose your output device(s).

In this particular configuration, output is sent to the Mac's internal speakers or an external speaker can be chosen.

You now should have your Mac set up so that you can speak to it or to a connected display.

Setting up Speakable Items

To use the Mac's built-in voice recognition software, you have to define its settings and then assign specific types of commands to your voice. You define the Speakable Items settings to choose how to turn on voice recognition and how your Mac will acknowledge that it received your voice commands correctly. For example, your Mac may wait until you press the Esc key or speak a certain word before it starts listening to voice commands. When it understands your command, it can beep.

To define the Speakable Items settings, follow these steps:

1. **Choose ⌘⇨System Preferences and click the Accessibility icon.**

2. **Click the Voice Control button in the left pane of the Accessibility settings, as shown in Figure 6-29.**

   A dialog box appears telling you that Dictation is trying to unlock Accessibility preferences.

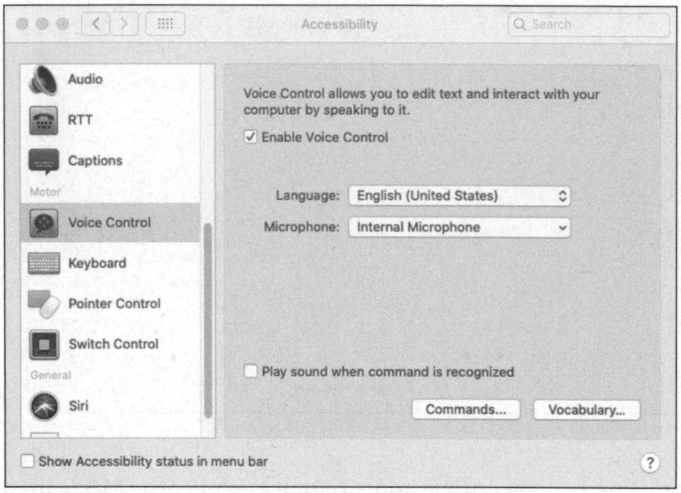

FIGURE 6-29:
Define how your
Mac recognizes
spoken
commands.

3. **Enter your password and click Unlock.**

   macOS installs Voice Control.

4. **Click the Play Sound When Command Is Recognized check box.**

   When this option is enabled, your computer will play a sound when Voice Control recognizes a command.

5. **Click the Commands button.**

   A list of commands you can enable with Voice Control is displayed, as shown in Figure 6-30. The first command is Open Siri. We suggest you copy the commands you'll use frequently, type them on a Pages document, print out a copy, and keep this list by your computer.

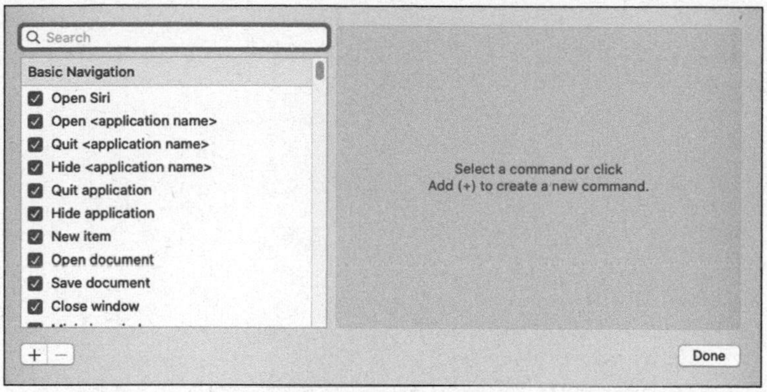

![Voice Control commands dialog showing a search field, Basic Navigation section with checkboxes for Open Siri, Open <application name>, Quit <application name>, Hide <application name>, Quit application, Hide application, New item, Open document, Save document, Close window, and a right panel reading "Select a command or click Add (+) to create a new command." with + - buttons and a Done button.]

FIGURE 6-30:
Voice Control
commands.

TIP

When you open an application and hover your cursor over a menu, a numbered list is displayed when Voice Control is enabled. Speak the number to perform the command.

6. **Click the Close button to exit System Preferences.**

2

Using the Internet

Contents at a Glance

CHAPTER 1: **Browsing the Web with Safari** 207
Browsing Websites 208
Organizing Your Website Experience 223
Storing Personal Info and Keeping It Private. 234
Saving and Sharing Web Pages 238
Viewing and Playing Multimedia Files 243
Downloading Files 244
Using Extensions 246

CHAPTER 2: **Corresponding with Mail** 249
Adding an Email Account to Mail. 250
Looking at the Mail Window 254
Writing Emails 257
Receiving and Reading Email 271
Organizing Email 276
Dealing with Junk Email 284
Deleting and Archiving Messages 290

CHAPTER 3: **Chatting with Messages and FaceTime** 293
Getting Started in Messages 294
Chatting with Others. 296
Making Calls with FaceTime. 302

CHAPTER 4: **Using Apple Pay and Apple Card** 307
Paying for Purchases with Apple Pay 308
Using Apple Card. 309

CHAPTER 5: **Moving Around with Maps** 311
Wherever You Go, There You Are 312
Asking for Directions. 315

IN THIS CHAPTER

» Browsing websites

» Managing bookmarks

» Creating a Reading List

» Securing your privacy

» Sharing web pages

» Viewing and playing multimedia files

» Downloading files

» Extending Safari's capabilities

Chapter **1**

Browsing the Web with Safari

The World Wide Web gives you entrance to a universe of fun facts, virtual museums around the world, and news from mainstream and obscure outlets, movies, radio stations, new apps, online shopping, local restaurants, and far-flung ferries. To access all this omnipresent goodness, you use a *web browser*, which is an app that lets you, well, browse, all the things stored on the web from around the globe.

In this chapter, we introduce you to *Safari*, which is the web browser app that comes with your Mac. We show you Safari's many features for browsing, searching, and reading on the Internet. Along the way, you'll find tips and tricks to make your surfing experience more fun and productive.

Browsing Websites

After you connect to the Internet (as explained in Book 1, Chapter 3), you can run a web browser app to browse online. The most popular browser for the Mac is the one that comes with it: Safari. However, you can download and run another web browser, such as

>> **Firefox:** www.mozilla.org/en-US/firefox/new

>> **Google Chrome:** www.google.com/chrome

>> **Opera:** www.opera.com

In this section, we tell you how to explore the web with Safari.

TIP

There are reasons for using other browsers, at least from time to time. If you're building a website, you (or your designer) should test it using every major browser you can find to make sure that no pages fail in some operating systems or browsers. In a somewhat similar vein, some web-based apps work only with certain browsers (Chrome and Internet Explorer come to mind) even though the web pages they create can be viewed from other browsers, including Safari.

Going on Safari

With macOS Safari, Safari is integrated with Siri (as so much of Catalina is), and you can place Siri suggestions on the home page — and change them as often as you want.

Figure 1-1 shows the first screen you see in Safari with macOS Catalina.

FIGURE 1-1:
Safari
(Dark Mode).

Figure 1-2 also shows the first screen you see — this time in the Light Mode

FIGURE 1-2:
Surfing the web with Safari in Light Mode.

Visiting websites

To visit a website, you use the website's *address* (also known as a *URL*, or Uniform Resource Locator). Most website addresses, such as `http://www.dummies.com`, consist of these parts:

>> `http://www:` Identifies the address as part of the web that uses the HyperText Transfer Protocol (HTTP). Some websites omit the www portion of the name and begin with http, or https, which is HTTP secure. Other websites use something else like mobile, which means the site is formatted for better viewing on mobile devices. Just keep in mind that www is common but not always necessary for many website addresses.

>> **The domain name of the website (such as** dummies**):** Most website names are abbreviations or smashed-together names of the website, such as whitehouse for the White House website.

>> **An identifying extension (such as** .com**):** The extension identifies the type of website, as shown in Table 1-1. Many websites in other countries end with a two-letter country address, such as .uk for the United Kingdom or .ch for Switzerland.

The domain extensions listed here are just the tip of the iceberg. For example, there's also .co, which is used by companies, .us for those who want a patriotic extension, and so on. There will be even more extensions as the web evolves.

TABLE 1-1

Common Web Address Extensions

Three-Letter Extension	Type of Website	Examples
.com	Often a commercial website, but can be another type of website	www.apple.com
.gov	Government website	www.nasa.gov
.edu	School website	www.mit.edu
.net	Network, sometimes used as an alternative to the .com extension	www.earthlink.net
.org	A nonprofit organization website	www.redcross.org
.mil	Military website	www.army.mil

REMEMBER

When visiting different web pages on a site, you might see additional text that identifies a specific web page, such as www.apple.com/iphone.

Opening a website you know

When you know the website address (URL) you want to visit, simply type it in to Safari. Follow these steps:

1. **Click the Safari icon (it looks like a compass) from the Dock or Launchpad to run Safari.**

2. **Click in the Search and Address field and type an address (such as www.dummies.com), as shown in Figure 1-1 and Figure 1-2, and then press Return.**

   As you begin to type an address, Safari auto-completes it with a likely match, usually based on your viewing history, and then highlights the part it added. In Figure 1-3, we typed **dum**, and Safari filled in the rest. You can see, too, other potential matches listed below; as you type more letters, the choices narrow. Press the Return key if the highlighted address is the one you want. Otherwise, continue typing or choose from the pop-up list that appears (if the website you want is listed there).

REMEMBER

   If you type a website address and see an error message, it might mean that you typed the website address incorrectly, your Internet connection isn't working, or the website is temporarily (or permanently) unavailable.

   Safari displays the website corresponding to the address you typed.

FIGURE 1-3:
Begin typing an
address, and
Safari suggests
potential
matches.

3. **Move about the web page (mouse, trackpad, or arrow keys) to scroll up
and down. Move the pointer over images, buttons, and bold text to click
links that open other web pages.**

TIP

Pinch your thumb and forefinger together on a trackpad to zoom in on a page,
or pinch them together to zoom out. This doesn't change the size of the Safari
window but makes everything on the web page larger. Click and drag a corner
or edge of the Safari window to resize it.

TIP

Press Control++ to zoom in on a page, or press Control+– to zoom out. Press
Control+0 to revert to the default magnification.

If you use a MacBook or a Magic Mouse or trackpad with a desktop Mac model,
use the two-finger scroll gesture to move back and forward between web
pages that you visited. Choose ⇨ System Preferences⇨Trackpad⇨More
Gestures. Click Swipe between Pages, and from the pop-up menu, choose
which finger and gesture combination you want to use for that gesture.

You may encounter a web page that has fields where you type limited
information, such as your name, address, and billing information to make an
online purchase. Other fields are meant for typing in longer passages, such as
comments about a blog post. Resize the second type of field by clicking and
dragging the bottom-right corner, allowing you to see more of what you type.

4. **When you finish, click the Close button (the red circle in the upper-left
corner) to simply close the Safari window.**

Or choose Safari⇨Quit Safari to completely exit the application.

Identifying Safari's tools

As with any software, you can get the most out of Safari web browser when you're
familiar with the tools it offers. Here we you tell you where to find each tool and
give you a general idea of each tool's purpose. Throughout this chapter, we give
you more information on how to use these tools.

Safari's Toolbar runs the width of the top of the browser. On the left side of the
Toolbar, shown in Figure 1-4, you see the following tools:

>> **Back:** Takes you to the previous web page (unless this is your first stop); click
again to go back another page, and so on, until you wind up on the first page
you viewed when you launched Safari.

FIGURE 1-4:
Check out your
surfing choices.

>> **Forward:** Moves you forward to a page you backed away from; click again to advance to the next page you backed away from, and so on, until you wind up on the last page you visited before you clicked the Back button.

>> **Search and Address:** Type a web address here or enter a search term.

>> **Show Sidebar:** In the Sidebar pane, see your bookmarks, Reading List, and Shared Links.

>> **Favorites Bar:** Your favorite sites, bookmarked in one convenient place. Click a bookmark to go to the site.

>> **Show Bookmarks:** Click this button to display your bookmarks below the Favorites Bar.

>> **Share:** Click this button to open a drop-down menu.

>> **Top Sites:** Your Mac keeps track of which sites you visit most frequently and helps you quickly return to them.

>> **Add:** Open a new tab.

On the Toolbar, you'll see these tools, shown in Figure 1-5:

>> **Reload:** Clicking the little arrowed-circle icon on the right side of the address bar reloads the current web page and displays any new information that changed since you arrived on the web page (such as breaking news on *The New York Times* home page). When Safari is loading or reloading a web page, the arrowed-circle turns into an X icon. Clicking the X icon stops Safari from loading or reloading the web page.

>> **Reader:** The reader is available in the sidebar, which is opened by clicking the Show Sidebar button. Figure 1-6 shows Safari after showing the sidebar.

>> **Favorites:** Your favorite sites — those you bookmarked, can also be viewed in the sidebar. After showing the sidebar, click the button that looks like a bookmark (see Figure 1-6), to display a list of your favorite websites.

>> **Full Screen view:** Safari supports full-screen view. Hover your cursor over the green button above the Back and Forward buttons and then choose Full Screen from the drop-down menu to take advantage of your entire screen. This option hides the menu as well. To return to partial-screen view, move your cursor to the top of the screen until the menu is revealed and then click the green button.

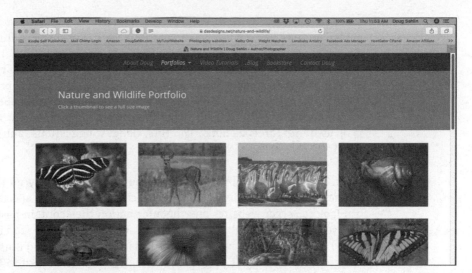

FIGURE 1-5:
More tools for
surfing the web.

TIP

Figures 1-4 and 1-5 show you the default Safari tools as of this writing. If your version looks different, you may need to visit the App Store and update Safari. To add or delete the buttons on the Safari Toolbar, choose View➪Customize Toolbar. A pane opens, as shown in Figure 1-6. Click and drag the icons to and from the toolbar and the pane to create a toolbar that meets your browsing needs. We tell you what each of the buttons does throughout the rest of this chapter.

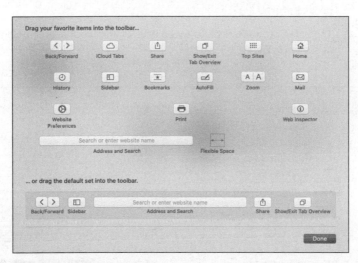

FIGURE 1-6:
Customize the
toolbar for
easier browsing
in Safari.

Searching for websites

The real power of the web is searching for, and finding, websites you don't know the address for. Whether you want to find the website for a specific company or person or more general information about a topic, the answers are literally at your fingertips. Just type a word or phrase that describes the information you want in the text field in the middle of the browser below the Menu Bar. If there's a website address in the field, select and delete it; then type your query, press Return, and a list of related web search results (*hits* or *links*) appears, probably offering more than you ever wanted to know about the subject of your search. The information is divided into three sections: Top Hits, Google Suggestions, and Bookmarks and History.

When you want to find something on the web, you usually go through a *search engine*, which is a behind-the-scenes technology used by special websites that can look for other websites and the information they contain based on a word or phrase you enter. Google is probably the most well-known search engine (and is Safari's default search engine), but others include Yahoo! and Bing, which you can designate as the default search engine. Here's how to use Safari to access search engines and then start your engine, um, er, search:

1. Click the Safari icon on the Dock or Launchpad to run Safari.

2. Click in the Search and Address field and enter the name of your favorite search engine such as bing.com and then press Return.

Safari refreshes and displays the home page of your search engine.

3. Enter your search query in the Search and Address field and then press Return.

The Safari browser displays a web page of links your search engine found, as shown in Figure 1-7.

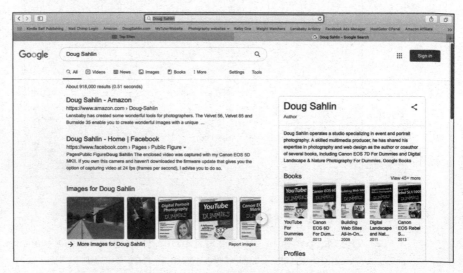

FIGURE 1-7:
Words or phrases you search for appear as web links in a new web page.

SEARCHING TIPS

Given the billions of websites on the web, your search can turn up more exact results if you better define your search terms. Here are a few ways you can specify your search terms:

- Use quotation marks around a phrase to find the words exactly as you typed them. For example, if you type **John Quincy Adams** in the Search field, your result contains references for **John** Smith and Jane **Adams** in **Quincy**, Massachusetts, as well as references to the former president. If you type **"John Quincy Adams",** your search results contain only websites that contain the name as you typed it.

- Use Boolean operations without quotes, for example, type **John AND Quincy AND Adams**.

- Confine your search to a specific website by adding site: *domain*. For example, if you want references to John Quincy Adams from the White House website, type **"John Quincy Adams" site:whitehouse.gov**.

- Exclude certain common usages by placing a minus sign before the word you want to exclude.

- Don't worry about using small articles and prepositions like *a, the, of, about;* or using capital letters.

- Check your spelling. If you mistype a word or phrase, the search engine might offer suggestions for the correct spelling and look for websites that contain that misspelled word or phrase, which probably won't be the website you really want to see.

Every time you type a word or phrase in the Search text box, Safari (and most other browsers) saves the last ten words or phrases you searched. To search for that same word or phrase later, just click the down arrow that appears in the left side of the Search text box to display a pull-down menu. Then click the word or phrase you want to search for again.

Click the website you want to visit or click one of the buttons at the top of the results web page to see results in other types of media, such as images, videos, shopping, news, or maps. Click the More button to see all the choices.

If you want to switch the default search engine from Google to Yahoo! or Bing, do the following:

1. Choose Safari⇨Preferences, and then click the Search tab.

2. Click the pop-up menu next to Search Engine and choose Yahoo!, Bing, or DuckDuckGo.

3. **Click the Close button in the upper-left corner of the Preferences window.**

TIP

If you search for websites and find yourself wandering down a number of blind alleys because the web pages you navigate to aren't what you're looking for, return to your search results and start afresh. Choose History ⇨ Search Results SnapBack, and the results instantly replace whatever page you were viewing.

Going back in time

If you visit a website and want to visit it again, Safari stores a list of your visited websites in its History menu, even for one year if you choose that option in Safari ⇨ Preferences ⇨ General.

To view a list of the websites you visited, follow these steps:

1. **In Safari, click History on the menu bar.**

   A drop-down menu appears, displaying the most recent websites you visited. Additionally, the History menu lists the past week's dates so you can view websites that you visited several days ago, and a list of Recently Closed pages, as shown in Figure 1-8.

2. **Choose a website to have Safari display your selected site.**

History	Bookmarks	Develop	Window	Help

Show All History	⌘Y
Back	⌘[
Forward	⌘]
Home	⇧⌘H
Search Results SnapBack	⌥⌘S
Recently Closed	▶
Reopen Last Closed Window	⇧⌘T
Reopen All Windows from Last Session	

Kelby One   HP Ink   Weight Watchers   Lensbaby Artistry   cPanel   Sarasota Writers Gr

G Hyphen - Google Search
G John Quincy-Adams - Google Search
G "John Quincy Adams"site:whitehouse.gov - Google Search
G "John Quincy Adams" - Google Search
G John Quincy Adams - Google Search
G Apple Match - Google Search
Home | Doug Sahlin
About | Doug Sahlin
Doug Sahlin | Author of the Yale Larsson Mystery Series
Strawberry Truffle - Bing
Bing
Sarasota Writers Group
Fine Art | Doug Sahlin - Author/Photographer
Portfolios | Doug Sahlin - Author/Photographer
Contact Doug | Doug Sahlin - Author/Photographer
About Doug | Doug Sahlin - Author/Photographer
Doug Sahlin - Author/Photograp...beautiful images is my passion!
d dummies - Learning Made Easy

Home | Doug Sahlin
Sarasota Writers Group
iTunes Connect
Lorem Ipsum Generator » Lorem Ipsum generated in paragraphs
Google Calendar - Week of September 1, 2019
Doug Sahlin - Author/Photograp...s my passion! (and 3 more tabs)
    Apple
    W Comma-separated values - Wikipedia
    G How to import facebook contacts to the mac - Google Search
    Doug Sahlin - Author/Photograp...beautiful images is my passion!
G Currents: Have Meaningful Discussions at Work | G Suite
Partners Imaging Centers - Home | Facebook
G Currents: Have Meaningful Discussions at Work | G Suite
Page Not Found | Facebook
Hurricane Dorian Stalls, Still Pu...t Tonight | The Weather Channel
YouTube
G archive folders in mac mail - Google Search
Is it me? — Nextdoor
Floridians Prepare for What Cou...onster' | The Weather Channel
G What does a folder icon with an arrow mean? - Google Search
G The volume mount sound on a Mac - Google Search
G How to save a document with Tags - Google Search
iCloud
Mac Pro - Apple

Earlier Today   ▶
Monday, September 16, 2019   ▶
Monday, September 9, 2019   ▶
Friday, September 6, 2019   ▶
Thursday, September 5, 2019   ▶
Wednesday, September 4, 2019   ▶
Monday, September 2, 2019   ▶

FIGURE 1-8:
The History menu lets you revisit previously viewed websites.

TIP

Although the History menu displays your web history from only the past seven days, you can choose History⇨Show All History to view a list of all the websites you visited after the last time your history was cleared. To establish the length of time you want to keep your browsing history, go to Safari⇨Preferences and click the General button on the toolbar. Choose a period specified by the Remove History Items pop-up menu, as shown in Figure 1-9.

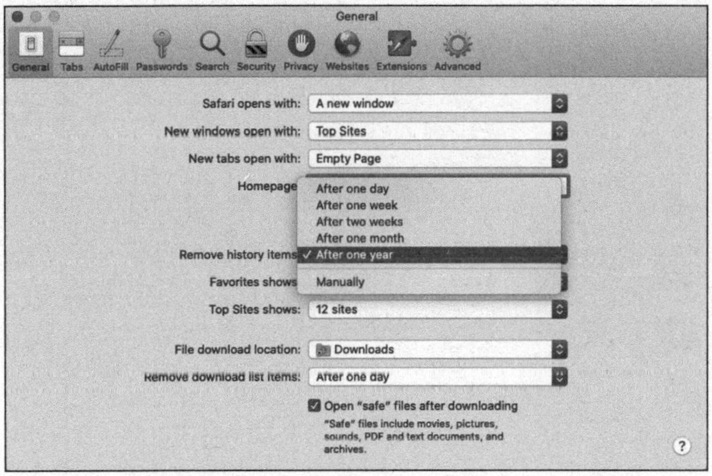

FIGURE 1-9:
Choose how often you want your browsing history erased.

You can also erase your web-browsing history at any time by choosing History⇨Clear History.

Reading in Reader

If a page you are viewing can be viewed in Reader, you have the option to add the page to your reading list. To do so, pause your cursor on the left side of the Search and Address text field. If the page can be viewed in reader, a plus sign appears and Add Page to Reading List appears in the text field. Click the plus sign to add the page to your Reading List.

To read a page you've saved, click the Sidebar button in the toolbar, and then click the Reading Glass button, shown in Figure 1-10. Click an item on the Reading List to view it. Safari aims to be elegant and clutter-free, so Reader removes all the ads, buttons, bells, and whistles from the web page and shows you only the article as one continuous page. To exit Reader, choose View⇨Hide Reader.

You can also view a website in Reader by typing the URL for the website in the Search or Enter Website Name text field and then pressing Return. After Safari refreshes, navigate to a site page you want to view in Reader and then choose Show ➪ Reader. After reading the page, you can exit Reader by choosing View ➪ Hide Reader.

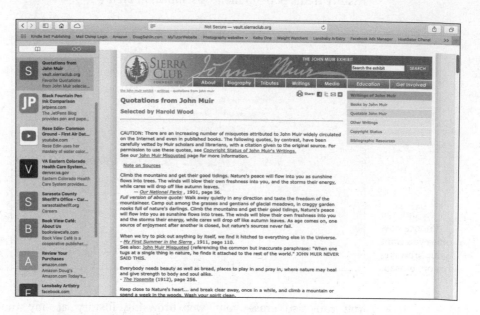

FIGURE 1-10:
Reader displays multipage articles as one continuous page.

TIP

In both Reader and normal Safari view, press ⌘+= to zoom in on the text or ⌘+− to zoom out. If you have a Magic Mouse or Trackpad or a MacBook that recognizes multitouch gestures, you can also pinch in or out to zoom. To revert to default magnification, press ⌘+0.

Using tabbed browsing

When you want to keep track of more than one website while browsing a second, third, or fourth site, you could open two (or three or four) separate browser windows. However, here's a more handy way. Safari and most other browsers offer a *tabbed browsing* feature, which allows you to easily jump around among multiple web pages in a single window. This is similar to the tabbed Finder window we explain in Book 1, Chapter 4. All you have to do is click the tab associated with the web page, as we discuss in these sections.

Creating new tabs

When you load Safari, you see a single web page displayed in a window. To add a tab, simply click the New Tab button (the plus sign on the right) to open a blank tab, and then open a website by typing a URL or search term in the Search and Address field.

TIP

Choose what type of tab you want to see when you click New Tab by going to Safari⇨Preferences and clicking the General button on the toolbar. Choose one of the four choices in the New Tabs Open With pop-up menu, as shown in Figure 1-11. We like to open in the Top Sites display, which we explain later in this chapter.

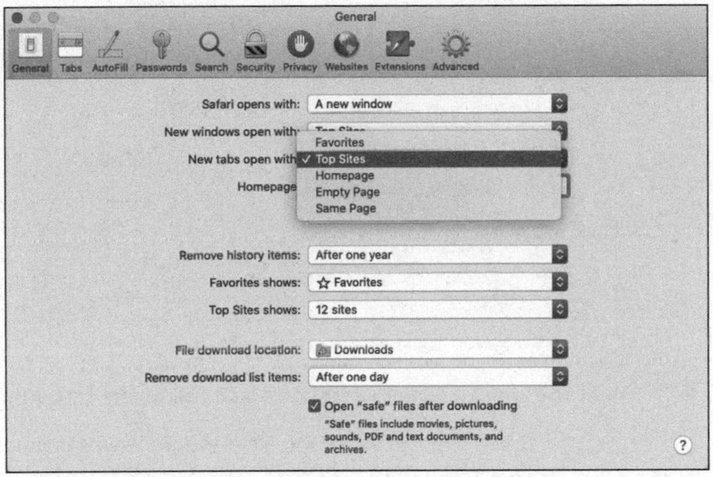

FIGURE 1-11:
Choose how you want to see new tabs.

If you turn on Safari in iCloud on your Mac and one or more iOS device, you can access tabs opened on one device from another. On your Mac, click the iCloud button on the toolbar to see the tabs open in Safari on your iPhone, iPad, or iPod touch, as shown in Figure 1-12. See Book 1, Chapter 3 to learn about iCloud. If the iCloud button is not on your toolbar, you can add it by choosing View⇨Customize toolbar and then dragging the button to the toolbar.

TIP

FIGURE 1-12:
Access web pages that are open on other devices with iCloud.

To work with tabs, set your preferences as explained here:

1. **Open Safari and choose Safari ⇨ Preferences.**

2. **Click the Tabs button on the toolbar.**

3. **From the pop-up menu shown in Figure 1-13, choose when you want tabs to open instead of windows.**

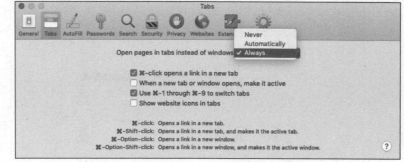

4. **Select the check boxes to activate one or all of the following choices:**

   - *⌘-click Opens a Link in a New Tab:* Rather than leave the current web page and replace it with the linked page, a ⌘-click will open the linked page in a new tab and leave the current web page open.

   - *When a New Tab or Window Opens, Make It Active:* When you click the New button, the tab or window that opens becomes the active one.

   - *Use ⌘+1 through ⌘+9 to switch tabs:* Choose this option and you can press the ⌘ key and a number to surf through your open tabs.

   - *Show website icons in tabs:* Choose this option and you see an icon to the left of the website name in each tab. If the site is a favorite, the icon is a star. Many commercial sites have a custom icon that appears to the left of the site name when you choose this option. For example, WordPress has an icon that is a stylized letter *W*.

5. **Click the Close button.**

Managing tabs

When you open multiple tabbed windows, as shown in Figure 1-14, you can rearrange how they're ordered, close them, or save a group of tabs as a bookmark that you can reopen all at once with a single click of your mouse or add them to your Reading List (which we explain shortly).

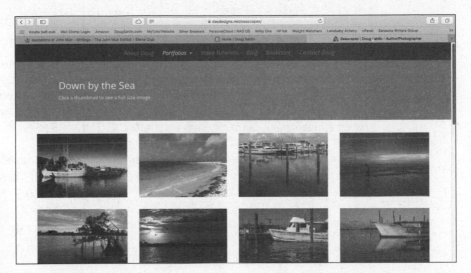

FIGURE 1-14:
Tabbed browsing lets you juggle multiple web pages inside a single window.

TIP

Some cool things you can try doing with tabbed windows include

» **Add a new tab.** Press ⌘+T or click the plus sign at the far right of the Tab bar.

» **Switch from tab to tab.** Press ⌘+Shift+→ or ⌘+Shift+←.

» **Close a tab.** Move your mouse over the tab and click the X that appears or press ⌘+W, although that will close the Safari window if you have only one tab open.

» **Rearrange the order of your tabs.** Drag and drop a tab to the left or right of another tab.

» **Move a tab to a new window.** Drag it below the Tab bar and then let go of your mouse button, or right-click a tab and choose Move Tab to New Window.

» **Save every currently loaded tabbed window as a bookmark.** Right-click any tab (or click the Bookmarks menu) and choose Add Bookmark for These ____ Tabs.

» **Save the articles of every currently loaded tabbed window in the Reading List.** Right-click any tab (or click the Bookmarks menu) and choose Add These ____ Tabs to Reading List.

» **Merge a bunch of open web page windows into a browser with tabs for each window.** Choose Window ➪ Merge All Windows.

» **Open a contextual menu that displays all the tab options.** Right-click a tab.

Setting your Safari home page

The first time you open Safari, the Apple website appears because it's set as the default home page. Subsequent times you open Safari, the website you were browsing when you last closed or quit Safari (or shut down and restarted your Mac) reopens. You can change your Safari home page to whatever you want — even a blank page, if that's what you prefer.

Throughout this chapter, all step-by-step instructions are given for Safari. Just keep in mind that other browsers (Firefox, Chrome, Internet Explorer, and so on) work in relatively similar ways.

To define a home page in Safari, follow these steps:

1. **Click the Safari icon on the Dock or Launchpad.**

2. **Click in the Search and Address field at the top of the Safari window and type the address of the web page you want to use as your home page.**

   If you have set the page as a bookmark, you can just click the bookmark to open the web page.

3. **Choose Safari ⇨ Preferences and click the General button on the toolbar.**

4. **Click the Set to Current Page button.**

   The website address of the page you are viewing automatically fills the Homepage field, as shown in Figure 1-15.

   You can also skip Step 2, go directly to Safari General preferences, and type the URL in the Homepage text field.

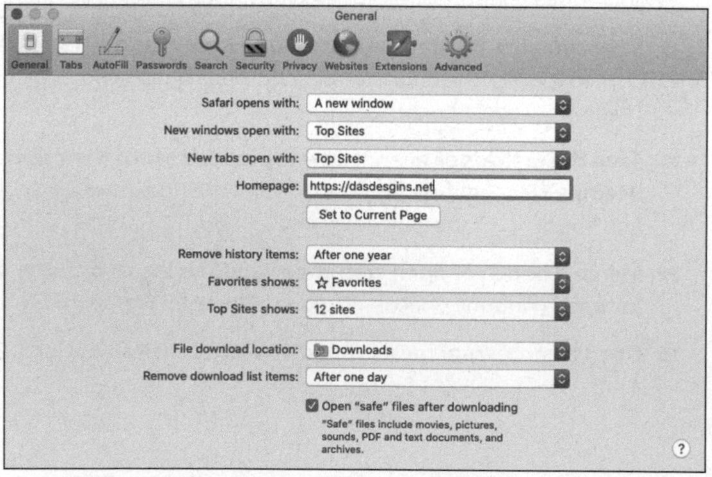

FIGURE 1-15:
Set your home page here.

If you want Safari to open to your home page or a blank page when you restart or reopen Safari (instead of opening the most recent web page you visited), choose Homepage or Empty Page from the New Windows Open With pop-up menu.

5. **Close the Safari preferences pane.**

Searching within a web page

You can search for a word or phrase within the text on a web page, and Safari will find and highlight each occurrence of the word or phrase. Here's how:

1. **From the web page you want to search, choose Edit ⇨ Find ⇨ Find.**

Under the toolbar, the Find text field appears.

2. **Type in the word or phrase you want to find.**

Safari highlights each occurrence of the search phrase, and a left and right arrow appear to the left of the search field. Safari also shows how many instances of the search word or phrase have been found. The first occurrence of your query is shown with a yellow highlight.

3. **Use the navigation arrows to go to the next or previous occurrence of the search term.**

4. **Click Done to close the Find banner or choose Edit ⇨ Find ⇨ Hide Find Banner.**

Organizing Your Website Experience

You can use Safari just to browse new websites and read articles at the moment you find them, but that doesn't take advantage of all Safari can do to help you manage your web browsing adventure — it's not named Safari for nothin'! In this section, we tell you how to use the Safari features that organize favorite websites you want to revisit, manage the articles you want to read later, and list links to articles your friends have posted on social media sites you use — namely, Bookmarks, Reading List, and Shared Links. You access all three from the Sidebar, which opens when you click the Sidebar button (the open book) or choose View ⇨ Show Sidebar.

TIP

To make the Sidebar pane wider or narrower, move the pointer to the right edge of the Sidebar until it becomes a vertical line with an arrow on one or both sides, and then click and drag.

Using bookmarks

Bookmarks are links to websites, such as a favorite news outlet or a reference source. Click a bookmark, and Safari opens to the bookmarked web page. What's more, bookmarks let you group likeminded websites, such as news sites, book review sites, gadgets sites, or sites related to one project you're working on, together in folders.

The Favorites bar, as shown in Figure 1-16, gives you quick access to websites you visit most frequently. The Favorites Bar is below the Search or Enter Website Name text field. This figure also shows the Favorites Sidebar in the locked-and-loaded-for-bear position.

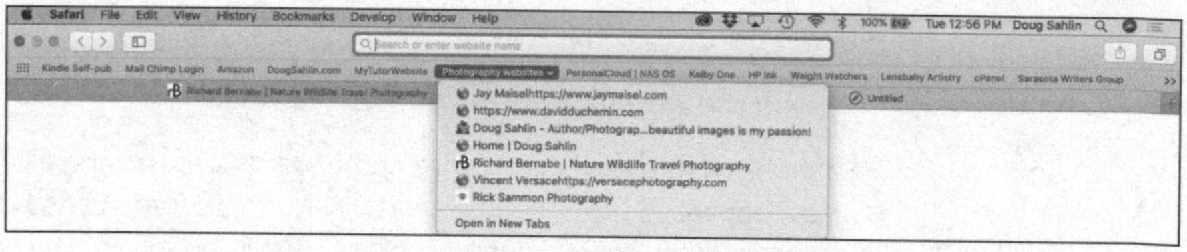

FIGURE 1-16: The Favorites bar displays bookmark quick-link buttons and folders.

Use the Favorites bar for one-click access to your favorite or frequently visited websites. You can place as many bookmarks and folders as you like on the Favorites bar, but you will see only the number that fit in the width of the Safari window; you have to click the arrows at the right end of the Favorites bar to open a menu that displays bookmarks that don't fit. You can get around that problem by placing folders on the Favorites bar.

The Bookmarks menu and the Sidebar, as shown in Figure 1-17, show all your bookmarks and folders.

Click the Sidebar button or choose View⇨Show Sidebar, and then click the Bookmarks tab. Alternatively, you can choose View⇨Show Bookmarks Sidebar. The Bookmarks section of the Sidebar displays the contents of your Favorites Bar and Bookmarks Menu folders that are displayed below your Favorites. Clicking the disclosure arrow to the left of a folder displays the bookmarks within or collapses them if it's already open. Click a bookmark to open that web page.

TIP

If you have lots of Favorites, click the disclosure arrow to the left of the title to hide favorites, making it easier for you to see folders.

REMEMBER

Bookmarks behave the same whether they appear in the Sidebar, on the Bookmarks menu, or on the Favorites bar. Simply click the bookmark, and it opens the linked web page. To open a bookmark from the menu, choose Bookmarks⇨Favorites and then choose the website you want to visit from the drop-down menu.

FIGURE 1-17:
The Sidebar shows your bookmarks and folders.

Adding bookmarks

By default, Safari comes with several bookmarks already placed on the Favorites bar and Bookmarks menu, all of which you see in Bookmarks on the Sidebar. You'll probably want to add your own choices to bookmarks. To bookmark a website address, follow these steps:

1. **In Safari, visit a website that you want to store as a bookmark.**

    REMEMBER

    A website is a collection of one or more web pages. If you want to bookmark a news website, for instance, you should use the top-level landing page as the bookmarked page instead of a web page that's linked to a specific article.

2. **Choose Bookmarks ⇨ Add Bookmark to open the dialog shown in Figure 1-18.**

    By default, the Name text box displays the current web page's title, which is typically the main website's name.

    TIP

    You can also add a bookmark by simply clicking the URL and dragging it down to the Favorites bar or into a folder in the Bookmarks section of the Sidebar.

3. **(Optional) Type a new name for the bookmark if you don't want to keep the default name.**

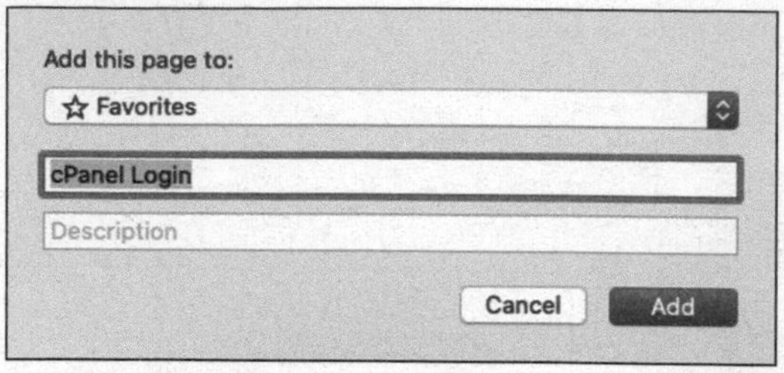

Add this page to:

☆ Favorites ⌄

cPanel Login

Description

Cancel   Add

FIGURE 1-18:
Accept or edit
a bookmark's
name.

4. **Click the Location pop-up menu and choose a location for storing your bookmark.**

You can choose the Favorites bar, the Bookmarks menu, or a specific folder stored on either. (You discover how to create a bookmark folder in the "Storing bookmarks in folders" section, later in this chapter.)

5. **Click the Add button.**

Your new bookmark appears where you placed it.

TIP

Turn on Safari in iCloud on your Mac and your iOS devices, or Safari on a Windows computer with iCloud, to sync your bookmarks across all devices. See Book 1, Chapter 3 to learn about using iCloud.

Storing bookmarks in folders

After you save many bookmarks, they can start to clutter the Bookmarks menu or Favorites bar. To organize your bookmarks, you can store related bookmarks in folders. There are two ways to create a bookmark folder: The first steps work in the Sidebar, and the second steps work in the Bookmark Editor.

Follow these steps to work in the Sidebar:

1. **Click the Sidebar button to open the sidebar and then click the Bookmarks Button (the open book) or choose View ➪ Show Bookmarks Sidebar.**

You see a list of the bookmarks that came with Safari along with any you added. (Refer to Figure 1-17.)

2. **Right-click anywhere in the sidebar and choose New Folder from the Context menu.**

Alternatively, you can choose Bookmarks ➪ Add Folder.

An Untitled Folder is added to the bottom of the list.

3. **Type a name for the folder and press Return.**

4. **Click the icon next to the bookmark you want to add to the folder and drag it to the folder.**

   If you click the name, the web page opens.

5. **Add additional bookmarks to the folder.**

   After you create a folder, you can add bookmarks at any time.

TIP

If you have tons of bookmarks, it will be difficult to drag them onto the folder. To solve this dilemma, choose File⇨New Window. Resize the new window and position it alongside another browser window. Open the Favorites sidebar on both windows, and drag bookmarks from one window onto the folder you want to populate in the other window.

Follow these steps to work in the Bookmark Editor:

1. **In Safari, choose Bookmarks⇨Edit Bookmarks to display your saved bookmarks.**

2. **Click the New Folder button at the upper-right side of the window, as shown in Figure 1-19.**

   An untitled folder is added to the bottom of the list.

   Click Favorites Bar, Bookmarks Menu, or another folder in the left column if you want the new folder to be placed inside an existing folder.

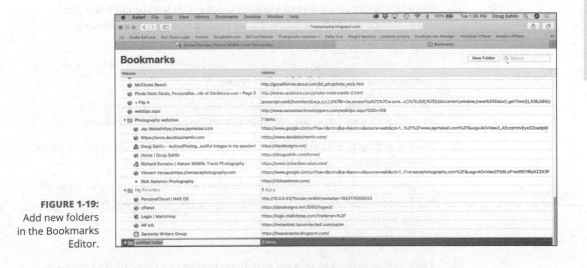

FIGURE 1-19: Add new folders in the Bookmarks Editor.

3. **Type a name for the folder and press Return.**

4. **(Optional) Click the disclosure triangle to the left of a folder name to display the bookmarks and folders within that folder.**

   This step is useful if you have bookmarks in another folder that you want to move to the new folder.

5. **Click and drag the bookmarks you want to move into the new folder.**

6. **Choose Bookmarks ⇨ Hide Bookmarks Editor.**

Rearranging or deleting bookmarks

Safari saves your bookmarks and bookmark folders in the order you create them, adding them to the bottom of an ever-growing list. If you continue to add bookmarks to the Bookmarks menu without placing them in folders, you may find that you have a gazillion bookmarks listed willy-nilly and can't remember what half of them link to (guilty, as charged). As time passes, you probably have bookmarks you don't use anymore — some may not even work anymore. The procedure is the same whether you work in the Sidebar or the Bookmarks Editor. Follow these steps to put your bookmarks in a more logical order and delete any you no longer want:

1. **In Safari, choose Bookmarks ⇨ Edit Bookmarks.**

   Or click the Sidebar button and then click the Bookmarks tab.

2. **Click the folder you want to move or delete (Sidebar) or click the disclosure triangle next to the folder name that contains the bookmark (Bookmarks Editor).**

   The contents, which might include bookmarks and additional folders that contain other bookmarks, are listed below.

   Click the additional folders to see the bookmarks contained within. You may need to repeat this step several times to find the bookmark you want.

3. **Click and drag the bookmark or bookmark folder you want to move up or down the list to a new folder or position.**

   Drag the bookmark or folder beyond the last item in a folder to move it out of the folder. A line shows where the item is being moved to; if you move it into a folder, the folder is highlighted.

   Safari moves your chosen bookmark to its new location.

4. **Click and drag bookmarks up and down within the collection or folder to change the order in which they are displayed.**

5. **In the Bookmarks Editor, click the bookmark that you want to delete and press Delete.**

Or, in the Sidebar, control-click the undesired bookmark and choose Delete from the context menu.

You can also delete a folder this way, but all the bookmarks and folders within the deleted folder will be deleted.

TIP

To restore a bookmark you mistakenly deleted, press ⌘+Z or choose Edit ⇨ Undo Remove Bookmark.

6. **Choose Bookmarks ⇨ Hide Bookmarks Editor to return to the most recent web page you viewed or click the Sidebar button to close the sidebar.**

Renaming bookmarks and folders

You may want to bookmark several web pages from the same website but have trouble differentiating them in the Bookmarks menu or Sidebar because the name that's displayed begins with the website and then the slashes and such to specify the web page. You can rename bookmarks and folders to something that's more meaningful to you, which will help you find your bookmarks more quickly. Here's how to rename in the Bookmarks Editor or the Sidebar:

» **Bookmarks Editor:** Choose Bookmarks ⇨ Edit Bookmarks. The Bookmarks Editor opens (refer to Figure 1-19). Click the bookmark or folder you want to rename, and then click it again. The pause between the two clicks is more pronounced than in a double-click. The name of the bookmark or folder is highlighted. Type the new name you want to use or click the text to edit it, and then press Return. After you finish editing your bookmarks, choose Bookmarks ⇨ Hide Bookmarks Editor.

» **Sidebar:** Click the Sidebar button, and then click the Bookmarks tab. Control-click the bookmark or folder you want to rename, and choose Rename Bookmark from the context menu. The name of the bookmark or folder is highlighted. Type the new name you want to use or click the text to edit it, and then press Return.

Importing and exporting bookmarks

After you collect and organize bookmarks, you might become dependent on your bookmarks to help you navigate the web. Fortunately, if you ever want to switch browsers, you can export bookmarks from one browser and import them into another browser.

To export bookmarks from Safari, follow these steps:

1. **In Safari, choose File ⇨ Export Bookmarks to open the Export Bookmarks dialog.**

2. **(Optional) Type a descriptive name for your bookmarks if you don't want to keep the default of Safari Bookmarks.**

3. **Click the Where pop-up menu to choose where you want to store your exported bookmarks file.**

If you click the arrow button that appears to the right of the Save As text box, a window appears displaying all the drives and folders that you can choose in which to store your bookmarks.

4. **Click Save.**

After you export bookmarks from one browser, it's usually a snap to import them into a second browser. To import bookmarks into Safari, follow these steps:

1. **In Safari, choose File ⇨ Import From, and then choose an option from the flyout menu.**

The options vary depending on which web browsers you have installed. On our working computer, we have a copy of Firefox, and the flyout menu gives us the option of importing Firefox bookmarks or importing a Bookmarks HTML file.

If you choose to import from another web browser on your computer, a dialog opens giving you the option of which type of bookmarks you want to import. For example, if you import from Firefox, you can import Bookmarks, History, and Passwords. After deciding which options you want to import, click the Import button.

If you choose Bookmarks HTML file, a dialog appears and you follow the next steps to complete the import.

2. **Navigate to the folder where the exported bookmarks file is stored.**

3. **Click the bookmark file you want to use and then click the Import button.**

Your imported bookmarks appear in an Imported folder that includes the date when you imported the folder. At this point, you can move this folder or its contents to the Bookmarks bar or Bookmarks menu to organize them. (See the earlier section, "Rearranging or deleting bookmarks.")

Creating a Reading List

Sometimes you find a great article that you really, really want to read but you just don't have time. Instead of bookmarking the page (we tell you all about bookmarks in the previous section), you can save the article to Reading List. And you can read those articles offline so you can get caught up on your reading while flying. Here's how to save and manage articles in the Reading List:

1. **In Safari, with the article or web page you want to read later open, click the One-Step Add button (the plus sign) at the left end of the Search and Address field.**

   The article is added to your reading list.

2. **When you're ready to read one or more of your saved articles, click the Sidebar icon in the toolbar (it looks like an open book) or choose View ⇨ Show Sidebar.**

3. **Click the Reading List tab to see the articles you placed there.**

   The Reading List, down the left side of the Safari window, shown in Figure 1-20, shows the title of the article, its source website, and the first few words of the article.

   Scroll through the list to see articles further down.

FIGURE 1-20:
The Reading List stores articles you want to read at a later date.

4. **Click the article you want to read.**

   It also could be a web page with more than one article, such as the cover page of a newspaper.

   The web page opens in the main part of the Safari window to the right of the Reading List.

   Click the Reader button for distraction-free reading.

REMEMBER

5. **Click the All or Unread buttons to change which articles you see in the Reading List.**

6. **To delete an article from the list, click the article and then click the X in the upper-right corner near the name of the selected article.**

7. **To delete the whole list, click the Clear All button.**

8. **Click the Sidebar button again to close the Sidebar.**

Displaying favorites in Top Sites

While you browse the web and go from one site to another to another, Safari pays attention behind the scenes to which websites you visit most. By tracking the websites you visit most frequently, Safari can display a selection of Top Sites that you can browse through to return to what Safari deems to be your favorite websites.

To display the Top Sites view of websites you visited, that Safari believes are your favorite websites, follow these steps:

1. **In the Safari window, click the Top Sites icon (it looks like a grid) on the Favorites bar to open the Top Sites display window.**

TIP

   If your toolbar does not have a Top Sites icon, you can add one by choosing View ⇨ Customize Toolbar, and then dragging and dropping the Top Sites icon to the Favorites bar.

   You see thumbnail views, shown in Figure 1-21, of the sites you visited most frequently. A star appears in the upper-right corner of the thumbnail of sites that have been updated since you last visited.

TIP

   You can modify the thumbnail view. Go to Safari ⇨ Preferences, click the General button, and then choose how many sites you want to see in Top Sites — 6, 12, or 24 — from the Top Sites Shows pop-up menu. When you change the size of the Safari window, the number of thumbnail images in Top Sites remains, but the size of each individual thumbnail changes to fit.

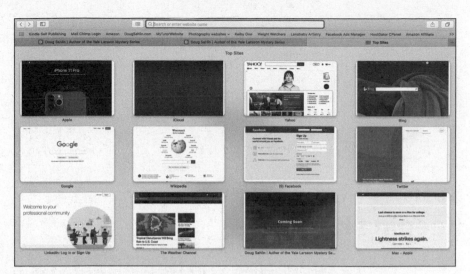

FIGURE 1-21:
Add or remove
Top Sites choices.

2. **Click a Top Sites thumbnail image of a website you want to visit.**

Safari goes to that web page.

3. **(Optional) Hover the cursor over the upper-left corner to see the Top Sites editing options:**

- *Exclude website.* To exclude a Top Sites selection that Safari deemed a Top Site, click the X in the upper-left corner of that Top Sites thumbnail image. As you delete one thumbnail, a new one is added in the lower-right corner of the Top Sites display.

- *Make a website permanent.* To mark a Top Sites selection as a permanent top site, click the pushpin icon next to the X in the upper-left corner of the Top Sites thumbnail image. The pushpin icon is highlighted to indicate that the website is a permanent top site. Click a highlighted pushpin icon to reverse the action: The page is no longer a permanent fixture in the Top Sites display and is replaced by a website you visit more frequently.

4. **(Optional) To rearrange the order in which your Top Sites thumbnail images appear, click a top site and drag and drop it to the location where you want it to appear.**

5. **(Optional) To add a new website to the Top Sites display window to Top Sites, do one of the following:**

- Press and hold the Add button to the left of the Search and Address field and then choose Add to Top Sites from the pop-up menu.

- Click and drag the URL icon to the Top Sites button, if you've added it to your toolbar.

Browsing the Web with Safari

6. **To exit the Top Sites display window, click one of the thumbnails to go to that website.**

   You can also type a web address in the Search and Address field and then press Return to go to that website or click a bookmark.

REMEMBER

   You can choose the Top Sites display as the default for a new tab (refer to Figure 1-11).

Storing Personal Info and Keeping It Private

Safari and iCloud have terrific built-in features that help you remember user names and passwords and credit card information. And Safari has security and privacy features to keep that personal information to yourself — or to your Mac. Here we tell you how to use AutoFill so Safari remembers passwords for you, and then we explain how to keep your information safe.

Using AutoFill to track passwords and more

If you don't share your Mac and you visit a lot of websites that require usernames and passwords, Safari can remember and automatically fill in the username and password for you when you open those websites. Safari can also automatically fill in forms with your name and address, credit card information, and information you've completed on an online form in the past. Safari encrypts this information, so even though it's remembered, it's safe.

In the following steps, we also show you how to add credit card information to Safari's brain trust. After adding card information, when you're making an online purchase and reach the credit card information fields, a drop-down field lets you choose which credit card you want to use from those you entered.

To use the AutoFill options, as shown in Figure 1-22, do the following:

1. **Choose Safari ⇨ Preferences and click the AutoFill button on the toolbar.**

2. **Select the Using Info from My Contacts Card check box.**

   Safari presents pre-filled drop-down fields in website forms that request information such as your address and telephone number, which will be taken from Contacts.

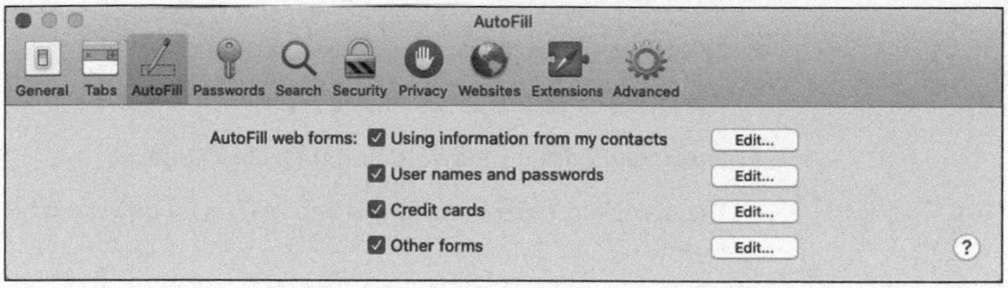

FIGURE 1-22:
AutoFill keeps track of passwords and fills in forms.

Click Edit to open Contacts and view the information that will be accessed. (See Book 5, Chapter 1 to learn more about Contacts.)

3. **Select the User Names and Passwords check box.**

The first time you visit a website that requires a username and password, Safari asks whether you want it remembered. If you choose Yes, your username and password are filled in automatically the next time you visit the website.

4. **(Optional) Click the Edit button next to User Names and Passwords.**

The Passwords Are Locked dialog appears.

5. **Enter your admin password.**

The Passwords Preferences dialog opens showing you a list that is divided into three columns: Websites, Username, and Password. The first column shows each website you've visited that requires a password. If you've allowed Safari to save your password for the site, a name or email address appears in the Username column and the password used is hidden by asterisks. After the Passwords Preferences dialog opens, you can do the following:

- Deselect AutoFill User Names and Passwords and Safari will not auto-fill usernames or passwords, nor will you be prompted by Safari to save website usernames and passwords. This also deselects usernames and passwords in AutoFill preferences.

- Click a website, and then click Details to display the username and password Safari saved for that site.

- Click a website (or Control-click multiple websites) and then click the Remove button to eliminate those usernames and passwords from Safari's memory.

- Click the Add button to open a dialog box into which you can enter a URL and the username and password required to access the site.

Then click the AutoFill button to return to the AutoFill Preferences.

6. Select the Credit Cards check box and then click Edit.

The Credit Cards Are Locked dialog appears.

7. Enter your admin password and then click Unlock.

The dialog box refreshes showing information for any credit cards you have saved.

8. To edit a credit card, select it and then modify the information.

You can edit the cardholder name, card number, expiration date, and cardholder name, or click Remove to delete the card information.

9. Click Add to add a card to the list.

A dialog appears in which you fill in the card description, card number, expiration date, and cardholder name.

WARNING

If you choose to use AutoFill for names, passwords — and especially credit cards — we highly recommend setting up your Mac to require a password whenever it is turned on or wakes from sleep. See Book 3, Chapter 2 to learn more about Mac security features.

10. Select the Other Forms check box, which will remember what you enter the first time you fill in a form and use it if the same website asks for the same information again.

Click the Edit button to see, and remove, websites for which AutoFill has been enabled.

REMEMBER

If you turn on the Keychain option in iCloud, the information you let AutoFill manage is available across all devices signed in to the same iCloud account with Keychain activated. See Book 1, Chapter 3 to learn about iCloud.

Protecting your web-browsing privacy

Safari encrypts your web browsing to help avoid Internet eavesdropping and potential digital theft. And, instead of letting websites access your information automatically when you fill out forms, Safari detects forms and presents your information in drop-down fields so you can choose which information to insert.

As a rule, Safari keeps track of your browsing history, but if you use Safari on a public Mac, perhaps in a library, you may not want to leave a trace of where you've been. Choose File ➪ New Private Window and Safari keeps your browsing secrets safe. When you enable Private Browsing, a new Safari window opens, and the Search or Enter Website Name field has a black background. In a nutshell, turning on the Private Browsing keeps your web-browsing history usage private by

>> Not tracking which websites you visit, which means they don't show up in History

>> Removing any files that you downloaded from the Downloads window (Window ⇨ Downloads)

>> Not saving names or passwords that you enter on websites

>> Not saving search words or terms that you enter in the Search and Address field

In other words, when you open a private window, Safari gets a case of amnesia, making Safari mind its own business until you close the private window. You know when Private Browsing is active because the Search or Enter Website Name field has a dark gray background. You can use the navigation buttons during the session, but when you close Safari, or close the private window, your viewing history is erased. In short, opening a private window is an excellent solution when you're surfing for your husband's anniversary present.

After you close a private window, Safari goes back to thoughtfully keeping track of the websites you visit and the terms you type into the search box so you can easily return to those sites or searches later.

In addition to surfing with a private window, Safari offers Security and Privacy preferences. Do the following to set these up:

1. **Choose Safari ⇨ Preferences and click the Security button on the toolbar.**

2. **Select the check box next to the options you want to activate:**

- *Fraudulent Sites:* When you open a website that Safari finds suspicious, you receive a warning that requires you to confirm or cancel opening the page. Safari uses Google Safe Browsing to determine if a site is fraudulent.

- *Web Content:* JavaScript is a language used for buttons, forms, and other website content; if this check box is left clear, some website functionality may be lost. Pop-up windows often contain advertising, so you may want to leave this check box clear. That said, some website functionality may be lost if you don't enable this feature. In both cases, if necessary, you'll receive a message from the website prompting you to activate the feature.

3. **Click the Privacy button on the toolbar to open Privacy preferences, as shown in Figure 1-23.**

4. **Protect your privacy by accepting the default Prevent Cross-Site Tracking.**

This option makes it harder for companies to track your browsing across multiple websites. We strongly suggest you do *not* deselect this option.

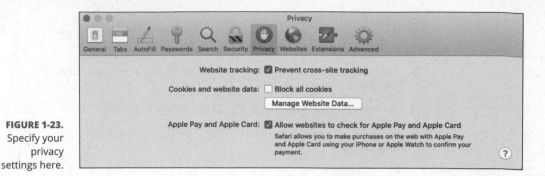

5. **Tighten your web-browsing security by clicking the Block All Cookies check box.**

If you select this option, Safari warns you that websites may not work if you enable this option. When this option is not selected, which is the default state, Safari keeps a list of websites that have stored data that can be used to track your browsing. You can click the Manage Website Data button and see who's tracking what, and then select specific sites you would like to remove, or remove all.

TIP

To enable quick surfing without interruptions, do not block all cookies, but visit the Privacy preferences frequently, click Manage Website Data, and remove suspect sites.

TECHNICAL STUFF

Cookies are pieces of information about you that websites you visit use to track your browser usage. Cookies may also be used for user authentication or specific information. When you sign up with a website, that site gives you a cookie so that the next time you go to that website, it recognizes you because it sees you have one of its cookies.

6. **Accept the default Apple Pay and Apple Card option.**

With the default option enabled, Safari lets you make purchases on the web with Apple Pay and Apple Card using your iPhone or Apple Watch to confirm payment. If you have none of the previously mentioned Apple baubles, feel free to deselect this option.

7. **Click the Close button.**

Saving and Sharing Web Pages

When you come upon a web page containing a story or a recipe that you want to save for later reference, you can add it to the Reading List, as we explain previously, or you can save the file. If you want to share that great recipe with friends, you have many options so they can have a look at what you find so interesting. We explain both saving and sharing here.

Saving a web page as a file

When you save a web page as a file, you store the complete text and graphics of that web page as a file on your Mac's hard drive. Safari gives you two ways to save a web page:

>> **As a Web Archive:** A *web archive* is meant for viewing a web page only in the Safari browser.

>> **As an HTML Source File (called Page Source):** If you view a web page saved as Page Source, you won't see any of the graphics, but you will see text references to the graphics and each one's associated URL. Saving a web page as an HTML source file lets you view and edit that file in any browser or web page authoring application, which is helpful if you want to figure out how someone designed that particular web page.

TECHNICAL STUFF

HTML stands for *HyperText Markup Language,* which is a special language used to specify the layout and behavior of web pages.

To save a web page as a file, follow these steps:

1. **In Safari, find the web page that you want to save and choose File ⇨ Save As.**

The Export As dialog opens, as shown in Figure 1-24.

2. **(Optional) Type a new descriptive name in the Export As field if you don't want to keep the one Safari automatically fills in for you.**

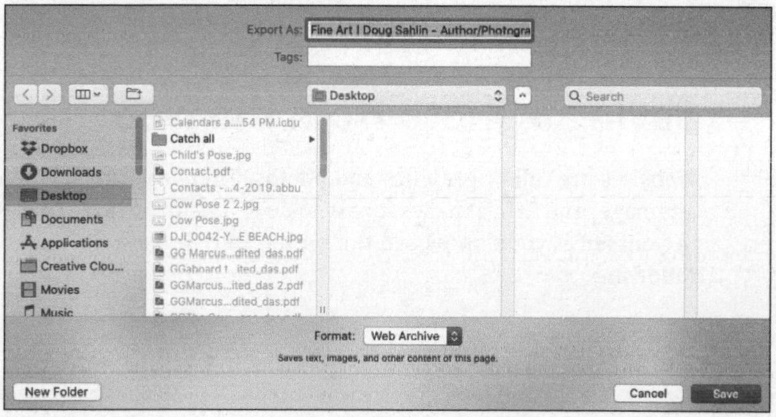

FIGURE 1-24:
Choose the file format and location.

REMEMBER

3. **(Optional) Add any tags you want to associate with the saved file.**

   Tags are keywords that help you find your file at a later date. See Book 1, Chapter 4 to learn about tags and tagging.

4. **From the Where pop-up menu, choose where you want to store your file on your Mac's hard drive.**

   Alternatively, you can click the New Folder button to create a new folder in which to store the exported file.

TIP

   If you click the Expand (downward-pointing arrow) button to the right of the Export As field, the Save As dialog expands to let you choose more folders to store your file.

5. **From the Format pop-up menu, choose Web Archive or Page Source, and then click Save.**

The other option you have is to export a page as a PDF. To do so, follow these steps:

1. **Choose File ⇨ Export as PDF.**

   The Export As dialog appears.

2. **Enter a descriptive name for the PDF and add any tags.**

3. **From the Where drop-down menu, navigate to the location where you'd like to save the PDF.**

   Alternatively, you can click the New Folder button to create a new folder in which to store the exported PDF.

4. **Click Save.**

REMEMBER

After you save a web page as a Web Archive, Page Source, or export a page as a PDF, you can view it by double-clicking the file icon in the folder where you saved it.

Saving a photo from the web

Websites are full of graphics and photos. There are times when you want to save an image, and Safari makes it easy to do — just make sure that you keep the image to yourself if you don't have the rights to it. To save an image to Photos, do the following:

1. **In Safari, find the image on a web page that you want to save.**

2. **Right-click the image and choose the Add Image to Photos option from the context menu shown in Figure 1-25.**

    Or choose one of the other saving options from the menu.

    Some websites "protect" against copying the images by using a transparent overlay that prevents your click from being on, and selecting, the image you want to copy.

    The image will be available in Photos the next time you launch the application.

    You can adjust, share, or print the image. (See Book 4, Chapter 4 for details on using Photos.)

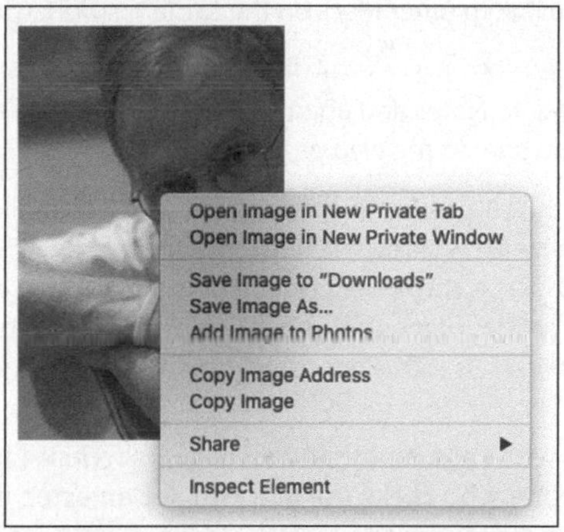

FIGURE 1-25:
Right-click to save an image from a web page.

Open image in New Private Tab
Open Image in New Private Window

Save Image to "Downloads"
Save Image As...
Add Image to Photos

Copy Image Address
Copy Image

Share   ▶

Inspect Element

Sharing a web page

If we had to choose one word to describe Apple apps, it would probably be "sharing." Whether it's text in Pages, an image in Photos, or a web page in Safari, the procedure for sharing is the same and as simple as a click.

To share a link to web page, do the following:

In Safari, click the Share button on the toolbar or choose File ⇨ Share; then choose one of these options, as shown in Figure 1-26:

>> **Email This Page:** Sends a link to the web page in an email message. The Mail application loads and opens a new email message containing your web page link. Fill in the address and subject fields, write an accompanying message, and click Send. (See Book 2, Chapter 2 to learn about Mail.)

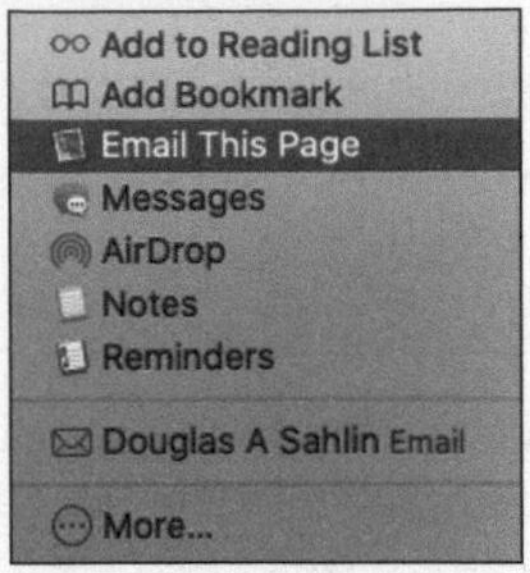

FIGURE 1-26:
Share news and discoveries with people you know.

» **Messages:** Sends a link to the web page that the recipient can click to open the web page with her web browser. A message bubble opens. Fill in the address field and click Send. (See Book 2, Chapter 3 to learn about Messages.)

» **AirDrop:** Sends the link to other Macs on the same network with AirDrop opened.

» **Notes:** Adds the URL to Notes and opens the application. Add any text to remind you why you shared the web page to Notes.

» **Reminders:** Adds the URL to Reminders and opens a Reminders window. Add any text to clarify why you shared the URL to reminders, and then set a date and a time. This may be a convenient way to save a page with an item you want to buy when payday comes around. In Reminders, you could have the application alert you when you've got some discretionary coin of the realm.

WARNING

If you send a link to a web page and that web page or website is changed or is no longer available, someone who clicks the link will see an error message instead of the web page you wanted him to see.

Printing a web page

Rather than saving or sharing a web page as a file, you might just want to print it instead: For example, you might want to print a press clip that lauds your latest art installation and mail it to your grandmother who doesn't have Internet access. To print a web page, follow these steps:

1. **In Safari, find the web page you want to print and choose File ➪ Print to open the Print dialog.**

2. **Open the Printer pop-up menu and choose the printer to use.**

3. **Use the other pop-up menus to choose print quality, number of copies, and page range.**

   Leave Print Backgrounds and Print Headers and Footers unchecked as this usually prints unnecessary information that only wastes ink.

4. **Click the Show Details button to see more options, with regard to page size, scale, and layout. Click Hide Details to close these options.**

   If you click the PDF button, you can save your web page as a PDF file.

5. **Click Print.**

Viewing and Playing Multimedia Files

The most basic web pages consist of mainly text and sometimes graphics. However, most websites offer robust content beyond simple words and pictures, including content stored as video, audio, and other types of common files, such as PDF files. Usually, you can just click the playback button, and the audio or video begins to roll. Sometimes you might need additional software — a plug-in — to view content, and you will be prompted to download the appropriate plug-in.

TECHNICAL STUFF

Since the advent of HTML5, the vast majority of videos on the web can be viewed cross platform on any browser.

Listening to streaming audio

Many websites offer audio that you can listen to, such as live interviews or radio shows. Such audio is often stored as *streaming audio,* which means that your computer downloads a temporary audio file and begins playing it almost instantly but doesn't actually save the radio app as a file on your hard drive.

Sometimes you can listen to streaming audio through the iTunes application, sometimes you need a copy of Windows Media Components, and sometimes you need a copy of RealPlayer.

Viewing PDF files

Many downloadable documents, booklets, brochures, e-book editions of *The New York Times* best-selling nonfiction and fiction titles, and user guides are offered as a PDF file. If a website offers a PDF file as a link you can click to open, you can view and scroll through it directly within Safari.

You can save a PDF document you're viewing to look at later by clicking the document displayed in the Safari web browser window and choosing File ⇨ Save As. You don't have to choose Export as PDF because the file already is a PDF. If you double-click a PDF file icon, you can view the contents of that PDF file by using the Preview application included with every Mac.

REMEMBER

You can also view PDF files by using the Adobe Reader application — a free download from Adobe (www.adobe.com) — which offers the basic features of the Preview application plus extra features for opening and viewing PDF documents. If you have problems printing certain PDF files with the Preview application, try printing them with the Adobe Reader application instead.

Downloading Files

Part of the web's appeal is that you can find interesting content — music tracks, or free demos of apps you can try before you buy, for example — that you can download and install on your own computer. (When you copy a file from the web and store it on your computer, that's *downloading*. When you copy a file from your computer to a website — such as your electronic tax forms that you file electronically on the IRS's website — that's *uploading*.)

WARNING

Download those files only if you trust the source. If you visit an unknown website, that unknown website might be trying to trick you into downloading a file that could do harmful things to your Mac, such as delete files, spy on your activities, or even bombard you with unwanted ads, so be careful. Safari has built-in protections that scan websites and downloads to warn you of potential dangers. To discover ways you can protect your Mac (and yourself) from potentially dangerous Internet threats, take a look at the earlier section on protecting your web-browsing privacy and consult Book 3, Chapter 2.

When you find a file you want to download, follow these steps:

1. **Click the Download link or button to begin downloading the file you want to save on your Mac's hard drive.**

If you've never downloaded from the website before, a dialog appears asking you if you want to allow downloads from the website.

2. **Click Allow or Cancel.**

If you allow downloads, an animated circle swoops to the Downloads icon on the dock. A Download icon appears to the left of the Share icon on the Safari toolbar. If you're downloading a large file, a blue progress bar appears below the icon indicating the progress of the download. When the bar disappears, your download is complete.

3. **When the file has completely downloaded, click the Downloads icon.**

A pop-up menu appears listing the files that have been downloaded (see Figure 1-27).

If the file is still downloading, you see a circular icon with an arrow, which indicates the progress of the download.

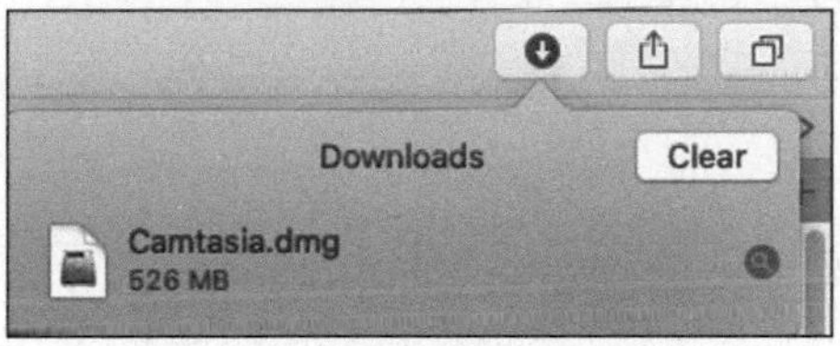

FIGURE 1-27:
Files you download can be viewed and installed from the Downloads icon.

4. **Double-click the file to open it, or if you downloaded an application, install it.**

Alternatively, you can go to the Downloads stack on the Dock and open the file from there.

If you click the magnifying glass icon to the right of a file displayed in the Downloads window, Safari opens a Finder window and displays the contents of the Downloads folder. The file you downloaded is highlighted.

5. **After opening a downloaded file, click the Downloads icon and then click the Clear button.**

The Downloads list is cleared, but the downloaded file still remains in the Downloads folder, or another location if you changed the default location in Safari Preferences.

TIP

By default, downloaded files are saved to the Downloads folder. To change the destination folder, choose Safari ➪ Preferences and click the General button. From the Save Downloaded Files To pop up menu, choose Other, and then click the destination folder in the Chooser. Alternatively, you can choose Ask for Each Download, and Safari will prompt you for the location where you want to save the file.

Browsing the Web with Safari

While the Safari Preferences are open, choose to open "safe" files, such as PDFs, photo, and movies, as soon as the download is finished by selecting the Open "Safe" Files After Downloading check box.

Using Extensions

You can enhance your Safari Internet navigation experience by adding *extensions*, which are add-on applets designed by developers and approved by Apple. To find and install extensions, follow these steps:

1. **Click the Safari icon on the Dock or Launchpad.**

2. **Choose Safari⇨Safari Extensions.**

The Safari Extensions Gallery on the App Store opens, as shown in Figure 1-28.

TIP

If you'd like to learn more about extensions, click the Learn to Use Safari Extensions link to open an informative web page that tells you everything you wanted to know about extensions but were afraid to ask.

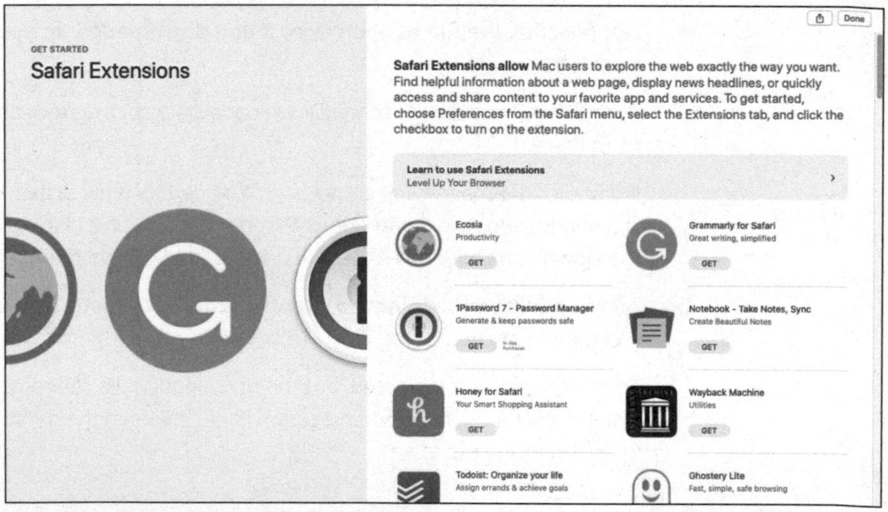

FIGURE 1-28: Safari Extensions automate and add features to your web browsing activities.

3. **Search for extensions by scrolling through the extensions on the opening page or clicking a category and scrolling through the results.**

When you find an extension that piques your curiosity, double-click its icon to learn more about the extension.

4. **When you find a useful or entertaining extension, click the Get button.**

The Get button become the Install button.

5. **Click the Install button.**

You're prompted for your Apple password. This is the same password you use for iCloud.

6. **Enter your password and click the Install button.**

The extension is installed in your Home directory's hidden Library folder to be accessed by Safari. (See Book 1, Chapter 4 to learn more about the Library folder.) Depending on the type of task the extension performs, it may appear as a banner under the toolbar or as a button on the toolbar, or it might show up on-call: for example, as password manager.

7. **To manage your extensions after you install them, choose Safari⇨ Preferences and click the Extensions tab.**

8. **Click the extension you want to manage and choose settings from the menus offered. Click Uninstall if you want to remove the extension.**

IN THIS CHAPTER

» **Configuring an email account**

» **Writing email**

» **Receiving and reading email**

» **Organizing mailboxes and mail**

» **Cleaning up junk email**

Chapter **2**

Corresponding with Mail

E mail has been in the news a lot recently. It used to be considered the profes-sional, not to mention private, secure, and trackable, method of electronic communication over the Internet. Email is fast, (almost always) free, and accessible to anyone with a computer, smartphone, tablet, or e-reader and an Internet connection.

The privacy of email has been shown to be an illusion in many cases. Many (most?) email messages are not encrypted, so anyone with access to them can read them. Some newer email systems do provide automatic end-to-end encryp-tion of messages. If you're concerned about security of email and other processes on your Mac, look at the iCloud security overview at https://support.apple. com/en-us/HT202303. (If you use Gmail, this link provides some information about encryption in that environment: https://support.google.com/mail/ answer/6330403?hl=en.)

A new breed of communication tools is emerging, exemplified by Slack (https:// slack.com) and WhatsApp (https://www.whatsapp.com). These tools have secu-rity built into them and are designed for sharing brief messages, images, and file references. (Look at Messages for an example of these new tools — you have it as part of the standard macOS installation.)

When you have an email account, you have two choices for reading and writing messages:

>> Through a web browser, such as Safari or Firefox (see the preceding chapter for the lowdown on Safari)

>> Through an email application, such as the Mac's free Mail application

Accessing an email account through a web browser is simple because you don't need to know how to use another application, and you don't have to worry about knowing the technical details of your email account. (You do need Internet access, though, to read or respond to messages.)

Accessing an email account through an email application lets you download messages so you can read or respond to them even if you aren't connected to the Internet. (Of course, you won't be able to send or receive any messages until you connect to the Internet again.)

If you plan to access your email account only through a browser, such as Safari, you can skip this entire chapter because this chapter explains how to use Mail. If you want to use Mail, read on. In this chapter, we explain how to send and receive email. First, though, we give you a quick review of how to set up an email account. (You can find the full rundown in Book 1, Chapter 3.) Then we take you through Mail, the email application that came with your Mac. Mail not only sends and receives messages but is also a veritable filing cabinet for your documents; you can use it to organize and store your correspondence to make later searches easier when you need to find an old "letter" or contract.

Adding an Email Account to Mail

We explain the down and dirty of connecting to the Internet and setting up Internet accounts with all those crazy acronyms like POP, IMAP, DNS, and ISP in Book 1, Chapter 3. Here we briefly take you through adding an email account from the Mail app. Before we begin, make sure you have the following information from your current email account(s):

>> **Username (or account name):** Typically a descriptive name (such as barackobama) or a collection of numbers and symbols (such as barack44). Your username plus the name of your email or Internet service provider (ISP) defines your complete email address, such as barackobama@gmail.com or barackobama@comcast.net.

>> **Password:** Any phrase that you choose to access your account. If someone sets up an email account for you, he might have already assigned a password that you can always change later.

If you use one of the common Internet email providers — such as Google, Yahoo!, or Apple's own iCloud — that's all you need. Mail takes care of the rest. And, if you use Apple's iCloud service and typed your icloud.com (or me.com) account name and password when you completed the Welcome setup process, Mail is already configured to access your iCloud email account.

If you use another service provider, you may also need the following, which you can find on your ISP website:

>> **Incoming server name:** This name may be a combination of POP or IMAP and your email account service provider, such as pop.comcast.net or imap.gmail.com.

>> **Outgoing server name:** This name may be a combination of SMTP (Simple Mail Transfer Protocol) and the name of the company that provides your email account, such as smtp.gmail.com or smtp.comcast.net.

These days, your ISP may be something other than one of the providers listed in this section. For many people, their ISP is their landlord; for people who set up an account on a mobile device, their ISP may be their telephone company or their cable TV provider. You normally have one ISP (one of these or other companies), and you access it from various devices. You may set up your Internet account as part of a package of telephone and TV services on a mobile device and then access it on your Mac. If your Internet access is through a company with which you have other dealings (your cable provider, for example), that company may help you configure your Mac. If you're writing a check every month for that service, they may help you with your email as well (because it's part of your bundle). You may want to consider whether your provider will provide setup support for you. If you have a MacBook, you can take it into your provider's local store. If email is provided through your company, your IT guru can set up an email account on your Mac.

REMEMBER

You can access your email from Mail (or a different email application) on your Mac, from a web browser on your Mac, or on another computer, such as at your friend's house or at an Internet café. You can also access your email from hand-held devices that have a Wi-Fi or cellular Internet connection. When you use a web browser, you go to the email provider's website.

You can set up your Mail account when you first set up your Mac (as we explain in Book 1, Chapter 3) or by setting up your email account within the Mail application.

Corresponding with Mail

After you collect the technical information needed to access your email account, you need to configure Mail to work with your email account by following these steps:

1. **Click the Mail icon (the postage stamp with the soaring bird on it) on the Dock.**

   The Add Account dialog prompts you to choose a service provider, as shown in Figure 2-1.

   TIP

   If you already added an email account — for example, iCloud, during the initial setup of your Mac — you can still add additional accounts by choosing Mail ⇨ Add Account and following these steps.

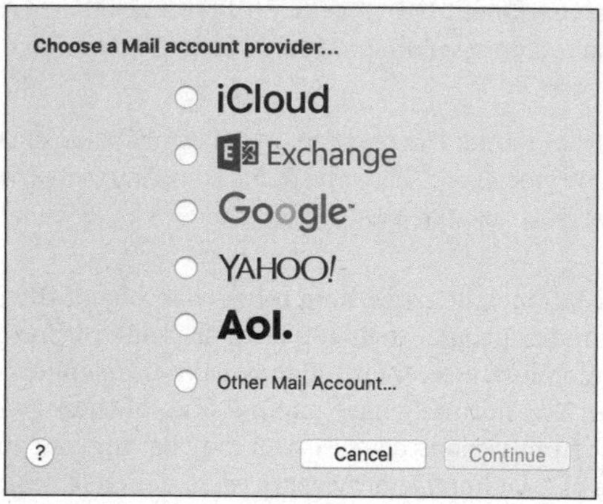

   Choose a Mail account provider...

   ○ **iCloud**

   ○ **E⊠ Exchange**

   ○ **Google**

   ○ **YAHOO!**

   ○ **Aol.**

   ○ Other Mail Account...

   ?   Cancel   Continue

FIGURE 2-1:
The New Account dialog displays common email service providers.

2. **Select the radio button for the ISP you use — for example, Google — and then click the Continue button.**

   If your ISP doesn't appear, select the Add Other Mail Account radio button and then click Continue.

3. **In the dialog that opens, enter the information requested (as shown in Figure 2-2), and then click the Set Up or Next button.**

   WARNING

   The dialog that appears differs depending on your ISP. If your server is not listed and you click the Other Mail Account radio button, a generic window appears into which you enter your information. This is one case where you may need help from a tech-savvy friend or your company's IT guru.

   The fields you need to enter change over time in general and, specifically, change depending on the account you're trying to use. These fields may include your name, phone number, age, or other data elements that help to establish your identity. The data you enter in the dialog varies from vendor to vendor and from time to time.

Note in Figure 2-2 that the instructions for the sign-in field not only ask for data, but describe how it will be used. That type of respect for and protection of identifiable user data is becoming increasingly common as people are becoming more sensitive to the use of their data.

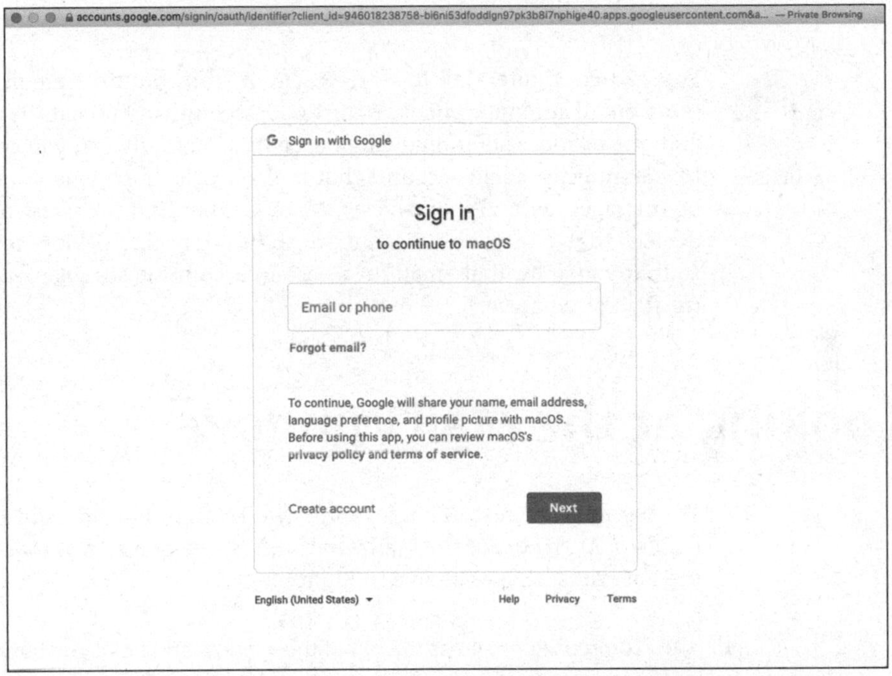

accounts.google.com/signin/oauth/identifier?client_id=946018238758-bi6ni53dfoddlgn97pk3b8i7nphige40.apps.googleusercontent.com&a... — Private Browsing

G Sign in with Google

Sign in

to continue to macOS

Email or phone

Forgot email?

To continue, Google will share your name, email address, language preference, and profile picture with macOS. Before using this app, you can review macOS's privacy policy and terms of service.

Create account   Next

English (United States) ▾   Help   Privacy   Terms

FIGURE 2-2:
Enter your new account info.

If you have issues, contact your email provider (often this is your ISP).

If you choose iCloud, use your Apple ID and password, and then click Sign In to add Mail to the iCloud services you use (see Book 1, Chapter 3).

Your full name is any name you want to associate with your messages. If you type **Lily, friend of frogs** in the Name text box, all your messages will include From: Lily, friend of frogs. Your email address includes your username plus ISP name, such as lilypond@gmail.com. Your password might be case-sensitive (most are), so type it exactly.

4. **A window appears asking you which apps you want to use with the account.**

   The options are Mail and Notes. Both are checked by default. To receive mail, you'll need to keep Mail checked, but you can uncheck Notes if you want. If you include Notes, a section for the email address you just added appears in the application. You'll then be able to create notes and send them via email.

Corresponding
with Mail

5. **Click Done and Mail connects to your email account and tries to fill in your account settings automatically.**

If Mail doesn't automatically detect your email account settings, continue following the onscreen steps to configure Mail to work with your email account. You will be prompted to add the other information mentioned earlier: the incoming and outgoing mail server names.

REMEMBER

You can configure Mail to retrieve email from multiple email accounts. To add more email accounts, choose Mail ⇨ Add Account and repeat the preceding steps to add one or more additional email accounts. Not only can you configure your Mac to use multiple email accounts, but it also works in reverse: An email account can be managed by multiple devices. Many people find it easiest to either set up all devices to use the same accounts or to limit specific devices to specific accounts so that you know that email for a certain account is always managed on your Mac (or iPad or whatever).

Looking at the Mail Window

Throughout the rest of the chapter, we refer to buttons and panes in the Mail window. At the top of the Mail window, you see two sets of tools (the Toolbar and the Favorites bar), as shown in Figure 2-3:

» **Toolbar:** Runs across the top of the window and holds the buttons that you click to take an action, such as write a new message, send a message, move a message to a different folder, mute a conversation, or even throw away a message.

» **Favorites bar:** Here you find buttons that quickly open your favorite mailboxes. To customize the Favorites bar, drag the mailboxes from the Mailboxes panel on the left side of the Mail app to the Favorites bar; to delete a button from the Favorites bar, click and drag the undesired button out of the Favorites bar, and it disappears in a puff of smoke.

FIGURE 2-3:
The Mail window has two main parts.

TIP

If the Favorites bar is not visible, choose View➪Show Favorites Bar.

You can customize the toolbar with the buttons you use most by choosing View➪Customize Toolbar to open the window shown in Figure 2-4. Click and drag the buttons until the toolbar has the tools you need. At the bottom, choose from the Show pop-up menu to display Icon and Text, Icon Only, or Text Only.

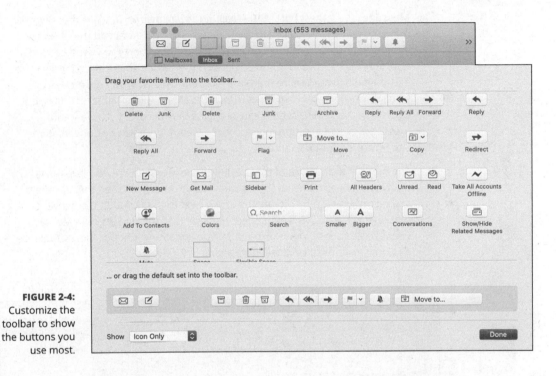

FIGURE 2-4: Customize the toolbar to show the buttons you use most.

Take a look at Mail on your Mac's screen while reviewing the following parts of the Mail window.

» **Mailboxes panel:** The first column on the left shows a list of your mailboxes. *Hint:* If you don't see this column, click the Mailboxes button on the left side of the Favorites bar. If you have more than one account, each account will have Inbox, Sent, Junk, and Trash sections. If you click the topmost button of the section — say, Inbox — you see all the messages in your Inbox listed in the center column. If you click an account, for example, your Gmail account in the Inbox section, you see only the messages sent to your Gmail email account. If you have just one email account, you will see only the categories. Click the disclosure triangle to the left of an email to show or hide the subcategories. After doing this, the subcategories for each account are not shown. Click the disclosure triangle again to reveal them.

TIP

>> **Message Preview list:** The second column (which is the first if the Mailboxes column is hidden) shows your messages. Click Sort By at the top of the column to choose how you want to sort your messages or choose View➪Sort By, and choose an option from the flyout menu.

Hover the pointer over the scroll bar on either column to show a vertical line with an arrow. Click and drag to make the columns wider or narrower.

>> **Message:** The largest part of the Mail window shows your active message: the message that you've clicked in the Message list. Mail gives you the option of viewing your messages in a Conversation format. When you view a conversation, you see the thread of messages with the same subject, even if they were exchanged between more than one recipient. This way, you don't have to scroll through to find responses from different people on different days, but can follow the "conversation" exchanges as they occurred. To view your messages in conversation mode, choose View➪Organize by Conversation. See Figure 2-5 for an example.

The number to the right of the preview in the Message Preview list shows how many exchanges make up the conversation. You can also see the "speakers" in the conversation by clicking the arrow next to the number; the active message in Figure 2-5 is expanded. To expand all the messages in Message Preview list, choose View➪Expand All Conversations. Choose View➪Collapse All Conversations to collapse them again.

FIGURE 2-5:
Viewing email messages as a conversation makes it easy to follow the sequence of exchanges.

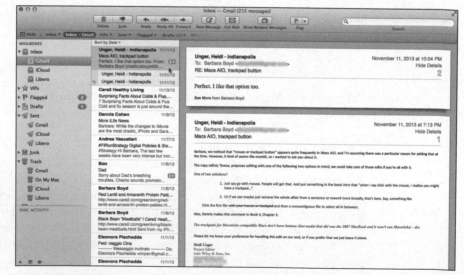

REMEMBER

Mail supports full-screen viewing. Just click the full-screen toggle switch in the upper-right corner and take advantage of your Mac's whole screen.

Writing Emails

After you configure your Mail account(s) and are familiar with the buttons and panes, you can start writing and sending email to anyone with an email address. In this section, we describe how to write and send an email, attach files and photos, and customize the appearance of your messages.

Creating a new email

When you write a message to someone for the first time, you have to create a new message. Follow these steps:

1. **In Mail, choose File⇨New Message or click the New Message button.**

The New Message button looks like a piece of paper with a pencil on it (refer to Figure 2-4).

A New Message window appears, as shown in Figure 2-6, in which all options are active — we tell you how to turn them on and off in the section, "Customizing your messages."

TIP

Although the steps here instruct you to click in each field, you can also press the tab key to move from field to field.

2. **Click the To text box and type an email address or do one of the following:**

- Click the Add button (the plus sign) at the right end of the field to open Contacts and select recipients from there.

- Begin typing a name you have stored in Contacts, and Mail will automatically fill in that person's email address (as long as it's part of the person's Contacts card). If a person has more than one email address, click the one you want from the list that appears. If the person you're sending the message to is not stored in Contacts, enter the email address and send the message.

Corresponding with Mail

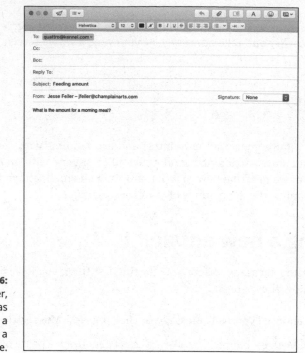

3. **(Optional) Click the Cc and/or Bcc text box and add an email address or addresses using one of the methods in Step 2.**

- *Carbon copy (Cc):* The Cc field is where you type email addresses of people whom you want to keep informed, but who don't necessarily need to write a reply. The email address you add to the Cc field will be visible to all recipients.

- *Blind carbon copy (Bcc):* The Bcc field sends a copy of your message to email addresses that you type here, but those email addresses will not be visible to other recipients.

TIP

When sending out a particularly important message, many people type the recipient's email address in the To field and their own email address in the Cc or Bcc fields. This way, they can verify that their message was sent correctly.

4. **(Optional) Type an email address in the Reply To field if replies should be sent to an email that's different than the address the message is being sent from.**

For example, if you send 1,000 invitations to a big event, you could create an email address specifically for the event on one of the common service providers. Although the invitation is sent from you, invitees respond to the special address, and your inbox isn't clogged with 1,000 responses. The Reply

To field is not visible by default. To view and use this field, select it from the Select Visible Header Fields drop-down list (the icon that looks like a bulleted list), which is to the right of the Send button that looks like a paper airplane.

5. **Click the Subject text box and type a brief description of your message for your recipient.**

6. **(Optional) Open the From pop-up menu to send the message from a different email account, if you have more than one.**

7. **(Optional) Open the Signature pop-up menu to choose a signature — if you created more than one — and use this option.**

   We show you how to create a signature in an upcoming section.

8. **(Optional) Open the Priority pop-up menu to add urgency to your message.**

   The priority options are High Priority, Normal Priority, and Low Priority.

   The Priority Field is not visible by default. To view and use this field, select it from the Select Visible Header Fields drop-down list (the icon that looks like a bulleted list), which is to the right of the Send button that looks like a paper airplane.

9. **Click in the Message field and type your message.**

   Use the font, size, and style pop-up menus to change the typeface of your message, or use more than one typeface in a message. (This works only if you choose Rich Text in the Composing section of Mail⇨Preferences.) Click the List button to format your text with bullets or numbers.

TIP

   You can copy text from another message or another app like Notes or Pages, and then choose Edit⇨Paste to insert the copied text.

10. **Click the Send button, which looks like a paper airplane, in the upper-left corner.**

Replying to or forwarding a message

You'll often find yourself responding to messages others send to you. When you reply to a message, your reply can contain the text that you originally received so the recipient can better understand the context of your reply.

To reply to a message, you need to receive a message first. To receive messages, just click the Get Mail button (refer to Figure 2-4), which looks like an envelope. You find out more about receiving messages later in this chapter.

To reply to or forward a message, follow these steps:

1. **In Mail, click the Inbox button in the Mailboxes section.**

The middle column lists all the messages stored in your Inbox folder. If the Mailboxes section is not visible, click the Mailboxes button on the Favorites toolbar. If you have more than one email account, click the account in which the message you want to reply to or forward appears.

2. **Select a message in the Inbox that you want to reply to.**

3. **Click one of the following buttons on the toolbar.**

Or you can click buttons on the heads-up display, which is revealed when you hover the pointer over the center of the line between the address information and message. The heads-up display that contains the Delete, Move Selected Messages to Junk, Reply, Reply All, and Forward buttons.

- *Reply:* Opens a response message addressed to the sender only.

- *Reply All:* If the message was sent to you and several other people, this option — the double left-pointing arrow — sends your response to everyone (except Bcc recipients whom you don't know about) who received the original message.

- *Forward:* To send the message to another person, without replying to the sender or other recipients, click the Forward button, which is a right-pointing arrow.

To both reply and forward the message, click Reply or Reply All. Then click in the Cc, or Bcc field, and type the email address of the person you want to forward the message to.

4. **Write your reply in the message that appears with the cursor blinking above the text of the original message.**

5. **Click Send.**

Customizing your messages

Like other Mac apps, Mail offers preferences that let you customize and personalize your messages. You access many settings from the Mail Preferences window and one group of settings from a New Message. We explain both here.

Keeping up appearances

In this section, we talk about how your outgoing messages appear. Whether you write a new message, reply to a message, or forward a message to another person, you have several choices about how that message appears. Go to Mail ➪ Preferences and set the following for your druthers:

1. **Click the Fonts & Colors button on the toolbar to choose the font for outgoing messages.**

2. **Click the Select button next to the Message Font field and scroll through the Fonts Chooser to choose a Collection, Family, Typeface, and Size, as shown in Figure 2-7.**

   You can also change the message font on individual messages using the pop-up menus above the message header (see Figure 2-7).

3. **(Optional) Click the Select button next to Message List Font and Fixed-width Font to change those.**

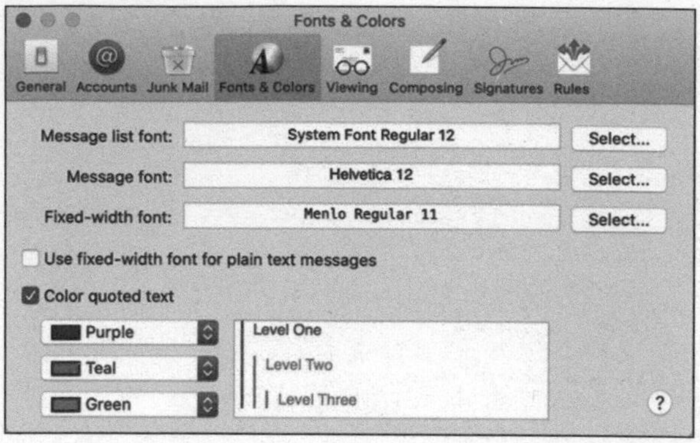

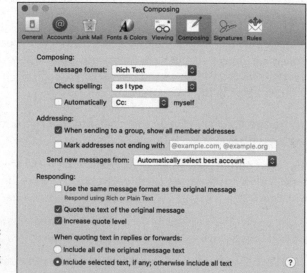

FIGURE 2-7:
Choose font
styles and sizes in
Mail Preferences.

4. **(Optional) Select the Color Quoted Text check box to change the color of text as it's quoted in an ongoing message conversation.**

Click the color swatch pop-up menus to change the color used for each level of a conversation. Click Other to open a color selector and choose a custom color.

5. **Click the Composing button on the toolbar to make choices about the appearance of outgoing messages, as shown in Figure 2-8.**

FIGURE 2-8:
Customize
how outgoing
messages look.

6. **In the Composing section, choose the following:**

- *Message Format:* Choose from Plain Text or *Rich Text,* which takes advantage of stylized text functions such as bold, italic, and underlining.

- *Check Spelling:* Activate one of the spell checking options: As I Type, When I Click Send, or Never.

- *Automatically Cc/Bcc Myself:* Select the check box to receive carbon copies (blind or viewed) for every message you send. The carbon copy will show up in your inbox in addition to the copy in your Sent messages folder.

7. **In the Addressing section, make the following choices:**

- *When Sending to a Group, Show All Member Addresses:* If this check box is left clear, group members see only the group name, not the addresses of individual members.

- *Mark Addresses Not Ending With:* Select the check box and type email address suffixes that you don't want marked. For example, if you type the suffix of your company email, all other messages will be marked, but company messages will not.

- *Send New Messages From:* If you have multiple email accounts, choose a specific account for sending all messages or choose Account of Selected Mailbox. You can always change the outgoing mailbox on individual messages as long as the From field is viewable. (See the upcoming section on showing and hiding address fields.)

8. **The options in the Responding section affect how your replies appear:**

- *Use the Same Message Format as the Original Message:* We suggest selecting this so you don't risk sending a formatted, rich text message that the recipient can't view properly.

- *Quote the Text of the Original Message:* Select this check box to show the original message in your reply.

- *Increase Quote Level:* Select this check box, and the original text will be indented one level. If you have an ongoing conversation, the original text indents one more level with each response.

- *When Quoting Text in Replies or Forwards:* You have two choices here:

  - *Include All of the Original Message Text:* The original text is included in forwarded messages as well as replies.

  - *Include Selected Text, If Any; Otherwise Include All Text:* If you want to include only a portion of the original message, highlight the portion of the message you want to appear in your reply, and then click the Reply or Forward button. Only the highlighted text appears in your message.

Signing your message

The signature block at the bottom of an outgoing message or reply gives you an opportunity to give a little extra information to the recipient, such as your phone number and website, or express your personality and wit with an image or citation. If you have multiple email accounts, you can assign a different signature to each account. You can also create multiple signature blocks and then choose which you want to use depending on the tone and occasion of your message. Here's how to create message signatures:

1. **Choose Mail⇨Preferences and then click the Signatures button on the toolbar.**

2. **As shown in Figure 2-9, click the account name in the first column and then click the + (plus sign) at the bottom of the second column.**

   Mail makes a signature suggestion, such as your first name or your first and last name with your email address.

3. **(Optional) To change the default signature that Mail chose, click the text to select it and retype what you want to appear as your signature block.**

You can also copy and paste an image from another app.

TIP

To insert a website link, leave the cursor in the Signature block but choose Edit➪Add Link. Type the URL (or copy and paste or click and drag from Safari) and then click OK. Recipients can click the link, and the website opens in the recipient's browser. You can also select typed text or an image and then choose Edit➪Add Link; the link is applied to the selected item (see Figure 2-9).

4. **Repeat Steps 2 and 3 to create other signatures: for example, a professional signature you use for work and another you use for messages sent to friends.**

Hint: Double-click the signature name (Signature #1, Signature #2, and so on) to give the signature a more meaningful name.

5. **(Optional) Click All Signatures, and then click and drag signatures from the second column to a different account name to use the same signature for different accounts.**

The number of signatures associated with each account is shown under the account name.

TIP

When you show the signature field in outgoing messages, you see only the signatures associated with the account you're using to send the message.

6. **Click the Close button.**

REMEMBER

Select and edit signature blocks within a message if it's not quite appropriate in that instance.

Showing and hiding address fields

Whenever you write a message, the To field is always visible because you need to send your message to at least one email address. However, Mail can hide and display the Header fields —Cc, Bcc, Reply To, and From — because you don't always want or need them in every message you write. A Priority and Signatures menu can be added, too, if those are something you find useful. Follow these steps:

1. **Click the New Message button (refer to Figure 2-4) to open a new message.**

2. **Click the Header Fields button to the right of the Send button to display the drop-down menu shown in Figure 2-10.**

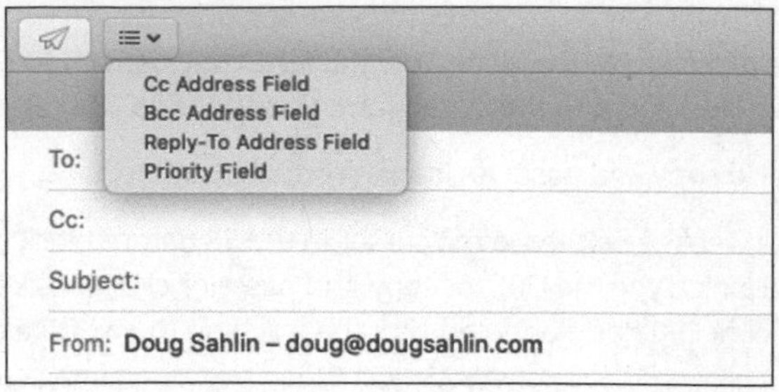

FIGURE 2-10:
Specify which header fields you see when you create new messages.

3. **Select the check boxes next to the fields you want to appear on your messages.**

   Those with a check mark appear in your new messages. Check Signature and/or Priority to see a menu for those items on new messages. Note that you have to click the Select Visible Header Fields button each time you want to add or delete a field from your messages. From now on, you see only the fields you selected in this and future new messages, replies, or forwarded messages that you create, until you decide to make a change by following these steps.

TIP

You don't have to send a new message to change the header fields that are visible in new messages. Follow the previous steps and then delete the message.

Sending a file or photo attachment

When you send an email, you're sending text. However, sometimes you might want to send pictures, documents, or videos. Anyone receiving your message and file attachment can then save the file attachment and open it later. Many people need to share files or digital images, and file attachments are one way to share files with others.

REMEMBER

Your email account may limit the maximum file size you can send, such as 10MB, and your recipients may have limits on the file size they can receive. If you have a file larger than 60 to 70 percent of the maximum limit, you might have to send your files through a free remote storage and file-sharing service, such as Hightail (www.hightail.com), SendThisFile (www.sendthisfile.com), or Dropbox (www.dropbox.com). As of this writing, the previously listed services have an option for a free account, but if you need to send humongous files, you'll have to upgrade your account. Refer to each site for current pricing.

Not only are there limits on the file size you can send, but there also are limits on the file size that your recipient can receive. Apple lets you send large files using Mail Drop. If your file is too big to send normally, it may be automatically passed to Mail Drop where it can be sent gradually to the user. Mail Drop is relatively new, so is may not work with all recipients. If you have trouble sending or receiving large files, you may want to switch over to Dropbox or one of the other services listed.

To attach a file to a message, follow these steps:

1. **In Mail, open a new Message window as described in one of the preceding sections.**

You can open a new Message window to create a new message, reply to an existing message, or forward an existing message.

2. **Choose File⇨Attach Files or click the Attach button, which looks like a paper clip.**

A browse dialog appears.

3. **Navigate through the folders to get to the file you want to send and then click it.**

TIP

To select multiple files, hold down the ⌘ key and click each file you want to send. To select a range of files, hold down the Shift key and click the first and last files you want to send.

4. **Click Choose File.**

If you have just one file, it is pasted into your message. If you paste multiple files, the file is particularly large or in a format that Mail can't display, such as FileMaker or ePub, you see an icon for the attached file in the message window.

TIP

By default, an Image attachment is sent full size. To change the size of the attached image, from the Image Size drop-down menu to the right of the Message Size, choose Small, Medium, Large, or Actual Size.

REMEMBER

The Options button at the bottom left of the Choose browser gives you the option to send Windows-friendly attachments, which is selected by default. You can either accept this option, or if you're sending the message to a fellow Macintosh user, deselect this option.

TIP

To send a single file as a file or to facilitate sending multiple files, select the file(s) in the Finder, and then choose File⇨Compress. The Finder creates a Zip file that comprises the selected files. If the Zip file is small enough, attach it to your message.

5. **Click the Message text box and type your message.**

6. **Click the Send button.**

You can set rules for all email attachments by choosing Edit ⇨ Attachments and selecting one or more of the following:

>> **Include Original Attachments In Reply:** Attaches the original attachment to your reply to the message it came with. This option is usually best left not selected because it only creates bigger messages that take longer to send, and the person who sent you the attachment should have it anyway.

>> **Send Windows-Friendly Attachments:** Makes sure that Windows users can read your attachment. This option is best selected because you can never be 100 percent sure which operating system your recipient will use to read your attachment.

>> **Insert Attachments at End:** Inserts the attachment at the bottom, so the recipient may have to scroll down to get to the attachment. Whether you select this option is really a personal preference. If you want the attachment in the middle of the message — a photo, for example — don't select this check box.

You could use the preceding steps to attach a photo to your message, or you can go directly to the Photo Browser, which shows photo previews instead of a list of names like DSC174 that don't mean anything to you until you open them. To use the Photo Browser, do the following:

1. **In Mail, open a new Message window, as described in one of the preceding sections.**

   You can open a new Message window to create a new message, reply to an existing message, or forward an existing message.

2. **Click the Photo Browser button, which has an image of a mountain with a tiny moon over it, as shown in Figure 2-11.**

3. **Click Photos to open the Photo Browser, shown in Figure 2-12.**

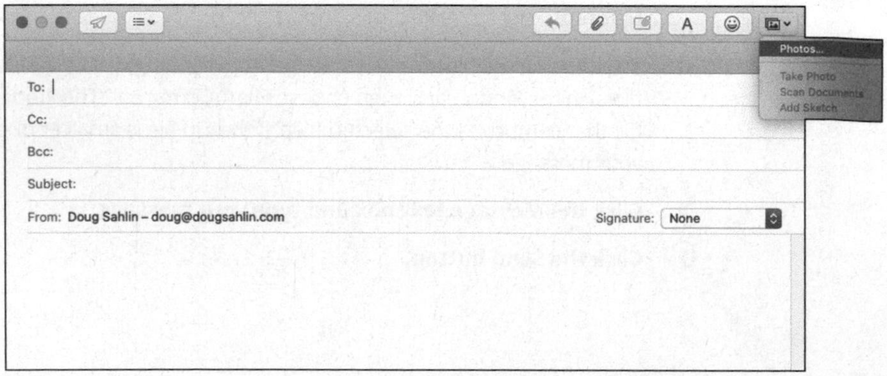

FIGURE 2-11: Click this button to browse for photos.

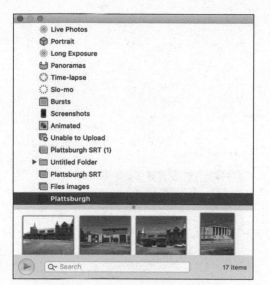

FIGURE 2-12:
Choose a photo
to attach to your
messages from
Photo Browser.

4. Click and drag the bottom-right corner to enlarge the browser and explore the images.

5. Scroll through thumbnails from your Photos and Photo Booth photos, events, and albums until you find the photo you want.

6. Double-click an event or album to see the photos in the event or album; double-click a photo to see an enlarged preview in the bottom half of the browser window.

TIP

To select multiple photos, hold down the ⌘ key and click each photo you want to send. To select a range of photos, hold down the Shift key and click the first and last photos you want to send.

7. Drag the selected photo or photos into your message.

The photos are pasted into your message.

8. Adjust the image size by selecting Small, Medium, Large, or Actual Size from the pop-up menu on the bottom right of the new message window, as shown in Figure 2-13.

The larger the photo, the larger the message file will be, making it potentially slower to send and receive, although the better resolution is useful if the photo is destined to be printed.

9. Click in the Message text box to type in a message.

10. Click the Send button.

TIP

In Book 4, Chapter 5, we explain how to send photos directly from Photos.

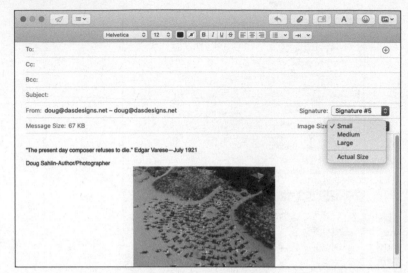

FIGURE 2-13:
Adjust the size of the photo you want to send.

Spelling and grammar checking

Although email is considered less formal than many other forms of communication (say, letters or a last will and testament), you probably don't want your email message riddled with spelling errors and typos that can make you look bad. That's why Mail provides a spelling and grammar checker.

If you have spell checking turned on while you type (Mail⇨Preferences⇨ Composing), the spell checker will underline suspected misspelled words in red to help you find potential problems easily as you create the message. To make sure this option is enabled, choose Edit⇨Spelling and Grammar⇨Check Spelling⇨ While Typing. Other Check Spelling options are: Before Sending and Never. Only choose the latter if you are a Nobel Laureate in Literature.

To nip spelling errors in the bud, follow these steps.

1. **Open a New Message window as described earlier in this chapter.**

You can open a New Message window to create a new message, reply to an existing message, or forward an existing message.

2. **Type your message.**

3. **Choose Edit⇨Spelling and Grammar⇨Show Spelling and Grammar.**

The spelling and grammar checker does it's thing, with a Spelling and Grammar dialog showing the first problem word.

4. **Click one of the following buttons:**

- *Change:* Changes the misspelled word with the spelling that you choose from the list box on the left

- *Find Next:* Finds the next misspelled word

- *Ignore:* Tells Mail that the word is correct

- *Learn:* Adds the word to the dictionary

- *Define:* Launches Mac's Dictionary application and looks up and displays the word's definition in the Dictionary's main window

- *Guess:* Offers best-guess word choices

5. **Click Send.**

REMEMBER

The spelling and grammar checker can't catch all possible errors (words like *fiend* and *friend* can slip past because the words are spelled correctly), so make sure that you proofread your message after you finish spell-checking and grammar-checking your message.

Receiving and Reading Email

To receive email, your email application must contact your incoming mail server and download the messages to your Mac. Then you can either check for new mail manually or have Mail check for new mail automatically.

Retrieving email

To check and retrieve email manually in Mail, choose Mailbox ⇨ Get New Mail or click the Get Mail icon that looks like an envelope. The number of new messages appears next to the Inbox icon, and in a red circle on the Mail icon on the Dock and Launchpad.

Checking for new email manually can get tedious, so you can configure Mail to check for new mail automatically at fixed intervals of time, such as every 5 or 15 minutes. To configure Mail to check for new messages automatically, follow these steps:

1. **In Mail, choose Mail ⇨ Preferences.**

2. **Click the General icon that looks like a light switch on the toolbar to display the General pane, as shown in Figure 2-14.**

Corresponding with Mail

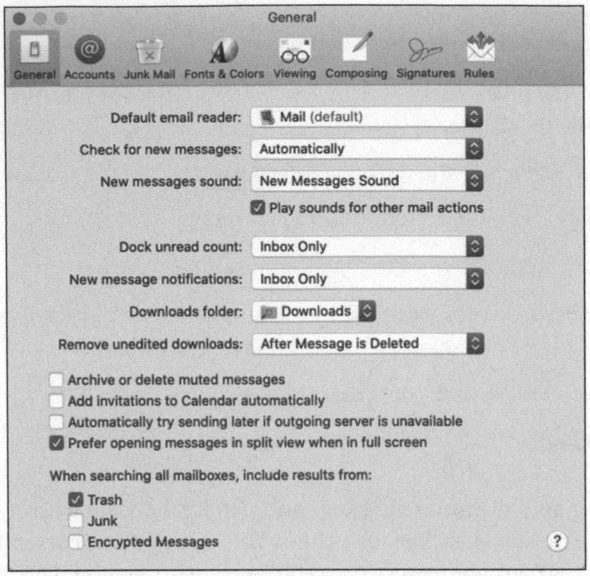

FIGURE 2-14:
Set how often to
check for new
email.

3. **From the Check for New Messages pop-up menu, choose an option to determine how often to check for new messages.**

Automatically will get your new mail whenever you open Mail and continuously as long as Mail remains open. Choose Every Minute, Every 5 Minutes, Every 15 Minutes, Every 30 Minutes, or Every Hour, to check at the chosen interval.

4. **(Optional) Choose a sound to play when you receive new messages from the New Messages Sound pop-up menu.**

By default, the New Messages Sound plays when a new message is received, or you can choose a different sound from the plethora of sounds on this menu. You can also choose None in case any sound bothers you.

5. **Use the pop-up menus to select your preferences for the following options:**

- *Dock Unread Count:* Choose whether the number in the badge on the Mail icon on the Dock reflects unread messages in your Inbox Only or in all mailboxes, or messages received today.

- *New Message Notifications:* Indicate which types of communications you want Notification Center to manage: Inbox Only, VIPs, Contacts, or All Mailboxes, or new messages received today. (See Book 1, Chapter 6 to learn about Notifications.)

- *Remove Unedited Downloads:* Indicate whether to remove them after the message is deleted, when Mail quits, or never.

6. **Choose other options.**

- *Archive or Delete Muted Messages:* Choose this option to archive muted messages. Deselect this option to delete muted messages.

- *Add Invitations to Calendar Automatically:* Choose this option, and Invitations sent in the iCal file format will be added automatically to the Calendar app. If you don't choose this option, you must manually add invitations to the calendar.

- *Automatically Try Sending Later If Server Is Unavailable:* Choose this option, and Mail stores unsent messages because the server is unavailable in the Outbox.

- *Prefer Opening Messages in Split View When in Full Screen:* Choose this option, and when Mail is full screen, open messages side-by-side with the message list. (If you're working with Mail and another app in Split View, messages open by sliding up from the bottom of the screen.)

  To always have messages slide up from the bottom of the screen, deselect the check box.

- *When Searching Mailboxes, Include Results From:* When performing a search you can include the following: Trash and/or Junk, and/or Encrypted Messages, or None.

7. **Click the Close button.**

REMEMBER

Mail can check for new messages only if you leave Mail running. If you quit Mail, it can't check for new messages periodically.

Reading email

After you start receiving email, you can start reading your messages. When you receive a new message, Mail flags it with a blue dot in the Message Preview list, as shown in Figure 2-15. If you have the Mailboxes list showing, the number next to each mailbox indicates the number of unread messages.

TIP

Your Mac can read your messages aloud to you. Just open a message and then choose Edit ➪ Speech ➪ Start Speaking.

To read a message, follow these steps:

1. **Launch Mail and review the Message Preview column.**

This is the second column, unless you've hidden the left column, which displays all mailboxes. If the Mailboxes column is visible, click Inbox to view all messages, or click an individual email account to view messages.

Corresponding with Mail

2. **Click a message to read the message in the message pane, or double-click a message to display and read a message in a separate window.**

When you choose this option, the screen splits in half and the message you double-clicked appears in a window on the right-hand side.

FIGURE 2-15:
Mail shows you which messages you haven't read yet.

The advantage of the message pane is that you can scan your messages quickly by clicking each one without having to open a separate window. The advantage of reading a message in a separate window is that you can resize that window and see more of the message without having to scroll as often as you would if you were reading that same message in the message pane.

Viewing and saving file attachments

When you receive a message that has a file attachment, you see a paper clip next to the sender's name in the Message Preview list and also on the actual message. To save a file attachment, follow these steps:

1. **Follow the steps in the previous section to review all messages or messages sent to a specific email account.**

2. **Click a message with an attachment icon (paper clip) in the Message Preview list.**

If the attachment is an image, it appears in the body of the email. If the attachment is a document, an icon for the document type is displayed with the name of the document.

3. **If the attachment is a document, double-click the attachment icon within the message, to view the attachment in the application it was created in.**

4. **Choose File ⇨ Save Attachments.**

   If the email message contains more than one attachment, all will be saved in the folder you specify in the next step.

5. **In the dialog that opens, choose the folder where you want to save the attachments.**

   By default, Mail saves your attachments into the Downloads stack on the Dock, unless you designate another folder in the General window of Mail preferences.

6. **Click Save.**

TIP

You can also just click and drag attachments from the message body to the Desktop or a Finder window or folder. To do so, hold down the ⌘ key to select more than one attachment; then click and drag any one of the selected attachments to the Desktop or a Finder window.

TIP

Right-click an attachment to display a context menu of options. The options differ depending on the file type of the attachments, but in most cases, you'll be able to preview the attachment, view it in its originating application, save the document, and so on.

WARNING

Before you download an attachment, make sure that you can trust it. That's easier said than done because if your computer has been compromised, the attachment may appear to come from one of the addresses in your contact list. A good way to check an email address is to hover over the name. Don't click it, but wait to see if the email address actually refers to the address you expect. Unfortunately, sometimes you discover that the true sender is not who you think it is. Fortunately, the Mac is less vulnerable to malware than other devices, but in today's world, you have to be extra careful.

Adding an email address to Contacts

Typing an email address every time you want to send a message can get tedious — if you can even remember the address. Mail searches your messages as well as Contacts for matches when you begin to type a name in an address field. Nonetheless, you may want to add the people behind those addresses to Contacts on your Mac so your addresses are all in one place.

Corresponding with Mail

When you receive an email from someone whose name and address you want to remember, you can store that person's email address in Contacts by following these steps:

1. **In Mail, click the Inbox button in the Mailboxes column on the far left.**

2. **In the Message Preview list, select a message sent by someone whose email address you want to save.**

3. **Choose Message ⇨ Add Sender to Contacts.**

   Although nothing appears to happen, your chosen email address is now stored in Contacts.

Adding an email contact to your VIPs list

If you have a business associate of a friend with whom you converse frequently, you can add this person to your VIPs list. When you add people to this list, their names appear below VIPs in the Mailboxes column of the Mail app. After adding someone to this list, any message from him that you don't delete is easily retrieved by clicking his name. To add a person to you VIPs list:

1. **In Mail, click the Inbox button in the Mailboxes column on the far left.**

2. **In the Message Preview list, open a message sent by someone who you'd like to add to your VIPs list.**

3. **Right-click the person's name in the From field, and from the context menu, choose Add to VIPs.**

   The person is added to your VIPs list. Click the person's name in your VIPs list, and every email he has sent (as well as ones he sends in the future) will appear in the Message Preview list.

REMEMBER

To view your list of stored names and email addresses, you can retrieve information from the Contacts application.

Organizing Email

To help you manage and organize your email messages, Mail lets you search and sort your messages. Spotlight (search) finds specific text stored in a particular message. When you find the messages you want, you may want to group them in a folder. You can also establish "smart mailboxes" so Mail automatically puts related messages in the same folder or establish rules for what mail goes to which mailbox. We also tell you how to use the Flag tool, which helps you sort emails related to specific tasks you'd like to attend to.

Searching through email

To manage your email effectively, you need to be able to search for one message (or more) you want to find and view. To search through your email for the names of senders, subjects, or text in a message, follow these steps:

1. **In Mail, click the Search text box in the upper-right corner.**

2. **Type a word, phrase, or partial phrase that you want to find.**

When you type, Mail displays a list of messages that match the text you're typing in the Message Preview list and indicates where the text was found (for example, People, Subject, Mailboxes, or Attachments), and the word Search appears next to the buttons on the Favorites bar, as shown in Figure 2-16.

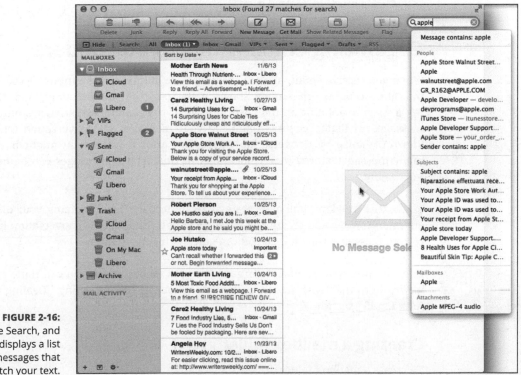

FIGURE 2-16: Use Search, and Mail displays a list of messages that match your text.

3. **Click one of the buttons on the Favorites bar or the mailboxes in the Mailboxes list to narrow your search.**

   Your options are to search through All mailboxes, the Inbox, or one of the account-specific inboxes, VIPs, Sent, or in Drafts or one of the account-specific outboxes.

TIP

   To include the Trash, Junk, or Encrypted Messages in your search, choose Mail⇨Preferences⇨General and select the Trash, Junk, and/or Encrypted Messages check boxes.

4. **(Optional) Click the Save button in the upper-right corner to open a Smart Mailbox window, and then customize your search.**

   Type in a name for your new Smart Mailbox search, choose any options you want to customize your search, and then click OK to save your Smart Mailbox search.

   We explain smart mailboxes in depth in the "Automatically organizing email with smart mailboxes" section, later in this chapter.

5. **Click a message to read it.**

Organizing email with mailbox folders

When you receive email, all your messages are dumped in the Inbox. If you have multiple accounts, the Inbox shows messages from all accounts, and clicking a specific account on the Favorites bar or the Mailboxes list shows only the messages in that account. Organizing your messages by conversation (choose View⇨Organize by Conversation) helps, but after a while, you might have so many messages stored there that trying to find related messages can be nearly impossible.

To fix this problem, you can create separate folders for organizing your different emails. After you create a folder, choosing to organize by conversation keeps related messages together so you can quickly find them later.

REMEMBER

One common type of email to organize is junk email, which you can route automatically to the Trash folder, as we write about in the upcoming "Dealing with Junk Email" section.

Creating a mailbox folder

To create a mailbox folder, follow these steps:

1. **In Mail, choose Mailbox⇨New Mailbox.**

   A New Mailbox dialog appears, as shown in Figure 2-17.

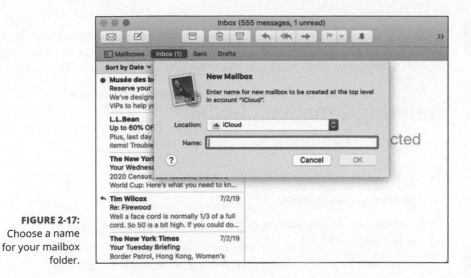

FIGURE 2-17:
Choose a name
for your mailbox
folder.

2. **Use the Location pop-up menu to choose a destination for your new folder.**

3. **In the Name text box, type a descriptive name for your mailbox folder and then click OK.**

   Your mailbox folder appears in the Mailboxes column of the Mail window.

4. **(Optional) Drag the folder onto the Favorites bar if you want.**

Storing messages in a mailbox folder

When you create a mailbox folder, it's completely empty. To store messages in a mailbox folder, you must drag those messages manually to the mailbox folder. Dragging moves your message from the Inbox folder to your designated mailbox folder.

To move a message to a mailbox folder, follow these steps:

1. **In Mail, click the Inbox icon in the Mailboxes list or on the Favorites bar to view your email messages.**

2. **Click a message and drag it to the mailbox folder you want and then release the mouse.**

   Your selected message now appears in the mailbox folder.

TIP

Perform a search for messages you want to store in a mailbox folder. For example, you can search for messages about a specific topic, or from a specific person. You can then drag and drop the search results into your new mailbox folder.

TIP

If you hold down the ⌘ key while clicking a message, you can select multiple messages. If you hold down the Shift key, you can click one message and then click another message to select those two messages and every message in between.

Deleting a mailbox folder

You can delete a mailbox folder by following these steps:

1. In Mail, click the mailbox folder you want to delete.

2. Choose Mailbox⇨Delete.

A confirmation dialog appears, asking whether you're sure that you want to delete your folder.

When you delete a mailbox folder, you delete all messages stored inside.

WARNING

3. Click Delete.

Automatically organizing email with smart mailboxes

Mailbox folders can help organize your messages, but you must manually drag messages into those folders or set up rules to automate the process. As an alternative, to make this process automatic, you can use *smart mailboxes*.

A smart mailbox differs from an ordinary mailbox in two ways:

» A smart mailbox lets you define the type of messages you want to store automatically; that way, Mail sorts your messages without any additional work from you.

» A smart mailbox doesn't actually contain a message but only a link to the actual message, which is still stored in the Inbox folder (or any folder that you move it to). Because smart mailboxes don't actually move messages, a single message can have links stored in multiple smart mailboxes.

Creating a smart mailbox

To create a smart mailbox, you need to define a name for your smart mailbox along with the criteria for the types of messages to store in your smart mailbox. To create a smart mailbox, follow these steps:

1. **In Mail, choose Mailbox⇨New Smart Mailbox Folder.**

   A New Smart Mailbox Folder dialog appears.

2. **Click the Smart Mailbox Folder text box and type a descriptive name for your smart mailbox.**

3. **Open the Match pop-up menu and choose All (of the Following Conditions) or Any (of the Following Conditions).**

4. **Open the first criterion pop-up menu and choose an option, such as From or Date Received, as shown in Figure 2-18.**

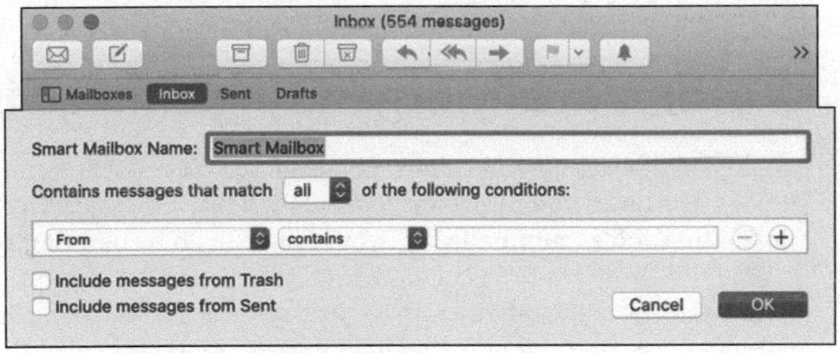

FIGURE 2-18:
The first pop-up menu lets you choose criteria for the type of messages to include.

5. **Open the second criterion pop-up menu and choose how to apply your first criterion (for example, Contains or Ends With).**

6. **In the Criteria text box, type a word or phrase that you want to use for your criterion.**

7. **(Optional) Click the Add Rule icon (the plus-sign button) and repeat Steps 3–6.**

8. **Click OK.**

   Your smart mailbox appears in the Mailboxes column of the Mail window. If any messages match your defined criteria, you can click your smart mailbox's icon to see a list of messages.

REMEMBER

The messages stored in a smart mailbox are just links to the actual messages stored in your Inbox folder. If you delete a message from a smart mailbox, the message remains in the Inbox; if you delete a message from the Inbox, it is also deleted from the smart mailbox.

Deleting a smart mailbox

Deleting a smart mailbox doesn't physically delete any messages because a smart mailbox only contains links to existing messages. To delete a smart mailbox, follow these steps:

1. **In Mail, click the smart mailbox folder you want to delete.**

2. **Choose Mailbox⇨Delete.**

   A confirmation dialog appears, asking whether you're sure that you want to delete your smart mailbox.

3. **Click Delete (or Cancel).**

Automatically organizing email with rules

Smart mailboxes provide links to email messages that remain in your Inbox folder. However, you may want to actually move a message from the Inbox folder to another folder automatically, which you can do by defining rules.

The basic idea behind rules is to pick criteria for selecting messages, such as all messages from specific email addresses or subject lines that contain certain phrases, and route them automatically into a folder.

To create a rule, follow these steps:

1. **Choose Mail⇨Preferences to open the Mail preferences window.**

2. **Click the Rules icon on the toolbar.**

   The Rules window appears.

3. **Click Add Rule.**

   The Rules window displays pop-up menus for defining a rule.

4. **Click the Description text box and type a description of what your rule does.**

5. **Open one or more pop-up menus to define how your rule works.**

   For instance, you might define what to look for or which folder to move the message to, as shown in Figure 2-19.

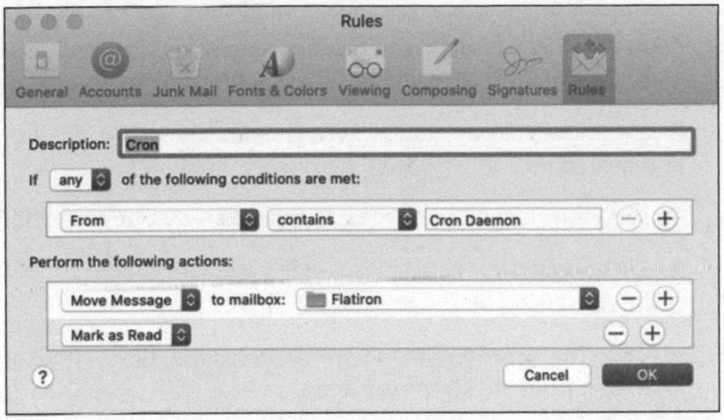

Rules

General | Accounts | Junk Mail | Fonts & Colors | Viewing | Composing | Signatures | Rules

Description: Cron

If [any ⟷] of the following conditions are met:

[From ⟷] [contains ⟷] [Cron Daemon] ⊖ ⊕

Perform the following actions:

[Move Message ⟷] to mailbox: [▓ Flatiron ⟷] ⊖ ⊕

[Mark as Read ⟷] ⊖ ⊕

[?] [Cancel] [OK]

FIGURE 2-19:
Actions for
your rule.

6. **(Optional) Click the plus sign button to define another sorting criterion for your rule and repeat Steps 5 and 6 as often as necessary.**

7. **Click OK when you finish defining your rule.**

    A confirmation dialog appears, asking whether you want to apply your new rule to your messages.

8. **Click Apply.**

    The rule is applied to your current messages and any new messages that meet the criteria you specify.

9. **Click the Close button of the Rules window.**

    Mail now displays your messages sorted into folders according to your defined rules.

REMEMBER

To modify an existing rule, click an existing rule and click Edit.

Flagging your messages

Sometimes you receive a message that contains a task you must attend to later. You could print the message and hang it on a bulletin board in your office or on your refrigerator so you don't forget, or you can flag it in Mail. You can choose from seven colors so you can use different colors for different types of emails: say, all emails related to one project, or to give the task a priority. Here's how to work with flags:

1. **Click Inbox from the Mailboxes list.**

2. **Select the message you want to flag.**

3. **Click the Flag pop-up menu on the toolbar, or choose Message⇨Flag, and select the color flag you want to assign to that message.**

   A little colored flag appears next to the message in the Message Preview list and next to the From field in the message itself.

4. **To see your flagged messages all together, do one of the following:**

   - Click Flagged in the Mailboxes list. (Click Show to the left of the Favorites bar to see the Mailboxes list.)

   - Click the Flagged button on the Favorites bar. (If you don't see the button, drag it from the Mailboxes list.)

   - Choose Flags from the Sort By menu at the top of the Message Preview list to see the flagged messages all together in the mailbox that you're viewing. Messages will be sorted by flag color.

5. **To remove the flag, select the message and choose Clear Flag from the flag pop-up menu.**

TIP

Flags are named by their color, but you can rename them; for example, name the red flag "Urgent" rather than "red." Click the disclosure triangle next to Flagged in the Mailboxes list. Double-click the flag name (the color) to select the word, and then type the name you want.

REMEMBER

You can set up rules (choose Mail⇨Preferences⇨Rules) to automatically flag messages that meet certain criteria.

Dealing with Junk Email

Just like you receive junk mail in your paper mailbox, soon after you get an email address, you're going to start receiving junk email (or *spam*). While you can't entirely stop it, Mail has filters that help limit the inevitable flow of junk email so you can keep your email account from getting overwhelmed, and — perhaps more important — limit the dispersion of your email address and the personal information on your computer that can be accessed through your email.

WARNING

Most junk email messages are advertisements trying to sell you various products, but some junk email messages are actually scams to trick you into visiting bogus websites that ask for your credit card number or (worse) try to trick you into giving your bank-account info. This form of spam is called *phishing*. Other times, junk email might contain an attachment masquerading as a free application that secretly contains a computer virus. Or, a junk email might try to trick you into clicking a web link that downloads and installs a computer virus on your Mac. By filtering out such malicious junk email, you can minimize potential threats that can jeopardize your Mac's integrity or your personal information.

Filtering junk email

Filtering means that Mail examines the content of messages and tries to determine whether the message is junk. To improve accuracy, Mail allows you to train it by manually identifying junk email that its existing rules didn't catch.

After a few weeks of watching you identify junk email, the Mail app's filters begin to recognize common junk email and route it automatically to a special Junk folder, keeping your Inbox free from most junk email so you can focus on reading the messages that matter to you.

To train Mail to recognize junk email, follow these steps:

1. In Mail, click the Mailboxes button on the Favorites bar or from the Mailboxes column, click the Inbox button.

A list of messages appears in the Message Preview list. Any messages Mail thinks are junk have brown text in the Mail Preview column.

2. Click a message that Mail filters as Junk.

You have three options:

- *Load Remote Content:* Click this button to load any remote content such as videos. This enable you to take a closer look at the message and decide whether it's junk.

- *Not Junk:* Choose this option, and the message text in the Mail Preview column becomes black.

- *Move to Junk:* Choose this option, and the message is moved to the Junk folder.

After sorting through the message Mail thinks are junk, you can make your own decisions on any remaining messages you think are suspect.

3. Click a message to review it.

If you think the message is junk, proceed to Step 4

4. Choose Message⇨Move to Junk or click the Move Selected Messages to Junk button on the toolbar.

This tells the Mail application's filters what you consider junk email. The message is moved to the Junk mailbox.

5. Click the Junk mailbox.

6. **If you have multiple email accounts, click the Inbox disclosure triangle and then choose the account from which you moved the message.**

Mail displays the messages in the Message Preview list, and the text for messages Mail thinks are junk is light brown.

7. **Click the message you marked as Junk.**

A banner runs across the top of the message, as shown in the top of Figure 2-20. If you accidentally marked the message as Junk, click the Move to Inbox button, and Mail moves the message to the appropriate Inbox. If the message is well and truly junk, don't do anything, except maybe empty the folder if it over-floweth with digital debris.

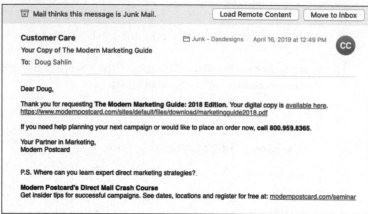

FIGURE 2-20:
Click Move to Inbox for legitimate messages.

REMEMBER

Sometimes legitimate email messages can wind up in Junk in Mail or in the Spam folders of web-based email providers, such as Gmail, Yahoo! Mail, and Microsoft Live Hotmail. If there are messages in your Junk or Spam mailboxes that shouldn't be there, click the message. A banner runs across the top of the message, as shown in Figure 2-20. Click the Not Junk button and drag the message to your Inbox. This way, Mail learns that messages from this sender are not junk mail.

WARNING

The cleverness and prowess of spammers and phishers increases daily. Keep an eye out for these tipoffs to counterfeit requests:

>> Misspelled words

>> Logo design, colors, or type that is slightly different than that of the legitimate company

>> Sender addresses that don't match the company name

TIP

To verify an email address you think is bogus, click the disclosure triangle to the right of the name in the From field. This displays the entire email address. If something is decidedly stinky in Helsinki, move the email to Junk.

Using advanced filter rules

If you find that you're still getting a lot of junk mail or that it arrives from a specific source, you can set the Junk mail preferences to better manage junk mail by following these steps:

1. **Choose Mail ⇨ Preferences and click the Junk Mail button.**

The Junk Mail preferences window shown in Figure 2-21 opens. You have two sections, Junk Mail Behaviors and Blocked.

2. **Click the Junk Mail Behaviors button.**

The Junk Mail Behaviors section of Junk Mail preferences is displayed, as shown in Figure 2-21.

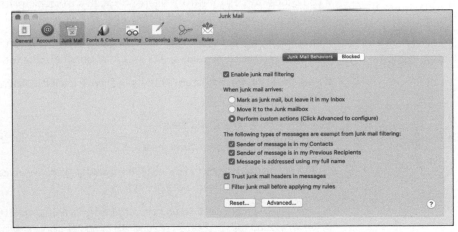

FIGURE 2-21: Help Mail learn which messages are Junk by setting Junk preferences.

3. **Make sure that the Enable Junk Mail Filtering check box is selected.**

4. **Select one of the following options from the When Junk Mail Arrives section:**

- *Mark as Junk Mail, But Leave It in My Inbox:* Puts junk mail in with all your good mail.

- *Move It to the Junk Mailbox:* This option nicely separates junk mail for you and puts it in its own mailbox.

- *Perform Custom Actions:* This option activates the Advanced button.

5. **Select one or more of the following choices for the types of messages to exempt from the junk mail filter.**

This helps keep legitimate messages out of your Junk mailbox.

- *Sender of Message Is in My Contacts*

- *Sender of Message Is in My Previous Recipients*

   Even if the sender isn't in your Contacts, if you received a message from the sender in the past, it won't be considered junk.

- *Message Is Addressed Using My Full Name*

6. **Select the Trust Junk Mail Headers in Messages check box.**

When you select this option, Mail trusts the mail that your email provider identifies as junk.

Many web-based email providers have special applications running on their email servers that try to sniff out junk email before it lands in your Inbox.

7. **Select Filter Junk Mail Before Applying Rules.**

If you choose this option, mail is filtered through Mail's junk mail filter before applying your custom filter rules.

TIP

If after modifying Mail's Junk Mail Behaviors, you decide to revert to the default settings, open Mail Preferences, click Junk Mail, and then click the Reset button.

8. **If you chose Perform Custom Actions in Step 4, click the Advanced button.**

A pane opens, as shown in Figure 2-22.

a. *Choose Any or All If drop-down menu.*

   This determines whether any or all of the following conditions must be met before Mail filters suspect messages as Junk.

b. *Use the pop-up menus to set up rules for filtering incoming mail. Use the plus and minus buttons to the right of each rule to add or delete a rule.*

c. *Use the pop-up menus in the Perform the Following Actions section. Indicate what you want Mail to do when a message arrives that meets the established rules.*

d. *Click OK.*

   Advanced Junk Mail settings have been applied.

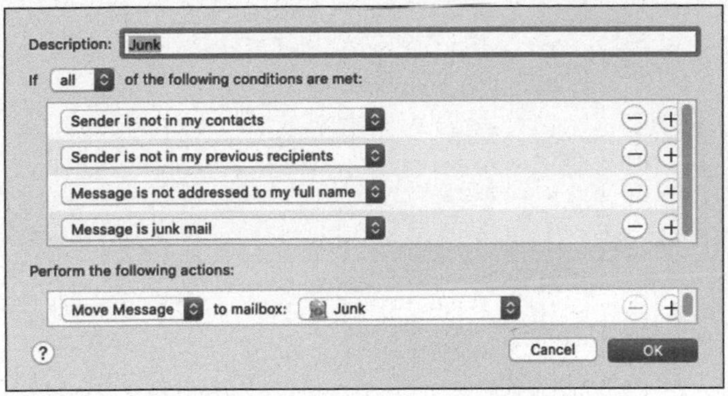

FIGURE 2-22:
Advanced Junk settings can better eliminate unwanted email.

Description: Junk

If all ⬍ of the following conditions are met:

Sender is not in my contacts	⬍	⊖ ⊕
Sender is not in my previous recipients	⬍	⊖ ⊕
Message is not addressed to my full name	⬍	⊖ ⊕
Message is junk mail	⬍	⊖ ⊕

Perform the following actions:

Move Message ⬍ to mailbox: 📥 Junk ⬍ ⊖ ⊕

?   Cancel   OK

TIP

Although Mail's built-in junk email filters can strip away most junk email, consider getting a special junk email filter as well. These email filters strip out most junk email better than Mail can do, but the Mail application's filters might later catch any junk email that slips past these separate filters, which essentially doubles your defenses against junk email. Some popular email filters are SpamSieve (http://c-command.com) and SPAMfighter (www.spamfighter.com). The latter is for PCs and should only be considered if you're using Boot Camp to run Windows on your Mac. Spam filters cost money and take time to configure, but if your email account is overrun by junk email, a separate junk email filter might be your only solution short of getting a new email account.

Remember the comment that it's a race between spammers and spam filters. That said, it doesn't hurt to periodically scan articles from reputable media and blogs to keep up to date with the state of the battle.

Using blocked sender rules

After you applying Junk Mail behaviors, senders of junk email are blocked. This is a good thing, but you have control over what gets blocked. In fact, you can add email address to the blocked sender list. To fine-tune what happens to blocked messages, follow these steps:

1. Choose Mail ▷ Preferences and then click the Junk Mail button.

The Junk Mail Behaviors dialog shown in Figure 2-21 appears.

2. Click the Blocked Button.

The Blocked dialog appears, as shown in Figure 2-23. Enable Blocked Mail Filtering is enabled by default. We strongly suggest you keep this option enabled; otherwise, blocked email will look just like normal email.

Corresponding with Mail

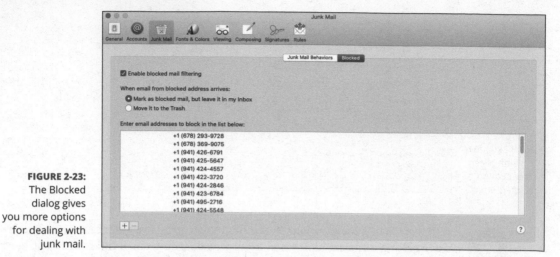

FIGURE 2-23:
The Blocked dialog gives you more options for dealing with junk mail.

3. **Choose one of the following When Email from Blocked Addresses Arrives options.**

- *Mark as Blocked Mail But Leave in My Inbox:* With the default options, Mail marks blocked messages with light brown text in the Message Preview list and displays buttons for dealing with the email. Disable this option if you trust Mail not to block any legitimate messages.

- *Move It to the Trash:* Choose this option and Mail automatically moves messages from blocked senders to Trash.

4. **Enter any email address you'd like blocked in the text box at the bottom of the dialog.**

5. **Click the Close button to exit the dialog.**

Deleting and Archiving Messages

After you read a message, you can leave it in your Inbox, delete it, or archive it for old time's sake. Generally, it's a good idea to delete messages you won't need again, such as an invitation to somebody's birthday party back in the summer of 2008. If you do delete a message that you shouldn't have, you can retrieve it, but only if the Trash folder hasn't been emptied.

Deleting messages

By deleting unnecessary messages, you can keep your Inbox organized and uncluttered — and if you're using an IMAP or Exchange account, free up space on the mail server where your email messages are stored.

To delete a message, follow these steps:

1. In Mail, click the Mailboxes button on the Favorites bar.

This displays the Mailboxes column. If this column is already displayed, go to Step 2.

2. Choose the account from which you want to delete messages.

3. Click the message you want to delete.

TIP

To select multiple messages, hold down the ⌘ key and click additional messages. To select a range of messages, hold down the Shift key, click the first message to delete, click the last message to delete, and then release the Shift key.

Sorting by From can make deleting messages from the same sender easier.

4. Choose Edit ⇨ Delete (or click the Delete button).

REMEMBER

Deleting a message doesn't immediately erase it but stores it in the Trash folder. If you don't "empty the trash," you still have the chance to retrieve deleted messages, as outlined in the next section.

Retrieving messages from the Trash folder

Each time you delete a message, Mail stores the deleted messages in the Trash folder. If you think you deleted a message by mistake, you can retrieve it by following these steps:

1. In Mail, click the Trash folder.

A list of deleted messages appears.

2. Click the message you want to retrieve.

3. Choose Message ⇨ Move To ⇨ Inbox.

If you have multiple inboxes, choose the one to which you want to move the message from the pop-up list.

TIP

You can set up Mail to automatically move deleted messages to the trash and permanently erase those trashed messages after a month, a week, a day, or upon quitting Mail. To configure this option, choose Mail ⇨ Preferences, click the Accounts button, click a mail account in the Accounts column, and then click Mailbox Behaviors and adjust the settings for Trash to suit your email housekeeping style.

Emptying the Trash folder

Messages stored in the Trash folder continue to take up space, so you should periodically empty the Trash folder by following these steps:

1. **In Mail, choose Mailbox⇨Erase Deleted Messages.**

A submenu appears, listing all the email accounts in Mail.

2. **Take one of the following actions.**

- Choose In All Accounts to erase all deleted messages.

- Choose the name of a specific email account to erase messages only from that particular account.

Archiving messages

If you want to reduce the number of messages you see in your mailboxes but not delete the messages — say, at the end of the year or when a project is complete — you can create an archive of those messages. Archived messages are kept in a folder in Mail but removed from active mailboxes. To archive messages, do the following:

1. **Click the mailbox that contains messages you want to archive.**

2. **Right-click the messages you want to archive or choose Edit⇨Select All if you want to archive all messages in the mailbox.**

3. **Choose Message⇨Archive.**

The selected messages are moved to the Archive file in Mail.

TIP

You can then click the Archive file, select the archived messages, and choose Mailbox⇨Export Mailbox. Select a destination in the window that opens and then click Choose. Your messages are exported to a file in the selected folder on the chosen external drive or directory. If you export the mailbox to an external drive, you can delete the exported messages from Mail to free up space on your Mac.

Chapter **3**

Chatting with Messages and FaceTime

The idea behind instant messaging (IM) is that you communicate with someone over the Internet by using text, audio, or video.

You can swap messages with your friends, chat in real time across the planet, and even see each other through live video windows while you speak. The application you use to chat on the Mac is called Messages, and it offers another way for you to communicate with almost anyone in the world, using an Internet connection.

By using your Mac's Messages app, you can exchange basic text chat messages with others instantly. And Messages also makes live video and audio chats and conferences, and file sharing, practically as easy as chatting over the telephone. If you have friends or family with a Mac or iPhone 4 or later, iPad 2 or later, or iPod touch (fourth generation or newer), you can use FaceTime to conduct a video chat from your Mac to your friend's Apple device.

In this chapter, we show you how to set up a Messages account and use Messages to have IM, audio, and video chats. We also explain how to share files, images, and even your Mac's screen with Messages. We give you all the tips and tricks to set up and use FaceTime, too.

We finish with a walk-through of emoji — a very cool communication tool.

Getting Started in Messages

Messages uses your Apple ID to send messages to other friends who have Messages installed on their computer or iOS device. Messages is a great way to stay in touch with friends and family who live far away. All you need with Messages is a Wi-Fi connection.

Setting up a Messages account

You can set up a Messages account by following these steps:

1. **Click the Messages icon (the speech bubbles) on the Dock or Launchpad to launch Messages.**

   A window opens with the prompts for signing in with your Apple ID. This launches Messages, which communicates with other Macs and iOS devices.

2. **Log in:**

   • *Type in your Apple ID and password and click Sign In.*

   Messages opens, ready to start messaging, as shown in Figure 3-1.

Keeping up appearances

You may be perfectly happy with how Messages looks, but check out the preferences that Messages offers for your chat window. Go to Messages⇨Preferences and do the following:

1. **Choose Messages⇨Preferences and then click the General button on the toolbar.**

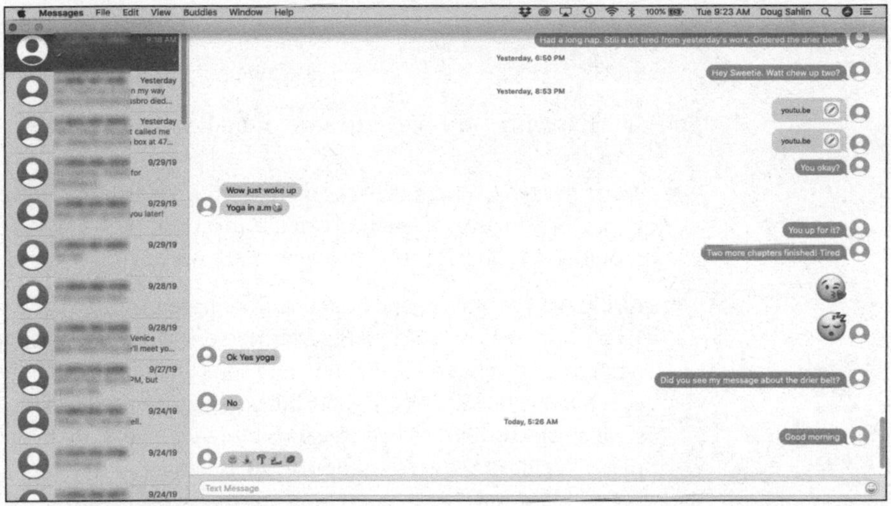

FIGURE 3-1:
Messages
enables you to
chat up a storm.

2. **Choose from the following options:**

- *Keep Messages:* Choose an option from the pop-up menu.

- *Application*: In this section, the default options are to notify you when messages from unknown contacts appear and to play sound effects when a message is received. Other options enable you to save history when conversations are closed and to be notified when your name is mentioned in a conversation.

WARNING

If you don't choose the Save History When Conversations Are Closed preference, closing a conversation deletes it.

- *Message Received Sound:* Open the pop-up menu to choose your preferred sound to indicate that a message has been received.

- *Save Received Files To:* Choose an option from the pop-up menu and choose the desired location in which files sent by friends are stored. We suggest you accept the default option to save the files in the Downloads folder.

3. **Drag the Text Size slider to increase or decrease the size of the text.**

4. **Click the Close button.**

Chatting with Others

You can chat with someone in five ways, and we tell you how in this section:

>> **Text:** You type messages back and forth to each other. Anyone on your Contacts (who uses Messages) can use text chatting — IM — because it requires only an Internet connection and a keyboard, virtual or mechanical.

>> **Audio:** You can talk to and hear the other person, much like a telephone. To participate in audio chatting, each person (there can be up to ten chat participants) needs a microphone and speakers or headphones. Most Macs come with a built-in microphone, but you might want an external microphone, such as one built into a headset, to capture your voice (and hear the other person's side of the conversation) more clearly.

>> **Video:** You can talk to, hear, and see the other person in a live video window. Participating in a video chat with a contact (or up to nine contacts in a multiperson video chat) requires a video camera, such as the FaceTime video camera built in to all new and recent iMacs, MacBooks, and Apple displays. If your Mac is a model without a video camera (or if you want to connect a different kind of video camera to your Mac that has a built-in FaceTime video camera), you can buy and connect an external video camera that is USB Video Class (UVC), such as one of the models offered by Microsoft (www.microsoft.com/hardware) or Logitech (www.logitech.com).

>> **Screen Sharing:** You can talk to and hear the other person while you take over her screen, mouse, and keyboard to fill your screen as though you're sitting in front of her computer. Likewise, your chat partner can take over your screen and control your keyboard or mouse as if she were sitting in front of your computer.

>> **File Sharing:** You can talk and hear each other while you share a file (or files), such as a document, a Keynote presentation, or photos in your Photos library. The files you want to share appear on your chatting partner's screen. Likewise, if your chatting partner is sharing photos (or other files) with you, you see the files she's sharing on your screen.

REMEMBER

If your Internet connection is too slow, Messages might refuse to let you start an audio or video chat.

Initiating a text chat

When you open Messages, the window has two parts (choose Window⇨Messages if you don't see it). The left pane shows a list of your previous and active chats divided by the name or number of each chat. You can have up to 32 contacts in a text chat. Click a name in the left column, and the conversation appears on the right pane, as shown in Figure 3-2.

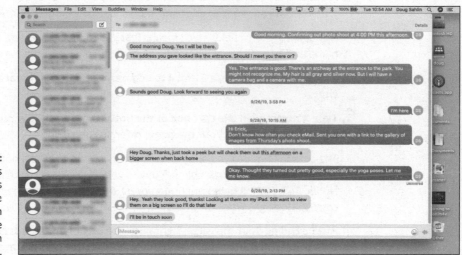

FIGURE 3-2:
The Messages window shows whom you've chatted with (left) and the conversation (right).

REMEMBER

Just because someone is connected to the Internet doesn't necessarily mean that he's in front of his computer and/or wants to chat. So if you find your messages falling on deaf ears (or fingertips) and the person isn't bothering to reply to your messages or chat requests, chances are that the person you're trying to chat with has gone fishing or is otherwise away from his computer.

To initiate a chat with someone, follow these steps:

1. **Click the Messages icon on the Dock or Launchpad.**

   The Messages app launches. Choose Window⇨Messages if you don't see the Messages window.

2. **Click the New Message button (looks like a pencil writing on a note pad) at the top of the chat list on the left side.**

   New Message appears at the top of the chat list, and a blank screen appears on the right.

3. **In the To text field, begin typing the name of the person to whom you want to send a message; potential matches from Contacts appear.**

Or, do the following:

Click the Add button (the plus sign) in the upper-right corner. This opens Contacts. In Contacts, you can open a group or search for a contact. Alternatively, you can scroll through each and every name in your Contacts app.

4. **From the suggestions list, or from Contacts, click the name of the person with whom you want to chat and then click the person's phone number.**

It appears in the To field, which means that you can initiate a chat. The person's name and avatar appear in the left column.

5. **(Optional) Repeat Steps 3 and 4 to add more people and create a group chat.**

6. **Type a message in the text box at the bottom of the chat window and press Return to send your message; refer to Figure 3-2.**

The person to whom you're sending the message will receive a notification (the default notification is a banner unless your recipient makes changes in the Notification section of System Preferences), and your message appears in their copy of Messages when they next launch the app.

7. **After sending your message, right-click the button in the left column with the recipient's names and choose Details from the Context menu.**

A window appears to the right of the button you right-clicked, as shown in Figure 3-3. Figure 3-3 shows details of a group chat. If you're only chatting with one person, the window does not include the option to name the group or add a member.

8. **(Optional) Click Add a Group Name.**

A blank text field appears where you clicked.

9. **(Optional) Type the group name and press Enter.**

10. **(Optional) Click Add Member.**

A blank text field appears where you clicked.

11. **Enter the name of the person you want to add to the group.**

As you type, a list of suggestions appears.

12. **Click the person you want to add to the group.**

13. **Continue adding members to the group as needed.**

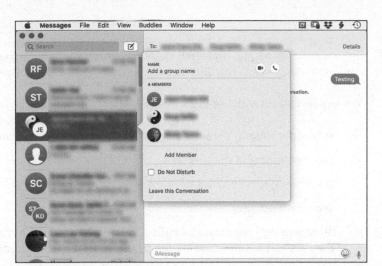

FIGURE 3-3:
The lowdown on
a group chat.

TIP

If you want to insert *emoticons* — those little smiley faces — in your text message, click the smiley face at the right end of the text-entry box (refer to Figure 3-2).

Initiating an audio or a video chat

To initiate an audio chat, everyone needs a microphone and speakers, which are standard equipment on iMacs and MacBooks (add-ons for Mac minis or Mac Pros) and on most Windows PCs (if that's what the person or people you want to chat with are using).

To initiate a video chat, everyone's computer needs a microphone and a video camera. Macs with a built-in FaceTime video camera can use that, but for older Macs without a built-in FaceTime or iSight camera, you have three options:

>> Plug a digital video camcorder into your Mac's FireWire port (if your Mac model has a FireWire port; some don't).

>> Buy a USB Video Class (UVC) video camera from Logitech (www.logitech.com) or Microsoft (www.microsoft.com/hardware), and plug it into your Mac.

>> Conduct a one-way video chat in which you see the other person but the other person only hears your voice. If the person you're chatting with doesn't have a video camera but you do, the opposite occurs in which she sees you, but you only hear her.

Including you, up to ten people can participate in an audio chat. Video chats are limited to nine people, and each must have a video camera connected to their computer along with a fast Internet connection (a minimum of 100 Kbps).

You can initiate an audio or video chat by following these steps:

1. **Follow the steps in the previous section to create a group chat.**

2. **Type something in the text field.**

Tell the recipients you want to have a video chat.

3. **Send the message.**

4. **After sending your message, right-click the button in the left column with the recipient's names and choose Details from the Context menu.**

A window appears to the right of the button you right-clicked, as shown in Figure 3-4.

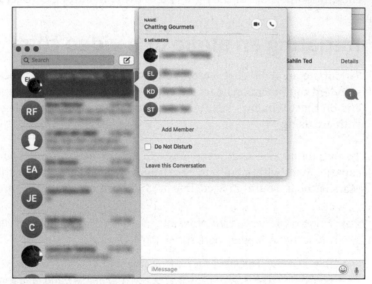

FIGURE 3-4:
Prelude to
an audio or
video chat.

5. **Click the Audio or Video icon at the top of the window.**

Your recipient will receive this call through FaceTime. In fact, it will be a FaceTime phone call or video call on your Mac as well. We cover FaceTime in detail in an upcoming section.

6. **Click the green button to expand the window.**

   This option fills the screen from top to bottom but does not alter the aspect ratio of the window, which would distort the video.

7. **Click the screen to drag it to a new location.**

REMEMBER

FaceTime doesn't have any controls to change volume. You can change the output audio by choosing ⬛ ⇨ System Preferences to open the System Preferences window, clicking the Sound icon, and then dragging the Output Volume slider until FaceTime recipients can hear you clearly. To adjust the volume of the system speakers, use the speaker function keys at the top of your keyboard.

REMEMBER

Even if your Mac has a camera and a fast Internet connection, someone you want to connect with in a video chat might not. In that case, you might be limited to using an audio or text chat instead.

Sharing files and photos

While you're chatting with Messages, sharing files, documents, and photos is as easy as dragging the file to the Messages text field and pressing Return. If you're in the middle of a video chat, drag the file to the video screen, and off it goes.

Saving or deleting your conversations

Messages saves your conversations until you delete them. When they get particularly long, though, you might like to save them and start fresh with the same person. Do the following to save and delete your text chats:

1. **Click the Messages icon on the Dock or Launchpad.**

2. **Click the buddy with whom you have an ongoing conversation you want to save.**

   Your conversation appears in the right pane of the Messages window.

3. **Choose File ⇨ Print.**

   The Print window appears.

4. **Click the PDF button at the bottom of the window and from the pop-up menu, choose Save as PDF.**

   Alternatively, if you want to share the message thread with your buddy, choose one of the send options to send the PDF.

5. **Type in a name for the file, choose a folder where you want to store it, and then click Save.**

6. **Choose File ⇨ Delete Conversation or hover the pointer over the chat list on the right end of the conversation you want to delete, and then click the X.**

   A dialog appears asking you if you want to delete the conversation.

7. **To delete the conversation, click Delete.**

Making Calls with FaceTime

Instant messaging gives you rapid responses and quick input, but sometimes seeing a friendly familiar face makes an exchange that much better. With *FaceTime*, the video chat app that comes with your Mac, you can communicate with people who use the following devices with FaceTime installed:

>> iPhone 4 and newer running iOS 4.1 or later

>> iPod touch fourth generation and newer running iOS 4.1 or later

>> iPad 2 and newer running (including iPad mini models) iOS 4.1 or later

>> Intel-based Mac running OS X 10.6.6 or later with camera and microphone

REMEMBER

FaceTime, like Messages, uses the Internet to communicate, so make sure you have a connection.

FaceTime uses the information in Contacts to call iPhone 4s and newer with a phone number and iPod touches, iPad 2s or newer, or other Macs with an email address. Any edits you make to Contacts in FaceTime appear when you open Contacts on its own; addresses in FaceTime reflect the preferences you set up in Contacts. (See Book 5, Chapter 1 to get a closer look at Contacts.) You also need an Internet connection and an Apple ID (your iTunes Store account or iCloud account works, too). If you don't have an Apple ID, you can set one up in FaceTime, or see Book 1, Chapter 3 for detailed instructions.

In this section, we show you how to sign in to FaceTime, call your friends, and accept incoming calls. We also tell you how to add your favorite peeps so you can call them lickety-split.

Signing in to FaceTime

To use FaceTime to make or receive calls on your Mac, you have to turn on FaceTime and sign in to your account. To sign in to FaceTime, follow these instructions:

1. **Click the FaceTime icon, which looks like a video camera with a phone in a circle on the side, on the Dock or Launchpad.**

The FaceTime window opens, and you see yourself in the video pane.

If this is the first time you've used FaceTime, go to Step 2. If not, go to the next section.

2. **Enter your Apple ID in the User Name field.**

If you don't have an Apple ID, click Create New Account and fill in the form that appears to the right of the video window, and then click Next to finish setting up an Apple ID.

3. **Click Next.**

4. **Enter your password in the Password field.**

5. **Click Next.**

The calling pane opens.

You can close the FaceTime window, but you remain signed in so you can receive calls.

Making a call with FaceTime

After you enable FaceTime and sign in to your account, you can make and receive calls. To make a call, follow these steps:

1. **Click the FaceTime icon on the Dock or Launchpad.**

The FaceTime window opens, and you see yourself in the video pane.

2. **Enter a name, email address, or phone number in the text field to the left of the video pane.**

FaceTime offers a list of suggestions.

3. **Click the name of the person you want to call.**

That person's name appears in the text field. The Audio and Video icons at the bottom of the window indicate the type of call you can make. If both Audio and Video are green, you can have an audio or video chat, as shown in Figure 3-5.

FIGURE 3-5:
Getting ready to
make a call.

4. **Click the Audio or Video button.**

    Your recipient's device rings, letting her know a FaceTime call is en route. If the
    person doesn't answer or declines the call, the person's name appears in the
    video window with the message "_____ is not available for FaceTime."

    If the person accepts your phone call, you see her face in the main part of your
    screen. A small window appears where you see yourself, which is what the
    person you called sees, as shown in Figure 3-6.

REMEMBER

    The person you're calling must have FaceTime activated on her computer or
    device (unless it's an iPhone) for the call to go through. If she doesn't have
    FaceTime enabled, you receive a message that she is unavailable.

5. **Use the buttons on the bottom of the screen (see Figure 3-6) to do the
    following:**

    - *View the Sidebar:* Shows the names and numbers of the people you're
      chatting with. We suggest you use this in full-screen mode. If you don't,
      part of the video window is hidden.

    - *Mute Audio:* Mutes your microphone so the person you're chatting with
      can't hear you. Click the button again to unmute your microphone.

    - *End Call:* Click this button to terminate the call.

End conversation

Pause video

Full Screen

Mute Audio   Take a picture

View the Sidebar

- *Pause Video:* Pauses the video on your recipients' screens.

- *Full Screen:* Click this button to expand the window to full screen. The video window will be centered onscreen with black borders to fill the width of the screen.

- *Take a Picture:* Click this button to take a picture of the person you're chatting with.

6. **To terminate your call, click the End button (the red circle with the X) or close the FaceTime window.**

Receiving a FaceTime call

You can receive calls when you launch FaceTime and sign in, as we describe earlier. If someone calls you, FaceTime automatically opens, and you see the following:

>> Yourself in the video pane

>> The name or phone number of the person who is calling you

>> Two buttons that give you the option to accept or decline the phone call, as shown in Figure 3-7

Click Accept to open the video call.

FIGURE 3-7:
You can accept
or decline
incoming calls.

REMEMBER

If you don't want to receive FaceTime video call invitations, choose either FaceTime ⇨ Turn Off FaceTime or FaceTime ⇨ Preferences and click Sign Out. After you sign out, you can sign in with another Apple ID.

Chapter **4**

Using Apple Pay and Apple Card

This book is about communications, and this chapter deals with one of the most crucial forms of communications: the exchange of money for goods and services. A very long time ago, there were financial institutions, like banks, which let you deposit and withdraw money. Many times, the withdrawals were for the purchase of items, and the deposits were payments for the goods and services that you provided to others.

Apple has become one of the largest corporations in the world, and part of its assets is its list of customers and credit card numbers. That list in and of itself is quite valuable. Close to a billion people have their credit cards on file with Apple. This means that, subject to their credit limits, they can easily make purchases from Apple.

Building up a customer list like this is a critical part of today's business world for any major corporation. After that list is built, the corporation can reach out to customers (and potential customers) to encourage purchases. Special offers can be made to customers, too.

Like many other companies, Apple has focused on making that list of customers and their credit cards as easy as possible for people to use. New techniques for processing credit cards have evolved. Apple has been a leader in that field because it relies on a specific type of technology to identify people who are trying to access Apple's resources (be they purchases or data from iCloud). In 2014, Apple launched Apple Pay, which was a major new way of handling these transactions. In 2019, Apple launched Apple Card — a new type of credit card.

Both of these technologies demonstrated Apple's tools for providing secure and private transactions. In many important ways, accessing iCloud data is pretty much the same as accessing your bank balance. (Some people would argue that the data in your bank balance is less critical than your personal data, but that's a discussion for another book.)

This chapter explores Apple Pay and Apple Card.

Paying for Purchases with Apple Pay

Apple Pay is a way to access your existing credit cards using what is called *contactless* payment technology. Apple didn't invent contactless payments, but it was able to become a leader in the field by building on the privacy and security mechanisms built into the iPhone.

When you present your credit card to a merchant for scanning or swiping, the information from the card goes to your financial institution along with the transaction amount; the transaction is then processed (or not).

Contactless payments work digitally. You're identified to your iPhone with an Apple ID, Touch ID, and perhaps Face ID if your device supports this feature. That identification means that the iPhone can transmit verified data to the financial institution, and the transaction can proceed (or not) just as if you had swiped your card.

This eliminates many of the problems with contact-based payments. If your credit card is lost or stolen, it can be used by the thief. However, if your contactless data is based on known information (your Face ID, Touch ID, Apple ID or some combination of these), losing your credit card doesn't matter.

Apple Pay allows you to carry a balance in your Apple Pay account. It also allows you to transfer from that balance to or from another iPhone user. Many Apple Pay transactions are for relatively small amounts.

Although commercial use of Apple Pay is not explicitly supported, many people do use it to pay small bills.

REMEMBER

Your Apple Pay account must be backed up by one or more credit card or bank accounts. Your credit card or bank account is what you access with Apple Pay. Apple Pay is only the mechanism for doing what you've been doing all along with credit cards that you swipe.

Using Apple Card

In 2019, Apple partnered with Goldman Sachs to jointly create a new credit card called the Apple Card. Although available for any purchase a credit card could be used for, Apple Card is specifically aimed at Apple Pay users. Perhaps the most important indication of this is that Apple Card has an option you can exercise to get a physical card. That's an option, not a requirement.

Experience with Apple Pay has introduced people to the idea of using their iPhones or other devices to receive or send money. As Apple Card launches, it's possible to see how this will continue and expand.

One common guess is that Apple will begin to use Apple Pay and/or Apple Card for the many, many funds transfers that it does every day. These transfers include purchases (and occasional refunds) in Apple Stores, but they don't stop there. When you purchase an app from the App Store, part of your payment goes to Apple, but the bulk of it goes to the developer. Periodically (normally once a month), Apple tallies up the amounts due to each of the over 20 million Apple app developers and issues a funds transfer to each developer's bank account. Not every developer gets a payment every month — in fact, between free apps and apps that don't sell well, it's reasonable to assume that more than half of the developers don't get monthly payments. Nevertheless, that's a lot of data processing and bank fees to keep the App Store running. If payments are made to an Apple Card and Goldman Sachs (as issuing bank for the credit card), Apple saves money.

Chapter 5

Moving Around with Maps

M aps may seem like an app that you just want on a mobile device such as an iPhone or iPad — and you find it there — but since Mac OS 10.9 Mavericks, Maps is available on your Mac, too, and with good reason. With an Internet connection, Maps can find your current location, provide directions between two locations, and calculate the travel time from where you are to your next appointment, taking traffic conditions into consideration, and give you that information in Notification Center — talk about app integration. What's more, with its built-in search function, you can find specific types of businesses that are near a location, such as restaurants near your hotel.

In this chapter, we tell you how to find your present location and locate an address you know. We talk about how to get directions from one place to another, and then make those indications available on your mobile device. We also explain how to share or save the locations and directions you use.

Wherever You Go, There You Are

When you first open the Maps app (click the Maps icon on the Dock or Launchpad), a map appears in the window. The default location is the United States if that's where you are, but the map you see may be different. (Look for the icon with a road map under a compass needle; that's the Maps icon.) In the following sections, we tell you how to find your location and use the Mac's gestures to navigate.

Finding your location

Maps uses network data to determine your location, and various apps, including Maps and Reminders, use a feature called Location Services to access your location to complete their tasks. If you want Maps to find your location, you have to enable Location Services by following these steps:

1. **Click the System Preferences icon on the Dock.**

   Or choose ➪ System Preferences.

2. **Click the Security & Privacy button.**

3. **Click the Privacy tab at the top of the window.**

4. **Click Location Services, as shown in Figure 5-1.**

5. **Select the check boxes for Enable Location Services and then for Maps.**

If the Location Services icons are dimmed and can't be selected, click the Lock button in the bottom-left corner, type an Administrator password for your Mac, and then select the check boxes. Click the Lock button again to prevent further changes.

TIP

Learn more about the Security & Privacy preferences in Book 3, Chapter 2.

6. **Click the Close button of the System Preferences window.**

When your Mac accesses Location Services, the Location Services icon appears on the status bar. Click the Current Position button in the upper-left corner, and a map of your neighborhood appears. Your exact location is the blue dot on the map, like you see in Figure 5-2. If there is a pulsing circle around the blue dot, your location is approximate; the smaller the circle, the more precise your exact (or nearly exact) location. A compass appears in the lower-right corner and points north.

REMEMBER

You need to give permission for an app to use Location Services. You can do that in System Preferences, but if you don't, when you actually try to use Location Services, the app will tell you what permission it needs and why it needs that permission. Either way, you give permission. Apple's emphasis on privacy extends to Location Services, which can be used for tremendously useful purposes and the reverse. When you see a message from an app requesting the use of Location Services, be aware that the description of why the app needs to access your location is checked by the app review team carefully.

Moving Around with
Maps

Navigating the Maps interface

Maps has buttons and menus to change the view and navigate the map, but Maps also takes advantage of the multitouch gestures offered by a trackpad. To change the style of the map, click one of the three buttons at the top of the window:

>> **Map:** Shows you a map with street names and route numbers. This is the default view. With this option, you can show traffic, air quality, and more from the Show menu.

>> **Transit:** Shows the street names and public transit information for your area. This map does not give you the option to show traffic.

>> **Satellite:** Shows a satellite view.

Choose View ⇨ Show Scale if you want to place a scale on the map. Change the orientation and size of the map by doing the following:

>> Click the plus and minus buttons below the compass to zoom in and out of the map. As you zoom in or out, the scale changes.

>> Double-click the mouse or trackpad to zoom in; hold the Option key while double-clicking to zoom out.

>> On a trackpad, use the spread and pinch gestures with your thumb and forefinger (or the two fingers that are comfortable for you) to zoom in and out of the map, respectively.

>> Scroll to move the map up, down, or sideways.

» Click the compass or the 3D button at the top of the window to switch to 3D view, which just tilts the map in Standard and Transit view but becomes 3D in Satellite view. After clicking the 3D button, it becomes a 2D button, which when clicked reverts the map to 2D.

» Click and hold the pointer on the compass and drag left or right to rotate the map.

» Press Option + ← to rotate the map counterclockwise or Option + → to rotate the map clockwise.

» Tap the Compass button that appears in the lower-left corner to return to a north-facing orientation.

TIP

Use the selections in the View menu as alternatives to Maps' buttons, or press ⌘+1 for Map view, ⌘+2 for Transit view, or ⌘+3 for Satellite view.

Asking for Directions

Even though you may not take your computer with you, or have Internet access while traveling, you can calmly plot your journey before grabbing your car keys or backpack. After planning your itinerary, print the directions or send them to your iPhone or iPad and be on your way, secure to find your way. First we show you how to find addresses or points of interest and store them in Maps, and then we show you how to get from one place to another.

Finding what you seek

You may know your way around your city or town but not know some of the street names — or perhaps you're headed to a city on business and want to find bookstores near your hotel. In these situations, you don't need directions as much as a location or information. Maps can work with a specific street name and number as well as inexact addresses, such as an intersection, a neighborhood, or a landmark. Use these steps to find either:

1. Click Maps on the Dock or Launchpad.

2. (Optional) Click the Current Position button if you want to find something right in your neighborhood.

3. Click the Search field at the top right of the window.

4. **Type one of the following in the search field. (If an address is already in the search field, click the X at the right end of the field to delete the text.)**

- *An address* in the form of a street name and number or an intersection, with the city and state or just the name of a city or town.

- *A neighborhood, landmark, or service* such as SOMA (South of Market) San Francisco, Liberty Bell, or bookstores Philadelphia.

- *The name* of a person or business that's stored in your Contacts. If you enter a common name, Maps will give you a list of Suggestions, as well a name or names from your Contacts app.

A list of potential matches from Contacts and the Maps database appears; when you type a word, the results list is divided by category such as Businesses (that contain those letters or word), Queries (potential words you could use to define your search), and Addresses (that contain those letters or word), as shown in Figure 5-3. In this case, we did a search for Books-A-Million in Venice, Florida. The locations are marked with red pins. Click one of the options in the left column, and then click Directions to show a route from your current location to the desired business.

TIP

After you search for addresses, Maps remembers them. In subsequent searches, they show up as suggestions.

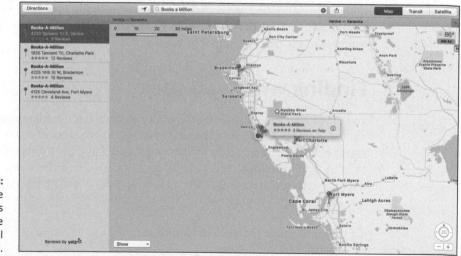

FIGURE 5-3:
Enter a name or address to generate potential matches.

5. **If you see the address you seek in the list, click it to show the location on the map.**

Otherwise, finish typing the complete search terms or address and press Return.

A red pin on the map indicates the address you seek, and multiple results and pins appear if you searched for a service in a location, as shown in Figure 5-4. The address is written on a flag attached to the pin.

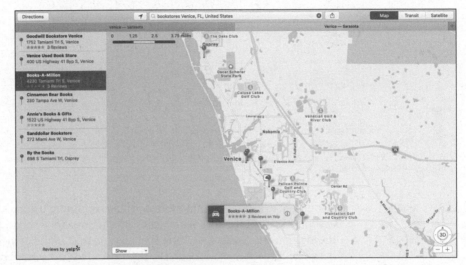

FIGURE 5-4:
A red pin and flag indicate the sought-after address.

6. **(Optional) Click the red push pin on the map to reveal minimal information about location; then click the Info button on the right end of the window or double-click the item in the results list to see information about the location.**

An information window opens that shows the distance of the location from your current location (determined by Location Services), along with information like the phone number and address of the selected site, the site's web address, or a link to Yelp, as shown in Figure 5-5. When available, you'll also see Reviews and Photos buttons that give you reviews to read and photos to look at of the location.

If listed, click the web page address to find out more about the location you found, such as the menu of a restaurant or special exhibits at a museum.

Moving Around with Maps

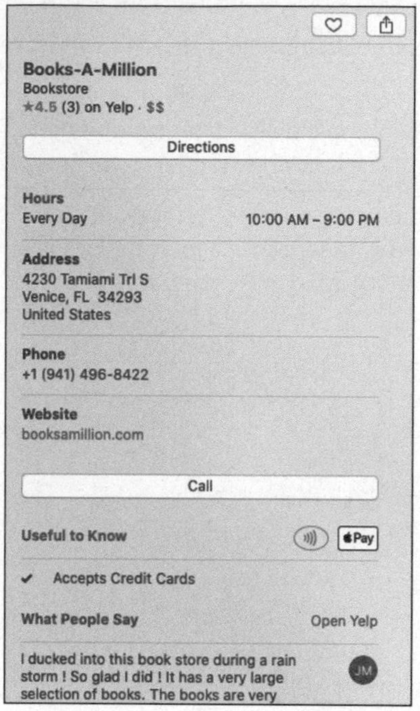

FIGURE 5-5:
The Info window
shows details.

Books-A-Million
Bookstore
★4.5 (3) on Yelp · $$

Directions

Hours
Every Day   10:00 AM – 9:00 PM

Address
4230 Tamiami Trl S
Venice, FL 34293
United States

Phone
+1 (941) 496-8422

Website
booksamillion.com

Call

Useful to Know

✓   Accepts Credit Cards

What People Say   Open Yelp

I ducked into this book store during a rain
storm ! So glad I did ! It has a very large
selection of books. The books are very

TIP

If you want to keep the found address in Maps for future use, click the Favorites button that looks like a heart in the information window to add the location as a Favorite. Click the Share button to the right of the Favorites button to reveal a menu of options including Add to Contacts. If you choose Add to Contacts, the Contacts app opens and creates a new card with the address and other pertinent information. Modify the information as needed and then click Done to save the information. You also have other sharing options, as we show you in the next section.

7. **Memorize what you found or go to the next section to learn how to save and share it.**

Sharing what you find

Oftentimes, a glance at a map is all you need to orient yourself to a location. Other times, you want to keep the location information you found. Two easy ways to keep the information are

>> Choose File➪Print to print a copy of the map and results list.

>> Choose File➪Export as PDF to save a PDF of the map and results.

To share the map and location information with yourself to your iPhone or iPad or with someone else, do the following:

1. **Find the address you want to share with someone, either by searching or choosing from a bookmark or Contacts.**

2. **Tap the Share button at the top of the screen or at the top of the information window for a location.**

   The Share menu opens, as shown in Figure 5-6.

   Or choose File⇨Share, and then choose an option from the drop-down menu. These options are the same as on the Share menu shown in Figure 5-6.

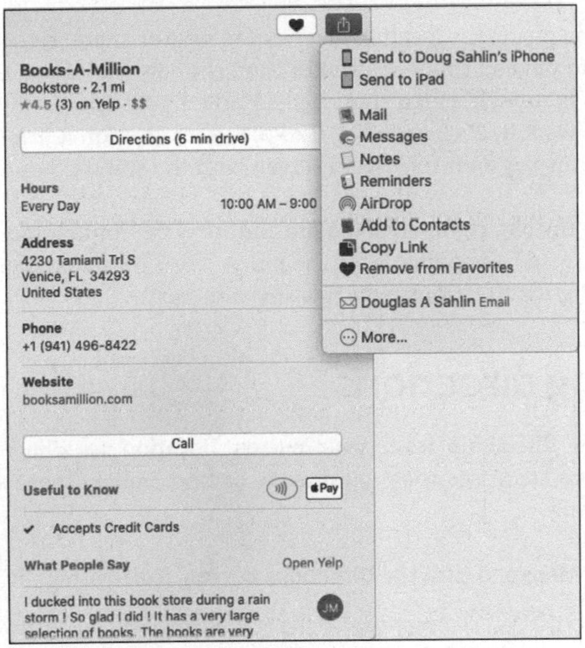

FIGURE 5-6: Share the location you found.

3. **Click one of the sharing options:**

   - *Send to phone or iPad:* This option appears is you have a phone or iPad linked with your computer.

   - *Email or Messages:* Click one of these to open an outgoing message that contains a map to the location. Fill in the email address for one or more recipients and then click Send. If you choose Messages, a dialog appears showing a map to the location. Add the recipients names in the To text field, add a message in the body, and then click Send. (See Book 2, Chapters 2 and 3 to learn about Mail and Messages, respectively.)

- *AirDrop:* Click to share the location with other people on your local network who use Macs with AirDrop access. (See Book 3, Chapter 4 to learn about AirDrop.)

- *Copy Link:* Copies the link to the system clipboard for use in another application.

- *Add to Favorites:* Adds the location to your Favorites list.

TIP

You can also click Copy Link, Add to Favorites, or Add to Contacts to save the location in either place.

Dropping a pin

If there's no pin on the location you want to save or share, right-click the location you want to pin and choose Drop Pin from the context menu. A purple pin shows up on the map with a flag that reads Marked Location. If the pin isn't exactly where you want it, click and drag it to the exact location. Click the Info button on the flag to display an information screen with the standard options.

To remove the pin, right-click the pin and from the context menu choose Remove Pin. You can add a bookmark for the pin and use it as a starting or ending point when asking for directions, which we explain next.

Getting directions

Maps finds directions from your current location to where you're going or between two addresses that you provide or find. Follow these steps to ask Maps for directions:

1. **Open Maps and click the Directions button, if it isn't highlighted.**

   The words *My Location* appear in the Start field, and the End field is blank or contains the placeholder *Search* in light gray.

TIP

   If My Location isn't listed in the Start text field, type **My** and Maps will fill in the blanks.

2. **Leave the Start field as your My Location or click the X on the right end of the field to create an empty field and type a new address for the starting point.**

   As you type, suggestions appear; click one or type the complete address.

TIP

A quick way to get directions from your current location is to click the Directions button once or twice until My Location shows in the Start field and then search for the address you want to go to. When the map is pinned (that is the pin and associated flag are shown), click the Info button on the right end of the flag and then click the Directions button. A route is immediately calculated, as shown in Figure 5-7.

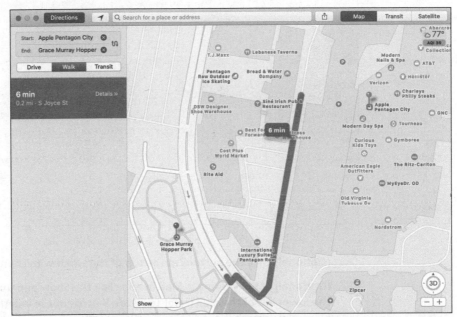

FIGURE 5-7:
Fill in the starting point and destination you want on the Directions screen.

3. **Click the End field and type the address of where you want to go.**

As you type, potential matches appear; click one or type the complete address.

Swap the Start and End points of the directions by clicking the Swap button to the left of the Start and End fields.

If you want directions and travel time for walking between destinations, click the Pedestrian button (next to the Driving button). You can also click the local transit button (it looks like a bus), which shows the bus route to the desired location. If you have to walk to a bus stop, or other mass transit location, such as a subway stop, the route is marked as a dashed line.

4. **Click the Directions button or click a match in the list.**

A list of point-to-point indications appears, and the map shows the route from your starting point to your destination, as shown in Figure 5-8.

Moving Around with Maps

The distance and estimated travel time are displayed above the directions. If more than one route is available, Maps displays alternate routes in light blue and the travel time for each. Click the route you want to follow to make it the main route.

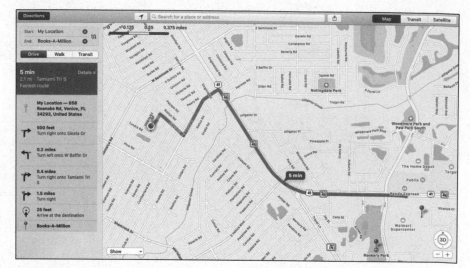

FIGURE 5-8:
Point-to-point directions are shown in a list and on the map.

5. **(Optional) Click the buttons at the top of the window to change the view.**

6. **(Optional) While viewing in Map mode, click the Show pop-up button at the lower left of the map (refer to Figure 5-8) to choose whether to show air quality, weather conditions, traffic, or a 3D map.**

REMEMBER

This feature is available in some locations only.

The roads on the map show you traffic conditions:

- *Red* shows where traffic is heavy and stop-and-go.

- *Orange* means traffic is moving slowly.

- *White dash in a red circle* (Road Closed) icons mean what they show — road closed.

- *A yellow icon with a man shoveling* indicates roadwork.

- *The front of a car in a red square* indicates accidents.

- *Yellow triangles with an exclamation point* indicate general alerts.

7. **(Optional) Print, save, or share the directions as we explain earlier.**

3
Beyond the Basics

Contents at a Glance

CHAPTER 1: **Backing Up and Restoring Your Data** 325

Using iCloud for Your Data. 326

Understanding Different Backup Options. 328

Blasting into the Past with Time Machine 332

Moving Your Backup from an Old Mac to a New Mac 344

Working with Data-Recovery Programs 345

Getting Rid of What You No Longer Need 348

CHAPTER 2: **Protecting Your Mac against Local and Remote Threats** 349

Locking Down Your Mac. 350

Using Passwords 350

Using Touch ID. 356

Encrypting Data with FileVault. 358

Using Firewalls. 362

Selecting Privacy Settings. 366

Creating Multiple Accounts 368

Defining Parental Controls. 371

A Few Final Security Tips 383

CHAPTER 3: **Networking Your Mac and Connecting Peripherals** 385

Creating a Wired Network 386

Creating a Wireless Network with a Router. 390

Connecting and Choosing a Printer 393

Biting into Bluetooth. 395

CHAPTER 4: **Sharing Files and Resources on a Network** 403

Sharing Files with People Near and Far 404

Sharing Printers. 415

Seeing Your Screen from Afar 416

CHAPTER 5: **Running Windows on a Mac**. 421

Working with BYOD and a Heterogeneous Computer Environment. 422

Using Boot Camp. 423

CHAPTER 6: **Maintenance and Troubleshooting** 427

Shutting Down Frozen or Hung-Up Programs 428

Handling Startup Troubles. 430

Repairing and Maintaining Storage Drives 434

Removing Jammed CDs or DVDs. 438

IN THIS CHAPTER

» Backing up with iCloud

» Considering your options for backing up

» Using Time Machine to recover files

» Transferring your data to a new Mac with Migration Assistant

» Recovering files you've lost

Chapter **1**

Backing Up and Restoring Your Data

B acking up data is something that many people routinely ignore, like changing the oil in the car on a regular basis. The only time most people think about backing up their data is after they've already lost something important, such as a business presentation or a folder full of close-to-the-heart family photos. Of course, by that time, it's already too late.

Backing up your data may not sound as exciting as playing video games or browsing the web, but it should be part of your everyday routine. If you can't risk losing your data, you must take the time to back it up. The good news is that your Mac came with Time Machine, the application that makes backing up a routine that your Mac can do on its own.

In this chapter, we explain some of the different backup options. Next, we show you how to set up Time Machine to perform regular automatic backups. We also talk about recovering an individual file and restoring your Mac with the Time Machine backup in the unfortunate event that you lose all your files (perhaps when your disk dies). We include a brief explanation of AutoSave and Versions, which you find in Apple apps such as Pages and Keynote, as well as in many third-party apps. We explore storing your data online with third-party services. If you purchase a new Mac, you'll want to make a backup of your old Mac and then move all your stuff to the new one — we show you how to do that, too.

Using iCloud for Your Data

One way to keep your data safe is to use iCloud to store it. When your data is in iCloud, Apple handles backups of iCloud data automatically. This means that you don't have to worry about backups yourself; however, there are many reasons for not relying solely on iCloud, so we discuss some other backup methods in this chapter.

One of the great features of iCloud is that, after it's set up, it just works — with one very big exception: iCloud relies on a network connection, so if you're not connected to the Internet, iCloud doesn't work.

iCloud offers 5GB of storage space for free, plus space for up to 1,000 photos and any purchased media, apps, and books. iCloud automatically synchronizes the contents of the Contacts, Calendar, Reminders, and Notes apps, as well as Safari bookmarks. This happens automatically when you turn on iCloud.

You can sync documents created with an iCloud-enabled app, such as Pages or Numbers, and stored on iCloud between multiple Macs or between your Mac and your iPhone, iPad, iPod touch, or Windows PC (which requires iCloud for Windows, a free download from the Apple website at https://support.apple.com/en-us/HT204283). Even if you don't sync with another device, you can turn on the iCloud and store your data remotely.

To turn on iCloud data, follow these steps:

1. **Choose ⇨ System Preferences, and then click Apple ID.**

2. **If you aren't already logged in with your Apple ID, log in.**

   The System Preferences dialog appears.

3. **Click Apple ID.**

   Your account information appears.

4. **Click the check box next to iCloud Drive, as shown in Figure 1-1.**

5. **(Optional) Turn on options for selected iCloud Drive as you see in Figure 1-2.**

REMEMBER

iCloud Drive doesn't back up apps not purchased in the App Store or Word documents or that 1,001st photo, so you should consider iCloud as a syncing tool for your Mac and a backup tool only for iOS devices.

FIGURE 1-1:
Turn on
iCloud Drive.

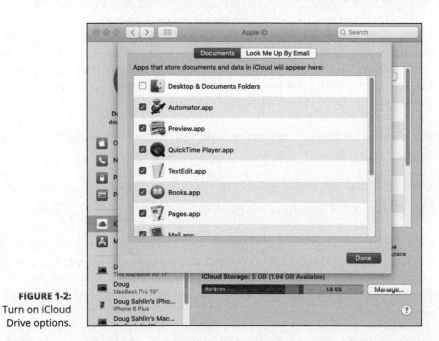

FIGURE 1-2:
Turn on iCloud
Drive options.

You can explore the various choices and options, but start with the defaults before you make too many changes. Many people select most of the options shown in Figure 1-2 so that all the documents for those apps (Automator, Preview, Quick-Time Player, and so forth) are backed up and shared to all your devices with the same Apple ID.

The first option, Desktop & Documents folder, is a little tricky. When you turn that option on, the Desktop and Documents folders on your Mac are backed up to your iCloud Drive continually. Each is named with the name of your Mac. Those folders are the relevant folders for your Mac, but using an app like Files and iCloud.com, you can see them all. Be careful about "cleaning up" apparently duplicate files because they may be copies that were created on a device other than the one you're running on now. Also, be careful about turning Desktop & Documents Folders on and off because you may accidentally create duplicate copies of the files. In general, turn that option on (or don't) and leave it.

Understanding Different Backup Options

Backing up is, essentially, duplicating your data — making a copy of every important file. You could duplicate each file as you create it and keep a copy on your hard drive, although this doesn't solve the problem if your hard drive crashes or your Mac is stolen. Ideally, you back up to one of the following external sources (we explain each of these in the following sections):

>> External hard drive — personal or networked, such as Time Capsule

>> Flash drive

>> Remote storage, such as Dropbox or SugarSync

>> CD-R or DVD-R with an external Apple USB SuperDrive

Each option has its pluses and minuses. Remote storage offers free options, but if you're backing up lots of files, or your entire system, you'll need to purchase extra storage. Flash drives are suitable for backing up small amounts of data or for transferring data to another computer, but they're too small for a complete system backup.

You must make sure to back up periodically, such as at the end of every week, or even every day if you update or create new files often. If you forget to back up your files, your backup copies could become woefully outdated, which can make them nearly useless.

Depending on the value of your files, you may want to consider using more than one backup method. For example, you may want to use Time Machine to completely back up your Mac on a weekly basis but depend on its hourly and daily backups for changes to the screenplay you're writing in Pages on iCloud. The idea here is that if catastrophe strikes and you lose your Mac, you can always replace the applications — *but* you can't retake family photos or rewrite your unfinished novel. The more backup copies you have of your critical files, the more likely it is that you'll never lose your data no matter what might happen to your Mac.

WARNING

The ideal backup solution requires at least two complete backups, with one of them stored at a remote location in case of a natural disaster like a hurricane or fire destroying the backup you keep in your office or home.

Backing up with external hard drives

To prevent the loss of all your data if your hard drive should suddenly bite the dust, you can connect an external hard drive to your Mac's USB or Thunderbolt port with a cable that's typically included with the hard drive.

TECHNICAL STUFF

USB and Thunderbolt ports connect peripherals to a computer. USB ports commonly connect a mouse, printer, or digital camera. Thunderbolt connects a display or storage device. The main advantage of using external hard drives is that copying large files is much faster and more convenient than copying the same files to CDs or DVDs. Additionally, external hard drives are easy to unplug from one Mac and plug into another Mac. No current Macs have built-in optical drives.

You can also put an external hard drive on your network. For example, Apple's Time Capsule provides external storage and functions as a Wi-Fi hub so multiple computers can back up to the Time Capsule. (There are 2TB and 3TB [terabyte] versions, so you probably won't have to worry about storage space unless you're a professional photographer with many thousands of images.) Time Capsule is no longer sold, but many people swear by their Time Capsule devices — until they wear out. This brings up a critical aspect of backups: You must have a backup of your backup. With a constant backup system such as Time Capsule or another product, this can mean doing a periodic backup of your backup — perhaps on a manual schedule (as long as you don't forget).

REMEMBER

Keep in mind the difference between archives and backups. Backups are at their best when they run automatically to back up all your data (or selected parts of your data). This means that you should have a copy of your data as it was at the last time the backup ran. This may be on an hourly basis, a daily basis, or whatever you choose. Backups are designed to let you go back to a known time that is usually recent.

On the other hand, archives are designed to be kept as a snapshot of data at a specific time. By a specific time, we don't mean the last hour or yesterday, but instead we mean a specific time — such as the end of the year. You may also do periodic archives when a major change is in store, such as when swapping in or out a disk drive.

Like so much technology, disk drives have come down in price recently. Apple no longer is in the disk drive business, but you can usually find disk drives at the Apple Store, as well as at many other online resources. Because the disk drives are such a critical part of your technology environment, you may want to pay attention to reviews and prices. Many people deliberately don't purchase the cheapest disk drives.

Any networked drive must use Apple Filing Protocol (AFP) file sharing.

Perhaps the biggest drawback of using external hard drives is that they can't protect against a catastrophe near your computer, such as a fire burning down your house or a flood soaking your computer desk and office. If a disaster wipes out the entire area around your computer, your external hard drive may be wiped out in the catastrophe as well.

You can treat an external hard drive as just another place to copy your files, but for greater convenience, you should use a special backup application, such as Time Machine, which we get to in shortly, in the section "Blasting into the Past with Time Machine." Backup applications can be set to run according to a schedule (for example, to back up your files every night at 6 p.m.).

If the files haven't changed since the last time you backed them up, the backup application saves time by skipping over those files rather than copying the same files to the external hard drive again.

WARNING

To retrieve files, you could just copy the files from your external hard drive back to your original hard drive — but be careful! If you changed a file on your original hard drive, copying the backup copy can wipe out the most recent changes and restore an old file to your hard drive, which probably isn't what you want. To keep you from accidentally wiping out new files with older versions of that same file, backup applications always compare the time and date a file was last modified to make sure that you always have copies of the latest file.

Storing backups on USB flash drives

Because of their low cost, fast copying speed, and ease of moving and plugging into any Mac, flash drives are a popular alternative for backing up files. Many USB flash drives have built-in key rings. Carrying one in your pocket or purse not only is convenient, but also ensures that your data is always safe and on your person should something happen to your Mac's hard drive at home or in the office, where your backup drive's original files are stored.

The biggest drawback of USB flash drives is their somewhat limited storage capacities, which typically range from 8GB to 128GB or sometimes more. USB flash drives in those capacity ranges can usually cost between $10 and $100. Whatever the capacity, USB flash drives are especially convenient for carrying your most critical files but not necessarily for backing up all your important files. In contrast to the hassles of writing (or *burning*) data to a CD or DVD, saving files to a USB flash drive is speedier and as simple as saving a file to a backup folder on your hard drive.

WARNING

Make sure the flash drive you choose uses USB 3.0, like the newest Macs. Of course, if you have an older Mac, you may have to use a USB 2.0 flash drive to match the USB port on your Mac, and it will seem much slower when you connect it to a new Mac.

WARNING

The convenience of flash drives is a double-edged sword. Using flash drives is often discouraged or even forbidden in some installations because they have been a very efficient way of introducing malware into your environment.

Storing backups off-site

Backing up your Mac's important files to an off-site storage service virtually guarantees that you'll never lose your data. We explain how they work here but keep in mind that doing a complete remote backup will be slower with a USB 2.0 flash drive and your ISP may limit file transfer sizes. You may want to use an external hard or flash drive for complete backups and then store particularly important documents on remote backup sites.

Low-cost (and even free) off-site storage options are available for Mac users. Many companies sell off-site storage space for a monthly fee. However, to entice you to try their services, they often provide a limited amount of free space that you can use for an unlimited period at no cost. To get your free off-site storage space, sign up with one or more of the following off-site data-backup sites, each of which offers a paid version with more storage space; most have a free option that offers from 2GB to 10GB of storage and then paid options for more storage or multiple users:

>> **Box** (www.box.com): Free 10GB storage space

>> **iDrive** (www.idrive.com): Free 5GB storage space

>> **Syncplicity** (www.syncplicity.com): Free 10GB storage space

Blasting into the Past with Time Machine

One problem with traditional backup applications is that they store the latest, or the last two or three previous, versions of your files. Normally, this is exactly what you want, but what if you want to see an earlier version of a short story you began working on two weeks ago? Trying to find files created on certain dates in the past is nearly impossible, unless you do one of the following:

>> **Keep a copy of the backup you made previously.**

>> **Save different versions of the document.**

>> **Work with applications that support Versions.** We explain this in the "Understanding Versions" section, later in this chapter.

Fortunately, that type of problem is trivial for your Mac's backup application, Time Machine. Unlike traditional backup applications that copy and store the latest or last one or two versions of files, Time Machine takes snapshots of your Mac's storage drive so that you can view its exact condition from two hours ago, two weeks ago, two months ago, or even farther back.

TIP

The external hard drive you use to back up your Mac with Time Machine should have oodles of storage space, and ideally, you use that drive *only* for Time Machine backups. The bigger the hard drive, the farther back in time you can go to recover old files and information.

REMEMBER

Time Machine only backs up changed files. If you have a 1TB drive on your Mac, a 4TB drive can accommodate many backups. You may think it can only handle four, but because it's only backing up the changes, it may back up many more. The actual number depends on what you're doing. If you're struggling to write and revise a 50-page document, your 1TB drive could probably store hundreds of such document versions.

By viewing the exact condition of what your Mac storage drive looked like in the past, you can see exactly what your files looked like at that time. After you find a specific file version from the past, you can easily restore it to the present with a click of the mouse.

Setting up Time Machine

To use Time Machine, you need to connect an external hard drive to your Mac with a USB or Thunderbolt cable, or you may have an additional hard drive installed in one of the additional drive bays inside an older Mac Pro desktop computer (the 2013 and upcoming Mac Pro models don't have multiple drive bays).

REMEMBER

If you use an external drive that doesn't have its own power supply, connect your Mac to a power supply. The drive will function when your Mac runs on its battery, but not as long as it will when your computer is plugged into a power source.

To set up Time Machine to back up the data on your Mac's primary hard drive to an external hard drive, follow these steps:

1. **Connect the external hard drive to your Mac.**

TIP

   When you plug in a new hard drive, the Time Machine application typically starts automatically and asks whether you want to use the hard drive to back up your Mac. Another choice asks whether you want to encrypt the backup disk, which will scramble the data until you access it. Otherwise anyone who gets his or her hands on your external backup drive can read your data.

   If Time Machine automatically runs and prompts you as described, skip to Step 4. If Time Machine does not prompt you, continue to the next step.

2. **Choose ⌘ ⇨ System Preferences and then click the Time Machine icon to open the Time Machine preferences pane, as shown in Figure 1-3.**

FIGURE 1-3:
To set up Time Machine, turn it on and choose an external drive to use.

3. **(Optional) If you want to exclude files from your backup or your backup disk has limited storage, skip to the section "Skipping files you don't want to back up" and then return to Step 4.**

4. **Accept the Back Up Automatically option.**

   If you deselect this option, you can manually back up your Mac as desired. This may be a good option if you have a MacBook Air with a small drive and use the computer infrequently.

Backing Up and
Restoring Your Data

If you deselect this option, and connect this disk to your computer, click the Time Machine icon in the menu bar, and choose Back Up Now from the drop-down menu.

5. **Click the Select Disk button.**

   A dialog appears, listing all available external hard drives you can use, as shown in Figure 1-4.

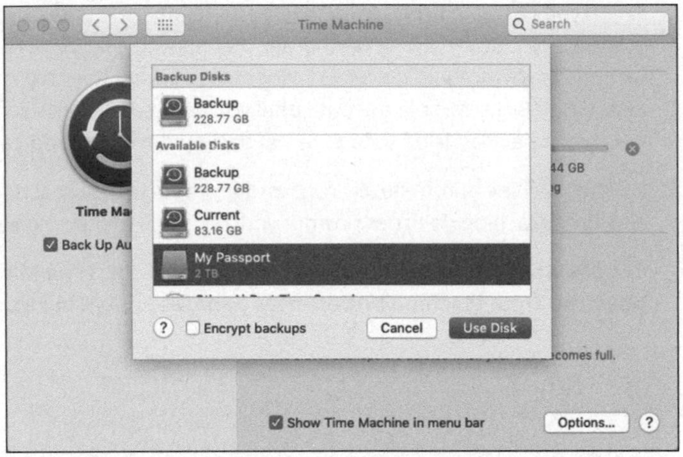

FIGURE 1-4:
You must choose
an external hard
drive to use with
Time Machine.

6. **Select an external hard drive and, optionally, select the Encrypt Backups check box if you want to encrypt the files saved to your backup drive. (See Book 3, Chapter 2 to discover more about encryption.)**

7. **Click the Use Disk button.**

   If you chose to encrypt your disk, the password creation screen opens. Do the following:

   a. *Click the key button to the right of the Backup Password text field if you want help creating a password or go directly to the next step.*

   Password Assistant (shown in Figure 1-5) opens and rates the security (quality) of your password. Select Manual from the pop-up menu, which lets you create your own password, or choose a type from the pop-up menu to see and select suggested passwords; drag the slider to define the password length. When you see a password you like, simply close the Password Assistant window and the selected password is assigned.

   b. *If you choose Manual, type a password in the first field and then type it again in the second field to verify it.*

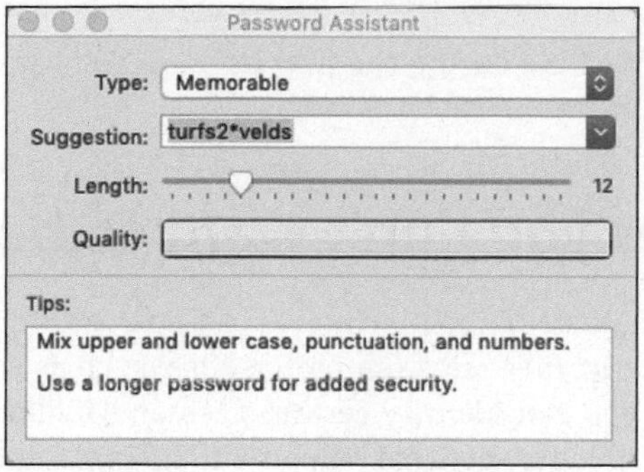

FIGURE 1-5:
Use Password
Assistant
to create a
memorable,
secure password.

Password Assistant

Type:	Memorable
Suggestion:	turfs2*velds
Length:	12
Quality:	

Tips:
Mix upper and lower case, punctuation, and numbers.
Use a longer password for added security.

WARNING

If you forget your password, you can't restore your Mac from your backup drive, so choose wisely. Better yet, copy the password and store it in a safe place.

c. *Type a password hint in the third field.*

d. *Click Encrypt Disk.*

Alternatively, you can click Choose Different Disk.

e. Time Machine prepares your backup disk for encryption.

After preparing the drive, the Time Machine pane appears again, listing your chosen external hard drive, and after a short amount of time, the Time Machine application begins backing up your Mac's data to the external hard drive you selected.

8. **(Optional) Select the Show Time Machine in Menu Bar check box if it isn't already checked.**

With this option checked, the Time Machine icon on the menu bar animates with a twirling arrow whenever Time Machine is backing up your Mac's data. Clicking the Time Machine icon at any time is how you can keep tabs on the status of an active backup, start or stop a backup, and choose the Enter Time Machine command to run the Time Machine recovery application (see Figure 1-6), as described in the upcoming section, "Retrieving files and folders."

9. **Click the Close button to close the Time Machine preferences pane.**

FIGURE 1-6:
Access your
Mac's backup
options from the
menu bar.

Latest Backup to "Backup":
Today, 11:12 AM

Back Up Now
Enter Time Machine

Open Time Machine Preferences...

WARNING

Don't interrupt Time Machine during the first backup. You can continue working while Time Machine runs in the background.

Skipping files you don't want to back up

Unless you specify otherwise, Time Machine backs up everything on your Mac to which your account has access except temporary files, such as your web browser's cache. To save space, you can identify certain files and folders you're not concerned about losing that you want Time Machine to ignore. For example, you may not want to back up your Applications folder if you already have all your applications stored on separate installation discs or you purchased them through the App Store, which lets you download them again if necessary. Or you may choose to skip backing up media you purchased and downloaded from iTunes because if you lose them you can download them again, so there's no need to waste that precious space on your Mac's backup drive.

To tell Time Machine which files or folders to skip, follow these steps:

1. Choose ⌘ ⇨ System Preferences and then click the Time Machine icon to open the Time Machine preferences pane (refer to Figure 1-1).

2. Click the Options button to open the Exclude These Items from Backups dialog.

3. Click the plus sign (+) and then navigate through the mini-Finder window to the file or folder you want Time Machine to ignore.

TIP

You can select multiple drives, files, and folders by holding down the ⌘ key and then clicking what you want Time Machine to ignore.

4. Click the Exclude button.

The Exclude These Items from Backups dialog appears again, as shown in Figure 1-7; you'll note that the Exclude button now is a Save button. Your backup disk appears first in the list. Next to each excluded item, you see the amount of storage it would occupy if you backed it up; below the list, you see the estimated size of your backup.

5. Select or deselect these additional optional Time Machine features if you want:

- *Back Up While on Battery Power:* This option allows Time Machine to back up your MacBook when it's running on battery power. Turning on this option will drain your MacBook's battery faster.

- *Exclude system files and applications:* This option excludes system files and applications from the backup, a useful option that conserves space on your Time Machine hard drive.

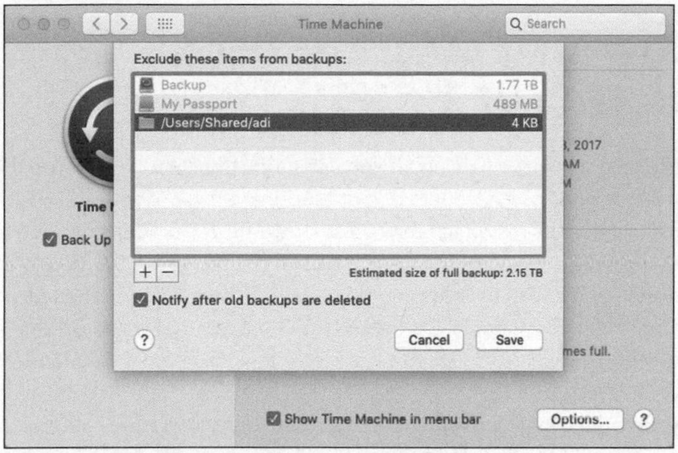

FIGURE 1-7:
Click the plus
sign (+) to choose
files you don't
want to back up.

6. **Click the Save button.**

7. **Click the Time Machine On button, if it's not clicked already.**

   Return to Step 4 of the previous instructions to continue.

> **TIP**
>
> You may want to control the time and frequency of Time Machine backups — a feature that Time Machine itself doesn't offer. Although you could just connect your external backup drive only when you want to perform a backup or go into the Plist (pronounced *pea-list*) of your Mac (a place where technical information is kept) and rewrite the instructions, you may be better purchasing an app called Backup Scheduler: Time Editor from the App Store ($6.99, https://itunes. apple.com/us/app/backup-scheduler-time-editor/id668331139?mt=12), which does the instructing for you.

Retrieving files and folders

Time Machine consists of two components:

» **The Time Machine preferences pane (described earlier in this chapter; refer to Figure 1-3):** Turn the Time Machine backup feature on or off, or adjust its settings.

» **The Time Machine restore application:** Recover files you deleted or changed from earlier backups. You run the restore application by clicking the Time Machine icon on the Dock or on the Launchpad, or by choosing the Enter Time Machine command from the Time Machine icon on the menu bar (refer to Figure 1-6).

HOW TIME MACHINE DOES ITS BACKUP THING

The first time you turn on and begin using Time Machine, it backs up the specified data from your user account on your Mac's hard drive (if you're the only user, it backs up everything), which can take a long time if your Mac's hard drive contains lots of applications and data. One thing you can do is start the Time Machine backup before going to bed so when you wake the next morning, your Mac will be completely (or almost completely) backed up — make sure PowerNap is on in ⇨ System Preferences ⇨ Energy Saver so Time Machine works even if your Mac falls asleep.

After its initial backup of your Mac's hard drive, Time Machine automatically performs an incremental backup of any data changed on your Mac's hard drive (providing the backup drive is attached) every hour. Time Machine saves hourly backups for the past 24 hours, daily backups for the past month, and weekly backups for everything older than a month. Time Machine skips backing up files you create and then delete before the next hourly backup.

When your external backup hard drive starts running out of free space for more backups, Time Machine deletes the oldest files it finds in order to make room for the newer ones.

If you use a portable Mac, when the external drive isn't connected, Time Machine saves a snapshot on your Mac's internal drive; the next time you connect the external drive, the backup resumes.

After you configure Time Machine to back up your Mac, you can use the Time Machine recovery application to retrieve old files or information you deleted or changed after Time Machine backed them up. The two ways to use the Time Machine recovery application to recover files, folders, or other pieces of information, such as address cards, email messages, or events from Calendar, are as follows:

>> By running an application and then clicking the Time Machine icon on the Dock or Launchpad, or choosing the Enter Time Machine command from the Time Machine icon on the menu bar

>> By opening a new Finder window and then clicking the Time Machine icon on the Dock (if the icon is present) or on the Launchpad, or choosing the Enter Time Machine command from the Time Machine icon on the menu bar

Recovering data from within an application

To use Time Machine to retrieve a specific piece of information from within an app (such as an address card from your Mac's Contacts app, which we use in this example), follow these steps:

1. **Click the Contacts icon on the Dock or on the Launchpad to launch Contacts.**

The Contacts app opens and displays the Contacts window, which lists all your contacts.

2. **Click the Time Machine icon on the Dock or Launchpad (or click the Time Machine icon on the menu bar and choose Enter Time Machine) to run the Time Machine restore app.**

Your Mac's screen will appear to space out while it launches the Time Machine restore app — into another dimension affectionately known as *The Time Machine Zone,* as shown in Figure 1-8.

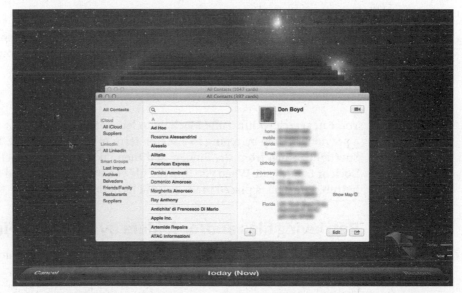

FIGURE 1-8:
The Time Machine restore application displays a far-out view of Contacts.

3. **Choose one of the following ways to select a contact card (or cards) that you want to restore from a past backup:**

- *Click the Backward and Forward arrow buttons near the bottom-right corner of the screen.* Click the Backward button to move the Contacts window backward in time to earlier Time Machine backups. Click the Forward button to move forward to more recent Time Machine backups.

- *Click a Contacts window in the stack of windows behind the frontmost Contacts window.* You can click the Contacts window directly behind the front Contacts window, or one behind it stretching farther back in time. Each time you click a Contacts window in the stack, Time Machine moves it to the front of the screen.

- *Move the pointer to the Time Machine timeline along the right edge of the screen.* The timeline bars expand to display a specific date. To choose a specific date, click it.

4. **When you locate the contact card you want to retrieve, click it, click the Restore button below the stack of windows, and then proceed to Step 6.**

TIP

To select more than one contact card, hold down the ⌘ key and click each additional contact you want to recover.

5. **If the contact you want to restore is nowhere to be found in the Contacts windows — or if you change your mind and don't want to recover a backed-up contact — click the Cancel button below the stack of windows (or press the Escape key).**

Time Machine closes and returns you to the present.

6. **The Time Machine Contacts window zooms forward and then closes, returning you to the Contacts application window, which now includes the recovered contact card (or cards).**

That's it — you've been saved!

TIP

You can search within Time Machine to locate the file you want to retrieve from a previous backup by typing in a search term in the search field. You can also use Spotlight Search from the Finder, and then click the Time Machine icon on the Dock or Launchpad. When you find the file you want, select it and click the Restore button. The item is placed in its original location.

Retrieving files and/or folders by using the Finder

To use the Finder window to retrieve files, folders, or a combination of both with the Time Machine restore app, follow these steps:

1. **Click the Time Machine icon on the Dock or on the Launchpad (or click the Time Machine icon on the menu bar and choose Enter Time Machine) to run the Time Machine restore app.**

2. **Choose one of the following ways to locate the file or folder from the past that you want to recover by using the Finder window:**

- *Click the Backward and Forward arrow buttons near the bottom-right corner of the screen.* Click the Backward button to move the Finder window backward in time to previous Time Machine backups. Click the Forward button to work your way forward to more recent Time Machine backups.

- *Click a Finder window behind the frontmost Finder window.* Each time you click a Finder window, Time Machine moves it forward to the front of the screen.

- *Move the pointer to the Time Machine timeline along the right edge of the screen.* The timeline bars expand to display a specific date. To choose a specific date, click it.

TIP

To take a peek at the contents of a particular document, picture, audio track, or other file, click it and then click the Quick Look button on the toolbar (see Figure 1-9), which gives you a speedy way to view the contents of your selected file to make sure that it's the one you really want to recover. The file type needs to be one that Quick Look understands. Quick Look can't read some database applications, such as FileMaker and Bento, nor most CAD documents.

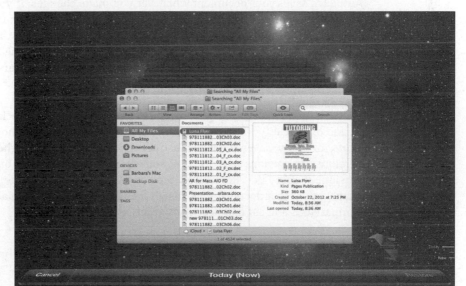

FIGURE 1-9:
Take a peek with
Quick Look view.

3. **When you locate the data you want to recover, select the file or folders, click the Restore button in the bottom-right corner of the screen, and then proceed to Step 5.**

TIP

To select more than one file or folder, hold down the ⌘ key and click each additional item you want to recover.

Backing Up and
Restoring Your Data

4. **If the data you want to recover is nowhere to be found in the Finder windows — or if you change your mind and don't want to recover backup data — click the Cancel button in the bottom-left corner (or press the Escape key).**

   The Time Machine recovery application closes, and you return to the present.

5. **The Time Machine Finder window zooms forward and then closes, safely returning you to a Finder window that now includes your recovered file or folder.**

   Consider yourself saved!

Understanding Versions

Some apps — such as Apple's iWork apps, TextEdit, and Preview — have Auto-Save and Versions functions, which automatically save your files while you work. AutoSave saves your document whenever you make changes. If you make a series of changes that you don't want to lose, you can choose to lock the document at that point. You have to unlock it to make future changes or use it as a template for a new document. To lock a document, hover the pointer near the file name at the top center of the window, click the disclosure triangle that appears, and then click the check box next to Locked.

Versions takes a snapshot of your document when it's new, each time you open it, and once hourly while you're working on it. Versions keeps those hourly snapshots for a day, saves the day's last version for a month, and then saves weekly versions for previous months. If at some point you want to go back to an earlier version, choose File ➪ Revert To ➪ Browse All Versions, and Time Machine shows snapshots of that document, as shown in Figure 1-10. You can make side-by-side comparisons and cut and paste between them.

Restoring your entire backup

If your system or startup disk is damaged, you may have to restore your entire backup to your Mac. If you use Time Machine, you're worry free. Here's how to restore your Mac with Time Machine:

1. **Connect the backup drive to your computer.**

   If you use a networked drive, make sure that your computer and the drive are on the same network.

FIGURE 1-10.
Versions is like
having a mini
Time Machine
inside an app.

2. **Choose ➪ Restart and hold down ⌘+R while your Mac restarts.**

If you can't access the menu — that is, your Mac is off and won't boot — hold down ⌘+R and press the On button. See Book 3, Chapter 6 for more information about troubleshooting.

3. **Select Restore from a Time Machine Backup and then click Continue.**

The Restore from Time Machine dialog appears with instructions and important information.

4. **Click Continue.**

The Select a Restore Source dialog appears showing you drives that are connected to your machine.

5. **Choose the drive where your backup is stored and click Continue.**

In most cases the drive will be called Time Machine.

6. **Select the date and time of the backup you want to use and then click Continue.**

The Select a Destination dialog appears. In most cases your system drive is the only drive shown.

7. **Click the drive and then click Continue.**

Time Machine begins copying your backup from the drive to your Mac.

8. **Breathe a sigh of relief that you back up regularly!**

Backing Up and
Restoring Your Data

Moving Your Backup from an Old Mac to a New Mac

Sooner or later, your Mac will be outdated, and you'll want to move your files to a new Mac. Apple has a handy Migration Assistant application to perform this task. You can transfer your files directly by connecting one Mac to the other with a Thunderbolt cable or over a network. If the old Mac is kaput, however, you can use your Time Machine backup. Follow these steps:

1. **On the new Mac, click the Launchpad icon on the Dock, open the Other folder, and then click the Migration Assistant icon.**

   The Migration Assistant Introduction dialog opens, as shown in Figure 1-11.

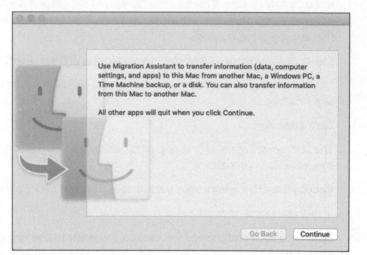

FIGURE 1-11:
Migration
Assistant
transfers your
existing files to
your new Mac.

2. **Click Continue.**

   Migration Assistant automatically quits any open apps, the Desktop closes, and a Migration Assistant window opens.

3. **Select the From Another Mac, Time Machine Backup, or Startup Disk option and then click Continue.**

   Enter the password for your computer, if asked. The Select a Migration Method dialog opens.

4. **Choose the From a Time Machine Backup or Other Disk option button and click Continue.**

   Migration Assistant searches for external drives.

5. **Select the drive from which you want to transfer your backup.**

6. **Select the information you want to transfer.**

   - *Users* includes all the user's media, documents, messages, contacts, and calendars.

   - *Applications* transfers applications that are compatible with the new Mac.

   - *Settings* transfers personal settings. Check Computer to transfer your desktop image and other personal settings; check Network (not shown in the figure) to transfer your network settings.

7. **Click Continue.**

   Migration Assistant begins transferring the selected files.

WARNING

If your new Mac has a newer operating system than your old Mac, applications that aren't compatible with the new operating system may not work or even be transferred. Choose ⇨ Software Update to find and install any application updates that are compatible with the operating system of your new Mac.

Working with Data-Recovery Programs

Data-recovery apps work by taking advantage of the way computers store and organize files by physically placing them in certain areas, known as *sectors*, on your Mac's internal storage drive (or removable storage device). To find out more about the nitty-gritty of how hard drives manage files, check out the nearby sidebar, "Hard drive: A tale of control, corruption, and redemption."

Suppose you're a well-protected Mac user who backs up your data regularly. You're completely safe, right, and you never have to worry about losing files you can't retrieve? Not exactly. Here are three situations where backup applications can't help you, and you may need to rely on special data-recovery applications instead:

» **Accidental deletion from the hard drive:** The most common way to lose a file is by accidentally deleting it. If you try to recover your lost file through a backup app, such as Time Machine, you may be shocked to find that your backup app can recover only a version of your file from the previous hour or older, but not from the span of time between Time Machine backups. So, if you spent the last 45 minutes changing a file and accidentally deleted it before Time Machine could run its next automatic backup, you're out of luck if you want to recover the changes you made in the last 45 minutes.

REMEMBER

Even if you format and erase your entire hard drive, your files may still physically remain on the hard drive, making it possible to recover those files.

>> **Hardware failure:** Another way to lose a file is through a hardware failure, such as your hard drive mangling portions of its disk surface. If a power outage or surge knocked out your Mac without properly shutting it down first, any open files that you were working on or that were stored may be corrupted. Such a failure can go unnoticed because the hard drive still works. As a result, your backup app copies and saves these mangled versions of your file. The moment you discover your file is corrupted, you also find that your backup app has been diligently copying and saving the same corrupted version of your file.

>> **Deletion from removable media:** You may lose data by deleting it from removable media, such as a USB flash drive or digital camera flash memory card (such as a Compact Flash [CF] or Secure Digital [SD] card, or Micro SD card). Most likely, your backup apps protect only your hard drive files, not any removable storage devices, which means that you could take 20 priceless pictures of your dog doing midair back-flip Frisbee catches, only to delete all those pictures by mistake (and tanking your dog's chances at YouTube stardom). Because your backup app may never have saved those files, you can't recover what was never saved.

Some popular data-recovery applications include

>> **Data Recovery for Mac** (www.data-photo-recovery-tips.com/data-recovery-for-mac; **$49.95**): Specializes in recovering files from corrupted or reformatted hard drives.

>> **Data Rescue** (www.prosofteng.com/data-rescue-mac-options; **$99**): Recovers and retrieves data from a hard drive your Mac can no longer access because of a hard disk failure.

>> **DiskWarrior** (www.alsoft.com/DiskWarrior; **$119.95**): Builds a new replacement directory, using data recovered from the original directory, thereby recovering files, folders, and documents that you thought were gone forever.

>> **Softtote Data Recovery Mac** (www.softtote.com; $69.99**):** Retrieves lost, formatted, deleted, corrupted, and infected files.

TIP

If you can't recover a file yourself by using a data-recovery application, you can often hire a professional service that can recover your data for you — but that data better be really important to you because data-recovery services are very expensive.

TECHNICAL STUFF

HARD DRIVE: A TALE OF CONTROL, CORRUPTION, AND REDEMPTION

To keep track of where each file is stored, your Mac maintains a directory that tells the computer the names of every file and the exact physical location where each file begins. Files are divided into blocks, and (typically) the end of each block contains a pointer to the next block of that file. This division is transparent to you, the user; when you open a file, you see all the blocks together. When different apps, such as word processors or spreadsheets, need to find and open a file, these apps depend on the Mac operating system to keep track of this directory so they know where to find a file.

When you delete a file, the computer simply removes that file's name from the directory. The blocks that make up your file still physically exist on the disk surface, but the computer can't find and assemble them again. Therefore data-recovery apps ignore the disk's directory listing and search for a file by examining every part of the entire storage device to find your missing files, locating the beginning of the first block and then following the pointers at the end of each block that indicate the beginning of the next one, creating a chain of blocks that make up the whole file.

If you didn't add any files since you last deleted the file you want to retrieve, a data-recovery app will likely retrieve your entire file again. If you saved and modified files since you last deleted a particular file, there's a good chance any new or modified files might have written over the area that contains your deleted file. In this case, your chances of recovering the entire file intact drops rapidly over time.

If a hardware failure corrupts a file, all or part of your file might be wiped out for good. However, in many cases, a hardware failure won't physically destroy all or part of a file. Instead, a hardware failure might physically scramble a file, much like throwing a pile of clothes all over the room. In this case, the file still physically exists, but the directory of the disk won't know where all the parts of the file have been scattered. So, to the computer, your files have effectively disappeared.

A data-recovery application can piece together scattered files by examining the physical surface of a disk, gathering up file fragments, and putting them back together again like Humpty Dumpty. Depending on how badly corrupted a file might be, collecting file fragments and putting them back together can recover an entire file or just part of a file, but sometimes recovering part of a file can be better than losing the whole file.

Getting Rid of What You No Longer Need

Although storage is getting cheaper all the time and you have room to store almost everything you want, there are limits. If you don't need files — and are certain that you won't need them — getting rid of them can free up space for new files.

You can use any of the storage strategies outlined in this chapter to move files to an external device that is devoted to out-of-date files (or to two such devices if you want a backup). Not only does this free up space, but it also gets rid of files that may actually cause harm if you keep them.

As people have become more and more concerned with computer security and privacy, they've realized that backups are often treasure troves of private data. (Unprotected backups have played key roles in many real-life crime sagas.) If you no longer need data, get rid of it — including any backups that may contain it.

IN THIS CHAPTER

» **Locking your Mac**

» **Adding passwords**

» **Using Touch ID**

» **Encrypting your documents with FileVault**

» **Configuring Firewall and Privacy settings**

» **Adding other users to your Mac**

Chapter **2**

Protecting Your Mac against Local and Remote Threats

O ne of the Mac's advantages is that it seems to be a minor target of viruses — but that certainly doesn't make it immune. With the worldwide connectivity of the Internet, everyone is vulnerable to everything, including malicious software (*malware*) and people with above-average computer skills, particularly those who use those skills for evil (*hackers*). Worse are those hackers who like to use email and websites to steal your personal identity information, such as credit card accounts or Social Security numbers (*phishing*), or those who send out software masquerading as one thing but as soon as you open it, you discover it's harmful (*Trojan horses* disseminating malware). Although threats over the Internet attract the most attention, your Mac is also vulnerable from mundane threats, such as thieves who may want to steal your computer.

No matter how much you know about computers, you can always become a victim if you're not careful. Therefore this chapter looks at the different ways to protect your Mac from threats — physical and cyber, local and remote.

Locking Down Your Mac

Most people lock their cars and house doors when they're away, and your Mac should be no exception to this practice. To protect your Mac physically, you can get a security cable that wraps around an immovable object (like that heavy roll-top desk you have in the den) and then attaches to your Mac. You can attach it by threading it through a handle or hole in your Macintosh case, or if you have a MacBook Pro, by connecting it to your Mac's built-in security slot, which is a tiny slot that a security cable plugs into. If you have a MacBook Air, don't bother searching because there is no security slot, but Maclocks makes an unobtrusive "security skin."

Some companies that sell security cables are

>> **Belkin:** www.belkin.com

>> **Kensington:** www.kensington.com

>> **Maclocks:** www.maclocks.com

>> **Targus:** www.targus.com

>> **Tryten:** www.tryten.com/categories/Mac-Computer-Locks

REMEMBER

Of course, security cables can be cut, although a security cable deters a thief who forgot his bolt cutters.

After protecting your Mac physically, you have other ways to lock down your Mac and keep other people out. Use a password to stop intruders from sneaking into your computer if you step away from your desk, encrypt the files, and use a software or hardware firewall, or both, to stop intruders from sneaking into your computer over the Internet.

WARNING

Anyone with enough time, determination, and skill can defeat passwords and firewalls. Security can only discourage and delay an intruder, but nothing can ever guarantee to stop one.

Using Passwords

Before you can ever use your Mac, you must configure it by creating an account name and password — an account on your Mac, not to be confused with your Apple ID, which can be used on multiple devices. The Setup Wizard walks you through this when you turn on your Mac for the first time. If you're the only person using your Mac, you'll probably have just one account (although we encourage you to have three — one for admin, one for everyday use, and a guest account).

A guest account gives your guests Internet privileges, but no access to your applications or file. If you disable automatic login, your password can keep others from using your Mac without your knowledge.

As a rule, your password should be difficult for someone to guess but easy for you to remember. Unfortunately, in practice, people often use simple — as in, lousy — passwords. To make your password difficult to guess but easy to remember, you should create a password that combines upper- and lowercase letters with numbers and/or symbols, such as OCHSa*co2010alum! (which abbreviates a phrase: in this case, *Ocean City High School all-star class of 2010 Alumnus!*). When you create your user accounts, take advantage of the Password Assistant to have your Mac create a password for you. Of course, it may be harder to remember but also harder to guess. When in doubt, record your password and store it in a safe place. For example, you could store all your passwords in a document, and then transfer them to a USB drive that you keep in a secure location.

TIP

One way to create passwords is to combine the first letters of the words in a phrase that you'll never forget with the name of a dearly departed pet. By picking a memorable phrase or lyric, such as "I'm walkin' on sunshine" and turning it into a nonsensical combination of letters, paired with the name of your long-gone pet hermit crab, Louise (Iw0sLou!se), you'll easily remember your password, but others won't easily guess it. Presumably, someone would have to know you very well to guess which phrase you use with which pet. Pairing these two things that are unique to you makes for a password that's easy for you to remember but hard for someone to guess.

Changing your password

Many online banking and credit card services require you to change your password every so often, some as often as once a month, which certainly keeps password-generating apps popular. Although it's a pain in the hindquarters, they have reason to require you to change — it increases security. To increase your file security, you should change the password on your Mac periodically, too. To change your password, follow these steps:

1. **Choose ⬦ System Preferences.**

   The System Preferences window appears.

2. **Click the Users & Groups icon to open the Users & Groups preferences pane, as shown in Figure 2-1.**

REMEMBER

   If the lock icon in the lower-left corner of the preferences window is locked, you must unlock it to make changes to your Mac's user account details. Click the lock icon, type your password in the dialog that appears, and then press Return to unlock your Mac's user account details.

FIGURE 2-1:
Users & Groups
preferences let
you change your
user account
details.

3. **Click your username under Current User in the left pane (or another account name under Other Users that you want to modify).**

   If you haven't created any additional users, you see only yourself listed.

4. **Click the Change Password button.**

   A dialog appears, displaying text boxes for typing your old password and typing a new password twice to verify that you typed your new password correctly.

5. **Enter your current password in the Old Password text box.**

6. **Enter your new password in the New Password text box.**

   If you want your Mac to evaluate your password or invent a password for you, click the key icon to the right of the New Password text box. The Password Assistant opens (see Figure 2-2).

   a. *Choose the type of password you want from the Type pop-up menu.* Manual lets you type in a password that you invent, and Password Assistant rates the security level of your password. The other five types offer various character combinations and security levels: Memorable; Letters & Numbers; Numbers Only; Random; or FIPS–181-compliant, which creates a password that meets federal standards.

   b. *Drag the Length slider to set how many characters you want your password to have.* The password appears in the Suggestion field, and the Quality bar shows how secure it is: The higher the quality, the safer the password.

   c. *Click the Close button.* The chosen suggestion is inserted as bullets in the New Password text box.

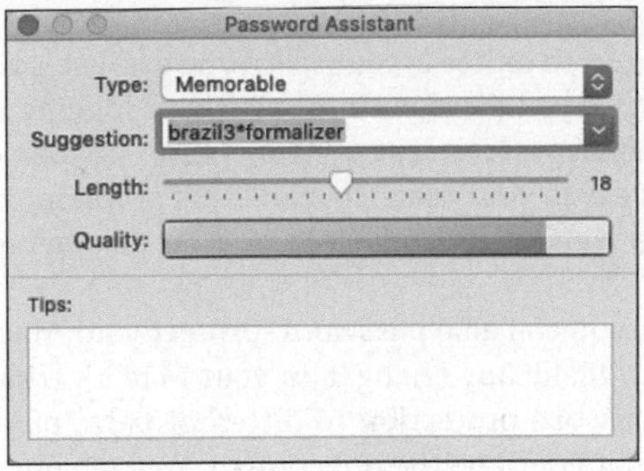

FIGURE 2-2:
Let Password
Assistant help
you choose a
password.

> Password Assistant
>
> Type: Memorable
> Suggestion: brazil3*formalizer
> Length: ——————18
> Quality: ——————
>
> Tips:

7. Enter your new password in the Verify text box.

8. Enter a descriptive phrase into the Password Hint text box.

WARNING

Adding a hint can help you remember your password, but it can also give an intruder a hint on what your password might be. Using our Iw0sLou!se example, you might use the phrase "favorite song crab." The intruder would have to know you pretty darn well to figure out that one!

9. Click Change Password.

The password dialog disappears.

10. Click the Close button to close the Users & Groups preferences window.

TIP

As more and more people pay attention to security (as they should), new standards and best practices are evolving. Long passwords (think a sentence or more) are more secure than short ones, but apps are behind the curve in many cases. You often will be asked to provide a password that is six to eight characters long with one uppercase character and one number, or some similar instructions. Some apps will require you to include at least one special character, such as a question mark; others will require you not to use such characters. This is the landscape of password security today, so we live with it until such time as everyone agrees on standards and best practices.

Applying password protection

Normally, you need your password to log in to your account. As we mention earlier, we recommend creating an admin account that you use to make changes to your Mac, such as installing new software or changing certain settings, and a user account with a different username and password for your day-to-day Mac activities and a guest account. Each account name and password should be different.

REMEMBER

Of course, after you log in to either account, anyone can use your Mac if you walk away and don't log out. If you leave your Mac without logging out, your Mac will either go to sleep or display a screen saver. At this time, anyone could tap the keyboard and have full access to your Mac. To avoid this problem, you can password-protect your Mac when waking up from sleep or after displaying a screen saver.

For further protection, you can also password-protect your Mac from allowing an unauthorized person to make any changes to your Mac's various System Preferences. By applying password protection to different parts of your Mac, you can increase the chances that you'll be the only one to control your computer.

REMEMBER

If you're the only person who has physical access to your Mac, you won't have to worry about password protection, but if your Mac is in an area where others can access it easily, password protection can be one extra step in keeping your Mac private.

All the choices here are optional, but we recommend choosing those that best meet your needs. To password-protect different parts of your Mac, follow these steps:

1. **Choose ⇨ System Preferences.**

   The System Preferences window appears.

2. **Click the Security & Privacy icon to open the Security & Privacy preferences pane.**

REMEMBER

   If the lock icon in the lower-left corner of the preferences window is locked, you must unlock it to make changes to your Mac's user account details. Click the lock icon, type your password in the dialog that appears, and then press Return to unlock your Mac's user account details.

3. **Click the Lock icon to enable changes.**

   A dialog appears telling you that System Preferences is trying to unlock Security and Privacy preferences.

4. **Enter your password and click Unlock.**

   The keys to the Security and Privacy kingdom are yours.

5. **Click the General tab.**

   The General preferences pane appears, as shown in Figure 2-3.

6. **Select (or deselect) the Require Password<*immediately*>after Sleep or Screen Saver Begins check box.**

   You can also choose to require the password at an interval between 5 seconds and 4 hours after your Mac goes to sleep.

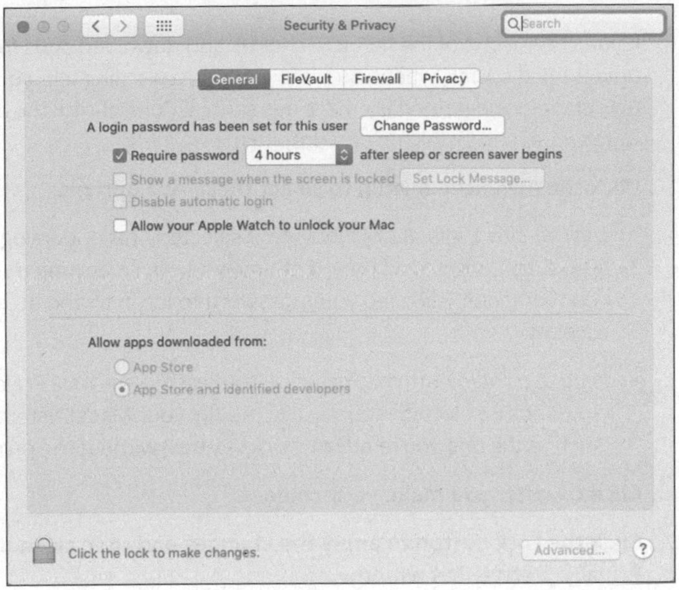

FIGURE 2-3:
General
Security &
Privacy
preferences
let you choose
different ways to
password-protect
your computer.

7. **Set a screen-lock message.**

   a. *Select the Show a Message When the Screen Is Locked check box.*

   b. *Click the Set Lock Message button.*

   c. *Type a message that will appear when your screen is locked, such as "Out to Lunch" or "Be Back at 2:30" or "Don't Even Think About Touching My Mac" or "You touch my Mac, I break your face."*

8. **Select (or deselect) the Disable Automatic Login check box.**

   If this check box is selected, your Mac asks for a user name and/or password before logging in to your account. If it's deselected, you don't enter a password to log in.

9. **Allow your Apple Watch to unlock your Mac.**

   If you choose this option, you must enter your password, and your watch will then be able to unlock your Mac when you hold it nearby.

10. **Click one of the gatekeeper choices under Allow Apps Downloaded From:**

    - *App Store:* Only apps from the App Store will be installed after being downloaded.

    - *App Store and Identified Developers:* Only apps from the App Store or signed with an Apple Developer ID will be installed after being downloaded.

TIP

If you choose one of the first two choices and download apps from an unidentified source, when you try to install it, a warning tells you it's from an unidentified and potentially malicious source. Control-click the app to override Gatekeeper and install the app despite the warning.

11. **Click the Advanced button to select these two options:**

- *Log Out after x Minutes of Inactivity:* If selected, this option logs off your account after the fixed period of time you set, so anyone trying to access your computer will need your password to log in to and access your account.

- *Require an Administrator Password to Access System-Wide Preferences:* If this check box is selected, nobody can modify your Mac's System Preferences (such as the one you're adjusting right now!) without the proper password.

12. **Click OK after you make your choices.**

13. **Click the Lock button to apply the changes and then close the Security & Privacy preferences window.**

Using Touch ID

Many people consider passwords to be less than ideal for security. To begin with, you have to remember them. The only sure way to make sure you don't forget or lose your password is to write it down and keep that piece of paper (or whatever you wrote on) safe.

There's a better way if you have a current MacBook Pro or MacBook Air that supports Touch ID. Instead of using a password, use yourself: your fingerprint with Touch ID. Touch ID will work to unlock your Mac, and it's secure enough to give you access to Apple Pay and other Apple services that involve money.

Touch ID is not a total replacement for passwords, so don't get your hopes up. After your restart your Mac, you'll need your password. After you've logged in with your password, you can then use Touch ID.

To use Touch ID, you need to set it up (usually a one-time process) and then be prepared to use it when you want.

Setting up Touch ID

Setting up your Mac for Touch ID is a fairly quick one-time process that takes just a few steps.

1. **Wash your hands and dry them.**

Wet hands don't work well with Touch ID.

2. **Choose ⌘ ⇨ System Preferences.**

The System Preferences window appears.

3. **In the System Preferences window, click Touch ID.**

4. **Click + to add a fingerprint.**

You're asked to enter your password.

5. **Enter your password.**

6. **Choose the Touch ID features you want to use on your MacBook.**

Your choices are:

- Unlocking your Mac
- Apple Pay
- iTunes and App Store

7. **Follow the instructions to register your fingerprint.**

You need to gently place your finger on the Touch ID button and keep it there until it has registered and you are instructed to move to another finger. You will need to register several fingerprints to complete the process.

Using Touch ID

If you have set up Touch ID, you'll be prompted to use it to unlock System Preferences, the Passwords section in Safari, or password-protected Notes in the Notes app. You can use either Touch ID or a password in these cases.

TIP

If you're traveling, you may want to disable Touch ID so that if security needs to turn on your Mac they can do so. In general, when planning a trip check with the authorities or http://support.apple.com because rules and technologies vary and change.

Encrypting Data with FileVault

Encryption physically scrambles your files so that even if people can access your files, they can't open or edit them unless they know the correct password. When you use FileVault, your Mac encrypts your entire drive, which means everything on your Mac is secure. If you have multiple users on your Mac, you must enable them so each can sign in with his password.

FileVault uses an encryption algorithm called Advanced Encryption Standard (AES), which is the latest U.S. government standard for scrambling data that even national governments with supercomputers can't crack — at least not in a realistic time frame.

Setting up FileVault

FileVault scrambles your files so that only your password (or the system's Master Password) can unlock the files so you — or someone you trust and give the password to — can read them. When you type in a password, you can access your files and use them normally, but as soon as you close a file, FileVault scrambles it once more. FileVault works in the background; you never even see it working.

1. **Choose ⇨ System Preferences.**

   The System Preferences window opens.

2. **Click Security & Privacy.**

   The Security & Privacy window opens.

3. **Click File Vault.**

   The File Vault window opens, as shown in Figure 2-4.

4. **Click the Lock button, enter your Password, and then click Unlock.**

5. **Click the Turn on FileVault button.**

   A dialog appears, as shown in Figure 2-5, giving you options for how to unlock your disk and reset your password if you forget it. Your choices are as follows:

   - *Allow my iCloud account to unlock my disk:* With this option, you use your iCloud password to unlock your disk. This is the simplest method.

   - *Create a recovery key and do not use my iCloud account:* With this option, a security key that you use to unlock your disk is created. You're prompted to record the key and save it in a safe place. If you choose this option, you see a dialog similar to Figure 2-6.

6. **If more than one person uses your Mac, a list of users appears, as shown in Figure 2-7.**

7. **Click the Enable User button next to the user(s) you want to give access to.**

8. **Enter the account password(s) and then click OK, as shown in Figure 2-8.**

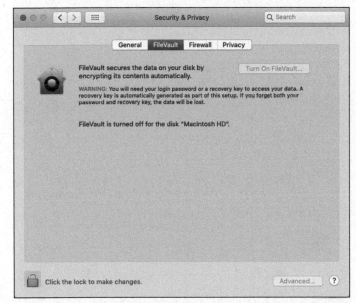

FIGURE 2-4:
The FileVault
pane lets
you turn on
FileVault and set
a password.

FIGURE 2-5:
Choose the
type of FileVault
security you want
to use.

FIGURE 2-6:
Securing your disk using a recovery key.

FIGURE 2-7:
You can set security separately for each user on your Mac.

FIGURE 2-8:
Verify the
password for
each user.

FileVault also works with external hard drives, so your data is safe wherever it's
stored.

TIP

Turning off FileVault

If you turned on FileVault and later change your mind, you can always turn it off:

1. Choose **** ➪ System Preferences and click the Security & Privacy icon.

2. Click the FileVault button to open the FileVault preferences pane (refer to
Figure 2-4).

3. Click the Lock button.

You're prompted for your password.

4. Enter your password and click Unlock.

When FileVault is turned on, the Turn Off FileVault button appears.

5. Click the Turn Off File Vault button, enter your Admin password, and
then click OK.

A confirmation dialog appears, informing you that you're about to turn off
FileVault.

6. Click the Turn Off FileVault button.

TIP

If you decide to sell or give your Mac to someone, you can use FileVault's Instant Wipe function to completely *clean* your Mac's drive. Technically, Instant Wipe eliminates the FileVault key, making the data inaccessible, and then overwrites the data with an illegible pattern.

Using Firewalls

Padlocks and FileVault protect your Mac against local threats, but when you connect your Mac to the Internet, you essentially open a door to remote threats. A highly technical person (such as a hacker) situated anywhere in the world could access your computer, copy or modify your files, or erase all your data. To keep out unwanted intruders, every computer needs a special program called a *firewall.*

A firewall simply blocks access to your computer, while still allowing you access to the Internet so you can browse websites or send and receive email. Every Mac comes with a software firewall that can protect you whenever your Mac connects to the Internet.

TECHNICAL STUFF

Many people use a special device — a *router* — to connect to the Internet. A router lets multiple computers use a single Internet connection, such as a high-speed broadband cable or DSL Internet connection. Routers include built-in hardware firewalls, and using one in combination with your Mac's software firewall can provide your Mac with twice the protection. For more about how to configure your router's firewall settings, refer to the router's user guide or look for more information in the support section of the router manufacturer's website. If all else fails, contact your ISP support staff.

Configuring the Mac firewall

Although the default setting for your Mac's firewall should be adequate for most people, you may want to configure your firewall to block additional Internet features for added security. For example, most people will likely need to access email and web pages, but never transfer files by using FTP (short for File Transfer Protocol). If you fall into this category, you can safely block this service.

WARNING

Don't configure your firewall unless you're sure that you know what you're doing. Otherwise, you may weaken the firewall or lock programs from accessing the Internet and not know how to repair those problems.

To configure your Mac's firewall, follow these steps:

1. **Choose ⌘ ⇨ System Preferences and then click the Security & Privacy icon.**

REMEMBER

   If the lock icon in the lower-left corner of the preferences window is locked, you must unlock it to make changes to your Mac's user account details. Click the lock icon, type your password in the dialog that appears, and then press Return to unlock your Mac's user account details.

2. **Click the Firewall tab.**

   The Firewall preferences pane appears.

3. **Click the Turn On Firewall button to turn on your Mac's firewall (if it isn't already turned on).**

4. **Click the Firewall Options button to display the firewall's custom settings, as shown in Figure 2-9.**

   In the center list box, you may see one or more sharing services you turned on by using the Sharing preferences pane (⌘ ⇨ System Preferences⇨Sharing). Find out how to share in Book 3, Chapter 4.

   The top half of the dialog enables you to block all incoming connections and enable printer sharing and incoming connections from apps or services you specify, such as Dropbox. The bottom half of the dialog that appears offers three check boxes. Incoming connections options are discussed in the next step.

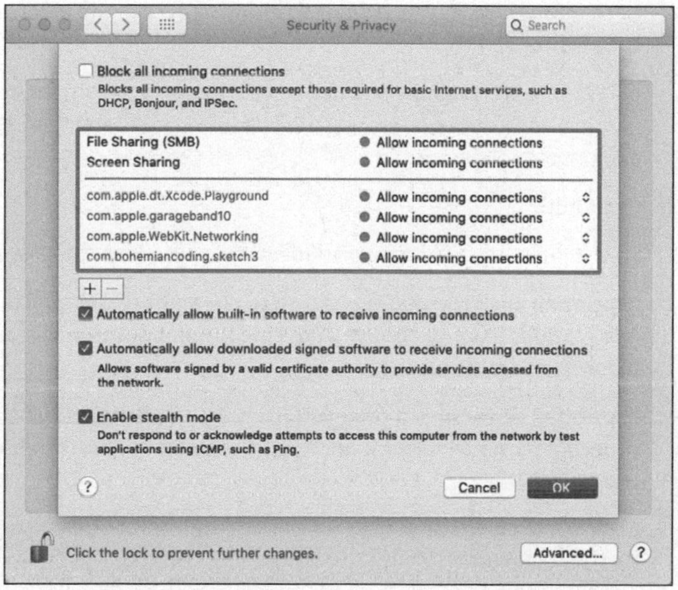

FIGURE 2-9:
This preferences pane offers additional firewall security options.

5. **Select (or deselect) the following check boxes:**

- *Block All Incoming Connections:* Allows only essential communications for basic Internet and Mail access; also blocks sharing services, such as Music sharing or Messages screen sharing. When you select this option, any services or applications listed in the pane disappear, replaced with a static warning that indicates all sharing services are being blocked.

- *Automatically Allow Built-In Software to Receive Incoming Connections:* The built-in software has been tested by Apple and millions of users. Problems can still creep through, but this option allows normal functioning of your Mac and its software.

- *Automatically Allow Downloaded Signed Software to Receive Incoming Connections:* Allows typical commercial applications such as Microsoft Word to check for software updates and Safari to access the web.

- *Enable Stealth Mode:* Makes the firewall refuse to respond to any outside attempts to contact it and gather information based on its responses.

Steps 6 through 10 are options and enable you to allow incoming connections for other software applications. If you're satisfied that no other applications will need incoming connections, go to Step 11.

6. **(Optional) Click the Add (+) button to add applications that you want to allow or block from communicating over the Internet.**

A dialog appears, listing the contents of the Applications folder.

7. **Click a program that you want to allow to access the Internet, such as Dropbox or Skype.**

If any other apps require an Internet connection, select them. You can select multiple applications by clicking the first application, and then ⌘-clicking additional applications.

8. **Click Add.**

Your chosen program appears under the Applications category.

9. **(Optional) Click the pop-up button to the right of an application in the applications list and choose Allow Incoming Communications or Block Incoming Communications.**

10. **(Optional) To remove a program from the applications list, click the program name to select it and click the Delete (–) button below the program list.**

11. **Click OK to close the dialog, and then click the Lock icon to prevent further changes.**

Buying a more robust firewall

Although the built-in Mac firewall blocks incoming connections well, it allows all outgoing connections — meaning that a malicious program you may inadvertently download could communicate via the Internet without your knowledge. To prevent this problem, you need a firewall that can block both incoming and outgoing connections.

WARNING

You should use only one software firewall at a time (although you *can* use one software firewall and a hardware firewall built into your router). If you use two or more software firewall programs, they may interfere with each other and cause your Mac to stop working correctly.

DEALING WITH NASTY MALWARE AND RATs

Two big threats exploit personal computers that aren't protected by properly configured firewall preferences or properly configured router firewall settings. The first of these threats — *malware* — consists of programs that sneak onto your computer and then secretly connect to the Internet to do merely annoying (and offensive) things (retrieve pornographic ads that appear all over your screen) or do more serious things (infect your computer with a virus that can erase your personal data). Or, they can keep track of every keystroke you type on your computer, which in turn is transmitted to a snooping program on a malevolent person's computer so the hacker can find out personal info such as credit card numbers, usernames, and passwords.

A second type of program that requires an outgoing Internet connection is a Remote Access Trojan (RAT). Malicious hackers often trick people into downloading and installing RATs on their computers. When installed, a RAT can connect to the Internet and allow the hacker to completely control the computer remotely over the Internet, including deleting or copying files, conducting attacks through this computer, or sending junk email (spam) through this computer.

Although computer malware and RATs written and released by hackers typically target PCs running Windows, security experts agree that it's only a matter of time before the same digital nastiness begins infecting Macs. To guard against potential viruses, spyware, and RATs, your Mac displays a dialog that alerts you when you run a program for the first time. This feature can alert you if a virus, spyware, or a RAT tries to infect a Mac. For further protection, consider purchasing a router with built-in firewall features, or installing an antivirus and antimalware program. (See the "Buying a more robust firewall" section for recommendations.)

If you want a more robust firewall than the one that comes with the Mac (and the added security of antivirus and antimalware protection), consider one of the following:

>> **ClamXAV:** Available at www.clamxav.com. You can download a free trial version of this software and use it for 30 days. After the trial period, the price for home use (protecting up to three Macs) is $29.95 per year.

>> **Intego Mac Internet Security X9:** Intego (www.intego.com) also offers a 30-day free trial. When the trial period ends, you can continue to protect one computer against Internet threats for $39.95 per year. Intego offers other products as well.

Selecting Privacy Settings

If you belong to a social network such as Facebook or LinkedIn, you may know a little bit about privacy settings and how confusing they can be. Seems like everyone wants to know where you are and what you're doing. Maybe that's okay with you, maybe it's not. Either way, you can set privacy settings on your Mac, too. Follow these steps:

1. **Choose ⚫⇨ System Preferences and then click the Security & Privacy icon.**

    REMEMBER

    If the lock icon in the lower-left corner of the preferences window is locked, you must unlock it to make changes to your preferences. Click the lock icon, type your password in the dialog that appears, and then press Return to unlock your preferences.

2. **Click the Privacy tab.**

    The Privacy preferences pane appears, as shown in Figure 2-10.

3. **Click the lock icon.**

    A dialog appears prompting you for your admin password to unlock Privacy settings.

FIGURE 2-10:
The Privacy
preferences let
you choose which
apps access data
from your Mac or
other apps.

4. **Click each app In the list to allow other apps to access that app's contents.**

   For example, click Contacts and then click the apps in the list on the right to give them access to Contacts. Each time an app requests access to information in another app, it will appear in the list for that app's Privacy preferences.

   Two other choices to consider in particular:

   - *Location Services:* Select the Enable Location Services check box, as shown in Figure 2-11, to allow applications that use your location to access it — for example, Weather, Maps, and HomeKit. You can selectively allow access only to certain applications or deselect the check box and prohibit access altogether.

   - *Analytics (scroll down the list of apps to find it):* Select the Share Mac Analytics check box if you want to send a message to Apple when you have a problem, such as Safari crashing, or to let your Mac send a message about how you're using it from time to time. The information is sent anonymously, so you don't have to worry about being spammed or anything. Your other options are to Share with App Developers and Share iCloud Analytics.

5. **Click the lock icon to prevent further changes.**

FIGURE 2-11:
Many apps use
Location Services
to complete
their tasks.

Creating Multiple Accounts

Every Mac has at least one account that allows you to use your computer. However, if multiple people need to use your Mac, you probably don't want to share the same account, which can be like trying to share the same pair of pants.

One problem with sharing the same account is that one person may change the screen saver or delete an app or file that someone else may want. To avoid people interfering with each other, you can divide your Mac into multiple accounts.

Essentially, having multiple accounts gives your Mac a split personality. Each account lets each person customize the same Mac while shielding other users from these changes. So, one account can display pink daffodils on the screen, and another account can display pictures of Mt. Rushmore.

To access any account, you need to log in to that account. To exit an account, you need to log out. Although two users may be logged in at the same time, you see only one user's Desktop, Finder, and setup.

Not only do separate accounts keep multiple users from accessing each other's files, but creating multiple accounts also gives you the ability to restrict what other accounts can do. That means you — parents, for example — can block

Internet access from an account, limit Internet access to specific times, or limit Internet access to specific websites. Such limits are *Parental Controls*.

Adding a new user account

To protect your files and settings, you should create a separate account for each person who uses your Mac. You can create four types of accounts:

>> **Administrator:** Gives the user access to create, modify, and delete accounts. Typically, you have only one Administrator account; however, another user you trust implicitly, such as your partner, spouse, or job-share colleague may also have an Administrator account.

>> **Standard:** Gives the user access to the computer and allows them to install programs or change their account settings, but doesn't let the user create, modify, or delete accounts or change any locked System Preferences settings.

>> **Managed with Parental Controls:** Gives the user restricted access to the computer based on the Parental Controls defined by an Administrator account.

>> **Sharing Only:** Gives the user remote access to shared files but not the access to log in or change settings on your computer.

TIP

Although each set of instructions begins with opening System Preferences and ends with closing System Preferences, you can open it once, go through each of the following sets of instructions, and then close System Preferences at the end.

You can set up a Managed with Parental Controls account from the Users & Groups System Preferences or directly from the Parental Controls System preferences. To set up a new user account, follow these steps:

1. Choose System Preferences and click the Users & Groups icon to show the Users & Groups preferences pane (see Figure 2-12).

REMEMBER

If the lock icon in the lower-left corner of the preferences window is locked, you must unlock it to make changes to your Mac's user account details. Click the lock icon, type your password in the dialog that appears, and then press Return to unlock your Mac's user account details.

2. Click the Add (+) button in the lower-left corner (above the lock icon).

A New Account dialog appears.

3. Choose the type of account you want to set up from the New Account pop-up menu, as shown in Figure 2-13.

Your choices are Administrator, Standard, Sharing Only, and Group.

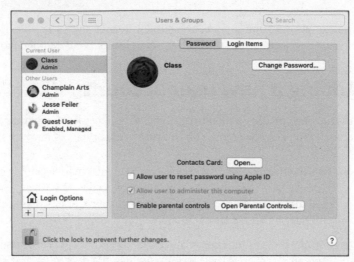

FIGURE 2-12:
Manage all single
accounts and
groups from the
Users & Groups
preferences.

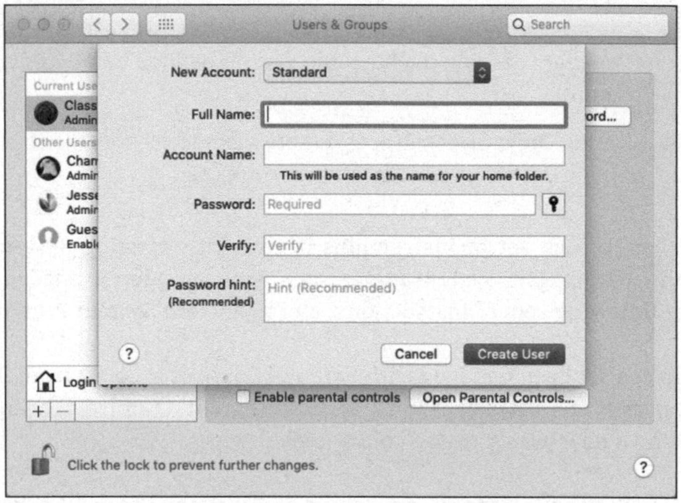

FIGURE 2-13:
The New Account
dialog lets you
define your new
account.

4. **Enter the name of the person who'll be using the account into the Full Name text box.**

5. **(Optional) In the Account Name text box, edit the short name that your Mac automatically creates.**

6. **Enter a password for this account into the Password text box.**

If you click the key to the right of the password text box, your Mac will generate a random password that may be more difficult to guess but also harder to remember.

7. Reenter the password you chose in Step 7 in the Verify text box.

8. (Optional) In the Password Hint text box, enter a descriptive phrase to help remind you of your password.

9. Click the Create User button.

The Users & Groups preferences pane displays the name of your new account.

10. (Optional) To assign an image to a user, follow these steps:

    a. Click the image (the Picture well) above the name to reveal a selection of images you can assign to that user.

    b. Click an image from the Defaults that are shown, click iCloud to choose a photo from Photo Stream, or click Camera to take a photo.

    c. Click Edit to zoom or add a special effect to the image or photo.

    d. When you have a photo you like, click the Done button to assign the photo to the user.

11. Select one or more of the choices in the pane (refer to Figure 2-12):

- *Allow User to Reset Password Using Apple ID:* The user can go into the Users & Groups pane on his Mac to set up and change the user password by identifying himself with his Apple ID.

- *Allow User to Administer This Computer:* Change the account type to Administrator.

- *Enable Parental Controls:* Click the Open Parental Controls button to assign the limits you want to apply to this user.

12. Click the lock at the bottom of the window to prevent changes.

13. Click the Close button of the Users & Groups preferences window.

Learn about Login Options later in this chapter, in the section "Enabling Fast User Switching."

TIP

Defining Parental Controls

You may want to use Parental Controls not only to protect your children from seeing things they may not be mature enough to see, but also to restrict what guest users can do with your Mac. You apply limits or restrictions to a Managed with Parental Controls account even if the person who accesses that account isn't your child. You can place several types of restrictions on an account. Following are the categories of limits you find in the Parental Controls preferences.

- ❯❯ **Apps:** Limits the apps the user may use and offers an option to simplify the appearance of the Finder.

- ❯❯ **Web:** Limits which websites the account can access.

- ❯❯ **Stores:** You can allow or restrict access to iTunes Store, Apple Books, and iTunes U. You can also restrict or allow access to explicit content, movies or TV shows with certain ratings (like TV-PG), and apps with age ratings such as 4+ or 17+.

- ❯❯ **Time Limits:** Prevents someone from accessing the account at certain times or on certain days.

- ❯❯ **Privacy:** Privacy is implemented by allowing you to specify data that can or cannot be changed in Contacts, Calendar, Reminders, or Diagnostics. (Diagnostics can report personal data access that is useful in troubleshooting performance issues but that also can reveal what the user is doing.)

- ❯❯ **Other:** Select the associated check boxes to hide profanity, prevent modifications to the printers connected to the Mac, prevent saving data to a CD or DVD, hiding explicit language in Dictionary, or modifying the Dock. You also can force the user to use Simple Finder, which is safer for young or inexperienced users to use without causing problems.

To apply Parental Controls to an account, follow these steps:

1. **Choose ⇨ System Preferences and then click the Users & Groups icon.**

Click the lock icon and enter your password to unlock the Users & Groups System Preferences.

2. **Click the Parental Controls button.**

The Parental Controls preferences window opens.

3. **Click the account to which you want to apply Parental Controls.**

4. **Click the tab you want to customize from the available tabs (Apps, Web, Stores, Time, Privacy, and Other), as shown in Figure 2-14.**

As is common with parental controls, you have a range of settings. For example you can allow or disallow the use of the camera and of specific apps. Multiplayer games can be limited, as well as email.

Limiting Web access, as shown in Figure 2-15, is possible for individual websites or types of websites. You can add to the list of permitted apps as you see fit.

FIGURE 2-14:
Choose the apps
the user can use.

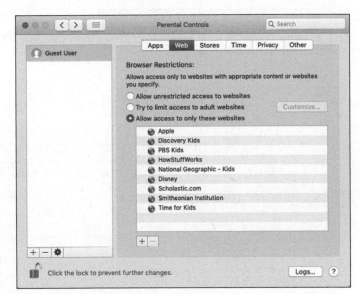

FIGURE 2-15:
Limiting access to
websites.

TIP

5. **Click the Logs button if you want to see a list of the apps or websites this user has used or visited in the past or contacts with whom Messages have been exchanged.**

Select one of the following radio buttons under the Website Restrictions section:

- *Allow Unrestricted Access to Websites:* Selecting this option allows users to access any website they want to visit.

- *Try to Limit Access to Adult Websites:* If you select this option, you can click the Customize button so that you can type the websites the account can always access and the websites that the account can never access.

  In both cases, you must type the address you chose to allow or block. Although this option can attempt to block most adult websites automatically, you need to enter additional addresses for particular websites that slip past the adult website filter.

- *Allow Access to Only These Websites:* If you select this option, you can then specify which websites the user can access by clicking the + button and adding websites you permit the user to visit. You can also remove websites you no longer want guest users to access by clicking the website in the list of allowed websites, and then clicking the – button to remove the website.

Most of the tabs in parental controls have a Logs button, as you see at the bottom right of Figure 2-15. This lets you see the apps or website that the user has accessed, as you see at the bottom right of Figure 2-16. This can be useful in keeping track of what people are visiting, as well as what they aren't visiting (think homework or time-wasting destinations).

Users can browse the various Apple Stores, and you can control what they can see or buy, as shown in Figure 2-17.

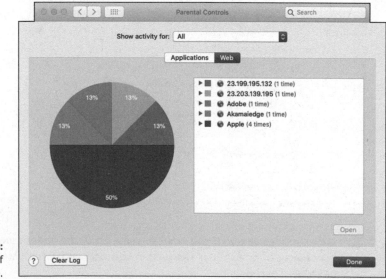

FIGURE 2-16:
View the log of
web usage.

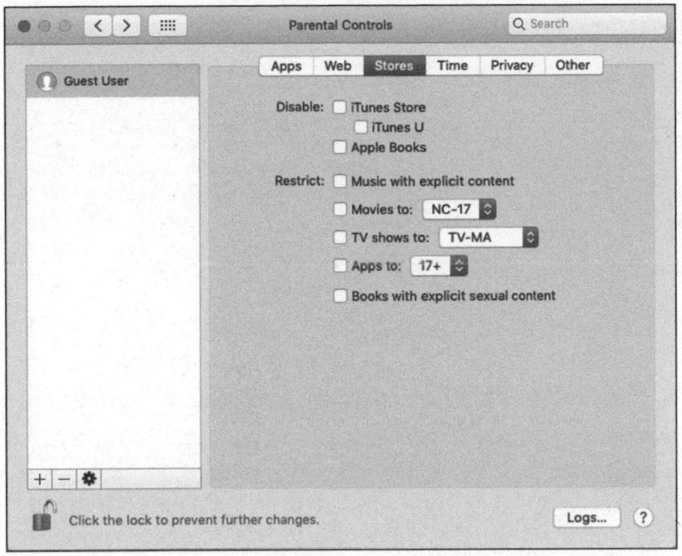

FIGURE 2-17:
Manage access to
the Apple Stores
on the web.

6. **Click the Time tab to open the Time Limits preferences pane, as shown in Figure 2-18, and choose from the following:**

    - *Limit Weekday Use To:* Select this Weekday Time Limits option and drag the slider to specify how much time the account can use your Mac.

    - *Limit Weekend Use To:* Select this Weekend Time Limits option and drag the slider to specify how much time the account can use your Mac.

    - *School Nights and Weekend:* Select one or both check boxes under the Bedtime category and set the start and end times of when you don't want the account to use your Mac, such as between 9 p.m. and 9 a.m.

    The School Nights option defines Sunday through Thursday. The Weekend option defines Friday and Saturday; however, this option pays no mind to exceptions such as holidays, school vacations, snow days, and other potential non-school-night calendar dates.

REMEMBER

7. **Click the Privacy tab to allow or prevent changes to Contacts, Calendars, Reminders, and Diagnostics.**

    It's important to note that check boxes shown in Figure 2-19 don't control *access:* They determine if the user can *change* the values.

    The tab in Parental Controls lets you manage others settings. It is — oddly enough — titled "Other."

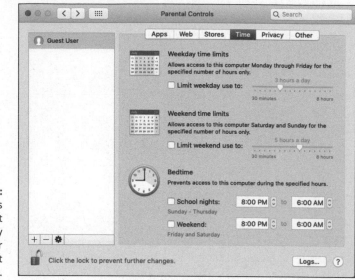

FIGURE 2-18:
Time Limits
preferences let
you specify
certain days or
times the account
can be used.

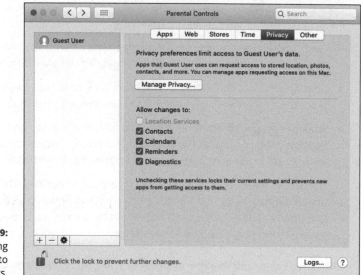

FIGURE 2-19:
Allowing
changes to
privacy settings.

8. **Click the Other tab to open the Other preferences pane.**

   Select the check boxes next to the limits you want to set. The effect each has is explained in the Other preferences window, as shown in Figure 2-20:

   - *Disable Built-In Camera*

   - *Disable Dictation*

- *Hide Profanity in Dictionary*
- *Limit Printer Administration*
- *Disable Changing the Password*
- *Limit CD and DVD Burning*

Click the lock icon at the bottom left of the window, and then click the Close button to quit System Preferences when you are finished setting or resetting the Parental Controls.

FIGURE 2-20:
The Other pane offers additional Parental Controls.

Activating a Sharing Only account

Your Mac comes with a preestablished Guest User account. This account lets friends or clients use your Mac temporarily, but nothing they do is saved on your Mac although it could be saved to a Shared file or to a remote storage site like Dropbox or an external hard or flash drive. By giving someone a Guest User desktop to use, your Desktop and everything you've so neatly organized doesn't get poked around or messed up.

Your Mac has only one Guest account because multiple users will access the same Guest account. To enable the Guest account, follow these steps:

1. **Choose ⇨ System Preferences, and then click the Users & Groups icon.**

   If the lock icon in the lower-left corner of the preferences window is locked, click to unlock it and then type your password in the dialog that appears. Press Return to unlock your Mac's user account details.

2. **Click the Guest User icon that appears in the list box on the left to open the Guest User dialog, as shown in Figure 2-21.**

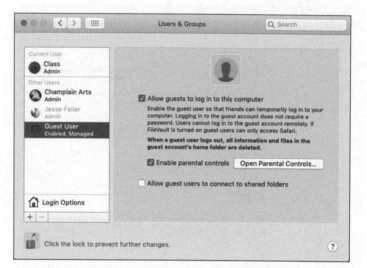

FIGURE 2-21: When you enable a Guest account, you can define additional options for how the Guest account works.

3. **Select the Allow Guests to Log In to This Computer check box, which allows anyone to use your Mac's Guest account without a password.**

4. **(Optional) Click the Open Parental Controls button if you want to specify which programs guests can use (or not use) and whether they can access the Internet.**

   Read about adjusting these settings in the earlier section, "Defining Parental Controls."

5. **(Optional) Select or deselect the Allow Guests to Connect to Shared Folders check box.**

   If this option is selected, a Guest account can read files created by other accounts and stored in a special shared folder or the other users' Public folder.

6. **Click the Close button of the Accounts preferences window.**

Switching between accounts

The Mac offers several ways to switch between accounts. The most straightforward way is to log out of one account and then log in to a different account. A faster and more convenient way is to use Fast User Switching, which essentially lets you switch accounts without having to log out of one account first.

To log out of an account, simply choose ⌂ Log Out (or press ⌘+Shift+Q) After you log out, the login window appears, listing the names and user icons of all accounts. At this time, you can click a different account name to log in to that account.

Before you can log out, a confirmation dialog appears as shown in Figure 2-22. Your open files and apps will be closed before logging out. Select the Reopen Windows When Logging Back In check box so when you log in, your Mac looks just like how you left it when you logged out.

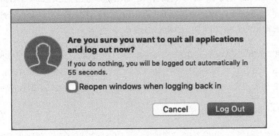

FIGURE 2-22:
Confirm that you
want to log out.

TIP

Hold the Option key while logging out to avoid the confirmation dialog.

If you use Fast User Switching, you won't have to bother with any of that because Fast User Switching gives the illusion of putting the currently active account in "suspended animation" mode while your Mac opens another account.

Enabling Fast User Switching

Before you can use Fast User Switching, you have to turn on this feature. Log in as Administrator and then follow these steps:

1. Choose ⌂ System Preferences, and then click the Users & Groups icon.

If the lock icon in the lower-left corner of the preferences window is locked, click to unlock it and then type your password in the dialog that appears. Press Return to unlock your Mac's user account details.

2. Click the Login Options icon at the bottom of the list of users on the left side of the pane to display the Login Options pane, as shown in Figure 2-23.

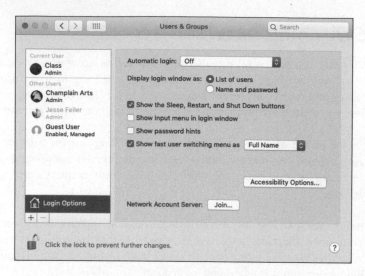

FIGURE 2-23:
Login Options is
where you can
turn on Fast User
Switching.

3. **Select the Show Fast User Switching Menu As check box, open the pop-up menu, and choose how you want to display the Fast User Switching Menu: Full Name, Short Name, or Icon.**

These options display what appears on the menulet. Full Name displays full account names, Short Name displays abbreviated account names, and Icon displays a generic icon that takes up the least amount of space in the menu bar.

4. **Select other Login Options:**

- *Automatic Login:* Leave this option Off or choose one user who will be automatically logged in when you restart your Mac, which is handy if you're the only user and your Mac is always in a safe place.

- *Display Login Window As:* Choose List of Users (from which you click a user and then type in the password) or Name and Password (which requires you to enter both your username and password).

- *Show the Sleep, Restart, and Shut Down Buttons:* Select this if you want to see these buttons on the login screen.

- *Show Input Menu in Login Window:* Allows users to choose the language they want to use when logging in.

- *Show Password Hints:* Users can click the question mark on the login screen to see a password hint, which you set up when you created the user account name and password.

- *Use VoiceOver in the Login Window:* Select this if you want VoiceOver to work during login. Learn more about VoiceOver in Book 1, Chapter 6.

5. **Click the Close button to close the Users & Groups preferences pane.**

Changing accounts with Fast User Switching

When you enable Fast User Switching, the Fast User Switching menulet appears in the right side of the menu bar, as shown in Figure 2-24. The menulet displays the names of accounts you can choose.

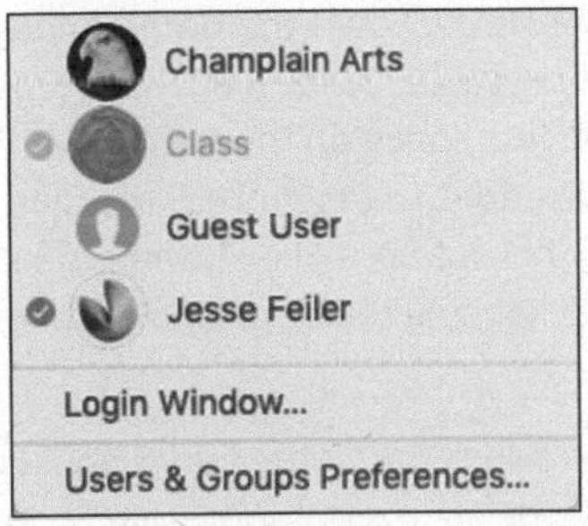

FIGURE 2-24: The Fast User Switching menulet.

To switch to a different account at any time, follow these steps:

1. **Click the Fast User Switching menulet on the right side of the menu bar and then click the account name you want to use.**

2. **Type the account password in the dialog that appears and press Return.**

   Your Mac switches you to your chosen account.

Deleting an account

After you create one or more accounts, you may want to delete an old or unused account. When you delete an account, your Mac gives you the option of retaining the account's Home folder, which may contain important files. To delete an account, follow these steps:

1. **Make sure that the account you want to delete is logged out and also that you're logged in to your Administrator account.**

2. **Choose ⌘ ➪ System Preferences, and then click the Users & Groups icon or click the Fast User Switching menulet and choose Users & Groups Preferences (refer to Figure 2-24).**

   If the lock icon in the lower-left corner of the preferences window is locked, click to unlock it, and then type your password in the dialog that appears. Press Return to unlock your Mac's user account details.

3. Select the account you want to delete in the accounts list and then click the Delete Account (–) button in the lower-left corner of the list.

A confirmation dialog appears, asking whether you really want to delete this account and presenting options to save the Home folder of the account, as shown in Figure 2-25. Select one of the following radio buttons:

- *Save the Home Folder in a Disk Image:* Saves the home folder and its contents in a compressed disk image (DMG) file. This keeps the files compressed, so they take up less space on the hard drive than if you choose the next option (which does not compress the files contained in the Home folder). Choosing this option is like stuffing things in an attic to get them out of sight but still keeping them around in case you need them later.

- *Don't Change the Home Folder:* Keeps the Home folder and its contents exactly as they are before you delete the account, so you can browse through the files contained within the folder at any time.

- *Delete the Home Folder:* Wipes out any files the user may have created in the account. Click the check box next to Erase Home Folder Securely to encrypt the files when they're erased, making them irretrievable.

4. Click Delete User.

Your Mac deletes the specified account.

FIGURE 2-25:
Do you really
want to delete?

382 BOOK 3 **Beyond the Basics**

A Few Final Security Tips

We want to give you a few extra security tips to keep your Mac and your documents safe:

» **Really take out the trash.** From the Desktop, choose Finder⇨Secure Empty Trash when eliminating old files, especially if you have sensitive documents. This feature is more incinerator than simple trash can.

» **Avoid suspicious websites.** If you open a website and then a gazillion other pages open, quit Safari and reopen it. Then choose History ⇨ Clear History to wipe out any memory of the pages that you opened. Your Mac will screen downloads from Safari, Mail, and Messages and offers to move potential malicious files directly to the trash — usually a good idea.

» **Mix it up.** Resist the temptation to use the same password for everything. Use Password Assistant to generate passwords, and then track those passwords by using Keychain Access (choose Go ⇨ Utilities and click Keychain Access). See the section "Changing your password" at the beginning of this chapter to learn more about Password Assistant.

» **Put junk in its place.** If an email arrives that *seems* to be from your bank or credit card provider, but the domain is @hotmail.com or @gmail.com or includes an overseas domain such as .es, don't respond! Mark it as Junk, and move on. Sorry to disappoint, but they really *didn't* find $14 million that belongs to you.

REMEMBER

Banks don't send or ask for sensitive financial information via email, maybe because they know that an ordinary email message is about as secure as a postcard — as in, *not secure.*

WARNING

Barbara recently received an email supposedly from Apple asking to sign in to her iCloud account to confirm information. Even the domain was @apple.com, but something didn't look quite right. The misspellings in the web page that opened were a tip-off, and upon closer inspection, the logo and colors were very close but not exact. Hovering the pointer over the domain revealed the real, non-Apple URL and a quick search on the Internet revealed that fake Apple email messages were in circulation!

Chapter **3**

Networking Your Mac and Connecting Peripherals

Most households and small businesses have a few computers, a printer or two, a scanner, an Internet service, and maybe even an external drive where files are backed up from each computer. (Be sure to read about the importance of backing up in Book 3, Chapter 1.) You can connect and disconnect *peripheral devices* (your printers, scanners, and such) to and from your computer when you want to use them — which would be a big hassle and time waster — or you can set up a network.

A *network* allows multiple computers to share files and devices, such as printers, modems, or back-up hard drives. Connecting two computers is the simplest of networks, but even a home setting today typically has a printer shared by two computers (more on that in the following chapter). And when multiple computers connect to a network, they can share files almost as quickly and easily as copying a file from one folder to another.

After you understand the concept of networking, networks aren't so difficult to set up. In this chapter, we show you how to set up a simple wired or wireless network — a few computers, a printer, and a modem. We then talk about another connectivity protocol — Bluetooth — which lets you connect peripherals (think keyboards and mice) wirelessly, as well as share files between devices. We delve into sharing in Book 3, Chapter 4.

Creating a Wired Network

Setting up networks is easy with Macs because of *Bonjour,* Apple's implementation of zero-configuration networking, which is part of your Mac's operating system. With Bonjour, your Mac seeks and discovers the peripheral devices and servers on your local network and you don't have to do any complicated configuring. You may see the word Bonjour in some of the networking preferences windows or when you set up chats (see Book 2, Chapter 3). Sometimes you hear this referred to as *plug and play* — plug in your computer and peripherals and it just works!

The simplest wired network connects two computers, using either a USB or Thunderbolt cable or a cable that conforms to a networking cable standard called *Ethernet.* Your Mac has an Ethernet or Thunderbolt port or both. If you plug a cable into the ports of two Macs, you have a simple network, as shown in Figure 3-1.

FIGURE 3-1:
A simple network connects two Macs via Ethernet or Thunderbolt cable.

Ethernet or Thunderbolt cable

TIP

All data transfer speeds in this section (and, in fact, in almost every article or book you read) are maximum possible speeds.

All recent Mac models have Thunderbolt ports, and many also have USB 3.0 ports. Thunderbolt 3 offers two-way 40 Gbps connections, making it faster than USB 3.0 where the top speed is 5 Gbps (and even faster than USB 3.1 where the top speed is 10 Gbps). (Older Macs have older versions of USB and — if they have Thunderbolt — it's older than Thunderbolt 3. What's critically important is that Thunderbolt 3 uses a USB-C cable, which is exactly what USB 3 can use. As you can see, there are still speed differences, but the two cables have made it possible to use more devices with more connections.

All desktop Mac models and the non–Retina MacBook Pro also have Ethernet ports. Other MacBook models without an Ethernet port rely on a wireless (Wi-Fi) connection, a USB-Ethernet adapter, or a Thunderbolt-Ethernet adapter.

TECHNICAL STUFF

Ethernet cables are often identified by the speeds at which they can send data. The earliest Ethernet cables were Category 3 (Cat 3) cables and could transfer data at 10 megabits per second (Mbps). The next generation of Ethernet cables was Category 5 and 5e (Cat 5/5e) cables, which could transfer data at 100 Mbps. Category 6 (Cat 6) cables transfer data at 1,000 Mbps or one gigabit per second (Gbit/s). With networking, speed is everything and Category 6a (Cat 6a) and Category 7 (Cat 7) transfer data at 10 Gbit/s. Category 7a supports transfer speeds of 100 Gbit/s.

Because it's physically impossible to connect more than two devices together with a single cable, wired networks use a *hub*. Each device connects to the hub, which indirectly connects each device to every other device also connected to the hub, as shown in Figure 3-2.

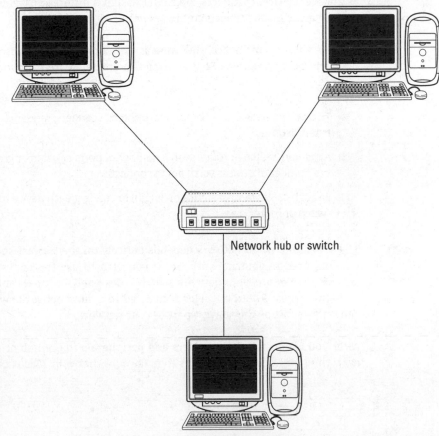

Network hub or switch

FIGURE 3-2:
A hub or switch allows multiple computers to connect together in a network.

An improved variation of a hub is a *switch*. Physically, a hub and a switch both connect multiple devices in a single point (refer to Figure 3-2).

With a hub, a network acts like one massive hallway that every computer shares. If many computers transfer data at the same time, the shared network can get crowded with data flowing everywhere, slowing the transfer of data throughout the network.

With a switch, the switch directs data between two devices. As a result, a switch can ensure that data transfers quickly, regardless of how much data the other devices on the network are transferring at the time.

A variation of a switch is a *router*, which often adds a firewall by using Network Address Translation (NAT) and Dynamic Host Configuration Protocol (DHCP). NAT uses one set of Internet Protocol (IP) addresses, which identify the computers and peripherals on the network for local network traffic, and another set for external traffic. This eliminates the risk of your device having the same address as another device. DHCP lets the router assign a different IP address to the same device each time it connects to the network.

Because routers cost nearly the same as ordinary hubs and switches, most wired networks rely on routers. So if you want to create a wired network of computers, you need

>> Two or more devices — computers, printers, scanners, modems, external drives

>> A network switch or router with a number of ports equal to or greater than the number of devices you want to connect

>> Enough cables (and of sufficient length) to connect each device to the network switch or router

REMEMBER

The speed of a wired network depends entirely on the slowest speed of the components used in your network. So, if you plan to use the fastest cables in your network, make sure your network switch is designed for those cables. If not, you'll have the fastest Ethernet cables connected to a slow network switch, which will run only as fast as the slowest part of your network.

After you connect your computers and peripherals to the hub or switch and turn everything on, follow these steps to make sure that your Mac is connected:

1. **Choose ⌘⇨System Preferences.**

   The System Preferences window opens.

2. **Click the Network icon.**

3. **Beside Ethernet or Thunderbolt, or whichever type of network cable or connection you use, you should see a green light and the word *Connected* underneath, as shown in Figure 3-3.**

   If you don't see a wired connection such as Ethernet or Thunderbolt, you may see the green light next to Wi-Fi, which is a wireless connection. If you don't see any green dots, you don't have any connection. Don't worry if you have several (or many) connections that are not enabled (they have red dots).

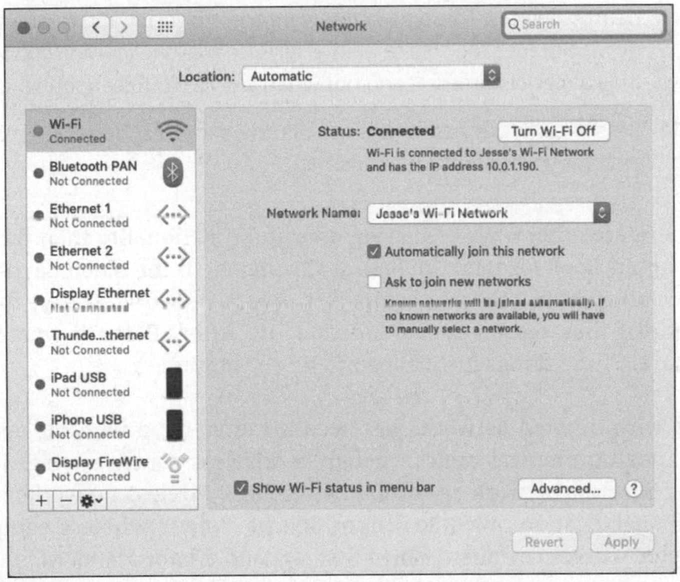

FIGURE 3-3:
Use Network preferences to connect to the network.

We explain how to set up file sharing in Book 3, Chapter 4. After you set up sharing, you see other computers on your network in the Finder under the Locations heading.

When you set up a wired network, the router may have wireless capabilities. If so, you can use an Ethernet cable to connect to the router a computer or printer that stays in one place, and then connect to the wireless network connection on your MacBook to work from your lawn chair in the garden or connect from a desktop Mac in another room in the house. To do so, turn on Wi-Fi and select the network, as we explain in the next section.

Creating a Wireless Network with a Router

Essentially, a wireless network is no different from a wired network, except (of course) that there are no wires. Instead, radio waves take their place. Wireless networks can be a bit slower than wired networks, but unless you transfer big files, going wireless is probably a tidier and more cost-effective alternative because there are no cables to buy or tack along the baseboard. We show you how to create wireless network that uses a wireless router and eventually a cable modem or DSL modem.

We'd be remiss if we didn't mention two downsides to wireless networks:

» Potential interference from cordless phones, microwave ovens, and other nearby devices. This type of interference is difficult and frustrating to track down because the source of interference may well be a cellphone that is on only at certain times — and not when you're troubleshooting interference.

» Less security because of the risk of others intercepting the signal unless you encrypt your communications.

TIP

There are other ways of sharing data and functionality than those you see in this chapter. Look for them in Book 3, Chapter 4. In the olden days (a few years ago), we talked about sharing computers over a network. Today, the emphasis is on sharing files, resources, and functionality. After all, that's what you really want to share. These things just happen to be on computers.

As with a wired network, you need a router for a wireless network. Instead of managing physical cables, though, a wireless router manages signals based on the wireless network protocols. The earliest wireless networks followed a technical specification called 802.11b or 802.11a. Newer wireless equipment followed a faster wireless standard called 802.11g, and a later standard is 802.11n. The most common current standard is 802.11ac. Most devices that support one of the 802.11 family protocols are compatible with one another to a large extent.

When setting up a wireless network, make sure that your router uses the same wireless standard as the built-in wireless radio or wireless adapter plugged into each of your devices. All new and recent Macs connect to Wi-Fi routers that use one to five types of the wireless 802.11 network standards.

You can buy any brand of wireless router to create a network, or rent one from your Internet service provider (ISP). Apple used to sell products such as Apple Time Capsule, Apple Express, and Airport Extreme, but it's no longer making new products in this line. Existing products work well for many people and are still available as new from a number of online vendors. Any router you choose will come with specific software and instructions for setting up your network. The basic steps are as follows:

1. **Name your network and base station so devices on the network can then find and connect to your Wi-Fi network.**

2. **Set up a password.**

   WPA2 provides the most security (see the nearby sidebar, "The hazards of wireless networking," for more information).

   TIP

3. **Define how you connect to the Internet.**

   You may need information from your Internet Service Provider (ISP) for this step (see Book 1, Chapter 3).

4. **Add printers and/or external hard drives.**

5. **Configure your Macs for sharing, as we explain in Book 3, Chapter 4.**

Because of physical obstacles, wireless networks don't always reach certain parts of a room or building, resulting in "dead spots" where you can't connect wirelessly. Walls or furniture can disrupt the wireless signals. You can add a device called an *access point*, also known as a *range extender*, which picks up the signal and rebroadcasts it beyond the reach of the Wi-Fi router, extending your wireless network range. The newest (but not widely distributed) Wi-Fi protocol — 802.11ac — uses a technology that is better at penetrating walls, which will make this problem less troublesome in the future.

TECHNICAL STUFF

The difference between an access point and a router is that the router is at the center of the network, allowing the computers to share printers (see the next chapter), Internet connections, and external hard drives. The *access point* is what allows the devices with wireless capabilities to connect to the network from a greater distance.

THE HAZARDS OF WIRELESS NETWORKING

To access a wired network, someone must physically connect a computer to the network with a cable. However, connecting to a wireless network can be done from another room, outside a building, or even across the street. As a result, wireless networks can be much less secure because a wireless network essentially shoves dozens of virtual cables out the window, so anyone can walk by and connect to the network.

When you create a wireless network, you can make your network more secure by taking advantage of a variety of security measures and options. The simplest security measure is to use a password that locks out people who don't know the password. Three types of passwords are used for wireless networks:

- **Wired Equivalent Privacy (WEP)** is an older protocol and offers minimal (almost useless) protection. Because it's an older protocol, it may not work on all your devices. Passwords use either 5 or 13 characters. WEP is no longer recommended; we're listing it here only so that you know what it is if you're working with a device that uses WEP.

- **Wi-Fi Protected Access (WPA)** is better than WEP because it changes the encryption key for each data transmission.

- **Wi-Fi Protected Access 2 (WPA2)** is the best choice because it uses the more secure Advanced Encryption Standard (AES) to encrypt the password when it's transmitted.

For further protection, you can also use encryption. *Encryption* scrambles the data sent to and from the wireless network. Without encryption, anyone can intercept information sent through a wireless network (including passwords). Still another security measure involves configuring your wireless network to let only specific computers connect to the network. By doing this, an intruder can't gain access to the wireless network because his or her computer is not approved to access the network.

Ultimately, wireless networking requires more security measures simply because it offers potential intruders the ability to access the network without physically being in the same room, house, or building. Wireless networks can be as safe as wired networks — as long as you turn on security options that can make your wireless network as secure as possible.

Connecting and Choosing a Printer

Out of the box, macOS comes with a number of special files called *printer drivers*, which tell your Mac how to communicate with most popular models of printer brands. When you buy a new printer, it often comes with a CD that contains a printer driver or a website address where you can download the appropriate driver. Put the CD aside and log onto the website, which will have more recent software for your printer. If there is no website available, you can use the CD (but it's usually out of date). With the downloaded software, you can install the printer driver to unlock special features that the Mac's built-in drivers may not take advantage of.

TECHNICAL STUFF

Periodically check the support section of the printer manufacturer's website to see whether a newer version of the printer installation software is available.

Some installers place a print utility on the Dock, and you may be able to set up the print utility to check automatically for updates.

Making your Mac work with your printer involves a two-step process:

1. **You connect your printer to your Mac, either physically with a USB cable or network connection (such as a USB or Ethernet connection to a router) or wirelessly to a Wi-Fi–enabled printer that's connected to the same Wi-Fi network your Mac connects to.**

2. **You must install the proper printer driver on your Mac (if you don't want to use the supplied driver that comes with macOS, or if your Mac doesn't have a driver for it). After you connect your printer to your Mac and install or select the correct printer driver, you can then print documents and control your printer's options.**

TIP

You can download additional printer drivers (and drivers for other types of hardware, such as scanners and pressure-sensitive tablets) directly from the Apple website (www.apple.com/downloads/macosx/drivers) or from the printer manufacturer's website. On this web page, enter **Printer Drivers**, or the name of your device into the search text box.

After you physically or wirelessly connect a printer to your Mac and install its printer driver, you may need to take one additional step and tell your Mac that this particular printer is connected. To get your Mac to recognize a connected printer, follow these steps:

1. **Power it on.**

2. **Choose ⌘⇨System Preferences.**

3. Click the Printers & Scanners icon.

The Printers & Scanners preferences window opens, as shown in Figure 3-4. Printers and scanners connected to your network are listed on the left.

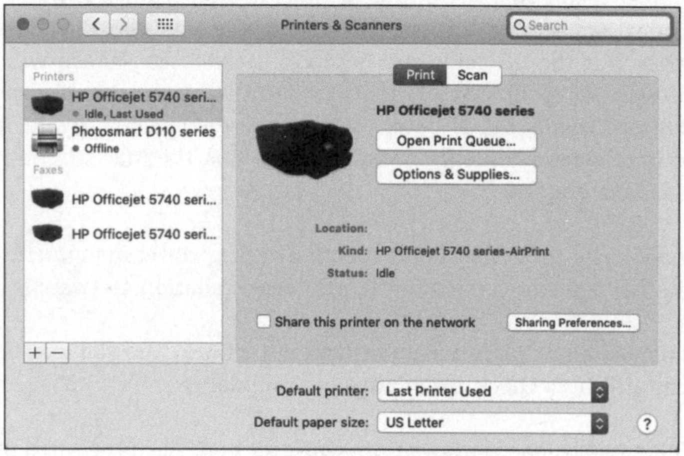

FIGURE 3-4:
See the printers connected to your network.

TIP

Printers may appear several times in the list if they're multipurpose printers. A multipurpose printer that can function as a printer, scanner, and fax machine may appear as three separate devices.

To add printers to your Mac, after they're connected and powered on, follow these steps:

1. Choose ⌘⇨ System Preferences and then click the Printers & Scanners icon to open the Printers & Scanners preferences pane (refer to Figure 3-4).

2. Click the Add (+) button at the bottom of the Printers list (refer to the left of Figure 3-4).

Note: Your Mac may list local printers (printers directly attached to your Mac) as well as printers linked to your Mac via a network. See Book 3, Chapter 4 to learn more about sharing printers.

3. In the Add dialog that appears (see Figure 3-5), you see a list of printers that are available on the network.

Click the Default tab if you don't see the printers.

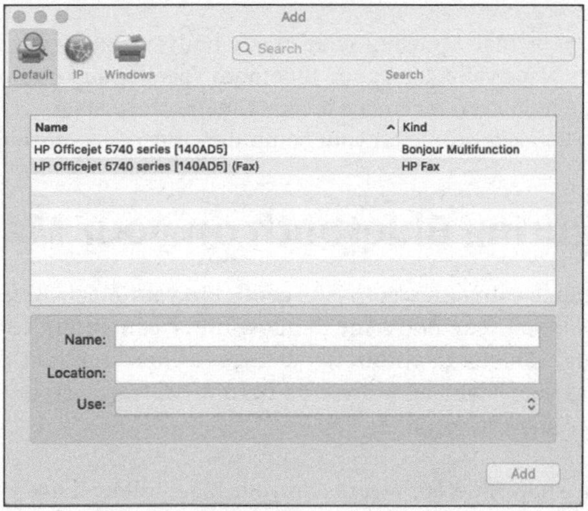

FIGURE 3-5:
Add a printer
from the list.

4. **In the list, click the printer you want your Mac's applications to always print to (unless you specify otherwise).**

5. **From the Use pop-up menu, choose the driver you want to use.**

6. **Click the Add button at the lower right of the Add window.**

7. **Click the Close button to quit System Preferences.**

Biting into Bluetooth

Bluetooth is a wireless technology standard designed primarily for connecting devices within a short distance of one another — up to 30 feet. Because of its short-range nature, Bluetooth is handy for connecting computers for short periods of time and for transferring small files, unlike faster wired or wireless (Wi-Fi) networks that connect computers on a more permanent basis.

TECHNICAL STUFF

If you think Bluetooth is a distant relative of Bluebeard or Babe the big blue ox, think again. Bluetooth was named after tenth-century Danish King Harald Gormsson, who during his short reign improved communication and merged the Danish and Norwegian tribes.

Most mobile phones and tablets have built-in Bluetooth capabilities, which makes it easy to wirelessly sync calendars and address books between a handheld device and a computer (as we explain in Book 1, Chapter 3). Bluetooth-enabled input devices, such as wireless keyboards, mice, and game consoles, as well as wireless headsets for chatting with FaceTime or using Internet phone services like Skype, connect to your Mac by using your Mac's built-in Bluetooth feature. Bluetooth speakers are also available. A good Bluetooth speaker and Apple's Music app are a match made in heaven for music lovers. Bluetooth speakers are also handy if you listen to audiobooks stored on your computer or accessed through the Kindle app.

Configuring Bluetooth on your Mac

The first step to using Bluetooth is to configure your Mac's Bluetooth preferences. For example, you may not want to allow other computers to browse your hard drive through Bluetooth without your express permission. Otherwise, someone could access your Mac and browse its hard drive from across the room, and you would never know it.

To configure how Bluetooth works on your Mac, follow these steps:

1. **Choose System Preferences, and then click the Sharing icon.**

   Alternatively, right-click (two-finger click on a trackpad) the System Preferences icon on the Dock and choose Sharing from the menu that appears.

2. **Select the Bluetooth Sharing check box and make sure that Bluetooth Sharing is highlighted.**

   The Sharing window opens, as shown in Figure 3-6.

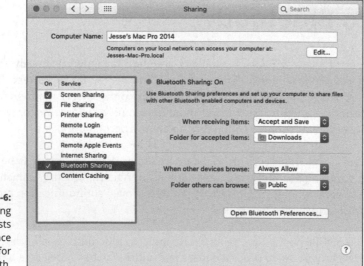

FIGURE 3-6:
The Sharing window lists preference choices for Bluetooth.

3. **Choose one of the following from the When Receiving Items pop-up menu:**

- *Accept and Save:* Automatically saves any files sent to you through Bluetooth. (We don't recommend this option because someone can send you a malicious application, such as a virus or Trojan Horse, which can wipe out your files when opened.)

- *Accept and Open:* Automatically saves and opens any files sent to you through Bluetooth. (We don't recommend this option because this — like the previous option — could automatically run a malicious application sent to your Mac through Bluetooth.)

- *Ask What to Do:* Displays a dialog that gives you the option of accepting or rejecting a file sent to you through Bluetooth. This option is probably your best choice.

- *Never Allow:* Always blocks anyone from sending you files through Bluetooth.

4. **Choose either Downloads (the default) or Other from the Folder for Accepted Items pop-up menu.**

If you choose Other, an Open dialog appears, letting you navigate to and click a folder where you want to store any files sent to you through Bluetooth.

5. **Choose one of the following from the When Other Devices Browse pop-up menu:**

- *Always Allow:* Automatically gives another (any) Bluetooth device full access to the contents of your Mac. (Not recommended — this allows others to mess up your files accidentally or deliberately.)

- *Ask What to Do:* Displays a dialog that gives you the option of accepting or rejecting another device's attempt to access your Mac through Bluetooth.

- *Never Allow:* Always blocks anyone from browsing through your Mac by using Bluetooth.

6. **Choose either Public or Other from the Folder Others Can Browse pop-up menu.**

If you choose Other, an Open dialog appears, letting you select a folder that you can share.

7. **Click the Open Bluetooth Preferences button and go on to the next section.**

Pairing a Bluetooth device

Pairing allows you to predetermine which Bluetooth-enabled devices can connect to your Mac. By pairing, you can keep strangers from trying to access your Mac without your knowledge. For additional security, paired devices require a password (also called a *passkey*) that further verifies that a specific device is allowed to connect to your Mac.

Pairing with your Mac

To pair a device with your Mac, follow these steps:

1. **Right-click (two-finger click on a trackpad) the System Preferences icon on the Dock and choose Bluetooth from the menu that appears.**

   Alternatively, choose ⌘⇨ System Preferences to open the System Preferences window and then click the Bluetooth icon.

   The Bluetooth preferences pane appears.

2. **If Bluetooth is off, click the Turn Bluetooth On button.**

   The Devices list shows Bluetooth-enabled devices in the vicinity and any devices you previously connected to.

3. **Click the Pair button next to the device you want to pair with your Mac.**

   A dialog shows a code that you should make sure matches the code on the device you're pairing. Click or tap Pair on the device to confirm, and the device appears as Connected in the Devices list, as shown in Figure 3-7.

FIGURE 3-7:
Bluetooth preferences let you pair a device with your Mac.

TIP

In the Bluetooth Preferences dialog, choose Show Bluetooth in Menu Bar. This enables you to click the icon and see which devices are within range and available for connection. You can also turn Bluetooth off from the icon's drop-down menu.

REMEMBER

If you're using a wireless keyboard or trackpad, Bluetooth Preferences is where you'll will see them.

TIP

To unpair a device or remove a previously paired device from the list, make sure Bluetooth is turned on and then hover the pointer to the right of the device you want to remove. Click the X that appears (refer to Figure 3-7).

If you connect Bluetooth-enabled input devices to your Mac, such as keyboards, mice, or trackpads, you should consider a few advanced settings. Choose ⇨ System Preferences and then click the Bluetooth icon or right-click (Control-click on a trackpad) the System Preferences icon on the Dock and choose Bluetooth. Click Advanced in the lower-right corner, and you see the window shown in Figure 3-8. Choose the settings that apply to the devices you use. For example, if you use a Bluetooth-enabled keyboard, you want to select the first and third options so that if your Mac doesn't see the keyboard, it opens Bluetooth Preferences automatically, and you can wake your Mac by touching the keyboard. If you have a wireless mouse but not a wireless keyboard, choose the second and third options.

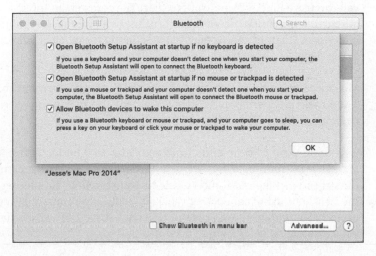

FIGURE 3-8:
Choose how your Mac interacts with input devices from the advanced Bluetooth settings.

Troubleshooting connections with Bluetooth-enabled devices

Sometimes you pair a device with your Mac, but the connection doesn't seem to hold when your Mac goes to sleep. If you connect a keyboard or headset to your computer and experience problems with the Bluetooth connection, power down the device by following this procedure:

1. **Shut down your Mac.**

2. **Turn off the keyboard or headset and hold the power button for 5 seconds.**

3. **Turn on your Mac.**

4. **When your Mac says there is no keyboard connected, turn on the keyboard and hold the power button for 10 seconds.**

    Alternatively, turn on the headset and hold the power button for 10 seconds.

5. **Pair the device with your Mac as explained in the preceding section.**

Sharing through Bluetooth

Because Bluetooth lets you create a simple, short-range network between Macs, you can use a Bluetooth network to share files or even an Internet connection with others. Such a simple network isn't meant to share massive numbers of files or a long-term Internet connection, but it is handy for quick email access or browsing a web page.

TECHNICAL STUFF

The speed of ordinary networks connected through Ethernet cables is 10, 100, or 1,000 megabits per second (Mbps), whereas the maximum speed of a Bluetooth network is only 1 Mbps.

When you want to copy a file from your Mac to another device, such as another Mac or a PC running Windows, you can set up a Bluetooth connection. Sharing files through Bluetooth allows you to transfer files to another device without the hassle of using connecting cables or mutually compatible removable storage devices like portable hard drives or USB flash drives. It's also a viable option when you're out of range of a Wi-Fi network.

To share files through Bluetooth, follow these steps:

1. **From the Finder, choose Go⇨Utilities.**

The contents of the Utilities folder appear.

2. **Double-click the Bluetooth File Exchange icon.**

A Select File to Send window appears.

TIP

Choose ⌘⇨System Preferences⇨Bluetooth and then click Show Bluetooth in Menu Bar. Then to quickly transfer files, click the Bluetooth icon on the menu bar to choose Send File to Device and then proceed.

3. **Select a file.**

TIP

To select multiple files, hold down the ⌘ key and click each file you want to send.

4. **Click Send.**

A Send File window appears, listing all Bluetooth-enabled devices near your Mac, as shown in Figure 3-9.

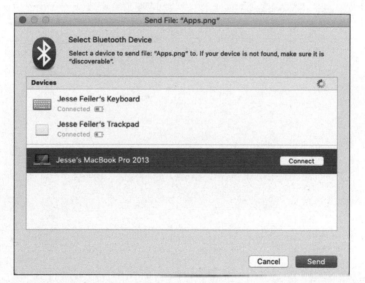

FIGURE 3-9:
The Send File window lets you choose a Bluetooth-enabled device to receive your file.

5. **Select a Bluetooth-enabled device and click Send.**

If you choose another Mac or mobile phone (but not an iPhone) to receive your files, a dialog may appear on the receiving device, asking the user to accept or decline the file transfer.

REMEMBER

If the receiving device has been configured to Accept and Save or Accept and Open (transferred files), the transfer will begin as you see in Figure 3-10. Otherwise, if the user has selected Ask What to Do (the default option) when configuring Bluetooth settings, you won't be asked to accept or reject the transfer each time.

See Book 3, Chapter 4 to learn about sharing an Internet connection with Bluetooth.

TIP

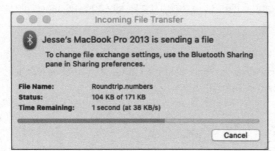

FIGURE 3-10:
Monitor the file transfer.

Chapter **4**

Sharing Files and Resources on a Network

The benefits of sharing over a network range from swapping files quickly and easily to sharing a single printer instead of having to buy a printer for every computer. Sharing files makes it easy for several people to work on the same project. Without a network, you could give someone a copy of a file, but then you may find yourself with three different versions of the same file, and deciphering which file contains the most accurate information would be difficult. (Read how to set up a network in the preceding chapter.)

Although networks allow others to share your files, other people connected to the network can't rummage through your Mac without your permission. Ideally, a network allows you to share files and equipment without risking the loss or corruption of crucial files on your own computer.

In this chapter, we talk about how to share files, printers, and Internet connections among computers on a network. We also show you how to access your Mac's screen from another computer with screen sharing.

Sharing Files with People Near and Far

If you want to share files with another Mac, you can set up a simple network, as we explain in the preceding chapter. Or, you can use *AirDrop*, which is a simple peer-to-peer (computer-to-computer) wireless network between Macs that sit near each other. An advantage of using AirDrop is sharing with many computers simultaneously without using a network hub.

Don't underestimate the significance of not having a network hub. Networks and their hubs often are built around a specific location (often a cable modem or shared file server). AirDrop and other hub-less connections enable you to make direct connections to a nearby computer. If you pick up your MacBook and take it with you to a meeting in a restaurant, you can establish another connection without plugging or unplugging anything (all subject to security, of course). This means that you and your colleague can continue your discussion about a new project in the restaurant even though it started in a meeting room. The people involved are the same as are the devices, but that annoying struggle with cables to reestablish connections just doesn't apply.

Using AirDrop

AirDrop lets you set up a peer-to-peer network between two or more Macs that are near to each other — more or less in the same room — the caveat being that you must have a Mac that supports AirDrop and a Wi-Fi connection. It doesn't work with Macs connected with an Ethernet cable. If your Mac is older than those listed here, AirDrop isn't for you:

- **iMac:** Early 2009

- **MacBook or MacBook Pro:** Late 2008

- **MacBook Air:** Mid-2010

- **Mac mini:** Mid-2010

- **Mac Pro:** Early 2009 with AirPort Extreme card or mid-2010

Don't despair, however — there are other solutions for peer-to-peer sharing even if you don't have AirDrop. Send files through Bluetooth or set up a peer-to-peer network (both explained in the preceding chapter), and then refer to the "Using a network" section in this chapter or use Messages, which we detail in Book 2, Chapter 3.

You don't have to have any kind of network already set up. You do have to have OS X 10.7 Lion or later installed on any Macs you want to use AirDrop with. You also need the recipient of your files to have File Sharing turned on in the Sharing pane of System Preferences, as shown in Figure 4-1.

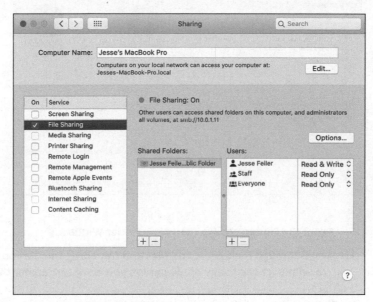

FIGURE 4-1:
Your recipient must have File Sharing turned on in System Preferences.

TIP

Sharing Preferences are shown and described in the "Using a network" section, later in this chapter. Consider this a sneak preview.

Here's how AirDrop works:

1. **From the Finder, choose Go ⇨ AirDrop.**

The AirDrop window opens, as shown in Figure 4-2. If you don't have Wi-Fi turned on, you're prompted to do so; when you do, you see the AirDrop window. Alternatively, you can click the AirDrop link in the sidebar of any Finder window.

You see the contact photos or other images of only those other Mac users who have AirDrop enabled; likewise, they only see you if you have AirDrop enabled. If your Mac goes to sleep, AirDrop disconnects.

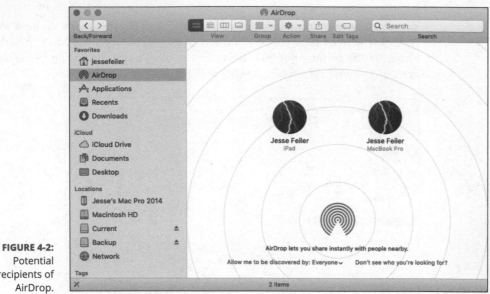

FIGURE 4-2:
Potential
recipients of
AirDrop.

2. **From the Finder, choose File ⇨ New Finder Window.**

3. **Scroll through the folders and files and then drag the file you want to transfer over the image of the person you want to transfer the file to.**

Handling an incoming AirDrop request depends on your settings and your choices. As you can see in Figure 4-3, when AirDrop is open on a Mac, you can choose who can discover you with AirDrop. In the case of Figure 4-3, everyone can. Note that you can choose who can discover you by choosing an option from the pop-up menu shown in Figure 4-3.

TIP

As long as the Mac user to which you want to send a file has AirDrop enabled, you can right-click the file and choose Share ⇨ AirDrop from the context menu.

That's not the end of the story. If the AirDrop request comes from someone logged in with another Apple ID, you have to decline or accept the AirDrop, as shown in Figure 4-3.

After you've accepted the AirDrop item (or if it comes from the same Apple ID), you can decide whether to open it, as shown in Figure 4-4. To decline accepting the file, simply click outside the box.

If you begin a download and want to cancel, open your Downloads folder and click the X next to the icon of the incoming file.

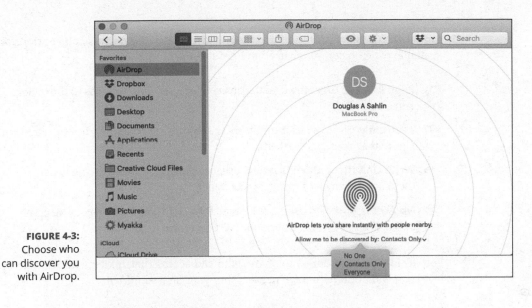

FIGURE 4-3:
FIGURE 4-3:
Choose who
can discover you
with AirDrop.

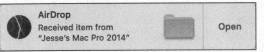

FIGURE 4-4:
Choose to open
an AirDrop item.

**TECHNICAL
STUFF**

In AirDrop, you don't have to worry about security. AirDrop automatically encrypts files and creates a *firewall* (an almost impenetrable barrier) between your Mac and the Mac you're sharing the file with. Other Macs on AirDrop can only see that you're on AirDrop; they can't peek into your Mac.

Using a network

Sharing files over the network is different from AirDrop in a few ways:

>> On the network, your Mac can be in a different room, a different building, even in a different country.

>> You set up the type of access you want others on the network to have.

>> Your connection to the network runs in the background where you don't see it — even while your Mac is sleeping.

When your Mac is connected to a network, you have the option of sharing one or more folders with everyone else on the network. To share folders, you need to define different permission levels — *privileges* — that allow or restrict what users

Sharing Files and
Resources on a Network

can do with a folder and the files inside it. The following permissions options are available for each computer user and group:

>> **Read & Write:** Gives the user the ability to see, retrieve, add files to the folder, and edit files.

>> **Read Only:** Gives the user the ability to see and open files, but they can't add files to the folder, or edit them.

>> **Write Only (Drop Box):** Gives the user the right to place files in the folder; they can't see any files stored in that folder.

>> **No Access:** Specified users are blocked from accessing files on your Mac. This option is only available when you select everyone.

You decide which folder(s) to share, who can access that folder, and what access level you want others to have in accessing your shared folder.

Each user on your Mac has his or her own Public folder that's created automatically when the user is added. By default, you can add and retrieve files to the Public folder (Read & Write privileges), and everyone can place files in the Drop Box folder (Write Only [Drop Box] privileges) stored within the Public folder. You can change the privileges for yourself or everyone, but you can delete neither user from the Public folder (although you can choose No Access for Everyone).

Turning on file sharing

The first step to sharing your files over a network is to turn on file sharing. Follow these steps:

1. **Choose ⌘⇨ System Preferences, and then click the Sharing icon or right-click (two-finger click on a trackpad) the System Preferences icon on the Dock and choose Sharing from the menu that appears.**

   Refer to Figure 4-1 to review the Sharing window.

2. **Click the File Sharing check box in the leftmost Service column.**

   This enables file sharing and you see a list of Public folders on your Mac. If you have more than one user account set up on your Mac, you see the Public folders for each account (see Figure 4-1).

3. **Click the plus-sign button underneath the Shared Folders column.**

4. **From the dialog that appears, displaying all the drives and folders on your Mac, scroll through to find the folder you want to share.**

The folder you want to share may be inside another folder.

REMEMBER

5. **Click the folder you want to share, and then Click Add.**

The folder appears in the list of Shared Folders.

6. **Repeat Steps 3–5 for each additional folder you want to share on the network.**

In the following section, you can see how to grant user privileges to your shared folders.

TIP

You don't have to share folders. If you don't turn on File Sharing, other people can't access your folders, but you can still use a network to access someone else's shared folders. You can also use devices, such as printers, that are on the network.

REMEMBER

It's always a good idea to share the least that you can. Don't share a folder if you can share a document. Don't provide Read & Write access if Read Only will do. Oversharing can lead to serious problems, particularly as people get used to broad access and ignore best practices of security.

Defining user access to shared folders

After you define one or more folders to share, you can also define the type of access people can have to your shared folders, such as giving certain people the capability to open and modify files and stopping other people from accessing your shared files.

The three types of network users are

» **Yourself:** Gives you Read & Write access (or else you won't be able to modify any files in your shared folders)

» **Everyone:** Allows others to access your shared folders as guests without requiring a password

» **Names of specific network users:** Allows you to give individuals access to your shared folders with a name and a password

If you trust everyone on a network, you can give everyone Read & Write privileges to your shared folders. However, it's probably best to give everyone Read Only privileges and only certain people Read & Write privileges.

DEFINING ACCESS PRIVILEGES FOR GUESTS

To define access privileges for guests, follow these steps:

1. **If Sharing isn't open, right-click the System Preferences icon on the Dock and choose Sharing from the menu that appears, or choose ⇨ System Preferences and then click the Sharing icon.**

2. **Click File Sharing in the Service list.**

3. **Click a folder in the Shared Folders list.**

   The Users list enumerates all the people allowed to access this particular shared folder (refer to Figure 4-5). You can add another.

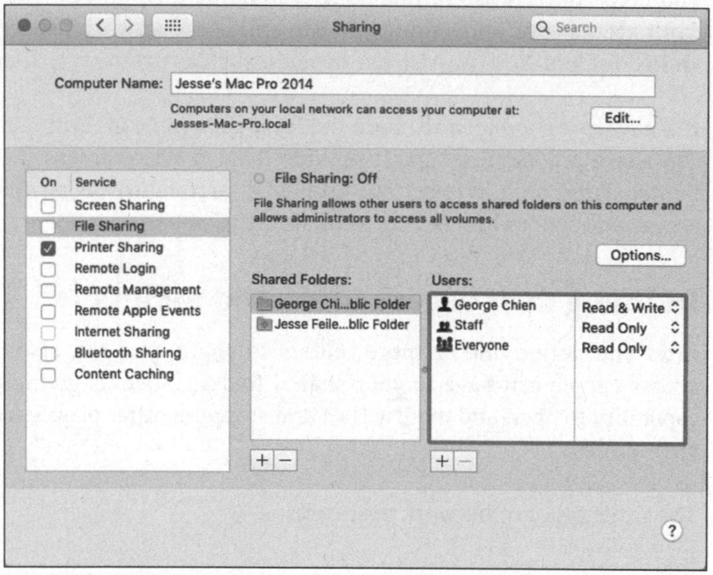

FIGURE 4-5:
Decide which
users can access
shared folders.

4. **Click a user to call up the access option pop-up menu, and then choose an access option, such as Read & Write, Read Only, Write Only (Drop Box), or No Access.**

5. **Repeat Steps 3 and 4 for each shared folder or user you want to configure.**

6. **Click the Close button of the System Preferences window.**

GIVING INDIVIDUALS ACCESS TO SHARED FOLDERS

The access level you give to the Everyone account for a shared folder means that anyone on the network has that level of access to your files — Read & Write, Read Only, Write Only. You probably want to give Everyone the minimum access (Read Only) to a shared folder and give specific individuals higher levels of access.

To define a username and password to access a shared folder, follow these steps:

1. **Choose ➪ System Preferences to open the System Preferences window and then click the Sharing icon.**

The Sharing pane appears.

2. **Click File Sharing in the Service list.**

3. **Click a folder in the Shared Folders list.**

The Users list enumerates all the people allowed to access this particular shared folder.

4. **Click the plus-sign button under the Users list, and then click the Contacts category or one of the groups from your Address Book in the left pane.**

A dialog appears, shown in Figure 4-6, where you can either choose the name of a person stored in Contacts or create a new user.

If the name of the person you want to add isn't a user in Contacts, add him to Contacts (see Book 5, Chapter 1) or as a Sharing Only user (see Book 3, Chapter 2).

TIP

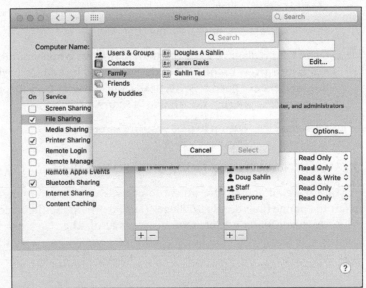

FIGURE 4-6:
Adding a person to the Users list.

5. **Click Contacts.**

Your list of contacts appears.

6. **Scroll through the list and click the name of the person to whom you want to grant privileges and then click Select.**

The Choose Password dialog appears, as shown in Figure 4-7.

7. **Enter a password in the Password text box.**

Be careful to note if the caps lock key is or isn't down. This is one of the areas where it matters.

8. **Reenter the password in the Verify text box.**

9. **Click the Create Account button.**

10. **In the dialog that appears, type your Admin password (the one you use to sign in to your Mac) to approve the configuration change and then click Modify Configuration.**

Your new user name appears in the Users list.

11. **Open the Privileges pop-up menu that appears when you click the disclosure arrow to the right of the name you just added to the Users box, and choose Read & Write, Read Only, or Write Only (Drop Box) to assign access privileges, as shown in Figure 4-5.**

12. **Click the Close button to quit System Preferences.**

REMOVING ACCOUNTS FROM SHARED FOLDERS

If you create an account for others to access your shared folders, you may later want to change their access privileges (such as changing their access from Read & Write to Read Only) or delete their accounts altogether.

To delete an account from a shared folder, follow these steps:

1. **Right-click (two-finger click on a trackpad) the System Preferences icon on the Dock and choose Sharing from the menu that appears, or choose ⇨ System Preferences to open the System Preferences window and then click the Sharing icon.**

2. **Click File Sharing in the Services list.**

3. **Click a folder in the Shared Folders list.**

   The Users list enumerates all the people allowed to access this particular shared folder.

4. **Click the name of the User for whom you want to change privileges.**

5. **Click the arrows next to the name to open the Privileges pop-up menu.**

6. **Select the new privileges you want the user to have.**

7. **Click the Close button of the System Preferences window.**

To delete a user, follow Steps 1–3 in the preceding list, and then follow these steps:

1. **In the Users list, click a name that you want to delete.**

2. **Click the minus-sign button under the Users list.**

   A confirmation dialog appears, asking whether you want to keep the account from accessing your shared folder.

3. **Click OK.**

4. **Click the Close button of the System Preferences window.**

File sharing in Sleep mode

Your Mac can share files even if you set up your Mac to sleep when it's inactive for a certain time. (You can use this feature if your wireless network supports the 802.11n or 802.11ac wireless protocol — see Book 1, Chapter 3 or Book 3, Chapter 3 for a brief explanation.) If you want your Mac to wake up when another user on the network wants to access your shared files, follow these steps:

1. **Right-click (two-finger click on a trackpad) the System Preferences icon on the Dock and choose Energy Saver from the menu that appears, or choose ⇨ System Preferences and then click the Energy Saver icon.**

2. **(MacBook model users) Click the Power Adapter tab.**

3. **Select the Wake for Wi-Fi Network Access check box.**

4. **Click the Close button of the System Preferences window.**

Accessing shared folders

You can share your folders with others on a network, and likewise, others may want to share their folders with you. To access a shared folder on someone else's computer, follow these steps:

1. **From the Finder, choose Go ➪ Network.**

   A Network window appears, listing all the computers that offer shared folders, as shown in Figure 4-8.

   Choose the view you prefer from the buttons on the toolbar.

REMEMBER

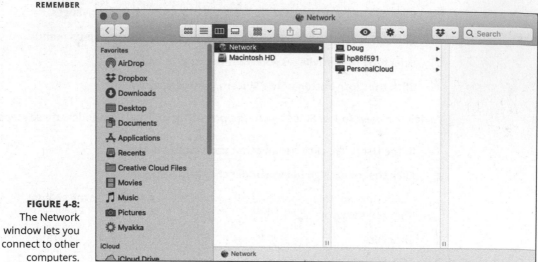

FIGURE 4-8: The Network window lets you connect to other computers.

2. **Double-click the computer you want to access to.**

   The settings you configured in Sharing (refer to Figure 4-1) come into play based on the user's Apple ID. On that basis you either get or are denied access.

TECHNICAL STUFF

   Earlier versions of macOS used a different strategy. This new version relies on your Apple ID (you don't enter a password at this point as you used to do). All access is controlled by Sharing, which makes it easier for most users and definitely more secure because it minimizes the number of places in the user interface that must deal with security.

Sharing Printers

Instead of buying a separate printer for each computer on your network — which is expensive and space-consuming — connect a single printer directly to one computer, and then configure that computer to share its printer with any computer connected to the same network. You can also share a network wireless printer. Depending on your printer, some special functions may be limited to the connected Mac so connect the printer to the Mac that you use for the most diverse functions. To share a printer, follow these steps:

1. **Choose ⟹ System Preferences and click the Sharing icon.**

2. **Click the Printer Sharing check box.**

   Printer sharing is now enabled and a list of printers connected to your Mac — physically or wirelessly — appears, as shown in Figure 4-9.

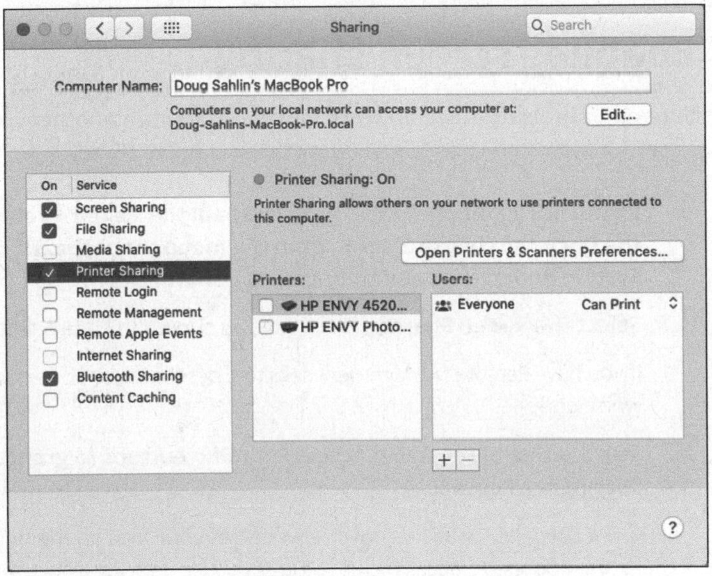

FIGURE 4-9: Each connected printer appears with a check box in the Sharing window.

3. **Select the check boxes of the printers you want to share.**

   Note that Everyone Can Print is the default in the Users column.

4. **(Optional) Add individual users just as you do for sharing files by clicking the plus-sign button beneath the Users column; choose No Access for Everyone and give selected users access to that printer.**

5. **Click the Close button to quit System Preferences.**

REMEMBER

When you choose File⇔Print in an application (say, Notes) to print a document or photo, a Print dialog appears. If you click the Printer pop-up menu, you see printers that you previously connected to your Mac. Choose Add Printer to choose a printer you haven't used, and a window appears (as we explain in Book 3, Chapter 3), listing all the available printers connected directly to your Mac (USB) or shared over the network. Click the Default tab if you don't see a list of printers.

Seeing Your Screen from Afar

Wouldn't it be great if while you're away from your office you could access your Mac? Or if you have a problem with your Mac and want to consult an expert, you can share your screen to show exactly what's going on? Screen Sharing lets you do this.

Enabling screen sharing

For you or others to see and work on your Mac from another computer, you need to set up access on your Mac. Follow these steps to do so:

1. **Right-click (two-finger click on a trackpad) the System Preferences icon on the Dock and choose Sharing from the menu that appears, or choose ⌘⇔ System Preferences and then click the Sharing icon.**

2. **Select the Screen Sharing check box, as shown in Figure 4-10.**

   If you have Remote Management selected, deselect it, or Screen Sharing won't work.

3. **Select either of the Allow Access For radio buttons to grant screen sharing privileges to**

   - *All Users,* which allows anyone who sees your Mac on the network or uses the address to access your computer.

   - *Only These Users,* which limits access to the people you add to the list. Click the Add (+) button to add users to the list as you do for file sharing, as we explain earlier in this chapter.

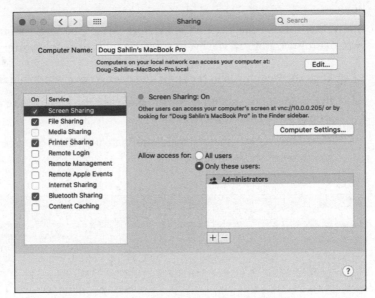

FIGURE 4-10:
Allow people to access your screen from another computer.

4. **Click the Computer Settings button.**

A dialog appears enabling you to choose which users may control the screen. Choose one of the following options:

- *Anyone May Request Control of the Screen.* Choose this option and anyone you share the screen with can request control of the screen.

- *VNC Viewers May Control Screen with Password.* Choose this option to enable virtual network computing (VNC) users to control the screen by entering the password you specify in the text field. VNC users access your computer remotely.

5. **Click OK to exit the Computer Settings dialog.**

6. **Click the Close button to exit System Preferences.**

Starting a screen-sharing session with another Mac

After you've enabled screen sharing, you can share your screen with another Mac on the network whose owner has also enabled screen sharing. Sharing a screen is beneficial for educational purposes such as showing a coworker how to do something. It's also useful for fun things, like sharing a video of your cat preening himself with someone else on the network. After enabling screen sharing, a network administrator can view your screen by doing the following:

1. **Click the Finder icon in the Dock and open a new Finder window.**

2. **In the Locations section of the sidebar, click the name of the computer whose screen you want to view.**

The Finder changes showing options to share the screen of the other computer, as shown in Figure 4-11.

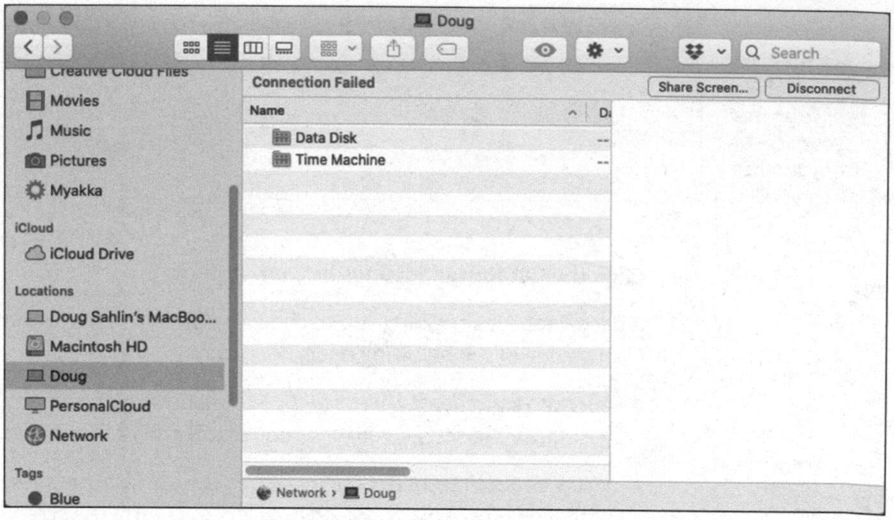

FIGURE 4-11: Connecting to another computer.

3. **Click the Share Screen button.**

The other computer's screen appears in a window, as shown in Figure 4-12. If a document is being authored on the computer whose screen you're sharing, that document opens in the same program being used on the originating computer. In this figure, the chapter as it was being written in Microsoft Word is being shared with another user's computer. The taskbar shows the name of the computer from which the screen is shared. The person sharing the computer can now work on the document or view what is happening on the originating computer:

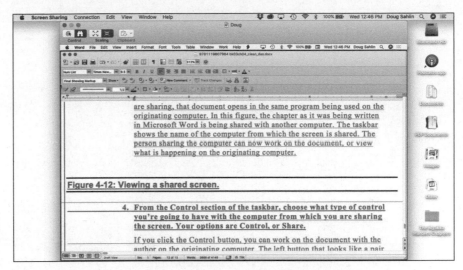

FIGURE 4-12:
Viewing a shared
screen.

4. **From the Control section of the taskbar, choose what type of control you're going to have with the computer from which you're sharing the screen; your options are Control and Share.**

   If you click the Control button, you can work on the document with the author on the originating computer. The right button that looks like a pair of binoculars enables you to only view the other screen. In either mode, your shared screen updates in real time as changes are made on the originating computer.

5. **Choose the desired scaling option.**

   The left Scaling button shows the document in full screen without the menu. The right Scaling button shows the document, taskbar, and menu bar.

REMEMBER

   When you have control of the screen, you can make changes to the document you're viewing. In this scenario, you'd be able to make changes to the Word document being authored on the screen you're sharing.

6. **To quit screen sharing, choose Screen Sharing ⇨ Quit Screen Sharing.**

Sharing Files and
Resources on a Network

Chapter **5**

Running Windows on a Mac

I n the 1990s, Microsoft Windows was *the* operating system for personal computers. Some other operating systems powered some computers, but by and large, the computing world — at least for business — was run on Intel processors using Windows.

People who used Macs were second-class citizens in many places. In fact, in many corporations, Macs were not allowed to be used. There was a certain logic to this because in those early days of personal computing, IT support staffs were just being formed and every nonstandard computer that came into the corporation was added work for the overstressed IT staff.

Still, some Mac users persevered. Some used their Macs at home for work and then switched to Windows in the office. With the passing of time, some people started noticing that those silly Macs that were considered nothing other than toys required less support than "real" computers running Windows.

Thus, the bring your own device (BYOD) movement came about. In many organizations, Macs didn't mean extra work for the IT staff — they often meant *less* work. (That "ease of use" mantra really showed its value.)

Working with BYOD and a Heterogeneous Computer Environment

In the early 2010s, thanks in large part to the phenomenal success of the iPhone, Apple devices began showing up in the corporate world. Mac developers started trying to adjust to no longer being laughed at by IT staff members saying, "Get a real computer."

The big takeaway from this summary of the 1990s and 2000s in the computer world was not that Apple superseded Windows in the business world. Instead, what happened was a mixture of several things:

>> Exclusive standards for personal computers were modified and sometimes repealed; they were often replaced by a list of approved products and required functionalities.

>> Pressure was exerted on all hardware and software developers and providers to encourage them to build interoperability into their products so that the brand names and gibberish code words were replaced by simple English phrases.

>> New standards and requirements were formalized so that some of the issues that come along with a multi-vendor environment were mitigated.

Bear these points in mind if your boss lets you know that you must get a Windows machine. This isn't 1995, so those reasons may no longer apply. If you can get the reasons down to specifics — what program has to run and what alternatives are there, for example — you may not need to run Windows, but if you do need to run Windows, this chapter is for you.

If you do need to run Windows, you have several choices:

>> For periodic use, a small and inexpensive Windows computer, for example, a small notebook PC, may be the simplest — particularly if you or other people in your organization already are comfortable with Windows.

>> Use one of the alternatives mentioned earlier (mobile devices, for example).

>> Use virtualization products such as Parallels (www.parallels.com). As of this writing, the Parallels Desktop software retails for $79.99.

Using Boot Camp

Boot Camp is part of the Mac operating system. You can use it to run Windows directly on your Mac. Boot Camp provides you with a simple way to switch back and forth between you Mac and Windows. Only one of them runs at a time. (Some third-party products, such as Parallels, allow you to transfer data between the two operating systems.)

TIP

If you're going to want to use Boot Camp (or any technology that is a bit complex), set it up before you need it. You may want to allow half an hour or even more to set up Boot Camp; when it's done, you'll be able to switch back and forth between Windows and macOS. It's easier to do that by yourself rather than in front of guests, clients, and other "helpful" people.

Setting up Boot Camp Assistant

Boot Camp Assistant is built into macOS; it's your guide to installing Boot Camp. The Boot Camp installation process is a bit complicated, even though most of it is hidden from you. The complications come because two operating systems need to be configured to work with one another in ways that they weren't built to do. Today, they do work together well. To install Boot Camp on your computer, follow these steps:

1. If you don't already have Windows 10, download it from www.microsoft.com/en-us/software-download/windows10ISO, **as shown in Figure 5-1.**

There are several versions you can buy. If you're part of an educational institution or corporation, check to see if you have a site license or other discount for the purchase.

2. In the Finder, double-click the Applications folder, double-click the Utilities folder, and double-click Boot Camp Assistant.

After starting the Boot Camp Assistant, you may be asked to download an update, an issue that occurred with the Mojave version of Boot Camp Assistant, as shown in Figure 5-2.

Boot Camp Assistant will keep you informed as the process continues. It will be reformatting your hard disk so that there is a separate area (called a *partition*) for your Windows software and data. Figure 5-3 shows the beginning of the process.

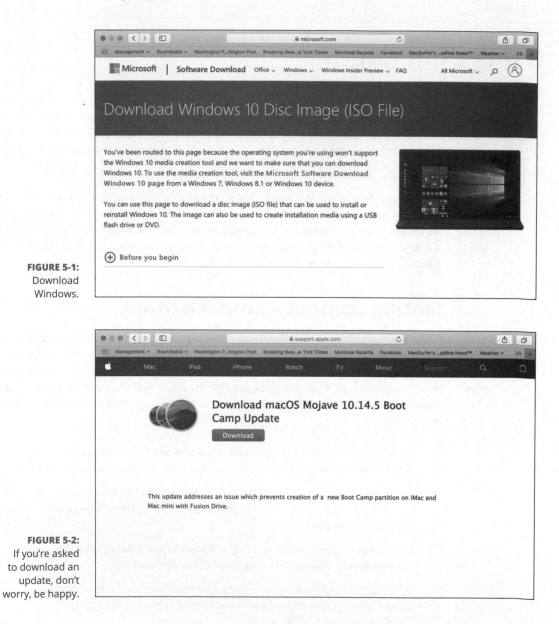

FIGURE 5-1:
Download
Windows.

FIGURE 5-2:
If you're asked
to download an
update, don't
worry, be happy.

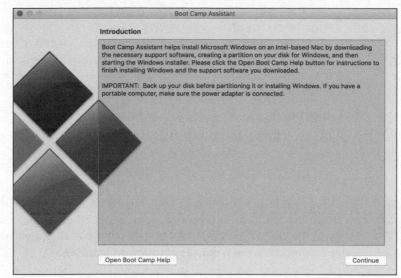

FIGURE 5-3:
Boot Camp keeps
you informed.

3. **When you're asked for Windows 10, select your downloaded Windows file from Step 2.**

4. **Set the size for the Windows partition by dragging the divider between Windows and macOS, as shown in Figure 5-4.**

   The divider represents your hard disk and you're setting the sizes for Windows and macOS. You can't redo it easily, so think about how you want to share your finite disk space.

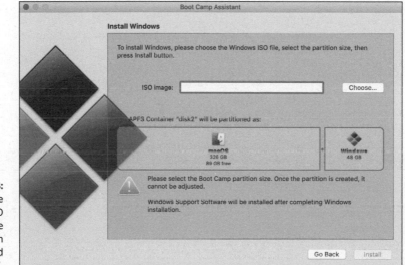

FIGURE 5-4:
Select the
Windows ISO
file, and set the
partition between
Windows and
macOS.

Running Windows on
a Mac

TIP

Consider the size of the applications you want to run in the Windows partition of your Mac; then add some space for system overhead (as of this writing, 20GB for Windows 10) and data files. Add 20 percent to this number to be on the safe side. This SWAG (Scientific Wild Ass Guess) gives you an idea of how much space you should allot for Windows.

5. **Click Install.**

Relax and have a sandwich and your favorite beverage while the Boot Camp Assistant installs Windows. On second thought, if it's almost 5 o'clock, have some chips and guacamole and your favorite beverage.

WARNING

Windows operating systems have been targets of hackers and virus creators. Plan on installing antivirus software on your Windows partition, and make sure to factor in the amount of space the software will take when figuring out how much space to allocate to the Windows partition on your Mac.

IN THIS CHAPTER

» **Taking care of application freezes and hang-ups**

» **Knowing what to do when you have trouble starting up**

» **Keeping your storage drives running smoothly**

» **Unjamming jammed CDs or DVDs**

» **Making your Mac perform routine maintenance**

Chapter **6**

Maintenance and Troubleshooting

No matter how well designed and well built a Mac is, it's still a machine, and all machines are liable to break down through no fault of yours. Many times, you can fix minor problems with a little bit of knowledge and willingness to poke and prod around your Mac. If your Mac isn't working correctly, you can check obvious things first, like making sure it's plugged in or that the battery is charged and that any connecting cables to your Mac are plugged in and secure. However, sometimes your Mac may be in more serious trouble than you can fix, so don't be afraid to take your Mac into your friendly neighborhood computer-repair store (one that specializes in repairing Macs, of course).

REMEMBER

Before you rush your Mac to the emergency room of Mac repairs, do some simple troubleshooting yourself. At the very least, be sure to back up your important files — before you have any troubles — so you won't lose them if you wind up sending your Mac to the repair shop. (Read about backing up in Book 3, Chapter 1.)

It's also worth pointing out a really important step to take when your Mac is not quite its usual perky self: Recognize that something may be wrong. Your nightly backups are great for restoring data, but if your first troubleshooting step is to see if the most recent backup is good, remember that you may be corrupting it by opening it. If you have the slightest suspicion of trouble, stop what you're doing, take a deep breath (or walk the dog), and assume that your Mac and everything it touches may be corrupted. Inadvertently corrupting backups is a remarkably common problem.

Luckily, Apple and third-party developers have created applications that analyze, diagnose, and repair problems on your Mac. In this chapter, we begin by addressing one of the most common problems: frozen apps. Then we get down to more serious problems related to your Mac not starting up properly or your hard drive acting strangely. We explain how to use the Recovery and Disk Utility applications that come with your Mac and give you suggestions for third-party applications to consider. We show you how to remove a jammed CD or DVD from the disc drive — in case you still have one of those. We close the chapter by giving you suggestions for preventive maintenance.

WARNING

Open your Mac *only if you know what you're doing.* If you open the case and start fiddling around with its electronic insides, you may damage your Mac — and invalidate your Mac's warranty. Besides, many of the most recent Macs are not user serviceable.

Shutting Down Frozen or Hung-Up Programs

Programs that always run perfectly may suddenly stop working for no apparent reason, and no matter which keys you press, where you click the mouse, or where you tap the trackpad, nothing happens. Sometimes you might see a spinning cursor (affectionately referred to as the "spinning beach ball of death"), which stays onscreen and refuses to go away until you take steps to unlock the frozen app.

Sometimes being patient and waiting a few minutes results in the hung-up app resolving whatever was ailing it as though nothing were wrong in the first place. More often, however, the spinning cursor keeps spinning in an oh-so-annoying fashion. To end the torment, you need to relaunch the Finder to refresh the Desktop or *force-quit* the frozen or hung-up app — basically, you shut down the app so that the rest of your Mac can get back to work. To force-quit an app, use one of the following methods:

>> Choose ⇨ Force Quit to display the Force Quit Applications dialog, as shown in Figure 6-1. If the Finder isn't responding, click Finder and then click the Relaunch button.

>> Right-click (two-finger click on the trackpad) the app's icon on the Dock and choose Force Quit from the menu that appears.

>> Choose ⌘ Force Quit to display the Force Quit Applications dialog. Then select the name of the hung-up application and click the Force Quit button (in place of the Relaunch button you see in Figure 6-1).

>> Press ⌘+Option+Esc to display the Force Quit Applications dialog. Then select the name of the hung-up application and click the Force Quit button.

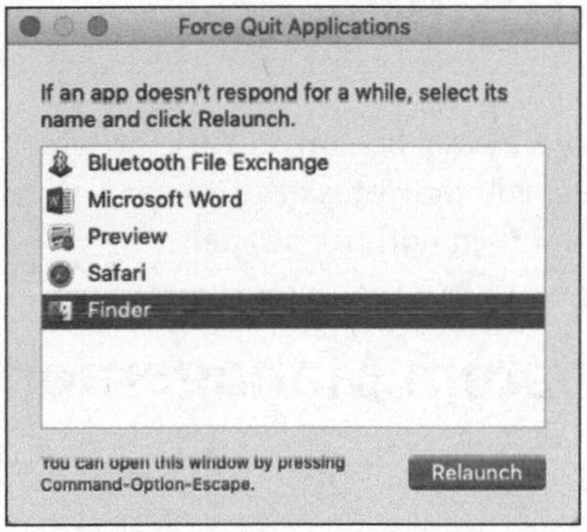

FIGURE 6-1:
Relaunch
the Finder
to unfreeze
your Mac.

Forcing the Finder to relaunch restarts it. Forcing other apps to quit (such as Microsoft Word) forces only that app to quit. If you know what you've been doing in a specific app, you can make an educated guess about whether you'll lose data with a force-quit. If you've saved your document's data very recently (and the save has completed successfully!), you may not lose data. Note that this is not a guarantee.

REMEMBER

One of the best ways to avoid problems with applications and the Mac operating system is to keep them updated. Set the App Store to check automatically for updates. Choose ⌘ System Preferences, and then click Software Update to open the Software Update preferences, as shown in Figure 6-2. Select the Check for Updates check box, and then choose any or all three options below. (See Book 1, Chapter 5 for information about the App Store.)

TIP

Many people believe that it is best not to install updates because they fear that updates can destabilize their system. That is certainly possible, but it isn't nearly as common as it was in earlier days of computers. On balance, the best practice is to install updates automatically using Software Update. An alternative is shown in Figure 6-2: Automatically install updates except for app updates from the App Store. The theory behind this approach is that if there is going to be a problem with a new version of software, it may be more likely in an app rather that in the operating system itself. (The reason for that is that the number of users of an app is much smaller than the number of users of the operating system.)

FIGURE 6-2:
FIGURE 6-2:
Keeping your
operating system
and applications
updated helps
avoid problems.

Handling Startup Troubles

Sometimes you may press the Power button to turn on your Mac, but nothing seems to happen. Other times, you may press the Power button and see the usual Apple logo on the screen — but *then* nothing happens.

Resetting the System Management Controller

If your Mac has a slight headache, and things just don't seem to be running right, before resorting to the more drastic solutions we show you in upcoming sections, you may consider resetting the System Management Controller (SMC). Resetting the SMC is easy-peasy, and it can solve problems like your computer running slowly, the battery on your MacBook Pro or MacBook air not charging properly, and so on. Resetting the SMC can fix a plethora of problems.

To reset the SMC on a desktop computer, follow these steps:

1. **Choose ⬤⇨Shut Down.**

2. **Unplug the power cord.**

3. **Wait 15 seconds.**

4. **Plug the power cord back in.**

5. **Wait 5 seconds and then press the power button to boot your Mac.**

You can also reset the SMC on a MacBook Pro or MacBook Air. However, if the computer has a removable battery, removing the battery is part of the process of resetting the SMC. If your MacBook Pro or MacBook Air has a removable battery, we suggest you have a competent computer repair center reset the SMC. If your

MacBook Pro or MacBook Air has a non-removable battery, you can rest the SMC by following these steps:

1. Choose Shut Down.

2. After your Mac shuts down, press Shift+Control+Option on the left side of the keyboard and press the power button at the same time. Hold this combination for 10 seconds.

TIP

If Your MacBook Pro has Touch ID, the Touch ID button is the power button.

3. Release all keys.

4. Press the power button to restart your Mac.

Resetting NVRAM and PRAM

If resetting the SMC doesn't work, you have another option before bringing in the cavalry with stainless-steel forceps and surgical masks: You can reset the non-volatile random access memory (NVRAM) and parameter RAM (PRAM). They take care of functions like sound volume, display resolutions, and other settings that need to be accessed rapidly by your computer.

To reset NVRAM and PRAM, follow these steps:

1. Choose Restart.

2. When the computer starts to reboot, hold down Option+⌘+P+R.

Your computer appears to restart.

3. Release the keys after 20 seconds, or when you hear the second Apple chime.

Booting up in Safe Mode

If you turn on your Mac and you can't see the familiar Desktop, menu bar, and Dock, don't panic. The first thing to do is try to boot up your Mac in *Safe Mode*, which is a boot sequence that loads the bare minimum of the OS X operating system — just enough to get your computer running.

Many startup problems occur when nonessential apps, such as appointment reminders that automatically load at login time and wind up interfering with other startup apps, preventing your Mac from booting up correctly. Other startup apps load before you see the login screen or the Desktop (if you've set your Mac to bypass the login window automatically and go directly to the Desktop when it

starts up). Booting up in Safe Mode cuts all the nonessential pre- and post-login apps out of the loop so that only your core apps load. A successful boot in Safe Mode at least tells you that your Mac's core system hasn't been compromised.

By booting up your Mac in Safe Mode, you can remove any applications you recently installed, turn off any startup options you may have activated, and then restart to see whether that fixes the boot-up problems. If you remove recently installed applications and deactivate startup options and problems persist, copy any important files from your hard drive to a backup drive to protect your crucial data in case the hard drive is starting to fail (see Book 3, Chapter 1). Follow these steps to determine the cause of the problem:

1. **Turn on your Mac, and then immediately hold down the Shift key until the Apple logo appears on the screen, indicating that your Mac is booting up.**

   If your Mac is on but not responding, hold down the Power button until your Mac restarts, and then immediately hold down the Shift key until the Apple logo appears on the screen.

   If your Mac starts up, you know at least that the problem isn't with the macOS itself but with something else on your Mac. Move on to Step 2 to repair it.

2. **To turn off startup options, go to System Preferences and click Users & Groups.**

   The Users & Groups window opens.

3. **Click your username in the column on the left.**

   If you have Admin privileges, you can set and reset other users' login options: Just select the name of the user you want to manage.

4. **Click the Login Items tab at the top of the right side of the window.**

   A list of the items that open automatically when you log in appears, as shown in Figure 6-3.

5. **Select a login item.**

6. **Click the minus sign button to delete it.**

   The application no longer starts when your computer boots up.

7. **Close the window.**

8. **Choose Restart.**

   If your Mac restarts without a problem, you know that the startup item you deselected was the problem.

   If your Mac doesn't restart, repeat Steps 1–5, each time deselecting the next login item on the list until your Mac restarts without a problem.

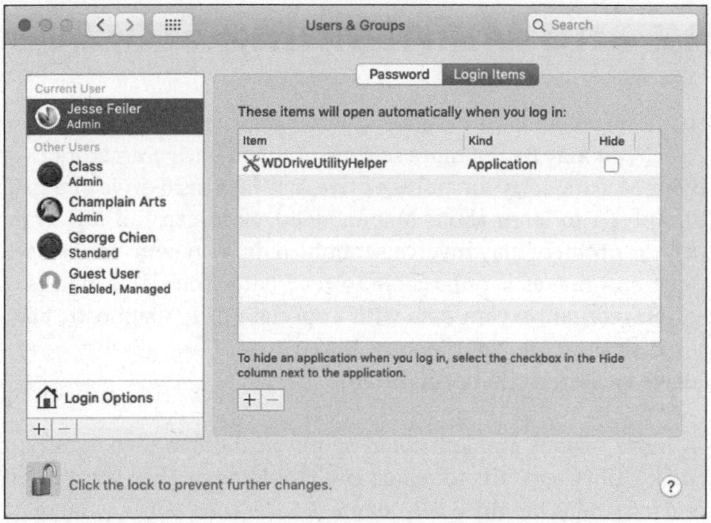

FIGURE 6-3:
Remove login items to determine which one may be causing problems.

Uninstalling apps

If the problem isn't resolved by removing startup items, the next thing to try is to uninstall any apps you recently installed. Although sometimes uninstalling is as simple as dragging the app icon from the Applications folder to the Trash (we talk about that in Book 1, Chapter 5), other times that's not the case. Just as there are *installers* that install apps on your Mac, there are also *uninstallers.*

When you install an app, you see the app icon in the Applications folder (and on the Launchpad), but there are also files associated with the app that the installer places in other folders on your Mac, such as the System and Library folders. To make sure that you throw away all the associated files, you need to run an uninstaller.

To find the uninstaller associated with the app you suspect is causing your problems, click the Spotlight Search button in the upper-right corner and enter **Uninstall**. Double-click the uninstaller you want to run. A window may open, asking for your login password or telling you that your Mac has to reboot. Either way, follow the onscreen instructions. Alternatively, you can enter Uninstaller.

If your Mac reboots successfully afterward, you know that the uninstalled app was causing the problems. At that point, before reinstalling, check the app in the App Store or visit the website of the problematic app to determine whether there's an update or information about incompatibility with your Mac model or operating system version. Try reinstalling from the disc if that's what you have; otherwise, try downloading the app anew and installing a new copy.

Repairing and Maintaining Storage Drives

If the problem isn't because of other apps trying to load when you turn on your Mac, you may have a more serious problem with your storage drive. Depending on your Mac model, your storage drive may be a hard drive or a flash drive (see Book 1, Chapter 1 to learn about Mac models). Both can fail for a number of reasons. A minor problem may involve scrambled data on your hard drive that confuses your Mac and makes it impossible to read data from it. If data is scrambled, you can often reorganize your data with a special utility diagnostic and repair app — such as Disk Utility on your Mac, or DiskWarrior (www.alsoft.com) — to get your hard drive back in working condition.

A more serious problem could be physical damage to your hard drive. If the Mac Disk Utility app fails to repair any problems on your hard drive, your hard drive's surface may be physically damaged. At that point, you may consider trying a third-party disk utility app. If either option doesn't work, your only option is to copy critical files from the damaged hard drive (if possible), replace the drive with a new one, and then restore your most recent Time Machine backup (you *are* backing up, aren't you?) to the new hard drive so you're back in business again as though nothing (or almost nothing) went kaput in the first place.

TIP

To find out how to use Time Machine to back up your Mac's hard drive, check out Book 3, Chapter 1.

The Disk Utility app that comes free with every Mac — tucked away in the Utilities folder inside the Applications folder or on the Launchpad — can examine your hard drive. However, to fix any problems it may find, you have to boot your Mac from a different hard drive or bootable USB flash drive, from the Recovery drive.

REMEMBER

Empty the Trash every now and then to eliminate files that you throw away from the Trash's temporary storage. Control-click or right-click (two-finger tap on the trackpad) the Trash icon on the Dock and choose Empty Trash or choose Finder ⇨ Empty Trash.

Running First Aid

If you suspect that your hard drive or another disk may be scrambled or physically damaged, you can run the Disk Utility app to verify your suspicions. Here's how to run First Aid:

1. **Run the Disk Utility app (stored inside the Utilities folder in the Applications folder).**

   The Disk Utility window appears.

2. **Select your Macintosh HD (or whatever disk you want to check) from the left pane of the Disk Utility window.**

3. **Click the First Aid button.**

4. **Click Run when you are asked if you want to run First Aid (see Figure 6-4).**

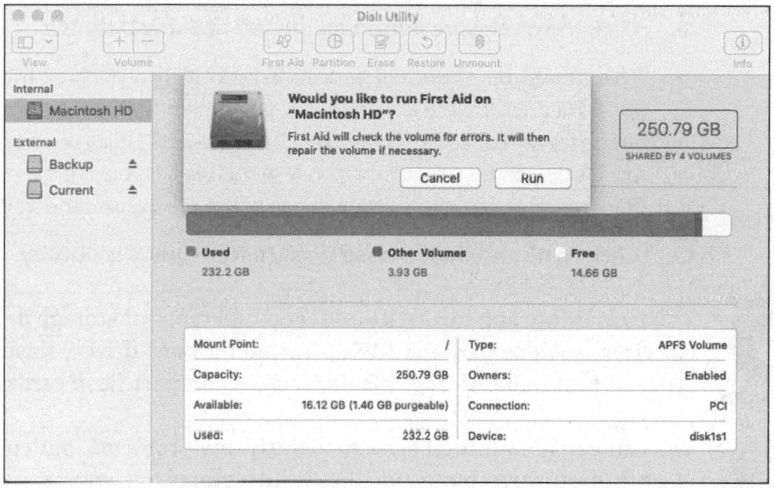

FIGURE 6-4:
Agree to run
First Aid.

If you're running First Aid on the startup disk, you'll be reminded that the startup disk will be locked during the process. Click Continue to proceed as shown in Figure 6-5.

TIP

Depending on the size of the disk, running First Aid can take a while. You may want to start it running before you quit for the day and then check it in the morning.

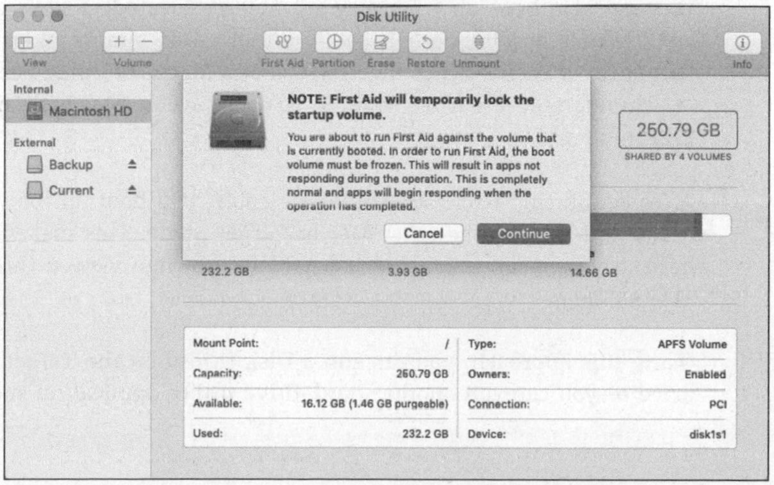

FIGURE 6-5:
If necessary, First
Aid will lock your
startup volume.

How long it will take depends on the size of your disk as well as the complexity of issues that may be discovered. Running First Aid overnight gives you the most flexibility. (You probably won't be able to run many apps during the process.)

When First Aid finishes running, a dialog appears telling you the First Aid process is complete.

5. **Click the disclosure button on the left of Show Details.**

    This shows you a bunch of geek stuff. Disk Utility reports on the problems found (if any). If there are problems, go to http://support.apple.com and chat with or call a support rep; have the Disk Utility report handy. Many problems can be solved fairly easily in this way. If you see the message "Operation Successful" at the bottom of the dialog, breathe a sigh of relief.

6. **Click Done and then choose Disk Utility ⇨ Quit Disk Utility.**

REMEMBER

The Disk Utility app can verify and repair all types of storage devices (except optical discs, such as CDs and DVDs), including hard drives, flash drives, and other types of removable storage media, such as compact flash cards.

REMEMBER

You can verify your hard drive to identify any problems, but you can't repair your startup hard drive by using Disk Utility stored on your startup hard drive. To repair your startup hard drive, you need to perform a Recovery Boot or reinstall the operating system, as described in the following sections or boot from another disk, as explained in the Tip.

Booting from another Mac through a Thunderbolt cable

You can also boot up from another Mac connected to your computer through an Ethernet or Thunderbolt cable. Either cable simply plugs into the respective ports of each Mac, connecting the two Macs. You may need a USB-Ethernet or Thunderbolt-Ethernet adapter if you have a MacBook model without an Ethernet port.

After connecting two Macs through a cable, you boot up the working Mac normally and boot up the other Mac in Target Mode. This makes the second Mac's hard drive appear as an external hard drive when viewed through the working Mac's Finder.

Using this approach, you can run a Disk Utility on the Target Mode Mac's hard drive or you can run another hard-drive utility application such as DiskWarrior (www.alsoft.com), Drive Genius (www.prosofteng.com), or Techtool Pro (www.micromat.com) on the working Mac to rescue the hard drive of the defective Mac. Starting a computer in Target Mode and using an app to repair it is much like jump-starting a car's dead battery by using a second car with a good battery.

To boot up from a second Mac connected by a cable, follow these steps:

1. Connect the second Mac to your Mac with an Ethernet or a Thunderbolt cable.

2. Turn on the working Mac.

3. Turn on the Mac that's having startup troubles and hold down the T key.

When the defective Mac's hard drive appears as an external drive on the working Mac, you can copy your important files from the hard drive or run a utility application to fix the hard drive on the defective Mac. After copying files or repairing the hard drive, you need to disconnect the cable and restart both Macs.

Using the Recovery Disk

The installation of a macOS system includes a hidden recovery disk that contains a stripped-down version of macOS. When you look at your disk with a tool such as Disk Utility, you normally don't see the recovery disk, but you can get to it following these instructions.

1. Choose Restart.

2. When you hear the Apple chime, press Cmd+R.

The Mac OS Recovery dialog appears prompting you to select a user you know the password for.

3. Select a user and click Next.

4. Enter your password.

The Mac OS Utilities dialog appears.

5. Choose one of the following options:

- *Restore From Time Machine Backup:* You can restore files from a Time Machine backup. The recovery disk has its own copy of Time Machine so that, as long as that disk is reachable, you can restore files to your Mac.

- *Reinstall macOS:* This option reinstalls a new copy of the OS. If you choose this option, follow the prompts to reinstall the operating system. When the reinstall is complete, connect the external hard drive that contains your Time Machine Backup and restore the backup.

- *Get Help Online:* This option enables you to access help from the Apple Support website.

- *Disk Utility:* This option enables you to repair the disk or erase it. The latter option permanently erases all data on the disk. If you choose this option, make sure you have a recent Time Machine backup available.

6. Click Continue.

What happens next differs depending on the option you choose. Follow the prompts to perform the selected task.

TIP

Another occasion when you may want to erase your hard drive and reinstall the operating system is if you plan on selling your Mac or giving it away. For security reasons, you want to wipe out your data with one of the secure-erase options in Disk Utility and return the Mac to its original condition so someone else can personalize the Mac.

Removing Jammed CDs or DVDs

Although Apple no longer ships optical drives in Macs, you may have an older Mac or even a new Apple SuperDrive. If so, this section is for you.

If a CD or DVD gets jammed in your Mac's internal or external CD/DVD drive, you can try one (or more) of the following methods to eject the stuck disc:

» If it has one, press the Eject key on your keyboard. (The MacBook Air, for example, does not have an Eject key, because it doesn't have an internal CD drive).

» Drag the CD/DVD icon on the Desktop to the Trash icon on the Dock. (The Trash icon turns into an Eject icon to let you know that your Mac wants to eject the disc but does not intend to delete the information on the disc.)

» Choose ⇨ Restart, and hold down the mouse or trackpad button while your Mac boots up.

» Click the Eject button next to the CD/DVD icon in the Sidebar of a Finder window. (Click the Finder icon on the Dock to open a new Finder window.)

» Click the Eject button next to the CD/DVD icon in iTunes.

» Choose Controls ⇨ Eject DVD from inside the DVD Player application.

» Load the Disk Utility application (located in the Utilities folder inside the Applications folder), click the CD/DVD icon, and click the Eject icon.

>> Select the CD/DVD icon on the Desktop and choose File ⇨ Eject from the main menu.

>> Select the CD/DVD icon on the Desktop and press ⌘+E.

>> Control-click the CD/DVD icon on the Desktop and choose Eject from the menu that appears.

WARNING

Although it may be tempting, don't jam tweezers, a flathead screwdriver, or any other object inside your CD/DVD drive to try to pry out a jammed disc. Not only can this scratch the disc surface, but it can also physically damage the CD/DVD drive.

Prevention is the best medicine, so here a few pointers on how to avoid getting discs jammed in the drive in the first place:

>> Do not use mini or business card CDs/DVDs or any other non-119mm optical discs in slot-loading drives, which you slide the disc into a slot.

>> Be careful of using discs with hand-applied labels in the drive. These labels can easily jam or make the disc too thick to eject properly.

>> If your Mac's disc drive is repeatedly acting strange or not working properly when you try to play a music CD or watch a DVD, your disc drive may be on its last legs and may have to be repaired or replaced. Stop using the drive and take (or send) your Mac to Apple or an authorized service provider for a checkup.

TIP

If you purchase an external optical disc drive, instead of Apple's SuperDrive, you may be happier with a tray-loading drive. They tend to be faster, have fewer problems, and last longer.

REMEMBER

This section about how to manage jammed discs is a good reminder why Apple (and most of the tech industries) adopt non-physical ways of managing data such as streaming music and video as well as Wi-Fi.

4

Using Your Mac as a Media Center

Contents at a Glance

CHAPTER 1: **Getting Acquainted with Media on Your Mac** 443

Using Your Apple ID to Enjoy and Share Media 443

Getting into the Media Apps in macOS Catalina 453

CHAPTER 2: **Tuning In and Listening with Music** 455

Getting to Know the Music App 456

Working with Playlists 458

Organizing Your Music 468

Adjusting Music Preferences 470

Playing Audio with Music 474

Listening to the Radio 484

Shopping at the iTunes Store 485

CHAPTER 3: **Enjoying Podcasts, News, and TV** 491

Finding and Playing Podcasts 491

Reading the News: Extra, Extra, Read All about It! 496

Watching TV on Your Mac 500

CHAPTER 4: **Reading and Listening to Books on Your Mac** 505

Thumbing through Books 505

CHAPTER 5: **Looking at Photos** 515

Understanding Digital Photography 515

Transferring Digital Images to the Mac 517

Organizing Your Photo Library 521

Capturing Photos with Photo Booth 534

Editing Photos with Photos 537

Sharing Photos 541

Chapter **1**

Getting Acquainted with Media on Your Mac

Computers started out as "calculation engines," but although plenty of people use them for mathematical and scientific research and analysis, they've become digital companions that let you browse and create many types of media. In fact, it's probably safe to say that the use of computers to perform complex calculations is less common that the use of computers for media development and enjoyment.

In this chapter, we show you how to share media with other family members using the Family Sharing feature.

Using Your Apple ID to Enjoy and Share Media

Your Apple ID is used to buy music or TV shows or anything else Apple is selling. In general, you should have only one Apple ID.

TECHNICAL STUFF

As of now, you can't merge two Apple IDs. But you may actually *want* more than one Apple ID. For example, developers use Apple IDs to manage their apps, and authors use Apple IDs to manage their books. But if you're an author or a developer, you need two different Apple IDs.

Whether it's because you have multiple Apple IDs or because you want to share media with a friend or family member, you may want to work with multiple Apple IDs at the same time.

Apple provides two ways for sharing Apple IDs: Media Sharing and Family Sharing. Both are accessed through System Preferences (see Figure 1-1). Family Sharing is at the upper right, and Media Sharing is part of Sharing in the fourth row.

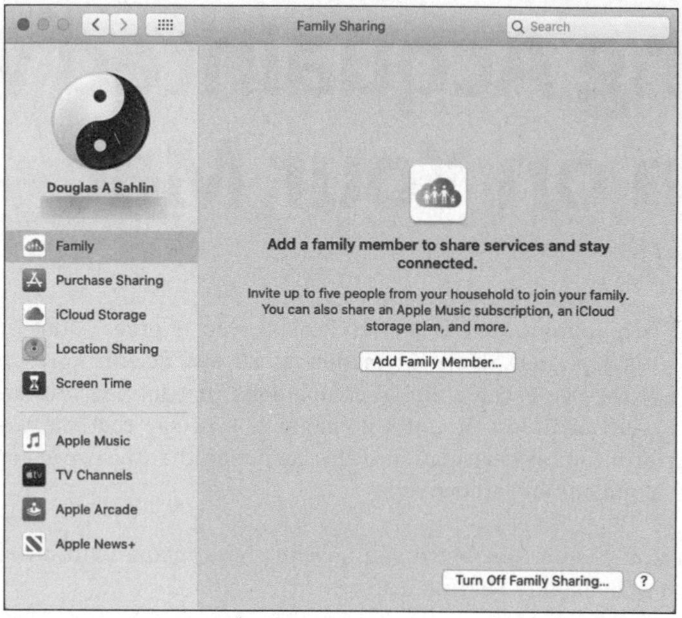

FIGURE 1-1:
Set Preferences for Family Sharing.

Media Sharing

Media Sharing (previously known as Home Sharing) lets you share your media with other devices on your Wi-Fi network. You set up Media Sharing through Sharing preferences. Choose ⇨ System Preferences, and click Sharing. This opens the Sharing pane, where you can set detailed Sharing preferences, as shown in Figure 1-2.

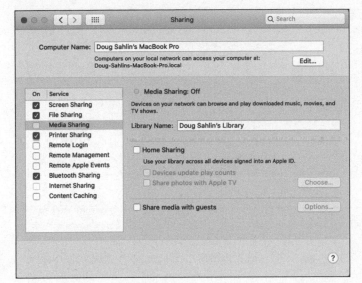

FIGURE 1-2:
Turn Media
Sharing on or off.

You can turn Media Sharing on or off. By default, you have a library created with your username, which can be shared across devices with an Apple ID. You also have an option to share your media with guests who may be signed in with another Apple ID.

Family Sharing

Family Sharing lets you share music, apps, movies, books, and TV shows with other members of your family. In addition to media, iCloud storage can be included in the family plan, as can your location, calendar, or reminders.

To use Family Sharing, follow these steps:

1. **Choose ⇨ System Preferences and click Family Sharing in the upper right.**

The Family Sharing pane, shown in Figure 1-3, appears.

2. **Click Next.**

The screen shown in Figure 1-4 appears.

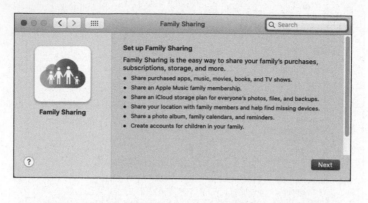

FIGURE 1-3:
Family Sharing
lets you share
many items.

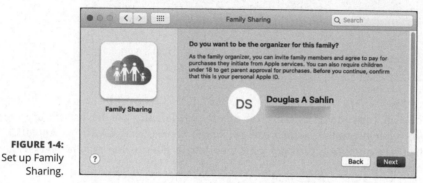

FIGURE 1-4:
Set up Family
Sharing.

3. **Select an organizer for the family and click Next.**

   The organizer must be someone with an Apple ID that is linked to a credit card.
   The organizer will pay for all family purchases.

4. **Decide whether you want to start sharing your Apple purchases right
   away or not now, as shown in Figure 1-5, and click Next.**

FIGURE 1-5:
Start sharing
(or not).

You're shown the specific credit card to be used for purchases (see Figure 1-6). You can change this credit card later.

FIGURE 1-6:
Accept the
credit card.

5. **Click Next.**

6. **The iTunes Terms and Conditions appears.**

   In order to enable Family Sharing, you must agree to iTunes Terms and Conditions.

7. **Click the I Agree to the iTunes Terms and Conditions check box and then click Agree.**

8. **Decide whether to share your location with family members (see Figure 1-7).**

   This feature enables you to share the location of your devices with family members in Find My iPhone. You can also share your location with family members when using Messages.

FIGURE 1-7:
Set location
privacy.

9. **Click Done.**

   The Family Sharing dialog refreshes (see Figure 1-8). Now you can add up to five family members by clicking the Add Family Member button and following the prompts.

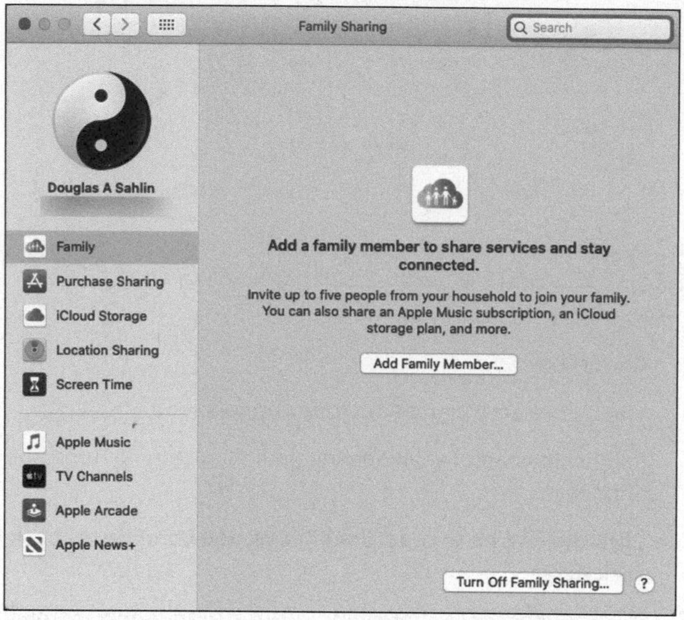

FIGURE 1-8: Set family members.

To change the Family Sharing settings later, choose ⇨ System Preferences and click Family Sharing. The left side of the Family Sharing preferences window lets you select each component individually.

Purchase Sharing (shown in Figure 1-9) lets you manage the payments for family purchases.

iCloud storage can be shared among family members; you can set it with the iCloud Storage tab shown in Figure 1-10.

When you come to location settings directly rather than in the sequence shown in Figure 1-7, you see the description shown in Figure 1-11.

FIGURE 1-9:
Manage purchase
payments.

FIGURE 1-10.
Share iCloud
storage.

FIGURE 1-11:
Share your
location.

Screen Time is a built-in app that lets you manage the amount of time you use on the screen of your device (and when you use it). You can set that for your family members through Family Sharing, as shown in Figure 1-12.

FIGURE 1-12:
Share Screen
Time.

Apple Music supports family memberships, which allow each family member to have a separate library. The cost of the Family Music account is billed through the organizer's credit card (as is everything). If you're not already a member of Apple Music, click the Start a Free Trial button, shown in Figure 1-13. Follow the prompts and you and your family members can rock on or Bach on.

FIGURE 1-13: Share Apple Music.

Apple TV is a subscription service that you can share with family members. It has really blossomed and now features many series. To learn more about Apple TV, click the Learn More button shown in Figure 1-14. You can subscribe to TV shows, purchase movies, and much more.

Apple Arcade is another new — as of this writing — Apple service. With a subscription to Apple Arcade, you have access to more than 100 games that are available on your Apple devices, such as the iPhone and iPad. For more information, click the Learn More button, shown in Figure 1-15.

Apple News made its debut in 2015. It has grown and evolved since then; in Catalina, it has significant new features. If you're not subscribed to Apple News, click the Learn More button shown in Figure 1-16.

FIGURE 1-14:
Apple TV,
the apple of
Apple's eye.

FIGURE 1-15:
Share games
when you
subscribe to
Apple Arcade.

FIGURE 1-16:
Share Apple
News.

Getting into the Media Apps in macOS Catalina

There are five types of media that you can use on your Mac: music, podcasts, books, photos, and TV and movies.

With the release of macOS Catalina in 2019, Apple has changed its approach to media. No longer do you buy most of your media from Apple on iTunes. Instead, you find five new specialized media apps in your Dock when you install Catalina. As is the case with all icons in the Dock, when you hover over an icon you see its name. Only one icon can be selected at a time, so you identify them in the Dock by their images. Figure 1-17 shows the Dock with the media apps labeled.

TIP

The media apps are available on macOS and iOS in comparable versions. Your music libraries and playlists are preserved using your Apple ID across your devices.

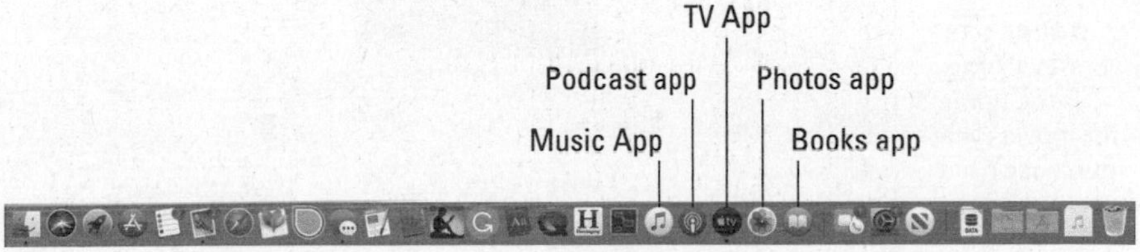

FIGURE 1-17:
The media apps
are at the left
of the Dock in
Catalina.

TV App

Podcast app   Photos app

Music App   Books app

Here are the media apps labeled in Figure 1–15:

- **Music:** It all started with iTunes and music. The original iTunes app has been simplified and streamlined. This is where you purchase music, set up your playlists, and play your music.

- **Podcasts:** Use this app to find podcasts that interest you, download them, and listen to them. You can see the top podcasts and download podcasts that may be suitable for a place without Wi-Fi.

- **Books:** You can buy books from the Book Store, and you can add new books in PDF format to your own library. PDF-based books, as well as books developed with Apple's authoring tools, work the same way, allowing you to read, bookmark, and annotate your book as you go along. There's a separate store for audiobooks.

- **Photos:** With Photos you can import images to your computer, edit them to pixel perfection, and organize them.

- **Apple TV:** Apple TV is the newest entry into Apple's media services. It comes along with Apple's launch of new shows on Apple TV. With Apple TV, you can view original Apple series, TV shows, and music you purchase. You can view Apple TV with the Apple TV app on your computer. You can also download the Apple TV app for iOS devices. Movies you purchase are added to your Apple TV Library, as shown in Figure 1-18.

FIGURE 1-18:
Your TV Library is the home for movies you purchase from Apple.

IN THIS CHAPTER

» **Looking at the Music app**

» **Creating playlists**

» **Keeping track of your music**

» **Setting your Music preferences**

» **Listening to audio in Music**

» **Tuning in to Music Radio**

» **Browsing and buying from the iTunes Store**

Chapter **2**

Tuning In and Listening with Music

iTunes changed the way people buy and play music. It's hard to overestimate the role that iTunes played in bringing music to digital devices around the world while support payments to artists. In 2019, with the announcement of macOS Catalina, Apple split iTunes into separate apps for Music, TV, and Podcasts (Books was already separate). This chapter covers Music from A to Z.

We tell you how Music is set up and how to listen to your music. We show you how to set up playlists on your own or let Music do it for you with Genius. We also give you a tour of the iTunes Store so you can find out how to add other media to your Mac — so have your Apple ID handy. Finally, we explain how to share media with other people.

Getting to Know the Music App

Your Mac (if it has macOS Catalina installed) comes with the new Music app. You use the Music app to organize, play, and convert audio and video formats. If you have an external Apple USB SuperDrive, you can also use Music to burn CDs or DVDs.

TECHNICAL STUFF

Apple has not sold a Mac with a built-in optical drive for several years. The last such Mac was discontinued in June 2012 and remained on sale in some locations until 2016.

The most recent version of Music (as of this writing) contains Apple Music, which with a subscription (as of this writing, you can subscribe for a free three-month trial) enables you to listen to music from Apple's huge library — 50 million songs as of this writing — and listen to Radio by clicking the Radio link in the Apple Music section in the left sidebar.

Music is simpler and more streamlined than iTunes was. This simplicity is also reflected in Podcasts and TV. Figure 2-1 shows the basics of the Music window.

FIGURE 2-1:
Manage your media from the Music app.

The Music window has two basic sections: the sidebar and the right section, known as the Music window, where you manage your music when perusing your Library or look for new music at the iTunes Store.

The sidebar

The sidebar (on the left) organizes your music. As you see in Figure 2-1, there are four sections to the sidebar: Apple Music, Library, Store, and Playlists. We cover each of these sections next.

Apple Music

Apple Music is a subscription-based product from Apple that lets you play any of 50 million tracks whenever and wherever you want, from any of your devices, without interruptions from ads. You can find out more about Apple Music at www. apple.com/apple-music/. The Apple Music section of the sidebar organizes the music in your Apple Music subscription.

As you see in Figure 2-1, your Apple Music subscription includes music suggested for you under the title "For You," as well as music you choose by browsing. Apple Radio is also part of the Apple Music sidebar section. You may see other sections of the Apple Music sidebar, depending on your choices and options.

You have three basic ways of listening to Apple Music:

>> **For You:** This section is constructed based on your previous browsing experiences. It's generally going to play the music you've liked. This is the tool to use if you want Apple Music to play music for you using your previous history.

>> **Browse:** This option lets you explore the 50 million Apple Music tracks. Here's how to find something new to you. This is the tool to use if you want to explore on your own.

>> **Radio:** Apple Music contains live radio stations built by Apple, such as Beats 1. This is the tool to use to listen to live content.

TIP

If you're not sure if Apple Music is your cup of tea, you can take a sip by clicking the Try It Free button (refer to Figure 2-1).

Library

As you see in Figure 2-2, the Music app makes it possible for you to manage a library of your music. It consists of music that you've purchased or added on your own. You can see recent additions, as well as browse by artist, album, or song, so that your view into your personal music library is as manageable as possible.

FIGURE 2-2:
Manage your
Library in the
Music app.

Playlists

You can use Music to select a group of songs and store those songs as a *playlist*. When you want to hear that group of songs, just select the playlist rather than having to select each song individually. Maybe you want to make a Sleep playlist, full of classical music to drift off to. Or maybe you want to make a Dinner Party playlist full of the kind of music you like to play for your favorite dinner guests. The possibilities are endless.

The Music window

To the right of the sidebar, is a vast piece of the Music app's real estate. And even if it were only half as large as it is, it wouldn't be half-vast. But we digress. What you see in the Music window depends on which link you click in the sidebar. Figure 2-1 shows content you see if you click Browse under Apple Music. Figure 2-2 shows the content when you click Albums in the Library section of the sidebar.

Working with Playlists

When you're ready to create a playlist, you have a few options:

>> **Ordinary playlist:** A list of favorite songs you select to include in that playlist.

>> **Smart Playlist:** You define rules for which songs to include, such as only songs recorded by a specific artist. As your audio file collection grows, a Smart

Playlist can automatically include any new songs by that specific artist or by whatever other criteria you define for that particular Smart Playlist.

All playlists are shown in the Playlists section of the sidebar.

Ordinary playlists

The simplest playlist to create is one that contains specific songs, such as a favorite album, a group of songs you want to listen to when you go for a run or workout, or perhaps every song by a particular artist.

Creating an ordinary playlist

To create a playlist of particular songs you want to group, follow these steps:

1. **In Music, choose File➪New➪ Playlist.**

   An untitled playlist appears, highlighted, in a new pane in the Music window, as shown in Figure 2-3.

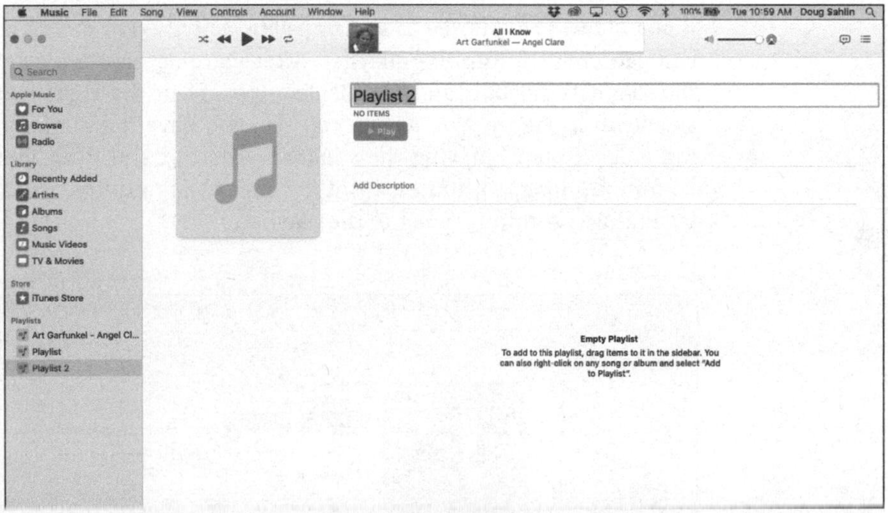

FIGURE 2-3: Click and drag songs to newly created playlists

2. **Type a name for your playlist and then press Return.**

3. **Click a Library link in the sidebar.**

   If you know the song you want in your playlist, click the songs link. If you want a playlist of specific albums, click the Albums link.

4. **Click and drag songs, albums, or artists from the Music window and drop them on your playlist.**

5. **Click the Done button.**

TIP

To make a quick playlist, hold down the ⌘ key, click the songs you want in the playlist, and then choose File⇨New⇨Playlist from Selection. Your new playlist appears in the Music window with the default name highlighted where you can type a more-identifying name.

TIP

To create a playlist of an album, click Albums in the Library section of the sidebar, choose the album you want as a playlist, right-click, and from the context menu choose Add to Playlist⇨New Playlist. Use the same technique to create a playlist of your favorite singer, by clicking Artists in the Library sidebar, right-clicking your favorite artist, and then choosing Add to Playlist⇨New Playlist.

Adding songs to an ordinary playlist

After you create a playlist, you can edit it. To add a song to a playlist, right-click the song and from the context menu, choose Add to Playlist⇨*Playlist Name.* The song you added appears in the playlist.

A playlist can be tailored to suit a specific activity. For example, if you're runner, you can create a Running playlist. After you populate a playlist, click its link in the Playlists sidebar, and the playlist appears in the right side of the interface, as shown in Figure 2-4. As you can see, you have many options, including adding a description, playing the songs in order, or shuffling them. This playlist is 26 minutes long, 4 minutes shy of the desired 30 minutes, which is easily rectified by adding a 4-minute song to the playlist.

FIGURE 2-4:
Open a playlist, and Music gives you many options.

Deleting songs from an ordinary playlist

To delete a song from a playlist, follow these steps:

1. **In Music, click the playlist that contains the songs you want to delete.**

   Your chosen playlist appears onscreen.

2. **Click a song to delete and then press the Delete key.**

   Alternatively, you can right-click a playlist song and from the context menu choose Remove from Playlist. After choosing either option, a confirmation dialog appears, asking whether you really want to remove the song from your playlist.

3. **Click Remove Song.**

REMEMBER

Deleting a song from a playlist doesn't delete the song from your Music library.

Smart Playlists

Manually adding and removing songs from a playlist can get tedious, especially if you regularly add new songs to your Music audio collection. Instead of placing specific songs in a playlist, a Smart Playlist lets you define specific criteria for the types of songs to store in that playlist, such as songs recorded earlier than 1990, or songs under a particular genre, such as Blues, Country, Hard Rock, or Folk. To create and use a Smart Playlist, you tag songs, define rules to determine which songs to include, and finally, edit existing playlists.

Tagging songs

To sort your song collection accurately into Smart Playlists, you can tag individual songs with descriptive information. Most songs stored as digital audio files already have some information stored in specific tags, such as the artist or album name. However, you may still want to edit or add new tags to help Smart Playlists sort your song collection.

To edit or add tags to a song, follow these steps:

1. **In Music, click a song that you want to tag and choose Song⇨Info (or press ⌘+I) to display the song track's information.**

2. **Click the Info tab to display text boxes where you can type in or change the song track's associated information, rate a song, or add comments as shown in Figure 2-5.**

   Alternatively, you can right-click a song and choose Get Info from the context menu.

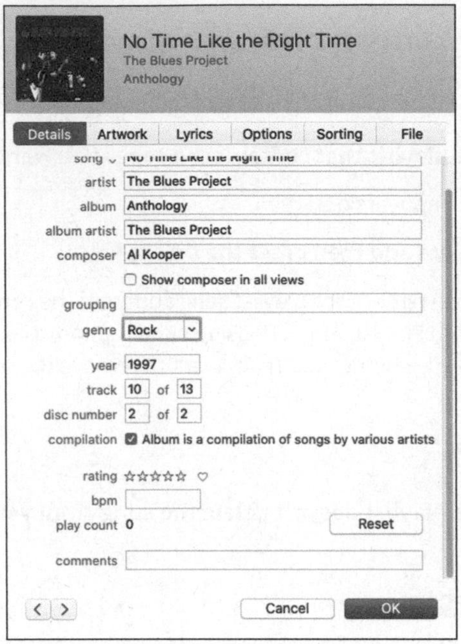

No Time Like the Right Time
The Blues Project
Anthology

| Details | Artwork | Lyrics | Options | Sorting | File |

song	No Time Like the Right Time
artist	The Blues Project
album	Anthology
album artist	The Blues Project
composer	Al Kooper
	☐ Show composer in all views
grouping	
genre	Rock
year	1997
track	10 of 13
disc number	2 of 2
compilation	☑ Album is a compilation of songs by various artists
rating	☆☆☆☆☆ ♡
bpm	
play count	0 Reset
comments	

< >   Cancel   OK

FIGURE 2-5:
Edit or enter
labels to identify
a song.

3. **Click a text field and edit or enter information.**

4. **In the same Info pane, open the Genre pop-up menu to add or change the song's genre.**

5. **Click the song track's other tabs, such as Sorting or Options, shown in Figure 2-4, to make additional adjustments to your selected audio file.**

6. **Assign a rating to the song.**

   You can choose a rating from one to five stars, or click the heart to love the song.

TIP

You can also love a song by clicking Songs in the sidebar which displays a list of songs in your Library, and then clicking the heart icon that appears next to the song's genre. To love an album, click Albums, which displays album covers; then click the album cover, click the three dots at the lower-right corner of the album, and choose Love from the context menu.

7. **When you finish tagging the song track, click OK to close the dialog and return to the main Music window.**

   The info for a song has many tabs, as shown in Figure 2-5. In the Options tab, shown in Figure 2-6, you can adjust the start and stop points of a song, adjust the volume, and choose whether to apply a digital equalizer to the song.

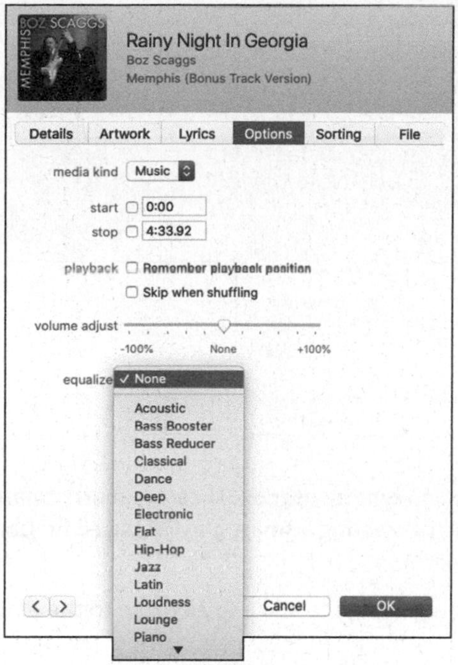

FIGURE 2-6:
Adjust volume,
choose an
equalizer setting,
and set playback
options here.

Creating a Smart Playlist

Smart Playlists use tags to sort and organize your song collection. You can use existing tags that are created for songs automatically (such as Artist and Album), as well as tags that you add to your songs to define the type of songs you want that Smart Playlist to store. A specific criterion for choosing a song is a *rule*.

To create a Smart Playlist, follow these steps:

1. **In Music, choose File⇨New⇨Smart Playlist.**

A Smart Playlist dialog appears, prompting you to define a rule for specifying which songs to store in the playlist.

2. **Choose an option from the Match pop-up menu.**

Your Smart Playlist can match all media, or just music.

3. **Open the first pop-up menu on the left and choose a category, such as Artist, Genre, or Date Added, for deciding which criteria will be used to automatically add songs to the Smart Playlist.**

4. **Open the second pop-up menu in the middle and choose an option.**

This option determines how Music uses the information you enter in the text field. The default option is Contains. In Figure 2-7, we're creating a Smart Playlist that contains songs by the artist Art Garfunkel.

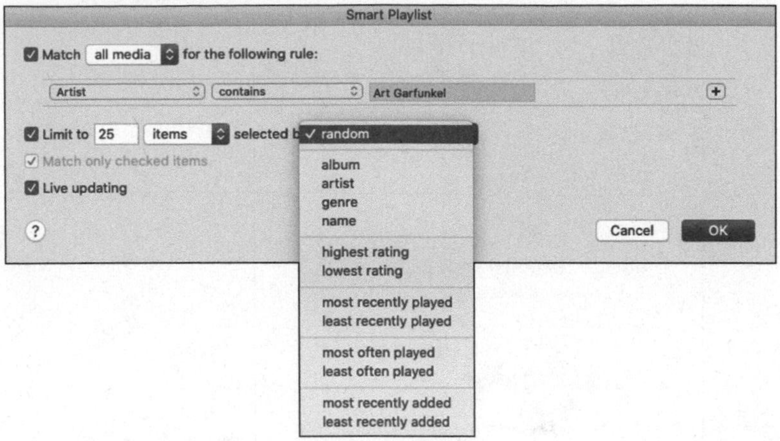

Smart Playlist

☑ Match all media ⇕ for the following rule:

    Artist ⇕ contains ⇕ Art Garfunkel ⊕

☑ Limit to 25 items ⇕ selected b ✓ random
☑ Match only checked items   album
☑ Live updating   artist
    genre
?   name   Cancel OK

highest rating
lowest rating

most recently played
least recently played

most often played
least often played

most recently added
least recently added

FIGURE 2-7:
Define a rule for
choosing songs.

5. **Click the text box and type a criterion, such as an artist name or a specific date if you're creating a smart playlist based on Date Added from the first pop-up menu.**

6. **(Optional) Click the plus sign to add another rule to the Playlist, as shown in Figure 2-7.**

After you add a second rule, the All or Any menu appears next to Match in the first line.

7. **(Optional) Make other selections in the Smart Playlist dialog:**

- *Limit To:* Select this check box and enter a number to define the maximum number of (choose one) songs/file size/minutes/hours/items the Smart Playlist can hold; then choose an option that suits your desired Smart Playlist criteria from the Selected By pop-up menu.

- *Selected By:* Choose an option from the pop-up menu shown in Figure 2-7.

- *Live Updating:* Select this check box if you want the Smart Playlist to update its list of songs automatically each time you add or remove a song from your Music song collection library or change a tag (on a song) that's used in the rule.

8. **Click OK.**

Your Smart Playlist appears in the list of playlists in the Playlists section of the sidebar. Smart Playlists have an icon that looks like a music symbol inside a circle to the left of the name.

TIP

To rename any playlist, double-click the name in the Playlist list to highlight the name, and then type in a new name to replace the existing name.

Editing a Smart Playlist

After you create a Smart Playlist, you can modify it, such as adding more rules or editing any existing rules. To edit a Smart Playlist, follow these steps:

1. **In the Playlists section of the sidebar, select the Smart Playlist that you want to edit.**

Smart Playlists have their own icons that appear to the left of the list's name and look like a music symbol with a circle around it.

2. **Double-click the Smart Playlist.**

The Smart Playlist appears in the Music window of the Music app interface (see Figure 2-8).

FIGURE 2-8:
This playlist ain't
no dummy.

3. **Click Edit Rules.**

The Smart Playlist dialog appears (refer to Figure 2-7).

4. **Make any changes to your Smart Playlist rule(s) and then click OK.**

If you want to cut to the chase when modifying a playlist, right-click its name and choose Edit Rules from the context menu.

TIP

If you have a lot of playlists, the Playlists list can get pretty crowded. You can streamline your playlist list by filing similar playlists in folders. Choose File ⇨ New Playlist Folder. Double-click the folder to rename it with a meaningful name, and then click and drag the playlists you want to file to the folder.

TIP

Genius playlists, shuffles, or mixes

If your guests are already ringing the doorbell and you don't have time to create the background music for your party, you can let Music create a Genius playlist, shuffle, or mix for you with songs Music thinks go well together.

Genius playlists

A Genius playlist is created based on a song you choose. Genius also suggests new songs for you to purchase that it thinks you'll like based on your purchase history.

Here's how to create a Genius playlist:

1. Choose File ⇨ Library ⇨ Turn On Genius.

The Genius options appear in the Music window of the Music app interface (see Figure 2-9). The Genius dialog gives you information about how to create a Genius playlist and more.

FIGURE 2-9:
Create a playlist like Einstein would create.

REMEMBER

You need an Internet connection for Genius to work.

2. Click the Turn on Genius button.

The dialog refreshing showing you the steps Genius is doing to create absolutely brilliant playlists.

Music accesses the iTunes Store so it can analyze your interests in music, movies, and TV shows, see what other users who have similar tastes have in their collections, and then make informed suggestions about media you may like.

3. **Click a song you like in your music collection and then choose File⇨ New⇨ Genius Playlist.**

   A playlist is created from your music library with songs that Music thinks go well with the song you selected.

   The Genius playlist is automatically named with the song it's based on and saved in the playlist list.

4. **Click the pull-down menu next to 25 Songs under the playlist name to change how many songs you want in your Genius playlist: 25, 50, 75, or 100.**

5. **Click the Refresh button to update your Genius playlist after you add more music to your Music library.**

WARNING

Sometimes instead of Create Genius Playlist (as in Step 2), you see No Genius Suggestions. Genius seems somewhat limited if you have non-English, classical, or pre-1960 music. Tagging your songs, as we explain previously in the "Tagging songs" section, can help Genius create playlists because tagging gives Music more information to work with.

DELETING A PLAYLIST

You may want to delete an ordinary playlist or a Smart Playlist you've created. To delete a playlist, follow these steps:

1. **In Music, click a playlist that you want to delete in the Playlists list and press the Delete key.**

   A confirmation dialog appears, asking whether you really want to delete your playlist.

   Remember: Deleting a playlist doesn't physically delete the audio files from your Music library.

2. **Click the Delete button.**

   The playlist is removed.

If Music created a Genius mix that you don't like, you can delete unwanted Genius mixes by using the same procedure.

Genius shuffles

A Genius shuffle is based on your existing collection. To create a Genius shuffle, simply choose Controls⇨Genius Shuffle, and Music goes to work. Click the Up Next button to see the songs in the shuffle. If you don't like the lineup, click Shuffle Again.

Organizing Your Music

You can use Music to play music on your Mac, but Music shows its real strength when you use it to organize your media files. Before we get into listening, watching, and learning, we want to explain how Music manages your media.

You have many ways to customize your view of content you keep in Music. Figure 2-10 shows one of them.

FIGURE 2-10:
Manage your media from the Music window.

>> **Toolbar:** Across the top, you find the playback controls, the now-playing display, volume control, and playback options.

>> **Left sidebar:** The left sidebar is divided into four categories, Apple Music, Library, Store, and Playlists. At the top of the sidebar is a Search text field.

To tweak the various views — for example, add or change the columns you see in Songs view — choose View⇨Show View Options, as shown in Figure 2-11, and select the things you want to see. Open the Sort By menu to change the order of the selections. Each view — Albums, Artists, Genres, Playlists, and

TIP

TIP

Internet — has different view options except for Radio, which has no view options.

To narrow the choices the Songs or Playlists view displays, right click the title bar directly above the first song in the list, and choose an option from the drop-down menu shown in Figure 2-12. With this menu, you can hide a column or display it.

FIGURE 2-11:
Customize the information you see with View Options.

TIP

To change the order in which items in a column are sorted, click the column. For example, Artists are sorted in alphabetical order. Click the column to change the sort from ascending to descending.

» **Devices:** When you connect a device (such as an iPhone, iPod, iPad, or MP3 player) to your Mac, it's listed in the left column. Click the device name and it appears on the right side of the interface. You can then sync the device with Music. After syncing the device with music, right-click the device's name and then choose Eject from the pop-up menu to safely eject it from your computer.

» **iTunes Store:** Click this button to go to the iTunes Store, which we discus later in this chapter.

FIGURE 2-12:
So many
columns, so
little time.

>> **Status bar:** Choose View ➪ Show Status Bar to see (across the bottom of the window) the number of items in a category, the playing time, and the amount of storage the media occupies.

Adjusting Music Preferences

Choosing how Music should respond when you insert a CD, what type of audio file format it uses to import your CD audio tracks, and which Library categories you want to display in the left-hand column of the Music application window are all options you can adjust by accessing the Music Preferences dialog. We go through the General and Parental Control preferences in this section, and throughout the chapter, we direct you to Preferences to adjust other aspects of Music. To open the Music Preferences dialog and adjust the settings, follow these steps:

1. Choose Music ➪ Preferences.

The Music Preferences window appears.

2. Click the General icon (if it isn't already selected) to display the General settings pane, as shown in Figure 2-13.

3. Select the check boxes for the items you want to see in the Library pop-up sidebar.

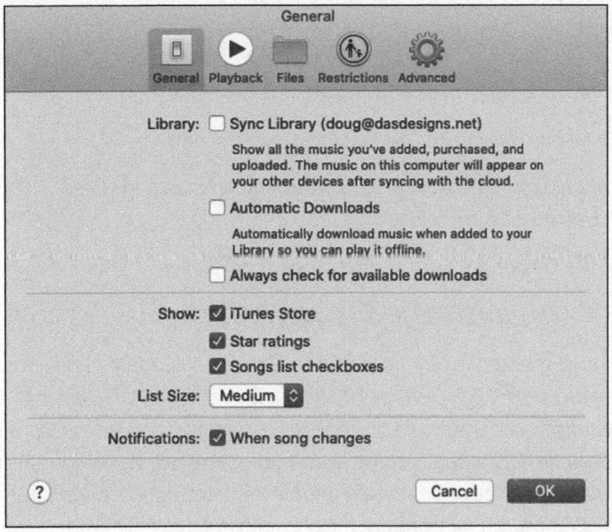

FIGURE 2-13:
Tailor Music to
your liking.

4. **Select or deselect the check boxes in the Notifications section to indicate whether you want to see song changes in Notification Center.**

5. **To specify what you want to happen whenever you insert an audio CD into your Mac, open the When a CD Is Inserted pop-up menu and choose one of the following:**

   - *Show CD:* Displays a list of audio tracks

   - *Play CD:* Displays a list of audio tracks and starts playing the first track

   - *Ask to Import CD:* Displays a dialog, asking whether you want to import all audio tracks from the CD (this is the default setting)

   - *Import CD:* Automatically converts all audio tracks into digital files

   - *Import CD and Eject:* Automatically converts all audio tracks into digital files and ejects the CD when it finishes without playing any tracks

6. **Select the Automatically Retrieve CD Track Names from Internet check box if you want Music to try to identify audio tracks by their song titles.**

   If this option isn't selected, each audio track will have a generic name (such as Track 1).

7. **To specify the file format and audio quality of the audio files Music will create when importing CD audio tracks, on the Files tab, click the Import Settings button.**

   The Import Settings preferences pane opens, as shown in Figure 2-14.

Tuning In and Listening with Music

a. Open the Import Using pop-up menu and choose one of the following:

AAC Encoder: Stores audio tracks as AAC files

AIFF Encoder: Stores audio tracks as AIFF files

Apple Lossless Encoder: Stores audio tracks as a lossless compressed .m4a file

MP3 Encoder: Stores audio tracks as MP3 files

WAV Encoder: Stores audio tracks as WAV files

b. Open the Setting pop-up menu and choose the audio quality for your files. Your choices are: High Quality (128 kbps), iTunes Plus (256 kbps, 44,100 kHz), Spoken Podcast, or Custom. If you choose Custom, you specify the Stereo Bit Rate, Sample Rate, and Channels from pop-up menus. When you specify Custom, you also have the option to use Variable Bit Rate Encoding (VBR), High Efficiency Encoding (HE), or Optimize the encoding for voice. The latter should only be chosen if all you encode are podcasts, or spoken-word tutorials.

REMEMBER

The higher the audio quality, the larger the file size.

c. Click OK to close the Import Settings preferences pane and return to the Files Preferences pane

d. (Optional) Select the Use Error Correction When Reading Audio CDs check box to increase the chances that Music can retrieve and convert audio tracks from a damaged or scratched CD.

e. Click OK to exit the Import Settings dialog and return to the General Preferences pane.

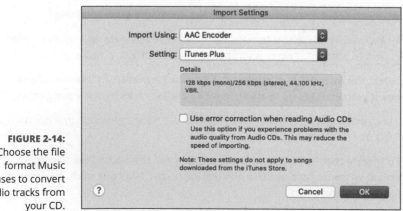

FIGURE 2-14:
Choose the file format Music uses to convert audio tracks from your CD.

8. (Optional) **If you share your Mac with children, you may want to set up some preferences which can limit the type of media that can be accessed in sharing or the iTunes Store. To do this, click the Restrictions button at the top of the Preferences window, as shown in Figure 2-15, and do the following in the Parental Controls window that opens:**

- *Disable:* Select Music Profiles, Apple Music, iTunes Store, Shared Libraries to deny access to those categories.

- *Ratings For:* Use the pop-up menu to change the country you want to see ratings for.

- *Restrict:* Choose limits you want to place on specific media, such as music with explicit content, movie ratings, and age ranges for TV shows. You choose the movie ratings and TV shows options from pop-up menus.

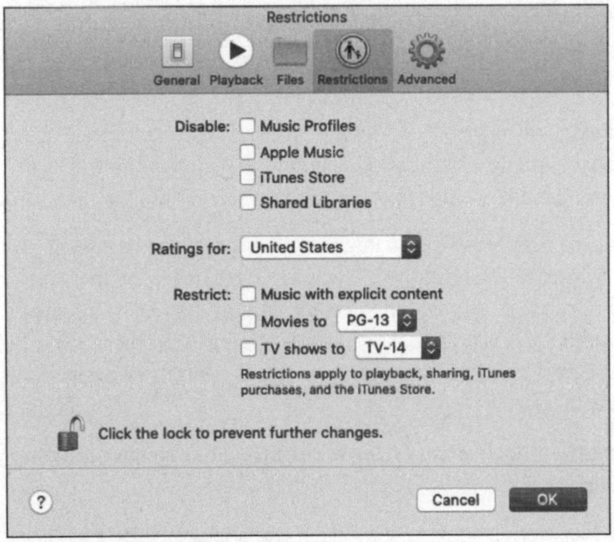

FIGURE 2-15:
Limit what media
can be accessed
in Music.

Then click the lock icon so no future changes can be made to the Restrictions preferences.

9. **Enter your admin password.**

The causes the lock icon to lock, and no further changes can be made until you access the Restrictions pane again, click the lock, and enter your admin password to add or remove restrictions.

10. **Click OK to close the Music Preferences dialog.**

You return to the main Music application window.

Tuning In and Listening with Music

Playing Audio with Music

Music turns your Mac into a stereo system and radio. You can play the most common audio files (MP3, WAV, AAC, and AIFF) on your Mac and connect headphones or external speakers to upgrade the playback quality and listening experience.

To launch Music, click the Music icon on the Dock or Launchpad.

Listening to CDs

You probably have audio CDs of your favorite albums, but rather than play them in a CD player, you can play them on your Mac — with an internal or external optical disc drive — by using Music. Much like a CD player, Music can play audio tracks on a CD in order or randomly. Even better, Music lets you choose which audio tracks you want to hear. To play an audio CD in Music, follow these steps:

1. **With Music open, insert an audio CD into your Mac.**

A dialog may appear (depending on the Music Preferences settings you choose), asking whether you want to import all audio tracks on the CD into Music. We discuss this process in the next section. For now, click No.

If you're connected to the Internet, Music searches a website called Gracenote for information about the CD you inserted, based on multiple criteria, including the number, order, and length of tracks on the CD. If Gracenote finds a match for your CD, Music displays that information, which can include the album name and artist, track titles, and (if available in the iTunes Store), the album's cover artwork.

2. **Click the Play button or press the spacebar to start playing your selected audio tracks.**

The Play button toggles to a Pause button (which you can click to pause the track you're listening to).

3. **When you finish listening to the CD, eject it by choosing Controls⇨ Eject Disc or by clicking the Eject Disc icon to the right of the CD icon.**

If you have a stereo, Music playback controls in the toolbar across the top of the window will look familiar (refer to Figure 2-2). You have a few extra options, which you access from the Music menu and preferences:

>> **Volume slider:** Drag the volume slider to adjust the sound.

>> **Adjust play:** Click one of the following buttons:

- *Shuffle:* Shuffles the songs from the list you choose from the sidebar.

- *Pause:* Temporarily stops playing audio. You can also press the spacebar to toggle the Play and Pause button.

- *Rewind:* Starts playing the selected audio track from the beginning. Clicking the Previous button a second time starts playing the previous audio track from the beginning.

- *Next:* Skips the selected audio track and starts playing the next audio track.

- *Continuous:* Plays songs in order from the list you choose from the sidebar.

» **Selective play:** Deselect the check boxes of any audio tracks you don't want to hear.

» **Random play:** Click the Shuffle button or choose Controls ➪ Shuffle ➪ On to play your audio tracks in random order. Choosing the Shuffle command again toggles off random play.

» **Repeat-selection play:** Choose Controls ➪ Repeat ➪ All to play the selected audio tracks continuously on the CD or Repeat ➪ One to repeat the same song. (Choose Controls ➪ Repeat ➪ Off to toggle off the Repeat Play feature.)

» **Equalizer:** Choose Window ➪ Equalizer and select one of the 22 preset frequency options closest to the type of media you're listening to, such as R&B, Classical, Rock, Small Speakers, or Spoken Word. When you choose a preset, the equalizer is automatically adjusted, or use the default Flat preset to manually adjust the equalizer settings (see Figure 2-16). Click the On check box to enable the preamp. The preamp determines how much gain is pumped into each channel. If you choose this option, adjust the preamp in small amounts, or you risk distorting the audio and possibly harming your computer speakers.

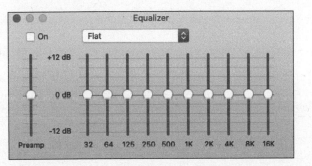

FIGURE 2-16:
Select the type of music with the Equalizer.

Tuning In and Listening with Music

>> **Preferences:** Choose Music⇨Preferences⇨Playback to adjust a few of your playback options.

- *Crossfade Songs*: Move the slider to set the length of silence between songs.

- *Sound Enhancer:* Move the slider from low to high to boost the sound quality.

- *Sound Check:* Sometimes songs play at different volumes. Select the Sound Check option so all songs are played at the same volume.

- *Video Playback Quality:* Choose an option from the pop-up menu. The best quality is the default setting, but if you're experiencing poor performance, choosing a lower quality may improve the speed at which the video plays back.

- *Video Download Quality:* Choose an option from the pop-up menu. This setting determines how well streaming video plays. Up to HD is the default setting, but if streaming video lags or stops until more is downloaded, choose a lower setting.

TIP

Control–click the Music icon on the Dock to bring up a playback controls menu.

Importing a CD's audio tracks into Music

If you have a CD that you often listen to, just import the music into Music. Converting audio tracks on a CD into digital audio files is *ripping.* After you adjust the Music import settings (see the earlier section, "Adjusting Music Preferences"), you're ready to rip.

TECHNICAL
STUFF

By default, Music saves songs imported from your CDs as high-quality iTunes Plus files in the 256 Kbps AAC format.

To convert an audio disc into digital files, open Music and follow these steps:

1. **Insert an audio CD into your Mac's optical disc drive, internal or external.**

Depending on how you set the Music preferences, a dialog may appear, asking whether you want to import all audio tracks on the CD into Music. Click Yes if you want to convert every audio track into a digital audio file and import to Music. If you want to import only some of the songs, click No and continue with the following steps.

If, in the Music Preferences dialog, you chose Play CD or Import CD, that action will take place automatically. If you chose Show CD, you see the window shown in Figure 2-17.

If the tracks of the CD don't appear in the central pane of Music, click the name of the CD in the Library pop-up menu.

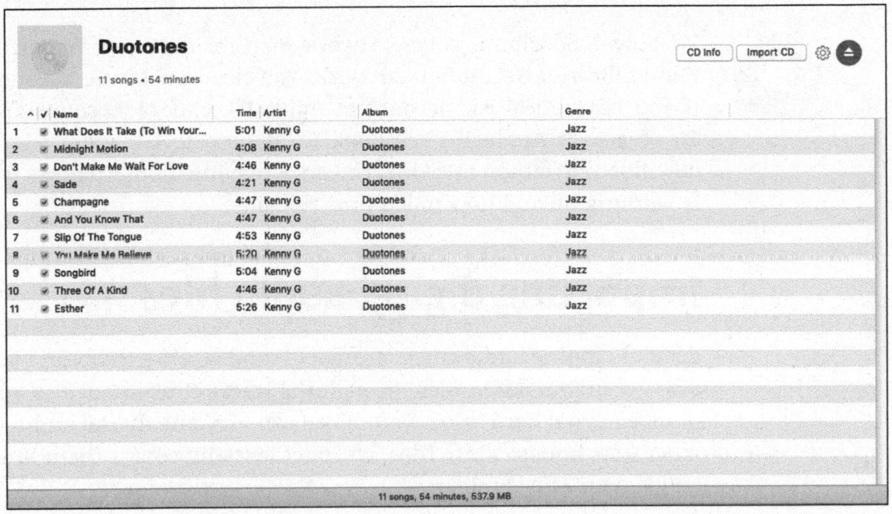

FIGURE 2-17:
Import all or some of the songs from a CD when you insert it.

2. **To choose which songs to import, deselect the check boxes of the tracks you don't want to import.**

   Check marks should appear in the check boxes of the audio tracks you want to import.

   If you don't see check boxes, choose Music⇨Preferences, click the General tab, and then select Songs List Checkboxes in the Show section.

   TIP

3. **Click the Options button and choose Get Track Names if you didn't select the automatic option in Music Preferences.**

4. **(Optional) Click the CD Info button to see information about the CD, such as the artist or year of publication.**

5. **Click the Import CD button in the upper-right corner of the Music window.**

   The Import Settings window opens (refer to Figure 2-14). AAC Encoder is the default encoding format; choose a different format from the pop-up menus if you prefer. Otherwise, click OK, and the Music app converts and copies all (or the selected) audio tracks into digital audio files and saves them to your Mac's hard drive in your Music folder.

   The now-playing display indicates which track is being copied and how long it will take to copy. It takes about ten minutes to import a full CD. A white check mark in a green circle appears next to tracks that have been successfully imported.

6. **When Music finishes importing your CD's audio tracks, eject the CD by choosing Controls⇨Eject Disc or by clicking the Eject Disc icon to the right of the CD name in the Import window.**

TIP

To download album cover artwork for CDs that you import to Music, choose File⇨Library⇨Get Album Artwork. You need an Music account or an Apple ID. If you have an Music account or Apple ID, choose Account⇨Sign In to sign in. To create an Apple ID, see Book 1, Chapter 3. After you sign in, Music begins downloading album artwork. The now-playing display shows which album Music is working on and how much time remains.

Importing digital audio files

Besides ripping audio tracks from a CD and storing them on your Mac, you might also get digital audio files through the Internet or handed to you on a flash drive or an external hard drive. Before you can play any digital audio files in Music, you must first import those files, which essentially copies them into the Music folder inside your Music folder.

You can simply drag files into your Music library, or you can follow these steps:

1. **In Music, choose File⇨Import to open a Finder window.**

2. **Navigate to and select the folder, audio files, or files you want to import into Music, and then click Open.**

   Music imports the folder, audio files, or files into your Music folder.

TIP

If you download music from an online source other than Music, select the Automatically Add to Music option when selecting the destination for saving a downloaded a file, and the file shows up in your Music library.

What's more, if you have lower-quality audio files from various sources, consider subscribing to iTunes Match. For $24.99 per year (as of this writing), iTunes Match looks at your Music library and upgrades songs that you own and that are available in the iTunes Store to iTunes Plus quality. Click the iTunes Store link in the sidebar to open the iTunes Store in the Music Window of the interface, scroll to the bottom of the page, and click the iTunes Match link; then follow the onscreen instructions to subscribe.

TECHNICAL
STUFF

If you poke around in your Mac's folders and files and see two Library files in Music, don't delete one just because it *looks* like a duplicate. Music stores your media in two Library folders. One holds the actual media files, and the other makes media available to other apps, such as Keynote or iMovie.

Searching your Music library

After you copy music (and eventually other media) into Music, you may not be able to find what you're looking for in your library. To find a song, podcast, TV show, or any other media you store on Music, you can search by typing some or all of a song, album, or show title, artist name, and so on. To search Music, follow these steps:

1. **Enter a search query in the Search text field in the sidebar.**

2. **Press Return.**

   Music displays all matches for your query in the Music Window. You get the whole enchilada showing top results, songs, and albums. Your results are segregated by Apple Music, Your Library, and iTunes Store, as shown in Figure 2-18.

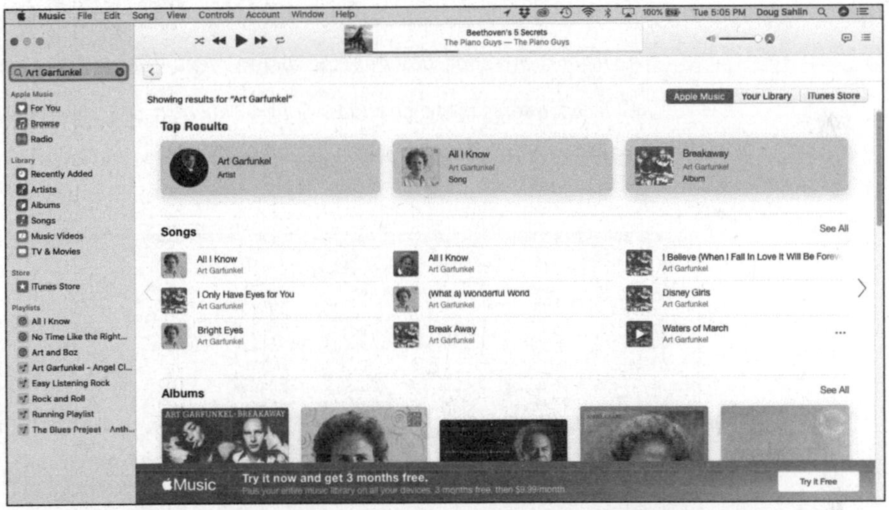

FIGURE 2-18:
Searching
for tunes.

3. **If you subscribe to Apple Music, click that button to play a song.**

4. **To see songs that match your query and purchase one, click the iTunes Store button.**

5. **Click Library to see matches in your Music Library.**

6. **Click the media you want to play.**

   Read the next section to find out more about playback.

Playing digital audio files

After you import one or more audio files into Music, you can view your list of audio files, as outlined in the beginning of this chapter in the "Getting to Know the Music Window" section. Refer to the earlier section, "Listening to CDs," for details on the playback controls. To play one or more audio files, follow these steps:

1. **Choose an option from the Library section of the sidebar, such as Songs, Albums, or Artists.**

2. **Select songs with one of the following methods.**

   - *Select the songs you want to play.* You can ⌘-click songs to select noncontiguous songs, or click the first song you want to play and then Shift-click the last song to select the first and last song.

   - *Drag a song from the list of songs in the Music Window and drop it on the Up Next window.* This method puts the song at the bottom of the list.

   - *Right-click a song, and from the context menu, choose Play Next or Play Later.*

   - *Select a song, and then choose Song⇨ Play Next or Song⇨ Play Later.*

   Your songs are added to the Up Next list, shown in Figure 2-19.

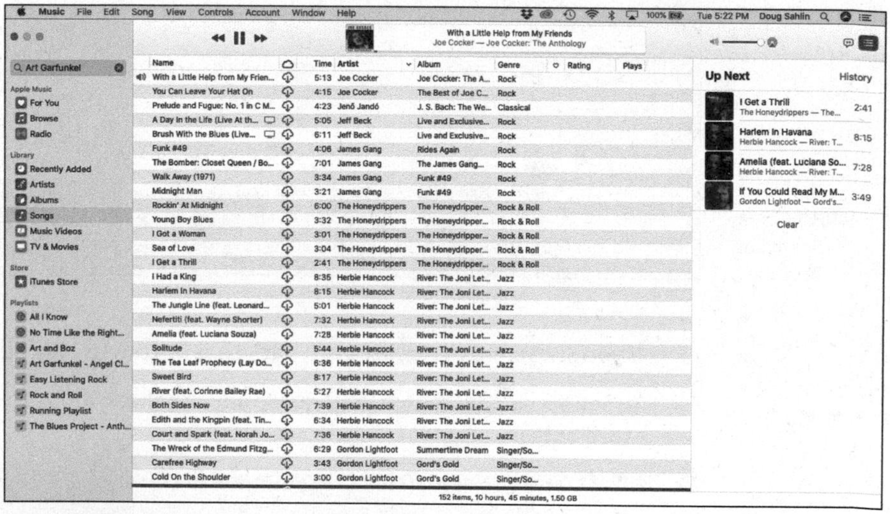

FIGURE 2-19: Playing a list of songs.

3. **Click the Play button or press the spacebar to start playing your selected audio tracks.**

   The Play button toggles to a Pause button.

4. **To manage the Up Next list, click the Up Next button in the upper-right corner or the Music window that looks like a bulleted list, and then choose what to do from the following:**

- *To delete all songs in the Up Next list:* Click the Clear button.

- *To show your listening history:* Click the History link, which becomes an Up Next link. Click Up Next to view the songs you've chosen to play.

- *To remove a song from Up Next:* Hover the pointer over a song and then click the red minus sign (–) that appears on the left side.

- *To move a song to a new (higher or lower) position on the Up Next list:* Click and drag the song to its new position in the Up Next list.

- *To see more options:* Click the three dots to the right of the song's name. From this list, you can remove a song from the Up Next list, get Genius suggestions, and much more, as shown in Figure 2-20. The Add To choice is for Playlist, which we talk about next.

FIGURE 2-20:
Manage the Up Next list.

TIP

If you have an iPhone, iPad, or iPod touch and a Wi-Fi network, you can download the Remote app from the App Store and control Music with your device.

To reduce the playback controls to a small window, choose Window ⇨ Switch to Mini Player. Click the Up Next button on the bottom of the Player. To hide the Mini Player and listen to your tunes while you do other things, swipe up with three fingers and park the Mini-Player on a vacant Desktop. Figure 2-21 shows the Mini-Player on a blank Desktop. For more information about Desktops, see Book 1, Chapter 5.

FIGURE 2-21:
The Mini Player puts controls on your Desktop.

Burning an audio CD

Ubiquitous Wi-Fi, broadband cellular networks, and Apple's iCloud service make accessing and sharing digital files between your Mac and other iOS devices (such as an iPod touch or iPhone) quick and easy. However, if you find that you still want your music on a CD, you can use the Music disc-burning feature to copy your favorite audio files to a CD that you can play whenever you don't have the option of listening to music with Music on your Mac or iOS device.

REMEMBER

CDs can hold approximately 70 to 80 minutes of audio. More stereos can recognize and play CD-Rs although newer stereos can recognize and play CD-RWs as well. (CD-Rs let you write to them only once, whereas CD-RWs allow you to erase and reuse them.)

To burn an audio CD, first create a playlist, and then instruct Music to copy all the songs in the playlist to an audio CD, as follows:

1. **Click the playlist you want to burn to CD.**

2. **(Optional) Deselect the check boxes of any songs you don't want to burn to the CD.**

3. **(Optional) Arrange the songs in the order you want them to play on the CD.**

   To arrange songs in a playlist, click in the first column (that displays the number of each song) and then drag a song up or down to a new position. You can also click the title of a song and drag it up or down the list.

4. Choose File⇨Burn Playlist to Disc.

The Burn Settings dialog appears, offering different radio buttons for choosing the type of CD you want to burn, such as Audio CD, MP3 CD, or Data CD, as shown in Figure 2-22. Audio CD is your best choice because some players don't recognize MP3 CDs, and Data CDs won't be playable.

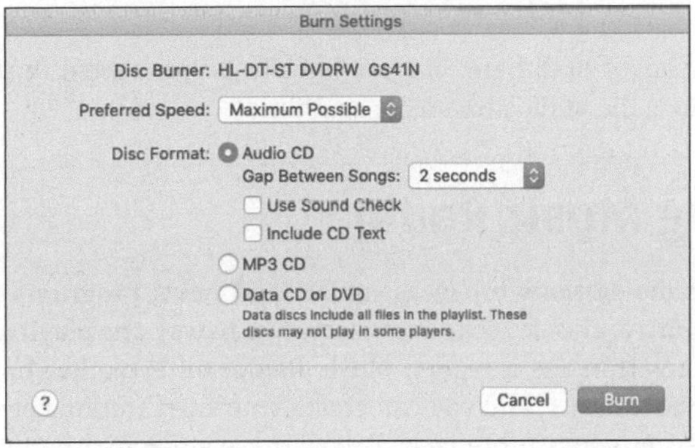

FIGURE 2-22:
Choose the type of CD you want to burn.

5. Select a Disc Format radio button (Audio CD, MP3 CD, or Data CD).

If you choose Audio CD, consider these additional options:

- (Optional) *Gap between Songs:* From this menu, choose None or from 1 to 5 Seconds to specify the amount of silence between song tracks.

- (Optional) *Use Sound Check:* Select this check box to instruct Music to ensure that all the song tracks play from the CD at the same volume level.

- (Optional) *Include CD Text:* Select this check box to display information about the CD on CD player models that offer a CD text information feature.

6. (Optional) Open the Preferred Speed pop-up menu and choose a disc burning speed, such as Maximum Possible or 24x.

If the CDs you burn on your Mac don't play correctly on other CD players, choose a slower burning speed. Otherwise, use the Maximum Possible option.

7. Click the Burn button.

8. When prompted, insert a blank CD-R or CD-RW into your Mac's internal or external optical disc drive.

The now-playing display of the Music window displays the progress of your disc burning. If you're burning more than one or two songs, you now have enough time to go get a cup of coffee, tea, or another beverage of your choosing.

Listening to the Radio

Music offers two types of radio listening:

>> **Music Radio:** Creates a station based on a genre or song you choose

>> **Internet radio:** Tunes in to radio stations through the Internet

We tell you about both here, but you have to be connected to the Internet to use either because the audio streams in real time.

Playing Music Radio

Although radio stations broadcast music and news programs within a category (such as country, classic rock, or conservative news), the playlists tend to be broad and flexible within the category. Music Radio, on the other hand, tends to offer more specific stations, and you can create your own stations based on songs, artists, and genres you want to hear. Follow these steps to use Music Radio:

1. **With Music open, click the Radio button at the bottom of the Apple Music section of the sidebar.**

   In the Music Window, you see a variety of radio shows from which to choose, as shown in Figure 2-23.

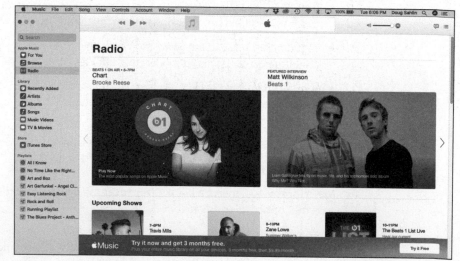

FIGURE 2-23: Choose a Music Radio station.

2. **Click an icon that piques your curiosity.**

   The music begins, sometimes with a brief spoken introduction about the station. Figure 2-24 shows a live radio station being played. Notice the controls at the top of the window. You can stop the show and continue playing. If you're playing a recorded show, you have the option to rewind or fast-forward.

REMEMBER

   In order to enjoy radio offered in the Music app, you must subscribe to Apple Music. As of this writing, Apple is offering a three-month Apple Music trial.

FIGURE 2-24:
Playing a radio station.

3. **Click the Pause button or Stop button to interrupt playback.**

4. **Click the Play button or press the spacebar to resume playing.**

5. **Choose Music⇨Quit Music (or press ⌘+Q) to leave the Music app altogether.**

REMEMBER

Internet radio is no longer available in Music. However, if you know the URL to a streaming radio station, launch the Music app and choose File⇨Open Stream. Select and copy the URL from Safari, and then paste the URL for the station in the URL field of the Open Stream window. It's now added to Internet radio.

Shopping at the iTunes Store

The iTunes Store offers a plethora of music. Whether you like classic rock or classical music, you can find it at the iTunes Store. You can purchase music and then download it to your Mac and listen to the songs you purchase on other devices.

In this section, we accompany you down the virtual aisles of the iTunes Store. The beauty of the iTunes Store is you don't need a shopping cart, and you can audition the music before you buy it.

REMEMBER

Have your Apple ID on hand when you want to shop the iTunes Store because that's what you use to sign in. If you don't have an Apple ID, you can create one by choosing Account ➪ Sign In to open a dialog box that enable you to sign in with your current ID, or click the Create Apple ID to create a new one.

TIP

For many purchases, you have to authorize your computer. This helps with copyright issues. You can authorize up to five computers, and you can also de-authorize computers, so don't worry about someone else using your Apple ID if you sell or give away your Mac. Other devices don't count as computers, so your iPad or iPhone aren't part of the five-computer limit. Choose Store ➪ Authorize This Computer. That's it.

To open the iTunes Store, click the iTunes Store link in the Store section of the sidebar.

With literally millions of digital media files to choose from, the initial impact can be overwhelming, but the iTunes Store organization helps you narrow your choices. When you first open the iTunes Store, the window you see is divided into sections that give you suggestions for different types of music you can purchase (see Figure 2-25).

At the top, you see a banner you can scroll to display new albums. Below the banner you find several sections you can scroll through. On the right side of the store, you see All Genres. Click the disclosure button to fine-tune your shopping experience by choosing a genre from the pop-up menu. After choosing a specific genre, the iTunes Store refreshes showing music from your chosen genre.

Down the right side, you see two sections:

>> **Music Quick Links:** This section is related to your Apple ID/Music account with buttons to access your account, redeem gift cards, send a gift, or request support. The next sections lists options for browsing and buying. If you choose a different genre from the All Genres pop-up menu (for example, Blues), this section becomes Blues Quick Links.

>> **Top Songs:** This section is divided into Singles, where you can preview or purchase songs. Click the chart title to see a full display of the list's contents.

FIGURE 2-25:
Browse the iTunes Store for music, music, and more music.

When you click an icon or name for any type of media from anywhere in the iTunes Store, the information window opens. These are the parts of an information screen, as shown in Figure 2-26:

>> **Buy button:** Click to download the media. Each option (for example, rent or buy, standard or high definition) has its own button. Songs can be purchased singly, or you can purchase the whole album. TV shows can be purchased singly or by season, and some movies have a rental option in addition to a buy option.

>> **Pop-up menu:** Click the disclosure button next to the price for a pop-up menu that has options to gift the app to a friend, add it to your own wish list, tell a friend about it, copy the link, or share the album info via Facebook or Twitter.

>> **Songs:** Lists all the tracks on the album. The price of the song is listed if you want to purchase an individual song and not the whole album. To the left of the song is a Play button that, when clicked, plays a preview of the song. There's even a preview all link at the bottom of the song list.

>> **iTunes Review:** The first few lines of the review are visible. If the entire review isn't visible, click the More button to read the whole review.

>> **Ratings and Reviews:** Click the tab to see what others have said about this item. Users can give a simple star rating, from zero to five, or write a review. Reviews help you decide whether the item is worth downloading or purchasing.

>> **Related:** Click this tab to see other albums similar to this one.

Tuning In and Listening with Music

To narrow your search, enter the name of your favorite artist, or genre, or album name — you get the idea — and the Music app refreshes and three buttons appear to the right showing search results for "your query": Apple Music, Your Library, and iTunes Store. Click the iTunes Store button to review music that matches your query.

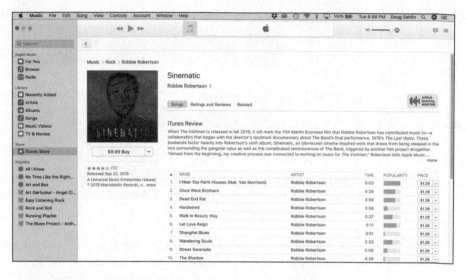

FIGURE 2-26:
Information about the album you select is displayed in Music.

Downloading media from Music

When you find something you like, click the Buy button, and the song or album is downloaded to Music on your Mac. If you have other Apple devices (such as an iPad or iPhone), you can sync your Library to other devices by choosing Music ⇨ Preferences ⇨ Sync Library.

REMEMBER

Don't worry if you have to interrupt the download process or it's interrupted unexpectedly. Music remembers the point it reached, and it will resume downloading when you open the Music app again and have an active Internet connection.

Of course, when you buy, you have to pay from your Apple ID account. This happens in either of two ways:

>> **Redeem:** You can redeem Apple or Music gift cards, gift certificates, or allowances (more on allowances shortly). Choose your Apple ID ⇨ Redeem. Type in the code from the card or certificate. The amount of the card or certificate is added to your account and appears to the left of the Apple ID account tab.

>> **Credit Card:** Your credit card information is stored with your account information. You can change your method of payment and even add money to your Apple ID by choosing Account⇨View My Account.

All songs on Music are currently in iTunes Plus format, which is 256 Kbps AAC without DRM limitations. Songs cost 69 cents, 99 cents, or $1.29, and album prices vary depending on the number of songs. If you buy a few songs from the same album and later decide you want the whole album, choose the Complete My Album option from the Quick Links section, and every album from which you purchased fewer songs than are on the album are listed with the price to complete the album. After you purchase and download songs from Music, they can be downloaded to any other devices that are associated with your account. If you choose Sync Library from General Preferences, purchases not downloaded to other devices have a cloud icon, which when clicked will download the song from the iTunes Store.

After you download the item, close the iTunes Store by clicking a button in the Library section of the Sidebar, which returns you to your Music library. To confirm your purchases, click the Purchased link under Music Quick Links in the iTunes Store.

TIP

To review your past purchases and download one again, click the iTunes Store link in the sidebar. Click Purchased in the Music Quick Links section to view a list of all tunes or albums you've downloaded. Click the link that looks like a cloud to download a song. If there is no cloud link, the song has already been downloaded to your computer.

Chapter **3**

Enjoying Podcasts, News, and TV

P odcasts are very popular on all devices, including the Mac. They're typically audio programs that are episodic in nature, either because they tell a story or provide information over time or because they're keyed to changing events. In previous versions of macOS, you viewed and subscribe to Podcasts in the iTunes app. In macOS Catalina, you view and subscribe to podcasts in the Podcasts app.

If you like movies and TV shows, you'll be happy to know that you no longer have to muck about iTunes to view movies and TV shows you purchase from the iTunes Store. They now reside in the TV app.

If you like to keep abreast of current events, you don't have to subscribe to news- papers. macOS Catalina is totally green. You can find your favorite news sources and much more in the News app. Rain forests throughout the world breathe a collective sigh of relief.

Finding and Playing Podcasts

The heart of podcasts on your Mac is the Podcasts app. You can find it in the Dock or Launchpad — it's purple with a white radio-wave kind of symbol from an antenna-like thing.

Exploring podcasts

Whether you download a single episode or subscribe to a series, you find the podcast in the Library on the Podcasts app. You can search for topics, titles, and presenters from within your Library, as shown in Figure 3-1.

TIP

If you find a podcast that you'd like to listen to and you can't find it by searching in the Podcasts app, copy the URL to your clipboard. Then open the Podcasts app and choose File⇨Add a Show by URL. In the Add Podcast window, paste the URL into the text field and click Subscribe. Each website is different. Look for a podcast or RSS icon and use that link to subscribe.

Listening to or watching podcasts

The controls for podcasts are similar to those for music. At the top of the main window, you see the basic controls. From left to right:

>> **Playback controls:** Here you find a Play button, a button that when clicked rewinds the episode 15 seconds and plays from that point forward, and a button that when clicked fast-forwards the episode 30 seconds and continues playing. The Play button become a Pause button when you're playing the episode.

>> **Episode window:** Shows information about the episode you're currently listening to. Inside the Episode window, you find a scrubber control. There are also two time indicators — one that shows how much time has elapsed since the start of the episode and that other that shows how much time is remaining. These numbers update in real time.

>> **Speaker controls:** Specify the device you want to use and control its volume, as shown in Figure 3-2.

>> **Episode notes (the Info button) and a list of podcasts, as well as what's next:** You can toggle the list between your podcasts and all podcasts.

FIGURE 3-2:
Select a speaker and set its volume.

When you click the Browse link in the left column, the main part of the right window shows the podcasts. The podcasts are divided into categories. You can also search for specific podcasts by entering a query in the Search text field.

Click a show's thumbnail image to find out more information about that show. After you review a show, you can subscribe to it and after you subscribe, you can view recent episodes, as shown in Figure 3-3.

The three dots to the right of the Subscribe button let you choose between subscribing to the show and sharing it with Mail, Messages, AirDrop, Notes, or other apps, as shown in Figure 3-4.

Enjoying Podcasts, News, and TV

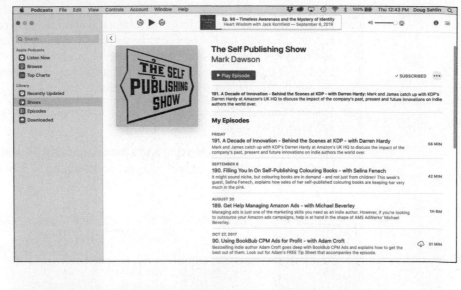

FIGURE 3-3:
View and
subscribe to
episodes.

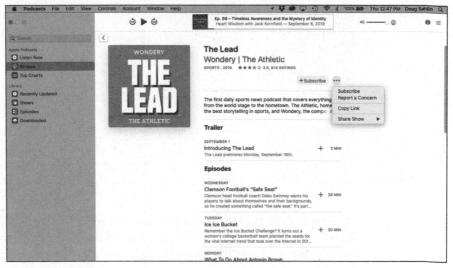

FIGURE 3-4:
Subscribe to or
share shows.

The + button for an episode lets you add the show to your library (or delete it), play the next episode, or go the main show, as shown in Figure 3-5.

Setting Podcast Preferences

As is the case with other apps, you can set preferences for podcasts. Figure 3-6 shows the General preferences. They let you choose how frequently podcasts are updated or downloaded.

FIGURE 3-5:
Options for an
episode you've
subscribed to.

FIGURE 3-6:
Set refresh and
download times.

General preferences

Remember that podcasts are continually updated and added to so you need to keep up to date with them.

Playback preferences

Figure 3-7 shows the Playback preferences you can set. Note that there are settings for how your podcasts behave with headphone controls. Many people listen to podcasts in the car or in other places where headphone controls are much easier to use than a Desktop.

Advanced preferences

The Advanced preferences (see Figure 3-8) apply to your entire podcast library and let you manage it as a whole.

Enjoying Podcasts,
News, and TV

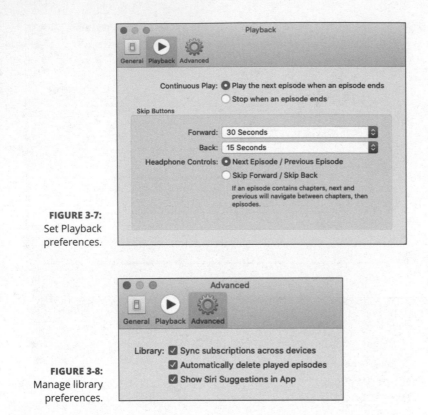

FIGURE 3-7:
Set Playback
preferences.

FIGURE 3-8:
Manage library
preferences.

Reading the News: Extra, Extra, Read All about It!

If you like to keep up with current events, you'll love the News app. You can read the latest news, check out news stories by choosing a topic, save stories you like, and peruse articles you've previously read. If keeping abreast of current affairs is your thing (and why wouldn't it be?), read on.

Reading the daily news

The Apple News app keeps you up to date on current events by including articles from major news sources such as *The Wall Street Journal, Los Angeles Times,* CNN Business, and much more. To read the daily news with your cuppa joe or other beverage, follow these steps:

1. **Click the News app icon (it looks like a stylized *N*) in the Dock or LaunchPad.**

   The News app opens showing the top stories for the day. The app is divided into two sections, the sidebar and the News pane, as shown in Figure 3-9.

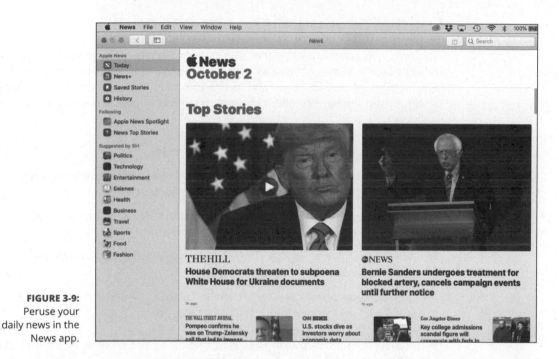

2. **Click a story you'd like to read.**

   The story opens in the News pane. After you open a story, it's added to your History.

   If you see a Play button on an image, click it to watch a video.

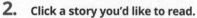

   TIP

3. **Click the Back button.**

   News shows the section you were on previously.

4. **Click a category in the sidebar to view articles you're interested in.**

   For example, if you're a sports fan, click Sports in the Suggested by Siri section, to view current sports news, or if you're a foodie, click Food.

5. **To view only the right pane of the interface, click the Hide Sidebar icon.**

   Click the icon again to view the sidebar.

REMEMBER

As of this writing, News+ is a subscription service that gives you access to your favorite magazines and newspapers. As of this writing, Apple is offering a 30-day free trial, after which you pay $9.99 per month. To learn more about News+, click its link in the sidebar.

Following a publisher or channel

The News app has more news than the average person could consume in a day, and let's face it, some of the news may not appeal to you. You can segregate your favorite types of news by topic and source into neat little links in the Following section of the sidebar. To add a channel or subject to the News sidebar, follow these steps:

1. **Click a link in the sidebar, and review the articles.**

2. **When you see an article by a publisher you'd like to follow, right-click the article and choose Follow Channel from the context menu.**

   A window appears with the word *Following* and a check mark. The publisher's name is added to the Following section of the sidebar.

3. **To follow a channel, right-click the title in Suggested by Siri, and choose Follow Channel from the context menu.**

   A window appears with the word *Following* and a check mark. The publisher's name is added to the Following section of the sidebar.

To unfollow a channel, in the Following section of the sidebar, right-click the channel and choose Unfollow from the context menu.

TIP

If for some reason, you don't want to see news from a specific source, or channel, right-click an article by a publisher and choose Block Channel from the context menu, or click a channel name in the Following section of the toolbar and choose Block Channel from the context menu.

Saving and sharing stories

So much news, so little time. If you're busy but you still like to stay in touch with what's happening in the news, you don't have to read every article that grabs your attention. You can save an article for reading on a rainy day. You can also share an article you think is interesting or would be interesting to a friend.

To save an article, do the following:

1. **Click a section you want to review in the sidebar.**

   The News pane refreshes showing articles in that category.

2. **Review the articles.**

   Don't read the article. For some reason, you can only save an article while reviewing all articles in a category.

3. **When you see an article you'd like to save, right-click it and from the context menu, choose Save Story.**

   The article is added to the Saved Stories category in the sidebar.

4. **To read a saved story, click Saved Stories in the sidebar.**

   A list of the stories you save appears in the News pane.

5. **Click the story you want to read.**

   The story appears in the News pane.

To remove a saved story, click the Saved Stories link in the sidebar, and then in the News pane, right-click the story and choose Unsave Story from the context menu.

To share a channel or story with a friend, right-click a story in the News pane, and from the context menu, choose Share and then choose an option from the flyout menu. You can share the store via Mail, Messages, Air Drop, Notes, or Reminders.

Setting News preferences

In previous sections, we show you how to read content that's important to you, as well as content you like. But let's face it, there are some things you may not want to read (for example, stories with explicit content). To fine-tune the content News makes available for you, do the following:

1. **Choose News⇨Preferences.**

   The News Preferences dialog appears, as shown in Figure 3-10.

2. **To limit the amount of content displayed in News today, click the Restrict Stories in Today check box.**

   News displays only stories from channels you follow in Today.

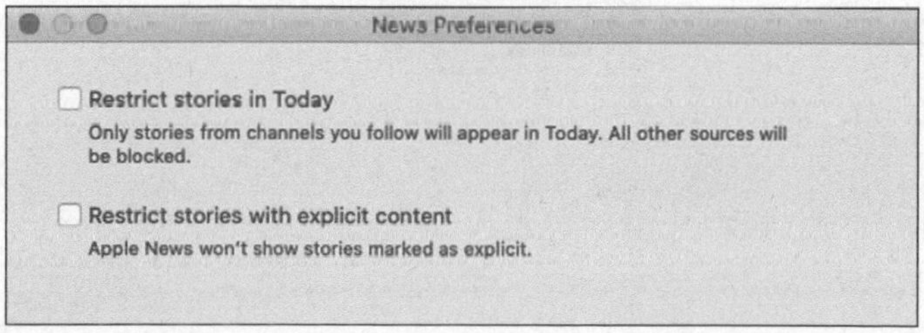

FIGURE 3-10:
Restricting the content News displays.

News Preferences

☐ Restrict stories in Today
Only stories from channels you follow will appear in Today. All other sources will be blocked.

☐ Restrict stories with explicit content
Apple News won't show stories marked as explicit.

3. **To restrict stories with potentially disturbing content, click the Restrict Stories with Explicit Content check box.**

News won't show stories with content marked as explicit.

Watching TV on Your Mac

Whether you're an author who spends eight hours or more behind a computer making stuff up, or an accountant working on your client's quarterly profit-and-loss statement, you need a break. And the TV app is the perfect source for watching a movie or TV show while you recharge your batteries. But first you need to launch the TV app as follows:

1. **Click the TV app icon (it looks like the Apple logo followed by *tv*) in the Dock or Launchpad.**

The TV app launches. The TV app is composed of a sidebar and the TV pane, as shown in Figure 3-11. The sidebar is divided into two sections:

- *Library:* Shows your purchases

- *Genres:* Shows the genres of the movies you've purchased

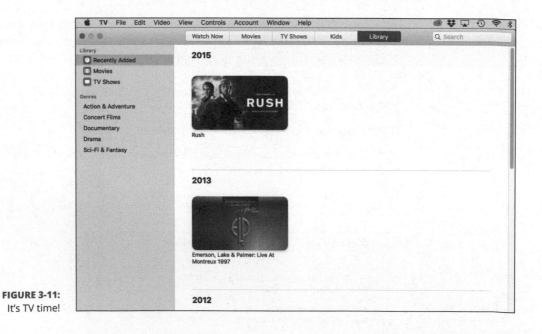

FIGURE 3-11:
It's TV time!

At the top of the interface are several buttons. The buttons on the left are used to purchase content from Apple, with the exception of the last button, which displays your Library.

2. **Click a link in your Library.**

Your options are Recently Added, Movies, and TV Shows or one of the genres you've purchased.

If you purchased movies or TV shows with the old iTunes app, they appear in your TV Library.

REMEMBER

3. **Hover your cursor over a title.**

Your options are Play or Download from the Cloud. Click the ellipses to see more options, as shown in Figure 3-12.

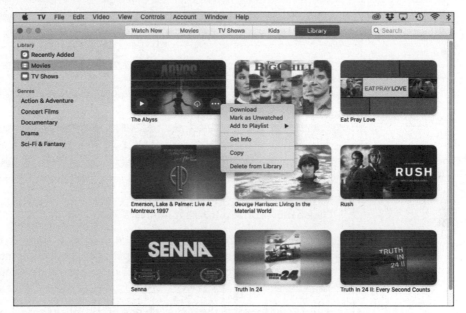

FIGURE 3-12:
Make a batch of popcorn.

4. **Click the Play button to view a movie or TV show.**

If you haven't downloaded the movie to your computer, it streams from the Apple Store and begins playing as soon as enough content has downloaded. The movie plays full screen on your computer.

Enjoying Podcasts, News, and TV

You can also purchase or rent movies from Apple. You do so from the TV app as follows:

1. **Launch the TV app as outlined in the previous section.**

2. **Click one of the links at the top of the interface.**

   Each link, except Library, lands you in the Apple Store. Figure 3-13 shows the movie section of the Apple Store. At the top of the screen is the featured movie for that section of the store.

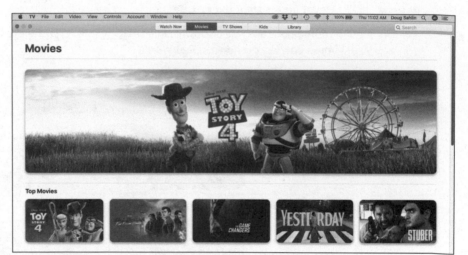

FIGURE 3-13:
Choosing a movie to buy or rent.

3. **Click a movie or TV show that interests you.**

   Information about the video appears in the TV pane, as shown in Figure 3-14. The amount of information displayed depends on the show or movie you're considering. Scroll down to see additional information and perhaps play a video trailer.

4. **If you want to watch the movie, do one of the following:**

   - *Click Buy.* Click this button to purchase the movie.

   - *Click Rent.* Click this button to rent the movie for 24 hours.

   - *Click In Up Next.* Click this button to add the movie to Watch Now.

   After choosing the first or second option, the Sign-in Required dialog appears. If you choose the third option, when you click the movie or show title in Watch Now, the movie or show information appears in the TV pane, and you have the option to buy or rent the movie.

FIGURE 3-14:
Getting
information
about a movie.

5. **Enter your Apple ID.**

   You've purchased or rented the movie.

REMEMBER

The TV app adds purchases to your Library. Unless you choose the option in TV General Preferences to automatically download TV shows and movies to your computer, the movie or TV show streams to your computer, which requires an Internet connection. If you want to watch a movie anytime, anywhere, choose the option to automatically download Library items to your computer.

TIP

To restrict the type of movies and shows that can be purchased through the TV app, choose TV⇨Preferences, and then click the Restrictions icon. After you unlock this tab and enter your admin password, you can disable purchases and restrict the type of content that can be purchased or viewed in the TV app.

IN THIS CHAPTER

» **Reading books**

» **Purchasing books**

» **Managing your books**

» **Listening to audiobooks**

Chapter **4**

Reading and Listening to Books on Your Mac

macOS Catalina has a number of changes in store for you: Overall, it provides improved performance and stability along with some simplifications to the user interface. Books is a perfect example of the simplifications. The Books app is what, prior to macOS Mojave, was known as the iBooks app; in keeping with today's reading trends, Books includes e-books, as well as audiobooks.

Thumbing through Books

When you first open Books, you see the Books welcome screen that invites you to Get Started. Click the Get Started button, and then sign in with your Apple ID and password (unless you're already signed in, in which case you won't be prompted to do this) and you're ready to download books from Apple Books. For a refresher on how to get an Apple ID, see Book 1, Chapter 3.

Any e-books or audiobooks you previously purchased from Apple Books will be automatically shown in Books. Books that have been downloaded to your Mac are accessible from Books. Books that you purchased but didn't download to your Mac have a cloud icon in the right corner of the book icon, which means they're available for download.

REMEMBER

Prior to macOS Mojave, you purchased books from iTunes. Any book purchased through iTunes is included in the Library on your Books app.

Figure 4-1 shows the basic Books window. If you've used previous versions of Books (such as iBooks on the Mac) you'll notice that this window is less cluttered. Have no fear: Your books are already there along with any PDFs you've manually added. Any audiobooks you purchased from Apple are moved automatically to Books. You can listen to them by clicking the Audiobooks link in the left column of your Library. Books are books regardless of whether you turn the pages or listen to a reader.

FIGURE 4-1:
Explore the Books window.

The three tabs at the top of the window let you look at your entire library, browse Apple Books, or browse the Audiobook Store. When you browse the Apple Books, the sidebar at the left shows you featured titles such as the top titles in sales charts, the *New York Times* best-sellers list, top authors, and categories of books. Tap a book to find out more about it or to buy it. Periodically, promotional links such as "Find a great book for less than $4" appear at the top of the screen when you browse the bookstore (refer to Figure 4-1).

You can see your books in a grid, as shown in Figure 4-1, or as a list, as shown in Figure 4-2. Switch between the two by choosing View➪View As Grid/List. Alternatively, you can click the icon that looks like a bulleted list to the right of the green dot to toggle between Grid and List views.

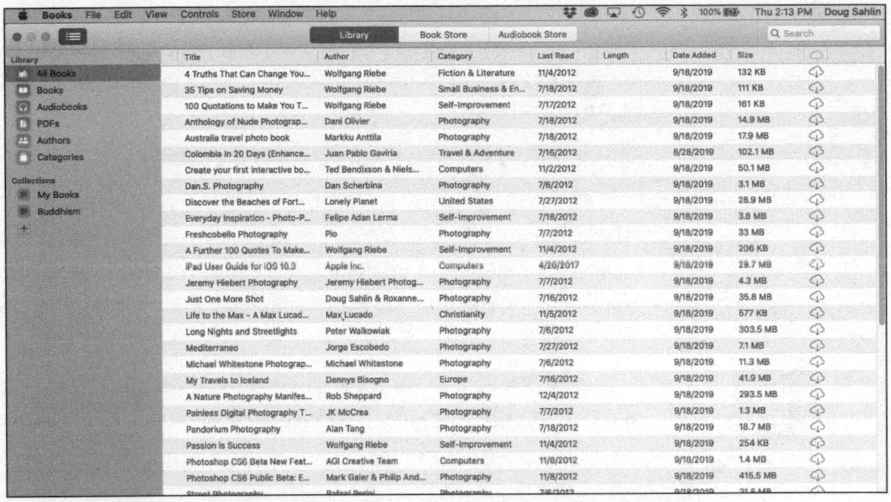

FIGURE 4-2:
Switch between Grid and List views.

Finding something to read at Apple Books

To shop for books and look for free books, just follow these steps:

1. **Click the Books icon on the Dock or from Launchpad.**

Your Library opens (refer to Figure 4-1) although you won't see any book icons if you haven't downloaded any books. Books you keep in the Books app are shown in your Library, even if you purchased them from other sources and manually added them.

2. **Click the Book Store button.**

Apple Books opens. The links in the left column enable you to browse specific categories of books. As of this writing the links are:

- *Featured:* Displays a list of featured books such as best sellers, popular categories, and so on.

- *Top Charts:* Displays a list of top paid books. Click the Free link to see a list of top free books. You can also narrow your search by choosing an option from the All Categories drop-down list.

- *NYTimes:* Displays a list of *New York Times* best sellers.

- *Categories:* Separates books into categories such as Biographies and Memoirs, Business and Personal Finance, and so on.

- *Top Authors:* Displays a list of top authors organized alphabetically.

3. **Click a tab that interests you to narrow your choices and then click a book that you might like to read, or click a promotional button on the Featured screen.**

   Alternatively, you can type a query into the Search text box to find a specific book or genre of books.

   After clicking a title, the info screen appears (see Figure 4-3) and shows the usual information: Details, Ratings and Reviews, and Related tabs; and Price and Get Sample buttons to either purchase the book or download a sample, respectively.

   If you're interested in audiobooks, click the Audiobooks button to peruse the Apple Books selection of books you can listen to.

FIGURE 4-3:
The info screen tells you everything you need to know to make an informed purchase.

4. **After you find something you want to try or purchase, click one of the following:**

   - *Buy Book:* Clicking this button confirms that you want to purchase the book.

   - *Get Sample:* Click this button to download a sample to your Mac. If you like it, you can purchase it later.

   As items are downloading, you can continue browsing. After the book downloads to your Mac, the book has a New or Sample banner across it in your Library.

5. **After clicking the Buy Book or Get Sample button, a dialog appears prompting you for your Apple password.**

   This is the same as your iCloud password. Enter your Apple ID and password, and then click OK to complete the purchase.

6. **(Optional) Click the disclosure arrow to the right of Buy Book and, from the pop-up menu shown in Figure 4-4, choose one of the following:**

   - *Gift This Book:* Click this link to give the book to a friend.

   - *Add to Wish List:* Click this link to add the book to your wish list.

   - *Mail:* Click this link to open a blank email window with the name of the book and the link to the book in Apple Books. Add a message to the email and send it to someone who might enjoy the book.

   - *Copy Link:* Click to copy the link to the book to your clipboard for other uses, such as adding the link to a letter you're writing.

FIGURE 4-4: Options for the book you're considering.

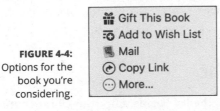

7. **(Optional) Do one of the following:**

   - *Click the Read or Read Sample button to open your recently downloaded item.*

   - *Click the Downloads button to the right of the Search text field to view a list of books you've recently downloaded. Click Open to open a book. After you view the list or open a book, the Downloads list is cleared.*

   - *Click the Back button (to the left of the Library button) to return to the category or chart you were perusing.*

   - *Click another tab at the top to go to a different category or chart.*

As long as you sign in to the same Apple ID on all your devices, the Books app syncs purchases from Apple Books across your iOS devices and Macs.

REMEMBER

Adding books and files from other sources

Books neatly keeps your digital reading material such as e-books in the ePub format and PDFs together in one place. To add your PDFs to Books, you can simply drag them from the Finder into the Books window or Books icon on the Dock. To add either PDFs or e-books in the ePub format that you obtained from sources other than Apple Books, do the following:

1. **Click the Books icon on the Dock or from Launchpad.**

2. **Choose File ⇨ Add to Library.**

   Click and scroll through the chooser window or use the Search field to find the PDF or ePub e-book you want to add.

3. **Click the Add button.**

   The file is added to Books.

   The books in your Books Library are separated into categories you find in the left column of your Library. You can view books by author, view PDFs, view books by category, and so on. You can even create collections of books, by clicking the plus sign (+) below Collections.

TECHNICAL
STUFF

When you click to open a PDF in Books on your Mac, Books defaults to Preview, or another PDF reading app such as Adobe Reader, to open the file. Books does, however, read PDFs on iOS devices.

Reading by screen light

After you download one or more books, the joy begins. Click the Library button, which is to the left of the center of the interface, and then click the book you want to read. The book opens in a separate window, as shown in Figure 4-5, usually to the cover but sometimes (as with a sample) to a random page. When you read a book you can use the following tools:

TIP

» **Library:** Click the Library button to return to the Library window.

   To quickly open a book you recently read, choose File ⇨ Open Recent and select the book you want from the submenu.

» **Table of Contents:** Click the Table of Contents button, which opens the table of contents as a pop-up menu. Click the chapter or section you want to go to.

» **Navigation:** Move your cursor to the middle of the right page and a right-pointing arrow appears. Click it to advance to the next page. To view the previous page, move your cursor to the middle of the left page to reveal a left-pointing arrow. Click it to read the previous page. You can also use the right and left arrow keys to navigate a book. If you have a trackpad, swipe left or right to turn the pages.

» **Readability:** Click the Font Size button in the upper-right corner, and a window opens, as shown in Figure 4-5.

- *Click the small or large* A *to adjust the size of text on the page. Click the button repeatedly until the text is easy to read.*

- *Click one of the color choices to change the page and type colors.*

- *Click a font name in the list to change the typeface.*

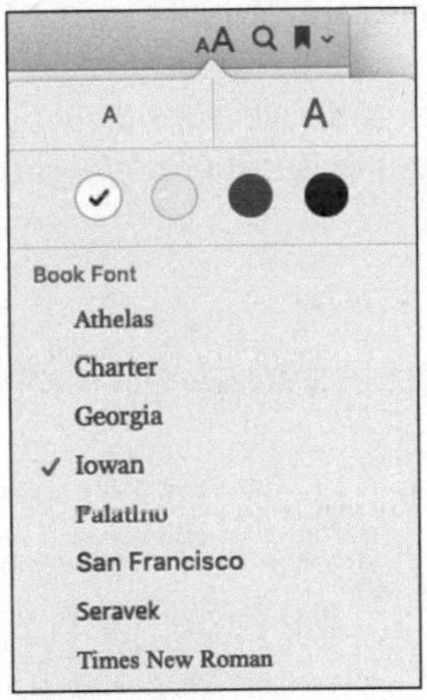

FIGURE 4-5:
Adjust the typeface style, size, and color to make for comfortable reading.

» **Search:** Click the Search button to look for a specific word or phrase or jump to a page number. Books offers a list of suggestions as you type. Click the desired item, and Books navigates to it.

» **Bookmarks:** Click the Bookmarks button to virtually dog-ear a page so you can find it later; click the disclosure triangle next to the bookmark to see a list of bookmarked pages.

» **Resizing:** Click the full-screen button to use your Mac's entire screen or click and drag one of the window edges or corners to resize the window.

» **Definitions:** Double-click a word to display the definition of the word in a new window.

» **Notes:** Create a note. Click and drag to select a phrase or section of text. When the contextual menu opens, as shown in Figure 4-6, do the following:

- *Choose a color to highlight the selected text or click the underlined* a *to underline it.*

- *Click Add Note to open a virtual sticky note where you can type your thoughts.*

- *Click Copy to temporarily save the selection to your Mac's Clipboard, and then paste it somewhere else.*

- *Click More to see additional options, such as searching the web or sharing the passage on a social network.*

- *Click the Notes button to see sections you highlighted or notes you added to the book. The notes appear in a column on the left side of the interface. Click a note to view the text you selected when you made the note. After viewing your notes, click the Notes button to hide the column.*

» **Preferences:** Choose Books ➪ Preferences, and then click the General button to turn on options, such as auto-hyphenation and justified text, as well as to turn on syncing bookmarks, highlights, and collections on your other devices. In Books Preferences, click the Store button set your preferences for shopping at Apple Books.

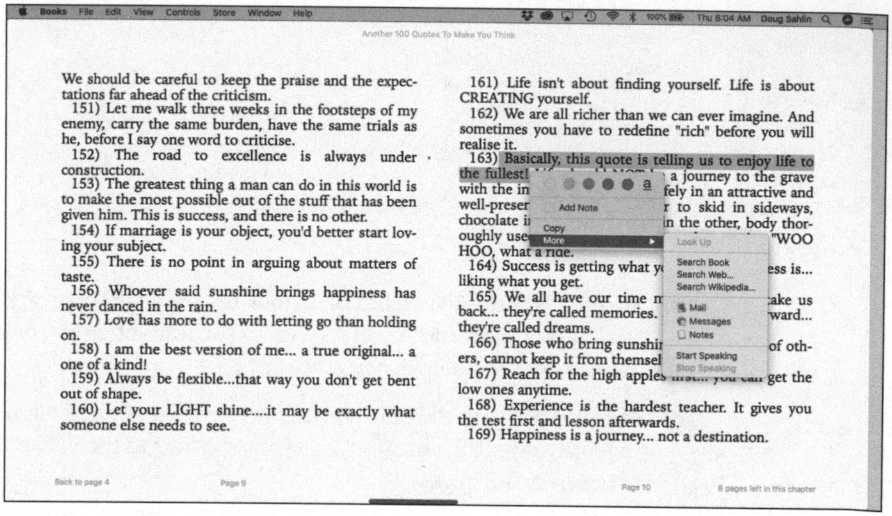

FIGURE 4-6:
Highlight text and take notes; click the Notes button to see them.

TIP

Enhanced or interactive books may have multimedia capabilities, such as clicking a three-dimensional item and then rotating it to view different angles, or watching a video that correlates with the book. These types of books can be read only in Books on Macs and iPads.

WARNING

Some authors have designed their books to work on iOS devices such as the iPad or iPhone. If your computer cannot use some of the features exclusive to iOS devices, a warning dialog appears. In spite of the warning dialog, you'll still be able to access many book features. When this dialog appears, click OK and read on.

Sorting your books

Books gives you choices of how you want to sort and view your books in your library. Access commands for sorting the books and seeing more information in the View menu:

>> Choose View ⇨ Sort By to re-order your books by Most Recent (those opened most recently), Title, or to Sort Manually, which lets you click and drag the books to the order you want.

>> Choose View ⇨ Show Title and Author to see that information beneath the book cover icon.

When you view you entire Library, the menu in the left column lets you view books by:

>> **All Books:** Shows you the covers of all your books.

>> **Collections:** This area is blank until you add a new collection, as shown in the following Tip. To view books in a collection, click the collection name.

TIP

Collections are a great way to group and sort your books. Choose File ⇨ New Collection, and then type in a new name in the highlighted item in the Collections list. After creating a collection, click All Books or one of the other sorting options, and then drag-and-drop a book onto the collection title to add it to the collection.

>> **Authors:** A list of authors appears down the left of the window (refer to Figure 4-1). Click an author's name in the list to see books only by that author, or click All Authors to see all your books.

>> **Categories:** A list of categories for which you have books appears down the left of the window. Click a category to see the books within it.

>> **List:** The icons disappear, and you see a spreadsheet-style list of your book titles, authors, and other information such as when you last read the book and the date it was added.

IN THIS CHAPTER

» **Seeing how digital photography works**

» **Getting your digital images onto your Mac**

» **Organizing your images**

» **Taking photos with Photo Booth**

» **Editing your images in Photos**

» **Sharing photos with family and friends**

Chapter **5**

Looking at Photos

More people are taking photos than ever before with digital cameras and mobile phones, and then using websites like Facebook, Instagram, and Twitter to share every moment and morsel. Of course, before you share your immortalized antics, you may want to edit the evidence with an image-editing app to make the subject or scene look better than it did in real life.

You can use Photos, which comes with macOS, not only for image editing but also for managing (an important part of digital photography because it's so easy to accumulate hundreds, if not thousands, of photos in a short time) and sharing your photos. From start to finish, Photos can take care of organizing your photos so you can focus on taking even more photos. We explain all these tasks in this chapter, but first, we provide a brief introduction — or refresher — on digital photography.

Understanding Digital Photography

Instead of using film, digital photography captures images as a collection of tiny dots called *pixels.* A single photo can comprise millions of pixels. To help you understand the capabilities of different digital cameras and mobile phones with built-in digital cameras, manufacturers identify the gadgets by how many millions of pixels they can capture in each photo. This total number of pixels — the *resolution* — ranges from as little as less than 4 megapixels (MP; a megapixel equals one million pixels) to 16MP or more. Figure 5-1 shows how pixels create an image.

FIGURE 5-1:
Every digital image contains lots of pixels.

One of the prime purposes of high-resolution images is that you can point and shoot and then do your cropping and organizing of the photo you want from the very large image you've captured. But it's always best to capture the best image you can in camera and then do a minimal amount of editing.

When you take photos, your digital camera stores those photos in a specific graphics file format. The two most common file formats available for capturing digital photographs are

>> **JPEG (Joint Photographic Experts Group):** JPEG is the most common file format because it is recognized by most computers and offers the ability to compress images to shrink the overall file size. (*Compressing* a JPEG file means decreasing the number of colors used in an image, which shrinks the file size but lowers the visual quality.)

>> **Raw:** Raw files are the equivalent of digital negatives. After capturing an image in a camera's Raw format, you can edit them to pixel perfection in Apple's Photos app. Every digital camera manufacturer offers its own Raw file format.

The biggest advantage of Raw files is that they allow for greater manipulation. As a result, professional photographers often use Raw files for greater control over manipulating their images. The biggest disadvantage is that Raw images take up a large amount of storage space, which means that you can't store as many images as photos captured in other formats.

Ultimately, there is no single "best" file format. If a digital camera lets you save images in different file formats, experiment to see which one you like best. You may prefer one type of file format, such as JPEG, for ordinary use, but prefer Raw for capturing images in special situations that don't require capturing images quickly, such as taking photos of a landscape.

TECHNICAL STUFF

Many cameras also offer the option to capture both Raw and JPEG images at the same time, giving you the best of both worlds. The JPEG images can be used immediately for the web and such, and the Raw images can be used for the special images you want to edit to perfection and print.

Transferring Digital Images to the Mac

To transfer photos from a device — digital camera, mobile phone, scanner, or tablet — to your Mac, you have several choices:

>> You can connect your device to your Mac by using a USB cable or wirelessly using AirDrop or your local network, if your device supports that option.

>> You can pop the flash memory card out of your device and plug it into your Mac's built-in SDxD card reader (if your camera uses SD cards and if your Mac has the reader) or a third-party card reader that connects to your Mac's USB port.

No matter which method you use, your Mac treats all the images stored on your device's flash memory card as just another external drive from which you can copy photos to your Mac's hard drive (such as into the Photos folder).

When you connect a device to your Mac, it can automatically load an app to retrieve those images. Photos and Image Capture, which both come preloaded on your Mac, can retrieve digital snapshots automatically. In this chapter, we focus on Photos. Use Image Capture if you just want to store photos on your Mac and use a different application to edit them. But most applications like Adobe Photoshop Elements and Adobe Lightroom can easily import your digital treasure.

If you organize photos in Photos, choose it as your default app to retrieve photos from a device. (You can specify another app as the external editor.) If you use a different app to organize your photos, such as Adobe Lightroom, you can make that app your default app. If you use more than one app to organize your photos, you can make Image Capture your default app and then use the Open With command to choose the app you want to use to edit your imported photos, deciding what to use on an image-by-image basis.

Retrieving photos using Photos

Photos will import both photos and videos from your camera or phone to your Mac. To import images to Photos, follow these steps:

1. **Connect your device to your Mac with the appropriate cable (or plug your memory card into your memory card reader).**

2. **Launch the Photos app by clicking the Photos icon in the Dock or the Launchpad.**

    The Photos app opens.

3. **Click the Full Screen button.**

    The Photos app displays a sidebar and a pane in which images are displayed.

4. **Click Devices in the sidebar.**

    The images on your card are displayed in the right pane.

5. **Click Open Photos for this device.**

    When you next connect this card or device to a card reader, Photos launches.

6. **Choose an option from the Import To pop-up menu.**

    The default option is to import them to the Library, but we suggest you choose New Album. This is an important first step to organizing your photo library. If you shoot lots of images, and store them all in the Library, you'll have a hard time finding images even though Photos separates images by the date they were photographed. Let's face it: Scrolling through hundreds of photographs shot on different dates is hard work.

7. **If you heed our sage advice, the New Album dialog appears, as shown in Figure 5-2.**

    When we name an album, we use the date and the place or person photographed. For example, if we shoot a card of images on October 3, 2019, in Venice, we name the folder 100319_Venice.

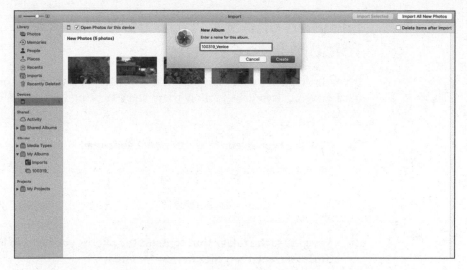

FIGURE 5-2:
Importing Images
to Photos.

8. **(Optional) Click and drag the Zoom slider in the upper-left corner of the Import toolbar left or right to increase or decrease the size of your photo thumbnails.**

9. **(Optional) Click the Delete Items after Import check box.**

   We suggest you do *not* do this unless you're importing images from a phone. It's always best to format your memory cards in the camera you use the card in.

10. **Select the photos you want to import.**

    We suggest you import all images. It's very hard to judge whether an image is in focus or not, or whether you like the image by just looking at a small thumbnail.

11. **Click Import All New Photos, or if you selected photos to import, click Import *x* Selected (where *x* is the number of images you selected).**

    Photos imports your images.

12. **If you imported images from a memory card, insert the card in your camera and format it.**

    As the risk of being redundant, It's always best to format a memory card in the camera in which it will be used to capture images.

WARNING

Never yank a memory card out of the card reader port, or pull a card reader with a card out of a USB port; doing so may cause your Mac to scramble the data on the memory card. Before physically removing a flash memory card from the port, eject the card safely from your Mac by clicking the Eject button that appears to the right of the flash memory icon in the Finder window sidebar.

Moving photos from other folders into Photos

If you have photos or image files in other folders on your Mac or on an external hard drive or flash drive, follow these steps to bring the photos and images into Photos:

1. **Click the Photos icon in the Dock or Launchpad.**

   The Photos app opens.

2. **Choose File⇨Import.**

   A Finder window opens.

3. **Navigate to the folder that contains the photos you want to import, click the folder, and then click Review for Import.**

   You could select individual images, but the thumbnails are so small, it's hard to determine which ones are keepers and which aren't.

   After choosing Review for Import, the images appear on the right side of the interface, as shown in Figure 5-3. Notice that Photos knows an image has already been imported.

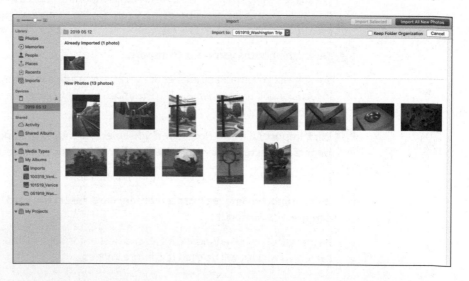

FIGURE 5-3:
Importing images from a folder on your computer.

4. **Choose an option from the Import To pop-up menu.**

   We strongly suggest you put the image in a new album as outlined in the previous section, unless they should be added to an existing album, in which case the album is listed on the pop-up menu.

5. **Click the images you want to import.**

   If you want to import all the images, go to Step 6.

6. **Click Import All New Photos, or if you selected specific images, click Import *x* Selected (where *x* is the number of images you'll be importing).**

   Photos imports the images into the Library or Album selected.

TIP

A fast way to import single photos into Photos is to drag and drop those photos to the Photos icon on the Dock, or to the Photos category under Library in the Photos Source list.

Organizing Your Photo Library

Photography is fun. But if you just keep adding images to Photos, you end up with a virtual shoebox full of photos with no idea how to find the image of Aunt June that you photographed on Mother's Day in 2016. Earlier in this chapter, we talk a little bit about organization. But there are a few more things you can do to have a squeaky clean library in Photos. Yes, we know this takes time. But the amount of time it takes pales in comparison to trying to find one treasured image among thousands.

Tagging images

If you get in the habit of tagging images after you import them, they'll be much easier to find in the future. The secret to tagging (also known as *keywording*) images is to use every conceivable keyword that fits an image. When we import images, we create a keyword for the place the image was photographed or the name of the person in the photography, the type of photography, and any other words that can help describe the image.

To add keywords to your images, follow these steps:

1. **Import the images as outlined in the "Transferring Digital Images to the Mac" section, earlier in this chapter.**

   We strongly suggest you create a folder for the images.

REMEMBER

2. **Select all the images you just imported.**

   Yep. You guessed it. You're gonna tag a bunch of images at once.

3. **Right-click and then choose Get Info from the context menu.**

   The Info dialog appears.

4. **Click inside the Add a Keyword text field, and enter a keyword.**

   We usually start with the name of the place the image was photographed. We use a separate keyword for the name of the town, and a separate keyword for the state.

5. **Press Return.**

   The keyword is added to the photos and the Info dialog is still open.

6. **Enter another keyword and press Return.**

   The new keyword is applied to the images, as shown in Figure 5-4.

TIP

If you really like an image, click the button shaped like a heart to tag the image as a Favorite. You can view these images, by clicking the Favorites link in the sidebar.

7. **Continue adding keywords that describe each image selected and then click the Close button.**

   The keywords are applied to the selected images.

FIGURE 5-4:
Keywording
images.

While you've still got the images you just imported in the Picture pane, you can fine-tune your keywords by selected an individual image, or a couple of images that are similar and add a keyword that applies to those images. For example, if you're adding keywords to vacation photos, and you've got some stellar images of Uncle Bob, select those images, right-click, choose Info from the context menu, and add the keyword *Uncle Bob* to them.

TIP

Another option for tagging images is tagging portraits of friends and family with a name. You do this in the Info panel by adding the person's name to the Face section of the Info window. Any photographs to which you add a person's name appear in the Faces section of the sidebar.

Using the Keyword Manager

The Keyword Manager stores all the keywords you've used. You use the Keyword Manager to add keywords and create shortcut keys for keywords. To use the Keyword Manager, follow these steps:

1. Choose Window ⇨ Keyword Manager.

The Keyword Manager appears, as shown in Figure 5-5.

FIGURE 5-5:
The Keyword Manager.

2. To create a hot key for a keyword you use frequently, drag it from the bottom window to the Quick Group window.

A Quick Group keyword uses the lowercase of the first letter as its shortcut. For example, if the keyword is *Florida,* the shortcut is *f.*

3. Click Edit Keywords.

The Keywords you've used are shown as a list.

4. Click the plus sign (+) to add a keyword to the list.

Enter the keyword in the text field and press Return.

5. Select a keyword and click the minus sign (–) to delete the keyword.

You can also rename a selected keyword, or assign a shortcut to the keyword.

6. **To assign a shortcut to a keyword, after clicking Edit Keywords, select the keyword and click Shortcut.**

A text field opens to the right of the keyword.

7. **Enter the desired keyword shortcut.**

For example, if the keyword is Virginia, *v* would be an excellent shortcut.

8. **Click OK.**

The keyword is added to the Quick Group.

9. **Click the Close button.**

To use a keyword from the Quick Group, choose Window ⇨ Keyword Manager, select the photo(s) to which you want to apply Quick Group keywords, and then drop the keyword on the photos or use its shortcut.

Manually adding information to photos

Your camera or phone adds information to images such as camera information, GPS information, and so on. In previous sections, we show you how to add keywords and location information to many photos. In this section, we show you how to manually add titles, keywords, and other information to your photos. To do so, follow these steps:

1. **Click any of the links in the Library section.**

Photos displays all images in that category.

2. **Right-click a photo to which you want add information and choose Get Info from the context menu.**

You can right-click a thumbnail or full-size image. After doing either, the Info window opens, as shown in Figure 5-6.

3. **Edit information for the photo(s) by clicking in the following fields:**

- *Add a Title:* Edit or type a title for the selected photo. If you've selected multiple images, the same title will be applied to all.

- *Add a Description:* Edit or type a descriptive word or words to describe the photo so you can search for it when you want to find it again. If you've selected multiple images, the same description will be applied to all.

- *Faces:* This option is only available if you right-click a full-size image. Enter the person's name in the text field, and the image appears in the People section.

FIGURE 5-6:
Add or modify
information
about a photo.

- *Keywords:* Click the Add Keyword field and begin typing a keyword. If you've used the keyword before, Photos lists suggestions. Click a keyword to add it to the photo's information. If Photos does not list suggestions, finish typing the keyword and it's added to the Keywords list, which you manage as outlined in a previous section.

4. **Click the Close button.**

Creating a Smart Album

If manually dragging photos in and out of albums is too tedious, you can set up a *Smart Album* from within Photos that will store photos automatically.

To create a Smart Album that can store photos automatically, follow these steps:

1. **Choose File ⇨ New Smart Album.**

A dialog appears, asking for a name for your Smart Album.

2. **Type a descriptive name for your album in the Smart Album Name text box.**

3. **Open the first pop-up menu and choose a criterion, such as Face or Favorite, or a camera setting like Aperture or Camera Model.**

4. **Open the second and third pop-up menus to refine the criterion you choose in Step 3, such as choosing only photos that are favorites.**

   After you define criterion for your Smart Album, the number of photos that match are listed at the bottom of the dialog.

5. **(Optional) Click the plus sign (+) button to define another criterion and repeat Steps 3 and 4.**

   You can add as many criteria to a Smart Album as you please, but in our humble estimation, one or two is plenty.

6. **Click OK.**

   Your Smart Album now stores photos based on your chosen criteria. New photos that match the criteria are added to the list.

Creating folders

Creating albums is a great way to organize your images, but if you're a prolific photographer, you end up with a long list of albums that you scroll through to find the one you want. You can make your life a lot easier by creating a folder and then adding albums to that folder. If you organize your folders by date and place, the obvious answer is to create a folder for each month of the year and put albums for each month in that folder.

To create a folder in which to store your images, follow these steps:

1. **In the Photos sidebar, click the plus sign (+) next to My Albums and choose Folder (see Figure 5-7).**

   A new folder is added to the My Albums section of the sidebar.

2. **Enter the desired name for the folder.**

FIGURE 5-7:
Creating a new folder.

3. Drag albums into the folder.

After you organize several albums into a folder, click the disclosure button to close the folder. Figure 5-8 shows Doug's My Albums section in Photos. The May 2019 folder is open, and one album is selected. Note the tag in the upper-right corner of each image, which shows the images that have keywords. Also notice that Doug has created a folder for each month of the year, in which albums containing photos created in that month are stored. Neat and tidy.

FIGURE 5-8: Folders keep you organized.

Deleting photos, albums, and folders

Many times, you'll import photos into Photos and decide that the photo isn't worth saving after all. To keep your Photos library from becoming too cluttered, you can delete the photos you don't need.

Besides deleting individual photos, you can also delete albums and folders that contain images you don't want. When you delete an album or folder (which contains albums), you don't physically delete the photos; you just delete the folder or album that contains the photos. The original photos are still stored in your Photos library.

To delete a photo, album, or folder, click the photo or the album or folder you want to delete and press the Delete key. If you delete a photo from an album, it's deleted only from that album, not from Photos.

Press ⌘+Z or choose Edit⇨Undo Delete right away if you want to recover your deleted items.

If you don't want to delete a photo but you want it out of sight, right-click the image and choose Hide from the context menu. The photo will be hidden from view but will still be visible in the Hidden album.

To bring your photos out of hiding, click the Hidden link in the sidebar, right-click the image, and choose Unhide from the context menu. The photo is back in its original spot.

Mapping your images

If you have a camera or phone that records the location in which the image was photographed as GPS data, you can see where the image was photographed on a map. If your camera or phone does not record GPS data, you can add the location to your image manually.

If your phone or camera records GPS data, right-click the image thumbnail or the full-size image, and choose Get Info from the context menu. You can see the location where the image was photographed and other information about the photo (see Figure 5-9). Notice the keywords and camera data.

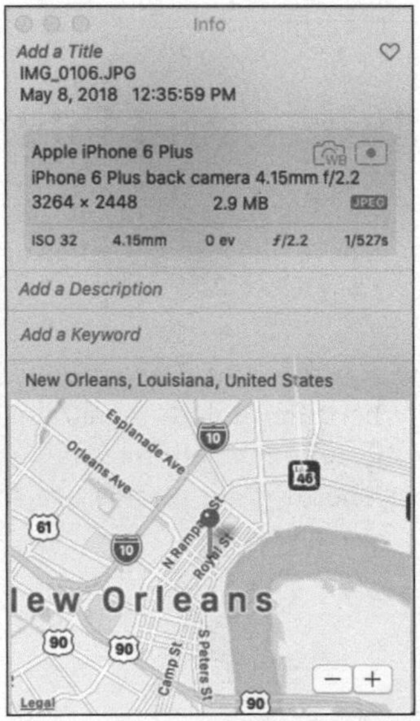

FIGURE 5-9: We know right where this photo was taken.

If your phone or camera does not record GPS data with the image's *metadata* (the info the camera stores with the photo), you can map the images as follows:

1. **Select the images you want to map.**

We suggest you do this immediately after importing them.

2. **Right-click and choose Get Info from the context menu.**

The Info window appears.

3. **Enter the name of the town in the Location text field.**

Photos will offer suggestions as you type, as shown in Figure 5-10. You may have to enter the state as well, if the town name is common.

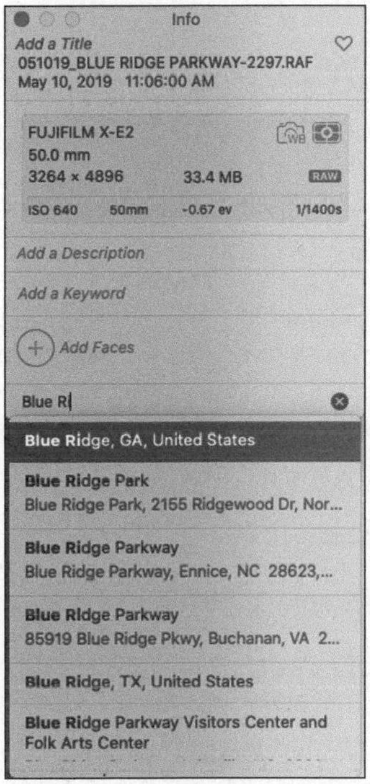

FIGURE 5-10:
Photos offers
location
suggestions.

4. **Choose a name from the suggestions list and press Return.**

A map appears, showing the location of the photos you just mapped, as shown in Figure 5-11.

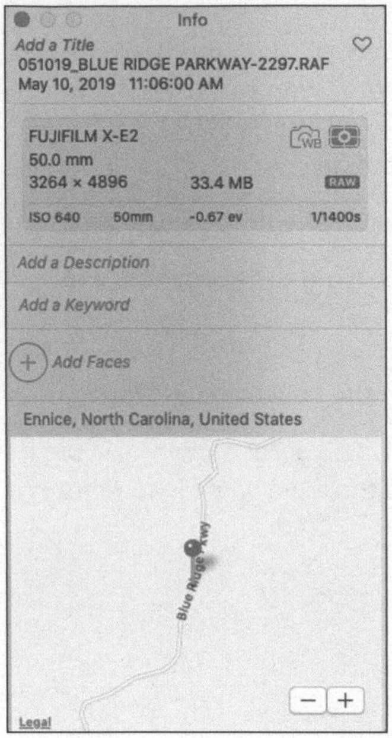

FIGURE 5-11:
We were here.

Creating Memories

Each day in your life is a gift, but some days are more special than others, like the day your child was born or the day you finally crossed Machu Picchu off your bucket list. You'll be happy to know you can create a memory of any special event that you photograph as a Memory. Any Memory you create is added to the Memories section of the sidebar.

To create a Memory, follow these steps:

1. **Select the images you want to add to the Memories section of the sidebar.**

2. **Click the Show as Memory button at the top of the Picture pane.**

   Photos shows you a preview of how the Memory will appear in the Memories section (see Figure 5-12).

3. **Scroll to the bottom of the window and click Add to Memories.**

   Photos adds the images to the Memories section. To see your Memories, click the Memories link in the sidebar. Click a Memory to expand it and view all the images, plus the slideshow Photos creates with your Memory.

To add a Memory to Favorite Memories, open a Memory, scroll to the bottom, and click Add to Favorite Memories.

TIP

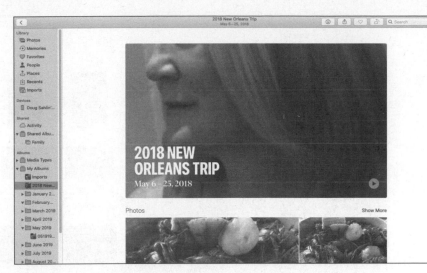

FIGURE 5-12:
Ah, such a sweet
memory.

Finding images

After you import hundreds of images into Photos, the time will come when you'll want to find certain images. If you've used keywords or given your images a unique description, finding the images you're looking for will be a piece of cake!

To find images, follow these steps:

1. Click the Photos link in the sidebar.

2. In the Search text field, enter text that will be associated with the images you want to find.

As you type, Photos offers a list of suggestions, as shown in Figure 5-13.

3. Click one of the suggestions.

The images are shown in the photo chooser.

Creating a slideshow

You may be a great photographer, but presentation is everything. To kick up the wow factor several notches, you can create slideshows by following these steps:

1. Click a link on the sidebar in which the images you want to create a slideshow with are stored.

The images are displayed in the photo chooser.

FIGURE 5-13:
Finding images.

2. **Select the images you want to appear in your slideshow.**

To select contiguous images, click the first image, and then Shift-click the last image. To select noncontiguous images ⌘+click the images you want in your slideshow.

3. **Right-click and, from the context menu, choose Create ⇨ Slideshow ⇨ Photos.**

The Add *x* Photos to Slideshow dialog appears (where *x* is the number of images you selected).

4. **Enter a name for the slideshow and click OK.**

The slideshow appears in the Projects window, as shown in Figure 5-14. There are three buttons on the right side of the Projects window: Themes, Music, and Duration.

5. **Click the Themes button and choose an option.**

Click the Play button to preview it. If you don't like the one you chose, chick the Themes button again and choose a different option.

6. **Click the Music button.**

Each theme has different music. If you don't like the default music, click Music Library to choose a tune from your Library in the Music app.

WARNING

If you choose a song from your Music app Library, it's probably copyrighted. You're technically not allowed to use copyrighted music in this way, but if the only people you're sharing it with are friends and family, it's probably okay. Just don't share the slideshow on social media, where you could be served a take-down notice for using copyrighted material illegally.

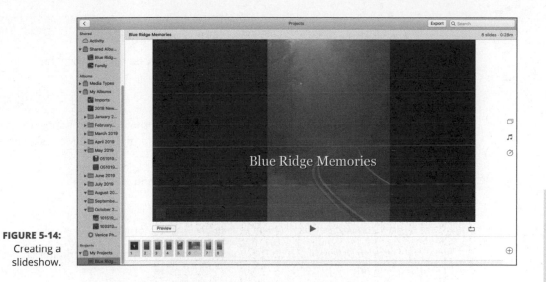

FIGURE 5-14:
Creating a
slideshow.

7. **Click the Duration button.**

The screen refreshes showing your duration options, as shown in Figure 5-15.

FIGURE 5-15:
Setting a
duration for
your slideshow.

8. **Choose your desired duration option.**

You can fit the slideshow to the music you've chosen, which can be a problem if the music is long, and you've only selected a few images. If you only selected a few images, Photos will automatically adjust the duration of the slideshow to the number of images. You can change this by dragging the slider to make the show longer or shorter.

9. **Accept the default Scale Photos to Fit Screen option.**

If you deselect this option, parts of the image may be hidden when the slideshow is played.

10. **Click Export.**

A Save As window appears. The default name for the slideshow is shown in the Save As field. The slideshow is saved in the .m4v format in your Movies folder. You can choose a different location if desired.

11. **Choose an option from the Format pop-up menu.**

Your choices are

- *Standard Definition (480p):* This option is good for sharing via email.

- *High Definition (720p):* This option is good for playing on a computer or iPad.

- *High Definition (1020p):* This option is also good for playing on a computer.

12. **(Optional) Click the Automatically Save to Music check box.**

Your slideshow will be saved to the Music app as well as the folder you specify.

13. **Click Save.**

The Exporting Slideshow dialog appears. After the slideshow is exported, it opens in Finder.

14. **Click the Play button to view your handiwork.**

Capturing Photos with Photo Booth

If your Mac has a built-in FaceTime camera, you can capture photos of yourself (or whoever or whatever is stationed in front of your Mac) by using the Photo Booth application. Photos you snap with Photo Booth save as JPEG files in a Photo Booth folder tucked inside your Photos folder.

TIP

You can plug in an optional external webcam, such as one of the models sold by Logitech (www.logitech.com) or Microsoft (www.microsoft.com/hardware), or plug in certain camcorders, to capture photos with Photo Booth. You can also use one of these optional external choices to conduct live, two-way video chats with friends and family, as we write about in Book 2, Chapter 3.

To capture photos with Photo Booth, follow these steps:

1. **Click the Photo Booth icon on the Dock or from Launchpad, or double-click the Photo Booth icon in the Applications folder.**

The Photo Booth window appears, displaying the image seen through the FaceTime camera. Click the zoom widget in the upper-right corner to use Photo Booth in full-screen mode, as shown in Figure 5-16. That way you have those nice red theater curtains framing your image.

TIP

If you click the Effects button, you can capture a photo by using visual effects (such as fish-eye).

FIGURE 5-16:
Use Photo Booth to capture photos with your Mac's built-in FaceTime camera.

2. **Use the three buttons on the lower-left side to choose from three formats:**

- *Four-up photo:* Click the left button to take four successive photos, just like an old-fashioned photo booth.

- *Single photo:* Click the middle button to take a single photo.

- *Video:* Click the right button to record video.

3. **Click the camera button in the middle of the Photo Booth window.**

Photo Booth counts down from 3 (in seconds) before capturing your photo. If you choose Four-up, Photo Booth snaps four successive shots. If you chose Video, Photo Booth begins recording video. Click the camera button again to stop recording video.

Each captured photo or video appears at the bottom of the Photo Booth window. Click a photo to see it in the Photo Booth viewing pane. Swipe left and right on the trackpad or with the Magic Mouse to move from one photo to the next.

If you hold down the Option key when you click the camera icon, Photo Booth snaps your photo right away without going through the three-second countdown.

4. **(Optional) Click a photo from the preview filmstrip, and then click one of the following choices from the Share pop-up menu:**

   - *Mail or Messages* opens a new message in Mail or Messages (respectively) with your selected photo pasted in the message. Address and send the message as you normally would with either app.

   - *AirDrop* makes your photo available to other AirDrop-capable Macs on the same network. See Book 3, Chapter 4 to learn about AirDrop.

   - *Notes:* Opens a window enabling you to add text for a note with which the image will be saved.

   - *Add to Photos* transfers the photo to your Photos library.

   - *Change Profile Picture* enables you to use the selected image as the new photo for your Contact Card.

5. **(Optional) Choose File⇨Export to export your photo to another folder, and then click the disclosure triangle next to the Save As field to see the Finder. Scroll through the directories and folders to choose the location to which you want to save the image.**

6. **(Optional) To print your photo, click the photo you want to print in the preview filmstrip and then choose File⇨Print. Adjust any necessary settings in the Print dialog that appears, and then click the Print button.**

7. **When you finish snapping and sharing photos, choose Photo Booth⇨Quit Photo Booth or press ⌘+Q to exit Photo Booth.**

   Images you export from Photo Booth to Photos are saved in the Photos section of your Library.

You can delete photos you take with Photo Booth as follows:

» **Single image:** In the preview filmstrip, click a photo that you want to delete, and then press the Delete key or click the "X" in the upper-left corner of the preview image.

» **All images:** To delete all your Photo Booth photos at one time, choose Edit⇨Delete All and click OK to confirm your choice.

TIP

The Save Image As option is the only one that lets you choose your own descriptive name for an image and specify the save location. All the other options save an image by using that image's original filename, which may be something cryptic like `wild_things_LJ-0187.jpg`, although you can always rename the file later if you want.

Editing Photos with Photos

Besides organizing your photos, Photos lets you edit them. Such editing can be as simple as rotating or cropping a photo, or it can be as intricate as removing red-eye from a photograph or modifying colors. When your photos look perfect, you can print them on your printer or through a printing service (which can actually cost less than what you may spend on ink cartridges and glossy photo paper!). And, because the digital format is universally web-friendly, you can share your photos in a Messages or Mail message, or on a social network like Facebook or Twitter, or create a shared Photo Stream on your iCloud account.

First, you want to make those photos as flawless as possible. To edit a photo, follow these steps:

1. **Click any link in your Library to see thumbnails of images in that section.**

2. **Click a photo and click the Edit button in the upper-right corner.**

   Photos displays your selected photo in the center pane, and an editing pane opens to the right of your photo, as shown in Figure 5-17. Note the buttons on the upper-right side. If you haven't done so already, you have the option to modify a photo's information and favorite a photo.

3. **Click the Rotate button to rotate the image in 90-degree increments.**

4. **To resize an image, click Crop.**

   The crop tools appear on the right side of the interface, as shown in Figure 5-18.

   REMEMBER

   You should always crop an image before applying other adjustments. When you crop, you can change the ratio of tonal values.

5. **If the image is not level, click Auto.**

   Photos straightens the image.

FIGURE 5-17:
The editing tools
appear in a pane
to the right of
your photo.

FIGURE 5-18:
Cropping an
image.

6. **If you're going to crop the image, choose an option from the Aspect menu.**

The default option is freeform, which lets you crop the image disproportionately, which is not a good thing if you're going to print the image. We suggest you choose an aspect that fits the paper you're going to print it on.

7. **Drag one of the handles to crop the image.**

As you drag, a grid appears on your image (see Figure 5-19). This grid is the so-called "rule of thirds." If you're going to crop according to the rule of thirds, make sure a focal point intersects with a point where the lines intersect.

When you're done cropping, you can exit the Edit pane by clicking Done, or perform the following steps if the image needs some enhancing.

FIGURE 5-19:
Cropping according to the rule of thirds.

8. **Click the Auto Enhance button that looks like a magic wand.**

   Photos attempts to enhance the image to pixel perfection. If you don't like the changes, click Revert to Original.

9. **Click the Effects tab of the Edit pane and click the effect you want, as shown in Figure 5-20.**

FIGURE 5-20:
Applying special effects.

10. **Click the Adjust tab of the Edit pane to adjust the image.**

Most of the options, except Retouch, have an Auto button. We suggest clicking that button to see if you like the results. If you don't, click the disclosure button for the adjustment you applied and tweak the settings. For example, if you press the Auto button to apply a vignette to an image, click the disclosure triangle and you can increase or decrease the strength and change the radius of the vignette.

Many of the adjustments have thumbnail previews of your image with varying degrees of the adjustment applied (for example, Black and White). If you like the looks of a thumbnail, click it to apply the adjustment to your image.

When you apply an adjustment to an image, the hollow blue dot next to the adjustment name is filled and has a check mark inside. If you don't like the results of a particular adjustment, but don't want to change the others, click the curved arrow to the right of the adjustment name to undo it.

To see how an image looks without an adjustment applied, click the blue circle with a check mark to temporarily remove the adjustment from the image. If you decide you like it, click the blue circle to reapply the adjustment.

You have the following adjustments from which to choose:

- *Light:* Lightens or darkens a photo.

- *Color:* Adjust the color balance of the image.

- *Black and White:* Converts the image to black and white.

- *Retouch:* Use this adjustment to remove sensor dust, or annoying things in your image like the telephone pole growing out of your friend's head. To use this option, click the disclosure triangle, drag the size slider to adjust the size of the brush, click the brush, and then drag over the offending part of your image. Photos attempts to repair it.

- *Red Eye:* Removes red-eye from photos where the flash reflected off your subject's eyes and made them look red. This does not work for the weird way animals' eyes often look in photos.

- *White Balance:* Click the Auto button if the whites in your image don't look white.

- *Curves:* Modifies tonal areas of your image to enhance it. Unless you're an experienced retoucher, we suggest you click the Auto button. Undo the adjustment if you don't like the results.

- *Levels:* This is helpful if the image is slightly underexposed. It stretches the brightness levels in the shadow and highlight areas of the image. Unless you're an experienced image editor, we suggest you try Auto.

- *Selective Color:* The adjustment gives you the ability to change the Hue, Saturation, and Luminance of individual colors in your image. You have an eyedropper, which can be used to select a color in the image, or you can click a color swatch. You can get some interesting results using selective color. If you go over the top, you can make this adjustment go away by clicking the blue dot with a check mark in it next to Selective Color.

- *Noise Reduction:* This option reduces digital noise in an image. Some people think digital noise looks like film grain. It doesn't. Use this option when you edit a photograph created in dark conditions, such as at night in a dimly lit restaurant.

- *Sharpen:* Enhance an image by increasing the sharpness of images with edges, such as windows. We suggest you click Auto with this adjustment, unless you've sharpened images in other photo-editing applications with good results.

- *Vignette:* Applies a circular vignette around the image, which draws viewers' attention to the center of the image.

TIP

If your photo ends up looking harsh or garish, and you've dabbled with any option in the Adjust section, click the Reset Adjustments button at the bottom of the Adjust section.

11. **Click the Done button to close the Edit pane.**

Sharing Photos

For many people, there's no point in taking photos if they don't share them with others. If you fall in this camp, you can publicize your photos to the world by printing them; posting them on a web page; uploading them directly to Facebook, Twitter, or Flickr; sending them to others via Mail or Messages; or burning them to a CD/DVD. For an added fee, you can print your photos as books, calendars, or greeting cards. In this section, we give you the rundown for sharing in each and every way.

Printing photos

You can print individual photos or groups of photos on your home printer by following these steps:

1. **Click an link in the sidebar to see images in the photo chooser.**

2. **Hold down the ⌘ key and click all the photos you want to print.**

If you choose multiple images, Photos arranges them to fit the page.

3. **Choose File⇨Print.**

   A Print dialog appears, as shown in Figure 5-21.

4. **Click the print styles to the right.**

   The photo appears as it will be printed.

5. **Choose the printer, paper size, and quality from the pop-up menus.**

6. **Click the Print button.**

FIGURE 5-21:
Choose from different ways to print your photos.

Sending photos in a message

If you want to share photos with family members or friends who have an email address or use Messages on a Mac, iPhone, iPad, or iPod touch, you can send photos by using the Mail or Messages app. You can send a photo by following these steps:

1. **Click any link in the sidebar to see the images in the photo chooser.**

2. **Hold down the ⌘ key and click the photo you want to send.**

   You can click up to ten photos to send in one email.

3. **Click the Share button and choose Mail.**

   Your photos appear as attachments in an email message.

4. **Enter an email address or addresses in the To text box.**

To send a photo with Messages, follow these steps:

1. **Select the photo you want to send as outlined in Steps 1 and 2 of the preceding list.**

2. **Click the Share button choose Messages from the fly-out menu.**

   A new message window appears with your photo attached to it.

3. **Address your message, type an accompanying note, and then click Send.**

You can also share images via AirDrop, Notes, and Reminders.

REMEMBER

Using Photo Stream

Photo Stream is part of Apple's iCloud service. If you activate Photo Stream, your last 30 days of new photos are uploaded to Photo Stream. To activate Photo Stream in Photos, choose Photos⇨Preferences and click the iCloud tab. Select the My Photo Stream and Shared Albums check boxes, as shown in Figure 5-22.

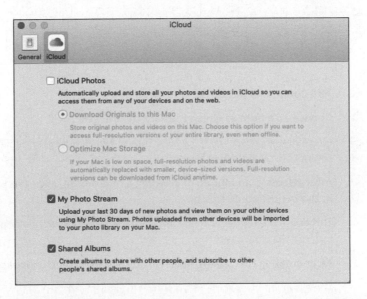

FIGURE 5-22:
Upload images to Photo Stream and share albums with others.

All the photos are synced to the devices you have connected to iCloud, such as your iPhone, iPad, or iPod touch. See Book 1, Chapter 3 to find out more about using iCloud.

To share photo streams with others, do the following:

1. **Click any link in the sidebar to see the images in the photo chooser.**

2. **Hold down the ⌘ key and click the photo(s) you want to upload.**

3. **Click the Share button and choose Shared Albums.**

   The Add to Shared Album dialog appears, as shown in Figure 5-23.

4. **Add Comments if desired.**

5. **Choose an album in which to share the images.**

   Alternatively, you can click the New Shared Album button and follow the prompts to create a new album.

6. **After choosing an album, or creating a new album, click the plus sign (+) in the Invite People text box.**

   This opens the Contacts app from which you can choose the people you want to share the album with.

7. **After creating the album, open it and click the icon that looks like a head.**

   The album info box appears, as shown in Figure 5-24.

8. **Select the Subscribers Can Post check box if you want others to be able to interact with your Photo Stream by adding their own photos and comments.**

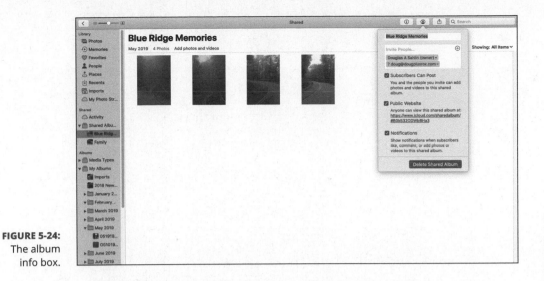

FIGURE 5-24:
The album
info box.

9. **Select the Public Website check box if you want to make your stream available to the general public.**

   Click the link to view the website.

10. **Click the Share button.**

    The selected photos are posted on iCloud as a Photo Stream, and a message is sent to the people you invited to view that stream.

TIP

Creating a book is a nice way to organize and view your photos on your computer. In full-screen view, click the My Projects button at the bottom of the window to see all your projects arranged as thumbnails in the photo pane. Double-click a project to open it.

TIP

To create a new project, click the plus sign (+), and choose one of the following options: Book, Calendar, Card, Wall Décor, Prints, Slideshow, or Other. Most of links connect you with the App Store, where you can choose a source to complete your project.

5

Taking Care of Business

Contents at a Glance

CHAPTER 1: **Managing Contacts** 549
Setting Up Contacts. 550
Working with Contacts 560
Sharing Your Contacts 568

CHAPTER 2: **Staying on Schedule with Calendar** 573
Getting Acquainted with Calendar 574
Working with Multiple Calendars 576
Creating and Modifying Events 585
Finding Events 595
Organizing Tasks with Reminders. 602

CHAPTER 3: **Creating Documents with Pages** 607
Working with Document Templates. 608
Working with Text 617
Creating and Placing Text Boxes. 629
Using Styles 631
Creating Charts and Tables. 635
Polishing Your Document. 642
Saving Your Documents on Your Mac or iCloud. 645
Printing Your Documents. 646
Exporting to a Different File Format. 646

CHAPTER 4: **Presenting with Keynote**. 649
Creating a Presentation 650
Manipulating Text 658
Adding Shapes, Charts, and Tables. 667
Adding Media Files 674
Rearranging Slides. 678
Creating Transitions and Effects 680
Using Masters to Customize Themes 686
Polishing Your Presentation. 687

CHAPTER 5: **Crunching with Numbers**. 695
Understanding the Parts of a Numbers Spreadsheet 696
Creating a Numbers Spreadsheet. 699
Working with Sheets 701
Typing Data into Tables 706
Making Your Spreadsheets Pretty. 720
Sharing Your Spreadsheet 722

CHAPTER 6: **Getting the Most Out of Pages,
Numbers, and Keynote**. 727
Collaborating with Keynote, Pages, and Numbers. 728
Inserting Media from Other Sources 731
Copying and Pasting 732
Modifying Photos. 732
Adding Comments. 737
Finding More Templates. 738

IN THIS CHAPTER

» **Setting up Contacts**

» **Editing, searching, deleting, and grouping contacts**

» **Sharing contacts**

Chapter **1**

Managing Contacts

Your Mac comes with a contact management app called (surprise!) Contacts. Here you store names of people and businesses along with all sorts of information about them: phone numbers; street addresses; virtual addresses, such as those used for email, instant messaging, or websites; social network usernames; and more intimate information, such as birthdays, anniversaries, and relations. Besides storing contact names and related contact information, Contacts can display contact information from more than one source, and it syncs with your iOS or Android devices — meaning that if you make a change to contact information on one device or computer, it's automatically updated on all your devices. Contacts also connects with other applications on your Mac so you can click someone's email address and immediately

>> Write and send an email or message to that person.

>> Open a FaceTime conversation.

>> Click the pin next to a street address and see it in Maps.

If by chance you still send letters or gifts the old-fashioned postal way, you can also print envelopes and mailing labels, and even the entire contacts list directly from Contacts.

Contacts is integrated with the other applications on your Mac that use addresses, including Mail (see Book 2, Chapter 2), Messages (Book 2, Chapter 3), and Calendar (Book 5, Chapter 2). When you enter or search for a physical or virtual address in those applications, they refer to Contacts. This way, you have to enter contact information only once.

In this chapter, we explain how to set up Contacts by customizing the contact template with fields you use most frequently. Then we outline three ways to enter information: manually, importing data from another contact management app, and syncing with other accounts. In the second half of the chapter, we show you how to set up groups of contacts as well as how to print and export your contacts.

Setting Up Contacts

Contacts acts like an electronic Rolodex (if you can remember such things). You save information about a person on a contact card so you can find that information again.

Each card contains information associated with one contact — be it a person or a company — such as telephone numbers and postal addresses, email addresses, URLs, birthdays, profile usernames, and photos. And most contact information links to something else. For example, click the red pin next to an address, and Maps opens to show you a map of that address. Or click the envelope icon next to an email address and open an outgoing email message addressed to that person or start a FaceTime conversation. Click the icon to the right of a URL, and the website opens in Safari. You get the picture.

Viewing Contacts

When you open Contacts, the window is divided into two or three columns, as shown in Figure 1-1. From left to right, the first column displays the Accounts list, which shows the sources and groups of your contacts although you can hide this column by choosing View➪Hide Groups. Clicking an item in the Accounts list then displays in the second column an alphabetized Contacts list of all contacts in the selected account or group. Click a contact in the Contacts list, and you see its card in the third column.

You have a few options for how the name on a contact card is displayed:

>> **Organize by company name.** When you create a contact card, Contacts assumes that you want to display that card in the alphabetized Contacts list by a person's name. To list a card by company name instead, click the card and choose Card➪Mark as a Company. (Or, you can select the Company check box when you're creating a new contact card; we mention this later in the

upcoming "Creating a contact" section and show it in Figure 1-4.) Your chosen card now displays a company name and icon. To change from a company name back to a person's name, choose Card➪Mark as a Person.

>> Sort by first or last name. To set whether your cards are sorted by first or last name, choose Contacts➪Preferences➪General and then select the sort and display options you prefer.

>> Change the display name of an individual card. To change the first name/ last name order for one card only, choose Card➪Show First/Last Name Before Last/First. That one card only will change, regardless of the General Preferences you set.

FIGURE 1-1:
Contacts displays accounts and groups, the Contacts list, and contact cards.

All Contacts	Q Search	Mr. Wardle
iCloud	Arabella Allen	
All iCloud	Benjamin Allen	message call video mail
Business	Martha Bardell	
Facebook List	Alfred Jingle	iPhone 1 (234) 567-890
Family	Samuel Pickwick	
Friends	Robert Sawyer	FaceTime
Mailing List	Augustus Snodgrass	birthday September 23, 1997
Media	Job Trotter	
Party	Tracy Tupman	home Manor Farm
Personal	Emily Wardle	Dingley Dell
Philmont	Mr. Wardle	England
Pickwickians	Rachael Wardle	note
Plattsburgh	Sam Weller	
Plattsburgh City Council	Tony Weller	
Plattsburgh Data Center	Nathaniel Winkle	
Plattsburgh Signs		
Postcards		
Public Group		
SRT Board		

TIP

You can view multiple cards by clicking names in the Contacts list, and then choose Card➪Open in Separate Window. Repeat until all the cards you want to see are open. You can view multiple cards by clicking the first card you want to display, and then Shift-clicking the last card you want to display. The option displays contiguous cards. To display noncontiguous cards, click the first card you want to display and then cmd+click additional cards you want to display.

Designing your Contacts template

Each time you add a new contact, Contacts displays a contact card with blank fields that represent a piece of information to fill in about that person or entity, such as first and last name, company, title, and email address. You may not want or need to store all that information about everyone, so you can define your Contacts card template to list only the fields you want to use, such as just name and email address. Remember that you can always add more fields to an individual card as needed.

To modify the Contacts template, follow these steps:

1. **Click the Contacts icon on the Dock or from Launchpad.**

2. **Choose Contacts⇨Preferences.**

A Preferences window appears.

3. **Click the Template tab.**

The Template pane appears, as shown in Figure 1-2.

4. **Remove or add fields as you want.**

- *To remove a field:* Click the minus sign to the left of the field and repeat for every field you want to remove.

- *To add a field:* Click the plus sign at the bottom of a contact cart to open the Add Field pop-up menu (see Figure 1-3) and choose a field to add, such as URL or Birthday, repeating for each field you want to add. Click More at the bottom of the menu to see other fields you can add.

TIP

Click the plus sign next to an existing field to add another field in that category — for example, the plus sign next to Mobile (refer to Figure 1-2) to add a field for another type of phone number, such as Home or Work.

FIGURE 1-3:
The Add Field menu provides more fields you can add to a template.

5. **(Optional) Click the label arrow next to the field name to change it or create a custom field name.**

   For example, click Work or Home and choose Change Address Format to select the address format of a particular country. Doing so affects the address format of your entire Contacts. You can make this change on individual cards, though, as we explain in Step 2 in the "Creating a contact" section.

   Or click Twitter, which is the default, and choose Facebook to set that as the default social network username field (refer to Figure 1-3).

6. **Click the Close button of the Template preferences pane.**

Entering contacts

After you define a Contacts card template, the next step is to enter actual names and information by creating cards for new contacts.

Contacts comes with two contact cards: one for Apple, Inc. and one for you. The card that's for you is called My Card, and this contact card always represents you. It contains your email address, phone number, address, photo or representative image, and any other information you want to put on it. If you want to send your information to someone — say, a new business associate — you send this card by clicking the Share button at the bottom of the contact card. When you edit My Card, you see a check box next to each field you fill in. Just deselect the check box next to any information you don't want to send out when you share your card.

- **To define a different card to represent you:** Click that card and choose Card⇨Make This My Card.
- **To view your card at any time:** Choose Card⇨Go to My Card.

There are three ways to add contacts, which we explain in the upcoming subsections:

- Create contacts and manually enter information.
- Import contacts from an older address book application.
- Access other cloud or remote accounts.

Creating a contact

Follow these steps whenever you want to add a contact, either when you're populating Contacts for the first time or when you want to add a contact to your existing Contacts.

1. **Choose File⇨New Card, or click the plus sign at the bottom of the Contacts window and choose New Contact from the pop-up menu.**

   The third column of the Contacts window displays a blank card for you to fill in, as shown in Figure 1-4.

TIP

The Contact card has a control that lets you choose between Info and Picture fields for the contact. By default, it's set to Info.

All Contacts
iCloud
All iCloud
Business
Facebook List
Family
Friends
Mailing List
Media
Party
Personal
Philmont
Pickwickians
Plattsburgh
Plattsburgh City Council
Plattsburgh Data Center
Plattsburgh Signs
Postcards
Public Group
SRT Board
Search
No Name
Arabella Allen
Benjamin Allen
Martha Bardell
Alfred Jingle
Samuel Pickwick
Robert Sawyer
Augustus Snodgrass
Job Trotter
Tracy Tupman
Emily Wardle
Mr. Wardle
Rachael Wardle
Sam Weller
Tony Weller
Nathaniel Winkle
First Last
Company
Company
Info
Picture
mobile Phone
home Email
ringtone Opening
text tone Note
home page URL
birthday month/day/year
home User Name AIM
Twitter User Name
home Street
City State ZIP
Country or Region
note
Done

FIGURE 1-4: Fill out a card to add a contact.

2. **Click the text fields (such as First, Last, or Home) and enter the information you want to save for your contact.**

You don't have to fill every field. And some fields — Birthday, for example — can have just one entry; others, such as those for phone numbers or addresses, can have many entries. When you enter data in the existing field, press Return to go to the next blank field. Alternatively, press Tab to navigate to the next blank field.

TIP

When adding information like phone numbers, don't be concerned with the formatting. Just enter the numbers and press Return, and Contacts formats the phone number for you. For example, if you enter 15555551212, the phone number is displayed as 1 (555) 555-1212.

If you want a contact to be sorted by its business name instead of a person's name, click the checkbox next to Company.

To change the address field format, click the field name — Home, Work, or Other — and choose Change Address Format from the pop-up menu. Choose the country for that address, and the card changes to reflect that country's address format.

REMEMBER

When you make changes to a field name or format on a card, the changes apply to that card only. To apply changes to *all* your contact cards, make the changes from Contacts➪Preferences➪Template.

3. **(Optional) To add a photo of your contact, switch to the Picture button and then click the plus sign below Change Profile Picture or choose Card➪Choose Custom Image, as shown in Figure 1-5.**

4. **To change the contact's image from his or her initials to an actual image, perform Step 3 again and choose an image from the pop-up menu, which enables you to take a picture with the FaceTime camera or choose an image you've already saved on your Mac.**

Alternatively, click Edit below the contact's initials to open the dialog shown in Figure 1-5.

A photo pane opens, as shown in Figure 1-6. Choose from the photos in your Photos app.

5. **(Optional) After you choose a photo, you can edit it as follows:**

- *Enlarge:* Use the zoom slider to enlarge the photo you want to use.

- *Position:* After zooming in, place your cursor over the image and click and drag the photo around in the photo box until it's where you like.

- *Embellish:* Click the Special Effects button (it looks like a fan) to add special effects, such as sepia tone or a controlled blurring of the photo.

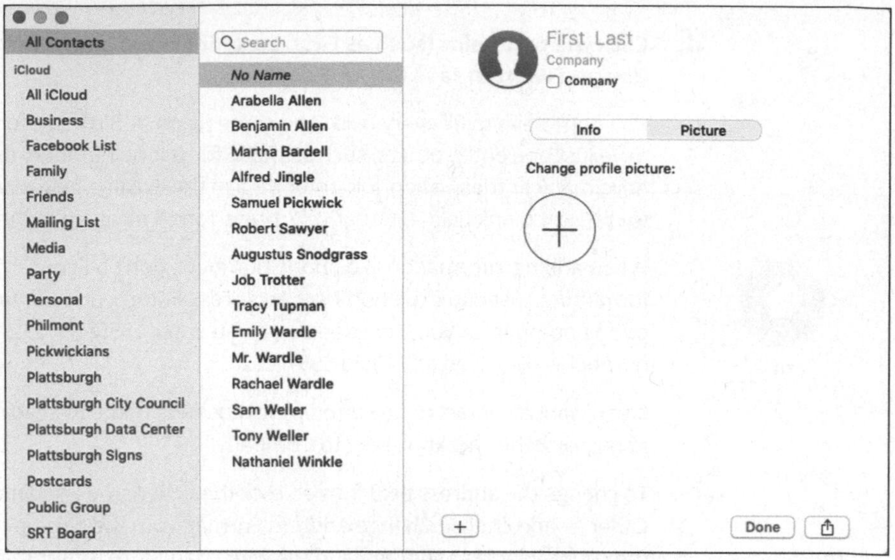

FIGURE 1-5:
Add a photo to
a contact to
connect names
with faces.

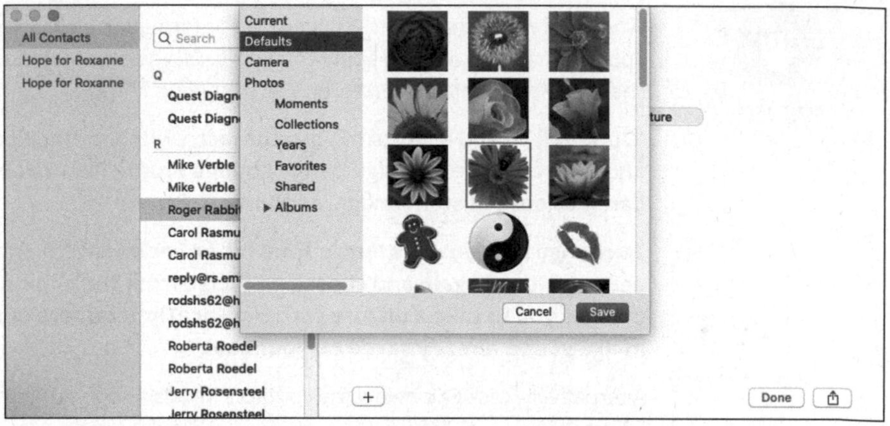

FIGURE 1-6:
Choose your
photo.

6. **Click Save when you're happy with the photo.**

The photo now appears to the left of the contact's name. If you're not happy with the results, click Edit underneath the image, and make the desired changes.

7. **(Optional) If you want to add a field to this card only, choose Card⇨Add Field. Or click the plus sign at the bottom of the card, and then from the menu, choose a field to add to the card, as shown in Figure 1-7.**

After you add a field to a card, you need to type information into that field.

REMEMBER

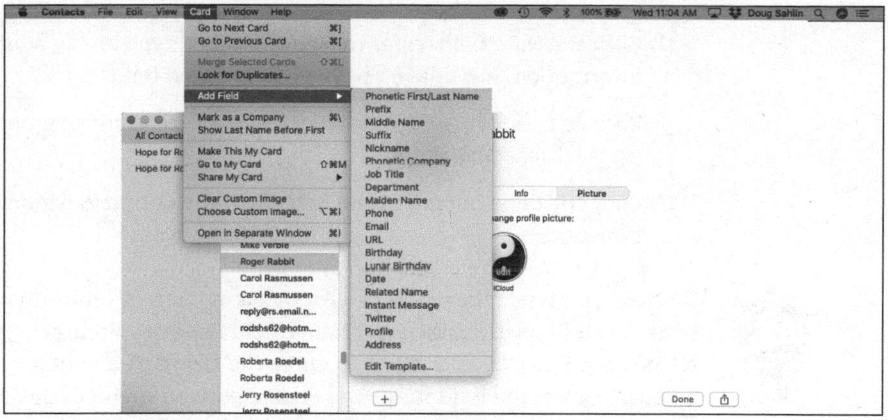

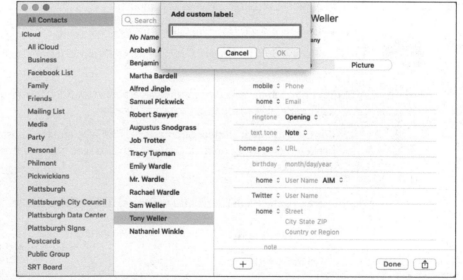

FIGURE 1-7:
Use the Add Field submenu to add a new field that appears only on the displayed card.

8. **To change the name of a field, click the name of the field and choose from the menu or scroll down to Custom.**

   The Add Custom Label dialog appears, as shown in Figure 1-8. Type in the name you want for the field and then click OK.

FIGURE 1-8:
Create custom names for fields.

9. **Click the Note field (refer to Figure 1-4) and type in any additional information that doesn't have an associated field.**

   Barbara uses this field to add a tag that she uses to create groups, which we explain later in this chapter.

10. **Click the Done button at the bottom of the Contacts window to save your new card.**

TIP

To help you remember how to pronounce names in unfamiliar languages, Contacts has a Phonetic First/Last Name field (refer to Figure 1-3). And the Related Names field gives you a place to enter the name of a contact's spouse, child, or assistant. Click the field name to reveal a pop-up menu of options.

Importing contacts

If your contacts are already in another application, there's no need to retype all that data. Just import the data into Contacts. Contacts understands the following four file formats:

TECHNICAL STUFF

» **vCard:** Standard file format used to store contact information; used by applications on different types of computers.

» **LDIF:** Standard data interchange file format.

   LDIF stands for Lightweight Directory Access Protocol (LDAP) Data Interchange Format.

» **Text file:** Tab-delimited or comma-separated value (CSV) format; comes from a database, spreadsheet, or contact application.

» **Contacts Archive:** Standard Contacts file format useful for transferring data between Macs with Contacts. Contacts can also read older Address Book archive files.

To import a contact's data file into Contacts, follow these steps:

1. **Choose File⇨Import.**

   A dialog appears.

2. **Select the file you want to import and then click Open.**

   If you import a CSV list, a dialog with the standard card template appears, listing the fields that will be imported.

3. **Accept or review duplicate cards:**

   • *To automatically accept duplicates:* Click Import.

   • *To see duplicates and resolve differences between the two:* Click Review.

4. **Click Next.**

The new contacts are imported and appear in a Last Import Smart Group. You can review all contacts in this group, and edit and delete them as needed until you import additional contacts.

TIP

If you're importing a text or CSV file, make sure that the correct field labels are associated with the data being imported. You can change the field labels if necessary.

When the import is finished, Contacts contains the new contact cards.

TIP

In applications that use the vCard format, you can export the contents to a vCard file and then email the file to yourself. Save the attached vCard file and then double-click it to import the contact into Contacts automatically without having to bother with the preceding steps.

Your newly imported contacts will appear in both the All Contacts group and the Last Import group under the Smart Group heading.

Accessing contacts from another device or server

We explain iCloud syncing in Book 1, Chapter 3, but it deserves attention here as well. If you have a mobile phone and keep contact information on a cloud server (such as iCloud or Google) or a social network (such as Facebook or LinkedIn), you can add that information to Contacts on your Mac, too. The accounts you add to Contacts are listed in the Accounts list.

Likewise, you may have access to address books on network servers — perhaps, the company directory at your place of employment. By adding the cloud or remote account information to Contacts, you can access the information. *Note:* Because the data is in a *remote* location (not on your Mac), you need to be online to access the information, and you may or may not have editing privileges. To add an account, follow these steps:

1. **Choose Contacts⇨Add Account.**

2. **Complete one of the following step lists:**

a. Select the radio button next to the service you want to add, such as iCloud (as shown in Figure 1-9), and then click Continue.

b. Type in your username and password.

Your account is verified.

c. Select the Contacts radio button (if it isn't already) selected and then click Done.

Or

d. *Select the Other Contacts Account radio button and then click Continue.*

e. *Choose CardDAV or LDAP from the pull-down menu.*

f. *Enter the requested information.*

You may have to ask the network administrator or a techie in your group for the information.

g. *Click Create.*

Your access is verified.

That account is added to the Accounts list on the Contacts window.

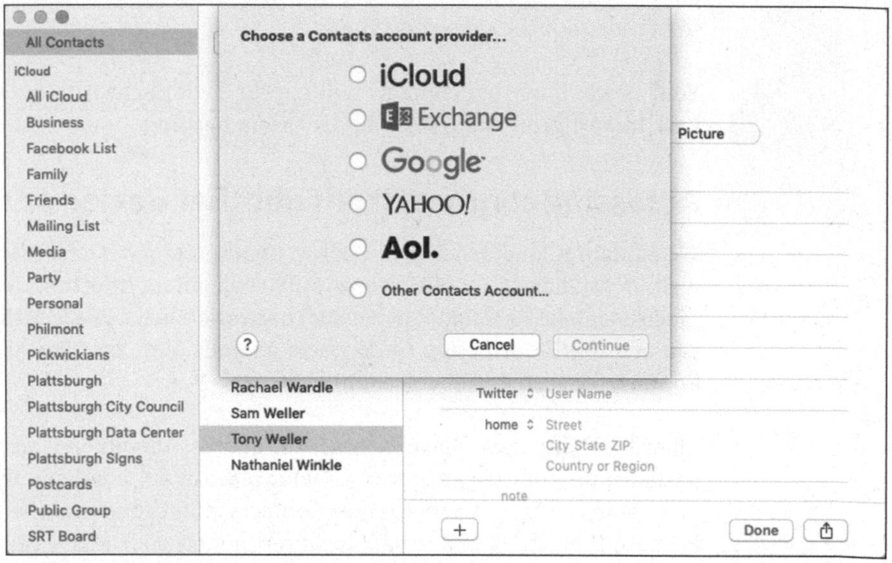

FIGURE 1-9:
Add an account to access address books stored on cloud or remote servers.

TIP

When you access multiple accounts, Contacts does its best to merge cards from different accounts onto one card. When a contact card contains information from more than one account, at the very bottom of the card you see a Cards field, which lists the accounts the card references.

Working with Contacts

There's no reason to add names and numbers to Contacts if you don't plan to use them. In this section, we explain all the different things you can do with Contacts: how to search for an number, edit a card when contact information changes, and create groups to make communicating with many people at once easier.

Searching contacts

The more contact cards you store in Contacts, the harder it is to find a particular contact you want. Instead of scrolling through every contact card to locate a certain one, you can search for specific contacts by following these steps:

1. **Click All Contacts or click the account or group you want to search from the Accounts list.**

2. **Click the search text field above the Contacts list.**

3. **Type a word or phrase that you want to find, such as a person's name or the company that person works for.**

The Contacts displays a list of contacts that match the text you typed.

4. **Click a contact to display the card for that person or company.**

TIP

To search for the occurrence of a contact's name on your Mac, Control-click the name of the contact in the Contacts list and choose Spotlight from the shortcut menu.

Editing a card

Life is dynamic; things change. When you need to update information on a card — a change of address, phone number, or company, for example — edit a card by following these steps:

1. **Find and open the card for the contact for whom you have new or updated information.**

TIP

You can edit contacts that are part of your personal accounts but probably not those you access through a company server. You can also add information to LinkedIn contacts, although you can't edit the information pulled from the contact's profile.

2. **Click the Edit button at the bottom of the window.**

A red circle with a minus sign appears to the left of all fields that contain information.

3. **Do one of the following:**

- Click the field in which you want to edit information, such as an out-of-date email address or phone number. The existing information is highlighted, and you can simply type the updated information to replace the existing information.

- Click an empty field and enter new information.

- Click the plus sign at the bottom of the page and select a field you want to add from the menu. (Click More Fields if you don't see what you're looking for and then choose from that expanded menu.) Type in the new information in the added field.

- Click the minus sign to delete the contents of a field.

If you delete the contents of a field by mistake, press cmd+Z.

4. **Repeat Step 3 to add additional fields or edit information.**

5. **Click the Done button.**

Contacts saves the updated contact information.

You can add or edit notes in the Note field without being in Edit mode. Just click in the Note field and type what you want.

Deleting a contact

Again, life is dynamic. When it's time for a little housekeeping, prune the contact cards you don't need any more.

You can delete only those contacts that are stored directly on your Mac or accounts that you access directly, such as via iCloud or Google. For example, you can't delete contacts on your company's server.

To delete a name from your Contacts, just click the contact and choose Edit⇨Delete Card, or press Delete. After doing so, a dialog appears asking you if you want to delete the contact. At this point, you can complete the deletion by pressing the Delete button, or press the Cancel button to cancel the deletion. If you accidentally delete a contact, press ⌘+Z or choose Edit⇨Undo to restore it.

To choose multiple contacts to delete, hold down the ⌘ key and click at will. If you hold down the Shift key, you can click two contiguous cards — or, select two noncontiguous cards, which selects all cards in between as well.

Creating groups

To help you organize your contacts, use Contacts to create groups of contacts, such as for your co-workers, friends, family members, restaurants, and so on. For greater convenience, you can even store the same contact in multiple groups. Although you don't have to use groups, this feature can help you manage your list of important contact cards. It's also a great way to send emails to a group of people without having to type in each name singly — just Control-click the group name and choose Send Email to *group name*.

Contacts has many more options than meet the eye. Most are revealed in pop-up or shortcut menus. Clicking field names in the Contact Card brings up shortcut menus, which present the options that vary depending on the apps that you have installed. Among the options you may see are

- **Telephone Number:** Show in Large Type, Send Message, and FaceTime. If you have Skype installed and configured to link with Contacts, you see two more options: Call with Skype and Send SMS with Skype.

- **Address:** Open in Maps, Copy Address, and Copy Map URL.

- **Email:** Send Email, FaceTime, Send Message, Send My Card, and Search with Spotlight.

- **Twitter Profile:** Tweet and Show Tweets.

- **Facebook Profile:** View Profile and View Photos.

- **LinkedIn/Myspace/Profile:** View Profile.

- **Flickr:** View Photostream.

- **Sina Weibo:** Post and View Posts.

- **Tencent Weibo:** Send Message and View Profile.

- **Related:** Show "relation's name" and Search with Spotlight.

Your Contacts initially contains one group: All Contacts. The All Contacts group automatically stores all contacts you've saved in Contacts. Even when a contact is assigned to a group, the contact remains in All Contacts.

REMEMBER

If your Mac is connected to a local area network (LAN), you may see a second group: Directories. The Directories group contains a list of contacts of everyone connected to that LAN. If you're using a Mac at home without a LAN, you won't see the Directories group.

Adding a group

You can create as many groups as you want, but for groups to be useful, you need to add contacts to that group. To create a new group, follow these steps:

1. **Choose File⇨New Group, or click the plus sign at the bottom of the screen and choose New Group from the pop-up menu.**

2. **Replace *untitled group* with a more descriptive name in the Accounts list, as shown in Figure 1-10, and then press Return.**

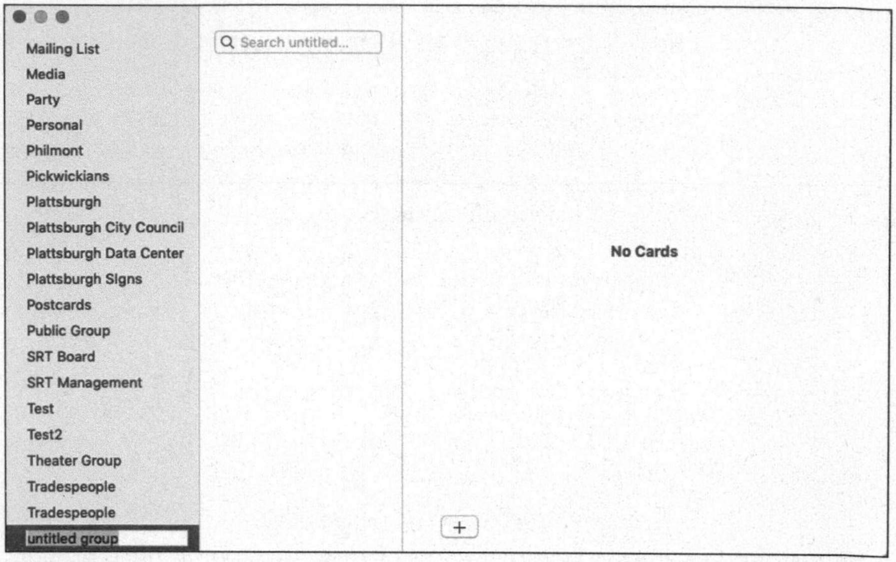

FIGURE 1-10:
Groups are subsets of your contacts in Contacts.

A window showing a list of groups: Mailing List, Media, Party, Personal, Philmont, Pickwickians, Plattsburgh, Plattsburgh City Council, Plattsburgh Data Center, Plattsburgh Signs, Postcards, Public Group, SRT Board, SRT Management, Test, Test2, Theater Group, Tradespeople, Tradespeople, untitled group. A search field labeled "Search untitled..." and "No Cards" displayed.

To add contacts to a group, follow these steps:

1. **Click All Contacts in the Accounts list to see all the contacts stored in Contacts.**

   When All Contacts is selected, the Contacts list displays contacts from all the accounts, so you may see duplicate names.

2. **Move the cursor over a contact, hold down the mouse or trackpad button until you see a contact card icon, and then drag the cursor over the group name where you want to store your contact.**

   TIP

   If you hold down the ⌘ key, you can click and choose multiple contacts. If you hold down the Shift key, you can click two noncontiguous contacts to select those two contacts and all contacts in between as well.

3. **Release the mouse or trackpad button when the group name appears highlighted.**

   Your chosen contact appears in your newly created group and in the All Contacts group.

TIP To see which groups a contact belongs to, click a name in the Contacts list and then hold down the Option key. The groups to which that contact belongs are highlighted in the Accounts list on the left.

Creating a group from a selection of contacts

If you already have a group of contacts selected that you want to organize, you can create a new group and store those contacts at the same time. To create a new group from a selection of contacts, follow these steps:

1. **Click All Contacts in the Accounts list to see all the names stored in Contacts.**

2. **Hold down the ⌘ key and click each contact you want to store in a group.**

   You can select a range of contacts by holding down the Shift key and clicking two noncontiguous contacts. Doing so selects those two contacts and all contacts in between.

3. **Choose File⇨New Group from Selection.**

   The group appears in the Accounts list with the moniker *untitled group*.

4. **Type a more descriptive name for your group and then press Return.**

   Your group now contains the contacts you selected in Step 2.

TIP

To send an email to a group, Control-click the group name and choose Send Email to *group name.*

Editing a distribution list

Say you have more than one phone number, email, or street address for the same person. To choose which fields to use for each contact in a group, edit the distribution list. For example, you can choose the same type of address for all members of the group — for example, using the work address — or you can select the information for each member of the group. Follow this procedure:

1. **Choose Edit⇨Edit Distribution List.**

2. **Select the group you want to edit.**

3. **Click the column header to open a pop-up menu that lets you choose which type of data you want to manage: Email, Phone, or Address.**

4. **Select the corresponding information you want to use for each member who has more than one entry.**

Adding contacts automatically with Smart Groups

Adding contacts manually or selecting them for a group is fine, but what if you frequently add and delete contacts? Doing all this manually can get old. To keep your group's contacts accurate and up to date more easily, you can use the Smart Groups feature.

With a Smart Group, you define the types of contacts you want to store, such as contacts for everyone who works at a certain company. Then the Smart Group automatically adds any contacts to the group from your Contacts.

To create a Smart Group, follow these steps:

1. **Choose File⇨New Smart Group.**

   A dialog appears, asking for a contact and rule for storing contacts in the group. A *rule* lets you group contacts based on certain criteria. For example, you may want to group the contacts of all people who work for Apple and live in Texas.

2. **Click the Smart Group Name text box and type a descriptive name for your Smart Group.**

3. **Click the first pop-up menu and choose the criteria for including a contact in your Smart Group, such as Company or City or just an entire card, as shown in Figure 1-11.**

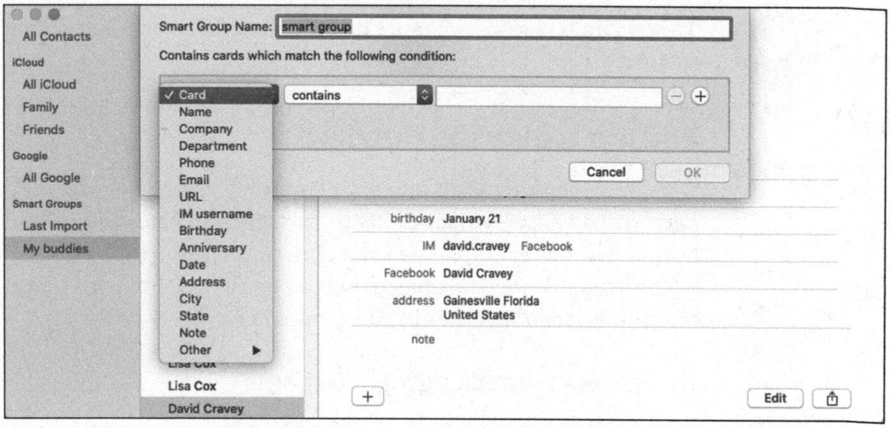

FIGURE 1-11:
This pop-up menu defines the criteria for storing contacts in your Smart Group.

4. **Click the second pop-up menu and choose how to use the criteria you defined in Step 3, such as Contains or Was Updated After.**

5. **Click the text box and type a word or phrase for your criteria to use.**

   For example, if you want to create a Smart Group that stores only contacts of people in the state of Florida on the card, your entire Smart Group rule may look like *State Contains Florida*.

6. **(Optional) Click the plus sign to the right of the text box to create any additional rules.**

If you create any additional rules and later decide you don't want them, you can always remove them by clicking the minus sign that appears next to the rule.

7. **Click OK.**

Creating a Smart Group from search results

Defining the criteria for storing names automatically in a Smart Group can be cumbersome when you aren't quite sure whether the defined criteria will work exactly the way you want. As an alternative, you can use Spotlight to search for the types of contacts you want to store, and *then* create a Smart Group based on your search results. Using this approach, you can see exactly which types of contacts appear in your Smart Group.

To create a Smart Group from search results, follow these steps:

1. **Click All Contacts, and in the search text field, type the text you want to find (such as the name of a company, a last name, or part of an email address), and press Return.**

The Contacts list shows the contacts that Spotlight found based on the text you typed in.

2. **Choose File⇨New Smart Group from Current Search.**

A Smart Group appears in the Group category, using the text you typed as the group name.

TIP

You can edit a Smart Group by right-clicking the name and choosing Edit Smart Group.

Deleting a group

If you create a group and no longer need it, you can delete it. When you delete a group, you delete only the group folder; you do not delete any contact cards stored in that group. To delete a group, click the group and choose Edit⇨Delete Group.

WARNING

You can delete a contact from the group by selecting the group, clicking the contact you want to delete, and then choosing Edit⇨Delete Card. A dialog box with two options appears: Delete, which deletes the contact from All Contacts and from the group, or Remove from Group, in which case, the contact is only removed from the group.

TIP

If you have both Contacts and Calendar open, from Contacts or a Group list, you can click and drag a contact (⌘-click to select more than one invitee) to the hour of an event to which you want to invite them. See Book 5, Chapter 2 to find out more about inviting contacts to an event by using Calendar.

Sharing Your Contacts

Sometimes you may need to share contact information with others. Contacts makes it easy to share one card or a group in the vCard format. A *vCard* is a standard format that many applications use to store contact information. By sharing contact data as a vCard, the information can be accessed by another application and computer, such as a Windows PC running Outlook.

Sending one contact at a time

To share a single card, click the Share button in the bottom-right corner of the contact card and select one of the following:

>> **Mail:** Opens a blank email message that contains a vCard attachment. Address the message to one or more recipients and click Send.

>> **Messages:** Opens a blank Messages message with a vCard attachment. Address the message and click Send.

>> **AirDrop:** Makes the vCard available on AirDrop to other Macs on your network that have AirDrop turned on.

>> **Notes:** Adds the contact information as a note in the Notes app. This stores the information in iCloud and is also available on other devices that are linked to your computer, such as your iPhone.

>> **More:** Click More at the bottom of the Share pop-up menu to open the Extensions dialog box, enabling you to select other extensions for sharing with others.

If you want to send your own card, choose Card⇨Share My Card and then choose one of the following options from the submenu:

>> **Mail My Card:** Opens a blank email message that contains a vCard attachment. Address the message to one or more recipients and click Send.

>> **Message My Card:** Opens a blank Messages message with a vCard attachment. Address the message and click Send.

>> **AirDrop My Card:** Makes the vCard available on AirDrop to other Macs on your network that have AirDrop turned on.

Exporting multiple cards

You have three choices for sharing multiple cards from Contacts:

>> Export contact data in the vCard format, which most contact management apps can import.

>> Export as an archive, which most Macs can read.

>> Export as a PDF, which most computers and hand-held devices can read.

Consider both the recipient's computer system and how the data will be used when exporting the cards. After the file is imported to another contact management app, either from the vCard or archive format, it can be edited. However, a PDF file is an image of the data, so it can be viewed or printed — but the data cannot be manipulated.

WARNING

When exporting contacts for use in another application, the application you're importing may not recognize every detail for the contact, such as a person's picture or notes you've added to a person's contact card.

Whichever file type you choose, the process is as follows for exporting contacts from Contacts:

1. **Select the names you want to export by doing one of the following:**

- Click All Contacts.

- Click an account or group name.

TIP

  To quickly export a group, Control-click a (non-Smart) group name and choose Export Group vCard.

- Select contacts from the Contacts list by holding the ⌘ key and clicking each one, or Shift-clicking the first one you want to select, and then Shift-clicking the last one you want to select. The latter option selects contiguous.

2. **Choose the file type to which you'd like to export the contacts.**

- *To export a PDF:* Choose File⇨Export as PDF.

- *To export as a vCard or an Archive:* Choose File⇨Export, and then choose Export vCard or Contacts Archive from the submenu.

  A Save As dialog appears.

3. **Type a descriptive name for your file in the Save As text box.**

4. **Choose the location to store your file; this can be an external drive or a folder on your Mac.**

5. **Click Save.**

   You can then treat the file as you would any other file you want to share: Send it to someone as an email attachment; copy it to a flash drive; or upload it to a cloud server, such as Dropbox.

TIP

Although your best bet for backing up Contacts is using iCloud, as explained in Book 1, Chapter 3, you can also use one of the sharing options to create a backup that you store on an external drive, a CD, or a remote storage server.

Printing your Contacts

You can export Contacts to a PDF file and then print the document, or you can print directly from Contacts. In addition to printing in list form, Contacts lets you print all or some of your contact information in different formats, such as mailing labels or cards that you can carry with you. To print your Contacts, follow these steps:

1. **Use one of the following methods to select the names you want to print:**

   - Click a single contact card.

   - Hold down the ⌘ key and click multiple contacts.

   - Hold down the Shift key, click a contact, and then click another contact elsewhere in the list. Selecting these two contacts highlights them both and all contacts in between.

   - To print all contact cards stored in an account or group, click the account or group name and then choose Edit⇨Select All or press ⌘+A.

   - Enter a name in the Search text field. Select a name to display the card.

2. **Choose File⇨Print.**

   A Print dialog appears.

3. **Click the Printer pop-up menu and choose a printer to use.**

4. **Click Show Details at the bottom of your printer dialog box.**

   The dialog expands, showing all printing options, as shown in Figure 1-12.

FIGURE 1-12:
The expanded
Print dialog lets
you choose how
to print your
selected contacts.

The figure shows a Print dialog with the following visible fields:

Printer:	HP Officejet 5740 series
Presets:	Default Settings
Copies:	1 ☐ Black & White ☑ Two-Sided
Pages:	⦿ All ⃝ From: 1 to: 1
	Contacts
Style:	Envelopes

Layout | Label | Orientation

Layout:	DL	Millimeters

Envelope Size:
Width: 220.000   Height: 110.000

Recipient:
Top: 44.000   Width: 124.944
Left: 88.000   Height: 58.944

Sender:
Top: 7.056   Width: 66.000
Left: 7.056   Height: 33.000

2 addresses (Wardle ...   Zoom:

? PDF Hide Details   Cancel   Print

5. **Click the Style pop-up menu and choose one of the following:**

- *Mailing Labels:* Prints names and addresses on different types of mailing labels

- *Envelopes:* Prints names and addresses on envelopes fed into your printer

- *Lists:* Prints your Contacts as a long list

WARNING

Make sure you have the right media in your printer for the option you choose in Step 5.

REMEMBER

Depending on the style that you choose in this step, you may need to pick additional options, such as defining the specific size of your mailing labels or choosing whether to print names in alphabetical order. You can also adjust other settings and options, such as number of copies and the font you want to use for your printed output.

6. **Click Print.**

Managing Contacts

IN THIS CHAPTER

» **Navigating the Calendar window**

» **Viewing calendars**

» **Creating and storing events**

» **Finding the events you're looking for**

» **Organizing tasks with Reminders**

Chapter **2**

Staying on Schedule with Calendar

You're busy. You may rely on a planner, random scraps of paper, sticky notes attached to your computer, or your memory to keep track of obligations, appointments, and commitments. Your Mac comes with an alternative: Calendar, which is Apple's calendar application. Calendar helps you track appointments and reminds you of tasks or deadlines.

In this chapter, first we introduce the Calendar interface. Then we show you how to create calendars and access them from different sources. Next, we explain how to put *events* (what Calendar calls anything such as an appointment, a birthday, or whatever else that requires a time/date reference) on your calendar(s). We talk about sharing your calendar with your other devices and with other people, both online and in print. And while we're on the subject of remembering, we present the task management app Reminders, which you use to create To Do lists and assign a time- or location-based alert to each task.

Getting Acquainted with Calendar

The Calendar toolbar displays the following items, as shown in Figure 2-1:

>> **Calendars:** This button hides or reveals the Calendars list to the left of the calendar itself.

>> **Add (+) button:** Clicking this button adds an event.

>> **Inbox:** Displays how many invitations you have.

>> **Views:** The buttons in the center give you access to the four Calendar views: Day, Week, Month, and Year.

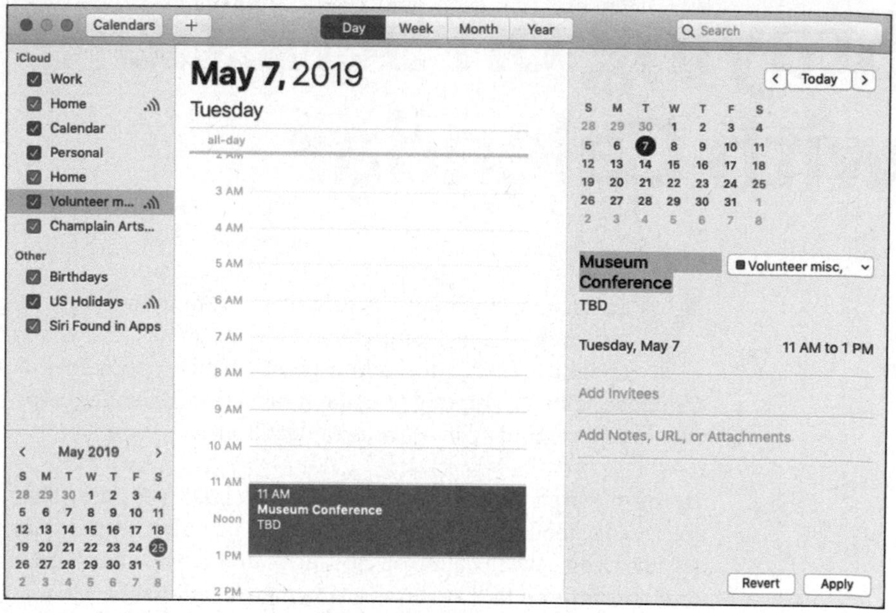

FIGURE 2-1:
The Calendar
toolbar helps you
view different
calendars and
choose the view
you want.

>> **Search:** Calendar looks for matches of text typed in the search field.

>> **Full-screen:** The button takes you to a full-screen view of Calendar.

>> **Today:** In the upper-left corner, just under the toolbar, the Today button takes you to the current day in the view you're using. The arrows to the left and right move one unit (day, week, month, or year) into the past or into the future (respectively) from the date where you are.

REMEMBER

Any scheduled activity, such as a doctor's appointment, a business meeting, or your kid's soccer practice, is an *event*.

Calendar offers four types of calendar views, each an electronic version of a familiar paper-based layout:

» **Day:** Shows a mini-month in the right window, a list of eight to ten upcoming events on the left, and a day-at-a-glance for the active day on the right below the mini calendar (refer to Figure 2-1).

» **Week:** Displays a week-at-a-glance version of your calendar, as shown in Figure 2-2. A column for each day is divided into half-hour time slots. You establish how many hours of the day you want to see.

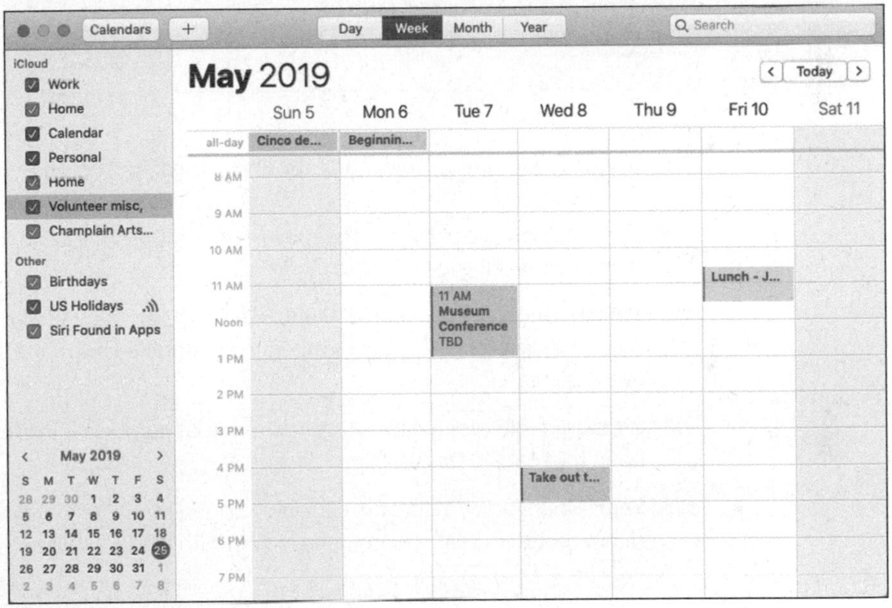

FIGURE 2-2:
Days are divided into half-hour segments in Week view.

When viewing the current day in Day or Week view, a line with a red ball at the left end (Day view) or under the day (Week view) indicates the current time of day.

TIP

» **Month:** Shows a month-at-a-glance with as much of the text of your events as possible on each day.

» **Year:** Displays the whole year in one pane, as shown in Figure 2-3. Click a date to see the appointments for that day.

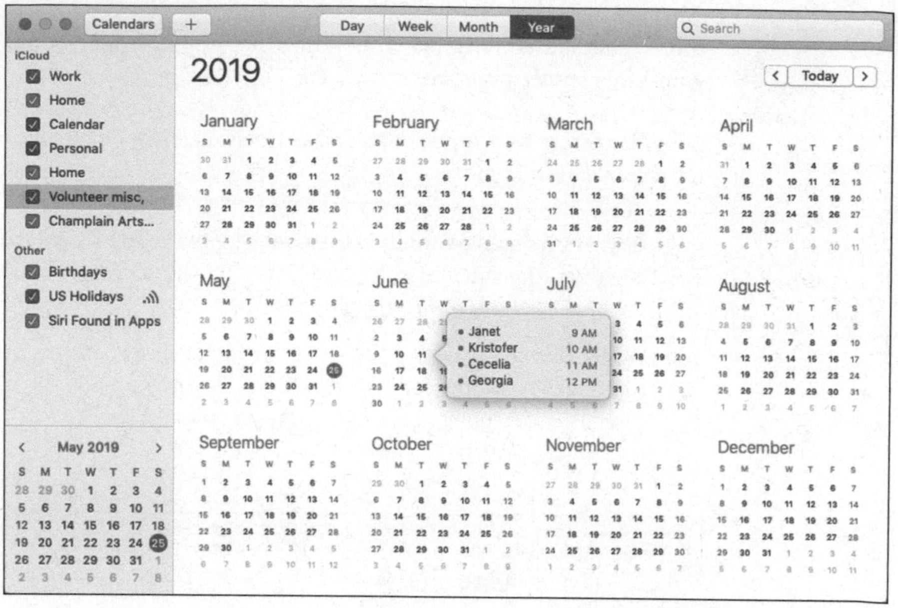

FIGURE 2-3:
Click a day in
Year view to
show its events.

You can move from one view and date to the next in the following ways:

» **Mini-month:** Click a date in the mini-month in Day view to go to the date clicked, remaining in Day view.

» **Month:** Double-click a date in Month view to open that date in Day view. You must double-click the actual number; if you double-click in the space, a new event is created.

» **Week:** Double-click a date — again, the actual number — in Week view to open that date in Day view.

» **Year:** Double-click a date in Year view to open that date in Day view. Double-click a month in Year view to open that month in Month view.

Working with Multiple Calendars

The great thing about Calendar is that calendars from different sources can be viewed in one app. Calendar accesses and manages multiple calendars from multiple sources or accounts, including your Mac or your iCloud account as well as online accounts where you keep (and perhaps share) calendars, such as Google or Microsoft Exchange.

TECHNICAL STUFF

As this is written, there are many concerns about privacy and the sharing of personal data. The list of calendars that you can share with Calendar changes over time, so check what options are available to you as you set up your calendars. Look for information under a Help tab in Calendar or the other calendars in which you're interested.

You can also import calendar data from another calendar or time management app.

When you click the Calendars button on the toolbar (refer to Figure 2-1), the Calendars list on the left side of Calendar displays the accounts you have activated. The calendars from each account are listed below its name. You can expand or collapse the list of calendars stored on each account by hovering the cursor to the right of the account name until Show or Hide appears and then clicking it.

By selecting or deselecting the check box next to each calendar in the Calendars list, you can selectively view specific events (say, only business events), or you can view business and personal events together.

Here we explain how to create a new calendar on your Mac or from iCloud, and then how to add calendars from other sources by accessing the related accounts.

Creating a new calendar

Calendar opens with a calendar to get you started. In the Calendars list, you see an On My Mac heading with Calendar listed under it. If you turned on Calendar in iCloud, you see iCloud — and any calendars you created on another device that use the same iCloud account — in the Calendars list. You may want or need to create additional calendars for other purposes. To create a new calendar, follow these steps:

1. **Click the Calendar icon on the Dock or from Launchpad.**

2. **Choose File ⇨ New Calendar.**

   If you don't add other accounts, that's all you have to do. If you do add other accounts, you have to drag the cursor one notch further to the right and choose On My Mac (or iCloud, if you use iCloud) or one of the remote servers where you keep calendars (if you use remote servers).

   An *Untitled* calendar appears in the Calendars pop-up list, as shown in Figure 2-4.

3. **Type a descriptive name for your calendar and then press Return.**

4. **Click a calendar in the Calendars list and choose Edit ⇨ Get Info.**

Staying on Schedule with Calendar

FIGURE 2-4:
New calendars
are added to your
Mac or iCloud
account.

5. **In the Info dialog that appears, click the color pop-up menu, choose a color, and (if you like) type a description of the calendar in the Description field.**

6. **Click OK.**

   Events stored on that calendar appear in the color you chose.

If you want to share or publish your calendar, refer to the section "Sharing your calendars" later in this chapter.

Accessing calendars from other accounts

Apple has made adding calendars from other accounts super easy. You can also add CalDAV or Exchange accounts, which are the formats most often used for shared corporate calendars. Events that you create or change at work with your company's calendar application, or events you create or change by using your Google or Yahoo! account, are added automatically to your calendar, and vice versa.

1. **Choose Calendar ⇨ Add Account.**

2. **Complete one of the following steps lists:**

   a. *Select the radio button next to the account you want to add (such as iCloud, as shown in Figure 2-5) and then click Continue.*

b. *Type in your username (it may be an email address) and password, and then click Create or Continue.*

Your account is verified.

c. *Select the radio button next to Calendar (if not already selected) and then click Done.*

Or

a. *Select the radio button next to Add CalDAV account and then click Continue.*

b. *Choose the account type from the pull-down menu: Automatic, Manual, or Advanced.*

TIP

We suggest leaving Automatic selected.

c. *Type the email address and password you use to access this calendar.*

d. *Click Create.*

Your access is verified.

That account is added to the Calendars list, and your online calendar's events appear in your Calendar window.

3. **After the account is set up, choose Calendar⇨Preferences and then click the Accounts tab.**

Staying on Schedule
with Calendar

4. **Click the name of the account you added.**

5. **From the Refresh Calendars pull-down menu, choose the interval at which you want Calendar to retrieve information from the account or update information you add on the server, as shown in Figure 2-6:**

   - *Push*: The calendar is updated as soon as a change occurs. This option may not be available for certain calendars that are accessed from the Internet.

   - *Every Minute/Hour*: This option lets you set the time interval from every 5 minutes to an hour. Calendar checks the server at the specified time interval and fetches any changes or sends changes you made.

   - *Manually:* Choose View ⇨ Refresh Calendars to fetch and send changes. If you use a MacBook and often run on battery power, this helps save the charge a bit.

6. **(Optional) Repeat to add more accounts.**

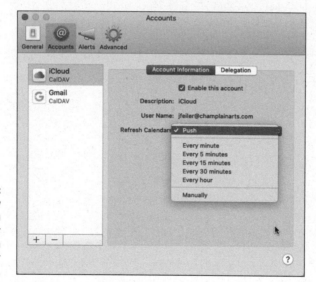

FIGURE 2-6:
Choose how often you want Calendar to refresh information for each account.

REMEMBER

When you use iCloud or another account–based online calendar (such as Google or Facebook), you can sign in to the same account, or accounts, on your smartphone, tablet, or from another computer. Your calendars are always at your fingertips.

Subscribing to online calendars

Another source of calendars for Calendar are those you can subscribe to online, such as a calendar of holidays, sports team schedules, bridge tournaments, or new DVD releases. Calendars you subscribe to appear under the Other category in the Calendars list. Events that appear in these calendars are added, deleted, and modified by whoever maintains the online calendar, which you can view but not change.

To subscribe to an online calendar

1. **Choose File ⇨ New Calendar Subscription to open the URL dialog.**

2. **Type the website URL for the calendar you want to subscribe to, as shown in Figure 2-7.**

For example, the link to a U.S. Holidays online calendar is `https://p06-calendars.icloud.com/holiday/US_en.ics`.

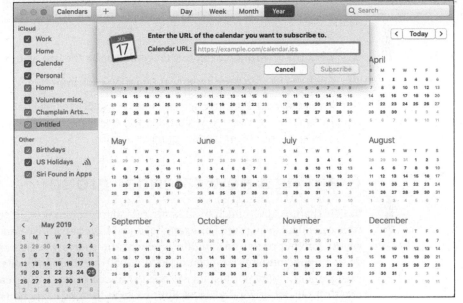

FIGURE 2-7:
You can subscribe to an online calendar.

3. **Click the Subscribe button.**

The name appears in the Calendars list under Other, and the calendar's events appear in the Calendar window.

TIP

Visit iCalShare (`www.icalshare.com`) to find calendars you can subscribe to.

Importing Calendar data

If you store calendar information in another application, or on another operating system and you're migrating to a Mac, you can export that data as a Calendar file or a vCalendar (.vcs) file, and then import that file into Calendar. If you're using Microsoft Outlook, save your calendar information as a separate file (as opposed to exporting it), and then import that file into Calendar.

After you save calendar data from another application, you can import that file into Calendar by following these steps:

1. **Choose File⇨Import and then choose Import or Import from Entourage.**

Although Outlook replaced Entourage in MS-Office for Mac 2011, if you use MS-Office 2008, you still have Entourage. When you choose Import from Entourage, Calendar scans your Mac's hard drive for your existing Entourage calendar data and imports those calendar events into Calendar, and you can skip the remaining steps.

2. **Click the drive and/or folder that contains the file you want to import.**

3. **Click the file you want to import and then click Import.**

Calendar imports your chosen calendar file's data into Calendar. You can then rename the calendar if you want, and add events or edit existing ones, as explained just a bit further along in this chapter.

Creating a new calendar group

Rather than create a bunch of separate calendars, you may want to organize multiple calendars in a group. For example, if you have separate calendars to schedule events for your son's and daughter's school and sporting events and your father's doctor's appointments, you could put all those calendars into a Family group. You may wonder, "Why not just create one Family calendar?" The reason we suggest creating separate calendars is because you can then print each one for the person it pertains to, and you can give your children access to their unique calendars. A calendar group doesn't store events; it simply stores one or more calendars.

WARNING

One caveat, however: Groups work only if you keep calendars on your Mac. That means if you use iCloud, you can't create groups. You may want to skip this section if that's your way of working with Calendar.

To create a calendar group, follow these steps:

1. **Click the Calendar icon on the Dock or from Launchpad.**

2. **Choose File⇨New Calendar Group.**

   The new group appears in the On My Mac section with the name *Group 1.*

REMEMBER

   You won't see this option if you turn on Calendar in iCloud. What's more, you may have to sign out of your other online calendars, such as Google or Facebook, create your groups, and then sign back in to the online calendars.

3. **Double-click the group name.**

   The name is highlighted in a text box that you can edit.

4. **Select the text and then type a descriptive name for your group and press Return.**

   A disclosure triangle appears to the left of the group name in the calendars list; click the triangle to hide or show the calendars in the group.

Adding a new calendar to a group

After you create a group, you can add new calendars to the group by following these steps:

1. **Choose File⇨New Calendar⇨On My Mac.**

   An Untitled Calendar appears in the On My Mac section.

2. **Type a descriptive name for your new calendar and press Return.**

3. **Move the pointer over the new calendar.**

4. **Click and drag the new calendar to the group you want to place the calendar in, and then release the mouse or trackpad button.**

   The name of your calendar now appears indented under the group.

TIP

Follow Steps 3 and 4 to move existing calendars to a group.

Moving a calendar out of a group

In case you don't want a calendar in a group, you can move it out of a group by following these steps:

1. **Click the Calendars button to open the Calendars list.**

2. **Move the cursor over the calendar you want to remove from a group.**

3. **Click and drag the calendar toward the left and up (or down) until it's out of the group.**

4. **Release the mouse or trackpad button.**

   Your existing calendar now appears outside any groups.

Moving a calendar or group

To help organize your calendars and groups, you may want to rearrange their order in the Calendar list by following these steps:

1. **Move the cursor to the calendar or group you want to move.**

2. **Hold down the mouse or trackpad button and drag the mouse or trackpad pointer up or down.**

   A thick horizontal line appears where your calendar or group will appear in the Calendar list, as shown in Figure 2-8.

3. **Release the mouse or trackpad button when you're happy with the new location of your calendar or group.**

Renaming and deleting calendars and groups

At any time, you can rename a calendar or group, whether it's on your Mac or on one of the online services (such as iCloud, Google, and Yahoo!). The name of a calendar or group is for your benefit and has no effect on the way Calendar works. To rename a calendar or group, double-click a calendar or group name, which highlights that name. Type a new name and press Return.

If you no longer need a particular calendar or group, click the one you want to delete and choose Edit⇨Delete. If you have any events stored on a calendar, a dialog appears, asking whether you really want to delete that calendar or group. Click Delete. If you delete a calendar or group by mistake, choose Edit⇨Undo or press ⌘+Z.

WARNING

When you delete a calendar, you also delete any events stored on that calendar. When you delete a group, you delete all calendars stored in that group along with all events stored on those calendars. Make sure that you really want to delete a calendar or group of calendars. You can also archive a copy before deleting so you have the reference without cluttering your calendar. We show you how to archive a calendar in an upcoming section.

Creating and Modifying Events

An *event* is any occurrence that has a specific time and date associated with it. Some common types of events are meetings, appointments with clients, times when you need to pick up someone (as at the airport), or recreational time (such as a concert or a two-week vacation). If you know that a particular event will occur on a specific date and time, you can store that event in Calendar so you won't forget or schedule a conflicting activity at that time.

Viewing events

As we list at the beginning of this chapter, Calendar lets you display time frames by day, week, month, or year, and shows all the events you've scheduled for the day, week, month, or year you choose to view. The amount of detail varies, depending on the view you choose. To change the time frame of your displayed events, click the Day, Week, Month, or Year button at the top of the Calendar window.

Creating an event

To create an event, start by deciding which calendar to store the event on, the date and time to schedule the event, and the event's duration. You also have options to create an event alert and whether to invite others to the event. Here, we show you how to create an event; in the next section, we explain your options.

There are two types of events — Quick Events, which let you quickly type a date, time, and event without much description such as "movie with Jim, Thursday at 7 pm," and full-blown Events, which have addresses, travel times, and other helpful information to get you to the right place at the right time. You have several ways to create an event:

>> **To create a Quick Event:** Click the Add Event button (the plus sign on the toolbar) or choose File⇨New Event. Then type in a phrase that defines your event in the Create Quick Event dialog that opens, as shown in Figure 2-9.

TECHNICAL STUFF

Calendar understands common phrases, such as "dinner on Tuesday" or "staff meeting Thursday from 9:00 a.m. to 1:00 p.m." Calendar uses the current date as the point of reference, and the default duration for an event is one hour. "Breakfast" or "morning" starts at 9:00 a.m. "Lunch" or "noon" begins at 12:00 p.m. "Dinner" or "night" starts at 8:00 p.m.

>> **In Day or Week view:** Double-click the hour you want the event to begin, and then type in a title for your event. Or, click and drag from the starting time to the ending time, and then type a title for your event.

>> **In Month view:** Double-click the date of the event, and type in the title and time, such as **Movie 7:00 p.m. – 9:00 p.m.**

>> **In Week or Month view:** Click and drag from the beginning to ending date for a multi-day event.

You can change the start and end time of an event by moving the pointer to the top or bottom of an event until it turns into a two-way-pointing arrow. Then hold down the mouse or trackpad button and move it up or down to change your start and end times by 15-minute increments.

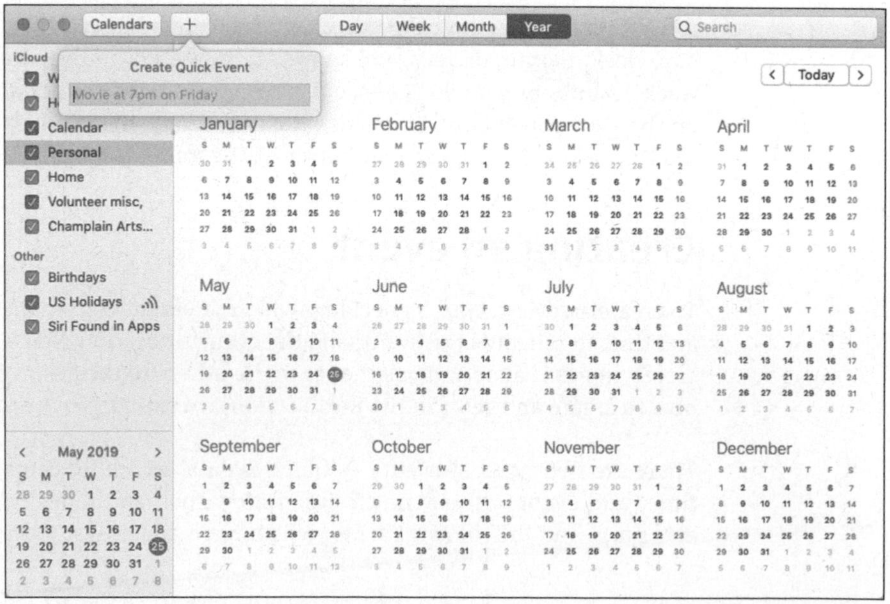

TIP

FIGURE 2-9:
Quickly create
an event.

Editing an event

Sometimes a title, time, and date are enough descriptors for an event. Other times, you want to add more information, or something changes and you have to change the date or time of an event. Editing an event lets you change the time, the date, or the description of an event. You can also add features to an event, such as setting an alert, inviting people to your event, or automatically opening a file.

Changing the description of an event

Each time you create an event, you type in a description of that event. To modify this description, follow these steps:

1. **Double-click the event you want to modify.**

Alternatively, click the event and choose Edit⇨Edit Event or press ⌘+E.

The event-editing dialog appears, as shown in Figure 2-10.

2. **Click the event description.**

In Figure 2-10, the description is *Pick up Ted at Airport.* Your cursor appears at the end of the description.

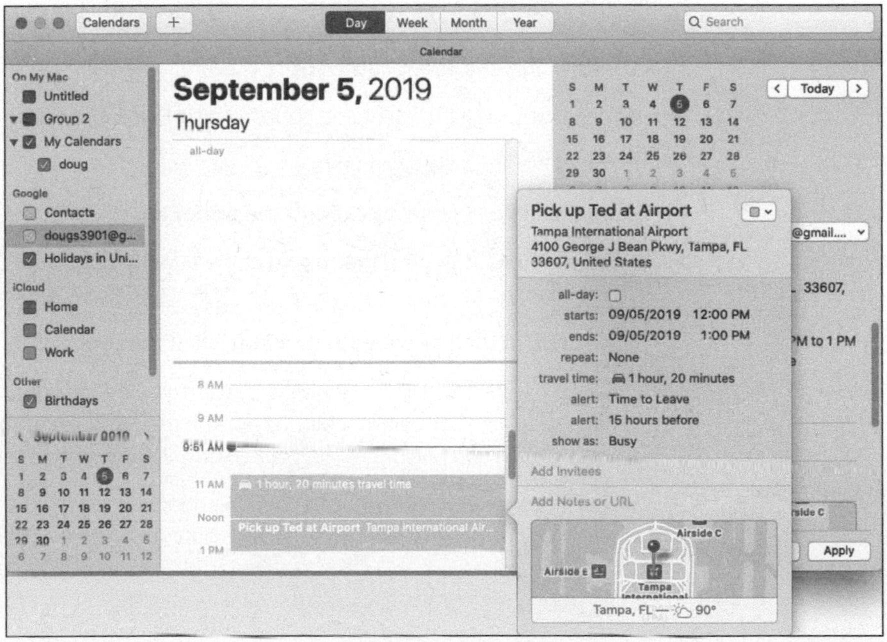

FIGURE 2-10: Define details for your event, create alerts, and invite others.

3. **Use the arrow and Delete keys to edit the event description; type any new text in the fields.**

   - Click the Location field to type a location where the event takes place.

   - Click the date and time to expand the options there, and then select the All-Day check box to create an event that lasts all day, like a birthday or vacation day. The From and To fields disappear if All Day is selected.

4. **Click the Travel Time pop-up menu to block out the necessary additional time to reach your appointment.**

   Choose the amount of time necessary from the listed options or click Custom to fill in a specific quantity.

   Choose View⇨Show Travel Time to see it reflected on the calendar. This helps you avoid scheduling appointments back to back.

5. **Click outside the event editing dialog when you're finished or make it a repeating event and add alerts, as we explain in the next two sections.**

Creating a recurring event

For an event that occurs regularly, such as every Monday or on the same day every month, you can create an event one time and then tell Calendar to display that event on a recurring basis. To create a recurring event, follow these steps:

1. **Double-click the event you want to modify.**

   Alternatively, click the event and choose Edit⇨Edit Event or press ⌘+E.

   The event-editing dialog appears.

2. **Click the time interval to expand the options.**

3. **Click the Repeat pop-up menu and choose an option, such as Every Day or Every Month.**

4. **(Optional) In the Repeat pop-up menu, click Custom.**

   A dialog appears, shown in Figure 2-11, letting you define specific days for the recurring event, such as every Monday or the first Wednesday of every month. Click OK when you finish creating your custom recurring event.

TIP

   If you share the calendar you create in Calendar with other iOS devices, use the Custom option on your Mac because the other iOS devices don't offer the same flexibility.

FIGURE 2-11:
Define custom parameters for a recurring event.

Laundry Day
Add Location

all-day: ☐
starts: 09/05/2019   8:00 AM
ends: 09/05/2019   9:00 AM

Frequency: Weekly ⌄

Every 1 week(s) on:

S M T W T F S

Cancel   OK

5. **Click the End Repeat pop-up menu to choose when the repeating should stop.**

- *Never:* If you want the event to repeat in perpetuity.

- *After:* The default is to end the event after it repeats one time. Click in the field to the right and type the number of times you want it to repeat.

- *On Date:* Type in the date you want the repeating event to end.

6. **Click outside the editing dialog to close it.**

Calendar automatically displays your recurring event throughout the rest of the calendar until you modify the event.

> **TIP**
> If a particular event occurs two or three times, you can set it up as a repeating event or you can just duplicate it, which is sometimes easier. To duplicate an event, click it and choose Edit ➪ Duplicate, or press ⌘+D (or hold down the Option key and then drag the event to the new time slot). When the duplicate appears, move the cursor to it, drag the event to a new date, and then release the mouse button.

Indicating your availability

If you share your calendar with others, you may want to indicate your availability during certain events. You can choose Busy or Free by selecting the pop-up menu next to Show As. Usually Calendar considers you Busy when you have an appointment, but if you show your attendance for three days at a conference, for instance, you may want to choose Free so those who view your calendar know that you're at the conference but free for appointments during that time. To indicate your availability:

1. **Double-click the event you want to edit.**

Alternatively after selecting the event, you can choose, Edit ➪ Event or press ⌘+E.

The event-editing dialog opens.

2. **Click the event duration.**

   The window changes to show time options, as shown in Figure 2-12.

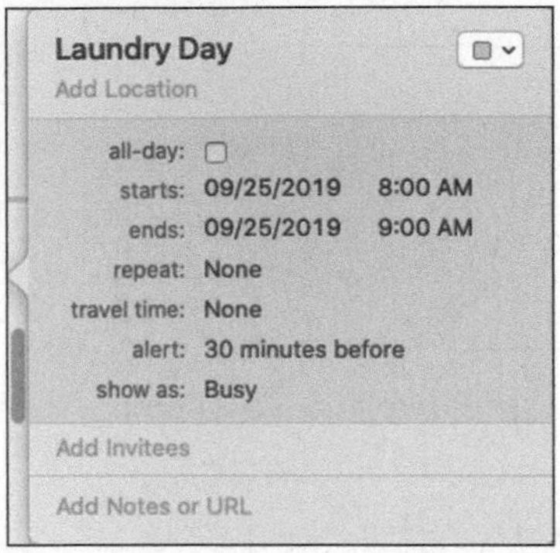

Laundry Day
Add Location

all-day:	☐		
starts:	09/25/2019	8:00 AM	
ends:	09/25/2019	9:00 AM	
repeat:	None		
travel time:	None		
alert:	30 minutes before		
show as:	Busy		

Add Invitees

Add Notes or URL

FIGURE 2-12:
Show your availability for an event.

3. **Choose an option from the Show As pop-up menu.**

   Your options are Free or Busy.

4. **Click outside the window when you finish editing the event.**

Setting an alert for an event

Scheduling an event is useless if you forget about it. That's why Calendar gives you the option of setting two types of alerts that can notify you of upcoming events:

» A message with or without an audible sound that shows up on your Mac, and looks like a dialog in the upper right corner, and, if you use iCloud, on your other devices

» A message that can be sent to you as an email or as a file that can be opened

You can choose more than one type of alert — or all of them — for each event.

To set an alert for an event, follow these steps:

1. **Double-click the event you want to be reminded about.**

   Alternatively, click it and then choose Edit ➪ Edit Event, or press ⌘+E.

   The event-editing dialog appears.

2. **Click the date and time to expand the Edit dialog.**

   An event-editing dialog appears (refer to Figure 2-12).

3. **Click the Alert pop-up menu and choose an option.**

The default option is to alert you at the time of the event.

4. **For other options, click Custom and then choose the alert type.**

- *Message with Sound:* The default option sends you a message with the default Calendar alert sound.

- *Email:* If you have more than one address, choose the one (from the pop-up menu) you want the alert sent to.

- *Open File:* This option opens the Calendar app. To open a different file, such as a report that you can review for an upcoming meeting, choose Other in the pop-up menu beneath the alert type menu and then scroll through the directories and folders of your Mac to select the file you want to open and then click Select.

5. **Click the time in the field after the start date to change the time at which you're alerted.**

If the alert is scheduled before noon, click AM and type P to change the alert to PM, or vice versa.

6. **(Optional) Add another alert by hovering the cursor over the alert and then click the plus button that appears to the right.**

An additional alert can be useful. For example, if the alert is for a business meeting, being alerted a day before lets you get your ducks in a row by preparing. A second alert an hour before the meeting enables you to make last-minute preparations.

7. **Click outside the event-editing dialog to close it.**

Moving an event to another calendar

You can always move an event from one calendar to another, such as from your Work calendar to your Home calendar. To move an event to another calendar, follow these steps:

1. **Double-click an event that you want to modify.**

Alternatively, click the event once and then choose Edit⇨ Edit Event, or press ⌘+E.

The event-editing dialog appears.

2. **Click the colored square in the upper right of the dialog to open the Calendar pop-up menu and then click the calendar name you want the event to appear in.**

Your event is moved.

Adding information to an event

To prepare for an event, you can also store information about that event's location, attendees, any important files related to the event (such as a presentation), a website URL, and any additional notes you want to jot down.

To add information to an event, follow these steps:

1. Double-click an event that you want to modify.

Alternatively, click it once and then choose Edit➪Edit Event, or press ⌘+E.

The event-editing dialog appears.

2. To add a location, click Add Location and type an address to remind yourself where the event will take place.

If the event occurs at a contact's location, start typing the contact's name, and a list of names from Contacts that match what you're typing appears. You can click a name to enter the related address.

3. Click Add Notes, URL, or Attachments.

The Add Notes, Add URL, and Add Attachment fields appear.

- *Add Note:* Click inside the text box and type any additional notes about your event.

- *Add URL:* Click inside the text box, and type a website address that's relevant to your event, such as a restaurant's website for an upcoming dinner.

- *Add Attachment:* Click to open the Chooser that shows the directories and folders on your Mac. Select a file to attach to the event, such as a business presentation that you need to give at the event, and then click Open.

4. Click outside the event-editing dialog to close it.

After you add information to your event, you can view it by clicking the event in Day, Week, or Month view. After the event info appears, you can peruse your notes, click a URL to view the website in Safari, or click the attachment to open it in its default application.

Inviting people to your event

Invitations for events ranging from staff meetings to birthday parties are often communicated electronically. Rather than type out a separate email with the details of your event, you can send the invitation directly from Calendar. And Calendar keeps track of the responses so you can see who has accepted, declined, or is still deciding. Follow these steps:

1. **Double-click an event to which you want to invite people.**

   Alternatively, you can click the event and then choose Edit⇨Edit Event or press ⌘+E.

   The event-editing dialog appears.

2. **Click Add Invitees and begin typing a name.**

   If the person you want to invite is in Contacts, Calendar automatically shows you a list of possible matches.

   The more you type, the narrower the list becomes.

3. **To invite another person to the event, click the plus sign (+) and type the person's name.**

   Calendar shows you matches for people you added to the Contacts app.

TIP

   If you created one or more groups in Contacts, start typing the name of the group in the Add Invitees window. Click the name of the group to invite all members of the group to your event.

TIP

   After the event appears in the event-editing dialog, choose Window⇨Open Contacts. Move the Contacts window so you can still see the event-editing dialog window, and then drag contacts to the Add Invitees window. You can select a contiguous group of contacts by clicking the first contact, and then Shift-clicking the last contacts to select all the contacts in between, or you can click the first contact and then ⌘+click additional contacts to select noncontiguous contacts.

4. **Repeat Step 3 for other people you want to invite to the event.**

5. **Click outside the window to apply the changes, and then click Send.**

   An invitation is sent to all invitees using the Calendar or ICS file format. If an invitee has Calendar or another calendar application associated with the email address, the invitation is sent directly to Calendar or the calendar application.

TECHNICAL STUFF

   ICS is the standard file type for exchanging calendar information. Calendar, Outlook, Google Calendar, and Calendar (on iOS devices) support the ICS standard. When you send or receive an email with an invitation attached, the invitation probably has the .ics filename extension. To add the event automatically to Calendar or the calendar application currently in use, you or the recipient simply click that attachment in the email message.

6. **The recipients have the option respond with a Yes, No, or Maybe.**

   You receive an email when recipients respond: A white check mark in a green circle appears next to the recipients who accept, a question mark in an orange circle indicates a Maybe response, and a red circle-with-slash means the recipient declined the invitation.

Responding to invitations

If someone sends you an invitation in Mail and you accept, it's added to your calendar automatically. Invitations appear in the Inbox on the toolbar. The number indicates the number of invitations you have. A badge with a number appears on the Calendar icon on the Dock, which also indicates the number of invitations you have in your Inbox.

When you click the Inbox, the invitations appear, as shown in Figure 2-13. Click Maybe, Decline, or Accept. The sender will be notified of your response. If you Accept, the event is added to Calendar.

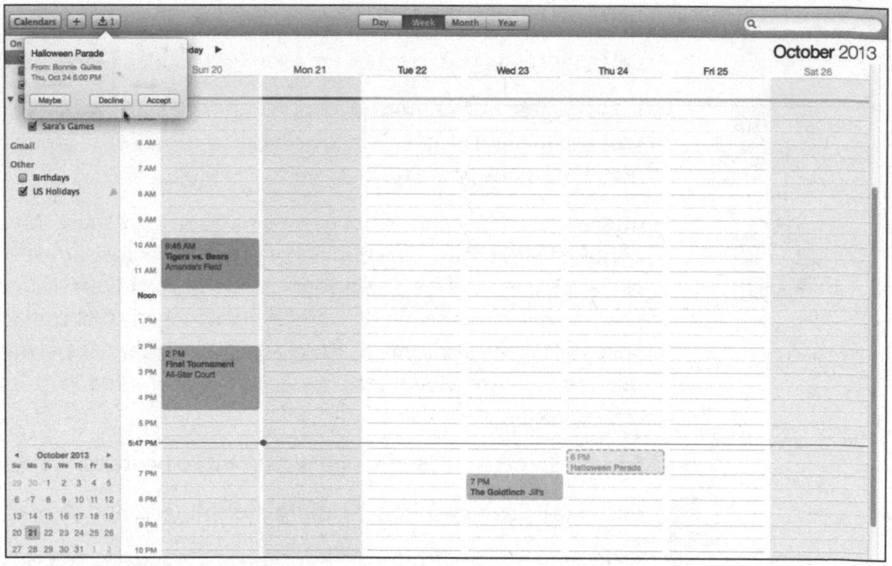

FIGURE 2-13: Invitations appear in the Inbox on the toolbar.

Moving an event

In case you store an event at the wrong date or time, you can change the date and time in the event-editing dialog, or move it to a new date and time by following these steps:

1. **Move the cursor to the middle of the event box.**

2. **Hold down the mouse button and drag the cursor to a new time or date.**

   The event moves with the cursor; the duration doesn't change.

3. **Release the mouse button when you're happy with the new date and time of the event.**

If you have to move the event to a date several months away, it's more prudent to double-click the event to open the event-editing dialog, and then type the new date in the Starts field. Click outside the window to apply the change.

Deleting an event

When you no longer need to remember an event, you can delete it. Just click it and choose Edit ⇨ Delete or right-click the event and choose Delete from the context menu. You may get a warning message if the event has attachments or invitees. If you delete an event by mistake, press ⌘+Z or choose Edit ⇨ Undo to retrieve your event.

If you delete an event with invitees, you don't have to notify them. The Calendar app sends an email to each invitee, letting them know the event has been cancelled.

Finding Events

Storing events is useful only if you can view upcoming events so you can prepare for them. To help you find and view events, Calendar offers several different methods that include using colors to identify different types of events and letting you search for a specific event by name.

Color-coding events

Events in a calendar reflect the color you assign to the calendar when you create the calendar. So if you assign the color blue to your Home calendar and the color red to your Work calendar, you can quickly identify which events on your calendar are home related (blue) or work related (red).

Use contrasting colors for multiple calendars to make it easy to tell which events belong to which calendar.

Selectively hiding events

Normally, Calendar displays all events, color-coding them so you can tell which events belong to which calendars. However, if you have too many events, you may find mixing Home and Work events too confusing. If you want to see only events stored on a specific calendar (such as Home or Work calendars), you can hide the events that are stored on other calendars.

To hide events stored on other calendars, deselect the check box of any of those calendars in the Calendar List. To view events stored on a calendar, make sure that a check mark appears in the check box of that calendar, as shown in Figure 2-14.

FIGURE 2-14: Hiding a calendar hides all events stored on that calendar.

Checking for today's events

Probably the most important events you need to keep an eye on are the ones you've scheduled for today. To see all events scheduled for today, click the Today button at the top of the Calendar window.

TIP Another quick way to review any upcoming events for today is to use the Calendar widget in Dashboard. To display today's events in the Calendar widget, click the current date (which appears in the left pane of the Calendar widget) until the events pane appears. (For more information about using the Dashboard, see Book 1, Chapter 2.)

Checking events for a specific date

Sometimes you may need to know whether you have any events scheduled on a certain date. To check a specific date, choose View➪Go to Date (or Go to Today if you're looking for that) or double-click the date in one of the calendar views.

REMEMBER

The Month view can show you the events scheduled for a particular date, but the Day and Week views can show you the specific times of your events for that day.

Searching for an event

If you scheduled an event several days ago, you may forget the exact date of that event. To help you find a specific event, Calendar lets you search for it by typing all or part of the information stored in that event — for example, the event name, the attendee names, or any notes you stored about the event.

To search for an event, follow these steps:

1. **Click the search text box in the upper-right corner of the Calendar window.**

2. **Type as much text as you can remember about the event you want to find, such as an attendee's name or the location of the event.**

The Calendar application displays a list of events that match the text you type. The list appears in a column on the right of the calendar window, as shown in Figure 2-15. If you have a recurring event, every instance that matches the search will appear. If the event you seek is on a hidden calendar (one that isn't selected), its contents won't appear in the search.

FIGURE 2-15:
You can search for and find events.

3. **Double-click an event from the list.**

    Your chosen event appears.

4. **Click the Clear button in the search text box to remove the list of matching events.**

Exporting Calendar data

To share your calendars with other applications (even those running on other operating systems, such as Windows or Linux), you need to export your Calendar file by following these steps:

1. **Choose File ⇨ Export ⇨ Export.**

    A dialog appears, giving you a chance to choose a filename and location to store your Calendar data, as shown in Figure 2-16.

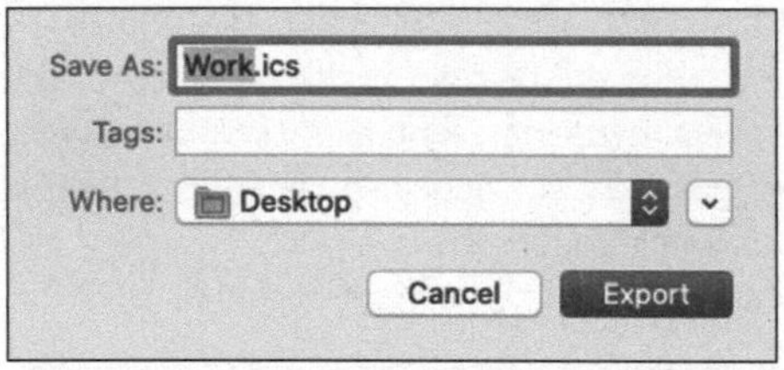

FIGURE 2-16:
Export your
calendars.

2. **In the Save As text box, type a name for your file.**

3. **Choose the location to store your file from the Where pop-up menu or click the disclosure triangle to expand the window and view the directories and folders on your Mac.**

4. **Click Export.**

Sharing your calendars

You can print your calendar and give a copy to people, but an easier way to share is to give others access to your calendar online. Your calendar will be a read-only file; the people who have access can view your calendar, but they can't change it. To share your calendar, follow these steps:

1. **Click the Calendar button to open the calendar list if it isn't in view.**

2. **Click the calendar you want to share.**

    You can share calendars only from On My Mac or iCloud.

3. **Choose Edit⇨Publish for a calendar on your Mac. Or, if you want to publish a calendar that's on iCloud, choose Edit⇨Share Calendar.**

A dialog opens, as shown in Figure 2-17 for Mac calendars and as Figure 2-18 for iCloud calendars.

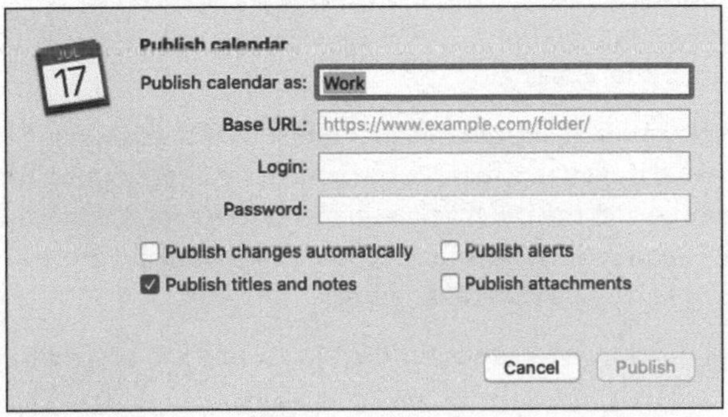

FIGURE 2-17:
Publish calendars stored on your Mac so other people can refer to them.

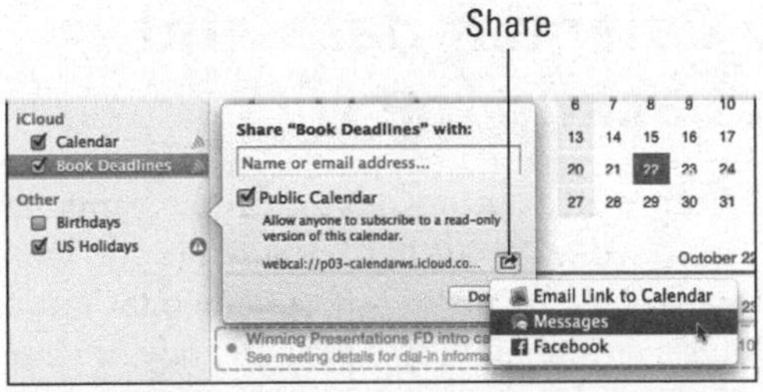

Publish calendar

Publish calendar as: Work

Base URL: https://www.example.com/folder/

Login:

Password:

☐ Publish changes automatically   ☐ Publish alerts
☑ Publish titles and notes   ☐ Publish attachments

Cancel   Publish

Share

FIGURE 2-18:
iCloud calendars can be shared privately or publicly.

iCloud
☑ Calendar
☑ Book Deadlines

Other
☐ Birthdays
☑ US Holidays

Share "Book Deadlines" with:

Name or email address…

☑ Public Calendar
Allow anyone to subscribe to a read-only version of this calendar.

webcal://p03-calendarws.icloud.co…

Email Link to Calendar
Messages
Facebook

October 22

Winning Presentations FD intro c
See meeting details for dial-in informa

6 7 8 9 10
13 14 15 16 17
20 21 22 23 24
27 28 29 30 31

4. **For calendars on your Mac, you can type a name for your calendar that will help those who have access understand what the calendar represents.**

This name is only for the shared calendar; it doesn't change the name of the calendar in Calendar.

REMEMBER

Shared iCloud calendars use the name they have in Calendar, so you should give your calendar a recognizable name.

5. **Do one of the following to publish your calendar:**

- *For calendars on your Mac* (refer to Figure 2-16): Type the URL web address of the server along with your login and password in the related fields. Select the options you want from the check boxes at the bottom of the dialog. Then click the Publish button.

- *For calendars on iCloud* (refer to Figure 2-17): If the people you want to share your calendar with are in Contacts, type the names and then choose the correct email addresses from the matches that appear. Otherwise, type the email addresses of the people you want to share the calendar with.

TIP

Choose Window ⇨ Contacts to display your contacts. Move the Contacts window so that it and the Share dialog are visible. You can now drag and drop contacts you want to share a calendar with from the Contacts window into the Share dialog.

If you want to make the calendar public, select the Public Calendar check box, and then share the URL by clicking the Share button (the curved arrow next to the URL). A pop-up menu gives you three ways to share the link — email, Messages, or Facebook. Click one and proceed as you would to send anything with those apps.

Click Done. You can also click the URL to select it, and then copy and paste somewhere else, such as on your website.

Backing up Calendar data and restoring a backup file

Because Calendar can store all your upcoming events (appointments, meetings, and so on), disaster could strike if your hard drive fails and wipes out your Calendar data. The best way to avoid this is to use the Calendar option in iCloud. If you prefer not to use iCloud, you should keep a backup copy of your Calendar data. To do so, follow these steps:

1. **Choose File ⇨ Export ⇨ Calendar Archive.**

   The Save dialog appears.

2. **In the Save As text box, type a descriptive name for your Calendar backup file.**

3. **Choose the location for storing your file from the Where pop-up menu.**

4. **Click Save.**

   Your archive is exported to the desired location. The resulting file has the `.icbu` extension.

TIP

Save your Calendar backup file on a separate drive, such as an external hard drive or a flash drive. That way, if your Mac hard drive fails, you won't lose both your original Calendar data and your backup file at the same time. (For more details on backing up files, see Book 3, Chapter 1.)

To retrieve your schedule from a backup file that you created earlier, choose File➪Import. In the Open dialog that appears, click the drive and folder where you saved your backup Calendar file. Then click Import. After you invoke the command, a warning dialog appears telling you the operation will replace the current data. To continue the import, click Restore. Calendar imports the backed-up file; any changes you made since the last backup will be lost.

Printing a Calendar file

Even if you have a laptop, you can't always have your computer with you, so you may want to print your calendar in the Day, Week, or Month view. To print a calendar, follow these steps:

1. **If you want to Print a calendar showing selected events, click the first event you want to include, and then ⌘+click additional events.**

    You could conceivably scroll through every month for the year to print a calendar showing all events for the years, but the most prudent use for this option is to print out events for the month.

2. **Choose File➪Print.**

    A Print dialog appears, as shown in Figure 2-19.

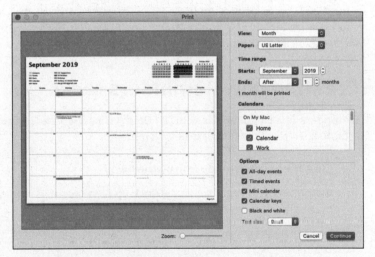

FIGURE 2-19:
The Print dialog shows you how your calendar will appear on paper.

3. **Click the View pop-up menu and choose Day, Week, Month, List, or Selected Events.**

    Selected Events shows only the event(s) you selected in Step 1.

4. **(Optional) Change any other settings, such as the paper size, time range, or calendars, and select the options you want from the Options section of the dialog box.**

   The options differ depending on the option you choose in Step 3.

5. **Click Continue.**

   Another Print dialog appears.

6. **Click the Printer pop-up menu, choose a printer and a printer preset if applicable, and then click Print.**

Organizing Tasks with Reminders

Although you can put an event on your calendar in Calendar and then set an alert so you don't forget it, not everything you need to remember is an event. For these items, which you may think of as to-do's with deadlines, you record in the Reminders app. (If you're familiar with earlier versions of Mac OS X, these items were part of iCal as the To Do or Reminders functions.)

A typical Reminders list contains goals or important tasks that you want to accomplish, usually by a specific date or time or based on when you leave or arrive at a location. You can create multiple Reminders lists and categorize them however you want. Like Contacts and Calendar, Reminders is also part of iCloud, so your tasks can be synced across all your devices signed in to the same iCloud account.

Creating new Reminders tasks

Reminders is a catch-all for your To Do lists, neatly divided into categories you establish. Here's how to create new Reminders:

1. **Click the Reminders app icon on the Dock.**

REMEMBER

   If the Reminders app is not on the Dock, you can open it using the Launchpad, or access it from the Applications folder.

   The Reminders app opens. The app is divided into two columns. In the left column are two buttons: Today and Scheduled. The right column is entitled reminders and shows a list of your current reminders and the number of completed reminders.

2. **Click Today in the left column and then click the plus sign to the upper right of Today.**

The cursor appears on the next available line — the first line if this is the first message for the day — and a radio button is to the left of the cursor with two buttons below it: Add Date and Add Location. You can enter the date and location by clicking these buttons and making choices from the pop-up menus, but it's easier to add the desired information after you enter the reminder.

You can also create a new task by clicking the Scheduled button. The results are the same.

REMEMBER

3. **Type the task you want to remember and press Return.**

   The task appears in the list with an info button to the right. The task is set to occur the day the task was written.

4. **Click the Info button.**

   The Details screen appears, as shown in Figure 2-20.

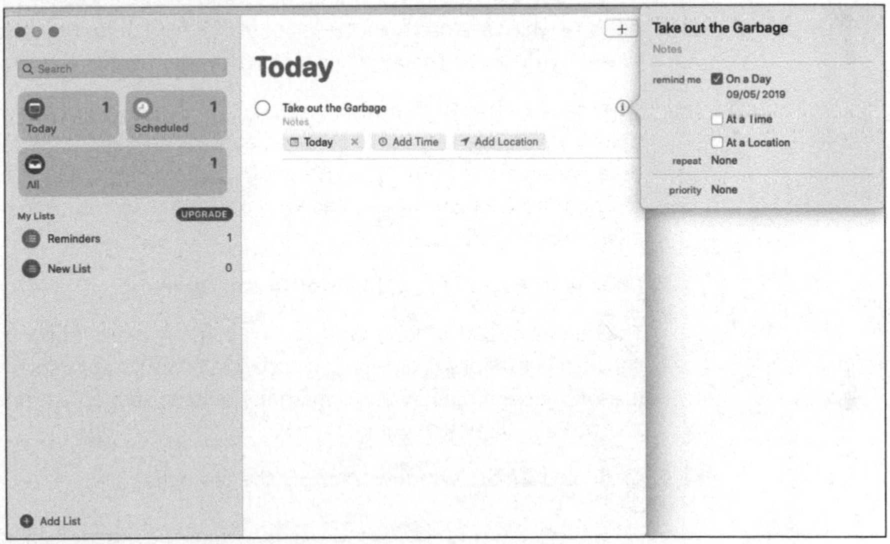

FIGURE 2-20:
Choose when and where Reminders should prod you to action.

5. **To change the date, click the current date.**

   A calendar appears. Click the date you want to be reminded, or edit the current date.

6. **Click At a Time if you want to be reminded at a certain time.**

   Edit the default time.

Staying on Schedule with Calendar

7. **If you want to be reminded when you're at a specific location, click At a Location.**

8. **Enter the desired location, or choose one from the suggestions that appear in the pop-up Suggestions list when you start typing.**

After you enter the location, a map appears in the window. By default, you're reminded when arriving at the location. If desired, select the Leaving radio button. If you choose this option, the reminder shows you leaving the location instead of arriving at it.

If you specify a location, Location Services must be enabled with any device or computer you use Reminders with.

WARNING

9. **(Optional) Choose an option from the Repeat pop-up menu.**

The default option is None. Your choices are Every Day, Every Week, Every Month, Every Year, or Custom. If you choose Custom, you can specify a frequency: Daily, Weekly, Monthly, or Yearly. Each choice gives you different options, which are pretty much self-explanatory. For example, it you choose Weekly, you can be reminded every 2 weeks on the day you choose.

You can also choose an option from the End Repeat pop-up menu. The default option is None, or you can choose On Date, in which case, Reminders enters a date based on the option you choose. Click the default date to reveal a calendar from which you can choose a date. Alternatively, you can manually edit the default date.

10. **Choose an option from the Priority pop-up menu.**

The default option is None, which is fine in many cases, but you can also choose Low, Medium, or High. An exclamation point appears to the left of a low-priority reminder, two exclamation points for a medium-priority reminder, and three exclamation points for a high-priority reminder.

11. **Click outside the window to apply the changes.**

Choose ➪ System Preferences ➪ Notifications and click the Reminders icon to choose the alert style you want Reminders to use, and click Sounds in System Preferences to select your preferred alert sound.

TIP

To rearrange, edit, or delete items in a list, do the following:

>> **To edit a task:** Click the item and then click the info button to the right of the task to open the Details screen. Edit the task following the steps you use to create a task.

>> **To delete an item:** Click it and then choose Edit ➪ Delete.

In the left-hand column, click one of the following icons: Today, Scheduled, All, or Flagged. This displays messages that fall into that category.

When you complete a task, select the radio button to the left of the task on the list (refer to Figure 2-20). The completed tasks show as completed after you click the Scheduled button. Click Hide to hide completed tasks, and then click Show to view them again. You can also view them by scrolling up to the top of the originating list to see the completed section.

Making new lists

Keeping all your tasks on the existing Reminders list somewhat defeats the purpose of the app, which is to divide your tasks by subject. There are three ways to create new lists:

>> Click the Add List button (refer to Figure 2-20) at the bottom of the window.

>> Choose File ⇨ New List.

When you create a new list, the default name is New List. Click the default title in the My Lists section on the left side of the Reminders window, and the text is highlighted in a text window. Enter the desired text and press Return.

When you have more than one list, choose Reminders ⇨ Preferences, and then choose an option from the Default List pop-up menu to select the list that you want to set as default. Then when you create new tasks outside of a list — for example, in Outlook or another app that syncs with Reminders — those tasks are added to the chosen list.

To delete an entire list, click it in My Lists and then choose Edit ⇨ Delete. A dialog confirms whether you're sure you want to delete the entire list; click Delete to proceed, or click Cancel if you change your mind.

To rearrange the order of lists in the My Lists section, click a list name and then drag it up or down to change the order in which your lists appear.

IN THIS CHAPTER

» **Using document templates**

» **Working with photos**

» **Creating and formatting text**

» **Saving time with formatting styles**

» **Adding text boxes, charts, and tables**

» **Putting the finishing touches on your document**

» **Saving your document**

» **Printing, exporting, and emailing your document**

Chapter **3**

Creating Documents with Pages

P ages is the word-processing and page-layout app of macOS. In Pages, you can type, edit, and format text to produce stationery-style documents, such as letters, envelopes, and business cards as well as longer text-heavy documents, such as reports and résumés. But Pages doesn't stop there. You can add and arrange graphics and text boxes on a page to create colorful newsletters, brochures, menus, flyers, and the like. And because Pages is part of macOS, you can add spreadsheets from Numbers and presentations from Keynote into your word-processing or page-layout document. (And the reverse is true: You can add word-processing or page-layout document sections to spreadsheets or presentations.)

This chapter shows Pages in Dark Mode on a Mac in many of the screenshots. If you haven't used Dark Mode before, it may look different from what you're used to. Just remember that in Dark Mode, your screen may be easier on your eyes; more important, the dark sections of the screen show a marked difference from the normal mode, which is normally the content of your document.

Working with Document Templates

To help you start writing, Pages supplies a variety of document templates. When you choose a document template, you just enter new text and customize the appearance of the template so you don't have to create everything from scratch. The following sections tell you how to get started.

Choosing a template

Pages offers nearly 100 templates although you find many more on the web, and we give you suggestions for websites to visit in Book 5, Chapter 6. Some templates, such as those for reports or letters, are designed mostly for writing (relatively) plain and simple documents, with the emphasis on content. In these templates, you type continuous text directly on the page in the document and can insert images or charts. Other templates, such as flyers or newsletters, are designed for mixing text and graphics when content and presentation have almost equal importance. The text in these templates goes into text boxes rather than a single page. When choosing a template, you want to select one that's closest to the type of document you want to create.

WARNING

After you create a document by using a template, you can't switch to a new template. If you want to use a different template, you have to create another document.

To choose a document template, follow these steps:

1. **Click the Pages icon on the Dock or Launchpad.**

If you've previously created documents in Pages, they appear when you launch the application. To create a new document, choose File➪New, and a dialog appears, displaying different templates you can choose, as shown in Figure 3-1.

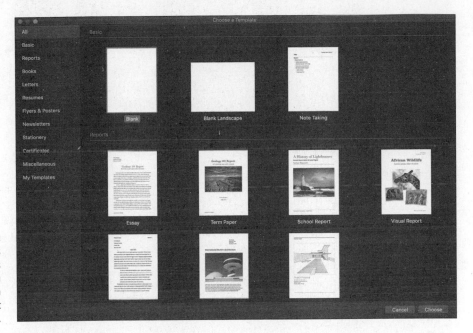

FIGURE 3-1:
Pages provides
various templates
to help you
create a
document
quickly.

2. **Click a template category in the list on the left to narrow your choices or scroll through the center pane.**

   If you want to start with a blank document, click the Blank portrait or landscape template, whichever best suits the type of document you want to create. Most of, but not all, the instructions apply to blank documents; we let you know when they don't.

3. **Select a template and then click the Choose button.**

   Or double-click the icon for the template you want to use.

   Pages opens your chosen template as a new, untitled document.

4. **Choose File⇨Save.**

   The Save As dialog opens. Type a name for your document and choose the folder where you want to store it. Pages supports Versions, which keeps a running backup of your document each time you change it. (We explain this feature in Book 1, Chapter 4, and Book 3, Chapter 1.)

TIP

To keep things simple, these instructions are for saving and storing the document on your Mac. You can also save and store your Pages documents on iCloud, which is a great option if you work from different devices. See the section "Saving Your Documents on Your Mac or iCloud" later in this chapter for details.

TEXT ON A PAGE VERSUS TEXT BOXES

You can quickly and easily create colorful documents on your Mac, but choosing the correct template can be confusing. For example, if you have to write a 100-page report, choose a report template that uses continuous text — not newsletter, which uses text boxes. Likewise, to publicize your garage sale, choose a flyer template, which will have only one box on a page, not letter, which will let you have continuous text that flows across several pages.

In continuous text documents (also known as word-processing), you type directly on a page with, um, continuous text. You can insert photos or tables if you want, but they complement the text and aren't the main focus of the document. In documents with text boxes (also known as *page layout*), you have to create a text box first and then place that text box somewhere on your page.

The advantage of continuous text is that you can keep typing, and Pages creates new pages automatically while you type. The disadvantage of this approach is that it's harder to define exactly where the text will appear on the page.

The advantage of using text boxes is that you can move those text boxes anywhere on a page (or to a different page). The disadvantage of typing text in text boxes is that they can display only a limited amount of text. If you need to type a larger chunk of text, you may need to link text boxes so that when your text overflows one text box, it flows automatically into another one.

Another difference between continuous text and text box documents is that you must manually add (or delete) pages when you use a template with text boxes by choosing Insert⇨Page. To delete a page, select it and choose Edit⇨Delete. With a continuous text template, Pages adds pages automatically while you type and deletes pages as necessary when you delete text.

Replacing placeholder text

Nearly every template, except for Blank, contains placeholder text (a mix of pseudo–Latin and gibberish that's been used in typesetting as dummy text since the sixteenth century), which you replace with your own text. To change placeholder text in a template, follow these steps:

1. **Double-click the placeholder text you want to change.**

   Pages selects the paragraph or text your cursor was over when you double-clicked, as shown in Figure 3-2.

2. **Type any new text you want to replace the placeholder text.**

FIGURE 3-2:
To replace
placeholder text,
double-click
it and type
new text.

Replacing placeholder photos and graphics

Many templates display placeholder photos and graphics. Unless you happen to like the image included with a template, you'll probably want to replace it with one of your own. Here we explain how to place photos from Photos; how to place images from other places on your computer; and how to insert a chart or table from Numbers, Apple's spreadsheet application.

Inserting photos from Photos

These steps work with both templates and blank documents to add or replace photos in Pages documents with photos from Photos:

1. **Click the photo icon on the placeholder image; Media Browser appears.**

2. **Click the Photos tab in the Media Browser to view all the photos stored in Photos, iCloud (If you're connected to the Internet), and your Photo Stream photos.**

   See Book 4, Chapter 5, to learn about Photos.

   If, like us, you have thousands of photos, click one of the subheads under Events in the Library list to narrow your choices. This makes it easier to find the photo you want to add to your document.

3. **Click the photo you want to insert.**

Pages replaces the placeholder image with the photo you choose from the Media Browser, as shown in Figure 3-3. The Media Browser closes automatically after the image is placed. In the next section, we explain how to manipulate photos in your documents.

FIGURE 3-3:
Use the Media Browser to insert photos directly.

TIP

To insert a photo without a placeholder, click the Media icon on the toolbar at the top of the Pages window, and repeat the previous Steps 2 and 3. The photo is added to your document. Move and resize as in the next section.

Moving and resizing a photo

After you place a photo in a document, you can move or resize it.

To move a photo, follow these steps:

1. **Drag the photo to a new position.**

If your document has continuous text, the paragraphs shift while you move the image so that the text runs before and after the image. If you're using a document with text boxes, the image moves directly over the text box.

2. **Release the mouse button or lift your finger from the trackpad when you're happy with the new location of the photo.**

To resize a photo, follow these steps:

1. **Click the photo you want to resize.**

   Handles appear around your chosen picture.

2. **Move the pointer to a handle until the pointer turns into a two-way pointing arrow.**

3. **Drag the handle to resize your photo.**

   The photo maintains its original aspect ratio.

4. **Release the mouse button or lift your finger from the trackpad when you're happy with the new size of the photo.**

Inserting other images

If the image you want to insert isn't stored in Photos, do the following:

1. **Choose Insert⇨Choose.**

   A Chooser opens, showing the folders and files on your Mac (as in Figure 3-4).

2. **Scroll through your folders and files until you find the image you want to insert.**

3. **Double-click the file.**

   Your image is added to your document.

4. **(Optional) To replace the placeholder image, click it, press Delete, and then drag the inserted image to the placeholder location, or resize it as shown in the previous section.**

TIP

You can also modify and mask images. We show you how to handle these tasks in Book 5, Chapter 6.

Inserting charts and tables from Numbers

You can insert charts or tables from Numbers (iWork's spreadsheet app, which we explore in Book 5, Chapter 5) directly in a document. (In the later section, "Creating Charts and Tables," we explain how to create a chart or table in Pages.)

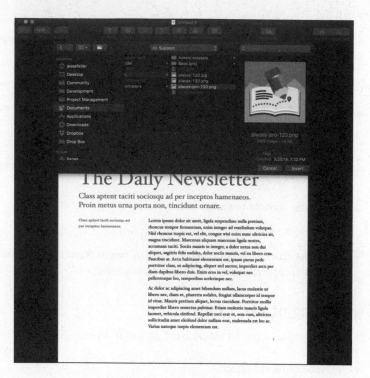

FIGURE 3-4:
Choose the file
you want to
insert in your
document.

1. **Open the Numbers document that has the chart or table you want to insert.**

2. **Select the chart or table you want to insert.**

   Depending on the document, you may have to select Rows and Columns.

3. **Choose Edit⇨Copy or press ⌘+C.**

4. **Return to your Pages document.**

5. **Choose Edit⇨Paste or press ⌘+V.**

6. **Drag the selection handles to resize the placeholder as needed to accommodate the table or chart.**

Adding pages or sections to your document

In continuous text documents, no matter how much text you type, pages are added. Each page has the same layout although some elements may be slightly changed. For example, when a second page is added to a letter, it has reduced header information (such as a smaller logo) and a page number instead of the address in the footer. In some documents, you may want to manually add a page break or create a section that has different margins than the rest of the document or begins a new chapter. For example, a financial report may have a cover page as

one section, a table of contents for the second section, and third section containing descriptive text with charts and graphs.

To add different pages to your document, follow these steps:

1. **Place the cursor at the end of the page that you want the additional page to follow.**

2. **Click the Insert Icon on the toolbar and choose the type of addition you want to make.**

   Available options will be bold; unavailable options will be dim in the pop-up menu.

   - *Page Break:* Appears in continuous text documents; creates a new page immediately after where you placed the cursor, which could be between two paragraphs or at the very end of your text.

   - *Column Break:* Appears if your document has columns; adds a column immediately after where you placed the cursor.

3. **To add a page to the document, click the Add Page button.**

You can add a new *section* to a document at any time without affecting the existing pages. Or, add a *section break* within an existing page, and then anything after the section break will move to the new section.

To add a new section to your document, simply choose Insert⇨Section, and a new section is added to the end of the document.

To add a section break, do the following:

1. **Click to place the cursor at the beginning of the text you want to move to the new section.**

2. **Choose Insert⇨Section Break.**

   The new section begins with the text that comes after where you placed the cursor.

3. **To see all the pages of your document, choose View⇨Page Thumbnails from the toolbar or the menu bar.**

   A left Sidebar opens, showing thumbnails of the pages or sections in your document, as shown in Figure 3-5. When you click a thumbnail, a colored background surrounds all the pages that are in the same section. The first page of a section is flush left, and subsequent pages in the section are indented to the right.

TIP

To hide page thumbnails, choose View⇨Show Document.

Zoom

FIGURE 3-5:
Thumbnails
show you all the
pages in your
document.

section

word count

Moving around your document

The page thumbnails not only show you how many pages are in a section, but they're also a way to jump from one page to another. Just click a thumbnail to move to that page.

Two other tools (refer to Figure 3-5) help you manage your document:

» **Zoom:** Click the pop-up menu, which lets you zoom in or out of your document to views that range from 25% to 400%. You can also choose to view one or two pages side by side at a time or to Fit Width or Fit Page. After you view two pages, Fit Spread is an option on the Zoom menu.

» **Word count:** Choose View⇨Show Character Count to display the number of characters in your document at the bottom center of your document, and then from the Character Count pop-up menu choose Words. Actually this displays the number of words already in the document. This updates as you add more text to your document.

REMEMBER

After you change Character Count to Word Count from the Character Count pop-up menu, Word Count is now shown on the View menu for the document you're editing. If you choose⇨Hide Word Count, you can display the word count again by choosing⇨Show Word Count.

TIP

When you create a new document, or edit an existing document that shows character count instead of word count, follow the previous steps.

TIP

Choose View⇨Hide Word Count to remove either of those from view.

Working with Text

Text can appear directly on a page or inside a text box. Although you type text directly on a page in continuous text documents (such as those created with the Blank template, letters, or reports), you can add text boxes and type text inside those text boxes, which you may choose to do if you want to insert a sidebar. In some templates, such as newsletters, posters, and business cards, you can type text *only* inside text boxes.

TIP

In many ways, text boxes behave like other objects placed in your document, such as photos or charts, and have a few different options than continuous text. We explain adding text boxes later in this chapter in the "Creating and Placing Text Boxes" section.

Either way, after you type your text, you probably want to make some changes. In the following subsections, we explain how to edit, format, and adjust the spacing of your text.

Editing text

Whether you're typing text directly on a page or inside a text box, you can edit text by adding, deleting, or rearranging it.

>> **Adding text:** Any new text you type appears wherever the cursor is located. To add text, just place the cursor where you want the new text to appear, click, and then type away.

REMEMBER

If you want to start your text on a new page or section of a continuous text document, choose Insert⇨Page Break or Insert⇨Section/Section Break, as we explain previously.

>> **Deleting text:** You can delete text in two ways:

- *Move the cursor to the right of the characters you want to erase and press Delete.* The Delete key appears to the right of the +/= key.

- *Select text and press Delete.* Select text by holding down the Shift key and moving the cursor with the arrow keys or by clicking and dragging the mouse over the text to select it, and then press Delete.

>> **Rearranging text:** After you write some text, you may need to rearrange it by copying or moving chunks of text from one location to another. You can copy and move text between two text boxes or from one part of a continuous text page to another part of the same page — or to another page all together.

To copy and move text, you can use the Cut, Copy, and Paste commands on the Edit menu, but you may find it quicker to select and drag text with the mouse. Here's how it's done:

a. *Select the text you want to copy or move.*

b. *Drag the selected text to a new location.*

If you want to copy text, hold down the Option key while dragging the selected text. If you want to move text, you don't need to hold down any keys.

c. *Release the mouse button or lift your finger from the trackpad to finish copying or moving your text.*

REMEMBER

Formatting text

The text styles and images you choose for your document create the tone of what you want to communicate — businesslike, fun, weird, and so on. You can format text by using fonts, styles, sizes, and colors. (Later in this chapter, in the "Using Styles" section, we tell you how to apply formatting in a different way.)

To give you fast access to the formatting options, Pages displays a Format pane (see Figure 3-6) down the right side of the Pages window. To view (or hide) the Format pane, click the Format icon on the toolbar or choose View➪Inspector➪Format.

To change selected text to another style included in the template, click the disclosure button next to the current style (*Body,* in the figure) to open the Paragraph Styles menu, and then click a different style, such as Title or Caption.

To format text in a way that isn't included in the template, select the text you want to format and then click the Style tab of the Format pane. Then, in the Font section, do any of the following:

FIGURE 3-6:
Choose fonts, styles, and sizes, text spacing, and alignment.

>> **Click the typeface (*Hoefler text*, in the figure).** Then choose a typeface from the menu that appears. Pages has "what-you-see-is-what-you-get" (affectionately known as WYSIWYG, pronounced *wizzy-wig*) menus so you see what the font looks like in the pop-up menu.

>> **Click the style (*Regular,* in the figure).** Then choose a style, such as Regular or Italic. You can also click the style buttons below this menu or make a selection from the Character Styles pop-up menu.

>> **Click the size arrows or type a number for the size you want (*11,* in the figure).**

>> **Click the color swatch or picker.** A color menu appears when you click the swatch, or a choice of color pickers appears when you click the color circle next to the swatch. Click a color to change the color of your selected text. If you're working with the color picker, choose a different color picker by clicking an icon at the top of the dialog box.

TIP

For more info on choosing colors, see Book 5, Chapter 4, where we tell you how to use these tools in Keynote. These tools are similar to each other in Pages and Keynote.

>> **Click the gear button to open the Advanced Options menu, as shown in Figure 3-7.** Use the pop-up menus to fine-tune character spacing, ligatures, and capitalization, or add a background color. When you select the Shadow check box, additional menus appear to adjust how your selected text will be shadowed.

FIGURE 3-7: Use Advanced Options to fine-tune your text.

TIP

To adjust text in a text box, select the desired text, and then click the Text tab of the Format pane. For example, if the text box has a header, click the text to select it and then change the format. Any other text in the text box is unchanged.

Adjusting line spacing, justification, and margins

You can change how characters look by playing with the font, but you can also change the way a block of text looks by changing how it's spaced on the page. In concrete terms, this means changing

>> **Alignment:** Define how text aligns within the left and right margins, in text boxes, and also between the top and bottom.

>> **Spacing:** Define how close together lines in a paragraph appear and how much space is between paragraphs.

>> **Margins:** Define the left and right boundaries that text can't go past.

Changing alignment

You may be more familiar with the term *justification*, which means how the text appears on the left and right edges. The Pages tools that adjust justification of your selected text are in the Alignment section of the Format pane, as follows:

>> **Align Left:** Text appears flush against the left margin but ragged along the right margin.

>> **Center:** Each line of text is centered within the left and right margins so that text appears ragged on both left and right margins.

>> **Align Right:** Text appears flush against the right margin but ragged along the left margin.

>> **Justify:** Text appears flush against both the left and right margins, but extra space appears between words and characters.

To align, or *justify*, your selected text, follow these steps:

1. Select the text you want to modify.

2. Click the Align Left, Center, Align Right, or Justify buttons of the Format pane.

3. (Optional) Click the left outdent or right indent buttons to move the selected text about half an inch to the left or right.

   The left outdent button is active only after you indent the selected text. Click the buttons more than once to further indent or outdent.

Changing line spacing

Line spacing used for most purposes typically varies from 0.5 to 2.0. (A value of 1.0 is single spacing, and a value of 2.0 is double spacing.) To change line spacing, follow these steps:

1. Select the line or lines of text you want to modify.

2. Click the disclosure triangle next to Spacing to open the Spacing pop-up menu and choose one of the following options: 1.0-single, 1.2, 1.5, or 2.0-Double.

3. Click the disclosure triangle to the left of Spacing and choose Lines if it isn't selected.

4. Click the up and down arrows for the spacing field to the right of the Spacing pop-up menu to change the line spacing value, or enter a value, such as 1.5.

5. (Optional) Choose one of the other options from the pop-up menu and then choose a value accordingly:

   - *At Least:* Sets a minimum of points for each line. This should be a minimum of the font size. For example, if you use a 10 point (pt) font, a 10 pt spacing is equal to a single-spaced paragraph.

   - *Exactly:* Sets the points to the exact number you choose. Oddly, if you set a 10 pt font to an exact 10 pt spacing, the lines almost overlap.

   - *Between:* Sets the number of points for the space between lines of text. The minimum is 1 pt and is equal to single spacing. A value equal to your font points creates double-spacing.

   The changes to your selected text occur immediately so you can try different solutions and see the effect they have on your text.

TIP

6. Click the up and down arrows next to the value fields for Before Paragraph and After Paragraph to set the amount of blank space that occurs there.

7. Click the Format icon on the toolbar to close the Format pane.

Defining margins for the whole document

The left and right margins define a document with only continuous text. Documents that use only text boxes are limited by the edges of the page.

To define the margins for the whole document, do the following:

1. Click the Document icon on the far right side of the toolbar or choose View➪Inspector➪Document Setup from the menu bar.

2. Click the Document tab, as shown in Figure 3-8.

3. Choose a paper size, such as US Letter or Legal, from the pop-up menu in the Printer & Paper Size section.

4. (Optional) Change the page orientation.

5. In the Document Margins section, type in the values you want for your left, right, top, and bottom margins.

   Or use the up and down arrows to choose a value.

FIGURE 3-8:
Set the margins
for the entire
document.

TIP

To set the units of measure for your rulers, choose Pages➪Preferences and then click Rulers. Use the pop-up menu next to Ruler Units to choose Inches, Centimeters, or Points.

Defining margins for a portion of text

To define the left and right margins of a portion of text — say a long citation from a book — you can use the ruler, which appears at the top of the Pages window when you choose View➪Show Ruler. The ruler lets you define an exact location for your margins, such as placing the left margin exactly 1.5 inches from the left edge of the page.

To define the left and right margins of selected text, follow these steps:

1. Select the text you want to modify.

2. Drag the Left Margin marker to a new position on the ruler and then release the mouse button or lift your finger from the trackpad.

The Left Margin marker is the blue triangle that appears on the left side of the ruler. If only the first lines of your paragraphs move, you've selected the Indent

REMEMBER

marker, which is at the very top of the Left Margin marker; grab the Left Margin marker from the bottom.

If the ruler isn't visible, choose View⇨Show Rulers.

3. **To indent the first line of a paragraph or paragraphs in your selected text, drag the Indent marker to a new position on the ruler and then release the mouse button or lift your finger from the trackpad.**

The Indent marker is the thin blue rectangle that appears over the Left Margin marker. Figure 3-9 shows the Left and Right Margin markers and the Indent marker.

If you drag the Left Margin marker after you move the Indent marker, the Indent marker moves with the Left Margin marker; dragging the Indent marker, however, moves the Indent marker by itself.

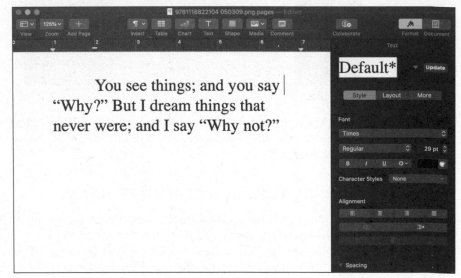

FIGURE 3-9:
Adjust paragraph margins and set first-line indents.

4. **Drag the Right Margin marker to a new position on the ruler and then release the mouse button or lift your finger from the trackpad.**

The Right Margin marker is the blue triangle that appears on the right side of the ruler.

Creating precise tabs and indents

Dragging the Left Margin and Right Margin markers on the ruler is a fast way to adjust the margins or first-line indents of a text selection. For a more precise way, follow these steps:

1. **Select the text you want to modify or click anywhere in the continuous text to apply the tabs to the entire document.**

2. **Click the Format icon on the toolbar or choose View⇨Inspector⇨Format.**

3. **Click the Layout tab.**

4. **Click the disclosure triangle next to Tabs.**

   The Text Inspector controls shown in Figure 3-10 appear.

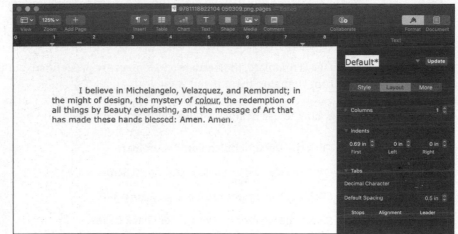

FIGURE 3-10:
Choose precise values for adjusting text margins.

5. **(Optional) Click in the Decimal Character field if you plan to use the tab for numbers with decimals.**

   For example, you could change a decimal to a comma if you're creating a European document.

6. **Enter a value or click the up and down arrows to choose a value in the Default Spacing field.**

7. **(Optional) If you want to add tab stops, click the plus button at the bottom of the window in the Tabs section and do the following:**

   a. *Click the number under Stops and indicate a precise position for the tab.*

   b. *Click the type of tab you want in the menu under Alignment: Left, Center, Right, or Decimal.*

   c. *Choose a Leader style from the pop-up menu: none, dashes, dots, a line, or arrows.*

   If you want to delete a tab, click the tab and then click the minus sign to delete it.

Click the disclosure triangle next to Indents to establish precise indent measurements for the first lines of paragraphs and also for the left and right margins of your selected text.

Adding headers and footers to a continuous text document

The header and footer is the space between the top (header) and bottom (footer) margin and the document body where you type your main text. The header and footer are where you usually place the date, page number, or document title; they contain information that repeats on each page. As with margins, documents that use text boxes don't have headers or footers.

If you use a template, the headers and footers are predefined, but that doesn't stop you from changing them if you want.

Here's how to use headers and footers:

1. **Click the Document icon on the toolbar.**

   Or, choose View⇨Inspector⇨Document Setup.

2. **Click the Document tab (refer to Figure 3-8).**

3. **Select the Header and/or Footer check boxes.**

   Text boxes for one or both will be added to your document.

4. **Choose how far from the edge of the page you want the header and footer to appear; type in a number or use the up and down arrows.**

   The header or footer text box moves according to the value you set. The top and bottom margins must be greater than the header and footer distance; otherwise, the document text will cover the header and footer. If you modify the header and footer, you need to modify the document margins.

5. **In the Document Margins section, enter a value in the Top and Bottom text fields, or use the arrows to specify each margin.**

   If your header is 1 inch, your top margin should be at least 1.5 inches. The header will begin 1 inch from the top of the page, and the main text — also known as the *document body* — will begin 1.5 inches from the top of the page or one-half inch below the header.

WARNING

6. **Leave the Document Body check box selected.**

Deselecting this box will convert your document to a page layout (text box only) document and may cause you to lose some of your work.

7. **Move the pointer near the top or bottom of the page, more or less where the header or footer should be, until an empty box appears, as shown in Figure 3-11.**

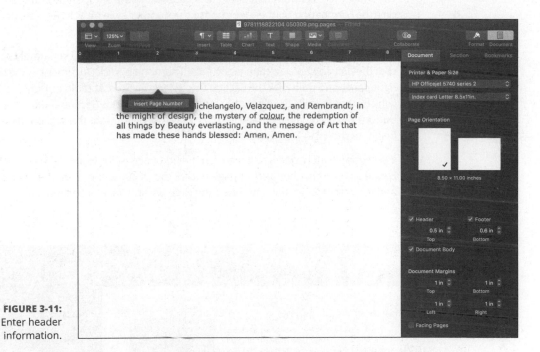

FIGURE 3-11: Enter header information.

8. **Click in the empty box.**

The cursor flashes in the empty box.

TIP

There are three boxes — one on the left, one in the center, and one on the right — into which you can enter distinct information in each and press Return independently in each one so text appears on different lines.

9. **Type the text you want to appear at the top or bottom of each page.**

Format the text as you would any other text, setting the typeface, size, and style or choosing a style associated with the template.

10. **To add the date or page number automatically, position the cursor where you want the text to appear, and then choose Insert⇨Page Number/Page Count/Date & Time from the Pages menu bar.**

To format the Date & Time, double-click the inserted text. A window opens, as shown in Figure 3-12, giving you format choices and the option to update the date whenever the file is opened.

To format the page numbers, click the Section tab in the Setup pane and then click the Format pop-up menu to choose the number style (Arabic, Roman, or letters).

If your document has multiple sections that you want numbered separately, click the first page of a section in the Page Thumbnails, click Document in the right panel, and then click the Section tab. Select the Start At radio button (which automatically deselects the Continue from Previous Section radio button) and then type the page number with which you want the section to begin, as shown in Figure 3-13.

If you don't want headers to appear on the first page — for example, you create a report that has a cover page — click the Document icon on the toolbar and then click the Section tab. Select the Hide on First Page of Section check box.

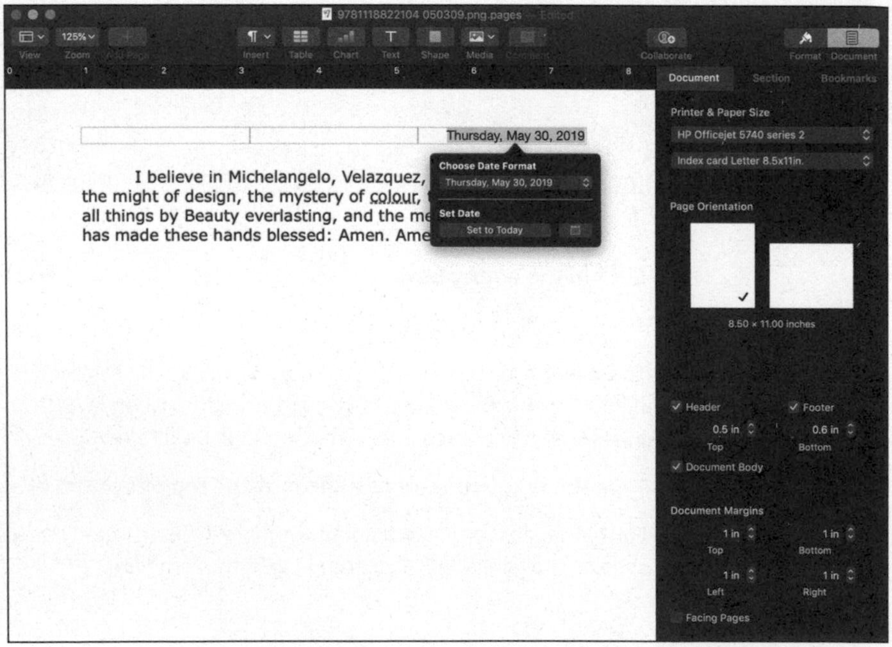

FIGURE 3-12:
Choose a format.

FIGURE 3-13:
Specify headers
and footers and
page numbering
for sections as
well as the entire
document.

Creating and Placing Text Boxes

As we mention earlier, text boxes hold text that you can place anywhere on a page (even in the middle of other text). You can create and place text boxes on any Pages document, whether created from a blank document or a template.

Creating a text box

When you create a text box, other text will wrap around it, making a text box an ideal candidate when you want to create a sidebar in a document. To create a text box, follow these steps:

1. **Click the Text icon on the toolbar.**

   A text box appears on the page.

2. **Click the Format icon and then choose the paragraph style you want to use for the text in the text box using the Text tab, as shown in Figure 3-14.**

FIGURE 3-14:
Choose the text
style for your new
text box.

3. **Type new text inside the text box.**

   Pages keeps your text within the boundaries of the text box.

You can also choose Insert⇨Text Box. The new text box will use the Body paragraph style.

TIP

Moving a text box

After you create a text box, you can move it. Simply drag the text box to a new
location, even to a different page. If your document is lengthy, you can click the
text box, choose Edit⇨Cut, click the destination page in the Pages pane (choose
View⇨Show Thumbnail Pages if you don't see it), and then choose Edit⇨Paste to
place your text box on the selected page.

Resizing a text box

Sometimes a text box is too large or small for the text you type inside. To fix this
problem, resize the text box:

1. **Click anywhere inside the text box.**

2. **Move the pointer to a handle until the pointer turns into a two-way
   arrow.**

3. **Drag a handle to resize the text box.**

   Handles on the sides resize vertically, making the box longer, or horizontally, making the box wider. Handles on the corners resize proportionally in both directions, making the overall box bigger.

4. **Release the mouse button or lift your finger from the trackpad when you're happy with the size of the text box.**

Uniting text boxes

If you type more text than a text box can display, you see a Clipping Indicator icon, which appears as a plus sign inside a square at the bottom of the text box. When you see the Clipping Indicator (it looks like a plus sign) at the bottom of a text box, you have two choices.

>> **Enlarge the text box.** You can resize the text box so it can display more text, as we describe in the preceding section. This may not always be practical because your page layout may not accommodate an expanded text box.

>> **Unite two text boxes.** If your text box is limited by the page margins, create another text box on the next page. Click one of the text boxes and then click the Arrange tab in the Format pane. Shift-click both text boxes, and then click the Unite button that appears at the bottom of the Format pane (when Arrange is selected). The two text boxes come together and your text flows from one to the next.

TIP

If two text boxes overlap each other, select them and in the Arrange tab of the Format pane, you can intersect the text boxes, subtract one text box from another, or exclude one text box from another.

REMEMBER

Depending on how much text you have, you can (and may need to) unite multiple text boxes.

Using Styles

You may have a favorite way to format text. Although you could manually change each formatting feature, you may find it faster and easier to use styles instead. Formatting styles store different types of formatting that you can apply to text. The Pages templates have formatting styles stored already. When you create your own documents, you can create formatting styles, too. By using formatting styles, you can format text quickly and consistently with minimum effort.

The following are the types of styles you can apply to text:

>> **Paragraph Styles:** Affect an entire paragraph (or many paragraphs) where the end of a paragraph is defined by a line that ends where you press Return.

>> **Image Styles:** Affect inserted images, applying special effects, borders, fill, and shadows.

>> **Text Box Styles:** Affect text inside a text box. There may be multiple paragraph styles inside a text box, in which case you want to follow the instructions for paragraph styles to apply them to each one in the text box.

Using a paragraph style

To apply a paragraph style, follow these steps:

1. **Drag to select the text you want to modify.**

2. **If you don't see the Format pane, click the Format icon on the toolbar.**

3. **If you're working with text in a text box, click the Text tab. If you chose continuous text, go to Step 4.**

4. **Click the disclosure triangle at the top of the Format pane to open the Paragraph Styles menu, as shown in Figure 3-15.**

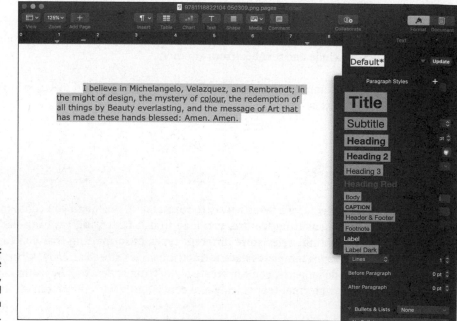

FIGURE 3-15: See the paragraph, character, and list styles used in the document.

5. **Choose a style that you want to use for your selected text.**

   Pages formats your selected text.

6. **(Optional) Use the Font tools (as we explain in the earlier section "Formatting text") to make changes to the paragraph style.**

   When you modify an existing text style, an asterisk appears to the right of the style name.

7. **To create a new paragraph style, click the disclosure triangle to open the Paragraph Styles menu, and then click the plus sign next to Paragraph Styles.**

   A new style is added to the menu with the name of the original style followed by a number 1.

8. **Click this new name in the menu and then click the arrow to the right to open a submenu. Choose Rename Style.**

   The name is highlighted, allowing you to type a new name.

9. **To apply the new formatting to the existing style, click Update Style.**

TIP

From the style pop-up menu, you can delete the style or choose Shortcut to assign a Hot Key so when you want to apply the style, instead of using the Format pane, you can just select the text and then press the Fn key associated with the style.

Using an image style

To apply a style to an image, follow these steps:

1. **Click the image you want to modify.**

2. **If you don't see the Format pane, click the Format icon on the toolbar.**

3. **Click the Style tab and then click one of the Image Styles, as shown in Figure 3-16.**

   Pages formats your selected image.

4. **(Optional) Use the following tools to make changes to the image style. Click the disclosure triangle to the left of each tool to reveal the available options.**

   - *Border:* Surrounds your image with a Line or Picture Frame; define the width, color, and scale of your choice. If the image already has a border, you use this tool to modify it.

FIGURE 3-16:
Choose from effects you can add to your images.

- *Shadow:* Creates one of three types of shadows — Drop, Contact, or Curved — behind the entire image. Blur, offset, and opacity settings add more special effects.

- *Reflection:* Adds a mirrored effect of your image under it.

- *Opacity:* Affects the entire image and changes the intensity of all components: the text, fills, and borders. This is a good tool if you want to use the image as a backdrop behind text.

5. **Click the left or right triangle to open a second Image Styles Chooser, and then click the plus sign to create a new image style.**

   A new style is added to the Chooser and the icon shows the effect.

Using a text box style

When you create a text box, you can format the text (as we explain in the earlier section, "Formatting text"), and you can format the box itself, adding a background fill color, border, and shadow. Follow these steps:

1. **Click the text box you want to modify.**

REMEMBER

   These actions apply to the text box and its contents so if there's more than one text style within the text box, you want to format those individually and then format the text box to apply a fill and/or border.

2. **If you don't see the Format pane, click the Format icon on the toolbar.**

3. **Click the Style tab and then click one of the Text Box Styles to apply a Pages preset to the text box.**

   There are five preset styles to apply a colored fill to the text box background.

4. **Use the Fill, Border, Shadow, and Opacity tools to make changes to the image style:**

   With the Fill tool, you can choose the color and style of the color you want behind your text. The Border tool gives you the option of highlighting the text box with a border. The Shadow tool enables you to create a drop shadow around the text box. The Opacity tool varies the fill opacity, letting more of the background show through.

5. **To save a modified text box style as a preset, click the left or right triangle to open a second Text Box Styles Chooser, and then click the plus sign to create a new text box style.**

   A new style is added to the Chooser and the icon shows the effect.

Creating Charts and Tables

As we mention earlier in this chapter, you can insert charts and tables directly from Numbers, which is great when you already have the charts and tables prepared or if you have complex data that's more easily worked with in Numbers. If you're starting from scratch, it may be quicker to build your chart or table directly in Pages. *Charts* are pie charts or bar charts that graphically represent data. *Tables* comprise rows and columns of information where the intersection of a row and a column is a *cell*.

Adding and removing a chart

Sometimes presenting your information as a chart makes your information easier to understand. To add a chart to a Pages document, follow these steps:

1. **Choose Insert⇨Chart⇨*Chart Type* or click the Charts icon on the Pages toolbar, and then choose the type of chart you want to create — bar, pie, 2-D or 3-D, for example.**

   A chart appears.

2. **Click the Edit Chart Data button at the bottom of the chart.**

   The Chart Data Editor appears, as shown in Figure 3-17.

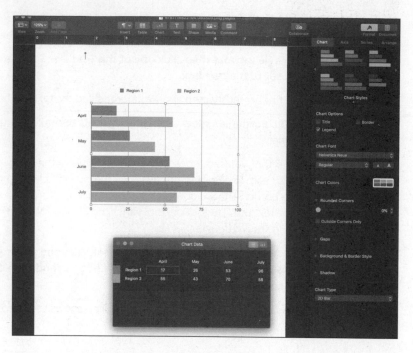

FIGURE 3-17:
Enter the data you want to display in the Chart Data Editor.

3. **Double-click the Row and Column field headers of the Chart Data Editor to select the placeholder text and enter the information you want on your chart.**

4. **Click the cells below the headers to enter the number values you want the chart to show.**

   The data entered appears in the chart and titles.

5. **Click the Switch Axis buttons in the upper-right corner of the Chart Data Editor to invert the axis.**

6. **Click the Format icon to open the Format pane and then click the following tabs to choose how you want the data to appear:**

   - *Chart:* Change the chart color scheme (Chart Styles), the typeface, and size; add gaps between columns; add backgrounds, borders, and shadow; and even change the chart type.

   - *Axis:* Edit the axis options and value labels on the axis.

   - *Series:* Edit value labels on the bars and add trendlines.

   - *Arrange:* Wrap text around the chart and align and distribute its position among other objects on your document, such as text boxes and images.

     See Book 5, Chapter 5, where we present Numbers. Read that chapter for detailed instructions about formatting charts.

TIP

To remove a chart, click it and press Delete.

Adding a table

Tables in Pages are *calculable*, which means that you can write formulas or insert functions in much the same way you would in Numbers. These are the steps for adding a table to your document:

1. Choose Insert⇨Table⇨*Table Type* or click the Table icon on the Pages toolbar.

A blank table appears on your document.

2. Edit the size of the rows and columns of your table by clicking the row and column headers. Then move your cursor over the right or left border until it becomes a double-headed arrow and drag to change the size of each header.

When you change the size of the header, the column is also resized.

3. Click the add rows or add columns button that looks like two parallel vertical lines next to the far ends of the row and column headers and use the up and down arrows on the pop-up menu to set the number of rows and columns, as shown in Figure 3-18.

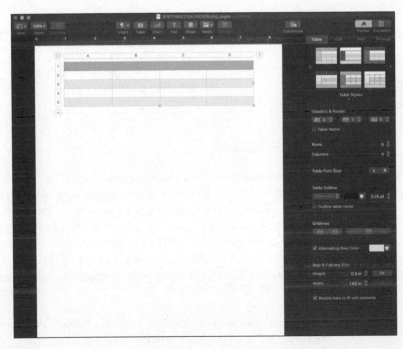

FIGURE 3-18: Set the number of rows and columns on your table.

4. **Click the Format icon on the toolbar to see the Format pane, if it's not open.**

5. **Click the tabs to edit the table as follows:**

   - *Table:* Change the table color and layout scheme (Table Styles), and use the menus to set the number of header rows and columns and footer rows, select the table font size, and add a table outline and grid lines.

   - *Cell:* Select all the cells or a portion of them and then choose the data format you want to use to fill the cells and add fill and border to the cells.

     To select a column of cells, click its header. To select a row of cells, click its number.

   - *Text:* Edit the font and text alignment. Alternatively, you can select a preset style by clicking the disclosure button to the right of the style and then choosing one from the menu.

   - *Arrange:* Wrap text around the table and align and distribute its position among other objects on your document, such as text boxes and images.

TIP

6. **Set up functions and conditional formats by entering numerical data in a row or column of cells.**

   Type an equals sign to open the Functions pane and then assign a function — for example, sum or average — to the cell at the bottom of a row, or end of a column.

TIP

   See Book 5, Chapter 5, where we present Numbers. Read that chapter for detailed instructions about formatting tables and writing formulas and using functions.

Adding shapes

Shapes add interest to your documents and make a good alternative to using background fill and border for your text. For example, you can create an interesting shape and then place a text box over it. (See the next section, "Arranging objects," to learn about positioning the two.) So rather than have a boring rectangle of text with a colored background, you can have a polygon with the text on it. If you use the Wrap Text tool that follows the contours of the shape, your text takes on the polygon shape, too. With your document open to the page where you want to insert a shape, follow these steps:

1. **Click the Shape icon on the toolbar and click the left and right arrows to flip through the selections, as shown in Figure 3-19.**

   Alternatively, you can choose Insert⇨Shape and then choose a shape from the flyout menu.

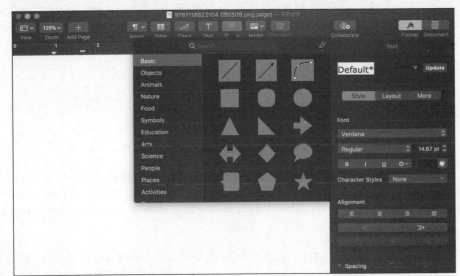

FIGURE 3-19:
Pages offers
shapes of many
sizes to add to
your documents.

2. **Choose the shape you want.**

   Your selected shape appears on the page with active resizing handles.

3. **Click the shape and grab a *resizing handle* — one of the squares on the box that surrounds the shape — to enlarge or reduce the shape to the size you want.**

4. **Modify the shape.**

   Many shapes have green grabber dots that you drag to change the shape or size of the shape. Hover the cursor over one of the green dots until it changes from an arrow to a plus sign, and then drag to see how the shape changes. For example, dragging clockwise or counterclockwise on the star or polygon increases or decreases the number of points on the star and the number of sides on the polygon. The grabber dot on the quote bubble or square moves the direction of the angle that points to another object.

   If the shape you're using doesn't have green grabber dots, choose Format⇨Shapes and Lines⇨Make Editable. When you invoke this command, red dots appear around the shape. Grab a dot and drag it to change the default shape. When you're done folding, spindling, or mutilating the shape, click outside it to apply the changes.

5. **Drag the shape to better position it on the page.**

6. **Click the shape, click the Format icon on the toolbar, and click the Style tab in the Format pane.**

7. **Click the options you see to choose a different shape style.**

From the Format pane, you can also change the fill, add a border, add a drop shadow to the shape, or add a reflection.

To add text to your shape, click the shape and begin typing.

Arranging objects

In your documents, you often have multiple shapes, objects, and images that may overlap. Sometimes one object even hides another and you almost go crazy trying to find it. Arranging and aligning objects can help keep everything in view and neatly . . . well . . . arranged.

Think of the shapes, objects, and so on as a stack of papers. If the bigger or darker sheet is on top, it hides what's underneath. You have to rearrange the order of your objects in order to see them all. To reveal objects that may be hidden by others, follow these steps:

1. **Click the object that you want to send to the bottom of the stack.**

2. **Choose Arrange⇨Send to Back.**

Anything that was hidden by that object now appears on top of it.

3. **Click the other objects one at a time and choose Arrange⇨Send Back, Arrange⇨Bring to Front, or Arrange⇨Bring Forward until you're satisfied with the appearance of your page.**

Text boxes are most useful when positioned as the top item on the stack, so most of the time, you want to choose Arrange⇨Bring to Front so your text boxes rest on top of other shapes or images.

After you have the objects in the positions you like, you can create groups or lock the objects.

4. **To create a group of objects, select your objects and then choose Arrange⇨Group.**

The objects stay together and move together.

You can edit individual objects in a group, by choosing Arrange⇨Ungroup. After you edit one or more objects that were in a group, regroup them by following the steps in this section.

To lock an object, group of objects, or a group, follow these steps:

1. **Select the object, objects, or groups that you want to lock.**

2. **Click the Format icon in the toolbar.**

The Format pane appears.

3. **In the Object Placement section, click Stay on Page.**

4. **In the Arrange section, click Lock.**

You can't move, delete, or edit the locked object(s) or group. To unlock the objects, click Unlock in the Format pane or choose Arrange⇨Unlock.

Alignment refers to how objects are placed in relationship to each other. To align your shapes or objects, do the following:

1. **Hold down the Shift key and click the objects you want to align.**

Resizing handles appear around each selected object.

2. **Choose Arrange⇨Align Objects or Arrange⇨Distribute Objects.**

- *Align Objects:* Lets you align the left, right, top, or bottom sides of the objects, or the vertical or horizontal centers.

- *Distribute Objects:* Evenly distributes three or more objects between the two farthest objects; choose horizontal or vertical.

Wrapping text around an object

When you insert a text box, photo, or chart inside continuous text or a text box, it sits on top of the existing text. To neatly separate the text and object, you want to *wrap* the text around the object. Follow these steps:

1. **Click the object, be it a text box, photo, or chart.**

2. **Click the Format icon on the toolbar or choose View⇨Inspector⇨Format.**

3. **Click the Arrange tab, as shown in Figure 3-20.**

4. **Click a text-wrap pop-up menu and choose one of the following:**

- *Automatic:* Pages determines the best distribution for the object in the text.

- *Around:* The text surrounds all sides of the object.

- *Above and Below:* The text appears above and below the object, but the space to the left and right is clear.

- *None:* The object will sit on top of the text.

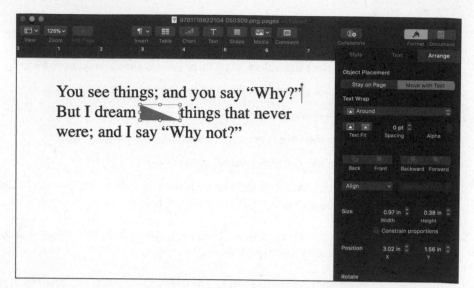

FIGURE 3-20:
Wrap text around
objects.

5. If you choose any of the choices in Step 4 except None and Inline with Text, click one of the Text Fit buttons to have the text create a rectangle around the object (left button) or flow around the contours of the object (right button).

6. Type in the Spacing field or use the up and down arrows to indicate the amount of space between the object and the text.

Polishing Your Document

When you finish designing your document, you're ready to show it to the world. Of course, before you show your document to others, you should proofread your document for grammar and spelling. Fortunately, Pages is happy to help you check a document's spelling.

Spell-checking a document

Pages can spell-check your entire document, including text trapped inside text boxes and shapes. To spell-check an entire document, follow these steps:

1. Choose Edit⇨Spelling and Grammar⇨Show Spelling and Grammar.

   If you choose Edit⇨Spelling and Grammar⇨Check Document Now, Pages underlines words it thinks are misspelled, but it doesn't offer any suggestions.

The first instance of a misspelled word is highlighted and the Spelling and Grammar dialog appears, as shown in Figure 3-21.

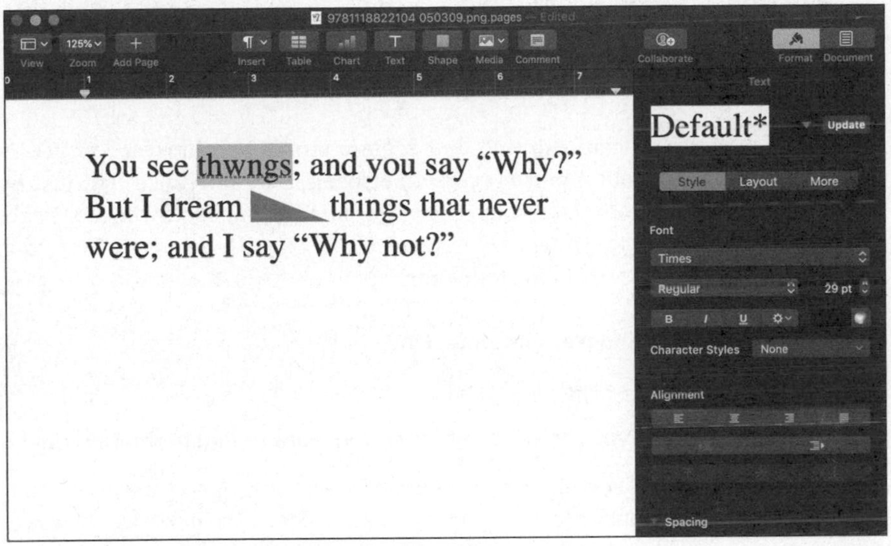

FIGURE 3-21:
Check spelling and grammar.

2. **Click one of the following:**

   - *Change:* Changes the misspelled word with the word selected in the list box. This option is not available if the word was not found in the Pages dictionary

   - *Find Next:* Looks for the next misspelled word

   - *Ignore:* Skips the misspelled word

   - *Learn:* Stores the selected word in the Pages dictionary

   - *Define:* Launches Mac's Dictionary application and displays the word's definition in the Dictionary's main window

   - *Guess:* Offers best-guess word choices

3. **Click the Close button of the Spelling dialog at any time to make it go away.**

TIP

By default, Pages checks your spelling while you type. When Pages identifies a misspelled word, it underlines it with a red dotted line. If you Control-click any word underlined with a red dotted line, Pages displays a shortcut menu of correctly spelled words that you can choose. If you want to turn off spell-checking while you type, choose Edit⇨Spelling and Grammar⇨Check Spelling While Typing to clear the check mark for this command.

REMEMBER

Proofreading your document is a good idea, even after spell-checking, because the spell checker only makes sure that the word is correctly spelled. If you type, "I have to dogs," when you really meant to type, "I have two dogs," no spell checker is going to flag that.

Finding and replacing text

Pages can also find and replace words or phrases. Say you're writing an article about a person named Swanson, only to realize that just before you send the article to your editor that the name is spelled Swansen. Pages will search your entire document and replace Swanson with Swansen. To find and replace a word or phrase, do the following:

1. **Choose Edit⇨Find⇨Find.**

   The Find dialog opens.

2. **Type the word or phrase you want to find in the Find field.**

   Pages displays the number found to the right of the word you type. The default option for this command is to find text. The next step shows you what you need to do to replace text along with two other useful options.

3. **Click the disclosure arrow to the right of the gear icon and choose Find and Replace.**

   There are two additional options on this menu.

   - *Match Case:* Select this option to have Pages distinguish uppercase and lowercase letters and find text *exactly* as you type it.

   - *Whole Words:* Select this option to ignore whole words that contain your text. If, for example, you search for *place* and select this option, *placemat* or *placement* won't be highlighted.

4. **Type the word or phrase you want to replace the found text with in the Replace field.**

   Pages highlights the word you want to find.

5. **Click Replace All to replace all instances of the old word with the new word, or click Replace and Find to replace this instance of the word and find the next instance of the word or phrase, and then click one of the following:**

   - *Replace:* Click this option to replace the old word with the new one. You have to click Next to highlight the next occurrence.

- *Replace All:* This is the only option if you choose Replace for the first instance of the word or phrase that Pages finds.

If you choose Replace and Find, you can examine each instance of the word or phrase you asked Pages to find. If you don't want to replace an instance of the word, click the right arrow to advance to the next instance of the word, or the left arrow to review the previous instance.

Saving Your Documents on Your Mac or iCloud

A handy feature of the iWork suite is that you can save your documents to iCloud and then access them from the apps on other devices where you have the Pages app installed and iCloud activated or from the iCloud website on other computers. This saves you from copying your document to a flash drive or emailing it to yourself.

Before you can use this feature, you have to turn on Pages in iCloud preferences by doing the following:

1. **Choose ⌘➪System Preferences and click the Apple ID icon.**

2. **Click the iCloud Options button.**

3. **Scroll down to Pages.app.**

4. **If the check box is not checked, click inside it.**

   You can now save Pages documents to iCloud.

5. **Click Done and then click Close to exit System Preferences.**

To save your Pages documents, choose File➪Save. In the Save As window that opens, type a name for your document, and then click the Where pop-up menu, as shown in Figure 3-22, from the iCloud section, choose Pages or iCloud or another destination folder, drive, or server. Click the disclosure triangle next to Save As to expand the window and scroll through your folders and directories.

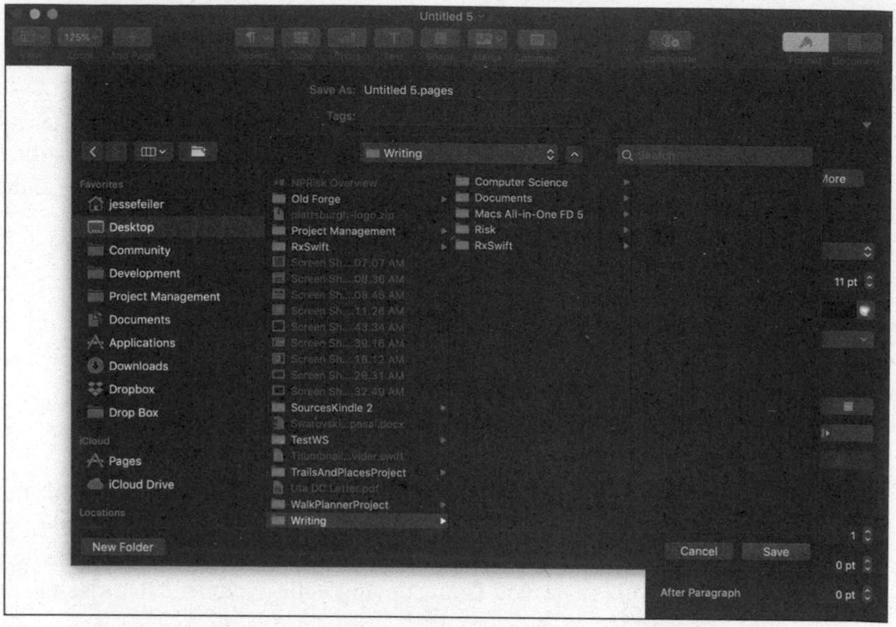

FIGURE 3-22:
Save your
documents to
your Mac or to
iCloud.

Printing Your Documents

You can print and distribute your document in the traditional way — as good old-fashioned hard copy — by following these steps:

1. **Choose File⇨Print.**

2. **Choose your printer, settings, number of copies, and page range.**

3. **Click the Print button.**

When your document comes out of the printer, you can hand it to someone, hang it up, or put a stamp on it and drop it in your local mailbox.

Exporting to a Different File Format

Chances are that you'll want to share your document electronically, too. However, as much as you love your Mac and Pages, not everyone uses the same types of computers or applications. Don't let that stop you from sharing your document files, though, because Pages can export files in diverse formats.

Although Pages saves documents in its own proprietary file format when you choose File⇨Save, if you want to share your Pages documents with others who don't have the Pages application, choose File⇨Export To and you can export your document in one of the following file formats:

- **PDF:** Saves your document as a series of static pages stored in the PDF Adobe Acrobat file format that can be viewed (but not necessarily edited) by any computer with a PDF viewing application.
- **Word:** Saves your document as a Microsoft Word file, which can be opened by any word processor that can read and edit Microsoft Word files.
- **ePub:** Saves your document in a format that can be read in Books on an iPad, iPod touch, or iPhone as well as on many electronic readers.
- **Plain Text:** Saves your document as text without any formatting or graphic effects.
- **Rich Text Format:** Saves your document as an RTF, which can be opened by most word-processing programs.
- **Pages '09:** Saves your document a Pages '09 document. If you're sharing your document with someone who hasn't upgraded to the latest version of Pages, this is a way to be sure they can access your document.

REMEMBER

The PDF file format preserves all formatting, but it doesn't let anyone edit that file unless they use a separate PDF-editing application, such as Adobe Acrobat Pro. If someone needs to edit your document, the Word option preserves Pages documents well. The Plain Text option is useful only if you can't transfer your Pages document to another application as a Word file.

To export a Pages document, follow these steps:

1. **Choose File⇨Export To⇨*File Type*.**

   A dialog appears. The document will be exported with the original filename.

2. **Select a format, such as Word or ePub, and then click Next.**

   Each format has different options. For example, if you export to ePub, you have cover options, layout options, and so on. You can require a password to open the document if you export to Word, PDF, or Pages '09.

3. **Select the folder where you want to store your document.**

   You may need to switch drives or folders until you find where you want to save your file.

4. **Click Export.**

REMEMBER

When you export a document, your original Pages document remains untouched in its original location.

You can also share your documents as a Mail or Messages attachment or make them available on iCloud or AirDrop, not to mention social networking sites. See the end of Book 5, Chapter 4, to learn about sharing with Keynote. It works the same for Pages as for Keynote.

IN THIS CHAPTER

» **Creating a presentation**

» **Adding, editing, and formatting text**

» **Working with shapes, charts, and tables**

» **Inserting photos and movies**

» **Changing the order of slides**

» **Using transitions and effects**

» **Customizing themes with masters**

» **Giving a presentation**

Chapter **4**

Presenting with Keynote

P resentations used to be confined to the realm of professional conferences and shareholder meetings. With or without a projector, the combination of your Mac and Keynote, makes it cost effective and time efficient to give presentations at weekly staff meetings, set up an interactive kiosk at the local small-business fair, or even post your presentation on your website. When you save Keynote presentations to iCloud, you can access your presentations on all your devices such as an iPhone or iPad or on another computer from the iCloud website. Keynote enhances your creativity with ready-made templates so you can concentrate more of your time on talking to an audience and less of your time fumbling around with jammed slide projectors, whiteboards, and felt markers that stain your fingertips.

Best of all, you can spice up your presentation with tables, charts, and audio and visual effects, from playing music and movies to showing visually interesting effects — stuff like text sliding across the display or dissolving away into noth-ingness. Such effects help get your point across and hold an audience's attention.

In this chapter, we begin our presentation (pardon the pun) with the Keynote basics: working with themes and slide layouts, replacing placeholder text and media with your text and media, and adding charts, tables, and animation. At the end of the chapter, we give you tips for practicing your presentation and tell you about the options you have for running the presentation even without being present. When you're up to speed on the basics, check out Book 5, Chapter 6, which shows you some nifty tricks that work with Pages, Keynote, and Numbers.

REMEMBER

Keynote is part of Catalina, along with Pages and Numbers. The apps are free for Mac owners and work well with one another. They also work well with the iOS apps that have the same names.

Creating a Presentation

A Keynote presentation consists of one or more slides, where typically each slide displays information to make a single point. Although our sample slide in Figure 4-1 shows only text and an image, a slide can include charts, graphics, photos, video, and audio as well.

FIGURE 4-1:
The appearance of a typical slide.

To make your presentation even more interesting to watch, you can add *transition* effects that appear when you switch from one slide to another. To emphasize the information on a particular slide, you can add individual visual effects, known as *builds,* to specific items, such as making text rotate or making a graphic image glide across the screen and halt in place.

We explain how to add all these embellishments to your presentation in the sections that follow; however, the basic steps to creating a presentation in Keynote are:

1. Launch the Keynote app by clicking its icon (it looks like a podium with a pie chart document on it) in the Dock or Launchpad.

2. Choose File➪New and then pick a theme to use for your presentation.

3. Create one or more slides.

4. Type text or place graphics and images on each slide.

5. (Optional) Add an audio or video file to each slide.

6. (Optional) Add visual effects to animate an entire slide or just the text or graphics that appear on that slide.

7. Save your presentation.

Choosing a theme and saving your presentation

A presentation consists of multiple slides. Although a black-and-white presentation can be elegant in a retro sort of way, color helps attract and keep your audience's attention. To make the creation of your presentation easier, Keynote provides *themes* that give your slides a consistent appearance, such as the font, size, style, and background color. Within each of the 33 themes (as of this writing), there are multiple *slide layouts*, which are templates for your slides. Each slide layout in a theme is a *master slide*, which defines the look of each slide you create based on the layout. We explain how to work with, and create, master slides in the section "Using Masters to Customize Themes" later in this chapter. Most themes have the following slide layouts:

>> Title, top or center

>> Title and subtitle

>> Title and bullets

>> Title, bullets, and photo

>> Bullet list

>> Photo (horizontal, vertical, three-up, or full-page photo)

>> Quote

>> Blank

Each theme offers a standard and wide (HD) format. Make sure you decide which you want to use before creating your presentation.

TIP

If you want to create a presentation without using a theme — say you want your presentation to reflect your corporate color scheme and font family — pick a simple theme, such as Black or White, to start so you have multiple slide layouts to which you can apply your desired color scheme, fonts, and so on.

To pick a theme, follow these steps:

1. **Open Keynote from the Dock or Launchpad and after the app launches, choose File⇨New.**

    The Choose a Theme dialog opens, as shown in Figure 4-2.

FIGURE 4-2:
Keynote provides a variety of themes for your presentations.

2. **Choose the slide format from the tabs at the top of the window: Standard (4:3) format or Wide (16:9) format.**

    Standard size slides echo traditional, square-ish 35mm slides and work well if you connect a projector to your Mac. Choose the Wide format when you plan to connect your Mac to a wide-screen HD monitor. If you're not sure which you'll be using, choose Wide, as most projectors can accommodate wide but you don't risk having black horizontal borders on your slides when projected on a wide-screen monitor.

3. **Click a theme and click the Choose button or double-click a theme.**

Keynote creates the first slide of your presentation, using your chosen theme. At this point, you can add text, graphics, audio, or video to the slide or you can add new slides.

4. **Choose File⇨Save.**

A Save As dialog opens.

5. **Type a name for your presentation.**

6. **Type any tags you want to attach to the file or choose existing ones from the pop-up menu.**

You can use tags to find files in Spotlight Search.

REMEMBER

7. **Click the Where pop-up menu and choose a destination for your file.**

You can save the presentation to a folder on your hard drive, external hard drive, iCloud Drive, or Keynote iCloud.

8. **Click Save.**

TIP

If, after saving a file or opening an existing file, you want to move the presentation from your Mac to iCloud or vice versa, or to an external disk or flash drive, choose File⇨Move To and then select the new location from the Where pop-up menu. This action removes the presentation from its original location and places it on the new one.

Opening an existing file

If you're working on a document on one source, such as your Mac, and you want to open a document from another source, such as iCloud or an external drive, choose File⇨Open, and choose one of the following locations:

» **Keynote:** You find Keynote listed as a subfolder of iCloud on the sidebar of the Finder window. Choose this option, click the file you want to work on and then click Open.

» **iCloud Drive:** You find your iCloud drive on the left sidebar of the Finder window. After choosing this option, click one of the documents on the list, and then click Open. (You need an Internet connection to work on iCloud documents.)

» **From your Mac or external drive:** From the Where pop-up menu, scroll through the directories and folders to find an existing document you want to work on, click it, and then click Open.

You can also use Keynote to open a presentation created in another presentation app, and then use it as is, make changes, even save it as a Keynote file. To open a non-Keynote presentation, such as Microsoft's PowerPoint, drag the file you want to open over the Keynote icon in the Dock or follow the steps outlined in the preceding paragraphs.

Finding your way around Keynote

After you create a presentation, the Keynote slide editor window opens as shown in Figure 4-3. Across the top of the Keynote window, you see the Toolbar, which holds buttons for the most frequently used functions. Below the Toolbar is the Format bar, which has pop-up menus for formatting the text and objects on your slides. We explain both the Toolbar and Format bar functions throughout this chapter.

FIGURE 4-3:
Navigator view gives you an overview of your presentation while working on a specific slide.

The window can have between one and three panels in the four available views. To switch to a different view, choose the View icon on the Keynote toolbar and then choose Navigator, Outline, Slide Only, or Light Table.

This is what you see in each view:

>> **Navigator:** Useful for editing individual slides and manipulating all the slides in an entire presentation. Referring to Figure 4-3, you can see that thumbnails of your slides are displayed in the Slide Navigator in the left pane, the slide you're editing is in the center panel, and the Format pane is on the right. To edit your presentation in this view, choose View➪Navigator.

>> **Slide Only:** Useful for editing the text and graphics of a single slide. The Slide Navigator pane closes, but you still have all the formatting tools available in the Format pane. To edit your presentation in this view, choose View⇨Slide Only.

>> **Light Table:** You see all your slides together, as in Figure 4-4. You can click and drag slides to a new position or change the slide layout by choosing a new one from the Format pane. Move the slider at the bottom of the left pane to show more, but smaller, slides or fewer, larger slides. When you double-click a slide in Light Table, it opens in the most recent of the three other views you used. This view is particularly useful for manipulating a large number of slides in a presentation. To edit your presentation in this view, choose View⇨Light Table.

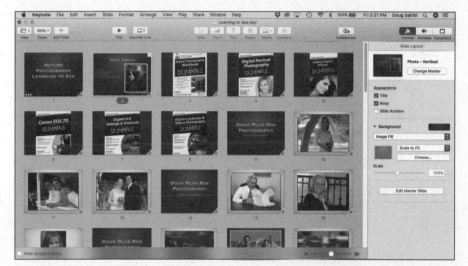

TIP

In both Navigator and Light Table views, slides with audio or movie media have three empty circles in the lower-left corner of the slide thumbnail image.

>> **Outline:** Similar to Navigator view but instead of seeing thumbnail images in the Slide Navigator, you see the text of each slide, which you can edit, and the edits are reflected on the slides. Choose Keynote⇨Preferences⇨General to choose the font size you want to use in Outline View. To edit your presentation in this view, choose View⇨Outline.

In addition to the presentation views, you can choose additional items you may want to see in the window. Choose View and then choose from these options:

>> **Show/Hide Rulers (not available in Light Table view):** Use the rulers as a reference when working with objects on your slide.

>> **Show/Hide Comments:** This is useful if other people comment on your presentation before or after you give it.

>> **Show/Hide Presenter Notes (not available in Light Table view):** These are notes that you can view when giving your presentation. You see the notes on your computer below the slide preview, which helps you remember what you want to say, but the projected presentation displays only your slides. When you select Show Presenter Notes, you can type your speech or reminders on each slide.

To change the font or create a list format of notes, click the Presenter Notes section, and then click the Format icon in the toolbar (refer to Figure 4-3); make your choices from the buttons and menus you see.

TIP

After using Keynote for a while, you may decide you need more buttons on the toolbar. To customize Keynote, choose View⇨Customize Toolbar, and then from the window that appears, drag the buttons you want to add to the toolbar, and drop them there.

Adding slides

When you create a new presentation, that presentation starts out containing just one slide. Because getting your idea across usually needs more than one slide, you probably want to add more slides. If you go overboard and add too many slides, you can always winnow a few.

Adding a blank slide

To add a blank slide to a presentation, do one of the following:

>> Choose Slide⇨New Slide on the menu bar (any view). The new, blank slide appears at the end of the presentation.

>> Control-click a slide thumbnail in the left panel, and choose New Slide (all but Full Slide view). The new blank slide appears after the slide you clicked.

>> Click a slide in the Slide Navigator or Light Table view and press Return. The new blank slide appears after the slide you clicked.

Adding predefined slides

Each Keynote theme has a selection of slide layouts that you can use to build your presentation. When you use a slide layout, you need only insert your text and images in the existing placeholders, and that makes presentation creation a snap. The slide layout structures are more or less the same for each theme, but the colors, style, and fonts that have been applied make each theme different.

To create a new slide with a slide layout, click the slide before the location where you want to insert a new slide, and then click the New (+) icon in Slide Navigator, Light Table, or Outline view. Choose the slide layout you want, as shown in Figure 4-5. You can change the slide layout later, even after you add your own text and images — we tell you how in just a bit.

FIGURE 4-5:
The Slide Layout menu is a quick way to create new slides.

Making duplicate slides

Making duplicate slides is helpful if you want to use the exact same header or layout on multiple slides. Even if you use slide layouts, you may tweak them and want to duplicate your efforts. Here's how:

>> **Duplicate one slide.** Click the slide you want to duplicate and choose Edit⇨Duplicate Selection, or Control-click and choose Duplicate. The new, duplicate slide appears immediately after the original.

>> **Duplicate multiple slides.** To duplicate more than one slide at once, hold down the Shift key and click the first and last slides of a series you want to duplicate, or hold the ⌘ key and click individual, noncontiguous slides; then do either of the previous commands to duplicate all the slides you chose. The dupes will be inserted after the last selected slide.

TIP

If you want to create a duplicate of your entire presentation, choose File⇨Duplicate.

Manipulating Text

Whether it's a title, subtitle, bulleted list, quote, or descriptive paragraph, text on a slide is written in a text box — although the box borders can be invisible. Most slides contain at least one text box that holds the title of the slide. Other text may be free-flowing or even a bulleted list that's inserted with an image.

Entering text

When you create a new slide, unless you choose the blank slide, the slide layout has text placeholders in text boxes and perhaps placeholder media, depending on the layout you choose. You replace the placeholders with your own words and images. For now, we're going to talk about text. To place text on a slide, follow these steps:

1. **Choose View⇨Navigator on the menu or toolbar.**

2. **In the Navigator, click the slide that you want to edit or create a new slide using one of the methods we outlined previously.**

   Your chosen slide appears.

3. **Double-click the placeholder text that appears in the Title, Subtitle, or Bullet Point text box.**

4. **Type text or use the arrow keys and Delete key to edit existing text.**

   The text style matches that shown in the placeholder text.

Inserting text boxes

Even when you work with a slide layout that contains text boxes, you can add your own. Click the slide where you want to place the text box. Click the Text icon in the Toolbar, and a text box appears on the slide. Then in the Format pane, click the text style you want to use. Click and drag the text box to the position you want on the slide. Resize the text box by clicking and dragging the resizing handles (those small boxes that appear on the corners and in the middle of each edge). Double-click the word *text* to erase it, and then type the text you want on your slide.

If you want to delete a text box, click it once and then press the Delete key on the keyboard.

Editing text

To edit text that you've already entered, you have two choices:

>> **In Outline view:** Select the slide you want to edit in the Slide Navigator, as shown in Figure 4-6, and then edit the text. You can change the titles, and add and delete bullets. Select a bulleted item and click and drag it by the bullet to move it up or down in the list or move it to another slide. Double-click the slide icon to collapse and hide the text.

>> **In Navigator or Slide Only view:** Double-click a word to highlight and change it or click and drag to select blocks of text you want to edit within the text boxes on the slide. Make the changes you want.

FIGURE 4-6:
Edit text in the Slide Navigator in Outline view.

TIP

To ensure that you don't give a presentation filled with typos and misspelled words, check the spelling in your presentation by choosing Edit⇨Spelling and Grammar⇨Check Spelling While Typing.

Formatting text and text boxes

Themes have predefined fonts, font sizes, and colors that create a coordinated design throughout the presentation and, quite frankly, make creating a presentation a snap. Nonetheless, you can format the text if you want by changing fonts, font sizes, or colors.

TIP

Use fonts and colors sparingly. Using too many fonts or colors can make text harder to read. When choosing text colors, make sure that you use colors that contrast with the slide's background color. For instance, light yellow text against a white or light-colored background is nearly impossible to read.

TIP

Any time you want to edit or change the style of an object, be it text, a shape, photo, chart, or table, click the object; then click the Format icon in the toolbar; and then click the tabs in the Format pane to see the editing and style options you can apply to the selected object. See the following sections for more details on formatting fonts, paragraphs, bullets, and backgrounds.

When you create a custom shape, it can be synced across the web with other documents.

Changing fonts

Most likely, you've changed fonts in other programs, and the procedure in Keynote is fairly similar. If you'd like to select a different font, and/or change the font size or color, follow the instructions here.

TIP

Changing a font on a slide will change only that slide. If you want to make the same change to all slides in your presentation, you want to change the master slide, and we dedicate a section to that topic further along in this chapter.

After you've selected the text, you can edit fonts with the Format menu or follow these steps:

1. **Click the Text tab and then the Style button in the Format pane.**

2. **If you want to use a different font style that's part of your chosen theme, click the disclosure triangle next to the sample font to open the Paragraph Styles menu.**

    A list of styles appears from which you can choose a different one.

    Or

3. **If you want to change the typeface, size, or style, in the Font section, scroll through the menus to select the options you want.**

The Font menu shows the typefaces as they are to help you imagine your presentation using that font.

4. **Click the font family when you find it, and then click the Typeface, Size, and Style menus and alignment buttons to make those changes to your type.**

The text on your slide changes to reflect the typeface, style, and size.

5. **(Optional) Click the gear icon to open the Advanced Options menu, as shown in Figure 4-7.**

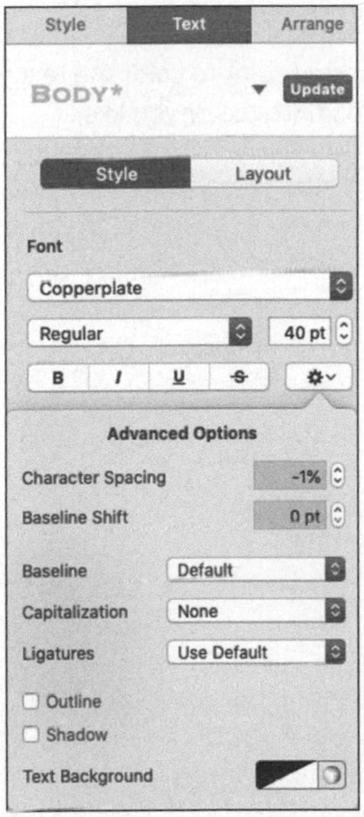

FIGURE 4-7:
The Text section of the Format pane lets you modify text.

6. **(Optional) Choose an option from the Text Color pop-up menu, and then click the Colors icon to change the color of the font.**

The first option lets you choose a different option such as a gradient fill or image fill. The color swatch opens a chooser that displays colors used in the theme. The color-wheel icon next to the color swatch opens the Color Wheel, as shown in Figure 4-8. Here's how to choose colors in the Color Wheel.

a. *Click the color picker you prefer: Color Wheel (which is the default), Slider, Palette, Spectrum, or Crayons. The color pickers give you different ways to choose colors. Click through to see which you're most comfortable using.*

b. *Click the desired color in the color picker that appears in the Colors window.*

c. *(Optional) In the Color Wheel, make the color lighter or darker by dragging the slider on the right side up and down.*

d. *(Optional) In any of the color pickers, adjust the opacity by dragging the Opacity slider left to decrease opacity, or right to increase opacity or type in a precise percentage in the text box to the right.*

e. *When you have a color you like, drag the color from the color box at the top to the color palette at the bottom. Your color is saved in the palette for future use.*

f. *Click the close window button or choose View⇨Close Colors.*

Keynote immediately uses your selected color to color the text you selected in Step 3. You can play around until you find a color you like.

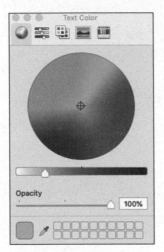

FIGURE 4-8:
The Colors
window lets you
choose a text
color.

The name in the Paragraph Styles menu changes to reflect the new settings you choose and an asterisk appears next to the name along with an Update button (refer to Figure 4-7). You can take the following actions:

>> **Click Update.** All slides that use that layout will reflect the changes you made.

>> **Click the name in the Paragraph Styles menu.** Choose the original style from the menu to revert to that style, or click the plus sign (+) at the top of the Paragraph Styles window to add the edited style as a new style. The latter option opens a blank text field in the Paragraph Styles window into which you type the name of the style. The new style is added to the paragraph styles menu for future use.

WARNING

Fonts aren't part of your presentation, but they reside on the computer from which you give the presentation. If you intend to use your presentation on a different computer, make sure that the fonts you use in your presentation are installed on the other computer, or Keynote will choose what it considers the closest font. So not only could the substitute font be ugly, but words may not fit within text boxes and may be cut off or dropped to a second line that could push lower text off the slide. If you use symbols or special characters, and they aren't available in the substitute font, they'll be replaced by a different symbol or an empty square.

TIP

GIVING YOUR PRESENTATION THAT SOMETHING EXTRA

Capitalizing whole words or phrases in your presentation, especially in titles, is EYE-CATCHING. With Keynote, you don't have to use Caps Lock and retype everything if you change your mind. Choose the text to which you want to add pizzazz and then choose Format⇨Font⇨Capitalization (or choose Capitalization in the Advanced Options window), then choose one of the following:

- **None:** The default option. You create a capital letter by holding down the Shift key and then pressing the letter you want to capitalize.

- **All Caps:** Capitalizes all the letters in your selected text.

- **Small Caps:** Capitalizes all the letters in your selected text — but in a small size. Any letters you type while holding the Shift key will be big capital letters.

- **Title Case:** Capitalizes the first letter of each word in your selected text, except articles, conjunctions, and prepositions.

- **Start Case:** Capitalizes the first letter of each word in your selected text.

You can also create a new text box and choose one of the previous capitalization options to apply the desired capitalization to any text you type.

If your text is just a little too long for the space it's in, you can scrunch it together, just barely, so that it fits without using a smaller font size. Choose Format⇨Font⇨Character Spacing⇨Tighten. For more precision, choose Character Spacing in the Advanced Options window and pick a specific percentage to tighten. If the typeface has a condensed variant, choose that for the best results.

Finally, **turn on font smoothing.** Choose ⌘⇨System Preferences⇨General and select the Use LCD Font Smoothing when Available option. Font smoothing makes the curves and lines of fonts seem less pixilated so they're more recognizable and easier on your eyes.

Formatting paragraphs

Although you may not create paragraphs with your text, Keynote considers even a single line a paragraph as far as formatting alignment and vertical spacing of the text in your text boxes. Select the text you'd like to modify and follow these steps:

1. **Click the Text tab and then the Style button in the Format pane.**

2. **Click the horizontal and vertical alignment buttons in the Alignment section and choose one of the following**

- *Left Alignment* (default): Text is aligned on the left and has a ragged edge on the right.

- *Center Alignment:* Moves your text to the center, but any bullets you have remain at the left edge of the text box.

- *Right Alignment:* Aligns your text on the right, and the left edge is ragged; bullets remain on the left edge of the text box.

- *Justified:* Adjusts the text to have straight edges on the left and right.

- *Minor adjustment:* Those two buttons below the alignment buttons shift the text one space at a time to the left or to the right.

- *Upper Alignment:* Moves the text to the top of the text box.

- *Middle Alignment:* Moves the text to the middle of the text box.

- *Lower Alignment:* Moves the text to the bottom of the text box.

3. **To change the vertical spacing between the lines of your text, click the disclosure triangle next to Spacing to see the menus shown in Figure 4-9, and choose the distance you want between the lines and before and after paragraphs, if your text box has more than one paragraph.**

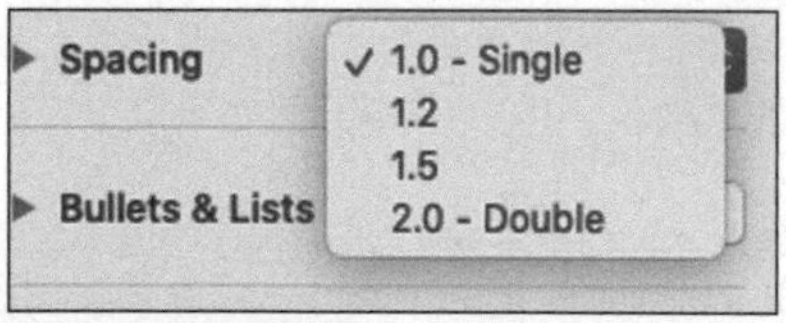

FIGURE 4-9:
Choose the distance between lines with the spacing menu.

▶ Spacing	✓ 1.0 - Single
	1.2
	1.5
▶ Bullets & Lists	2.0 - Double

TIP

Text boxes adjust to the amount of text you type, so if you type more text than space allows, the text box grows as much as it can and then the font size begins to shrink to accommodate the text; delete text, and the font size grows again.

Formatting bullets

As we mention earlier in this chapter, themes come with predefined fonts, colors, styles, and bullets as part of the package. But Keynote offers such a variety of bullets, you may want to have some fun and change them. Select the text and follow these steps to change bullets:

1. **Click the Text tab and then the Style button in the Format pane.**

2. **Click the disclosure triangle next to Bullets & Lists and choose one of the options shown in Figure 4-10:**

   - *Bullet:* Creates a standard bullet (a period) before each item on your list.

   - *Image:* Creates an image bullet before each item on your list. This option opens the Image Bullets menu from which an image, specify image size, and alignment. You also have the option to use a custom image.

   - *Lettered:* Creates a letter before each item in your list starting with A. This option opens a menu from which you can choose the letter style and the letter shown before the first item in your list.

   - *Numbered:* Creates a number before each item in your list starting with 1. This option opens a menu from which you can choose the number style and the number shown before the first item in your list.

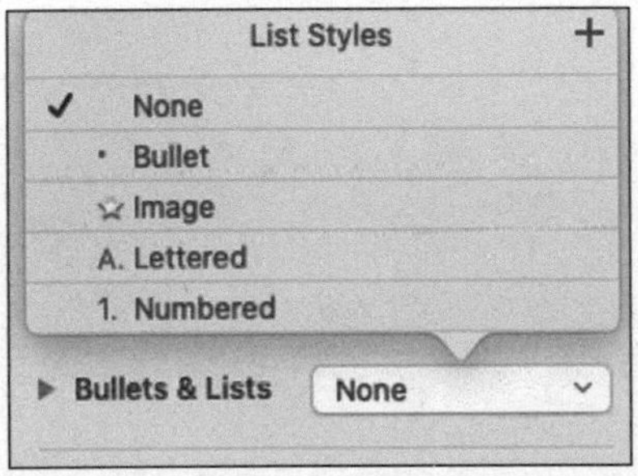

FIGURE 4-10:
Choosing a style for your Bullet List.

3. **Click the next menu to choose the bullet style: None, Text, Image, or Numbers.**

4. **Use the other pop-up menus to make adjustments; menus differ slightly from one bullet style to another:**

   - *Bullet/Number Indent:* Adjusts the distance from the outer edge of the text box and the bullet. The text moves with the bullet.

   - *Text Indent:* Adjusts the distance from the outer edge of the text box and the text. The greater the difference between the bullet indent and the text indent, the farther the text is from the bullet.

- *Align:* Sets the vertical position of the bullet in relation to the text.

- *Size:* Alters the size of the bullet.

- *Color/Image:* Lets you edit the color of text or number bullets and the icon used for image bullets.

- *Numbered bullets:* Lets you choose from Arabic, Roman, and outline format, with and without parentheses.

Changing backgrounds and borders

Some text boxes have a background color that's different from the slide background or the box may be outlined by a border or frame. Again, the preset styles are in keeping with the theme you choose, but if you want to change them or you're creating your own custom theme, select the text box and follow these steps:

1. Click the Style tab in the Format pane.

2. Click the disclosure triangles next to each option and then choose the options you want from the pop-up menus.

Choose from the preset style at the top of the Format pane, which formats the background of the cell and text, or choose an option from the pop-up menus. You see a preview of your choices on the slide. Figure 4-11 shows a cell formatted with a light gray background.

FIGURE 4-11: Fills, borders, and shadows make text boxes stand out.

- *Fill:* Puts a color, gradient, or image behind your text. Depending on the choice, you're presented with tools for choosing the color, the spectrum and direction (gradient), and scaling (image).

- *Border:* Surrounds your text with a Line and Picture Frame; define the width, color, and scale of your choice.

- *Shadow:* Creates one of three types of shadows — Drop, Contact, or Curved — behind the entire text box. Blur, offset, and opacity settings add more special effects. If you choose the Curved option, you can specify whether the shadow appears on the left side, bows inward, or bows outward.

- *Reflection:* Adds a mirrored effect of your text box under it. After choosing this option, you specify how visible the reflection is.

- *Opacity:* Affects the entire text box and changes the intensity of all components: the text, fills, and borders and reflections.

Presenting with Keynote

Adding Shapes, Charts, and Tables

One basic principle of a good presentation is giving the audience something interesting to look at. Here's where you get a look at how to use the visual-aid options offered in Keynote.

Inserting predefined shapes

Shapes can help draw your viewers' eyes to the thing you want them to notice. An arrow can connect your first point to your second; a star makes a key success stand out visually. Keynote comes with three types of simple, straightforward lines, and 12 ready-to-go basic shapes that you can stretch, shrink, and twist like Silly Putty. If you're an artistic type, there's also a tool for drawing your own shape. Each theme offers the three lines and 12 shapes in a selection of colors associated with the theme, as well as clear. Follow these steps to insert a shape on your slide:

1. Create a new slide or select the slide you want to put the shape on.

2. Click the Shape icon in the Toolbar and click the left and right arrows to flip through the color selection. Choose the shape you want, as shown in Figure 4-12.

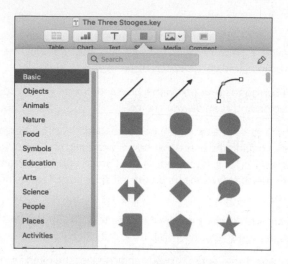

FIGURE 4-12:
Keynote offers a dozen shapes to add to your presentation.

Your selected shape appears on the slide with active resizing handles.

Some shapes have green grabber dots that you drag to change the shape or size of the shape. For example, dragging clockwise or counterclockwise on the star or polygon increases or decreases the number of points on the star and the number of sides on the polygon. The star also has a grabber you use to change the radius of the circle from which the star points emanate. Hover the cursor over one of the green dots until it changes from an arrow to a plus sign, and then click and drag to see how the shape changes.

3. **Click the shape and grab a resizing handle — one of the squares on the box that surrounds the shape — to enlarge or reduce the shape to the size you want.**

   All shapes have eight resizing dots. Drag a corner dot to resize the width and height of the shape simultaneously. Hold down the Shift key while dragging a corner dot to resize the shape proportionally. Grab a dot for the top center or bottom center to change the height of the shape. Grab a dot from the left center or right center to change the width of the shape.

4. **Click and drag the shape to where you want it on your slide.**

5. **Click the shape and then click the Format icon in the Toolbar and the Style tab in the Format pane.**

   Click the options you see to change the color of the shape or add special effects such as fill, shadow, and borders to the shape.

TIP

To add text to your shape, double-click the shape and start typing. As you type, the text wraps to the outline of the shape. If you enter more text than the size of the shape can accommodate, you can either enlarge the shape or change the font size in the Text section of the Format pane.

You can create custom shapes; if you do, you can sync them from one document to another using iCloud.

Aligning and arranging objects

When working with multiple shapes, objects, images, and text boxes, you may want to align or overlap them. To align your shapes or objects, do the following:

1. **Hold down the Shift key and click the objects you want to align.**

Resizing handles appear around each selected object.

2. **Choose Arrange⇨Align Objects to align the left, right, top, or bottom sides of the objects, or the vertical or horizontal centers.**

Do it twice to choose the vertical alignment and then the horizontal alignment.

3. **Choose Arrange⇨Distribute Objects to evenly distribute the centers of the selected objects (whatever their size) between the two farthest objects; choose horizontal or vertical.**

Think about the objects on your slide as single pieces of paper, one on top of the other. If the largest piece is on top of the others, you can't see the others. On the other hand, if the largest piece is transparent, you can see what's underneath. You have to rearrange the order in which overlapping objects are stacked. For instance, in Figure 4-13, you can't see the text because the rectangle and arrow are stacked above the text box. If either of the shapes were opaque (by lowering the shape's opacity in the Format pane), you'd be able to see the text.

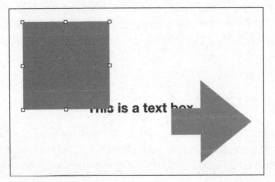

FIGURE 4-13:
Rearrange and group objects to your liking.

To reveal objects that may be hidden by others, follow these steps:

1. **Click the object that you want to send to the bottom of the stack.**

2. **Choose Arrange⇨Send to Back.**

   Anything that was hidden by that object now appears on top of it.

3. **Click the other objects one at a time and choose Arrange⇨Send to Back or Arrange⇨Bring to Front, Arrange⇨Bring Forward, or Arrange⇨Bring Forward until you're satisfied with the appearance of your slide.**

   Text boxes work best as the top item on the stack, so most of the time you want to choose Arrange⇨Bring to Front for text boxes that rest on top of other shapes or images.

4. **After you have the objects in the positions you like, you can create groups or lock the objects.**

   You have these options:

   - *Select your objects, and then choose Arrange⇨Group.*

     The objects stay together and move together.

   - *Select a single object, a group, or multiple objects, and then choose Arrange⇨Lock.*

     Locked objects become unmovable, undeletable, and uneditable. You can, however, copy or duplicate the locked object.

Choose Arrange⇨Unlock to unlock previously locked objects.

Instead of using the menus, click the text boxes and shapes you want to work with and then click Format in the toolbar and the Arrange tab in the Format pane. Use the buttons and menus to make adjustments to how the objects are aligned and arranged, as shown earlier in Figure 4-13. You can also resize, reposition, rotate, or flip the objects.

Adding a chart

Sometimes presenting your information as a chart makes your information easier to understand. Essentially, you choose a chart type and then input the information you want to represent. To add a chart to a presentation, follow these steps:

1. **Create a new slide or open an existing slide.**

2. **Click the Chart icon in the Toolbar and click the left and right arrows to flip through the selections. First click a tab for the type of chart you want (2D, 3D, or Interactive); then choose the chart you want, as shown in Figure 4-14.**

   The chart appears on your slide.

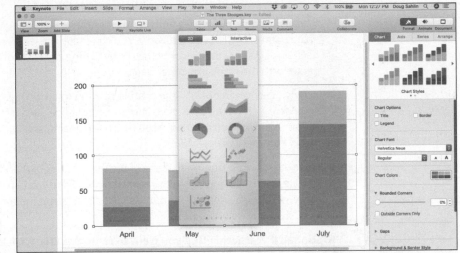

FIGURE 4-14:
Charts can make
your data easier
to understand.

3. **Click the chart on the slide, and then click the Edit Chart Data button.**

A grid appears where you enter the data for your chart.

4. **Double-click the Row and Column field headers of the Chart Data Editor
to select the placeholder text and enter the information you want on
your chart.**

5. **Click the cells below the headers to enter the number values you want
the chart to show.**

The data entered appears in the chart and titles on the slide.

TIP

Interactive charts are created the same way as 2D or 3D charts but during the
presentation, the data is animated. While preparing the animated chart, use
the slider at the bottom to see how each part will be displayed. Click the Play
button in the toolbar to preview the animation; press Return when the slide
presentation opens and press Esc to return to the Keynote editing screen.

6. **Click Format in the toolbar and then go through the tabs in the Format
pane to edit the appearance and position of the chart and data:**

- *Chart:* Gives you tools for changing the colors and fonts of the chart, as well
  as adding special effects such as a title, border, and/or legend. At the top of
  the panel you find a Chart Type menu; click to change to a different type of
  chart — any data you entered will appear on the new type.

- *Axis:* Lets you name the axes and change the scale. (This tab is available for
  all charts except pie charts.) Here you also find the menus for defining the
  value labels with percentage, currency, or others.

- *Series:* Offers menus for displaying and choosing the label format the value
  labels on charts, excluding pie charts.

- *Wedges:* Shows check boxes and menus for adding labels and defining the value data format in pie charts only. You can move the labels off the chart itself and separate the pieces of the pie by setting a greater distance from center with the respective slider bars.

- *Arrange:* Lets you reposition the chart in relation to other objects on the slide or align it on the slide itself. This doesn't change parts of the chart. (Refer to the previous section "Aligning and arranging objects" to understand how this works.)

- *Axis/Wedge Labels:* Double-click any of the text on the chart and the Axis or Wedge Labels tab appears in the Format panel. Here you can define the label (number, percentage, and so on) and also change the font family, size, style, and color.

7. **(Optional) If you decide that you want to remove a chart, click it, and then press Delete.**

Adding a table

When you add a table in Keynote, it's a fully functioning, calculable table, much as if it had been created in Numbers. These are the steps for adding a table to a slide in your presentation:

1. **Click the Table icon in the Toolbar and click the left and right arrows to flip through the color selection. Click the table you like, and it appears on your slide.**

2. **Change the size of your table by clicking the table and then doing the following:**

   - *Resize the table.* Click the button in the upper-left corner to display the resizing handle. Click the handle in the lower-left corner to resize width and height simultaneously. Hold down the Shift key while dragging this handle to resize proportionately. Click the bottom handle to change the height of the table and the middle-left handle to change the width. This doesn't add rows and columns but changes the table size.

   - *Move the table.* After resizing the table, click the button in the upper-left corner and drag the table to a new location.

   - *Add a row or column.* Click the add button (it has two parallel lines in a circle) at the bottom-left corner to add rows or the upper-right corner to add columns. A mini menu appears. The number indicates the current number of rows or columns; use the up and down arrows to increase or decrease the number. Rows and columns are added to the chart automatically.

- *Insert or delete a row or column.* Hover the cursor over the row or column identifier (letters for columns, numbers for rows) of the column to the left of, or above, where you want to insert a new row or column. Click the disclosure arrow that appears to open a menu that gives you choices to insert a row or column before or after the one you selected. You can also delete the row or column you selected.

- *Adjust row height or column width.* Follow the steps for inserting, but choose Fit Height/Width to Content to adjust the height or width of the row or column to accommodate the contents of the cells in that row or column. Or, click the column or row and then hover the cursor over one of the edges of the row or column header until the cursor becomes a double-sided arrow. Click and drag the cursor/arrow to adjust the height or width of the row or column.

3. **Edit the appearance of your table with the fields in the Format pane. Select the cells, rows, or columns you want to edit and click the tab for the things you want to change:**

   - *Table:* Has menus and buttons to adjust the color, font size, grid lines, and number of header and footer cells. These changes affect the entire table.

   - *Cell:* Makes changes to the cells, rows, or columns you select either singly or in multiples. Define how the data is formatted, such as currency or percentage, and assign fill and border colors and styles.

   - *Text:* Lets you define the font face, text color, style, and alignment of text in selected cells, rows, or columns.

   - *Arrange:* Lets you reposition the table in relation to other objects on the slide or align it on the slide itself. (Refer to the previous section "Aligning and arranging objects" to understand how this works.) In this tab, you also have the option to resize the table manually.

4. **To place formulas or functions in a cell, press the equals (=) key.**

   The functions menu appears in the Format pane.

5. **(Optional) If you decide that you want to remove a table, click the button in the table's upper-left corner, and then press Delete.**

REMEMBER

You can also use the Keynote menu to add objects to your slides. Choose Insert➪Table/Chart/Shape/Line, and then choose the specific type from the sub-menu that opens.

Adding Media Files

Text by itself can be as monotonous and confusing to read as the flight arrival and departure displays at an airport. Adding sound, still images, and movies makes your presentation appealing and communicative. Sound can be an audio recording of a song stored in Music; photos can be digital photographs stored in Photos; and movies can be short video clips.

Adding sound

You can add any audio file stored in Music or stored on your computer to a slide in your presentation or to the entire presentation. To add sound to a slide, follow these steps:

1. **Click the slide with which you want to play an audio file.**

2. **Click the Media button on the Keynote toolbar.**

3. **Click the Music button.**

   Your Music library is displayed, as shown in Figure 4-15. You can choose a song from the library or from a playlist.

FIGURE 4-15: The browser lets you choose an audio file from Music.

4. **Click the library, playlist, or folder where your audio resides.**

   The available files from which you can choose are displayed.

5. **Click the audio file you want to use and drag it onto the slide.**

   Keynote displays an audio icon directly on your slide to let you know audio is inserted here. If desired, you can drag the icon to a different location.

6. **Click the audio icon on the slide and then select or deselect Start Audio On Click on the Audio tab of the Format pane.**

   When deselected, the audio will begin as soon as the slide appears in the presentation; when selected, you have to click any key to start playback.

   TIP

   In the Format pane, you can also replace the audio with a different file, set the playback volume, and trim the audio file so only a portion plays with your slide.

7. **To delete the audio, click it, and then press the Delete button.**

To add background audio that plays during the entire slideshow, do the following:

1. **Click the Document icon on the toolbar.**

2. **Click the Audio tab in the Document pane, shown in Figure 4-16.**

FIGURE 4-16:
Add background audio to your entire presentation.

3. **Click the plus sign (+) button at the bottom right of the Soundtrack section.**

The browser opens displaying your Music library and playlists.

4. **Select the audio you want, as explained in the preceding steps list.**

5. **Choose Play Once or Loop from the pop-up menu next to Soundtrack.**

- *Play Once:* The track stops playing if the audio ends before the presentation is over.

- *Loop:* Plays the audio again from the beginning if the track ends before the presentation is over.

TIP

To play more than one audio file in an application, after adding one song to your presentation, repeat Steps 3 through 5. The songs will play in the order they appear in the Audio tab of the Document pane. When you have multiple songs in a presentation, you can change the order in which they play by dragging them to different locations on the Audio tab.

TIP

You can add voiceover to accompany your presentation so when people view it without you, they have the benefit of hearing what you want to say about each slide. Choose Play⇨Record Slideshow and begin speaking. Click the right arrow to move to the next slide. Click the Esc key when you finish. Choose Play⇨Play Slideshow to hear how you did.

Adding photos or movies

If you store digital photos in Photos, you can place those photos on any slide in a Keynote presentation by following these steps:

1. **Create a new slide or click the slide where you want to insert a photo.**

2. **Click the Media icon in the toolbar and then click Photos.**

Your Photos library is displayed in the browser.

3. **Click the Photos or Movies tab.**

The browser displays all the pictures and movies stored in Photos. Click an album or event to narrow your choices and more easily find the image or movie you want, as shown in Figure 4-17.

4. **Click the photo or movie you want from the Media Browser.**

If there is no placeholder media, the photo or movie fills your slide. Resize the photo or movie by clicking it and then dragging the resize handles. Click and drag to position the photo where you want it. If there is, the photo immediately replaces the placeholder image, maintaining any border, shadow, and fill styles.

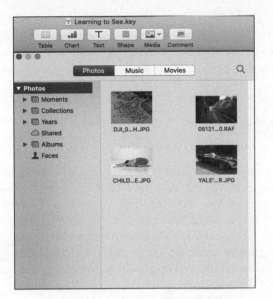

FIGURE 4-17:
Use the Photos
pane in the
browser to
choose a picture
from Photos.

With movies, you may be asked if you want to optimize the file (depending on your preferences in Keynote⇨Preferences⇨General). Optimizing the file will make adjustments so it displays nicely on an iOS device — if you plan to show your presentation on an iPad, this is a good idea; otherwise, it's a step you can probably skip.

5. **Edit the photo or movie by clicking it and then clicking Format in the toolbar. Click the tabs as follows:**

- *Style:* Offers menus to choose one of the predefined image styles associated with the theme or change the borders, shadows, opacity, and reflection in the same way as explained for text boxes.

- *Image:* Gives options for replacing the photo, masking and adjusting it, which we explain in Book 5, Chapter 6 because it's a task that is the same in Pages, Keynote, and Numbers.

- *Movie:* Lets you replace the movie, adjust the volume, trim the movie, and choose the *poster frame* (the frame displayed in your presentation). You can also select or deselect Start Movie On Click. When deselected, the movie will begin as soon as the slide appears in the presentation; when selected, press the spacebar or click the movie to start playback.

TIP

If the movie you add to your presentation has a black frame at the start, in the Edit Movie section of the Format pane's Movie tab, click Edit Movie and drag the Poster Frame slider until you see the frame you want displayed in your presentation.

- *Arrange:* Gives you the option to arrange where the media appears in the stacking order.

TIP

If you plan to use your presentation on a different computer, choose Key-note➪Preferences➪General. Next to Saving, select the Copy Audio and Movies into Document check box so your media files are part of the presentation.

Rearranging Slides

After you create your slides, chances are, they aren't in the exact order you want to give your presentation, or you may have a few that you aren't sure you want to use but aren't ready to delete. Keynote displays slides in the order they appear in the Navigator, Outline, or Light Table view. In Navigator and Outline view, the top slide appears first, followed by the slide directly beneath it, and so on, whereas in Light Table view, they're arranged left to right in a grid. After you create two or more slides in a presentation, you may want to rearrange their positions.

To rearrange slides in a presentation, follow these steps:

1. **Choose one of the following:**

   - View➪Navigator or Outline (displays slides vertically in the Slide Organizer pane)

   - View➪Light Table (displays slides in rows and columns)

2. **Click and drag a slide in the Slide Navigator, Outline, or Light Table to its new position.**

   In Light Table view, Keynote moves slide icons out of the way to show you where your new slide will appear, but a grayed rectangle remains in the original position until you release the mouse button or lift your finger from the trackpad.

3. **Release the mouse button or lift your finger from the trackpad when you're happy with the new position of the slide in your presentation.**

Creating groups of slides

Keynote offers you the possibility of creating groups of slides within your presentation. You may want to create a group of related slides, much like an outline that has topics and subtopics. Groups make editing your presentation easier because you can move a group of related slides from one place to another without losing the order of the individual slides within the group.

To create a group, follow these steps:

1. **Choose View⇨Navigator.**

2. **Click the slide you want to be the first of the group, and then click the last slide you want in the group.**

3. **Press Tab.**

4. **Press Tab or click and drag the slide toward the right.**

   A disclosure triangle appears next to the first slide in the group, and subsequent slides are indented. You can also have subgroups, as shown in Figure 4-18; Slide 1 is the head, Slide 2 is in the group, and Slide 3 is the first of a subgroup of Slide 2.

FIGURE 4-18: Create groups and subgroups of slides within your presentation.

5. **Repeat for other slides.**

   Clicking the disclosure triangle opens and closes the group.

To move a slide out of a group, click and drag the slide to the left or click the slide, and then hold down the Shift key and press Tab; the slide moves to the left.

Deleting a slide

Eventually, you may find that you don't need a slide anymore. Deleting a slide is easy, and deleting a slide group is, perhaps, too easy.

WARNING

In groups, if you delete the head slide when the group is closed, the entire group is deleted. If you delete the head slide when the group is open, only that slide is deleted; slides in the group or subgroups move one step to the left.

To delete a slide, go to the Navigator, Outline, or Light Table view, select the slide(s) that you want to delete, and then do one of the following:

>> Press Delete.

>> Choose Edit⇨Delete on the menu bar.

>> Control-click a slide and choose Delete.

TIP

If you delete a slide by mistake, choose Edit⇨Undo Delete on the menu bar (or press ⌘+Z).

Skipping a slide

You may use the same presentation multiple times but with different audiences or time allowances, so you may not want to use every slide every time. You can suppress slides without deleting them, which gives you the flexibility of using the same presentation in different settings. To skip a slide, go to Navigator, Outline, or Light Table view, select the slide(s) you want to skip, and then Control-click the slide and choose Skip Slide. To add the skipped slide back in the presentation, Control-click the slide and choose Don't Skip Slide.

Creating Transitions and Effects

To make your presentations visually interesting to watch, you can add transitions and effects. *Slide transitions* define how a slide appears and disappears from the display. *Text and graphic effects* define how the text or graphic initially appears on or disappears from the slide and how it moves around a slide. You can also add hyperlinks to your presentation.

Creating a slide transition

To create a slide transition, follow these steps:

1. **Choose View⇨Navigator on the menu bar.**

2. **In the Slide Navigator, click the slide that you want to display with a transition.**

3. **Click the Animate icon to open the Transitions pane.**

4. **Click the Add an Effect button to see the Transitions menu (as shown in Figure 4-19).**

FIGURE 4-19:
Use the
Transitions
tab in the
Slide Inspector
to define a
transition.

5. **Choose an effect that piques your curiosity**

   Depending on the transition effect you choose, you may need to define other options, such as the direction or duration of your transition.

   The Magic Move effect lets you add animation to your presentation without hiring a designer. It animates an object, moving it from its location on one slide to a new location on the next slide. The object must be the same on both slides. Place the object at the starting point on the first slide and then on the end point on the second slide. The Magic Move feature moves the object when the slide transitions from the first slide to the second slide.

A preview of your transition in action appears in the central slide pane.

Transition options will vary depending on the effect you choose. You choose options such as the direction from which the transition begins, the duration of the transition, and how the transition starts from pop-up menus.

Click the Change button to use a different transition or add another one; choose None in the Effect pop-up menu to remove a transition.

6. **Click the Animate button to close the Transitions pane.**

Creating text and graphic effects

Sometimes you want your bullets to show up one at a time. Instead of creating separate slides — the first with one bullet, the second with two bullets, the third with three, and so on — create your slide with the bullets you want, and then choose how Keynote "builds" your slide during your presentation. Keynote offers three ways to create text and graphic effects in over 25 types of transitions:

>> **Build In:** Defines how text and graphics enter a slide. (If you choose the Build In transition, initially, the text and graphics won't appear on the slide.)

>> **Action:** Defines how text and graphics move on a slide.

>> **Build Out:** Defines how text and graphics exit a slide.

Creating builds

To define an effect for text or graphics, follow these steps:

1. **Choose View⇨Navigator on the menu or toolbar.**

2. **In the Navigator, click the slide that contains the text or graphic you want to display with a visual effect.**

3. **Click the text or graphic you want to modify; for example, a text box with a bulleted list or a table with several rows.**

   Choose animated charts to add action to those.

4. **Click Animate in the toolbar.**

5. **Click the Build In or Build Out tab.**

6. **Click Add an Effect and choose an option from the pop-up menu.**

7. **Set the Delivery options to build your bullet list, chart, or table, one item at a time.**

Delivery options vary depending on the Effect you choose. The options you specify determine how each bullet from a list is delivered during the presentation, or how an individual word is delivered.

8. **Click Preview to see how the build will display during your presentation.**

9. **Click Change to use a different effect or delete the effect (None).**

10. **(Optional) Click another object and assign a build to that object as in Steps 6 and 7.**

a. Click the Build Order button to open the Build Order window (refer to Figure 4-20).

b. Click and drag the objects in the list to set the order they'll be added to the slide.

c. Click an object, and then in the Build In section of the Animate pane, choose when to start the builds and the delay between each object.

d. Click Preview to see how it will look during your presentation.

e. Click the Close button to exit the Build Order window.

FIGURE 4-20: Builds are a great way to show information one piece at a time.

11. **Click Animate in the Toolbar to close the Builds pane.**

Making text and graphics move on a slide

If you choose the Action button for text or graphics, you can choose the Move Effect, which lets you define a line that the text or graphic follows as it moves across a slide. To define a line to move text or graphics on a slide, follow these steps:

1. **Follow Steps 1 through 4 in the preceding section for creating builds.**

2. **Click the Action tab.**

3. **Click Add an Effect.**

4. **Choose Move from the Effect pop-up menu.**

Keynote displays a red line that shows how your chosen text or graphic will move, as shown in Figure 4-21.

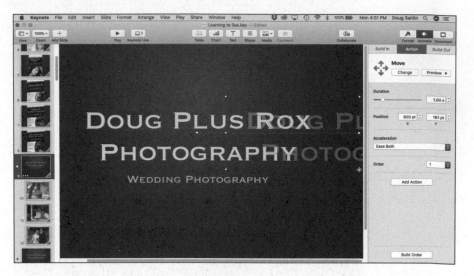

FIGURE 4-21:
Keynote displays the path connecting text or graphics on a slide.

5. **(Optional) Click and drag the handle at the beginning or end of the red line to move the line or change the line length.**

Moving the red line changes the direction your chosen text or graphic moves. Changing the line length determines how far your chosen text or graphic moves.

6. **(Optional) Click the Add Action button to add another action to the same object.**

7. **(Optional) Click another object to add an action or build to that object.**

For example, you could have an easel slide across the slide, bounce, or jiggle, and then the bulleted list appears on the easel, building one item at a time with the blur effect. Use the Build Order window to adjust the order in which the action and builds take place (refer to Figure 4-20).

The Action feature moves an object or text on a slide. The Magic Move feature animates objects or text from one slide to the next during the slide transition.

Adding hyperlinks to your presentation

Like links in a web page, hyperlinks within your presentation connect to another point in the presentation, connect to a website, or open an outgoing email message. They're particularly useful for creating presentations that a viewer will watch alone — say, at a kiosk or even on your website. You don't have to be present for the viewer to see your presentation. Hyperlinks are also helpful if you want to access media stored remotely, such as a video that would take up storage on your computer.

Here's how to create a hyperlink:

1. Choose View⇨Navigator on the menu or toolbar.

2. Click the slide that contains the text or graphic you want to use as the departure point for the hyperlink.

3. Select the text or graphic that will act as the hyperlink button.

4. Click Format⇨Add Link to open the link window, shown in Figure 4-22.

Figure 4-22 shows the available options for linking to a slide. Options for the other links are self-explanatory.

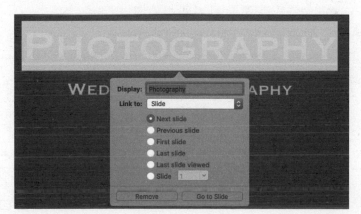

FIGURE 4-22: Link to another slide, website, or email address.

5. Choose one of the following options from the Link to: pop-up menu:

- *Slide:* Use the check boxes to choose another slide within the presentation, or fill in the slide number.

- *Webpage:* Type in the URL of the web page you want to link to.

- *Email:* If the hyperlink is for an outgoing email message, type in the address to whom the message should be sent, along with a subject line.

- *Exit Slideshow:* Clicking the hyperlink will close the presentation.

To delete the hyperlink, click the hyperlink button on the object (a right-pointing arrow), and then click Remove.

Using Masters to Customize Themes

Instead of tweaking a slide layout and then duplicating the slide or duplicating a whole presentation and then redoing the text and images, you can make changes to the slide master or create a new Keynote theme. *Masters* are the templates used to create new slides based on the layout of the master slide. When you change a master, you can then update all slides that use that master within the presentation. Changes you make to slide masters within a presentation only affect that specific presentation. See the tip after these steps about how to create a new theme. To edit masters, follow these steps:

1. **In any view, choose View⇨ Edit Master Slide.**

   The first master slide appears. In the same view, you see the master slide and the format tools. We find Navigator view easiest for editing masters because you can see all the slide layouts in the left panel.

2. **Click the master slide you want to edit.**

3. **Click the part you want to change (text or image), and then make the changes you want in the Format pane.**

   For example, you can simply choose a different predefined style for that placeholder by clicking the menus in the Format pane, or you can change the font itself, the color, size, and alignment.

   For text, you can also add new styles to the list or rename or delete existing styles, and then use those new or renamed styles on subsequent slide masters. Click text on any slide, and then click the Text tab in the Format pane. Click the text name to open the paragraph styles menu and then click the plus sign at the top to add a new style or click a style to delete or rename it, as shown in Figure 4-23.

   For text boxes or image placeholders, you can change the borders and shadows. Click and drag to change the position of placeholders.

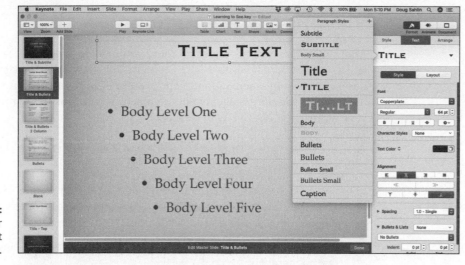

FIGURE 4-23:
Create your
own slide layout
masters.

4. Repeat Steps 2 and 3 for other slides.

5. Rename the slide by clicking to select the name in the master slide navigator and type a new name.

6. Create a new master slide by right-clicking a slide and then choosing New Master Slide from the context menu.

For example, if you frequently use a specific type of chart, you could add a master slide to the theme you use most often and insert a chart on that master slide.

The new master slide appears below the slide from which it was created, the default name appended by copy. Edit the slide as shown in the previous steps; if you want, rename it.

7. Click Done when you finish.

TIP

To make your own personalized theme, create a new presentation from a plain theme or one that's similar to the end result you want. Edit the master slides, and then save it as a new theme by choosing File⇨Save Theme. If you're creating a theme you'll use often, consider putting your company name or logo in the theme so it's one less task you have to do when creating presentations.

Polishing Your Presentation

When you finish modifying the slides in your presentation, you need to show your presentation to others. You may give a presentation in person or post it on You-Tube or your website so people can view it at their leisure.

Presenting with
Keynote

Viewing a presentation

After you finish creating a presentation, you need to view it to see how it actually looks and if needed, edit it to fine-tune it. The slide order or visual effects may have looked good when you put your presentation together, but when viewed in its entirety, you may suddenly notice gaps or repetitions in your presentation. To view a presentation, follow these steps:

1. **In the Navigator, Outline, or Light Table view, click the first slide you want to view.**

   If you click the first slide of your presentation, you'll view your entire presentation. If you click a slide in the middle of your presentation, your slideshow begins from that slide and proceeds until it reaches the last slide.

2. **Click the Play icon on the Keynote toolbar or choose Play⇨Play Slideshow on the menu bar.**

   The slide you chose in Step 1 appears.

3. **Click the mouse button or trackpad, press the spacebar, or use the right arrow key to view each successive slide — the left arrow key takes you back a slide.**

   If you're at the last slide of your presentation, click the mouse button or trackpad, or press the spacebar, to exit your presentation.

4. **(Optional) Press Esc if you want to stop viewing your presentation before reaching the last slide.**

TIP

If you don't want to click through the presentation, click the Setup icon in the toolbar and choose Self-Playing in the Presentation Type pop-up menu.

Rehearsing a presentation

Viewing a presentation lets you make sure that all the slides are in the right order and that all effects and transitions work as you expect. Before giving your presentation, you may want to rehearse it and let Keynote approximate how much time you spend on each slide.

REMEMBER

Rehearsing can give you only a general estimate of the time needed to give your presentation. In real life, various conditions — for example, an impatient audience sitting in a stuffy conference room where the air conditioning suddenly breaks down — may make you nervous or speed up your timing.

To rehearse a presentation, follow these steps:

1. **In the Navigator, Outline, or Light Table view, click the first slide you want to view.**

2. **Choose Play⇨Rehearse Slideshow on the menu bar.**

   Keynote displays your slides. Click the tool button in the upper right and you see the tools windows, as shown in Figure 4-24. We activated all the viewing options except the clock, so you see how much time has elapsed, the current and upcoming slide, the slide navigator, and presenter notes.

   To add presenter notes, click in the Presenter Notes text box shown in Figure 4-24, and enter some notes to prompt you what to say to your audience. Presenter Notes are a huge benefit the first time you present your handiwork to a live audience, especially if you're not a seasoned public speaker.

3. **Practice what you're going to say when presenting each slide and press the spacebar or click the mouse button to advance to the next slide.**

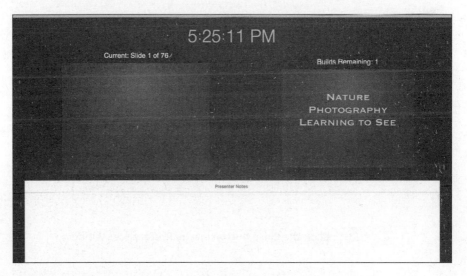

FIGURE 4-24: Keynote tracks how much time you spend on each slide.

Preparing for your big event

When the day arrives that you have to give your presentation, Keynote has some tools to help you there, too. As long as your presentation will be presented with a second projection system — that is, not viewed directly on your Mac while you're giving it — you can display your notes and stopwatch next to your slides on your Mac while the audience sees only your slides.

To set up the Presenter Display, follow these steps:

1. **Choose Keynote⇨Preferences.**

2. **Click the Slideshow tab.**

3. **Click Enable Presenter Display.**

   When your computer is connected to a projection system, you see the presenter display, which looks like Figure 4-24.

4. **Select the items you see onscreen, such as the pointer, in the Interacting section as shown in Figure 4-25.**

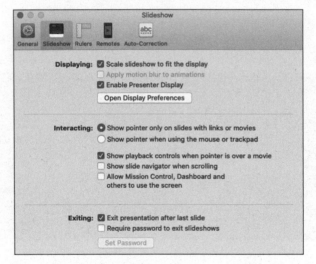

FIGURE 4-25:
Choose how you want to interact with your presentation.

5. **Click the Close button on the Preferences window.**

Controlling your presentation remotely

If you're a social kind of gal who likes to mingle with her audience while giving a presentation, you'll be happy to know that you can use your iOS device to play your presentation while interacting with your audience. To play your presentation remotely:

1. **Download the iOS version of Keynote from the App Store.**

2. **On your Mac, choose Keynote⇨Preferences, and click the Remotes tab.**

3. **Click Enable.**

   Do not close Preferences.

4. Launch Keynote on your iOS device, and then tap the Remote icon in the upper-right corner of the interface.

A window appears telling you your device can be used to remotely control Keynote presentations.

5. Click Continue.

An expanding blue dot appears.

6. Click the blue dot.

7. On your Mac the Remotes dialog refreshes showing you the remote device, as shown in Figure 4-26.

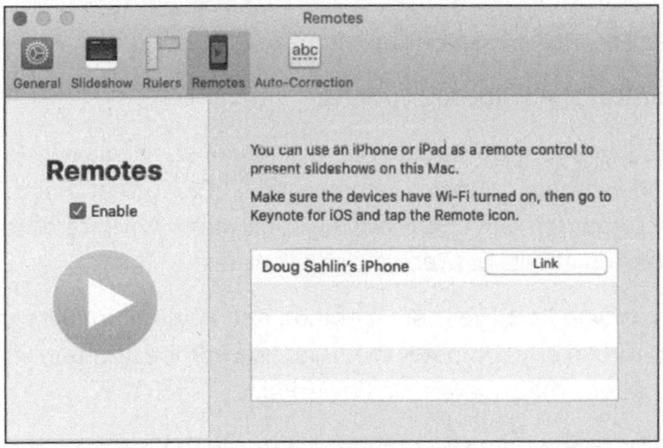

FIGURE 4-26:
Linking an iOS device to use as a remote control.

8. Click Link.

A four-digit verify code appears on your Mac and iOS device.

9. Click Confirm.

Your iOS device is linked to your Mac and can be used to play your presentations remotely.

10. Click the Close button to exit Keynote Preferences.

To play a presentation remotely, your Mac and iOS device must be connected wirelessly to a Wi-Fi network. After you launch Keynote and open your presentation, launch Keynote on your iOS device and a huge green Play button appears in the middle of your screen. Click the button, and as long as you don't wander too far from your Mac, you can shows your slides and interact with your audience.

TIP

If you use an Android or Windows handheld device, you'll find remote control apps in their stores too.

Letting others run your presentation

When you give a presentation, you'll probably do it directly from your Mac. However, there may come a time when you need to save your presentation to run on a different type of computer or you want to give others the opportunity to see your presentation on your website, on YouTube, or on one of the presentation sharing websites like SlideShare (www.slideshare.net). Fortunately, Keynote lets you *export* a Keynote presentation in six different formats and share your presentation in several ways, such as by email or on social media sites.

Exporting your Keynote presentation

To export a Keynote presentation, follow these steps:

1. **Choose File⇨Export To on the menu bar.**

2. **Click one of the following options:**

- *PDF:* Saves your presentation as a series of static images stored in the Adobe Acrobat Portable Document File (PDF) format that can be viewed by any computer with a PDF viewing application. Any interesting visual or transition effects between slides will be lost.

- *PowerPoint:* Saves your presentation as a PowerPoint file that you can edit and run on any computer that runs PowerPoint. (Certain visual effects and transitions may not work in PowerPoint.)

- *Movie:* Saves your presentation as a movie that can play on a Windows PC or Mac computer that has the free QuickTime player. This movie preserves all transitions and visual effects.

- *HTML:* Saves each slide as a separate web page. Any interesting visual or transition effects between slides will be lost.

- *Images:* Saves each slide as a separate graphic file.

- *Keynote '09:* Saves your presentation as a file that's compatible with the previous version of Keynote.

TIP

If you want to preserve your visual effects and transitions, save your presentation as a movie, which also allows you to play your presentation on a TV connected to an iOS device. If you want to preserve and edit your presentation on a Mac or Windows PC running Microsoft PowerPoint, save your presentation as a PowerPoint file.

3. **(Optional) The Export Your Presentation dialog opens, as shown in Figure 4-27.**

Depending on the option you choose in Step 2, you may see additional ways to customize your presentation.

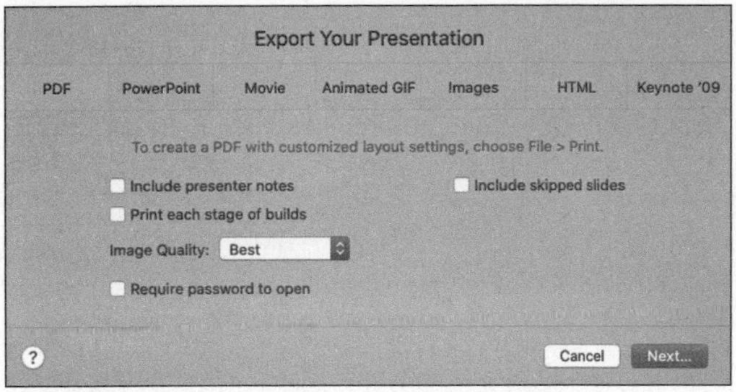

Export Your Presentation

| PDF | PowerPoint | Movie | Animated GIF | Images | HTML | Keynote '09 |

To create a PDF with customized layout settings, choose File > Print.

- [ ] Include presenter notes   - [ ] Include skipped slides
- [ ] Print each stage of builds

Image Quality: [Best ▾]

- [ ] Require password to open

[?]   [Cancel] [Next...]

FIGURE 4-27:
Choose a format
in which to save
your Keynote
presentation.

4. **Click Next.**

Another dialog appears, showing all the drives and folders on your hard drive.

5. **Click the folder where you want to store your presentation.**

You may need to switch drives or folders until you find where you want to save your file.

6. **Click the Export button.**

REMEMBER

When you export a presentation, your original Keynote presentation remains untouched in its original location.

Sharing your Keynote presentation

You have two ways to share your presentation: Save the presentation to your iCloud.com and then share the link, or share the actual presentation. When you share the link, anyone who opens it can make changes to it, and those changes will sync to your Mac and iOS devices that access the presentation.

Here's how you can share your presentation via iCloud:

1. **Make sure that you've saved your presentation on iCloud.**

If you aren't sure how to save your presentation on iCloud, see the "Choosing a theme and saving your presentation" section.

Your presentation must be saved on iCloud for this option to work.

REMEMBER

2. **Click Collaborate in the toolbar.**

If your presentation isn't saved on your iCloud Drive, a dialog notifies you and gives you the option to move your presentation to iCloud. Choose this option.

If your presentation is saved to iCloud, choose one of the following options:

- *Mail:* Opens a new message with a link to your presentation. Address the message and click Send.

- *Messages:* Opens a new message with a link to your presentation. Address the message and click Send.

- *Copy Link:* Places the link in the Clipboard so you can paste it somewhere else, such as on your website or in another presentation.

- *AirDrop*: Give you the option to collaborate with other people on your network who have AirDrop enabled.

3. **Click the Share Options disclosure button and choose the following options for:**

- *Who can access:* Choose an option from the pop-up menu. Your choices are: Only people you invite, or Anyone with the link.

- *Permission:* Choose an option from the pop-up menu. Your choices are: Can make changes, or View only.

4. **Click Share.**

Your next step vary depending on which option you choose in Step 2. The options are self-explanatory.

TIP

Click View Share Settings to see the link as well as who else is editing it, click the Stop Sharing button to remove the link from any place that you've shared it, or click the Send Link button to share it via Mail, Message, Twitter, Facebook, or LinkedIn.

REMEMBER

For more tips on using Keynote, go to Book 5, Chapter 6.

IN THIS CHAPTER

» Getting to know the Numbers app

» Creating a spreadsheet

» Using sheets

» Working with tables and charts

» Polishing a spreadsheet

» Printing and sharing your spreadsheet

Chapter **5**

Crunching with Numbers

N umbers is a spreadsheet application designed to help you manipulate and calculate numbers for a wide variety of tasks, such as balancing a budget, calculating a loan, or creating an invoice. The Numbers application also lets you create line, bar, and pie charts that help you analyze your data visually. What's more, Numbers offers organizational and layout capabilities that you won't find in other spreadsheet apps.

In this chapter, we explain the parts of a spreadsheet; then we explain how to create a new spreadsheet, or open an existing spreadsheet created in a different application. We show you how to work with your data on a spreadsheet, including setting up tables, entering data, and using formulas. We give you some tips for personalizing a spreadsheet to make it aesthetically pleasing. At the end of the chapter, we go over printing and sharing your spreadsheet, even if the person you want to share with doesn't use Numbers.

Understanding the Parts of a Numbers Spreadsheet

The Numbers window is divided into two main sections: the sheet and the Format/Filter pane. You place charts, tables, data, functions, and even graphics and media on the sheet. The Format pane is where you apply styles and color to the fonts and data you select in the worksheet, and the Organize pane is where you establish criteria to sort data on tables. Other things you can see on the Numbers window are

>> **Toolbar:** Across the top is the toolbar, which has buttons for frequently performed tasks.

TIP

To customize the Toolbar to suit your working preferences, choose View⇨ Customize Toolbar and then from the window that appears, drag your favorite buttons to the toolbar.

>> **Sheet tabs:** As you add new sheets to the file, tabs appear across the top, which you click to move from one sheet to another.

>> **Rulers:** If you choose View⇨Show Rulers, you see rulers above and to the left of the active sheet, which help you determine the final size of your spreadsheet, especially if you want to print it.

A sheet may have zero or more *tables*, which are distinct gridworks comprising *rows* (identified by incremental numbers down the left margin) and *columns* (in alphabetical order by a letter at the top). The intersection of a row and column is a *cell*, and that's where you type and store numbers, text, and formulas, as shown in Figure 5-1. A cell has the coordinates of the row and column; E4, for example, is the intersection of the fifth column (E) and the fourth row (4).

Besides the mundane-but-fundamental cells that form the backbone of any spreadsheet, you can also place the following eye-catching (and useful) items in your sheets by clicking the buttons on the toolbar, as shown in Figure 5-2:

>> **Table:** A *table* consists of rows and columns that can contain words, numbers, calculated results, or a combination of these types of contents.

>> **Chart:** A *chart* displays data stored in a table. Common types of charts are line, bar, pie, and column. With Numbers, you can build two-axis and mixed charts as well as 2D, 3D, and interactive charts.

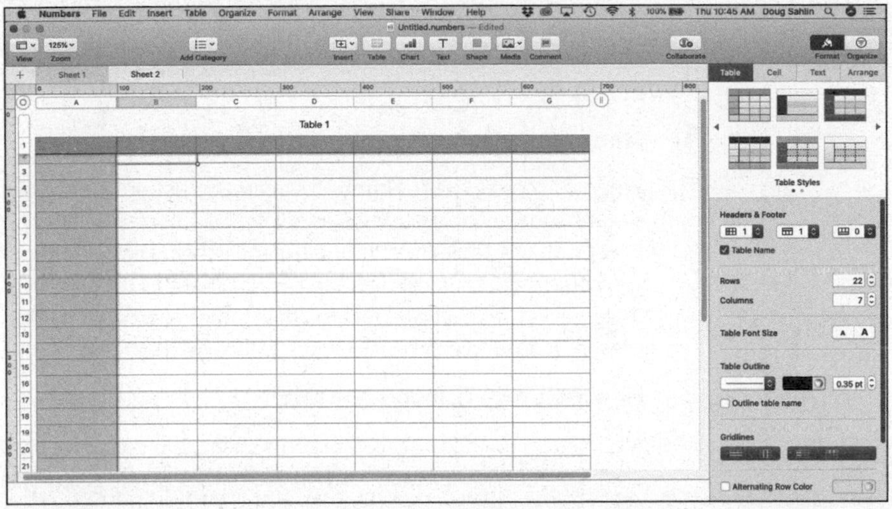

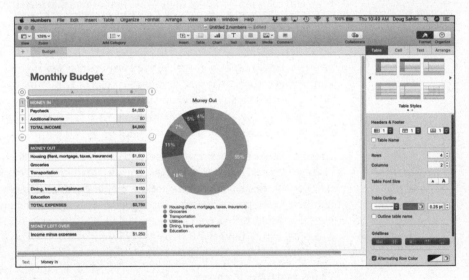

FIGURE 5-1:
The parts of a Numbers window and table.

FIGURE 5-2:
A sheet can have tables, charts, text boxes, and images.

>> **Text:** Text serves both decorative and informative functions. In a text box, you type and store text independent of the rows and columns in a table.

>> **Shape:** Choose from three line styles and a dozen shapes to add pizzazz to your sheet.

>> **Media:** Add photos, music, or movies to your sheet.

>> **Comment:** Comments are particularly useful when you share your sheets because others can give you feedback without changing the sheet itself.

Putting together a spreadsheet is a simple process. The following list points out the basic steps:

1. **Start with a sheet.**

When you create a new Numbers document, either from scratch by choosing a blank sheet or by choosing a template, Numbers automatically creates one sheet with one table on it. Your job is to fill that table with data — although you could delete it if you want to use that sheet as a cover page. Add more tables — yes, a sheet can hold multiple tables — or start spicing up your data presentation with charts or pictures. (More on that later.)

2. **Fill a table with numbers and text.**

After setting up at least one table on a sheet, you can move the table around on the sheet and/or resize it. When you're happy with the table's position on the sheet and the table's size, you can start entering numbers into the table's rows and columns. Add titles to the rows and columns to identify what those numbers mean, such as *August Sales* or *Car Payments*.

3. **Create formulas and use functions.**

After you enter numbers in a table, you'll want to manipulate one or more numbers in certain ways, such as totaling a column of numbers. Numbers offers 250 predefined functions to take your numbers or text and calculate a result, such as how much your company made in sales last month or how a salesperson's sales results have changed.

REMEMBER

Functions are pre-loaded in Numbers and use one or more variables to calculate a result. You write formulas. Both are mathematical expressions that not only calculate useful results, but they also let you enter hypothetical numbers to see possible results. For example, if every salesperson improved her sales results by 5 percent every month, how much profit increase would that bring to the company? By typing in different values, you can ask, "What if?" questions with your data and formulas.

4. **Visualize data with charts.**

Just glancing at a dozen numbers in a row or column might not show you much of anything. By turning numeric data into line, bar, or pie charts, Numbers can help you spot trends in your data.

5. **Polish your sheets.**

Most spreadsheets consist of rows and columns of numbers with a bit of descriptive text thrown in for good measure. Although functional, such spreadsheets are boring to look at. That's why Numbers gives you the chance to place text and images on your sheets to make your information (tables and charts) compelling. You can even add audio effects!

Creating a Numbers Spreadsheet

To help you create a spreadsheet, Numbers provides dozens of templates that you can use as–is or modify. Templates contain preset tables with formulas, which calculate the task at hand. For example, in the Personal Savings template, you enter your goal, the length of time for your investment, and the interest rate, and then the template calculates how much you have to save each month to reach your goal. Changing those values changes the results.

Templates also have predefined font styles and color schemes. You can alter anything you want in a template — tables, charts, colors — but finding a template that is close to what you want to do gives you a head start. That way, you don't have to spend time designing, so you can concentrate on your figures.

TIP

If you prefer, use the Blank template to create a spreadsheet (one sheet with one table) from scratch. If you design a particularly useful spreadsheet, you can save it as a custom template (by choosing File ⇨ Save as Template).

Creating a new spreadsheet with a template

To create a spreadsheet based on a template, follow these steps:

1. **Double-click the Numbers icon the looks like a 3D bar chart in Launchpad or click the Numbers icon on the Dock and choose File ⇨ New.**

   The Choose a Template window appears, as shown in Figure 5-3.

2. **Click a template category in the list on the left (or click All if you want to see all currently available templates).**

   Choose a template that is closest to what you want to do: for example, a schedule or a personal budget.

3. **Double-click the template that you want to use. Alternatively, click the template you like in the main pane and then click the Choose button.**

   Numbers opens your chosen template.

REMEMBER

If you want to start with a blank spreadsheet, click Blank, which is the first template under Basic.

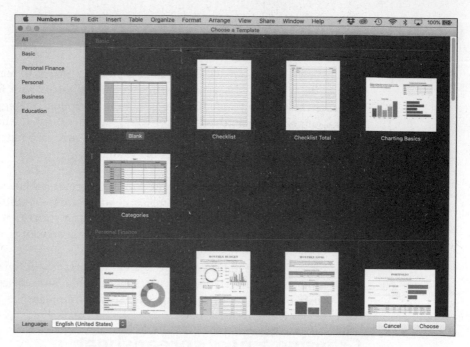

FIGURE 5-3:
Templates are
organized in
categories, such
as Personal or
Business.

4. **Choose File⇨Save.**

The Save As dialog opens.

5. **Type a name for your spreadsheet and choose the folder where you want
to store it on your Mac or save it to your iCloud Drive, or the Numbers
folder on your iCloud Drive.**

Opening an existing file

If you're working on a Numbers document on one source (such as your Mac) and
you want to open a document from another source (such as iCloud or an external
drive), choose File⇨Open, and do one of the following:

>> Click Numbers in the iCloud section of the sidebar, click one of the documents
in the list, and then click Open.

>> Click Open Recent and choose a file from the flyout menu.

You need an Internet connection to work on iCloud Drive documents.

REMEMBER

>> Browse the folders on your Mac or external drive in which the document is
stored, select the desired document, and then click Open.

You might have spreadsheets that were created in a different application (such as Microsoft Excel, Quicken Open Financial Exchange [OFX], or AppleWorks 6), or you may have raw data that you want to bring into Numbers (such as comma-separated value [CSV] or tab-delimited text). You can open the file in Numbers, and Numbers will create sheets and tables with the data supplied. To open a non-Numbers file, drag the file you want to open over the Numbers icon on the Dock or follow the steps outlined earlier for opening a file stored on your computer.

Working with Sheets

Every Numbers spreadsheet needs at least one sheet, although you can have many (refer to Figure 5-1, which has two sheets). A sheet acts like a limitless page that can hold any number of tables, charts, and other objects. You want to use sheets to organize the information in your document, such as using one sheet to hold January sales results, a second sheet to hold February sales results, and a third sheet to hold a line chart that shows each salesperson's results for the first two months.

To help organize your sheets, Numbers stores the names of all your sheets in the tabs at the top of the sheet. Clicking the disclosure triangle on the right end of a sheet tab opens a list of all tables and charts stored on that particular sheet, along with options for copying, deleting, or renaming the sheet, as shown in Figure 5-4.

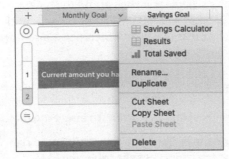

FIGURE 5-4:
View a sheet's elements.

To view the contents of a specific sheet, click that sheet name at the top of the sheet. To view a particular table or chart, find the sheet that contains that table or chart. Then click that specific table or chart.

Adding a sheet

You can always add another sheet. When you add a sheet, Numbers creates one table on that sheet automatically. To add a sheet, choose one of the following:

>> Choose Insert ⇨ Sheet from the menu bar.

>> Click the Add Sheet icon (a + sign) that appears at the far left of the row of sheet tabs.

Deleting a sheet

If you need a sheet to go away, clear out, disappear, whatever, you can delete it.

WARNING

When you delete a sheet, you also delete any tables or charts stored on that sheet.

To delete a sheet, hover the cursor over the right end of the tab for the sheet you want to delete. Click the disclosure triangle when you see it, and then choose Delete from the pop-up menu (refer to Figure 5-4).

Adding or removing a table

As we mention earlier, a sheet can hold one or more tables, and the data you put in a table can be used as data references for charts you add to sheets. When you add a table, it uses the color scheme you choose and the typefaces associated with the template you're using, but it's empty — you have to input the data. Here, we show you how to add and format tables and then delve into how to use them to manipulate and display your data.

To add a table, follow these steps:

1. **Click the tab for the sheet where you want to insert the table.**

2. **Click the Table icon on the toolbar and click the left and right arrows to flip through the color selection. Click the table you like.**

   The table appears on your spreadsheet.

TIP

To remove a table, click the Resize button and then press Delete.

Resizing a table

You have a variety of options for changing the size of your table:

>> **Resize handles:** Click the table and then click the Select Table button in the upper-left corner. Drag the handles around the edges to resize the table. This doesn't add rows and columns, just proportionately changes the table size.

>> **Resize corner:** Click inside the table, and then click and drag the button in the bottom-right corner to add or remove columns and rows, and define the overall size and shape of your table.

>> **Adding row/column button:** Click the Add button (two parallel lines in a circle) at the bottom-left corner to add rows or at the upper-right corner to add columns. Rows and columns are added to the table automatically.

>> **Inserting or delete a row or column:** Hover the cursor by the row or column identifier (letters for columns, numbers for rows) before or after where you want to insert a row or column until you see a disclosure arrow. Click the arrow to open a menu that gives you choices to insert a row or column before or after the one you selected. You can also delete or hide the row or column you selected.

TIP

Delete multiple columns or rows by highlighting those column or row headings, clicking the Table menu, and then choosing Delete Columns or Delete Rows.

If you click the disclosure arrow of column A or B or row 1 or 2, you also have choices to insert header rows or columns or to convert the selected row or column into a header row or column. (See the Inserting headers and resizing rows and columns section for more information.)

>> **Adjusting row height or column width:** Follow the steps for inserting but choose Fit Height/Width to Content to adjust the height or width of the row or column to accommodate the contents of the cells in that row or column. Or, click the column or row and then hover the cursor over one of the edges of the row or column header until the cursor becomes a double-sided arrow. Click and drag the cursor/arrow to adjust the height or width of the row or column.

Changing the appearance of a table

Click the Format button on the toolbar to open the Format pane and see the tools you can use to edit the appearance of your table. Select the cells, rows, or columns you want to edit, and click the tab of the Format pane for the things you want to change:

>> **Table:** Use this tab's menus and buttons to adjust the color, font size, grid lines, and number of header and footer cells. These changes affect the entire table.

>> **Cell:** Make changes to the cells, rows, or columns you select either singly or in multiples. Define how the data is formatted, such as currency or percentage, and assign fill and border colors and styles.

>> **Text:** Define the text color, style, and alignment of text in selected cells, rows, or columns.

>> **Arrange:** Reposition the table in relation to other objects on the sheet or align it on the sheet itself.

Inserting headers and resizing rows and columns

Headers are the first rows and columns of your table, where you usually type the names of the rows and columns. Footers are the final rows of the table, where you can repeat header names in particularly large tables. You can have header rows and columns that span up to five rows or columns, which is a handy way to use titles and subtitles for each row or column. Another way to insert header rows and columns is the following:

1. Click the table, click the Format button on the toolbar, and then click the Table tab of the Format pane.

2. In the Headers & Footer section, use the pop-up menus to choose the number of row and column headers and column footers you want, up to five for each.

3. To make your header rows and columns stay put while you scroll through the rest of your table, click Freeze Header Row/Column in the pop-up menu.

To insert header rows or columns after you already have data in your table, follow these steps:

1. Click a cell in one of the header rows or columns, either before or after where you want to insert another header row or column.

2. Click the Table menu and choose from the following:

- *Add Header Row Above:* Inserts an additional header row directly above the selected cell

- *Add Header Row Below:* Inserts an additional header row directly below the selected cell

- *Add Header Column Before:* Inserts an additional header column to the left of the selected cell

- *Add Header Column After:* Inserts a new column to the right of the selected cell

3. **(Optional) Click a cell and in the Row and Column Size section in the Table section of the Format pane, use the arrows in the Width and Height fields to specify the width and height of the cell, or click the Fit button to size the cell to its contents. Alternatively, you can enter values in each text field.**

To emphasize the header rows and columns and footers and make them stand out from the contents of the table, you can outline single cells — or the entire row or column — with a border and/or fill the cells with a background color. Select the cells you want to emphasize and then do the following:

1. **Click the Cell tab in the Format pane (click the Format icon on the toolbar if you don't see the Format pane).**

2. **Click the disclosure triangle next to Fill to add a background color to the headers or footers.**

   a. *If the cell is not filled, choose an option from the Color Fill pop-up such as Gradient. Choose an option from the Fill pop-up menu. If the cell is filled with a color or gradient, go to Step b.*

   b. *Click the color swatch to choose a standard color or click the button next to the swatch to open the color pickers and choose a color from the Color Wheel. If the cell is filled with a gradient, you have two color swatches, one for the first color of the gradient, and one for the second.*

3. **Click the disclosure triangle next to Border Style to see the border options.**

   a. *Click the Border button, and choose a border style.*

      If you select one cell in the table and then choose the four-sided border, the four sides of that one cell will have the border.

      If you select several cells, and then choose the four-sided border, the border surrounds the group but the lines between the cells remain unchanged.

      If you want to add a border around all the selected cells, choose the border style that has both the outline and the inner lines emphasized.

b. Click the Border Styles button and choose an option from the pop-up menu. The options in this menu determine the width and color of the border based on the table style you choose for the table.

c. Click the pop-up menu beneath the Border Styles section to change the border style from line to dash or dot.

d. Use the up and down arrows beneath that pop-up menu to change the thickness of the border.

e. Click the color swatch to choose a standard color or click the button next to the swatch to open the color pickers and choose a color from the Color Wheel.

Typing Data into Tables

Now we get into the numbers part of Numbers. You need to know about the three types of data you can store inside a table: numbers, text, and formulas. You can also store images in a cell, which doesn't work as data per se but is useful to create documents such as an inventory or real estate listing.

We give you details about working with each type of data in the next three sections. However, in summary, to type anything into a table, follow these steps:

1. **Select a cell by clicking it or by pressing the arrow keys.**

2. **Type a number, text, or formula.**

   If you want to use a predefined function or create a formula of your own, type an equal sign (=) in the cell. The Function panel opens on the right side of the window.

3. **Press Return to select the cell below, press Tab to select the cell to the right, or click any cell into which you want to type new data.**

4. **Repeat Steps 2 and 3 for each additional formula or item of data you want to type into the table.**

To enter text on a new line in a cell, press Shift+Option+Return, and type the text you want on a new line. As you enter new lines, the height of the cell increases to accommodate the new text.

Triple-click a cell to edit its contents.

Formatting numbers and text

When you type a number in a cell, the number will look plain — 45 or 60.3. To make your numbers more meaningful, you should format them. For example, the number 39 might mean nothing, but if you format it to appear as $39.00, your number now clearly represents a dollar amount.

To format numbers, follow these steps:

1. **Click to select one cell or click and drag to select multiple cells.**

Numbers draws a border around your selected cell(s).

If you select empty cells, Numbers remembers the assigned format and automatically formats any numbers you type into those cells in the future.

REMEMBER

2. **Click the Format button on the toolbar, and then click the Cell tab of the Format pane.**

3. **Choose how you want the data to appear in the Data Format pop-up menu, as shown in Figure 5-5.**

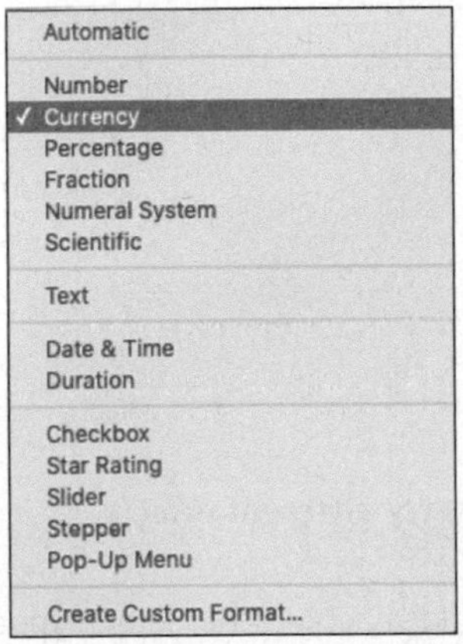

FIGURE 5-5:
Data looks, and works, differently depending on how it's formatted.

Automatic

Number
✓ Currency
Percentage
Fraction
Numeral System
Scientific

Text

Date & Time
Duration

Checkbox
Star Rating
Slider
Stepper
Pop-Up Menu

Create Custom Format...

Each choice has options that appear in the Format pane:

- The numeric choices have submenus with further choices, such as how many decimals or the currency symbol.

- When cells are formatted as Text, numbers have no numeric values. This is useful for typing in zip codes and phone numbers.

- The Date & Time and Duration choices offer formatting options such as spelling out the month or using a number. Here, too, numbers are considered text.

- The last set of choices are neither numeric nor text but instead let you create data entry cells that require an action, such as clicking to place a check mark in the box or limit your choices, such as a pop-up menu. (See "Formatting data entry cells," later in this chapter.)

To add color to your cells and/or definition to them, click the disclosure triangles next to the Fill and Border options. Choose the options you want from the pop-up menus, as shown in Figure 5-6.

FIGURE 5-6:
Add background colors and borders to cells.

The cells automatically change as you try different effects.

» *Fill* puts a color, a gradient, or an image behind characters typed in the cell. Depending on the choice, you're presented with tools for choosing the color, the spectrum and direction (gradient), and scaling (image).

» *Border* surrounds your cell(s) with a line; define the width and color, and choose whether you want a border around each cell or around the group of cells or only on one side or in between.

» Click the *Colors icon* in either section to change the color of the fill or border. The color block opens a Chooser that displays colors used in the theme; the Color Wheel opens the Colors window.

- Click the color picker you prefer: Wheel (which is the default), Slider, Palette, Spectrum, or Crayons.

- Click the desired color in the color picker that appears in the Colors window.

- (Optional) In the Color Wheel, make the color lighter or darker by dragging the slider on the bottom left or right. For example, if the cell background is black, drag the slider left to fill the background with a gray color.

- (Optional) In any of the color pickers, adjust the opacity by dragging the opacity slider left and right or type in a precise percentage in the text box to the right.

- When you have a color you like, drag the color from the color box at the top to the color palette at the bottom. Your color is saved in the palette for future use.

- Click the red Close window button or choose View ⇨ Hide Colors.

To format the style of the characters in the selected cell(s) — whether they're formatted as numbers, text, or data entry — click the Text tab in the Format pane and then the Style button.

>> *To use a different font in the theme:* Click the Paragraph Styles menu and choose a different font.

>> *To change the font style:* In the Font section, scroll through the Family menus to select the options you want.

- Click the disclosure triangle to the right of the Font menu to reveal a pop-up menu of all fonts installed on your system. The name of each font is displayed using the font face, which gives you a visual representation of how it will look in your spreadsheet.

- Click the font you like to format the cell, and then click the Typeface, Size, and Style menus and buttons to fine-tune the look of the cell.

- Change the font color by clicking the Color Wheel and following the steps mentioned previously.

>> *To choose how you want your text to appear in the cell:* Choose an option from the Alignment buttons. The button with the A automatically aligns numbers to the right and text to the left.

>> *Accept the default Wrap Text in Cell option.* With this option, when the text you enter exceeds the width of the cell, it wraps to a new line and the height of the cell changes to accommodate the text.

Entering formulas

The main purpose of a table is to use the data (numbers, textual data, dates, and times) you store in cells to calculate a new result, such as adding a row or column of numbers. To calculate and display a result, you need to store a formula in the cell where you want the result to appear.

Numbers provides three ways to create formulas in a cell:

>> Quick Formula

>> Typed formulas

>> Advanced functions

Using Quick Formula

To help you calculate numbers in a hurry, Numbers Quick Formula feature offers a variety of formulas that can calculate common results, such as

>> **Sum:** Adds numbers

>> **Average:** Calculates the arithmetic mean

>> **Minimum:** Displays the smallest number

>> **Maximum:** Displays the largest number

>> **Count:** Displays how many cells you select

>> **Product:** Multiplies numbers

To use a Quick Formula, follow these steps:

1. **Click the empty cell at the bottom or to the right of cells that contain the numbers you want to operate the function on.**

2. **Choose Insert⇨Formula on the menu bar.**

3. **From the flyout menu choose Sum, Average, Minimum, Maximum, Count, or Product.**

   Numbers displays your calculated results.

Typing a formula

Quick Formula is handy when it offers the formula you need, such as when you add up rows or columns of numbers with the Sum formula. Often, however, you need to create your own formula.

Every formula consists of two parts:

>> **Operators:** Perform calculations, such as addition (+), subtraction (–), multiplication (*), and division (/).

>> **Cell references:** Define where to find the data to use for calculations.

A typical formula looks like this:

```
= A3 + A4
```

This formula tells Numbers to take the number stored in column A, row 3 and add it to the number stored in column A, row 4.

To type a formula, follow these steps:

1. **Click (or use the arrow keys to highlight) the cell where you want the formula results to appear.**

2. **Type =.**

The Formula Editor appears.

3. **Click a cell that contains the data you want to include in your calculation.**

4. **Type an operator, such as * for multiplication or / for division.**

5. **Click another cell that contains the data you want to include in your calculation.**

TIP

To apply a formula to a range of cells in a column, perform Steps 1 and 2; click inside the first cell you want to include in the calculation, and then drag to the last cell you want to include in the calculation; then click the Accept button (the green check mark) to complete the formula.

6. **Repeat Steps 4 and 5 as needed.**

7. **Click the Accept button (green check mark) or the Cancel button (red X) in the Formula Editor when you're done.**

Numbers displays the results of your formula. If you change the numbers in the cells you define in Steps 3 and 5, Numbers calculates a new result instantly.

TIP

For a fast way to calculate values without having to type a formula in a cell, use Instant Calculations. Just select two or more cells that contain numbers, and you can see the results in the Instant Calculations results tabs along the bottom of the Numbers window, as shown in Figure 5-7. You can change the types of results you see in the Instant Calculations Results tabs by clicking the Action button (it looks like a gear) and selecting the functions you want to see from the pop-up menu.

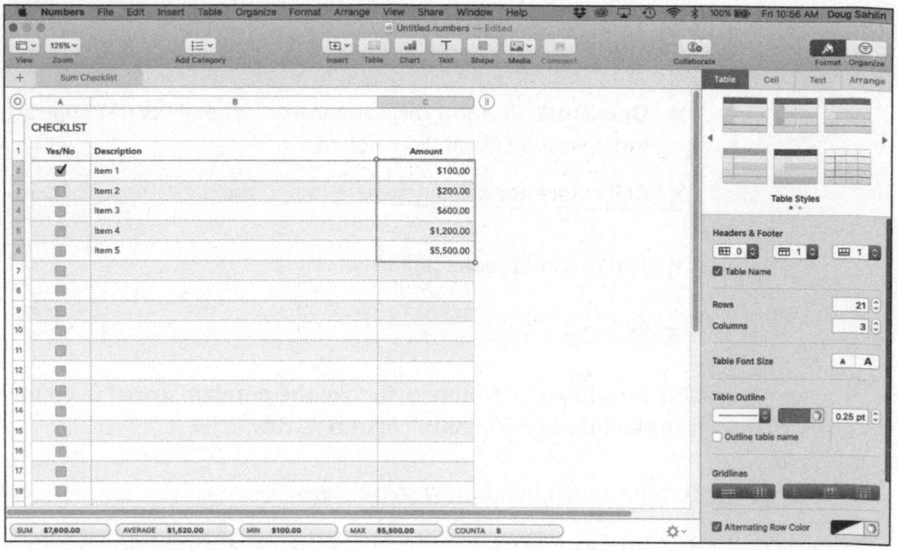

FIGURE 5-7:
Instant calculations can show results without typing a formula first.

Using functions

Typing simple formulas that add or multiply is easy. However, many calculations can get more complicated, such as trying to calculate the amount of interest paid on a loan with a specific interest rate over a defined period.

To help you calculate commonly used formulas, Numbers provides a library of 250 *functions*, which are prebuilt formulas that you can plug into your table and define what data to use without having to create the formula yourself.

To use a function, follow these steps:

1. **Click (or use the arrow keys to highlight) the cell where you want the function results to appear.**

REMEMBER

Some functions operate on data typed into the cell where the function is inserted. For example, if you insert the sine function, the sine of numbers you type into that cell will be calculated. Other functions use data in several cells to calculate a result, such as depreciation, which uses original cost, time in service, and some other business-y information. That type of information must be typed into the cells that the function refers to in order for it to work.

2. **Press the equal (=) key.**

The Formula Editor appears, and the Functions pane opens, as shown in Figure 5-8.

TIP

You can move the Formula Editor if you move the pointer to the left end of the Formula Editor. When the pointer turns into a hand, click and drag the Formula Editor to a new location so it doesn't hide the cells you're working on.

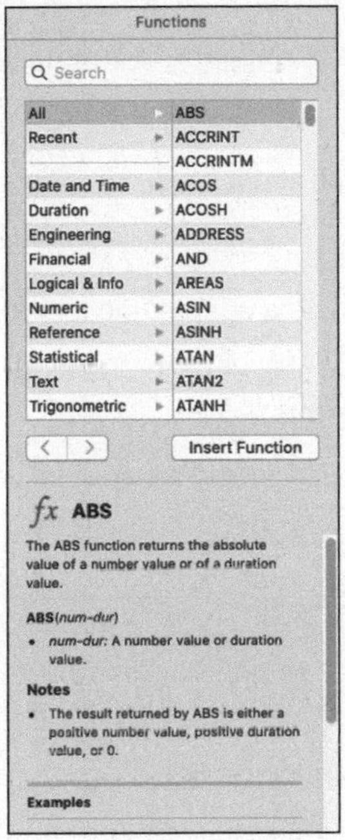

FIGURE 5-8:
The Functions pane displays all available functions in Numbers.

3. **Choose the type of function you want from the left column (or click All), and then scroll through the functions on the right and click the one you want to insert.**

   A definition for the selected function is shown at the bottom of the pane, along with an explanation of the types of data needed to complete the operation and an example of how it works.

4. **Click the Insert Function button.**

   The Formula Editor now contains your chosen function.

5. **Edit the formula by typing the cell names (such as C4) or clicking the cells that contain the data the function needs to calculate.**

6. **Click the Accept (green check mark) or Cancel (red X) button on the Formula Editor.**

   Numbers shows your result.

Formatting data entry cells

After you create formulas or functions in cells, you can type new data in the cells defined by a formula or function and watch Numbers calculate a new result instantly. Typing a new number in a cell is easy to do, but sometimes a formula or function requires a specific range of values. For example, if you have a formula that calculates sales tax, you may not want someone to enter a sales tax more than 10 percent or less than 5 percent.

To limit the types of values someone can enter in a cell, you can use one of the following methods, as shown in Figure 5-9:

» **Sliders:** Users can drag a slider to choose a value within a fixed range.

» **Steppers:** Users can click up and down arrows to choose a value that increases or decreases in fixed increments.

» **Pop-up menus:** Users can choose from a limited range of choices.

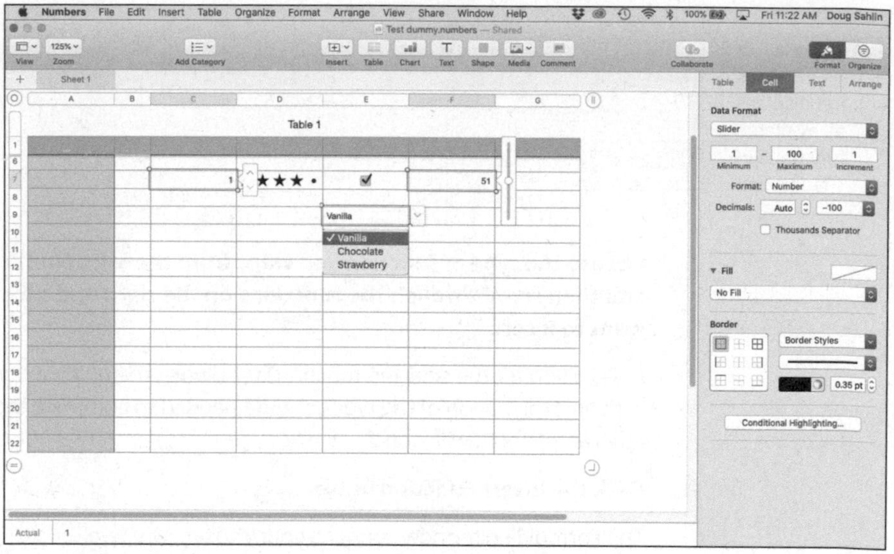

FIGURE 5-9:
Sliders, steppers, and pop-up menus restrict the types of values a cell can hold.

You can also format the cell with a check box or star rating, as shown in Figure 5-9.

Formatting a cell with a slider or a stepper

Using a slider or stepper is useful when you want to restrict a cell to a range of values, such as 1–45. The main difference is that a slider appears *next to* a cell, whereas a stepper appears *inside* a cell.

To format a cell with a slider or stepper, follow these steps:

1. **Click a cell that you want to restrict to a range of values.**

2. **Click the Format button on the toolbar, and then click the Cell tab of the Format pane.**

3. Choose Slider or Stepper from the Data Format pop-up menu.

4. Enter the minimum acceptable value.

5. Enter the maximum acceptable value.

6. Enter a value in the Increment text box to increase or decrease by when the user drags the slider or clicks the up- and down-arrows of the stepper.

7. Use the Format and Decimals menus to edit the displayed number.

Numbers displays a slider next to the cell. Users have a choice of typing a value or using the slider to define a value. If you choose a value outside the minimum and maximum range defined in Steps 3 and 4, the cell won't accept the invalid data.

Formatting a cell with a pop-up menu

A pop-up menu restricts a cell to a limited number of choices. To format a cell with a pop-up menu, follow these steps:

1. Repeat Steps 1 and 2 for inserting a slider or stepper (see the preceding section).

2. Click the list box under the Data Format pop-up menu and choose Pop-Up Menu.

3. Click the plus (+) sign button to add an item to the pop-up menu associated with the cell, and then type in the number or text you want added.

Repeat to add other items.

4. To remove an item from the list, click the item and then click the minus (–) sign button.

Repeat to delete other items.

5. Choose Start with First Item or Start with Blank from the pop-up menu next to the add/delete items buttons.

This determines what will be shown in the cell.

Numbers displays a pop-up menu that lists choices when users click that cell.

You can also set a *conditional highlight* so that if your data meets a certain criterion or condition, Numbers will highlight the number or text in a color you want. Say you create a spreadsheet to track office supply inventory, and you want to know when you have fewer than five black pens. Set the conditional formatting of the cell to "less than or equal to 5." Then, when there are five pens or fewer, the cell changes color. Now, at a glance, you see pertinent information. To use conditional formatting, follow these steps:

1. **Select the cell(s) where you want to use conditional formatting.**

2. **Click the Format button on the toolbar, and then click the Cell tab of the Format pane.**

3. **Click the Conditional Highlighting button at the bottom of the pane.**

   You may have to scroll to find it.

4. **Click the Add a Rule button.**

   The Conditional Formatting window opens.

5. **Peruse the tabs and select the rule you want to use, as shown in Figure 5-10.**

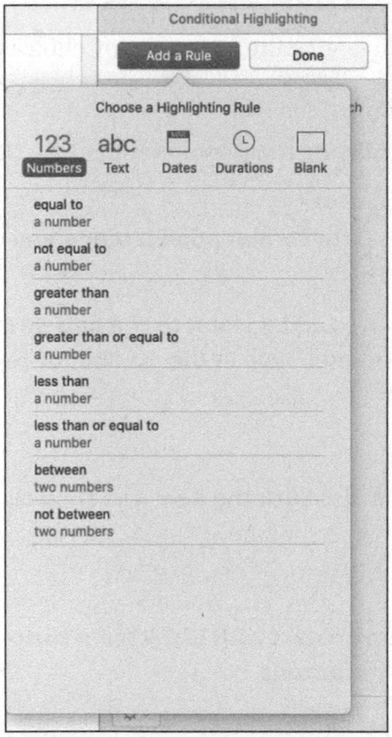

FIGURE 5-10:
Numbers formats cells that meet Conditional Formatting criteria.

A field appears where you can type in a value.

- *If you want to refer to another cell:* Click the blue circle on the right end of the field and type in a cell reference. Or, click the cell in your sheet, and its reference appears in the field.

- *To change the value:* Click in the field and press the Delete key, and then type another value or enter a different cell reference.

6. Click the pop-up menu to format how you want the data highlighted.

The sample box shows how the cell will appear if the data in it meet the conditional rule you set.

7. (Optional) To add another rule, repeat Steps 4–6.

8. (Optional) To delete a rule, click the Trash icon to the right of the rule name.

9. (Optional) To rearrange the order of the rules, hover the cursor to the left of the rule name and click and drag the Rearrange button (it looks like three horizontal lines).

10. Click Done.

Sorting data

When you enter your data, you don't always do so in the order you want to see it. For example, to track invoices, you create a column for each piece of data, such as invoice number, date of purchase, customer name, and total, and then you enter the data from a stack of invoices so each row holds the data for one invoice. You may enter the data by invoice number first but then want to sort by customer name to see which customers have more than one outstanding invoice or by total to see who spent the most. You can sort the data by one of those columns. Here's how you do it:

1. Click the table you want to sort or select a group of cells you want to sort.

2. Hover the cursor over the column indicator (the letters) that you want to use to define the sort.

3. Click the disclosure triangle that appears to open the pop-up menu.

4. Select Sort Ascending or Sort Descending to establish the order in which you want the data.

Numbers will sort your data by the column you chose.

TIP

By default, Numbers sorts the entire table when you sort a column. To choose different sort options, click the Organize button on the toolbar to display the Organize pane. From here, you can choose to sort only selected rows, add a column, sort by categories, and so on. The available options differ depending on the content of your table.

Deleting data in cells

If you ever want to delete data in a cell, Numbers provides two ways:

>> Delete data but retain any formatting.

>> Delete data and formatting.

To delete data but retain any formatting, follow these steps:

1. **Select one or more cells that contain data you want to delete.**

2. **Press Delete or choose Edit ⇨ Delete from the menu bar.**

To delete both data and formatting in cells, follow these steps:

1. **Select one or more cells that contain data and formatting you want to delete.**

2. **Choose Edit ⇨ Clear All from the menu bar.**

Adding a chart

Charts are a graphical representation of data. Before you add a chart to your sheet, create a table and enter the data you want the chart to represent. Then, do the following:

1. **On the table where you input the data for your chart, click and drag to select the data, including row and column headers.**

2. **Click the Chart icon on the toolbar and then click the left and right arrows to flip through the color selection. First, click a tab for the type of chart you want — 2D, 3D, or Interactive — and, then choose the chart you want.**

    The chart with your data appears on your sheet.

If the data is on one sheet but you want to place the table on another sheet, do the following (you can also use these steps to create charts on the same sheet, if you want):

1. **Click that sheet where you want to place the chart.**

2. **Click the Chart icon on the toolbar and then click the left and right arrows to flip through the color selection. First, click a tab for the type of chart you want — 2D, 3D, or Interactive — and, then choose the chart you want.**

3. Click **Edit Data References** at the bottom of the chart.

4. Click the sheet that holds the data.

5. Click and drag to select the cells, including headers, that contain the data you want in the chart.

6. Click the **Done** button.

The data selected from the table flows into the chart on the other sheet.

TIP

Interactive charts are created the same way as 2D or 3D charts. Here's the difference. Rather than see, for example, eight columns that represent two types of data for four months, you see two columns at a time, and clicking the playback arrows animates the data.

7. Click **Format** on the toolbar and then go through the tabs of the Format pane to edit the appearance and position of the chart and data:

- *Chart* gives you tools for changing the colors and fonts of the chart, as well as adding special effects such as shadow or opacity and a title and/or legend. At the bottom of the panel is the Chart Type menu. Click to change to a different type of chart, and any data you entered will appear on the new type.

- *Axis* (all but pie charts) lets you name the axes and change the scale. Here you also find the menus for defining the value labels with percentage, currency, or others.

- *Series* (all but pie charts) offers menus for naming the value labels.

- *Wedges* (only pie charts) shows check boxes and menus for adding labels and defining the value data format. You can move the labels off the chart itself and separate the pieces of the pie by setting a greater distance from center with the respective slider bars.

- *Arrange* lets you reposition the chart in relation to other objects on the slide or align it on the sheet itself. This doesn't change parts of the chart.

- *Axis/Wedge Labels* lets you can define the label (number, percentage, and so on) and also change the font family, size, style, and color. Double-click any of the text on the chart, and the Axis or Wedge Labels tab appears in the Format pane.

8. (Optional) To remove a chart, click it and then press Delete.

REMEMBER

You can also use the Numbers menu to add objects to your spreadsheets; choose Insert➪Chart/Shape/Line and then choose the specific type from the submenu that opens.

Naming sheets, tables, and charts

Numbers gives each sheet, table, and chart a generic name, such as Sheet 2, Table 1, or Chart 3. To help you better understand the type of information stored on each sheet, table, and chart, use more descriptive names, especially when you add multiple tables and charts. The sheet name appears on the sheet tab, and table and chart names appear when you click the disclosure triangle on the sheet tab.

To name a sheet, double-click the name on the sheet tab to select it and type a new name, or click the disclosure triangle and choose Rename from the sheet tab pop-up menu and then rename it.

Although you don't have to have a name for your charts and tables, it does help if you have more than one chart or table on a sheet. To name a table or chart, double-click the placeholder text to type a name for the table or chart. If you don't see the placeholder text, click the table or chart, and then click the Format button on the toolbar. Click the Table or Chart tab in the Format pane, and then select the check box next to Table Name or Title (for charts). Click the Table tab and Outline Table Name to put a box around the table name.

TIP

To move a table or chart from one sheet to another, click the table or chart and choose Edit⇨Cut. Click the sheet you want to move the table or chart to, and then choose Edit⇨Paste. Data and calculations remain unchanged. Click and drag the table or chart to the position you want on the sheet.

Making Your Spreadsheets Pretty

Tables and charts are the two most crucial objects you can place and arrange on a sheet. However, Numbers also lets you place text boxes, shapes, and pictures on a sheet. Text boxes can contain titles or short descriptions of the information displayed on the sheet. Shapes can add color or indicate navigational cues, such as arrows. Photos can make your entire sheet look more interesting, or they may be the focus of your sheet if you're creating an inventory.

TIP

Click the Table tab in the Format pane, and choose Alternating Row Color to have that effect in your table. The colors will reflect those of the theme you chose, but you can change them with the color tool, which we explain in detail in the "Formatting numbers and text" section.

Adding a text box

To add a text box to a sheet, follow these steps:

1. **Click the sheet tab to which you want to add the text box.**

   Numbers displays your chosen sheet and any additional objects that may already be on that sheet, such as tables or charts.

2. **Click the Text icon (T) on the toolbar. Alternatively, you can choose Insert ⇨ Text Box.**

   A text box appears on the sheet.

3. **Type any text that you want to appear in the text box. Press Return to type text on a new line.**

   While you type, your text box lengthens to accommodate your text. You can widen the text box by clicking the text box and dragging the handles on its sides.

4. **(Optional) Select any text and choose any formatting options from the Format pane, as we explain earlier for formatting text in tables and cells.**

5. **(Optional) In the Layout section of the Format pane, you can divide text into columns, add an inset, specify indents, add borders, specify text position, and add a background.**

TIP

To create a bulleted or numbered list in a text box, place your cursor where you want the list to begin, and then choose an option from the Bullets & Lists pop-up menu in the Text tab of the Format pane. Start typing. When you press Return to start a new line, Numbers inserts the bullet or number. To finish the list, press Return twice.

Adding media

To add a photo, a movie, or audio file to a sheet, follow these steps:

1. **Click the sheet tab to which you want to add media.**

2. **Click the Media icon on the toolbar, choose an option from the flyout menu, and choose one of the following:**

   - *Photos:* Opens a window showing image files you stored in the Photos app. Click an image to add it to the spreadsheet.

   - *Image Gallery:* Opens a window onto which you drag an image file. Alternatively, you can click the icon in the lower-left corner of the window to open a Finder window you use to navigate through your folders, select an image, and then click Open.

- *Movies:* Opens a window showing movies you stored in the Photos app. Click a Movie to add it to the spreadsheet.

- *Music:* Opens a window that shows audio files stored on your computer. Click a file to add it to your spreadsheet.

Numbers displays your chosen image or movie on the sheet. If you added an audio or movie file, a play icon indicates that. You can move the media around the sheet, resize photos and movies with the resizing handles, and use the editing tools of the Format pane to add borders or fills.

3. **(Optional) To delete inserted media, click it and press Delete.**

TIP

If you want to use an image as a background for a cell or group of cells, select the cell or cells and then use the Fill tool of the Format pane and choose Image Fill. After filling the cells with an image, choose an option from the Scale pop-up menu.

Sharing Your Spreadsheet

You put a lot of effort into making your spreadsheet presentable. When you're ready to actually present it, you can share your spreadsheet with others by printing it or saving it as a file for electronic distribution.

Printing a spreadsheet

In other spreadsheet applications, it's not uncommon to print your spreadsheet and chart only to find that part of your chart or spreadsheet is cut off by the edge of the paper. To avoid this problem, Numbers displays a Content Scale, which lets you magnify or shrink an entire sheet so it fits and prints perfectly on a page.

To shrink or magnify a sheet to print, follow these steps:

1. **Click the sheet tab you want to print.**

2. **Choose File ⇨ Print.**

Numbers displays a page and shows how the charts and tables on your sheet will print (see Figure 5-11).

3. **Drag the Content Scale slider to magnify or shrink your data until it fits exactly the way you want on the page, or select the Fit button if you want Numbers to do the work for you.**

The Content Scale slider is located at the bottom center of the Print Preview pane.

4. **Choose any other print options you want and click the Print button.**

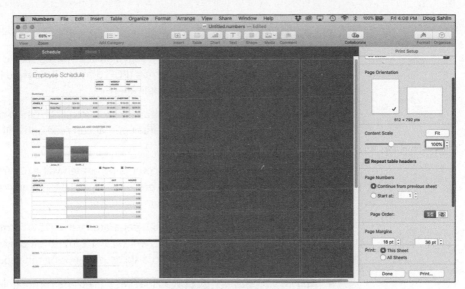

FIGURE 5-11:
Use Print Preview
to see how your
sheet will print.

Exporting a spreadsheet

When you choose File ⇨ Save, Numbers saves your spreadsheet in its own proprietary file format. If you want to share your spreadsheets with others who don't
have Numbers, export your spreadsheet into another file format by following
these steps:

**1. Choose File ⇨ Export to ⇨ PDF/Excel/CSV/TSV/Numbers '09 on the
menu bar.**

The Export Your Spreadsheet dialog appears, as shown in Figure 5-12.

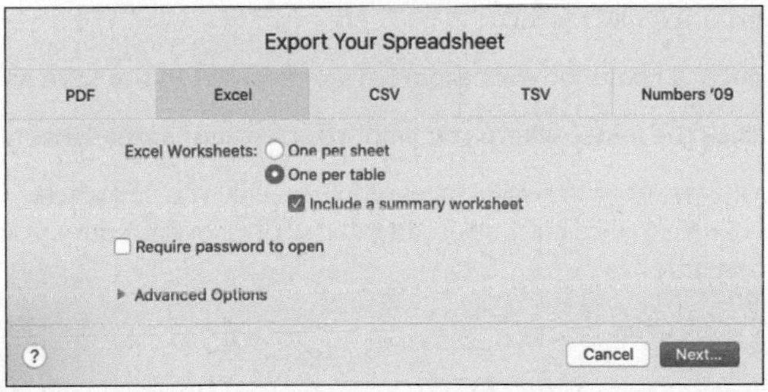

	Export Your Spreadsheet			
PDF	Excel	CSV	TSV	Numbers '09

Excel Worksheets: ○ One per sheet
● One per table
☑ Include a summary worksheet

☐ Require password to open

▸ Advanced Options

Cancel   Next...

FIGURE 5-12:
Choose a format
to save your
spreadsheets.

2. **Choose one of the following formats:**

- *PDF:* Saves your spreadsheet as a series of static pages stored in the Adobe Acrobat Portable Document Format (PDF) that can be viewed by any computer with a PDF viewing application.

- *Excel:* Saves your spreadsheet as a Microsoft Excel file, which can be opened and edited by any spreadsheet that can read and edit Microsoft Excel files.

- *CSV:* Saves your spreadsheet in comma-separated value (CSV) format, which is a universal format that preserves only data, not any charts or pictures you have stored on your spreadsheet.

- *TSV:* Saves your spreadsheet in tab-separated value (TSV) format, which saves data in a tabular structure, which can be interpreted by spreadsheet applications that can reconstruct a spreadsheet using tab separated values.

- *Numbers '09:* Saves your spreadsheet as a file that's compatible with the previous version of Numbers.

REMEMBER

The PDF file format preserves formatting 100 percent, but you need extra software to edit it. Generally, if someone needs to edit your spreadsheet and doesn't use Numbers, choose File ⇨ Export to ⇨ Excel. The CSV option is useful only for transferring your data to another application that can't read Excel files.

The format you choose is highlighted, but you can switch to another one by clicking a different tab.

3. **(Optional) If you want to add a password to open the document, select the Require Password to Open check box (all except CSV).**

4. **Click Next.**

A dialog appears, where you choose a name and location to save your exported spreadsheet.

5. **Enter a name for your exported spreadsheet in the Save As text box.**

6. **Click the folder where you want to store your spreadsheet.**

You may need to switch drives or folders until you find where you want to save your file. You can also select an external drive or flash drive from the Devices section.

7. **Click Export.**

REMEMBER

When you export a spreadsheet, your original Numbers spreadsheet remains untouched in its original location.

Sharing files directly from Numbers

You have two more ways to share your spreadsheet:

>> **Upload the spreadsheet to iCloud.com and then share the link.**

When you share the link, anyone who opens it can make changes to it, and those changes will sync to your Mac and iOS devices that access the spreadsheet.

>> **Share the spreadsheet itself.**

Either way, when you share the link or spreadsheet, all the sheets contained in the spreadsheet are included.

Here's how you can share your presentation:

1. **Choose Share ⇨ Send a Copy, and then choose one of the following options from the flyout menu:**

   - *Mail:* Choose this option to send a copy of your spreadsheet via email.

   - *Messages:* Choose this option to send a copy of your spreadsheet via Messages.

   - *AirDrop:* Choose this option to send a copy of your spreadsheet via AirDrop.

   All these choices open a dialog that lets you send the spreadsheet as a Numbers file or as a PDF, an Excel file, a CSV file, or a TSV file. This dialog is identical to the one shown in Figure 5-12.

2. **Choose the file type and then click Next.**

   The file is converted if you chose an option other than Numbers.

   A new Message opens.

3. **Type in the address(es) to which you want to send the spreadsheet and then click Send.**

   For AirDrop, a file is created that other people on your local network with Macs using AirDrop can see and access. See Book 3, Chapter 4 to learn more about AirDrop.

   After you share a spreadsheet, the Share button on the toolbar changes from an arrow to two bodies.

REMEMBER

You can also use Numbers to collaborate with others, a task we show you in Book 5, Chapter 6.

IN THIS CHAPTER

» Collaborating with Pages, Numbers and Keynote

» Inserting photos, movies, and music in your documents

» Copying and pasting into your documents

» Finding text and replacing it

» Editing photos

» Making comments in your documents

» Tracking down third-party templates

Chapter **6**

Getting the Most Out of Pages, Numbers, and Keynote

I f you read the last few chapters about using Apple's flagship applications — Pages, Numbers, and Keynote — you may have noticed that the window layout, the commands, and the tools are similar for them all. Some actions are exactly the same, and that's where this chapter comes in. We take you through some of the lesser-known (and some more advanced) functions of the applications discussed in the previous chapters that work the same whether you're writing a newsletter in Pages, preparing a presentation in Keynote, or building a budget in Numbers.

One of the most important commonalities of the these apps is the fact that you can collaborate with other people. As the saying goes, "Many hands make light work," so join forces with friends or colleagues to create and edit your projects.

Collaborating with Keynote, Pages, and Numbers

The collaboration process is similar to other collaboration processes you may have encountered (although it's simpler than many of them). The basic idea is that you *create* a document. Then, using your Internet connection, you *invite* one or more other people to share the document. Either of you can *make changes* to the document, and the other will see the changes. That's the basic outline.

REMEMBER

You must have an Internet connection and a cloud account such as iCloud or a third-party cloud product such as Box or Dropbox. The person you're sharing with doesn't need iCloud or even a Mac for basic viewing and some editing of the document, but Internet is non-negotiable.

As you see in the following steps, there are some additional options you can use, but "create, invite, make changes" is the basic process. Here are the details:

1. **Create or open a document created in Numbers, Keynote, or Pages.**

2. **Click the Collaborate button in the toolbar, as shown in Figure 6-1.**

3. **If your document isn't already in iCloud, you'll be prompted to move it there, as shown in Figure 6-2.**

FIGURE 6-1:
Start collaborating by clicking the Collaborate button.

FIGURE 6-2:
Move your
document to
iCloud.

4. **Decide how to invite your collaborators, as shown in Figure 6-3.**

   Mail is the most common way of communicating with people these days.
   Messages is perhaps the second most common way. You can send a link for
   people to open when they have a chance, and you can also use AirDrop with
   another Mac user or someone who's using an iOS device. For the sake of this
   discussion, we show you how to start a collaboration via email.

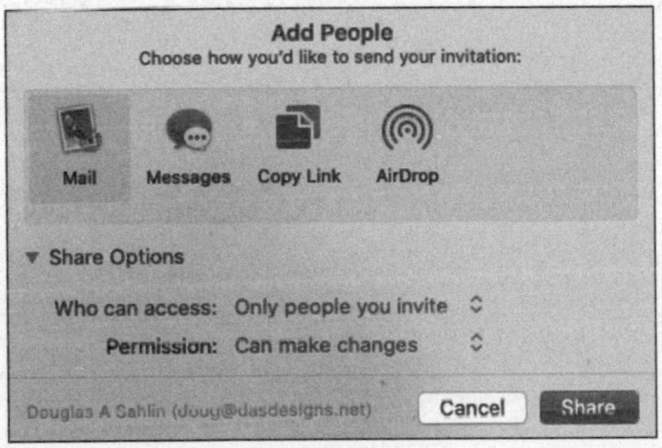

Add People
Choose how you'd like to send your invitation:

Mail   Messages   Copy Link   AirDrop

▼ Share Options

Who can access: Only people you invite ◇
Permission: Can make changes ◇

Douglas A Sahlin (doug@dasdesigns.net)   Cancel   Share

FIGURE 6-3:
Send your
invitation.

5. **Click Mail and then choose from the Share Options menu shown in Figure 6-3.**

6. **Click Share.**

   A Mail form opens. The title of your document is the subject, and the document is attached.

7. **Add the email address of the person you want to collaborate with, as shown in Figure 6-4, and then click Send.**

   Your invitation is sent.

   When a collaborator receives an invitation, she double-clicks the document to open it in the Apple application (Pages, Numbers, or Keynote) from which it was sent. If the owner of the document gave invitees permission to make changes, an invitee can then make the desired changes to the document. When she saves the document, it's saved to iCloud with her changes. The next time the owner opens the document, he sees the changes collaborators have made. If the owner chooses Revert ➪ Browse All Versions, all versions of the document are tiled in a manner similar to viewing a Time Machine backup. The owner can click through the versions, download and view them, and if desired, restore the document to a previous version.

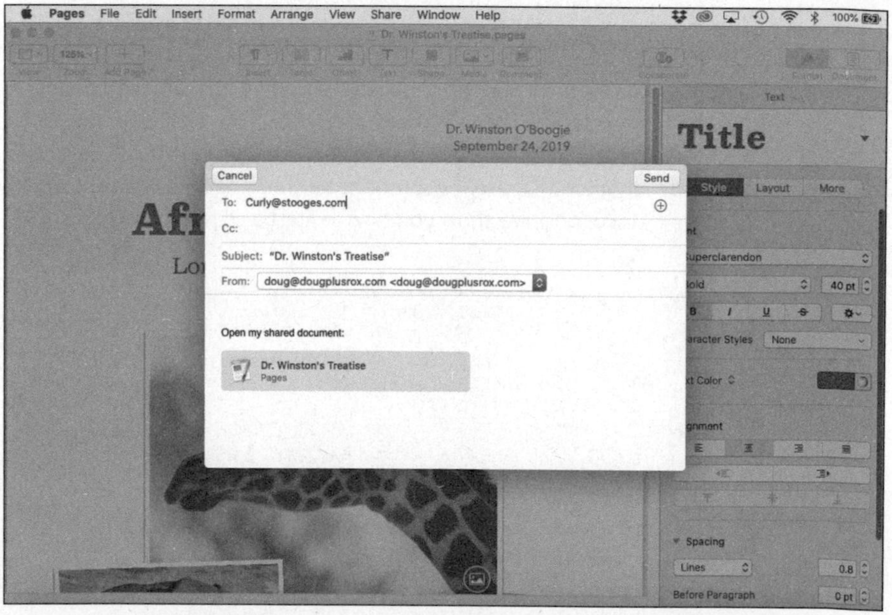

FIGURE 6-4: Sending the document to collaborators.

Inserting Media from Other Sources

Because documents are often shared electronically and viewed on a computer, media can be a fun — and informative — addition to any kind of document. A song might seem an odd addition to a spreadsheet, but a sound effect that screams "Wow!" when sales totals are over the top can be a way to compliment your sales team. Respectively, we show you how to insert photos, movies, and music from Music and Photos into your newsletters, presentations, and spreadsheets in Book 5, Chapters 3, 4, and 5, but you can also add media from other sources by following these steps:

1. **In any of the Apple apps — Pages, Numbers, or Keynote — choose Insert ⇨ Choose.**

   A browser dialog opens, as shown in Figure 6-5.

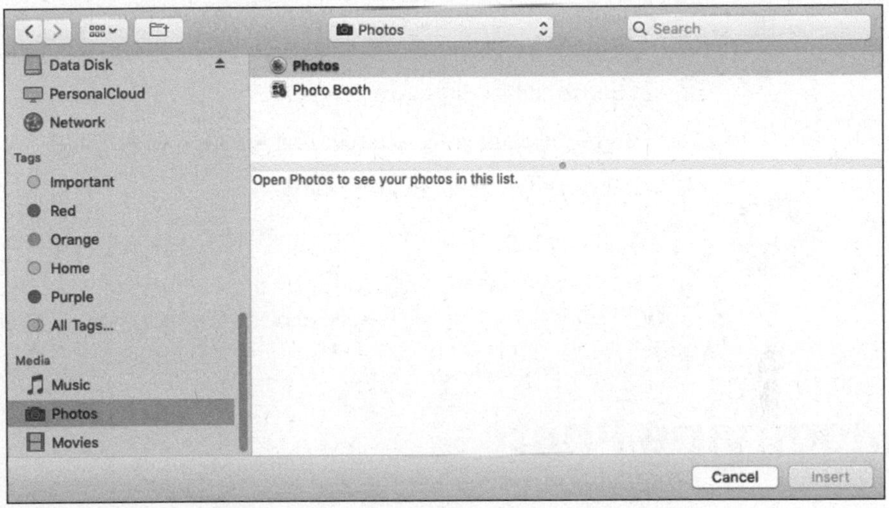

◀ ▶ ⬚⬚ ⬇ 🗁	📷 Photos ⬍ 🔍 Search

🖥 Data Disk ⏏	● **Photos**
🖥 PersonalCloud	📷 Photo Booth
🌐 Network	
Tags	
○ Important	Open Photos to see your photos in this list.
● Red	
● Orange	
○ Home	
● Purple	
○ All Tags...	
Media	
♫ Music	
📷 Photos	
⊟ Movies	
	Cancel Insert

FIGURE 6-5: Insert media from sources other than Photos and Music.

2. **Browse the directories and folders until you find the file you want to insert.**

   If the file is on a flash drive or another external drive, click that drive in the Devices section to see files stored there.

3. **Click the file, and then click the Insert button.**

   The media file is inserted in your document.

REMEMBER

Audio and video can only be truly appreciated in electronically distributed documents — they don't do much for printed matter.

TIP

You can also insert a supported file by opening an Apple application like Photos or Music on the same desktop where you're working on Pages, Numbers, or Keynote. Move your cursor over the green dot and choose Tile to Left of Screen. In Pages, move your cursor over the green dot and choose Tile to Right of Screen. Drag a supported file such as an image or audio file, and drop it into Pages, Numbers, or Keynote.

Copying and Pasting

Two of the most helpful functions when working with documents on computers are Copy and Paste. In Pages, Numbers, and Keynote, you can copy just about any text, image, object, table, or chart and then paste it somewhere else in the same document, in a new document in the same app, or in a different app. Here are the few simple steps it takes:

1. **Click the item you want to copy.**

2. **Choose Edit ➪ Copy or press ⌘+C.**

3. **Go to the place you want to insert the item you copied.**

4. **Choose Edit ➪ Paste or press ⌘+V.**

TIP

- If the item you copied is formatted, choose Edit ➪ Paste and Match Style.

- If you copied cells from Numbers that contain formulas, choose Edit ➪ Paste Formula Results to paste the data instead of the formulas.

Modifying Photos

Pages, Numbers, Keynote, and Preview provide some quick and easy ways to modify the appearance of a photo:

» **Masking:** Masking lets you display just a portion of an image, such as an oval or star-shaped area. Masking hides the other parts of the image; if you unmask an image, you see the whole thing again. This is different from cropping, which actually cuts off the portion of the image you don't want.

» **Instant Alpha:** Instant Alpha lets you make part of an image transparent, making the image seem cut out against the background of your document.

» **Adjust Image:** You can adjust contrast, exposure, and sharpness.

Masking a photo

A mask acts like a cookie cutter that you plop over a photo to save anything *inside* the cookie-cutter shape but hide anything *outside* the shape. Pages, Numbers, and Keynote provide a variety of shaped masks, such as ovals, stars, arrows, and triangles. For example, in your school newspaper you could put the face of a sports winner in a star shape.

To apply a mask to a photo, follow these steps:

1. **Click the photo you want to mask.**

Handles appear around your chosen photo.

2. **Choose Format ⇨ Image ⇨ Mask with Shape, and then choose a shape from the flyout menu, such as Polygon or Diamond.**

Your chosen mask appears over your photo, as shown in Figure 6-6. The parts of the image outside of the mask are dimmed. An editing tool appears at the bottom of the image.

FIGURE 6-6:
Use a mask to save a portion of a photo.

3. **(Optional) Resize the photo or the mask or both.**

- *Photo:* Click the photo button on the editing tool and then resize the photo with the slider.

- *Mask:* Click the mask button on the editing tool to resize the mask with the slider.

TIP

You can also use the handles to resize the image or mask. Holding down the Shift key while dragging a mask handle retains the height and width aspect ratio.

4. **To choose which part of the picture appears within the mask, move the pointer to the dimmed portion of the photo outside the mask and then drag the dimmed portion.**

TIP

You move the photo to position it within the mask: You don't move the mask over the photo.

5. **Click the Done button or click outside the image.**

The Mask is applied to your photo, as shown in Figure 6-7.

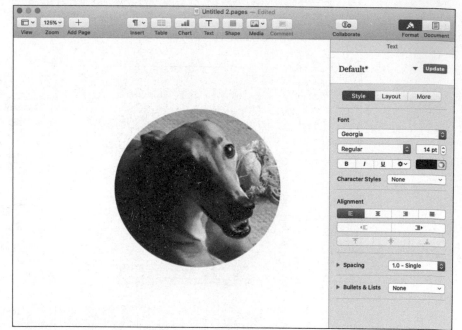

FIGURE 6-7:
View the masked photo.

WARNING

You can apply only one mask at a time to a photo. If you want to apply a different mask over a photo, you must remove the first mask by choosing Format ⇨ Image ⇨ Reset Mask.

TIP

If you apply a mask to an image, and you're not satisfied with the results, choose Format ⇨ Image ⇨ Edit Mask.

Making parts of a picture transparent with Instant Alpha

The Instant Alpha feature lets you remove an irregular portion of a photo. This can create unusual visual effects by stripping unwanted portions of a photo and keeping the parts you like. This differs from cropping, which is when you cut the edges off but the image remains rectangular. Look at these steps and the figure, and you'll see what we mean.

To use the Instant Alpha feature, follow these steps:

1. **Click the photo you want to modify.**

Handles appear around your chosen photo.

2. **Choose Format ➪ Image ➪ Instant Alpha from the menu bar.**

A dialog appears over your photo, telling you how to use the Instant Alpha feature.

3. **Place the pointer over the portion of your photo that you want to make transparent and then drag the mouse or on the trackpad.**

TECHNICAL STUFF

A common use of Instant Alpha is to eliminate a background and make the main subject stand out, maybe even then paste it over a different background. Instant Alpha uses color to identify the part you want to eliminate, so you may have to do Step 3 more than once to eliminate more parts. It highlights all parts of your photo that are similar in color to the area that you originally pointed to.

4. **Release the mouse button or trackpad when you're happy with the portion of the photo that the Instant Alpha feature has highlighted and made transparent.**

5. **Click Done to save the changes or Reset to try again.**

TIP

You can use the Instant Alpha feature multiple times to remove different colors from the same photo. If you make a mistake, choose Edit ➪ Undo Instant Alpha on the menu bar or press ⌘+Z.

Using Adjust Image

Another way to tweak your photos is to choose View ➪ Show Adjust Image, which opens the window shown in Figure 6-8. Use the sliders to adjust contrast, exposure, sharpness, and other aspects of your photo. Click the Enhance button if you want the Adjust Image tool to auto-correct the image. You see the effects immediately on your image and need only click the Close button to accept them. Click the Reset Image button if you don't like the changes you made; doing so returns your image to its original state.

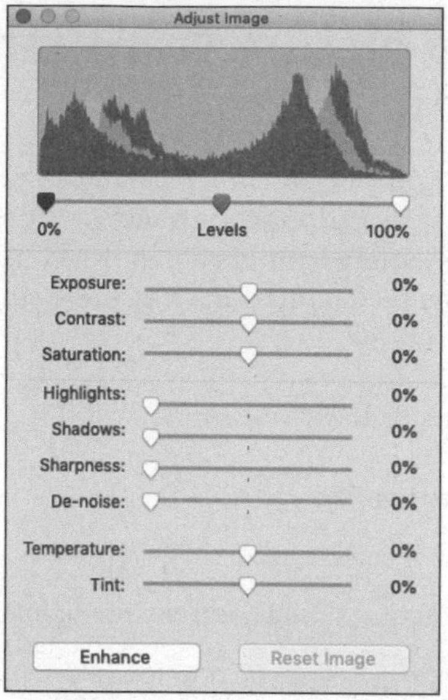

FIGURE 6-8:
Use Adjust Image
to tweak photos.

A common way to adjust the image is to *desaturate* it (drag the Saturation slider all the way to the left). This removes the color from the image, as shown in Figure 6-9.

FIGURE 6-9:
Desaturate
the image.

Adding Comments

Comments are like sticky notes in your document. You can leave notes for yourself or someone else reading your document, and other people can leave comments for you, too. To add comments, do the following:

1. **In an open document, click the Comment icon on the toolbar.**

A virtual sticky note appears on your document.

2. **Type the comment you want to make, as shown in Figure 6-10.**

FIGURE 6-10:
Add comments
as reminders
or notes.

That's it. In Pages, a yellow square appears in the document to indicate where you inserted a comment, while in Keynote and Numbers, your comment remains on the window, unless you hide it as explained next. To manage your comments, try these techniques:

>> **Edit:** Click the comment (in Pages, click the icon in the document to open it) and edit or add more to it.

>> **Hide or display:** Choose View⇨Comments (Comments and Changes in Pages)⇨Hide Comments to hide all comments. (This won't delete it.) Choose View⇨Comments/Comments and Changes⇨Show Comment to see it again.

>> **View additional comments:** Choose View⇨Comments (Comments and Changes in Pages)⇨Show Next Comment (Show Next Comment or Change in Pages), or Choose View⇨Comments (Comments and Changes in Pages)⇨Show Previous Comment (Show Previous Comments and Changes in Pages).

>> **View the Comments pane:** Choose View⇨Show Comments Pane.

>> **Delete:** Open the comment and click Delete.

>> **Reply:** If you're collaborating with others and you add a comment to a document, others can respond by opening the comment and clicking Reply.

TIP

So you can track whose comments belong to whom, you — and other people with whom you share documents and who make comments on your documents — can add an author name to the comments. For each commenter, choose *App Name*⇨Preferences⇨General and type a name in the Author field. As extra ID-help, choose View⇨Comments⇨Author Color to assign a color to each comment author.

Finding More Templates

If the standard templates and typefaces offered in Pages, Numbers, and Keynote don't satisfy your creative needs, several third-party software developers offer free or sell templates that work with these applications. We list a few here, but make sure to check out the App Store and search the Internet for others.

>> **Graphic Node** (`http://graphicnode.com/bundle-for-iwork`): Offers still and motion themes and animations.

>> **KeynotePro** (`www.keynotepro.com/index.aspx`): Sells stylized templates for traditional presentations and kiosks.

>> **Keynote Themes Plus** (`www.keynotethemesplus.com/home.html`): Produces high-definition themes and presentations.

>> **StockLayouts** (`www.stocklayouts.com`): Free and paid Pages templates are available in various formats and specific to different industries such as health care, sports, and education.

Index

A

About This Mac window, 20
access point, 391
access privileges, defining for guests, 410
Accessibility features
    about, 187
    for hearing, 191–192
    keyboard limitations, 193–196
    mouse options, 196–198
    trackpad options, 196–198
    for vision, 188–191
accessing
    accounts, 368
    calendars from other accounts, 578–580
    contacts from other devices/servers, 559–560
    email from Mail, 78
    files
        about, 90, 144–145
        from Dock, 144–145
    folders, 90, 414
    help, 55–56
    Location Services, 313
    shared folders, 414
    tags from Finder menu, 105
account name
    email accounts, 250
    Mail, 78
accounts
    accessing
        about, 368
        calendars from other, 578–580
    adjusting with Fast User Switching, 381
    CalDAV, 578
    configuring, 79–81
    creating multiple, 368–371
    deleting, 381–382
    email, 77–81
    Exchange, 578

    logging out of, 379
    removing from shared folders, 412–413
    social network, 77–81
    switching between, 379–381
acquiring apps, 152–157
Action feature (Keynote), 684–685
activating
    Fast User Switching, 379–380
    File Sharing, 408–409
    First Aid, 434–436
    iCloud data, 326
    Media Sharing, 445
    Pages in iCloud preferences, 645
    Photo Stream, 543
    Screen Sharing, 416–417
    Sharing Only accounts, 377–378
    Switch Control, 199
    Windows, 421–426
active app, 129
Add (+) button (Calendar), 574
Add tool (Safari), 212
adding
    app icons, 130
    bookmarks, 225–226
    books from other sources, 509–510
    calendars to groups, 582
    charts
        about, 635–636
        in Keynote, 667–673
        in Numbers, 718–719
    column buttons in Numbers, 703
    comments in Keynote, Pages and Numbers, 737–738
    contacts automatically with Smart Groups, 565–567
    email accounts
        about, 77–78
        to Mail, 250–254
    email addresses to Contacts, 275–276
    email contacts to VIPs list, 276
    file aliases to Dock, 144–146

adding *(continued)*

   files from other sources, 509–510

   folder aliases to Dock, 144–146

   footers, 626–629

   groups, 563–564

   headers, 626–629

   hyperlinks to presentations in Keynote, 685–686

   information

      to events, 592

      to photos manually, 524–525

   keywords, 521–522

   media

      in Keynote, 674–678

      in Numbers, 721–722

   Memories to Favorite Memories, 530

   movies in Keynote, 676–678

   pages to documents, 614–616

   photos in Keynote, 676–678

   row buttons in Numbers, 703

   sections to documents, 614–616

   shapes

      about, 638–640

      in Keynote, 667–673

   sheets in Numbers, 702

   slides, 656–658

   songs to ordinary playlists, 460

   sound in Keynote, 674–676

   tables

      about, 637–638

      in Keynote, 667–673

      in Numbers, 702

   tabs, 221

   text

      about, 617

      to shapes in Keynote, 668

   text boxes in Numbers, 721

   user accounts, 369–371

address fields, showing/hiding, 265–266

Address option (Contacts), 563

Adjust Image, in Keynote, Pages and Numbers, 735–736

Adjust play buttons (Music app), 474–475

adjusting

   accounts with Fast User Switching, 381

   alignment, 621

   appearance

      about, 171–175

      of Dock, 45–46

      of tables in Numbers, 703–704

   backgrounds in Keynote, 666–667

   borders in Keynote, 666–667

   colors of user interface, 173–175

   column width in Numbers, 703

   Contacts template, 552–553

   date, 175–178

   description of events, 587–588

   Desktop, 48, 166–168

   display, 171–175

   events, 585–595

   Family Sharing settings, 448

   fonts in Keynote, 660–663

   justification, 620–629

   line spacing, 620–629

   margins, 620–629

   Music preferences, 470–473

   passwords, 351–353

   photos in Keynote, Pages and Numbers, 732–736

   row height in Numbers, 703

   screen resolution, 171–172

   sleep options, 14–16

   sounds, 178–181

   tag color, 105

   text in text boxes, 620

   time, 175–178

   view options, 99–100

   views in App Store, 155

adjustments, for photos, 540–541

Administrator account, 369

Adobe (website), 244

Adobe Lightroom, 518

Adobe Photoshop Elements, 518

Advanced Encryption Standard (AES), 115

advanced filter rules, 287–289

Advanced preferences (Podcast app), 495

AES (Advanced Encryption Standard), 115

AFP (Apple Filing Protocol), 330

AirDrop

   about, 242, 404

   sending location information via, 320

   sharing contacts via, 568

   using, 404–407

AirDrop My Card option, 568
AirPlay Display menu, 172
AirPort Wi-Fi feature, 59
albums
  creating playlists of, 460
  deleting, 527–528
  downloading cover artwork for, 478
alerts
  about, 182
  setting for events, 590–591
alias icons
  about, 134
  creating, 142–143
  deleting, 143
  moving, 142
  removing from Dock/Desktop, 162
  storing, 143
aliases
  about, 110
  Dock, 143–147
Align Left option, 621
Align Right option, 621
alignment
  changing, 621
  defined, 620
  of objects in Keynote, 669–670
All Caps option (Keynote), 663
All Contacts group, 563
all-in-one desktop category, of Macs, 8
analog, 58
animating text/graphics on slides in Keynote, 684–685
app icons, 44–45
app menus, 25
App Store
  downloading apps from, 156–157
  shopping in, 153–156
App Store icon, 158
app windows, moving to different Desktops, 150–151
appearance
  changing
    about, 171–175
    of Dock, 45–46
    of tables in Numbers, 703–704
  Messages app, 294–295
  of spreadsheets in Numbers, 720–722

Apple Arcade, 451, 452
Apple Books
  about, 505
  shopping for books at, 507–509
Apple Card
  about, 308
  using, 309
Apple compatible devices, 60
Apple Filing Protocol (AFP), 330
Apple ID
  about, 12, 63–64
  for App Store, 153
  Books app and, 509
  creating
    in iCloud, 66–70
    during Mac setup, 64–65
  establishing, 63–71
  iTunes Store, 486
  legacy, 71
  media and, 443–453
  merging, 444
  sharing, 444
  two-factor authentication, 65–66
  website, 64
Apple Inc., 553
Apple Magic Mouse, 33–34
Apple menu, 25, 132–133
Apple Music, 77, 451, 457
Apple News
  about, 451, 453, 496
  following publishers/channels, 498
  reading daily news, 496–498
  saving stories, 498–499
  setting preferences, 499–500
  sharing stories, 498–499
Apple Pay
  about, 307–308
  paying for purchases with, 308–309
Apple Store (website), 19
Apple SuperDrive, 438–439
Apple Support, 11, 326
Apple TV, 451, 452, 454
Application files, 134
Application icons, 134
Application Switcher, 137

Applications folder, 86

applying
  Parental Controls, 372–377
  password protection, 353–356

apps
  about, 127–128
  acquiring, 152–157
  active, 129
  data-recovery, 345–346
  Dock aliases, 143–147
  downloading from App Store, 156–157
  force-quitting, 140–141, 428–429
  free, 152
  freemium, 153
  installing, 158
  launching, 128–136
  managing, 127–164
  media player, 192
  opening, 132
  organizing
    into folders, 44–45
    multiple desktops with Spaces, 148–152
  quitting, 139–141
  recovering data from within, 339–340
  security of, 163–164
  shutting down, 139–140
  subscription, 153
  switching between, 137–139
  uninstalling, 160–163, 433
  updating, 158–159

Apps and Games We Love Right Now section (App Store), 154

Apps limit (Parental Controls), 372

AppZapper (website), 163

archive format, 569

archiving
  about, 329–330
  defined, 112
  files, 112–117
  folders, 112–117
  messages, 292

Arrange tab
  Format pane, 672, 719
  Numbers, 704

arranging
  icons within Icon view, 95–96
  objects
    about, 640–641
    in Keynote, 669–670

arrow keys, 42–43

asking for directions, 315–322

assigned commands, 37

attachments, file/photo, 266–270

audio CDs, burning, 482–483

audio chats
  about, 296, 299–301
  playing with Music app, 474–483

audio files
  about, 474
  importing tracks from CDs into Music app, 476–478
  playing, 676

Audiobooks button (Apple Books), 508

authorizing computers, 486

authors, viewing books by, 513

AutoFill, tracking passwords using, 234–236

Automatically Add to Music option (Music app), 478

Auto-Save functions, 342

Average formula, 710

Axis tab (Format pane), 671, 719

Axis/Wedge Labels tab (Format pane), 672, 719

B

Back command, 92, 93

Back tool (Safari), 211

backgrounds, changing in Keynote, 666–667

backing up
  data
    about, 325–348
    in Calendar, 600–601
  with external hard drives, 329–330
  freeing up space, 348
  hard drive, 347
  moving between Macs, 344–345
  options for, 328–331
  restoring backup files, 600–601
  skipping files during, 336–337

storing
off-site, 331
on USB flash drives, 330–331
with Time Machine, 332–343
Backup Scheduler: Time Editor, 337
badges, 182
balance, adjusting, 178
banners, 182
Belkin (website), 350
biometric security, 65
Black and White adjustment (Photos), 540
blocked sender rules, 289–290
blocking channels in news app, 498
Bluetooth
about, 395–396
configuring, 396–397
pairing devices, 398–400
sharing through, 400–402
Bluetooth Preferences dialog, 399
Bonjour, 386
book icon, 505
Bookmark Editor, 227–228
bookmarks
about, 224–225
adding, 225–226
deleting, 228–229
exporting, 229–230
importing, 229–230
rearranging, 228–229
renaming, 229
storing in folders, 226–228
Bookmarks button (Books app), 511
Bookmarks Editor, 229
Books app
about, 454, 505–507
adding books/files from other sources, 509–510
reading by screen light, 510–512
shopping for books, 507–509
sorting books, 513
Books app window, 506
Boot Camp
about, 423
setting up Boot Camp Assistant, 423–426

booting up
defined, 11
from other Macs through Thunderbolt cable, 436–437
in Safe Mode, 431–433
Border option
Keynote, 667
Numbers, 708
borders, changing in Keynote, 666–667
Box (website), 331
bring your own device (BYOD), 422–423
broadband, 58
Browse option (Apple Music), 457
browsing
tabbed
about, 218
creating tabs, 218–220
managing tabs, 220–221
websites, 208–223 (See also Safari)
building
alias icons, 142–143
Apple IDs
in iCloud, 66–70
during Mac setup, 64–65
builds in Keynote, 682–683
bulleted lists in Numbers, 721
calendar groups, 582–584
calendars, 577–578
charts, 635–642
contacts, 554–558
Desktops, 148–149
DMG files, 113, 114–116
effects in Keynote, 680–686
emails, 257–259
events, 585–595
folders, 102–104, 112, 526–527
Genius playlists, 466–467
Genius shuffles, 468
graphic effects in Keynote, 682–685
groups
in Contacts, 562–568
from selections of contacts, 565
of slides in Keynote, 678–679

building *(continued)*
  indents, 624–626
  mailbox folders, 278–279
  Memories, 530–531
  multiple accounts, 368–371
  numbered lists in Numbers, 721
  ordinary playlists, 459–460
  presentations, 650–658
  projects, 545
  Quick Events, 586
  quick playlists, 460
  Reading list, 230–232
  recurring events, 588–589
  rules, 282–283
  slideshows, 531–534
  Smart Albums, 525–526
  Smart Folders, 122–123
  Smart Groups from search results, 567
  smart mailboxes, 280–281
  Smart Playlists, 463–464
  spreadsheets
    in Numbers, 699–701
    with templates, 699–700
  Stacks on Dock, 145
  tables, 635–642
  tabs, 218–220, 624–626
  tasks in Reminders, 602–605
  text boxes, 629–630
  text effects in Keynote, 682–685
  transitions in Keynote, 680–686
  wired networks, 386–389
  wireless networks with routers, 390–391
  Zip files, 113–114
builds, creating in Keynote, 682–683
built-in optical drive, 456
bulleted lists, 721
bullets, formatting in Keynote, 665–666
burning audio CDs, 482–483
Buy button (iTunes Store information screen), 487
buying stronger firewalls, 365–366
BYOD (bring your own device), 422–423

C

CalDAV account, 578
Calendar
  about, 568, 573–576
  accessing calendars from other accounts, 578–580
  adding
    calendars to groups, 582
    information to events, 592
  adjusting
    description of events, 587–588
    events, 585–595
  backing up data in, 600–601
  color-coding events, 595
  creating
    calendar groups, 582–584
    calendars, 577–578
    events, 585–595
    recurring events, 588–589
  deleting
    calendars, 584–585
    events, 595
    groups, 584–585
  duplicating events, 589
  editing events, 587–595
  exporting Calendar data, 598
  finding events, 595–602
  hiding events, 595–596
  importing calendar data, 582
  indicating availability in, 589–590
  inviting people to events, 592–593
  moving
    calendars, 584
    calendars out of groups, 582–584
    events, 591, 594–595
    events to other calendars, 591
    groups, 584
  printing Calendar files, 601–602
  renaming calendars/groups, 584–585
  responding to invitations, 594
  restoring backup files, 600–601
  searching for events, 597–598

setting alerts for events, 590–591

sharing calendars, 598–600

subscribing to online calendars, 580–581

toolbar, 574

verifying

   events for specific dates, 596–597

   for today's events, 596

viewing events, 585

views, 586

working with multiple calendars, 576–585

Calendar widget, 596

Calendars button (Calendar), 574

calls, making with FaceTime, 302–306

capitalization, in Keynote, 663

Caps Lock key, 42, 663

capturing photos with Photo Booth, 534–537

cards

   editing in Contacts, 561–562

   exporting, 569–570

   viewing in Contacts, 551

Cataline version, 12

categories, viewing books by, 513

Categories category (Apple Books), 507

CDs

   burning audio, 482–483

   importing audio tracks into Music app, 476–478

   listening to, 474–476

   removing jammed, 438–439

cell references, in Numbers formulas, 711

Cell tab (Numbers), 704

cellular data modem, 63

Center option, 621

changing

   accounts with Fast User Switching, 381

   alignment, 621

   appearance

     about, 171–175

     of Dock, 45–46

     of tables in Numbers, 703–704

   backgrounds in Keynote, 666–667

   borders in Keynote, 666–667

   colors of user interface, 173–175

column width in Numbers, 703

Contacts template, 552–553

date, 175–178

description of events, 587–588

Desktop, 48, 166–168

display, 171–175

events, 585–595

Family Sharing settings, 448

fonts in Keynote, 660–663

justification, 620–629

line spacing, 620–629

margins, 620–629

Music preferences, 470–473

passwords, 351–353

photos in Keynote, Pages and Numbers, 732–736

row height in Numbers, 703

screen resolution, 171–172

sleep options, 14–16

sounds, 178–181

tag color, 105

text in text boxes, 620

time, 175–178

view options, 99–100

views in App Store, 155

channels, following in News app, 498

Character Count tool (Pages), 617

characters

   restrictions in file/folder names, 108

   typing, 39–40

Chart tab (Format pane), 671, 719

charts

   adding

     about, 635–636

     in Keynote, 667–673

     in Numbers, 718–719

   creating, 635–642

   inserting from Numbers, 613–614

   interactive, 671

   naming in Numbers, 720

   Numbers, 696

   removing, 635–636

Cheat Sheet (website), 4

choosing
  application-specific function keys, 38
  Desktop image, 166–168
  items in Finder, 94
  printers, 393–395
  privacy settings, 366–368
  templates, 608–609
  themes in Keynote, 651–653
  wireless router, 59–61
ClamXAV, 366
click and drag gesture, 35
clicking
  mouse, 33
  in scroll bar, 32
closing
  documents, 139
  tabs, 91, 221
  windows, 30
cloud icon, 505
cloud storage, 157
Collection, viewing books by, 513
Color adjustment (Photos), 540
color-coding events, 595
colors
  changing for user interface, 173–175
  tags, 105
Colors icon (numbers), 708
Column view, 85, 92, 93, 97–98, 99
column width, resizing, 96–97
commands
  assigned, 37
  shortcut, 38
  Siri, 51–52
comments
  adding in Keynote, Pages and Numbers, 737–738
  Numbers, 697
company name, organizing contacts by, 550–551
compatibility, of wireless routers, 60
Compressed format, 115, 516
computers, authorizing, 486
condensing dialogs, 27
conditional formatting, 716–717
conditional highlight, 715

configuring
  accounts, 79–81
  Bluetooth, 396–397
  firewalls, 362–364
  iCloud preferences, 72–74
  Mail, 254
  Siri, 53
confirming Internet connection, 59
connections. *See also* Internet connections
  printers, 393–395
  removable devices, 85
contactless payment technology, 308
Contacts
  about, 549–550
  accessing contacts from other devices/servers, 559–560
  adding
    contacts automatically with Smart Groups, 565–567
    email addresses to, 275–276
    groups, 563–564
  creating
    contacts, 554–558
    groups, 562–568
    groups from selections of contacts, 565
    Smart Groups from search results, 567
  deleting
    contacts, 562
    groups, 567–568
  designing Contacts template, 551–553
  editing
    cards, 561–562
    distribution lists, 565
    Smart Groups, 567
  entering contacts, 553–560
  exporting cards, 569–570
  importing contacts, 558–559
  printing contacts, 570–571
  searching contacts, 561
  sending contacts, 568
  setting up, 550–560
  sharing contacts, 568–571
  shortcut menus, 563
  viewing contacts, 550–551
  working with contacts, 560–568

Contacts Archive file format, 558
Contacts template, designing, 551–553
contextual menus, 33, 563
Continuous button (Music app), 475
control-click gesture, 35
control-clicking mouse, 33
controlling
  apps, 127–164
  devices, 85–86
  files, 107–112
  folders, 107–112
  malware, 365
  presentations remotely in Keynote, 690–691
  tabs, 220–221
  text, 658–667
  windows, 27–32
controls
  Music app, 474–476
  playback (Podcasts app), 492
  speaker (Podcasts app), 493
conversations, deleting/saving, 301–302
converting audio discs into digital files, 476–477
cookies, 238
Copy Link (Maps app), 320
copying and pasting in Keynote, Pages and
    Numbers, 732
copying files/folders, 110–111
copyright, 532
Core 2 Duo processor, 19
Core Duo processor, 19
Core Solo processor, 19
corners, resizing in Numbers, 703
Count formula, 710
Cover Flow view, 85, 92, 93
creating
  alias icons, 142–143
  Apple IDs
    in iCloud, 66–70
    during Mac setup, 64–65
  builds in Keynote, 682–683
  bulleted lists in Numbers, 721
  calendar groups, 582–584
  calendars, 577–578
  charts, 635–642
  contacts, 554–558

Desktops, 148–149
DMG files, 113, 114–116
effects in Keynote, 680–686
emails, 257–259
events, 585–595
folders, 102–104, 112, 526–527
Genius playlists, 466–467
Genius shuffles, 468
graphic effects in Keynote, 682–685
groups
  in Contacts, 562–568
  from selections of contacts, 565
  of slides in Keynote, 678–679
indents, 624–626
mailbox folders, 278–279
Memories, 530–531
multiple accounts, 368–371
numbered lists in Numbers, 721
ordinary playlists, 459–460
presentations, 650–658
projects, 545
Quick Events, 586
quick playlists, 460
Reading list, 230–232
recurring events, 588–589
rules, 282–283
slideshows, 531–534
Smart Albums, 525–526
Smart Folders, 122–123
Smart Groups from search results, 567
smart mailboxes, 280–281
Smart Playlists, 463–464
spreadsheets
  in Numbers, 699–701
  with templates, 699–700
Stacks on Dock, 145
tables, 635–642
tabs, 218–220, 624–626
tasks in Reminders, 602–605
text boxes, 629–630
text effects in Keynote, 682–685
transitions in Keynote, 680–686
wired networks, 386–389
wireless networks with routers, 390–391
Zip files, 113–114

credit cards
  in App Store, 156
  in iTunes Store, 489
Crossfade Songs (Music app), 476
CSV file format, 724
Ctrl+-, 211
Ctrl++, 211
cursors
  control keys for, 42–43
  moving, 39
Curves adjustment (Photos), 540
customizing
  about, 165–166
  accessibility features, 187–198
  appearance, 171–175
  choosing Desktop image, 166–168
  colors of user interface, 173–175
  date, 175–178
  display, 171–175
  enabling Switch Control, 199
  function keys, 38
  messages, 261–266
  Night Shift, 172–173
  notifications, 181–186
  screen resolution, 171–172
  screen saver, 168–170
  sounds, 178–181
  Speakable Items feature, 199–203
  Split-View mode, 186–187
  System Preference window layout, 170
  themes using Masters, 686–687
  time, 175–178

D

Dashboard (Calendar), 596
data
  backing up, 325–348
  deleting in cells in Numbers, 718
  encrypting with FileVault, 358–362
  recovering from within apps, 339–340
  restoring, 325–348
  sorting in Numbers, 717

typing into tables in Numbers, 706–720
  using iCloud for, 326–328
data entry cells, formatting in Numbers, 713–717
Data Recovery for Mac, 346
Data Rescue, 346
data storage
  about, 8
  keeping in iCloud, 71–76
data transfer
  about, 8
  speed for, 386
data-recovery apps, 345–346
date, changing, 175–178
Day layout (Calendar), 575
Day view (Calendar), 586
dead spots, 391
defining
  access privileges for guests, 410
  margins, 622–624
definitions, in Books app, 511
Delete key, 40, 43
deleting
  accounts
    about, 381–382
    from shared folders, 412–413
  albums, 527–528
  alias icons, 143, 162
  app icons, 130
  bookmarks, 228–229
  calendars, 584–585
  charts, 635–636
  columns in Numbers, 703
  contacts, 562
  conversations, 301–302
  data in cells in Numbers, 718
  events, 595
  files, 86, 115–117, 123–125
  folders, 86, 115–117, 123–125, 527–528
  groups, 567–568, 584–585
  hyperlinks in Keynote, 686
  icons from Dock, 147
  jammed CDs/DVDs, 438–439
  mailbox folders, 280

memory card, 519

menulets, 26

messages, 290–291

photos, 527–528, 536

playlists, 467

removable devices, 86

rows in Numbers, 703

saved stories in News app, 499

sheets in Numbers, 702

slides in Keynote, 680

smart mailboxes, 282

songs from ordinary playlists, 461

tables in Numbers, 702

tasks in Reminders, 604

text, 618

user setting files, 162–163

designing Contacts template, 551–553

Desktop

about, 43–44

changing, 48, 166–168

choosing image, 166–168

creating, 148–149

Dock, 44–46

Finder, 46–48

moving app windows to different, 150–151

organizing with Spaces, 148–152

removing app alias icons from, 162

switching, 150

desktop category, of Macs, 8, 14

Desktop & Documents folder, 87, 328

Desktop Space. *See* Space

Detect Displays button, 172

devices

accessing contacts from other, 559–560

managing, 85–86

Music app, 469

syncing with other, 74–75

Devices category, 85–86

DHCP (Dynamic Host Configuration Protocol), 59, 388

dialogs

about, 24–25

condensing, 27

expanding, 27

dial-up, 58

digital audio files

importing, 478

playing, 479–482

digital images, transferring to Macs, 517

digital photography, 515–517

directions, asking for, 315–322

directories. *See* folders

Directories group, 563

disabling

FileVault, 361–362

Macs, 13–18

Media Sharing, 445

notifications, 186

disclosure button, 486

disclosure triangle, 21, 97

disk image, 113

Disk Utility app, 113, 434, 436

DiskWarrior, 346, 434, 436

display, changing, 171–175

Display option, 188

displaying

address fields, 265–266

favorites in Top Sites, 232–234

folder contents, 92

tags in Sidebar, 105

Displays tab, 20

distribution lists, editing, 565

DMG files, creating, 113, 114–116

Dock

about, 44–46, 128

accessing files from, 144–145

adding file/folder aliases to, 144–146

creating Stacks on, 145

hiding, 129

launching apps from, 129–130

rearranging icons on, 146–147

removing

app alias icons from, 162

icons from, 147

switching among apps using, 137

Dock aliases, 143 147

Dock preference pane, 45

document body, 626
Document files, 134
Document icons, 134
document templates, 608–617
documents
  adding pages/sections to, 614–616
  closing, 139
  enhancing, 642–645
  moving around, 616–617
  opening, 134–136
  printing, 646
  saving
    about, 645–646
    multiple versions of, 104
  spell-checking, 642–644
Documents folder, 87
domain name, 209
double-clicking mouse, 33
downloading
  album cover artwork, 478
  apps from App Store, 156–157
  files, 244–246
  media from Music app, 488–489
  Remote app, 481
Downloads folder, 44, 87, 245
dragging
  files, 111
  folders, 111
  mouse, 33
  in scroll box, 32
  windows, 151
Drive Genius (website), 437
Drop Box folder, 408
Dropbox (website), 266
drop-down menus, 41
dropping pins in Maps app, 320
dual-core i3 processor, 19
dual-core i5 processor, 19
Duplicate command, 102
duplicate slides, 658
duplicating
  events, 589
  filenames, 108
DVD/CS Master format, 115
DVDs, removing jammed, 438–439
Dynamic Host Configuration Protocol (DHCP), 59, 388

E

Edit menu, 26
editing
  cards in Contacts, 561–562
  distribution lists, 565
  events, 587–595
  photos with Photos, 537–541
  Smart Groups, 567
  Smart Playlists, 465
  tasks in Reminders, 604
  text
    about, 617–618
    in Keynote, 659–660
Editor's Choice section (App Store), 154
effects, creating in Keynote, 680–686
Effects button (Photo Booth), 535
Eject button, 519
Eject icon, 438
Eject key, 38, 438
ejecting removable devices, 85
email
  about, 249–250
  accessing from Mail, 78
  adding
    accounts to Mail, 250–254
    addresses to Contacts, 275–276
    contacts to VIPs list, 276
  creating, 257–259
  location information, 319
  setting up accounts, 77–81
  verifying addresses, 287
  web pages, 241
  writing, 257–271
Email option (Contacts), 563
emoticons, 299
empowering Siri, 53–54
emptying Trash, 124–125, 292, 383, 434
enabling
  Fast User Switching, 379–380
  File Sharing, 408–409
  First Aid, 434–436
  iCoud data, 326
  Media Sharing, 445
  Pages in iCloud preferences, 645
  Photo Stream, 543

Screen Sharing, 416–417
Sharing Only accounts, 377–378
Switch Control, 199
Windows, 421–426
Enclosing Folder command, 93
encrypted wireless network, 62
encrypting
about, 392
data with FileVault, 358–362
End key, 43
Energy Saver setting, 168
enhanced books, 512
enhancing
documents, 642–645
presentations in Keynote, 687–694
entering
contacts, 553–560
formulas in Numbers, 710–713
text in Keynote, 658
Episode window (Podcasts app), 493
ePub files, 647
Equalizer (Music app), 475
ergonomic input devices, 198
Esc key, 38
establishing Apple ID, 63–71
Ethernet cables, 387
Ethernet connection, 58–59, 386
Ethernet port, 386, 387
events
adding information to, 592
adjusting description of, 587–588
color-coding, 595
creating, 585–595
deleting, 595
duplicating, 589
editing, 587–595
finding, 595–602
hiding, 595–596
inviting people to, 592–593
modifying, 585–595
moving
about, 594–595
to other calendars, 591
preparing for in Keynote, 689–690
recurring, 588–589
searching for, 597–598

setting alerts for, 590–591
verifying
specific dates, 596–597
today's, 596
viewing, 585
Excel file format, 724
Exchange account, 77–78, 578
Exclude These Items from Backups dialog, 336–337
expanding dialogs, 27
exporting
bookmarks, 229–230
Calendar data, 598
cards, 569–570
to different file formats, 646–648
presentations in Keynote, 692–693
spreadsheets in Numbers, 723–724
extensions, 246–247
external hard drives
backing up, 329–330
opening files from, 653
external optical disc drive, 439

F

Facebook Profile option (Contacts), 563
FaceTime. *See also* Messages
making calls with, 302–306
volume controls for, 301
Family Sharing, 445–453
Fast User Switching, 379–381
Favorite Memories, 530
favorites, displaying in Top Sites, 232–234
Favorites bar, 224, 254–255
Favorites Bar, 212
Favorites category (Sidebar), 47
Featured category (Apple Books), 507
file aliases, adding to Dock, 144–146
file attachments
saving, 274–275
sending, 266–270
viewing, 274–275
file formats
about, 108, 209–210
for contacts, 558
exporting to different, 646–648
for photos, 516–517

File icon, 44–45
File menu, 26
File Sharing
  about, 296, 301
  in Sleep mode, 413
  turning on, 408–409
File Transfer Protocol (FTP), 362
files
  about, 83–84
  accessing
    about, 90
    from Dock, 144–145
  adding from other sources, 509–510
  archiving, 112–117
  audio, 474
  Calendar, 601–602
  classifying, 105–107
  compressing, 516
  copying, 110–111
  creating folders, 102–104
  deleting, 115–117, 123–125
  downloading, 244–246
  dragging, 111
  Finder, 84–93
  grouping, 112
  manipulating, 107–112
  moving, 111–112
  opening
    in Keynote, 653–654
    in Numbers, 700–701
    in Stacks, 146
  organizing into folders, 44–45, 93–101
  renaming, 108–109
  retrieving
    about, 337–342
    from Trash, 124
  saving
    multiple versions of documents, 104
    web pages as, 239–240
  searching, 117–123
  sharing
    directly in Numbers, 725
    on networks, 403–419

  skipping during backup, 336–337
  user setting, 162–163
  viewing
    contents of with Quick Look, 100–101
    folders, 93–101
FileVault
  encrypting data with, 358–362
  setting up, 358–361
  turning off, 361–362
Fill option
  Keynote, 667
  Numbers, 708
filtering junk email, 285–287
Find and Replace dialog, 38
Finder
  about, 46–48, 84–85
  adjusting view options, 99–100
  Column view, 97–98, 99
  creating folders, 102–104
  defined, 83
  Devices category, 85–86
  folders, 86–87
  Gallery view, 98, 99
  Icon view, 94–96, 99
  launching apps from, 133, 134
  List view, 96–97, 99
  navigating, 90–93
  opening, 90
  organizing folders, 93–101
  retrieving files/folders using, 340–342
  selecting items in, 94
  setting preferences, 88–89
  tags, 105–107
  viewing folders, 93–101
Finder menu
  accessing tags from, 105
  creating folders from, 102
finding
  events, 595–602
  images, 531
  podcasts, 491–496
  templates in Keynote, Pages and Numbers, 738
  your location, 312–313

finding and replacing text, 644–645

Firefox (website), 208

firewalls
    about, 362
    buying stronger, 365–366
    configuring, 362–364
    defined, 407

FireWire port, 299

First Aid, running, 434–436

flagging messages, 283–284

flash drives, 328

flash memory card, removing, 519

Flash Storage, 20

Flickr option (Contacts), 563

Fn key, 37–38, 43

folder aliases, adding to Dock, 144–146

folders
    about, 83–84, 86–87
    accessing, 90
    archiving, 112–117
    classifying, 105–107
    copying, 110–111
    creating, 102–104, 112, 526–527
    defined, 83
    deleting, 115–117, 123–125, 527–528
    displaying contents of, 92
    dragging, 111
    Finder, 84–93
    following path for, 93
    hierarchy of, 87
    jumping between, 91–92
    manipulating, 107–112
    moving
        about, 111–112
        to higher, 92–93
        photos between, 520–521
    opening, 90
    organizing
        about, 93–101
        apps/files into, 44–45
    renaming, 108–109, 229
    retrieving
        about, 337–342
        from Trash, 124
    saving multiple versions of documents, 104

searching files, 117–123

storing bookmarks in, 226–228

viewing, 93–101

following
    channels in news app, 498
    folder path, 93
    publishers in news app, 498

font smoothing, 663

fonts, changing in Keynote, 660–663

footers, adding, 626–629

For You option (Apple Music), 457

force shutdown, 18

force-quitting apps, 140–141, 428–429

Format pane
    Keynote, 666–667, 669, 670, 671–672
    Numbers, 704

formatting
    bullets in Keynote, 665–666
    cells with sliders/steppers, 714–715
    conditional, 716–717
    data entry cells in Numbers, 713–717
    numbers in Numbers, 707–709
    paragraphs in Keynote, 664
    text
        about, 618–620
        in Keynote, 660–667
        in Numbers, 707–709
    text boxes in Keynote, 660–667

Formula Editor, 712–713

formulas
    entering in Numbers, 710–713
    typing in Numbers, 710–712

Forward command, 92

Forward tool (Safari), 212

forwarding messages, 259–260

free apps, 152

freemium apps, 153

frozen apps, 18

frozen programs, shutting down, 428–430

FTP (File Transfer Protocol), 362

Full Screen view tool (Safari), 212

Full-screen button (Calendar), 574

full-screen view, 31

function keys, 36–38

functions, using in Numbers, 712–713

G

Gallery view, 98, 99
General preferences (Podcast app), 495
generating
  alias icons, 142–143
  Apple IDs
    in iCloud, 66–70
    during Mac setup, 64–65
  builds in Keynote, 682–683
  bulleted lists in Numbers, 721
  calendar groups, 582–584
  calendars, 577–578
  charts, 635–642
  contacts, 554–558
  Desktops, 148–149
  DMG files, 113, 114–116
  effects in Keynote, 680–686
  emails, 257–259
  events, 585–595
  folders, 102–104, 112, 526–527
  Genius playlists, 466–467
  Genius shuffles, 468
  graphic effects in Keynote, 682–685
  groups
    in Contacts, 562–568
    from selections of contacts, 565
    of slides in Keynote, 678–679
  indents, 624–626
  mailbox folders, 278–279
  Memories, 530–531
  multiple accounts, 368–371
  numbered lists in Numbers, 721
  ordinary playlists, 459–460
  presentations, 650–658
  projects, 545
  Quick Events, 586
  quick playlists, 460
  Reading list, 230–232
  recurring events, 588–589
  rules, 282–283
  slideshows, 531–534
  Smart Albums, 525–526
  Smart Folders, 122–123
  Smart Groups from search results, 567
  smart mailboxes, 280–281
  Smart Playlists, 463–464
  spreadsheets
    in Numbers, 699–701
    with templates, 699–700
  Stacks on Dock, 145
  tables, 635–642
  tabs, 218–220, 624–626
  tasks in Reminders, 602–605
  text boxes, 629–630
  text effects in Keynote, 682–685
  transitions in Keynote, 680–686
  wired networks, 386–389
  wireless networks with routers, 390–391
  Zip files, 113–114
Genius playlist, 466–467
Genius shuffles, 468
gestures, 35–36
getting started
  with Macs, 54–56
  with Messages app, 294–295
gift cards, in App Store, 156
Go menu, 91–92
Google Chrome (website), 208
GPS data, 528–529
grammar, checking, 270–271
Graphic Node, 738
graphics
  animating on slides in Keynote, 684–685
  creating effects in Keynote, 682–685
grouping files, 112
groups
  adding
    about, 563–564
    calendars to, 582
  creating
    for calendars, 582–584
    in Contacts, 562–568
    from selections of contacts, 565
    for slides in Keynote, 678–679
  deleting, 567–568, 584–585
  moving
    about, 584
    calendars out of, 582–584
  renaming, 584–585
guests, defining access privileges for, 410

H

hackers, 349

handles, resizing in Numbers, 703

handling

apps, 127–164

devices, 85–86

files, 107–112

folders, 107–112

malware, 365

presentations remotely in Keynote, 690–691

tabs, 220–221

text, 658–667

windows, 27–32

hard disk drive (HDD), 85

hard drives

about, 347

accidental deletion from, 345–346

external, 329–330

space on, 157

verifying, 436

hardware

failure of, 346

repairing, 17

HDD (hard disk drive), 85

headers

adding, 626–629

inserting in Numbers, 704–706

hearing, Accessibility features for, 191–192

help, getting, 54–56

hiding

address fields, 265–266

Dock, 129

events, 595–596

photos, 528

thumbnails, 615

windows, 130

hierarchy of folders, 87

Hightail (website), 266

History menu, 216–217

Home key, 43

home page, setting in Safari, 222–223

Home Sharing. *See* Media Sharing

Hopper, Grace Murray (computer programmer), 312

Hot Corners button, 152

Hot Key, 633

hotspots, 58, 59, 63

HTML (HyperText Markup Language), 239

HTTP (Hypertext Transfer Protocol), 209

hub, 387

hung-up programs, shutting down, 428–430

Hybrid Image (HFS + ISO/UDF) format, 115

hyperlinks

adding to presentations in Keynote, 685–686

deleting in Keynote, 686

HyperText Markup Language (HTML), 239

Hypertext Transfer Protocol (HTTP), 209

I

iBooks app. *See* Books app

iCalShare (website), 581

iCloud

about, 71–72

configuring preferences, 72–74

creating Apple ID in, 66–70

keeping data in, 71–76

Keychain option, 236

preferences, 645

saving documents on, 645–646

sharing storage in, 448, 449

syncing with other devices, 74–75

turning on data, 326

using for data, 326–328

website, 75–76

iCloud category (Sidebar), 47

iCloud Control Panel 3.0 for Windows, 72

iCloud Drive, 326, 653

Icon view (Finder), 94–96, 99

icons

alias, 134, 142–143, 162

app, 44–45

App Store, 158

Application icons, 134

arranging within Icon view, 95–96

book, 505

cloud, 505

Document, 134

Eject, 438

explained, 3–4

icons *(continued)*
  File, 44–45
  Language & Region, 178
  Launchpad, 131
  lock, 62
  menulets, 26
  Music, 476
  Notification Center, 26
  rearranging on Dock, 146–147
  removing from Dock, 147
  Setup (Keynote), 688
  Spotlight Search, 26
  Stack, 146
  Trash, 44, 438
  Wi-Fi, 61–62
ICS filename extension, 593
identifying
  parts and capabilities of Macs, 20–22
  processor types, 19
iDrive (website), 331
iMac
  about, 9–10
  AirDrop and, 404
Image Capture, 517–518
image styles, 632, 633–634
images
  adding
    information to manually, 524–525
    in Keynote, 676–678
    keywords to, 521–522
  creating
    folders, 526–527
    Memories, 530–531
    slideshows, 531–534
    Smart Albums, 525–526
  deleting, 527–528
  Desktop, 166–168
  digital photography, 515–517
  editing, 537–541
  finding, 531
  hiding, 528
  inserting from, 611–612
  Keyword Manager, 523–524
  mapping, 528–530
  masking in Keynote, Pages and Numbers, 732–734

  modifying in Keynote, Pages and Numbers, 732–736
  moving between folders, 520–521
  organizing library, 521–534
  printing, 541–542
  retrieving using, 518–519
  saving from web, 240–241
  sending in messages, 542–543
  sharing, 296, 301, 541–545
  tagging, 521–523
  transferring to Macs, 517
  unhiding, 528
IMAP (Internet Message Access Protocol), 77–78
importing
  bookmarks, 229–230
  calendar data, 582
  CD audio tracks into Music app, 476–478
  contacts, 558–559
  digital audio files, 478
Inbox button (Calendar), 574
incoming server name, 251
indents, creating, 624–626
information, 27
information window (iTunes Store), 487
initiating
  audio chats, 299–301
  text chats, 297–299
  video chats, 299–301
input, adjusting, 178
inserting
  charts from Numbers, 613–614
  columns in Numbers, 703
  headers in Numbers, 704–706
  images, 613
  media from others sources in Keynote, Pages and Numbers, 730–731
  photos from Photos, 611–612
  predefined shapes in Keynote, 667–669
  rows in Numbers, 703
  tables from Numbers, 613–614
  text boxes in Keynote, 659
installing apps, 158
Instant Alpha feature, 732, 735
Instant Calculation, 711
Instant Wipe function (FileVault), 362
Intego Mac Internet Security X9, 366

Intel processors, 19
interactions, Siri, 49–51
interactive books, 512
interactive charts, 671
Internet connections
  about, 57
  Apple ID, 63–71
  Apple Music, 77
  cellular data modem, 63
  Ethernet, 58–59
  iCloud, 71–76
  setting up
    about, 58–63
    email/social network accounts, 77–81
  wireless, 58, 59–63
Internet Message Access Protocol (IMAP), 77–78
Internet Protocol (IP), 388
Internet radio, 484, 485
Internet resources
  Accessibility features, 187
  Adobe, 244
  Apple compatible devices, 60
  Apple ID, 64
  Apple Store, 19
  Apple Support, 11, 326
  AppZapper, 163
  Backup Scheduler: Time Editor, 337
  Belkin, 350
  Box, 331
  Cheat Sheet, 4
  ClamXAV, 366
  Data Recovery for Mac, 346
  Data Rescue, 346
  DiskWarrior, 346, 434, 436
  Drive Genius, 437
  Dropbox, 266
  encryption, 249
  Firefox, 208
  Google Chrome, 208
  Graphic Node, 738
  Hightail, 266
  iCalShare, 581
  iCloud, 75–76
  iCloud Control Panel 3.0 for Windows, 72

iCloud security overview, 249
iDrive, 331
Intego Mac Internet Security X9, 366
Kensington, 350
Keynote Themes Plus, 738
KeynotePro, 738
Logitech, 296, 299, 534
Maclocks, 350
Mailsmith, 78
Microsoft, 296, 299, 534
New York Times, 63
opening, 210–211
Opera, 208
organizing, 223–234
Parallels, 423
Power Nap feature, 16
searching for, 213–216
SendThisFile, 266
Slack, 249
Softtote Data Recovery Mac, 346
SPAMfighter, 289
SpamSieve, 289
Spring Cleaning, 163
StockLayouts, 738
Syncplicity, 331
Targus, 350
Techtool Pro, 437
Thunderbird, 78
Tryten, 350
Uninstaller, 163
viewing history of, 216–217
viewing in Reader, 218
visiting, 209–217
WhatsApp, 249
inviting people to events, 592–593
iOS devices, books for, 512
IP (Internet Protocol), 388
iSight camera, 299
iTunes, 455. See also Books app; Music; Podcasts; TV app
iTunes Match, 77, 478
iTunes Plus format, 489
iTunes Review, 487
iTunes Store, 469, 485–489
iWork suite, 645

J

Jaguar version, 12
Joint Photographic Experts Group (JPEG), 516
JPEG (Joint Photographic Experts Group), 516
junk email
  about, 284–285
  advanced filter rules, 287–289
  blocked sender rules, 289–290
  filtering, 285–287
justification, adjusting, 620–629
Justify option, 621

K

Kensington (website), 350
keyboard
  about, 36
  arrow keys, 42–43
  cursor control keys, 42–43
  function keys, 36–38
  limitations to, 193–196
  modifier keys, 40–42
  numeric keypad, 42
  special feature keys, 36–38
  typewriter keys, 38–40
Keyboard tab, 38
Keychain option (iCloud), 236
Keynote
  about, 649–650, 727
  adding
    charts, 667–673
    comments, 737–738
    hyperlinks to presentations, 685–686
    media files, 674–678
    movies, 676–678
    photos, 676–678
    shapes, 667–673
    slides, 656–658
    sound, 674–676
    tables, 667–673
    text to shapes, 668
  Adjust Image, 735–736

adjusting
  backgrounds, 666–667
  borders, 666–667
  fonts, 660–663
  photos, 732–736
aligning objects, 669–670
animating text/graphics on slides, 684–685
arranging objects, 669–670
capitalization in, 663
collaborating with Pages, Numbers and, 728–730
controlling presentations remotely, 690–691
copying and pasting, 732
creating
  builds, 682–683
  effects, 680–686
  graphic effects, 682–685
  groups of slides, 678–679
  presentations, 650–658
  text effects, 682–685
  transitions, 680–686
customizing themes using Masters, 686–687
deleting
  hyperlinks, 686
  slides, 680
editing text in Keynote, 659–660
enhancing presentations, 687–694
entering text, 658
exporting presentations, 692–693
finding templates, 738
formatting
  bullets, 665–666
  paragraphs, 664
  text, 660–667
  text boxes, 660–667
inserting
  media from other sources, 730–731
  predefined shapes, 667–669
  text boxes, 659
Instant Alpha feature, 735
manipulating text, 658–667
masking photos, 732–734
navigating, 654–656

opening files, 653–654

preparing for events, 689–690

rearranging slides, 678–680

rehearsing presentations, 688–689

saving presentations, 651–653

selecting themes, 651–653

sharing presentations, 693–694

skipping slides, 680

viewing presentations, 688

Keynote Themes Plus, 738

KeynotePro, 738

keystroke shortcuts, 41, 42

Keyword Manager, 523–524

keywords, adding, 521–522

L

LAN (local area network), 563

Language & Region icon, 178

launching

apps, 128–136

Fast User Switching, 379–380

File Sharing, 408–409

First Aid, 434–436

iCoud data, 326

Macs, 11–12

Media Sharing, 445

Pages in iCloud preferences, 645

Photo Stream, 543

Screen Sharing, 416–417

Screen-Sharing sessions with other Macs, 417–419

Sharing Only accounts, 377–378

Switch Control, 199

Windows, 421–426

Launchpad

deleting apps from, 161

launching apps from, 131–132

Launchpad icon, 131

LCD (liquid crystal display), 10

LDIF file format, 558

leasing modems, 59

legacy Apple ID, 71

Levels adjustment (Photos), 540

library (Music app), 457–458, 478–479

Library button (Books app), 510

Library folder, 86, 87

Light adjustment (Photos), 540

Light Table view (Keynote), 655

line spacing, adjusting, 620–629

LinkedIn/MySpace/Profile option (Contacts), 563

liquid crystal display (LCD), 10

List view, 85, 92, 93, 96 97, 99

listening

to CDs, 474–476

to podcasts, 492–494

to radio, 484–485

to streaming audio, 243

lists

in Reminders, 605

viewing books by, 513

local area network (LAN), 563

locating

events, 595–602

images, 531

podcasts, 491–496

templates in Keynote, Pages and Numbers, 738

your location, 312–313

location, finding your, 312–313

Location Services, accessing, 313

Locations category (Sidebar), 47

lock icon, 62

locking down Macs, 350

logging out, of accounts, 379

Logitech (website), 296, 299, 534

M

Mac mini

about, 9

AirDrop and, 404

microphone, 49

power/sleep indicator light on, 10

Mac Pro

about, 9

AirDrop and, 404

microphone, 49

MacBook, AirDrop and, 404
MacBook Air
  about, 10
  AirDrop and, 404
  Eject key, 438
  Ethernet connections with, 58
  resetting SMC on, 430–431
MacBook Pro
  about, 10
  AirDrop and, 404
  Ethernet connections with, 58
  power/sleep indicator light on, 16
  resetting SMC on, 430–431
Maclocks (website), 350
macOS Catalina, media apps with, 453–454
macOS versions, 12
Macs. *See also specific topics*
  booting from through Thunderbolt cable, 436–437
  identifying parts and capabilities of, 20–22
  locking down, 350
  models, 7–10
  moving backups between, 344–345
  opening files from, 653
  pairing with, 398–399
  restarting, 18
  saving documents on, 645–646
  shutting down, 16–18
  starting
    about, 11–12
    Screen-Sharing sessions with other, 417–419
  transferring digital images to, 517
  turning off, 13–18
  watching TV on, 500–503
Magic Mouse (Apple), 33–34
Magic Move feature (Keynote), 684–685
Magic Trackpad, 8, 34–36
magnification, 45
Mail
  about, 249–250
  accessing email from, 78
  adding
    email accounts to, 250–254
    email addresses to Contacts, 275–276
    email contacts to VIPs list, 276

archiving messages, 292
configuring, 254
deleting messages, 290–291
emptying Trash folder, 292
gathering account information for, 78–79
junk email, 284–290
organizing email, 276–284
reading email, 273–274
receiving email, 271–273
retrieving messages from Trash folder, 291
saving file attachments, 274–275
sending photos in messages, 542–543
sharing
  contacts via, 568
  documents via, 648
viewing file attachments, 274–275
window, 254–257
writing emails, 257–271
Mail My Card option, 568
mailbox folders
  creating, 278–279
  deleting, 280
  organizing email with, 278–280
  storing messages in, 279–280
Mailboxes panel (Mail window), 255
Mailsmith (website), 78
maintenance. *See also* troubleshooting
  about, 427–428, 434
  storage drives, 434–438
malware
  defined, 349
  handling, 365
Managed with Parental Controls account, 369
managing
  apps, 127–164
  devices, 85–86
  files, 107–112
  folders, 107–112
  malware, 365
  presentations remotely in Keynote, 690–691
  tabs, 220–221
  text, 658–667
  windows, 27–32
Map button (Maps app), 314

mapping images, 528–530

Maps
about, 311
asking for directions, 315–322
dropping pins, 320
finding your location, 312–313
navigating, 314–315
sharing location information, 318–320

margins
adjusting, 620–629
defined, 621
defining, 622–624

masking photos in Keynote, Pages and Numbers, 732–734

Masters, customizing themes using, 686–687

Maximum formula, 710

media
about, 443
adding
files in Keynote, 674–678
in Numbers, 721–722
Apple ID and, 443–453
downloading from Music app, 488–489
Family Sharing, 445–453
inserting from other sources in Keynote, Pages and Numbers, 730–731
macOS Catalina, 453–454
Media Sharing, 444–445
Numbers, 697

media player apps, 192

Media Sharing, 444–445

Memories, creating, 530–531

memory card, removing, 519

Memory tab, 20

menu bar
about, 25–26
launching apps from, 134

menu commands, 26

menulets, 25–26

menus
about, 24–25
menu bar, 25–26
using to copy files/folders, 110

merging Apple IDs, 444

mesh Wi-Fi systems, 59

Message (Mail window), 256

Message My Card option, 568

Message Preview list (Mail window), 256

messages
archiving, 292
customizing, 261–266
deleting, 290–291
flagging, 283–284
forwarding, 259–260
retrieving from Trash folder, 291
sending photos in, 542–543
signing, 264–265
storing in mailbox folders, 279–280

Messages. See also FaceTime
about, 293–294
getting started, 294–295
sending
location information via, 319
photos in messages, 542–543
sharing
contacts via, 568
documents via, 648
ways to chat, 296–302
web pages in, 242

microphones
built-in, 49
setting up, 200–201

Microsoft (website), 296, 299, 534

Microsoft Word
filenames in, 108
Home key in, 43
selecting application-specific function keys in, 38

Migration Assistant Introduction dialog, 344

Minimize window button, 46

minimized windows, 130

minimizing
playback controls, 481
windows, 30–31

Minimum formula, 710

Mission Control
moving windows via, 150
opening, 35, 138
setting preferences, 151–152
switching
among apps using, 137
Desktops using, 150

models (Macs), 7–10

modems, leasing, 59

modifier keys, 40–42

modifying

  accounts with Fast User Switching, 381

  alignment, 621

  appearance

    about, 171–175

    of Dock, 45–46

    of tables in Numbers, 703–704

  backgrounds in Keynote, 666–667

  borders in Keynote, 666–667

  colors of user interface, 173–175

  column width in Numbers, 703

  Contacts template, 552–553

  date, 175–178

  description of events, 587–588

  Desktop, 48, 166–168

  display, 171–175

  events, 585–595

  Family Sharing settings, 448

  fonts in Keynote, 660–663

  justification, 620–629

  line spacing, 620–629

  margins, 620–629

  Music preferences, 470–473

  passwords, 351–353

  photos in Keynote, Pages and Numbers, 732–736

  row height in Numbers, 703

  screen resolution, 171–172

  sleep options, 14–16

  sounds, 178–181

  tag color, 105

  text in text boxes, 620

  time, 175–178

  view options, 99–100

  views in App Store, 155

Month layout (Calendar), 575

Month view (Calendar), 586

Mountain Lion version, 12

mouse

  options for, 196–198

  scrolling windows with, 32

  using, 33–34

  using to copy files/folders, 110–111

movies, adding in Keynote, 676–678

Movies folder, 87

moving

  alias icons, 142

  app windows to different Desktops, 150–151

  around documents, 616–617

  backups, 344–345

  calendars

    about, 584

    out of groups, 582–584

  cursors, 39

  events

    about, 594–595

    to other calendars, 591

  files, 86, 111–112

  folders, 86, 111–112

  groups, 584

  to higher folders, 92–93

  maps, 314

  photos

    about, 612–613

    between folders, 520–521

  tabs, 221

  text boxes, 630

  windows with title bar, 28–29

multimedia files, viewing and playing, 243–244

Music

  about, 454, 455–456

  adjusting preferences, 470–473

  burning audio CDs, 482–483

  components of, 456–458

  downloading media from, 488–489

  importing

    CD audio tracks into, 476–478

    digital audio files, 478

  listening to radio, 484–485

  organizing music, 468–470

  playing

    audio with, 474–483

    digital audio files, 479–482

  playlists, 458–468

  searching library, 478–479

  shopping at iTunes Store, 485–489

music, copyright for, 532

Music folder, 87

Music icon, 476
Music Quick Links section, 486
Music Radio, 484–485
Music window (Music app), 458
My Card, 553

N

name, sorting contacts by, 551
naming charts, sheets and tables in Numbers, 720
NAT (Network Address Translation), 388
navigating
  in Books app, 510
  in Finder, 90–93
  in Keynote, 654–656
  in Maps app, 314–315
Navigator view (Keynote), 654, 659
Network Address Translation (NAT), 388
networks
  about, 385–386
  Bluetooth, 395–402
  creating
    wired networks, 386–389
    wireless networks with routers, 390–391
  hazards of wireless, 392
  sharing files/resources on, 403–419
  using, 407–414
New York Times (website), 63
News+, 498
Next button (Music app), 475
Night Shift tab, 172–173
No Access permission, 408
Noise Reduction adjustment (Photos), 541
None option (Keynote), 663
non-volatile random access memory (NVAM),
    resetting, 431
notebook category, of Macs, 8, 14
Notes
  in Books app, 511–512
  sharing contacts via, 568
  web pages in, 242
Notification Center, 182
Notification Center icon, 26
notifications
  about, 181–186
  disabling, 186

receiving, 182–186
  types of, 182
numbered lists, 721
Numbers
  about, 695, 727
  adding
    charts, 718–719
    comments, 737–738
    media, 721–722
    sheets, 702
    tables, 702
    text boxes, 721
  Adjust Image, 735–736
  adjusting
    appearance of tables, 703–704
    photos, 732–736
  appearance of spreadsheets, 720–722
  collaborating with Keynote, Pages and, 728–730
  copying and pasting, 732
  creating
    bulleted lists, 721
    numbered lists, 721
    spreadsheets, 699–701
    spreadsheets with templates, 699–700
  deleting
    data in cells, 718
    sheets, 702
  entering formulas, 710–713
  exporting spreadsheets, 723–724
  finding templates, 738
  formatting
    cells with pop-up menus, 715–717
    cells with sliders/steppers, 714–715
    data entry cells, 713–717
    numbers, 707–709
    text, 707–709
  inserting
    charts/tables from, 613–614
    headers, 704–706
    media from other sources, 730–731
  Instant Alpha feature, 735
  masking photos, 732–734
  naming charts, sheets and tables, 720
  opening files, 700–701
  printing spreadsheets, 722–723
  Quick Formula, 710–713

Numbers *(continued)*
  removing tables, 702
  resizing
    columns, 704–706
    rows, 704–706
    tables, 703
  sharing
    files directly, 725
    spreadsheets, 722–725
  sorting data, 717
  spreadsheet components, 696–698
  typing
    data into tables, 706–720
    formulas, 710–712
  using functions, 712–713
  working with spreadsheets, 701–706
numbers, formatting in Numbers, 707–709
Numbers '09 file format, 724
numeric keypad, 42
NVAM (non-volatile random access memory),
  resetting, 431
NYTimes category (Apple Books), 507

O

objects
  aligning in Keynote, 669–670
  arranging
    about, 640–641
    in Keynote, 669–670
  wrapping text around, 641–642
off-site backups, 331
one-finger drag gesture, 36
online calendars, subscribing to, 580–581
Opacity option (Keynote), 667
opening
  apps, 132
  documents, 134–136
  files
    in Keynote, 653–654
    in Numbers, 700–701
    stored in Stacks, 146
  Finder, 90
  Finder windows, 47
  folders, 90

iTunes Store, 486
  minimized windows, 31
  Mission Control, 35, 138
  PDFs, 510
  System Preferences window, 301
  tabs, 91
  websites, 210–211
  Zip files, 113
Opera (website), 208
operating system, 12
operators, in Numbers formulas, 711
optical disc drive, 439
ordinary playlists, 458, 459–461
organizing
  apps into folders, 44–45
  contacts by company name, 550–551
  email, 276–284
  files into folders, 44–45
  folders, 93–101
  multiple desktops with Spaces, 148–152
  music, 468–470
  Photo library, 521–534
  websites, 223–234
OS X Mavericks, 83–84
outgoing server name, 251
Outline view (Keynote), 655, 659
output, adjusting, 178
Overview tab, 20

P

Page Up/Down keys, 32, 43
Pages
  about, 607–608, 727
  adding
    charts, 635–636
    comments, 737–738
    footers, 626–629
    headers, 626–629
    pages to documents, 614–616
    sections to documents, 614–616
    shapes, 638–640
    tables, 637–638
    text, 617
  Adjust Image, 735–736

adjusting
  alignment, 621
  justification, 620–629
  line spacing, 620–629
  margins, 620–629
  photos, 732–736
  text in text boxes, 620
arranging objects, 640–641
choosing templates, 608–609
collaborating with Keynote, Numbers and, 728–730
copying and pasting, 732
creating
  charts, 635–642
  indents, 624–626
  tables, 635–642
  tabs, 624–626
  text boxes, 629–630
defining margins, 622–623
deleting text, 618
document templates, 608–617
editing text, 617–618
enhancing documents, 642–645
exporting to different file formats, 646–648
finding and replacing text, 644–645
finding templates, 738
formatting text, 618–620
hiding thumbnails, 615
image style, 633–634
inserting
  charts from Numbers, 613–614
  images, 613
  media from other sources, 730–731
  photos from Photos, 611–612
  tables from Numbers, 613–614
Instant Alpha feature, 735
masking photos, 732–734
moving
  around documents, 616–617
  photos, 612–613
  text boxes, 630
printing documents, 646
rearranging text, 618

removing charts, 635–636
replacing
  placeholder photos/graphics, 611–614
  placeholder text, 610–611
resizing
  photos, 612–613
  text boxes, 630–631
saving documents, 645–646
setting units of measurement, 623
spell-checking documents, 642–644
styles, 631–635
  text and, 610
text box style, 634–635
turning on in iCloud preferences, 645
uniting text boxes, 631
using paragraph styles, 632–633
working with text, 617–629
wrapping text around objects, 641–642
Pages '09 files, 647
pairing Bluetooth devices, 398–400
paragraph styles, 632–633
Paragraph Styles menu, 662
paragraphs, formatting in Keynote, 664
Parallels, 423
parameter (PRAM), resetting, 431
Parental Controls
  about, 371–377
  preferences for, 372
passwords
  about, 350–351
  applying protection, 353–356
  changing, 351–353
  email accounts, 251
  for Mac, 12
  Mail, 78
  tracking using AutoFill, 234–236
  wireless network, 62
Pause button (Music app), 475
paying for purchases with Apple Pay, 308–309
PDF files
  about, 647, 724
  opening, 510
  viewing, 243–244

peripheral devices
    about, 385–386
    Bluetooth, 395–402
    printers, 393–395
permissions, for Location Services, 313
personal information, storing, 234–239
personalizing
    about, 165–166
    accessibility features, 187–198
    appearance, 171–175
    choosing Desktop image, 166–168
    colors of user interface, 173–175
    date, 175–178
    display, 171–175
    enabling Switch Control, 199
    function keys, 38
    messages, 261–266
    Night Shift, 172–173
    notifications, 181–186
    screen resolution, 171–172
    screen saver, 168–170
    sounds, 178–181
    Speakable Items feature, 199–203
    Split-View mode, 186–187
    System Preference window layout, 170
    themes using Masters, 686–687
    time, 175–178
phishing, 284, 349
Phonetic First/Last Name field (Contacts), 558
photo attachments, sending, 266–270
Photo Booth
    capturing photos with, 534–537
    deleting photos, 536
Photo Browser, 268–269
Photo Stream, 543–545
photos
    adding
        information to manually, 524–525
        in Keynote, 676–678
        keywords to, 521–522
    creating
        folders, 526–527
        Memories, 530–531
        slideshows, 531–534
        Smart Albums, 525–526

    deleting, 527–528
    Desktop, 166–168
    digital photography, 515–517
    editing, 537–541
    finding, 531
    hiding, 528
    inserting from, 611–612
    Keyword Manager, 523–524
    mapping, 528–530
    masking in Keynote, Pages and Numbers, 732–734
    modifying in Keynote, Pages and Numbers, 732–736
    moving between folders, 520–521
    organizing library, 521–534
    printing, 541–542
    retrieving using, 518–519
    saving from web, 240–241
    sending in messages, 542–543
    sharing, 296, 301, 541–545
    tagging, 521–523
    transferring to Macs, 517
    unhiding, 528
Photos
    about, 454, 515
    adding
        information to photos manually, 524–525
        keywords, 521–522
    creating
        folders, 526–527
        Memories, 530–531
        slideshows, 531–534
        Smart Albums, 525–526
    deleting photos/albums/folders, 527–528
    digital photography, 515–517
    editing photos, 537–541
    finding images, 531
    hiding photos, 528
    inserting photos from, 611–612
    Keyword Manager, 523–524
    mapping images, 528–530
    moving photos between folders, 520=521
    organizing library, 521–534
    printing photos, 541–542
    retrieving photos using, 518–519
    sending photos in messages, 542–543
    sharing photos, 541–545

tagging images, 521–523
transferring digital images to Macs, 517
unhiding photos, 528
pictures
adding
information to manually, 524–525
in Keynote, 676–678
keywords to, 521–522
creating
folders, 526–527
Memories, 530–531
slideshows, 531–534
Smart Albums, 525–526
deleting, 527–528
Desktop, 166–168
digital photography, 515–517
editing, 537–541
finding, 531
hiding, 528
inserting from, 611–612
Keyword Manager, 523–524
mapping, 528–530
masking in Keynote, Pages and Numbers, 732–734
modifying in Keynote, Pages and Numbers, 732–736
moving between folders, 520–521
organizing library, 521–534
printing, 541–542
retrieving using, 518–519
saving from web, 240–241
sending in messages, 542–543
sharing, 296, 301, 541–545
tagging, 521–523
transferring to Macs, 517
unhiding, 528
Pictures folder, 87
pinch gesture, 35
pins, dropping in maps app, 320
pixels, 515–516
placeholder photos/graphics, replacing, 611–614
placeholder text, replacing, 610–611
placing scales on maps, 314
plain text files, 647
playback controls, Podcasts app, 492
Playback preferences (Podcast app), 495
playing

audio files, 676
audio with Music app, 474–483
digital audio files, 479–482
multimedia files, 243–244
Music Radio, 484–485
podcasts, 491–496
playlists
about, 458–459
deleting, 467
Genius, 466–467
Music app, 458
ordinary, 458, 459–461
renaming, 464
Smart Playlists, 458, 461–465
Plist, 337
plug and play, 63, 386
Podcasts
about, 454, 491
exploring podcasts, 492
finding podcasts, 491–496
listening to podcasts, 492–494
playing podcasts, 491–496
setting preferences, 494–496
watching podcasts, 492–494
point-and-click, 35
POP (Post Office Protocol), 77–78
pop-up menu (iTunes Store information screen), 487
pop-up menus method, 714, 715–717
Post Office Protocol (POP), 77–78
PowerNap feature, 16, 338
power/sleep indicator light, 16
PRAM (parameter), resetting, 431
predefined slides, 657
preferences
Books app, 512
Finder, 88–89
iCloud, 72–74, 645
Mission Control, 151–152
Music app, 470–473, 476
Parental Controls, 372
Podcast app, 494–496
setting in News app, 499–500
sharing, 405–406
Spotlight Search, 120–121
for tags, 105

preferences pane (Time Machine), 337

preparing for events in Keynote, 689–690

presentations

  adding hyperlinks to in Keynote, 685–686

  controlling remotely in Keynote, 690–691

  creating, 650–658

  enhancing in Keynote, 687–694

  exporting in Keynote, 692–693

  rehearsing in Keynote, 688–689

  saving in KeyNote, 651–653

  sharing in Keynote, 693–694

  viewing in Keynote, 688

Preview app, 101

Print dialog, 26, 416

printing

  Calendar files, 601–602

  choosing printers, 393–395

  connecting printers, 393–395

  contacts, 570–571

  documents, 646

  photos, 541–542

  sharing printers, 415–416

  spreadsheets in Numbers, 722–723

  web pages, 242–243

privacy

  calendars and, 577

  selecting settings for, 366–368

Privacy limit (Parental Controls), 372

privileges, 407–408

processors, 19–20

Product formula, 710

projects, creating, 545

proofreading, 644

protecting web-browsing privacy, 236–238

Public folder, 87, 408

publishers, following in News app, 498

Purchase Sharing, 448, 449

purging, 157

Q

quad-core i7 processor, 19

quad-core Xeon processor, 19

Quick Events, 585–586

Quick Formula (Numbers), 710–713

Quick Links section (App Store), 154

Quick Look, viewing file contents with, 100–101

quick playlists, 460

quitting apps, 139–141

R

radio, listening to, 484–485

Radio option (Apple Music), 457

random play (Music app), 475

range extender, 391

RAT (Remote Access Trojan), 365

Ratings and Reviews (iTunes Store information screen), 487

Raw files, 517

Read Only permission, 408

Read & Write permission, 408, 409

readability, in Books app, 511

Reader tool (Safari), 212, 217–218

reading

  email, 273–274

  news, 496–498

  by screen light, 510–512

Reading list, creating, 230–232

Read-Only format, 115

Read-Write format, 115

Ready, Set, Play section (App Store), 154

rearranging

  bookmarks, 228–229

  icons on Dock, 146–147

  slides in Keynote, 678–680

  tabs, 221

  text, 618

receiving

  FaceTime calls, 305–306

  notifications, 182–186

Recent Items (Apple menu), launching apps from, 132–133

recovering data from within apps, 339–340

Recovery Boot, 436

Recovery Disk, 437–438

recurring events, creating, 588–589

Red Eye adjustment (Photos), 540

redeeming, in iTunes Store, 488

Reflection option (Keynote), 667

rehearsing presentations in Keynote, 688–689

Related option (Contacts), 563

Related tab (iTunes Store information screen), 487
Reload tool (Safari), 212
Remember icon, 3
Reminders
  about, 602
  creating tasks, 602–605
  deleting tasks, 604
  editing tasks, 604
  making lists, 605
  web pages in, 242
Remote Access Trojan (RAT), 365
Remote app, downloading, 481
remote storage, 328
removable devices
  connecting, 85
  ejecting, 85
  removing, 86
removable media, deletion from, 346
removing
  accounts
    about, 381–382
    from shared folders, 412–413
  albums, 527–528
  alias icons, 143, 162
  app icons, 130
  bookmarks, 228–229
  calendars, 584–585
  charts, 635–636
  columns in Numbers, 703
  contacts, 562
  conversations, 301–302
  data in cells in Numbers, 718
  events, 595
  files, 86, 115–117, 123–125
  folders, 86, 115–117, 123–125, 527–528
  groups, 567–568, 584–585
  hyperlinks in Keynote, 686
  icons from Dock, 147
  jammed CDs/DVDs, 438–439
  mailbox folders, 280
  memory card, 519
  menulets, 26
  messages, 290–291
  photos, 527–528, 536

playlists, 467
removable devices, 86
rows in Numbers, 703
saved stories in News app, 499
sheets in Numbers, 702
slides in Keynote, 680
smart mailboxes, 282
songs from ordinary playlists, 461
tables in Numbers, 702
tasks in Reminders, 604
text, 618
user setting files, 162–163
renaming
  bookmarks, 229
  calendars, 584–585
  files, 86, 108–109
  folders, 86, 108–109, 229
  groups, 584–585
  playlists, 464
  Zip files, 113
repairing
  hardware, 17
  storage devices, 434–438
repeat-selection play (Music app), 475
replacing
  placeholder photos/graphics, 611–614
  placeholder text, 610–611
replying, to messages, 259–260
resetting
  non-volatile random access memory (NVAM), 431
  parameter (PRAM), 431
  System Management Controller (SMC), 430–431
resizing
  in Books app, 511
  column width, 96–97
  columns in Numbers, 704–706
  corners in Numbers, 703
  handles in Numbers, 703
  photos, 612–613
  rows in Numbers, 704–706
  tables in Numbers, 703
  text boxes, 630–631
  windows, 29–30
resolution, 516

resources
  Internet
    Accessibility features, 187
    Adobe, 244
    Apple compatible devices, 60
    Apple ID, 64
    Apple Store, 19
    Apple Support, 11, 326
    AppZapper, 163
    Backup Scheduler: Time Editor, 337
    Belkin, 350
    Box, 331
    Cheat Sheet, 4
    ClamXAV, 366
    Data Recovery for Mac, 346
    Data Rescue, 346
    DiskWarrior, 346, 434, 436
    Drive Genius, 437
    Dropbox, 266
    encryption, 249
    Firefox, 208
    Google Chrome, 208
    Graphic Node, 738
    Hightail, 266
    iCalShare, 581
    iCloud, 75–76
    iCloud Control Panel 3.0 for Windows, 72
    iCloud security overview, 249
    iDrive, 331
    Intego Mac Internet Security X9, 366
    Kensington, 350
    Keynote Themes Plus, 738
    KeynotePro, 738
    Logitech, 296, 299, 534
    Maclocks, 350
    Mailsmith, 78
    Microsoft, 296, 299, 534
    New York Times, 63
    opening, 210–211
    Opera, 208
    organizing, 223–234
    Parallels, 423
    Power Nap feature, 16
    searching for, 213–216

    SendThisFile, 266
    Slack, 249
    Softtote Data Recovery Mac, 346
    SPAMfighter, 289
    SpamSieve, 289
    Spring Cleaning, 163
    StockLayouts, 738
    Syncplicity, 331
    Targus, 350
    Techtool Pro, 437
    Thunderbird, 78
    Tryten, 350
    Uninstaller, 163
    viewing history of, 216–217
    viewing in Reader, 218
    visiting, 209–217
    WhatsApp, 249
  sharing on networks, 403–419
responding, to invitations, 594
restarting, 17, 18
restore application (Time Machine), 337
restoring
  backup files, 600–601
  data, 325–348
  data-recovery programs, 345–346
  entire backup, 342–343
restrictions, TV app, 503
Retina display, 10
Retouch adjustment (Photos), 540
retrieving
  email, 271–273
  files
    about, 337–342
    from Trash, 124
  folders
    about, 337–342
    from Trash, 124
  messages from Trash folder, 291
  photos using Photos, 518–519
Return key, 40
Rewind button (Music app), 475
Rich Text Format files, 647
right-clicking mouse, 33
rotate gesture, 35

rotating maps, 315
routers
    about, 388
    abouts, 362
    creating wireless networks with, 390–391
rule of thirds, 538
Rulers (Numbers), 696
rules, automatically organizing email with, 282–283
running
    First Aid, 434–436
    Windows, 421–426

S

Safari
    about, 207
    browsing websites, 208–223
    downloading files, 244–246
    organizing on, 223–234
    playing multimedia files, 243–244
    privacy of information, 234–238
    saving web pages, 238–241
    setting home page, 222–223
    sharing web pages, 238–239, 241–243
    storing personal info, 234–238
    tools, 211–213
    using extensions, 246–247
    viewing multimedia files, 243–244
Safe Mode, booting up in, 431–433
Satellite button (Maps app), 314
Save As command, creating folders using, 102–104
Save command, creating folders using, 102–104
Save dialog, 26
Save Image As option (Photo Booth), 537
saving
    conversations, 301–302
    documents, 645–646
    file attachments, 274–275
    multiple versions of documents, 104
    presentations in Keynote, 651–653
    stories in News app, 498–499
    web pages, 238–241
scales, placing on maps, 314
screen light, reading by, 510–512
screen resolution, changing, 171–172

screen saver, 15, 168–170
Screen Sharing
    about, 296
    enabling, 416–417
    starting sessions with other Macs, 417–419
Screen Time app, 450
screenshot, 40
scroll bars, 32
scroll gesture, 35
scrolling
    with mouse, 34
    windows, 32
Search and Address tool (Safari), 212
Search button
    Books app, 511
    Calendar, 574
search engine
    about, 214
    switching default, 215–216
searching
    contacts, 561
    for events, 597–598
    files, 117–123
    Music library, 478–479
    through email, 277–278
    tips for, 215
    within web pages, 223
    for websites, 213–216
sections, adding to documents, 614–616
sectors, 345
secured wireless network, 62
security
    about, 349
    of apps, 163–164
    creating multiple accounts, 368–371
    encrypting data with FileVault, 358–362
    firewalls, 362–366
    locking down Mac, 350
    Parental Controls, 371–382
    passwords, 350–356
    selecting privacy settings, 366–368
    tips for, 383
    Touch ID, 356–357
    wireless networks, 63

selecting
  application-specific function keys, 38
  Desktop image, 166–168
  items in Finder, 94
  printers, 393–395
  privacy settings, 366–368
  templates, 608–609
  themes in Keynote, 651–653
  wireless router, 59–61
Selective Color adjustment (Photos), 541
selective play (Music app), 475
sending
  contacts, 568
  file attachments, 266–270
  photo attachments, 266–270
  photos in messages, 542–543
SendThisFile (website), 266
Series tab (Format pane), 671, 719
server name, 78–79, 251
servers, accessing contacts from other, 559–560
Service tab, 20
setting(s)
  alerts for events, 590–591
  Family Sharing, 448
  Finder preferences, 88–89
  Mission Control preferences, 151–152
  Podcast app preferences, 494–496
  preferences
    in News app, 499–500
    for Spotlight Search, 120
  privacy, 366–368
  Safari home page, 222–223
  tag preferences, 105
  units of measurement, 623
setup
  Boot Camp Assistant, 423–426
  Contacts, 550–560
  email account, 77–81
  FileVault, 358–361
  Internet connections, 58–63
  Messages account, 294
  microphones, 200–201
  social network accounts, 77–81
  Speakable Items, 202–203
  Time Machine, 332–336
  Touch ID, 357

Setup icon (Keynote), 688
Shadow option (Keynote), 667
shapes
  adding
    about, 638–640
    in Keynote, 667–673
    text to in Keynote, 668
  Numbers, 697
Share tool (Safari), 212
sharing
  Apple IDs, 444
  calendars, 598–600
  contacts, 568–571
  files
    about, 301
    directly in Numbers, 725
    on networks, 403–419
  location information, 318–320
  photo streams, 544–545
  photos, 296, 301, 541–545
  presentations in Keynote, 693–694
  printers, 415–416
  resources on networks, 403–419
  spreadsheets in Numbers, 722–725
  stories in News app, 498–499
  through Bluetooth, 400–402
  web pages, 238–239, 241–243
Sharing Only account, 369, 377–378
Sharing Preferences, 405–406
Sharpen adjustment (Photos), 541
Sheet tabs (Numbers), 696
shopping
  in App Store, 153–156
  for books at Apple Books, 507–509
  at iTunes Store, 485–489
shortcut commands, 38
shortcut menus. See contextual menu
shortcuts, keystroke, 41, 42
Show Bookmarks tool (Safari), 212
Show Sidebar tool (Safari), 212
showing
  address fields, 265–266
  favorites in Top Sites, 232–234
  folder contents, 92
  tags in Sidebar, 105
Shuffle button (Music app), 475

shutting down
    apps, 139–140
    frozen programs, 428–430
    hung-up programs, 428–430
    Macs, 16–18
Sidebar
    about, 84, 229
    displaying tags in, 105
    in Finder, 47
    Music app, 457–458, 468–469
signing in, to FaceTime, 303
signing messages, 264–265
SIM card, 63
Sina Weibo option (Contacts), 563
single-clicking mouse, 33
Siri
    about, 48–49
    commands, 51–52
    configuring, 53
    empowering, 53–54
    interactions with, 49–51
six-core Xeon processor, 19
skipping
    files during backup, 336–337
    slides in Keynote, 680
Slack (website), 249
Sleep mode
    file sharing in, 413
    putting Macs into, 13–16
Slide Only view (Keynote), 655, 659
sliders
    formatting cells with in Numbers, 714–715
    method, 714
slides
    adding, 656–658
    animating text/graphics on in Keynote, 684–685
    creating groups of in Keynote, 678–679
    deleting in Keynote, 680
    rearranging in Keynote, 678–680
    skipping in Keynote, 680
slideshows, creating, 531–534
Small Caps option (Keynote), 663
Smart Albums, creating, 525–526
Smart Folders, 121–123
Smart Groups

adding contacts automatically with, 565–567
    creating from search results, 567
    editing, 567
smart mailboxes
    automatically organizing email with, 280–282
    creating, 280–281
    deleting, 282
Smart Playlists
    about, 458, 461
    creating, 463–464
    deleting, 467
    editing, 465
    tagging songs, 461–463
SMC (System Management Controller), resetting, 430–431
Snow Leopard version, 12
social networks, setting up accounts, 77–81
Softtote Data Recovery Mac, 346
software. See apps
solid state drive (SSD), 85
songs
    adding to ordinary playlists, 460
    deleting from ordinary playlists, 461
    iTunes Store information screen, 487
    tagging, 461–463
sorting
    books, 513
    contacts by name, 551
    data in Numbers, 717
sound, adding in Keynote, 674–676
Sound Check (Music app), 476
Sound Effects tab, 179–181
Sound Enhancer (Music app), 476
sounds, 178–181, 182
Spaces
    about, 148
    organizing multiple desktops with, 148–152
spacing, 621
SPAMfighter (website), 289
SpamSieve (website), 289
Speakable Items feature
    about, 199–200
    setting up
        microphones, 200–201
        Speakable Items, 202–203

speaker controls (Podcasts app), 493

special feature keys, 36–38

speed

of ordinary networks, 400

of wired networks, 388

of wireless routers, 60–61

spell-checking documents, 270–271, 642–644

"spinning beach ball of death," 428

Split-View mode, 186–187

Spotlight Search

about, 117

launching apps from, 134

preferences, 120–121

Smart Folders, 121–123

using, 118–120

Spotlight Search icon, 26

spreadsheets. *See also* Numbers

adding in Numbers, 702

appearance of in Numbers, 720–722

creating

in Numbers, 699–701

with templates, 699–700

deleting in Numbers, 702

exporting in Numbers, 723–724

naming in Numbers, 720

printing in Numbers, 722–723

sharing in Numbers, 722–725

working with, 701–706

Spring Cleaning (website), 163

spring-loaded folders feature, 111

SSD (solid state drive), 85

Stack icon, 146

Stacks

creating on Dock, 145

opening files stored in, 146

Standard account, 369

standards, 390

Start Case option (Keynote), 663

starting

Fast User Switching, 379–380

File Sharing, 408–409

First Aid, 434–436

iCloud data, 326

Media Sharing, 445

Pages in iCloud preferences, 645

Photo Stream, 543

Screen Sharing, 416–417

Sharing Only accounts, 377–378

Switch Control, 199

Windows, 421–426

startup, troubleshooting, 430–433

Status Bar, 470

steppers method, 714–715

StockLayouts, 738

storage devices, repairing, 434–438

Storage tab, 20

Stores limit (Parental Control), 372

stories, saving/sharing in News app, 498–499

storing

alias icons, 143

backups

off-site, 331

on USB flash drives, 330–331

bookmarks in folders, 226–228

messages in mailbox folders, 279–280

personal information, 234–239

streaming audio, listening to, 243

styles, 631–635

subscribing, to online calendars, 580–581

subscription apps, 153

Sum formula, 710

Support tab, 20

swipe gesture, 35

swiping, with mouse, 34

switch, 388

Switch Control, enabling, 199

switching

between accounts, 379–381

between apps, 130, 137–139

default search engine, 215–216

Desktops, 150

between folders, 91–92

between tabs, 221

views

in Calendar, 576

in Finder, 93

in Maps app, 315

syncing
  defined, 71
  with other devices, 74–75
Syncplicity (website), 331
System folder, 86–87
System Information, 22
System Management Controller (SMC), resetting, 430–431
System Preferences
  about, 165–166
  opening window, 301
System Report window, 21
system software, updating, 158–159

T

Tab key, 40
tabbed browsing
  about, 218
  creating tabs, 218–220
  managing tabs, 220–221
Table of Contents button (Books app), 510
Table tab (Numbers), 704, 720
tables
  adding
    about, 637–638
    in keynote, 667–673
    in Keynote, 672–673
    in Numbers, 702
  changing appearance of in Numbers, 703–704
  creating, 635–642
  inserting from Numbers, 613–614
  naming in Numbers, 720
  Numbers, 696
  removing in Numbers, 702
  resizing in Numbers, 703
  typing data into in Numbers, 706–720
tabs
  about, 85
  creating, 218–220, 624–626
  managing, 220–221
  working with, 90–91
tagging
  images, 521–523
  songs, 461–463

tags
  about, 83–84, 105
  of files and folders, 105–107
  setting preferences, 105
Tags button, 105
Tags category (Sidebar), 47
Target Mode, 436–437
Targus (website), 350
tasks
  creating in Reminders, 602–605
  deleting in Reminders, 604
  editing in Reminders, 604
Technical Stuff icon, 3
Techtool Pro (website), 437
Telephone Number option (Contacts), 563
templates
  choosing, 608–609
  creating spreadsheets with, 699–700
  document, 608–617
  finding in Keynote, Pages and Numbers, 738
Tencent Weibo option (Contacts), 563
text
  adding
    about, 617
    to shapes in Keynote, 668
  adjusting in text boxes, 620
  animating on slides in Keynote, 684–685
  creating effects in Keynote, 682–685
  deleting, 618
  editing
    about, 617–618
    in Keynote, 659–660
  entering in Keynote, 658
  finding and replacing, 644–645
  formatting
    about, 618–620
    in Keynote, 660–667
    in Numbers, 707–709
  manipulating, 658–667
  Numbers, 697
  rearranging, 618
  working with, 617–629
  wrapping around objects, 641–642
text box styles, 632, 634–635

text boxes
  about, 610, 620
  adding in Numbers, 721
  creating, 629–630
  formatting in Keynote, 660–667
  inserting in Keynote, 659
  moving, 630
  resizing, 630–631
  uniting, 631
text chatting, 296, 297–299
text file, 558
Text tab (Numbers), 704
themes
  choosing in Keynote, 651–653
  customizing using Masters, 686–687
3D button (Maps app), 315
3D charts, 671
thumbnails, hiding, 615
Thunderbird (website), 78
Thunderbolt cable, booting from other Macs through, 436–437
Thunderbolt port, 8, 329, 386
time, changing, 175–178
Time Capsule, 329
Time Limits limit (Parental Controls), 372
Time Machine
  about, 332
  backing up with, 332–343
  how it works, 338
  setting up, 332–336
Tip icon, 3
title bar, moving windows with, 28–29
Title Case option (Keynote), 663
Today button (Calendar), 574
toolbar
  about, 84
  Calendar, 574
  Mail window, 254
  Music app, 468
  Numbers, 696
tools, Safari, 211–213
Top Authors category (Apple Books), 507
Top Charts category (Apple Books), 507
Top Free Games and Apps section (App Store), 154

Top Paid Games and Apps section (App Store), 154
Top Sites tool (Safari), 212, 232–234
Top Songs section, 486
Touch Bar, 11
Touch ID
  about, 11, 65, 356
  setting up, 357
  using, 357
trackball, 34
tracking passwords using AutoFill, 234–236
trackpad
  operating, 34–36
  options for, 196–198
  scrolling windows with, 32
  switching Desktops using, 150
  using to copy files/folders, 110–111
transferring digital images to Macs, 517
Transit button (Maps app), 314
transitions, creating in Keynote, 680–686
Trash folder
  emptying, 124–125, 292, 383, 434
  retrieving
    files from, 124
    folders from, 124
    messages from, 291
Trash icon, 44, 123, 438
traveling, with Macs, 17
Trojan horses, 349
troubleshooting. *See also* maintenance
  about, 427–428
  CDs, 438–439
  connections with Bluetooth-enabled devices, 400
  data recovery, 345–346
  DVDs, 438–439
  purchases in App Store, 157
  shutting down frozen/hung-up programs, 428–430
  startup, 430–433
  storage drives, 434–438
Try It Free button (Apple Music), 457
Tryten (website), 350
TSV file format, 724
turning off
  FileVault, 361–362
  Macs, 13–18

Media Sharing, 445
notifications, 186
turning on
Fast User Switching, 379–380
File Sharing, 408–409
First Aid, 434–436
iCoud data, 326
Media Sharing, 445
Pages in iCloud preferences, 645
Photo Stream, 543
Screen Sharing, 416–417
Sharing Only accounts, 377–378
Switch Control, 199
Windows, 421–426
TV app, 500–503
Twitter Profile option (Contacts), 563
2D charts, 671
two-factor authentication, 65–66
two-finger double-tap gesture, 36
two-finger tap gesture, 36
typewriter keys, 38–40
typing
characters, 39–40
data into tables in Numbers, 706–720
formulas in Numbers, 710–712

U

UI (user interface)
about, 23–24
changing colors for, 173–175
desktop, 43–48
dialogs, 24–25, 26–27
help, 54–56
keyboard, 36–43
menu bar, 25–26
menu commands, 26
menus, 24–26
mouse, 33–34
Siri, 48–54
trackpad, 34–36
windows, 24–25, 27–32
unfollowing channels in News app, 498

unhiding photos, 528
Uniform Resource Locator (URL), 209
Uninstaller (website), 163
uninstallers, 433
uninstalling apps, 160–163, 433
uniting text boxes, 631
units of measurement, setting, 623
unpairing devices, 399
unpinch gesture, 35
updating
apps, 158–159
system software, 158–159
uploading, 244
URL (Uniform Resource Locator), 209
USB flash drives, 330–331
USB port, 8, 329
USB Video Class (UVC), 299
USB-to-Ethernet adapter, 58
user accounts, adding, 369–371
user interface (UI)
about, 23–24
changing colors for, 173–175
desktop, 43–48
dialogs, 24–25, 26–27
help, 54–56
keyboard, 36–43
menu bar, 25–26
menu commands, 26
menus, 24–26
mouse, 33–34
Siri, 48–54
trackpad, 34–36
windows, 24–25, 27–32
username
email accounts, 250
for Mac, 12
Mail, 78
users
removing settings files, 162–163
for shared folders, 409–413
Users folder, 87
Utilities folder, 93
UVC (USB Video Class), 299

V

vCard file format, 558, 559, 569
verifying
  email addresses, 287
  events for specific dates, 596–597
  hard drive, 436
  for today's events, 596
versions, macOS, 12
Versions feature, 104, 342
video chats, 296, 299–301
Video Download Quality (Music app), 476
Video Playback Quality (Music app), 476
View menu, 26, 315
View Options window, 99–100
viewing
  active apps, 129
  app windows, 130
  books, 513
  cards in Contacts, 551
  contacts, 550–551
  events, 585
  file attachments, 274–275
  file contents with Quick Look, 100–101
  file extensions, 108
  folders, 93–101
  minimized windows, 130
  multimedia files, 243–244
  PDF files, 243–244
  presentations in Keynote, 688
  website history, 216–217
  websites in Reader, 218
views
  Books app, 506
  Calendar, 575, 586
  changing
    in App Store, 155
    options for, 99–100
  Column, 97–98, 99
  Finder, 93
  Gallery, 98, 99
  Icon, 94–96, 99
  Keynote, 654–655
  List, 96–97, 99
  Music app, 468

Quick Look, 100–101
switching
  in Calendar, 576
  in Maps app, 315
Views button (Calendar), 574
Vignette adjustment (Photos), 541
VIPs list, adding email contacts to, 276
virtual assistant, 49
vision, Accessibility features for, 188–191
Voiceover option, 676
VoiceOver option, 188, 676
volume, adjusting, 178
Volume Slider (Music app), 474

W

waking sleeping Macs, 16
Warning icon, 4
watching
  podcasts, 492–494
  TV on Macs, 500–503
web browsing. *See* Safari
Web limit (Parental Controls), 372
web pages
  printing, 242–243
  saving, 238–241
  searching within, 223
  sharing, 238–239, 241–243
web-browsing privacy, protecting, 236–238
websites
  Accessibility features, 187
  Adobe, 244
  Apple compatible devices, 60
  Apple ID, 64
  Apple Store, 19
  Apple Support, 11, 326
  AppZapper, 163
  Backup Scheduler: Time Editor, 337
  Belkin, 350
  Box, 331
  Cheat Sheet, 4
  ClamXAV, 366
  Data Recovery for Mac, 346
  Data Rescue, 346
  DiskWarrior, 346, 434, 436

Drive Genius, 437
Dropbox, 266
encryption, 249
Firefox, 208
Google Chrome, 208
Graphic Node, 738
Hightail, 266
iCalShare, 581
iCloud, 75–76
iCloud Control Panel 3.0 for Windows, 72
iCloud security overview, 249
iDrive, 331
Intego Mac Internet Security X9, 366
Kensington, 350
Keynote Themes Plus, 738
KeynotePro, 738
Logitech, 296, 299, 534
Maclocks, 350
Mailsmith, 78
Microsoft, 296, 299, 534
New York Times, 63
opening, 210–211
Opera, 208
organizing, 223–234
Parallels, 423
Power Nap feature, 16
searching for, 213–216
SendThisFile, 266
Slack, 249
Softtote Data Recovery Mac, 346
SPAMfighter, 289
SpamSieve, 289
Spring Cleaning, 163
StockLayouts, 738
Syncplicity, 331
Targus, 350
Techtool Pro, 437
Thunderbird, 78
Tryten, 350
Uninstaller, 163
viewing history of, 216–217
viewing in Reader, 218
visiting, 209–217
WhatsApp, 249

websprinter drivers, 393
Wedges tab (Format pane), 672, 719
Week layout (Calendar), 575
Week view (Calendar), 586
WEP (Wired Equivalent Privacy), 392
WhatsApp (website), 249
White Balance adjustment (Photos), 540
Wi-Fi icon, 61–62
Wi-Fi Protected Access 2 (WPA2), 392
Wi-Fi-Protected Access (WPA), 392
windows
    about, 24–25
    About This Mac, 20
    Books app, 506
    closing, 30
    dragging, 151
    Episode (Podcasts app), 493
    Finder, 47
    full-screen view, 31
    hiding, 130
    Mail, 254–257
    managing, 27–32
    minimizing, 30–31, 130
    moving with title bar, 28–29
    Music, 458
    resizing, 29–30
    scrolling, 32
    System Report, 21
    View Options, 99–100
    zooming, 31
Windows (Microsoft)
    about, 421–422
    Boot Camp, 423–426
    bring your own device (BYOD), 422–423
    running, 421–426
Wired Equivalent Privacy (WEP), 392
wired networks, creating, 386–389
wireless (Wi-Fi) connection
    about, 58, 59–63
    creating with routers, 390–391
    hazards of, 392
wireless router, choosing, 59–61
wireless standard, 60
Word Count tool (Pages), 616, 617

Word files, 647

WPA (Wi-Fi-Protected Access), 392

WPA2 (Wi-Fi Protected Access 2), 392

wrapping text around objects, 641–642

Write Only permission, 408

writing emails, 257–271

Y

Year layout (Calendar), 575

Z

Zip files, creating, 113–114

Zoom button, 31

Zoom option, 188

Zoom tool (Pages), 616

zooming

  maps, 314

  windows, 31

About the Authors

Joe Hutsko: Joe is the author of *Green Gadgets For Dummies, Flip Video For Dummies* (with Drew Davidson), and *iPhone All-in-One For Dummies* (with Barbara Boyd). For more than two decades, he has written about computers, gadgets, video games, trends, and high-tech movers and shakers for numerous publications and websites, including *The New York Times, Macworld, PC World, Fortune, Newsweek, Popular Science, TV Guide,* the *Washington Post, Wired,* Gamespot, MSNBC, Engadget, TechCrunch, and Salon. You can find links to Joe's stories on his blog, at www.joehutsko.com.

Barbara Boyd: Barbara writes mostly about technology and occasionally about food, gardens, and travel. She's the co-author, with Joe Hutsko, of the first, second, and third editions of *iPhone All-in-One For Dummies,* and the author of *AARP iPad: Tech to Connect* and *iCloud and iTunes Match in a Day For Dummies.* She also co-authored (with Christina Martinez) *The Complete Idiot's Guide to Pinterest Marketing* and *Innovative Presentations For Dummies* (with Ray Anthony). Presently, Barbara stays busy writing, keeping up with technology, and tending her garden and olive trees. Barbara divides her time between city life in Rome and country life on an olive farm in Calabria, the toe of Italy's boot.

Jesse Feiler: Jesse writes apps and books about building and using them. As the worlds of publishing and development have changed, he, too, has changed, and now is a publisher. His company, Champlain Arts, has published a number of Jesse's apps, including Minutes Machine, The Nonprofit Risk App, Saranac River Trail, Better Choices (for Clinton County Health Department), and Trails & Places: The Guide to Presenting and Exploring Trails. Champlain Arts has also published *The Studio Story* by three-time Tony Award winner Uta Hagen, as well as her memoir *Sources.* His website is www.champlainarts.com.

Doug Sahlin: Doug is the author of more than 20 how-to books, many of them bestsellers. He is a professional photographer specializing in landscape and fine art photography. From 2006 to 2010, he was president of Superb Images, a company specializing in wedding and event photography. Sahlin shares his knowledge of photography as administrator of the Lensbaby Artistry Facebook group, which has more than 3,500 members. He also shares video tutorials on his YouTube Digital Photo Guru channel (www.youtube.com/c/digitalphotoguru). To view some of Doug's photography, go to https://dasdesigns.net/portfolios.

Authors' Acknowledgments

You see the authors' names on the cover, but these books (like any books) are really a collaboration, an effort of a many-membered team. Thanks go to Ashley Coffey at Wiley for commissioning the fifth edition of this book.

Thanks to our literary agents, Carole Jelen and Margot Hutchison, for their astute representation and moral support. And finally, thanks to the folks at Apple who developed such cool products.

Publisher's Acknowledgments

Senior Acquisitions Editor: Tracy Boggier

Project Editor: Elizabeth Kuball

Copy Editor: Elizabeth Kuball

Technical Editor: Ryan Williams

Sr. Editorial Assistant: Cherie Case

Proofreader: Debbye Butler

Production Editor: Magesh Elangovan

Cover Image: © sdecoret/Shutterstock; (screenshot) Courtesy of Jesse Feiler